Radio Drama
and Comedy Writers,
1928–1962

ALSO BY RYAN ELLETT

*Encyclopedia of Black Radio in the United States,
1921–1955* (McFarland, 2012)

Radio Drama and Comedy Writers, 1928–1962

RYAN ELLETT

McFarland & Company, Inc., Publishers
Jefferson, North Carolina

ISBN (print) 978-1-4766-6593-1 ∞
ISBN (ebook) 978-1-4766-2980-3

LIBRARY OF CONGRESS CATALOGUING DATA ARE AVAILABLE

BRITISH LIBRARY CATALOGUING DATA ARE AVAILABLE

© 2017 Ryan Ellett. All rights reserved

No part of this book may be reproduced or transmitted in any form or by any means, electronic or mechanical, including photocopying or recording, or by any information storage and retrieval system, without permission in writing from the publisher.

Front cover photograph by Hal Bergman (iStock)

Printed in the United States of America

*McFarland & Company, Inc., Publishers
Box 611, Jefferson, North Carolina 28640
www.mcfarlandpub.com*

For Don Frey,
whose enthusiasm and passion
for old-time radio exemplifies the joy
so many find in these historical recordings.

And for David Siegel (1932–2016),
whose legacy in preserving and researching
the Golden Age of radio is unsurpassed.

Acknowledgments

This book has been many years in the making with a number of delays along the way. Because of its scope I have received input and feedback from many individuals who themselves spend countless hours documenting the history of old-time radio programs. Some of the genres' most stalwart historians have provided documentation, explanation, and clarification about individuals and matters included here: Jim Cox, Jack French, Martin Grams, Jr., Ian Grieves, Jay Hickerson, Doug Hopkinson, Elizabeth McLeod, Randy Riddle, Karl Schadow, David Siegel, Derek Tague, Joe Webb, Jim Widner, and Stewart Wright. I'm also indebted to editors of the hobby's magazines, Bob Burchett, Tom Cheree, French, Patrick Luciano, Bob Newman, and Frank Rosin who published some early findings that led to further discoveries and refinement. The librarians at the University of Kansas, University of Missouri–Kansas City, Iowa State University, and Lawrence Public Libraries always went out of their way to track down articles and obscure titles so crucial to this scholarship. Jim Beshires, Don Frey, and Bruce Frey provided not only resources but, more importantly, regular encouragement throughout this project's creation.

My family deserves an abundance of gratitude for allowing me the time to pursue this book. The number of hours such a work takes is practically incalculable and many of those hours surely would have been spent with my wife and children.

Writing this has been a labor of love and I hope the entire old-time radio community finds it as valuable as I do.

Table of Contents

Acknowledgments vi

Preface 1

Introduction: The Broadcast Scribes 3

Writers, A to Z 9

Bibliography 201

Index 207

Preface

The field of documenting radio drama stretches back to the early 1970s and includes entries touching on nearly every facet of the industry. The era's biggest stars such as Jack Benny and Fred Allen have numerous works devoted to them and dozens of aural performers have been documented in volumes published by presses of all size and focus. A number of individual programs such as *Gunsmoke* and *Fibber McGee & Molly* have books dedicated to exploring every facet of their broadcast runs. Even sound effects artists, announcers, and the ad men have received in-depth scholarly attention. Interestingly, however, the most overlooked contributors to the Golden Age of radio drama—commonly known as old-time radio—are surely the scriptwriters, without whom the early airwaves would have been little more than crudely adapted stage productions and poorly improvised banter.

In a literature that includes hundreds of books and even more articles penned by professional historians and devoted amateur enthusiasts, the writers of those old-time radio programs lack a resource with a singular focus on their output. This book attempts to remedy that oversight and begin the process of recognizing these authors who entertained and informed the nation's listeners during the depths of the Great Depression, the darkest years of World War II, and the beginning of the Cold War.

The old-time radio era, dating roughly from the debut of *Amos 'n' Andy* in 1928 to the demise of *Suspense* and *Yours Truly, Johnny Dollar* in 1962, is far too wide in scope to be explored exhaustively in one volume. Nevertheless, it is possible to offer a thorough survey of the medium's most revered, groundbreaking, successful, and prolific writers. For the reader generally unfamiliar with radio drama, this book offers biographical and bibliographical background about many of the primary and secondary industry scribes behind the biggest comedic and dramatic broadcasts. For the reader with a wider knowledge of radio's Golden Age, these entries will explore both the many obscure writers behind the blockbuster series and the big-name writers behind many lost and forgotten programs.

It would be impossible to document every individual who ever typed out copy that made its way to the ether at some point during the 1930s, 40s, and 50s. Hundreds are identified here and undoubtedly thousands more could claim some broadcasting authorial credits. While the major networks and largest advertising agencies employed many of these writers, independent production companies and nearly every station from New York City to the smallest town had employees tasked with creating copy to fill precious air time.

Scriptwriters were initially identified for inclusion in this book due to their references in publications by the fields most prominent historians including Jim Cox, John Dunning, and Martin Grams. That selection was then expanded by further readings in the industry trade magazines of the 1930s, 40s, and 50s. An imperfect methodology to be sure, but one I feel provides a solid overview of the medium's most important contributors and a deep sampling of the unsung work horses who toiled in anonymity even during their working years.

Because old-time radio enthusiasts tend to gravitate toward the dramatic broadcasts (a wide genre that includes most plot-driven stories including comedies and soap operas), only token representatives are included among copywriters employed within other genres such as newscasts, musical-variety shows, talk programming, and sportscasts. At times these individuals made unique or notable contributions to their field or also commonly wrote dramatic fare as well.

Many writers in these pages earned greater fame for work on Broadway, television, and motion pictures. Often their radio career is underexplored or even unknown; this volume attempts to more fully describe the entirety of theses artists' careers. While trying to acknowledge the non-radio portions of authors' bodies of work, an exhaustive review of non-aural work would both detract from the focus of this book and often unnecessarily replicate information that can easily be obtained elsewhere. My goal was to place a writer's radio scripts within the context of his or her overall career output.

The wide survey of authors precluded in-depth analysis of any individual's writing style and career output; Indeed, most radio writers took what work they could get and did not concern themselves with grander artistic visions and philosophies. A script was a paycheck and rarely was the creator concerned with anything more. However, these entries provide a jumping-off point for the scholar interested in diving deeper into the study of any particular scribe included in these pages. Further, the collections noted in the bibliography offer opportunity for many lifetimes of more detailed, dedicated research.

If the reader is disappointed in the biographical or bibliographical information provided in certain entries, be assured this writer was as well. My hope is that it will spark others to dig deeper into the written record, whether research collections, historical publications, or papers and documentation tucked away in private hands, and shed light on the innumerable craftsmen who left a mark—great or small—on the Golden Age of radio broadcasting.

Introduction:
The Broadcast Scribes

The so-called Golden Age of radio was short, generally identified by radio drama enthusiasts as a period that began approximately in 1926 with the founding of the National Broadcasting Company and ended in 1962 with the final broadcasts of *Yours Truly, Johnny Dollar* and *Suspense*, in reality it was a much shorter era.

More realistically, the medium's Golden Age began around 1930 when *Amos 'n' Andy* became a national craze and ended in the Post-War period of the late 1940s as television began its ascent. If generously ascribed a two-decade span, the heyday of dramatic radio was "the shortest Golden Age in history" according to one of the medium's most respected wordsmiths, Norman Corwin.

This relatively brief flash of mass media dominance, in contrast to over a century of motion pictures and nearly three-quarters of a century of television, certainly accounts for the paucity of historical works on the subject. It surely must go far in explaining why so little attention has been given to the hundreds and even thousands of men and women who wrote the words that were subsequently aired across the nation and even around the globe.

Despite numerous volumes that have been published since the late 1960s focusing on the actors, actresses, and even sound effects artists whose talents made radio the theater of the mind, scriptwriters have rarely received more than cursory attention in the field's literature. Many modern listeners may struggle to name more than a dozen of these authors.

Working in the Shadows

Unfortunately for those authors a number of factors have contributed to their neglected recognition. First, the poorly documented nature of the early decades of radio's development make it very difficult to identify many "firsts" in the field, a favorite activity of historians. Though radio technology was discovered in the late 1800s and used for communication (via morse code) by both amateur and commercial operators, the general public was not widely knowledgeable about it.

Therefore, up until the technology could readily handle the transmission of human voices, music, and sound beginning in the late 1910s and early 1920s, historians must rely on sparse notes in early publications focused far more on the technical aspects of broadcasting than the actual content of those broadcasts. They must also scour printed news outlets that viewed radio as little more than a curiosity, generally only worthy of the occasional mention. This scarcity of written records for the industry's first years has thus made it impossible to identify radio's first writer, regardless of how the term "writer" might be considered in a broadcasting context.

As the medium matured, however, scriptwriters often failed to get their share of attention and credit. A second force working against proper commemoration of the vast majority of radio's earliest writers was their low level of recognition even from peers and publications knowledgeable about the industry. In radio's heyday—the Golden Age defined above—the authors behind America's favorite programs remained largely anonymous. The on-air credits some received late in the genre's era due to union demands did little to cement the names of the wordsmiths in the public imagination. Instead, the performers and to lesser extent directors were given credit for the success or failure of particular programs through their interpretations of the scripted word.

Finally, even if specific individuals could be put forth as worthy of such recognition, disagreement about what constitutes radio writing would prevent any consensus on the choices. A lack of a common understanding of who was considered a broadcast author further stands in the way of proper historical recognition.

A Vague Profession

Rome Cowgill, a professional radio script writer and scholar of the art of broadcast writing asked in 1949 "Who was a radio writer?" Was it only the author behind the 15-, 30-, and 60-minute dramas and comedies that fueled a multi-million dollar industry? Was it the copywriter on the local small-town station filling air space between programs? What about news broadcasters, rural farm reporters, or educators who created scripts for high school or university stations? Is it necessary to go back even further and suggest the pioneering scientists who experimented with radio technology and surely wrote down specific messages as part of controlled experiments? Or subsequent early amateur radio operator who jotted down information to be shared over the airwaves with likeminded hobbyists?

Taken in the widest scope, some level of writing was necessary for nearly every type of program that appeared on radio. Musical shows, whether featuring classical, opera, or popular tunes, required commentary unique to each genre of music. Talk programs, including speeches, interviews, and round-table formats, required very different scripts. Variety, children's, and news broadcasts called for yet even more diverse writing approaches from each other and also from the previously mentioned genres. Sports broadcasting, incredibly popular even in radio's earliest days, required still another skill set with its unique combination of on-air ad-libbing in conjunction with a tremendous amount of background research and preparatory writing. Even radio drama, the area of most interest to old-time radio enthusiasts, required numerous writing styles; from mysteries, soap operas, and sitcoms to romance and juvenile adventures.

Considering this book's narrower focus of radio drama, pointing to one author or group of authors who first set about purposefully adapting or writing original material intended to entertain listeners can never be done with any degree of certainty. The earliest original broadcast story yet uncovered may be a drama penned in 1919, documented in a 1944 doctoral dissertation by Donald Riley. Further records indicate that many of the earliest dramatic radio productions were simply performances of stage plays over the air. However, the limitations of this strategy were soon apparent to audiences listening to works that were also meant to be seen. Even then plays and short stories remained prominent sources of radio material, though the increased skill in adaptation was more of an art of translation, argued Max Wylie in 1939, than an act of original creation.

The Art Form of Radio Drama

By necessity, no single work could hope to be authoritative on the vast field of broadcast authorship. Though the individuals who cranked out countless lines of commentary and continuity for late-night poetry readings, Sunday afternoon easy listening concerts, and collegiate basketball games were no less professional writers than those penning scripts for the top Hooper-rated shows, they will not be given consideration in these pages unless they also made contributions to the dramatic radio genres.

Within ten years the art of writing for radio matured from a novelty to a step in a rapidly expanding industry. Within another decade and a half scholars were publishing textbooks for college courses outlining the best methods for writing for radio, an outlet for writers that hadn't even existed when the then-students were born. Nevertheless, broadcast script writing was recognized and described even in its time by Max Wylie as the "orphan child of accepted literature."

In numerous ways, writing for radio was unlike most other types of writing. Most obviously it lacked the visual element, a centerpiece of the art of drama for millennia. Up until this point there were no forms of live mass entertainment or storytelling that, at their core, relied only upon words and sounds. Public performance was enhanced by gestures, expressions, movement, and the overall presence of the presenter. Published writings in the form of books or magazines or something similar, though relying only on words, were free to use as many words as necessary to convey images and impressions to the reader. Not so with radio writing, or at least *good* radio writing; writing with something to say and a good way to say it. Numerous publications from the era highlight the many unique challenges facing any scribe who hoped to hear his or her story on the airwaves and some of the best techniques available to meet those challenges.

As noted above, the huge library of English-language plays was the initial source for early radio sketches. Though at first even the crudest enactments held the attention of listeners still enthralled by the strange technology, by the mid–1920s industry executives were realizing that many of these previously published works required considerable skill to be adapted well to radio, and some simply were not appropriate for translation. Stories that were built around character introspection were notoriously difficult to adapt, though writers learned various tricks for including compelling voice-over narrative or introducing a secondary character who could be the focus of the main character's talks.

Complicated plots, too, presented many problems of adaptation. But classic literature offered too many story ideas for the radio industry to ignore so writers grew adept at pruning off all but the most central storylines of novels that sometimes ran hundreds of pages (compressed to approximately 30 pages for a half-hour show). Subplots could be combined or compressed in a montage sequence. The number of characters often had to be reduced as well for reasons of economy. Thus, adapters learned to skillfully eliminate parts or merge multiple characters into just a couple. Dialog, too, usually had to be rewritten, a task that may have excited or vexed any particular writer.

Most difficult for the writer may have been adapting a high quality story that featured little action. Radio, after all, required action to keep the audience tuned it. The average scripter found it much easier to cut than to add; padding scenes was rarely beneficial and inserting new scenes ran the risk of compromising the integrity of the original source material. Writers in these cases sought out single sentences that could be expanded to full scenes, perhaps elaborating some backstory or emphasizing a unique, powerful setting.

Radio required a specialized style of dialog and narration, different from the spoken word of live theater and written word of books that came before its development. Most often, conversation had to set the scene, convey actions, and move the plot. To top it off, of course, this conversation had to sound natural, like people talking in the real world. This preferably meant using short, broken sentences, communicating in short bursts, even interrupting other characters.

Yet at the same time, clarity reigned supreme; listeners could not go back and re-listen in the event of confusion, nor could they observe the action to bring them up to speed on a story. Character names needed to be used frequently for identification, and everybody in a scene had to be identified in some manner even if some didn't or couldn't talk. Only of slightly less importance was creating the scene of the action. If not done properly, audiences would create backgrounds in their own minds and writers risked shattering those illusions if later describing the scene differently than envisioned by listeners.

Both short and long lines of dialog could be effective and a mixture helped to keep listeners on their toes. Too many qualifying phrases, however, obscured a line of dialog and risked losing the audience. Economy was king; according to one expert, the writer had approximately one minute to establish the characters, setting, and premise before risking losing listeners.

Similarly, the best writing was descriptive to avoid trite and tired phrases but not so unique that it distracted listeners from the story at hand. Specific and concrete words were of utmost importance within the time constraints imposed by radio, as were short and forceful words. As with good poetry, onomatopoetic words were valuable. Each word and sentence has to contribute to a story, serving some purpose; describing the setting, moving the plot, or illuminating a character.

Conciseness was of the utmost importance in the industry. Radio's time limits were non-negotiable; a complete story had to be told within a fifteen- or thirty-minute (occasionally a full hour) span. While many stories could be worked into these parameters, some simply could not and an author was wise to realistically assess a story's time needs before investing too many hours writing an unworkable script. Ace scriptwriters also had to be proficient with sound and not just words. Just as motion picture scripters have to recognize how visuals and actions will work with the written word to carry a scene, so the radio scripters had to recognize sounds that would punctuate and complement the written word to convey a scene.

There were additional numerous unique challenges for writing radio plays. They started with the very beginning of a program; each broadcast needed an opening that identifies the show, gives sponsor information, and creates an opening scene that immediately grabs the listeners' interest. The opening scene, too, was critical. As mentioned above, a writer had approximately one minute to establish the setting, introduce characters, and reveal an engaging plot hook.

Scene endings and transitions were presented problems for writers more versed in stage production. They had to create aural devices to replace the stage's visual curtain that clearly indicated a transition, possibly of time, place, or both. Music, narration, and sound fades became the common methods used by the medium's writers to solve this dilemma.

Similarly, bringing characters into and out of a story was often tricky. The audience could not see a silent character waiting in the wing or entering a scene. Entrance and exit lines were a necessity, but they needed to be inserted naturally without disrupting the flow of the story.

Other story writing elements that caused problems were allowing sufficient time to pass for particular actions. Whether through the use of transitions or other tools, the passage of time needs to be plausible. A character couldn't run out to the corner store and be back in a few seconds without disrupting the listeners' sense of timing.

Different genres also posed their own

unique challenges to writers. The daily soap operas required slight conflict to end each episode, complicated by the fact that the story could only be advanced a very little bit during each broadcast. Storylines needed careful timing, generally wrapping up in no more than three months but allowing new plots to be introduced and developed without distracting from the primary plot. Story points had to be reiterated constantly and characters reintroduced frequently because writers could not assume they had a consistent audience. The necessary daily synopsis and recap were tedious but critical components of a serial script, and were a challenge for the writer who wished to liven up the process.

While the most popular of the different drama genres, the weekly episodic series (i.e. *Big Town* and *The Adventures of Sam Spade*), had their own pitfalls of which writers needed to be aware. Most of them had established characters and settings, so stories had to take place and needed to be plausible within those confines. Introductions could still be tricky, as they needed to introduce the main characters to new listeners without turning off established listeners with needlessly repetitive details. The done-in-one nature of these episodes offered advantages over the endless storylines of the serials, but it did impose limits on story ideas and long-term story development.

The anthology series contained some of the constraints of the weekly episodic dramas, especially the strict time limits. Additionally, authors needed to establish characters quickly as the listener did not have a history with them as with episodic series' main heroes.

Yet for all this, scripting an engaging radio play was the same as writing a story or play that enthralled a reader. A good story was supreme. Mastery of all radio's conventions would not cover a weak story.

Conclusion

By 1938 one professional estimated there were several hundred writers across the nation producing the roughly one million words spoken across the four major networks every day on the air. Just one year later a one radio writer opined that the medium had produced almost none of its own writers. Rather, it had called on the talents of established playwrights, short story writers, and poets to produce much of the air's high quality work.

Established authors tended to avoid radio for a number of reasons. First, inertia is a powerful force and writers who had achieved any level of success in theater, books, or periodicals had little incentive to learn the ins and outs of the new medium, many of which are outlined above. Second, and perhaps no less important, while one could earn a basic living as a radio script writer, the job usually involved a disproportionate amount of work for the same pay as could be found in other mediums. By 1950 when writing for the airwaves had become a fully developed art, one veteran bemoaned that fact that radio was quite possibly the hardest writing field to break into, yet at the same time offered far less compensation. This may inevitably have led to a third reason that quality authors shied away from broadcasting, that the business developed a bit of a shabby reputation among the literati and serious artistic circles. The intense commercial nature of radio placed many demands and constraints on authors that were less prominent in other mediums.

Overlooked as they were, there was no Golden-Age of dramatic radio without the writer. The entire production, as sensational and star-filled as any may have been, all had at their center a script; lines pounded out on a simple typewriter on plain white paper. These lines told actors and announcers when to speak, sound effects artists when to cue a noise, and orchestras when to play some notes. Talented actors, musicians, and sound artists made immeasurable contributions, of course, but before this multitude of professionals could do their job, there had to be a script from which to start.

This volume, therefore, is intended to highlight those few creators already widely recognized for their contributions to the field of radio, while also expanding general knowledge of hundreds more obscure writers and even introducing formerly forgotten authors to the historical record.

REFERENCES

Cowgill, Rome. *Fundamentals of Writing for Radio: Drama, Talks, Continuities, and Nondramatic Features with Guidance in Program Planning, Production, and Marketing.* NY: Rinehart & Company, Inc., 1949.

Crews, Albert. *Professional Radio Writing.* Boston: Houghton Mifflin Co., 1946.

Mackey, David R. *Drama on the Air.* NY: Prentice-Hall, Inc., 1951.

Seymour, Katharine and John T. W. Martin. *Practical Radio Writing: The Technique of Writing for Broadcasting Simply and Thoroughly Explained.* NY: Longmans, Green and Co., 1938.

Wagner, Paul H. *Radio Journalism.* Minneapolis, MN: Burgess Publishing Co., 1940.

Weaver, Luther. *The Technique of Radio Writing.* NY: Prentice-Hall, Inc., 1948.

Wylie, Max. *Radio Writing.* New York: Farrar & Rinehart, 1939.

Writers, A to Z

Ace, Goodman

One of a number of network radio professionals who got started at Kansas City's CBS affiliate KMBC, Goodman Ace (January 15, 1899–March 25, 1982) started on radio reviewing the legitimate theater, a job he held for the *Kansas City Journal-Post* newspaper. In 1928 he married Jane Sherwood, a dancing school classmate.

In August 1930, Ace began a regular radio feature on KMBC called *The Movie Man* in which he reviewed new film releases. One evening as he was preparing to sign off, Ace got the signal to keep going: the following act had failed to show up. Totally unprepared, he motioned for Jane to join him in the studio where, after a brief preparation during a broadcasting break, they proceeded to talk about a game of bridge they played the night before.

Listeners liked what they heard, wrote in to the station, and the Aces were given some regular airtime to continue their chats. Ace wrote the sketches for *Easy Aces* and over the course of the following year gradually expanded his scripts beyond the narrow topic of playing bridge. In 1931 KMBC contracted with WGN in Chicago to let the husband and wife broadcast their program from the Windy City. The Blackett-Sample agency, which would grow into one of the most powerful in the industry, kept *Easy Aces* sponsored and eventually moved the program to New York.

Never a ratings smash, *Easy Aces* nevertheless ran until 1944 when Goodman ran afoul of his sponsor, Anacin. When a representative from the aspirin-maker objected to a portion of one of his shows, Ace sarcastically replied that he didn't care for Anacin's packaging. The program was dropped soon after.

Ace's humor was greatly appreciated by comedians in the industry and it didn't take long for Danny Kaye to hire Ace as his lead writer at a whopping $3,500 per week.

The Kaye series ran for just a year (1945–1946) but didn't find much audience favor. Goodman clashed with fellow writer—and Kaye's wife—**Sylvia Fine** and eventually left the job. Goodman supplemented his writing income with $75,000 annual payments from Ziv Productions, which bought old *Easy Aces* recordings and sold them into syndication.

After leaving *The Danny Kaye Show* Ace was hired by CBS to work as "supervisor of comedy and variety" which involved leading a network team of writers to work on programs in need of improvement. During his time in the position this included *Little Show* and *CBS Is There* and in 1947 the network debuted his new creation *You Are There*.

Goodman and Jane returned to the air in their original *Easy Aces* characters in 1948 on a series called *mr. ace and JANE*, a half-hour version of their older quarter-hour program. The pair couldn't rekindle their original magic and the new show lasted just a single season.

Recognized as one of the top wits in radio, Goodman was charged with ensuring *The Big Show* was successful in turning back the rising tide of television in 1950 as well as returning NBC to the top of the ratings after having both Jack Benny and Edgar Bergen lured away by CBS. Despite the massive amounts of money thrown at the series—a veritable who's who of stars of whom NBC still had many on staff—*The Big Show* was a ratings disappointment and left the air after eighteen months. For all his talent even Ace could not craft it into a winner.

Well after dramatic radio had faded and Ace had moved on to television, a few of the *Easy Aces* scripts were dusted off the shelf and reprinted in a hardback book published by Doubleday & Company. Unfortunately, a relatively small number of *Easy Aces* recordings survive of the thousands aired through the 1930s, the core of his radio work.

Ace made his name in radio but his money in television, at one point finding himself the highest paid writer in the industry. He wrote for some of the biggest names in the industry's early days including Milton Berle, Sid Caesar, and Perry Como. In his later years Ace appeared on WPAT and wrote a weekly column for *The Saturday Review*.

Books: *The Book of Little Knowledge: More Than You Want to Know About Television* (1955); *How Are You? or The Fine Art of Hypochondria* (1966); *Ladies and Gentlemen—Easy Aces* (1970).

Sources: *Ladies and Gentlemen—Easy Aces*; Arthur Church Collection.

Acree, Chuck

Chuck Acree, a performer and M.C. for Chicago radios stations in the 1930s and 1940s, scripted WLS' *Something to Talk About* for several years before and during World War II. He adapted the show to a newspaper column that he syndicated for years afterwards.

Sources: *Radio Daily* December 29, 1949, p. 6; *Variety* July 14, 1943, p. 82.

Adair, Lynn

Lynn (Eva Donaldson) Adair, the wife of a Chicago banker, was selling original radio scripts such as *Mother and Dad* as early as 1933. Among her work that eventually reached the air were stories for *The Sacred Flame* (1936–1937), *Junior Thriller* (1937), and *Young Widder Jones* (1938).

Sources: *Broadcasting* March 15, 1933, p. 30; *Radio Daily* May 19, 1937, p. 8, September 22, 1937, p. 5.

Adams, Paul

Paul Adams, a writer and director for Young & Rubicam, scripted *We, the People* (1940–1943, interrupted by service in the Army), an untitled U.S. Treasury program (ca. 1946), and *Hopalong Cassidy* (1950–1951).

Sources: *Broadcasting* April 12, 1943, p. 35; *Variety* May 22, 1946, p. 23.

Adamson, Ed

Ed Adamson (January 28, 1915–October 1, 1972), according to writer Norman Katkov who worked with him in television in the 1960s, was "warm, friendly, witty" and in many ways a thorough "New Yorker." He was a twin and the son of **Hans Christian Adamson** who also did some writing for radio in the 1930s and 1940s.

Adamson managed to carve a steady career writing in radio and, later, television, despite the brutally competitive nature of the field and the fact that he never had a successful series that he could call his own. In radio Adamson focused on mystery and detective shows and was active for about a decade from the late 1940s to the late 1950s. Shows with which he is more closely associated are *Counterspy* (1949–1950), *The Private Files of Rex Saunders* (1951), and *That Hammer Guy* (1953). The latter was written under the supervision of Mike Hammer creator Mickey Spillane. Other radio work came with *Abbott Mysteries*, stories adapted from Frances Crane's series of novels, *Inner Sanctum* (1949), and *FBI in Peace and War* (1957).

As television ceded popularity to television, Adamson smoothly made the transition and by the mid–1950s was seeing his scripts aired with some regularity. Among the more well-known series for which he contributed scripts are *The Outer Limits*, *The Virginian*, *The Rifleman*, *Richard Diamond*, and *The Untouchables*. Not all of his work panned out, such as a pilot episode he co-scripted with Bernie Fein for a proposed series called *The Prince on Center Street*.

In 1959 Adamson left his contract writing position with CBS and signed with Four Star Productions, a television production company founded by former film and radio star Dick Powell among others. Adamson was hired to serve as an associate producer and head writer for the company's *Richard Diamond* series. A year later he was assigned to work on *Wanted: Dead or*

Alive, a western featuring Steve McQueen. Adamson and McQueen disagreed on different facets of the show and production meetings frequently turned tense. There was professional respect between the two, however, and Adamson allowed that McQueen better understood the Josh Randall character than he did. In return, McQueen later gave in to Adamson's insistence that Dick Donner be hired as director for several episodes over McQueen's heated objections.

After spending many years writing scripts for detectives developed by others, in the early 1970s Ed Adamson finally saw one of his own creations brought to the airwaves. His private eye was Miles Banyon, a hard-boiled gumshoe of the old school, a throwback to those of Adamson's younger days in the 1930s and 1940s. Banyon debuted to audiences in a made-for-television film simply called *Banyon* that aired in 1971. It starred Robert Forster, who Adamson specifically envisioned in the role as he wrote the teleplay, against a gritty 1930s Los Angeles background. The film was a successful pilot and NBC ordered fifteen hour-long episodes of a Banyon television series for the 1972–1973 season.

Unfortunately, what should have been a crowning achievement for Adamson's writing career turned into a series of frustrations and disappointments. When NBC decided to turn the Banyon pilot into a regular series, network executives hired QM Productions to turn out the fifteen-episode order. After working for so many years with others' characters, however, Adamson did not take kindly to others tinkering with his beloved creation. The disagreements started during development of the pilot film; Adamson and co-writer **Richard Alan Simmons** had differing opinions as to how to approach it and director Robert Day recalled that the two "did not get along well." The problems continued when QM Productions began working with the property in preparation for the new series. Adamson wanted to do Banyon his way and took considerable umbrage when the production company made changes and told him what needed to be done.

Tragedy struck and Adamson didn't live to see his Mike Banyon's first and only season on the small screen. During filming of the initial fifteen episodes Adamson died of a heart attack while the thirteenth episode was being shot. Adamson "was made for radio and television" Norman Katkov recalled. He was fast, able to dictate entire scripts at one setting, sometimes acting out the characters and scenes while pacing the room. He was a writer until the end, which came at the relatively young age of 57.

Sources: Bruce Geller Papers; Brunsdale; Cox, "Drama! Thrills! Action!"; Etter; McQueen p. 87–90; Royce; Takamoto; *Broadcasting* April 13, 1959, p. 91, July 25, 1960, p. 78; *Sponsor* Feb. 1948, p. 90–91; Bowie, interview; thrillingdetective.com.

Adamson, Hans Christian

Hans Christian Adamson (July 20, 1890– September 11, 1968) was Danish-born but spent his adulthood in the United States. He left his wife while his twin boys, one of whom was **Ed Adamson**, were young. Adamson worked as a writer much of his life and his work appeared in a number of mediums, including newspapers, radio, and books. In the mid–1930s Adamson stepped away from journalism to work as an assistant to the president of New York City's American Museum of Natural History as well as to be in charge of the institution's PR department. As part of his responsibilities Adamson became editor of the Hayden Planetarium's monthly bulletin that he turned into a regular magazine called *The Sky*. Within a couple years he passed on editorial duties to Clyde Fisher.

It is likely that Adamson got involved with radio in the late 1930s via his position with the Museum of Natural History. His first known broadcasting project was CBS' 1937 series *Adventures in Exploration* that was produced in conjunction with the Museum. A year later he is credited with writing contributions to CBS' *American School of the Air*, broadcast daily from 1930 to 1948 and directed at school teachers and children. Every Wednesday during the 1939–1940 season Adamson wrote a piece called "New Horizons" which focused on different geographical areas highlighted in the Museum of Natural History's exhibits. He also created classroom manuals to accompany his scripts. During the

1941–1942 season the show's Wednesday segment was renamed "Lands of New-World Neighbors" which was aligned with Adamson's 1941 book of the same name. His writing skill was such that his script "Man-Made Waterways" was chosen as one the year's ten best radio dramas by Norman Weiser, editor of *Writer's Radio Theatre* 1940–1941.

During World War II Adamson was shot down over the Pacific while in a B-17 with revered World War I pilot Eddie Rickenbacker, a harrowing experience related a number of places in the decades since, including on radio and film. Adamson, Rickenbacker, and the other crew members survived over three weeks on the open sea before being rescued by a United States naval patrol. Before the war's end he reached the rank of colonel in the U.S. Army Air Corps.

After the war Adamson retired from the military and returned to radio, penning scripts for air-themed programs including *The World's Most Famous Flights* (1946), *The World's Most Honored Flights* (1946) hosted by Eddie Rickenbacker, and *The National Air Travel Club* (1947). On May 1, 1951, NBC's *Cavalcade of America* dramatized Rickenbacker's story of being stranded on the high seas and Adamson provided the script. Much of Adamson's surviving writing exists in the form of naval history novels set in World War II.

Books: *The Empire of the Snakes* (1935) with Frederic Grosvenor Carnochan; *Out of Africa* (1935) with Frederic Grosvenor Carnochan; *Lands of New World Neighbors* (1941); *Eddie Rickenbacker* (1946); *Keepers of the Lights* (1955); *Hellcats of the Sea* (1955) with Charles A. Lockwood; *Through Hell and Deep Water* (1956) with Charles A. Lockwood; *Zoomies, Subs, and Zeros* (1956) with Charles A. Lockwood; *Admiral Thunderbolt* (1959); *Tragedy at Honda* (1960) with Charles A. Lockwood; *Rebellion in Missouri, 1861: Nathaniel Lyon and His Army of the West* (1961); *Hell at 50 Fathoms* (1962) with Charles A. Lockwood; *Blood on the Midnight Sun* (1964) with Per Klem; *Halsey's Typhoons* (1967) with G. F. Kosco; *Battles of the Philippine Sea* (1967) with Charles A. Lockwood; *Down to the Sea in Subs* (1967) with Charles A. Lockwood; *Guerrilla Submarines* (1974) with E. F. Dissette. Notable additions to his book output are some cookbooks written with his wife, Helen Lyon Adamson: *Sportsman's Game and Fish Cookbook* (1957) and *The Galley Cookbook* (1961).

Sources: Charles A. Lockwood Papers, 1904–1967; Bryson; Dunning; Robinson; *Broadcasting* May 5, 1942, p. 7, October 15, 1945, p. 74; *Variety* July 14, 1937, p. 46, November 8, 1939, p. 21; Eugene (OR) *Register Guard* September 12, 1968, p. 4A; Bowie, interview.

Alexander, Harmon J. (Hyman Joseph, also Hy, Hi)

Harmon Alexander (February 27, 1904–September 3, 1960), who commonly went by Hi Alexander in the industry trades, spent several years writing radio material and earned credits on some top-talent shows. His earliest known writing gigs were for the New York theater scene in the mid–1930s. By 1937 he was providing scripts for Teddy Bergman's (aka Blubber Bergman or Alan Reed) transcribed 26-episode series produced by Radio Events, Inc. and sponsored by Bigelow-Sanford Carpet Co. At the time he was also contributing material to The Script Library, a venture partially run by his wife **Georgia Backus** (married 1935), actress and writer in radio and motion pictures. The Script Library rented out scripts to smaller stations for production using their own local staff members.

In the mid–1930s Alexander ran a summer stock theater company in Craryville, NY, that counted Lucien La Dievere, Allen Boretz, Lee Brody, Lupan Fine, Jack Albertson, and Roslyn Kirkland among its members. By 1938 he was creating material for Ken Murray as well as running a theater at Camp Coake in Craryville, NY. Alexander's most notable credits came in the 1940s during which he provided scripts for *Duffy's Tavern* 1944 summer replacement *Nit Wit Court* with co-writers Phil Cole, Ben Perry, David Kohnhorst, *The Hallmark Charlotte Greenwood Show* (1945), *The Mel Torme Show* (1948) with Ben Perry, and most impressively the long-running *Burns & Allen Show* (beginning in 1943 with **Hank Garson**). His stature among his writing peers was demonstrated in 1946 when he was chosen to serve on the Radio Writers Guild Hollywood council along with such luminaries as Harry Bartell, **Sam Moore**, and **Don Quinn**. In the early 1950s Alexander was identified as a Communist sympathizer when the Red Scare swept through the entertainment industry.

Film: *Chase Me, Charlie* (1948), a six-reel Charlie Chaplin picture produced by Capitol Pictures, Corp.
Theatre: *Cut the Cards* (1932, 2-act play with Mack Swift); *Speak of the Devil* (1934, 3-act play with Georgia Backus).
Sources: Reed; *Billboard* November 23, 1946, p. 10–11, October 11, 1952, p. 8; *The Educational Screen* September 1941, p. 318; *Motion Picture Daily* June 10, 1937, p. 17, August 30, 1937, p. 10; *Radio Daily* February 15, 1937, p. 5, February 16, 1937, p. 1, 3; *The Screen Writer* March 1946, p. 46; *Variety* January 29, 1936, p. 54, July 28, 1937, p. 35, May 4, 1938, p. 28, December 22, 1943, p. 32, July 12, 1944, p. 28; July 14, 1948, p. 30; *The New York Herald Tribune* June 2, 1935, p. D3.

Alexander, Martha

Martha Alexander wrote for various radio series but specialized in the serials, a genre which garnered little respect, though she was singled out by one industry magazine for her talent. Former *Romance of Helen Trent* actress Mary Jane Higby insisted that Alexander was the best writer the series ever had. Alexander left *Trent* to write for *The Second Mrs. Burton* between 1946 and 1947 but felt strongly enough about her work that she quit the series over a disagreement with the sponsor regarding the overall tone they desired in the storylines.

During an overseas vacation in 1952 Alexander wrote a television series for production in England, *Willow Cottage*, as well as three plays and a significant portion of a novel. Later that year she took over writing chores for the television version of the serial *Valiant Lady*. She called Georgetown, CT, home during these years.

Radio: Alexander is known to have contributed at least one story to the Kellogg-sponsored *Hollywood Story* (1947), *Armstrong Theatre*, *Aunt Jenny*, *CBS Starlight Theatre*, *The First Nighter Program*, *Grand Central Station*, *Lucky Strike Theatre*, and *Somerset Maugham Theatre*.
Sources: Cox *A to Z* p. 201–202; Cox *Great Radio Soap Operas*; Higby p. 128; Cox "Same Time, Same Station"; Cox "Soap Opera Superwriters"; *Bulletin* (Wilton, CT) November 17, 1952, p. 26; *Sponsor* May 23, 1949, p. 58; *Radio Annual* 1946 p. 813; *Variety* August 27, 1947, p. 24.

Alexander, Michael

A little known radio writer, Michael Alexander has left his name in radio history books for penning *The Romance of Helen Trent* and at least three episodes of *Cavalcade of America* in 1949.
Source: Dunning.

Aley, Albert

New York–born Albert Aley (April 25, 1919– January 1, 1986) entered show business as a child actor on radio in the 1930s and appeared on numerous programs over CBS, NBC, and WNEW, most notably CBS' children's series *Let's Pretend*. Within a few years Aley had moved into writing broadcast scripts and is credited with working on several series during the 1940s. These programs included *Don Winslow of the Navy* (which he took over from original writer **Al Barker** in 1942), the soap opera *Stella Dallas* (ca. 1941–1942), *Superman* (ca. 1946, 1949), *Mr. Keen, Tracer of Lost Persons*, and *Have Gun, Will Travel*.

Aley is most remembered in radio circles for his long run writing the popular juvenile aviation show *Hop Harrigan* on which he also acted. He collaborated with **Wilfred Moore** and **Robert Burtt**, creators of earlier juvenile air thrillers *The Air Adventures of Jimmie Allen* and *Captain Midnight*, to bring *Harrigan* to the air. Aley's run on that show lasted its duration, from 1942 to 1948. Aley also produced at least one radio series, *Mark Trail*, before he moved into television in the early 1950s.

Television was a rewarding field for Aley and his work appeared on the air into the early 1980s. Working for Rockhill Radio in New York in the early days of television, Aley was one of the major forces bringing *Tom Corbett, Space Cadet* to TV in 1951. As a producer with Rockhill he produced several radio, television, and film packages. He continued his writing by contributing over two dozen scripts to various Westerns in the early 1960s including *The Rifleman, Have Gun, Will Travel, Laramie*, and *Rawhide*. Aley's career culminated with Emmy nominations for producing the television series *Ironside* (1970 and 1971) and *The Paperchase* (1979). His final scripts aired in 1980 on *Vega$* and *Barnaby Jones*.

Film: Screenplay for Walt Disney's *Ugly Dachshund* (1966).
Sources: Anderson, *An Actor's Odyssey* p. 62; Cox *Radio Crime Fighters* p. 102; Cox *Mr. Keen* p. 253; French "Keep 'Em Flying"; *The Radio Annual* 1938 p. 583, 1939 p. 611, 1943 p. 709, 1945 p. 824, 1946 p. 739, 811, 1949 p. 911, 1953 p. 770; *Radio and Television Mirror* November 1941 p. 20; *Variety* October 21, 1942, p. 34.

Alland, William (Bill)

Bill Alland's (March 4, 1916–November 11, 1997) radio writing credits are slim but they belie a robust career in both radio and film, areas in which he stayed much busier as an actor. Alland was a member of Orson Welles' Mercury Theater troupe between 1938 and 1940 and appeared in a number of their radio plays on their self-titled series, including the legendary "War of the Worlds" broadcast. Alland continued with the group after they picked up Campbell Soup's sponsorship and changed the program name to *The Campbell Playhouse*.

Alland's association with Welles likely facilitated his move into motion pictures, including on-screen and off-screen work in *Citizen Kane*. He placed his professional career on hiatus to enlist with the Army Air Corps during World War II during which he flew over 50 combat missions in the South Pacific. It was reported in *Variety* that the war-time series *G.I. Jive* was at least partially his idea.

After the war Alland made a brief return to his radio roots producing and writing the series *Doorway to Life* (1947–1948), his most notable radio contribution. He is widely credited in many sources with winning a Peabody Award for the series, but there is questionable evidence supporting this. It would appear to be a claim without merit that Alland made during his career that has subsequently been repeated in the years since.

By the early 1950s Alland was moving into the heyday of his career during which he would produce over two dozen B-movies, primarily science fiction. Foremost among them were features such as *The Creature from the Black Lagoon* (1954) and *Tarantula* (1955). He also received writing credits for a number of the films. In the middle of this film work Alland found time for acting jobs in radio, two decades after his debut with the Mercury Theater. These roles were mainly on the era's adult Westerns including *Frontier Gentleman* and *Have Gun, Will Travel*.

Sources: Weaver p. 7–8; *Variety* July 15, 1942, p. 39, December 30, 1942, p. 30.

Allen, Fred

Fred Allen (May 31, 1894–March 17, 1956), born John Florence Sullivan, was one of the most highly regarded radio comics of his time by critics and fellow comedians alike. His early years were grim; his mother died when he was three and his father when he was fourteen. One of Allen's father's last acts for the boy was to get him a job in the Boston Public Library. The small sum he earned at that job mostly went to his aunt, with whom Allen and his brother Bob, had move in with upon their father's death.

Allen began spending time at local theaters and amateur nights and was so inspired by what he saw that he checked out a book on juggling and began to learn the skill. At 18 he got his first opportunities to perform with Sam Cohen's circuit of amateur nights throughout New England. Amateur work eventually turned to professional work and for a time he was known as Paul Huckle, European Entertainer, Fred St. James (from the St. James Hotel located on Bowdoin Square) and Freddy James, the World's Worst Juggler.

No matter the name, Allen worked in obscurity and lived in poverty, subsisting on fare from cheap "hash houses." Still, he managed to move beyond New England and get bookings in the upper Midwest. Seen at one performance by an Australian promoter, Allen headed down under for an uninspiring tour that lasted nearly a year. During the tour he added a dummy, Jake, to his act.

In 1916 Allen returned to the West Coast and slowly made his way back East. His agent felt that Fred Allen had made considerable growth as a comedian in recent years but as Freddy James he was too associated with second-rate bookings to break into bigger theaters. Purely by accident Allen finally acquired the name by which he gained his greatest fame. Upon arriving for a booking he found himself billed as Fred Allen, his Freddy James stage name confused with an old agent named Edgar Allen.

Fred Allen met Portland Hoffa in 1922 while performing in *The Passing Show of 1922*. Hoffa, named for her Oregon birth city, was in the chorus. Several years later, in 1927, the two were married. It was another five years before Allen went on the air on his own radio program, *The*

Linit Bath Club Revue. The sponsor initially paid him $1,000 per week, out of which Allen was to pay for all talent, including the script. He could either write his own material or pay others to do it for him; Allen chose to do it himself. Recognized as a master wit both by critics and fellow comedians, even his considerable talent was not enough for a weekly radio program. It didn't take long for Allen to realize that writing thirty minutes of original material week in and week out was not sustainable. By way of a friend Allen was put in contact with **Harry Tugend**, a critic for the *Motion Picture Herald* who was planning to move into radio. The pair worked together for four years.

After only six months with Linit Allen's show was dropped and subsequently picked up by Hellmann's Mayonnaise and dubbed *The Salad Bowl Revue.* Along with the change in sponsor came a change in weekly budget, to $4,000. In early 1934 his sponsor changed yet again, this time to the laxative Sal Hepatica. *The Sal Hepatica Revue* quickly earned enviable ratings and he was given a full hour of time, renamed *Town Hall Tonight.* An hour of comedy required massive amounts of raw material to be winnowed and edited down. During this successful run Tugend left the radio grind to go to work in motion pictures.

By the end of the 1930s, Fred Allen's show was reduced to thirty minutes, the common length of prime time comedy programs. **Arnold Auerbach** and **Herman Wouk** labored to produce the weekly scripts that Allen still insisted on rewriting himself. In 1944 years of stress and inattention to his health led to hypertension and Allen was forced to take a hiatus from the air.

Allen was back in 1945 and he returned to the top tier of radio programs for a few short years before a precipitous plunge in 1948. Variously ascribed to game show competition *Stop the Music* and to a program formula that grew stale with listeners, Fred Allen lost his show in 1949. While he made appearances on other radio shows in following years, he was done writing for the air.

Sources: Allen *Much Ado*; *Treadmill*; Dunning.

Alsberg, Arthur

Son of a Wall Street stock broker and a graduate of the University of Pennsylvania, Arthur Alsberg (July 25, 1917–August 7, 2004) had a lengthy writing career that started on radio and continued many decades on television. In the early 1940s Alsberg worked at Rockhill Radio, Inc., first as a scriptwriter and then, beginning in 1942, as a vice-president. The company offered scripts, transcriptions, and other services to its clients. Alsberg is credited by one contemporary industry trade publication with writing for the *Fred Allen Show* in his early writing days. In the mid–1940s Alsberg was hired to work on the writing team for Danny Kaye's radio program (1945–1946), headed by **Goodman Ace**. On this show he worked alongside **Hal Kanter**, **Arnold Auerbach**, and Herbert Baker.

A number of sources indicate Alsberg also wrote for Milton Berle's radio program (1947–1948) but there is no primary evidence to support this contention. However, Goodman Ace also worked as the head writer for Berle's show and very possibly brought Alsberg with him to the new series. He received writing credit for some episodes of *A Day in the Life of Dennis Day*, a spin-off of the perennially popular *Jack Benny Show.*

In the early 1950s Alsberg was hired to write *Our Miss Brooks,* a popular series that followed the exploits of a high school English teacher featuring Eve Arden. Alsberg would stay with the show as it transitioned from radio television.

Alsberg transitioned easily to television, where he earned writing responsibilities on many programs from the 1950s all the way into the 1990s. Some of the earliest were *Bachelor Father* and *Pete and Gladys* and some of the most popular were *Our Miss Brooks*, *I Dream of Jeannie*, and *The Jetsons.* He served as a board member of the Writers Guild of America West in the late 1950s.

Theater: *Timid Tiger, Lusty Lamb* (1964 A two-act comedy written with John O'Dea); *Happiness Is Just a Little Thing Called a Rolls Royce* (1968, with Robert Fisher).

Sources: Kanter p. 84–88; *Broadcasting* October 26, 1942, p. 28, June 2, 1958, p. 84, May 24, 1965, p. 93; *Radio Annual*, 1943 p. 657; *Radio Annual and Television Yearbook* 1959 p. 1201.

Anderson, James Maxwell

Maxwell Anderson (December 15, 1888–February 28, 1959) was a prominent playwright of the early 20th century who also wrote for nearly every medium available during his lengthy writing career. Educated at the University of North Dakota and Stanford, Anderson turned to journalism after a couple short stints in the education field. After a few years writing for a number of newspapers and periodicals, Anderson turned full-time to writing plays.

Anderson's work was well-received, earning him a Pulitzer Prize for Drama in 1933 for *Both Your Houses*, the New York Drama Critics Circle Award for *Winterset* (1936) and *High Tor* (1937), and an Academy Award nomination for *All Quiet on the Western Front* (1930). A number of his plays were adapted to film including *Joan of Lorraine* as *Joan of Arc* (1948) and *Elizabeth the Queen* as *The Private Lives of Elizabeth and Essex* (1939). Anderson also did film adaptations, most prominent among them the previously mentioned *All Quiet on the Western Front* (1930) and *The Wrong Man* (1957) for Alfred Hitchcock.

Despite all his theater success, in 1937 Anderson dipped his toe in radio with a play written especially for the air, "The Feast of Ortolans," which was set during the French Revolution and was heard on NBC in September. This was followed in January 1938 with "Second Overture," a radio play set during another revolution, Russia's in 1918. The broadcast, too, was aired over NBC. Just a few months later, on May 28, 1938, his work "The Bastion Saint-Gervais" about the Spanish Civil War and written especially for radio, was broadcast.

Anderson did not move full time into radio or even get attached to any particular series. His patriotism, however, did lead him to contribute a few scripts to various series during World War II in support of the war effort. Among these was "The Miracle of the Danube," performed over CBS in the spring of 1941 for *Free Company*, featuring Burgess Meredith and Paul Muni. Yet another was "Our Navy," written for *This Is War!* and broadcast during February 1942.

A number of his plays were adapted to radio during the 1930s and 1940s, appearing on such prestigious programs as *Fleischmann's Yeast Hour, Lux Radio Theatre, Cavalcade of America,* and *The Theatre Guild on the Air*. NBC Blue network's wartime sitcom *Captain Flagg and Sergeant Quirt* (1941–1942) was based on Anderson's play *What Price Glory?*

Musicals: *Knickerbocker Holiday* and *Lost in the Stars*, both with Kurt Weill.

Sources: Balk p. 196, 198, 202, 256; Buxton & Owens p. 46; Dunning *Tune in Yesterday* p. 346; Shivers p. 155, 181, 187; *The Atlanta Constitution*, April 27, 1941, p. 12C; *The New York Tribune*, January 23, 1938, p. E10; *The Pittsburgh Press*, August 23, 1937, p. 16; *The Washington Post*, September 19, 1937, p. F4, March 1, 1942, p. L5.

Anderson, Sherwood

The Ohio-born Sherwood Anderson (September 13, 1876–March 8, 1941) was an influential novelist and short story writer who had little interest in radio, a medium that came into its own only during the last years of his life. During the 1930s Anderson expressed disdain for radio as a whole, considering it "dull, materialistic, and corrupt" because of its commercial basis. He wasn't averse to allowing his plays to be adapted for the air, however, which occurred as early as 1925 and he appeared on the air a number of times to discuss his work through the 1930s.

In 1936 Anderson was talked into contributing a radio play for Lucile Charles' proposed CBS series entitled *Land of Plenty*. Other contributors approached for the project were Langston Hughes and **Irwin Shaw**. After much coaxing and the receipt of CBS' $250 check, Anderson wrote his first draft of "Textiles," a mixture of speeches and musical chants. Ultimately, *Land of Plenty* was shelved by CBS and only the premier episode, a story penned by Irwin Shaw called "Supply and Demand," was aired in May 1937. Anderson received a slight bit of consolation when the script was included in a 1938 book of contemporary radio plays.

Anderson is only known to have returned to radio again near the end of his life. In the fall of 1940 he talked with Jacques Chambrun about preparing a script for the *Big Town* radio series, about a crusading newspaper editor. Time constraints, however, prevented Anderson from moving ahead with the idea. Anderson, toward the end of the year, returned again to radio, a medium that was increasingly intriguing to him. He spent some time outlining a possible series that pulled from the themes and ideas that helped establish his professional reputation in works such as *Winesburg, OH*. Anderson described it to Chambrun as "a very absorbing weekly program of the very day life in an imaginary American small town," with stories that would feed the "hunger in people to get back nearer to the soil." Neither did this project come to fruition.

In the early weeks of 1941 Anderson began working on his only radio script that would make it to the air. Titled "Above Suspicion," the play was to be a part of the *Free Company* CBS series celebrating different American freedoms. Tasked with writing about freedom from police persecution, the original draft was left incomplete at the time of his death in March 1941. Other members of the *Free Company* project, including **Maxwell Anderson**, finished the radio play.

Sources: Rideout; Wertheim p. 181; *The Los Angeles Times* September 2, 1936, p. 16; *The New York Tribune* February 22, 1925, p. SM16.

Andrews, Charles Robert Hardy Douglas

Bearing one of the longest names of any radio writer, Charles Andrews (often known as Robert Hardy Andrews professionally) was born in Kansas in 1903 and apparently was writing prodigiously as a child, cranking out a 100,000-word serial for a newspaper contest at 16. Andrews moved to Minnesota by the time he was 20 where he became an editor at *The Minneapolis Journal*. Within a few years he married Vi Bradley and moved to Chicago, went to work for the *Chicago Daily News*, and earned a name for himself writing newspaper serials.

Based on his success with the *Daily News*, Frank Hummert hired Andrews to write an early radio serial, *The Stolen Husband* (1931) and *Skippy* (1931–1935). The former originally featured only one performer (later expanded to a full cast), and the latter was based on a comic strip. Neither was a smash, though *Skippy* was eventually picked up for national broadcast, and Andrews worked with Hummert to develop more serials including *Betty and Bob* and *Judy and Jane* (1932–1935). What these series lacked in popularity they made up for in providing Hummert and Andrews experience in finding serial formulas that clicked with audiences. Within a short time the pair (with Hummert's future wife, Anne Ashenhurst) created *Just Plain Bill* (1932–1955), *The Romance of Helen Trent* (1933–1960), and *Ma Perkins* (1933–1960), all soap opera series that would each run for more than twenty years.

In Chicago Andrews found himself writing up to five radio scripts per day. Besides the soap operas, he was closely involved in the development of *Jack Armstrong, All-American Boy* in 1933, a juvenile-oriented program intended to replace the declining *Skippy*. Andrews reportedly had a hand in yet another popular juvenile serial a few years later, *Terry and the Pirates*. Based on Milton Caniff's newspaper strip, the series ran from 1937 to 1948. In the 1930s Andrews relocated to New York where his writing output increased even more, up to seven series at one time. To maintain a pace that could produce 100,000 words per week at a peak, he reportedly guzzled 40 cups of coffee and smoked 100 cigarettes every day of the week during his working sessions from noon to midnight. Andrews claimed that his personal record was 32,000 words in one 20-hour marathon day.

Stories of Andrews' writing stamina have been passed down through the years. At one point a storyline was changed at the last minute and Andrews had to write 25 scripts in five days. Another story claims that when a batch of his scripts was lost in a plane crash, he dictated one day's episode over the phone to the studio where it was written down and taken to actors who were on the air. Other than a few more pauses than normal, the episode went off without a hitch. Perhaps it comes as no surprise that after years of keeping several series on the air simultaneously, Andrews eventually opted for a change. A man of few spoken words, he left his job with the Hummerts with the understated explanation, "Got tired." A reported output of 30 million words over 39 radio series would, indeed, tire out most writers.

Leaving radio did not slow down Andrews' writing, however. In the mid-1930s he signed with Warner Bros. studios to create screenplays and in 1942 moved to Universal Studios. His total film count is unknown (not all were produced) but 1949's *I Married a Communist* was documented as his 55th released film. Just his film work added an estimated 1.5 million words to Andrews' writing count.

If Andrews was not considered a literary star, he clearly had a knack for writing stories that audiences wanted to hear and watch. That his work was described as "weak" by one major magazine and that he was dismissed as simply a "hired gun" or even a one-man "writing syndicate" by other critics did not diminish the respect Andrews held among radio, television, and motion picture producers who needed a dependable stream of scripts to keep the lights on.

While rumors persisted over the years that Andrews voiced the Shadow on the classic radio program for a short time, this claim has been thoroughly debunked as Andrews was still writing in Chicago when *The Shadow* was airing from New York. Andrews wasn't sentimental about writing professionally: "A writer should sit at his typewriter and write." Write he did, penning television and film scripts up until the last few years of his life before he passed away November 11, 1976.

Radio: *Alias Jimmy Valentine*; *Aunt Jenny*; *Mary Noble, Backstage Wife*; *Mr. Keen, Tracer of Lost Persons*; *Terry and Mary*; *Maxwell House Show Boat* (ca. 1937); *Mrs. Wiggs of the Cabbage Patch* (ca. 1938); *Young Widder Jones* (ca. 1939); *Big Town* (1940); *March of Time* (1942); *Family Theatre* (1953, 1954); *Lux Radio Theatre* (1954, 1955).

Television: *Adventures of Don Renegale*; *The Millionaire* (Writer and writing consultant for 158 episodes between 1955–1959); *Death Valley Days* (15 episodes between 1963–1970); *Thriller* (1961–1962); *The Ford Television Theatre* (1953–1954); *The Texan* (1958), *The Barbara Stanwyck Show* (1961), *87th Precinct* (1962), *Combat!* (1962), *Going My Way* (1962).

Books: Several, including *Burning Gold* (1945), *Legend of a Lady: The Story of Rita Martin* (1950), and *A Corner of Chicago* (autobiography, 1963).

Films: Dozens of screenplays from *Three Girls Lost* (1931) to *Khyber Pass* (1966), some of which were not produced.

Sources: Balk 100–101, 175, 176–177, 192; Buxton & Owen p. 121, 130, 148, 211, 217, 226, 234; Cox *Great Radio Soap Operas* p. 15, 77, 81, 111, 113; Cox *Radio Factory* p. 45, 82, 85, 86, 88, 90, 100–101; Grams *The Shadow* p. 53–54; Harmon *The Great Radio Heroes* p. 196; *Broadcasting* July 15, 193, p. 46, August 22 1960; *Hollywood* November 1935 p. 39; *Motion Picture Herald* November 23, 1935, p. 64; *Variety* May 4, 1938, p. 29, February 18, 1942, p. 6; *The Hartford Courant* July 24, 1949, p. D8; *The Los Angeles Times* April 11, 1950, p. B3.

Angel, Buckley

Buckley Angel was the writer and director along with **Joel Murcott** for *The Adventures of Frank Race*, a syndicated program that ran in different areas from 1949 to 1952. Between 1950 and 1951 Angel contributed scripts to another syndicate series, *Hopalong Cassidy*, featuring William Boyd. He had a handful of scripts broadcast in the late 1940s but *Frank Race* and *Hopalong Cassidy* were his two most notable assignments in radio. Angel is crediting with writing some scripts that were the basis for the *Mystery Harbor* television series in 1956, though it is not clear if the series was ever aired.

Radio: *The Whistler* (1946); *Suspense* (1948).
Film: *The Devil and the Deep Six* (1957).
Plays: *Tobago* (1960).
Sources: Cox *Radio Crime Fighters* p. 132–134; Grams *Suspense*; *The Los Angeles Times* February 14, 1956, p. B6, April 23, 1957, p. C5, August 10, 1960, p. 23.

Arent, Arthur

Recipient of a Guggenheim Fellowship in 1938, Arthur Arent (September 29, 1904–May 18, 1972) wrote a number of plays for the Federal Theatre Project in the late 1930s. Throughout the 1940s and early 1950s Arent penned more than 30 episodes of DuPont's *Cavalcade of America* series and more than a dozen episodes of United States Steel's *Theatre Guild on the Air*. He is credited with contributing at least two scripts to *The Eternal Light* and in 1947 Arent was hired to write a script for an anti-syphilis transcribed series directed by **Erik Barnouw**.

Television: *The United States Steel Hour* (1953–1955); *General Electric Theater* (1956); *Matinee Theatre* (1957); *Suspicion* (1958).

Books: *Gravedigger's Funeral* (1969); *The Laying on of Hands* (1970).

Theater: Writer and managing editor for the Federal Theatre Project's *The Living Newspaper* series of plays: *Ethiopia* (1935, never publicly performed); *Triple-A Plowed Under* (1936, one of 15 contributors); *Injunction Granted* (1936, one of 15 contributors); *Power* (1937); *Pins and Needles* (1937, book); *One Third of a Nation* (1938); *It's Up to You* (1943), a patriotic piece written in cooperation with the Food Distribution Administration of the U.S. Department of Agriculture.

Sources: Arthur Arent; Isaac; Segal; *The Film Daily* April 1, 1943, p. 4; *Variety* July 25, 1945, p. 36, December 17, 1947, p. 39, September 8, 1948; *New York Herald Tribune* April 4, 1938, p. 9; John Simon Guggenheim Memorial Foundation website.

Arthur, Robert A., Jr.

Robert Arthur (November 10, 1909–May 2, 1969) was an award-winning radio scriptwriter who specialized in mysteries. Philippines-born and a graduate of the University of Michigan, Arthur wrote many mystery stories during the 1930s that appeared in the era's pulp magazines such as *Amazing Stories*, *Black Mask*, and *The Shadow*.

A 1940 course on radio writing introduced Arthur to the medium and he kept busy writing stories for various series during the 1940s. In that class he met **David Kogan** who would become his writing partner for many years. Arthur's biggest contribution to classic radio was the creation of *The Mysterious Traveler* (1944–1953) for which he also wrote many episodes. The series won the 1953 Edgar Allen Poe Award for Best Radio Drama (with Kogan) and received two additional nominations in 1949 and 1951. Arthur and Kogan first won the award in 1950 with their series *Murder by Experts* (1949–1951). He also contributed to classic chiller shows *The Sealed Book* (which he created with Kogan in 1945), *The Shadow*, and *The Strange Dr. Weird* (1944–1945). Arthur's busy radio career came to a quick end in the early 1950s due to his association with the Radio Writers Guild, which came under suspicion during the Red Scare.

With his sudden departure from radio drama in the 1950s, Arthur turned to books as an outlet for his stories. He created the children's series *Alfred Hitchcock and the Three Investigators* and wrote ten of the first eleven volumes between 1964 and 1969. A total of 43 books appeared in the series, the rest written by other authors though Arthur outlined ideas for a few of them. During the 1960s he also wrote more than a dozen collections of short stories published under the Alfred Hitchcock moniker.

Radio: *Just Five Lines* (ca. 1943); *Nick Carter, Master Detective* (ca. 1944), *Appointment With Life* (editor, ca. 1944); *Kate Smith Show* (ca. 1946); *ABC Mystery Time* (1957); *Suspense* (1960–1962); *Theatre Five* (1965).

Sources: *Broadcasting* June 5, 1944, p. 48, November 5, 1945, p. 56; *Radio Mirror* August 1943 p. 36; *Variety* October 9, 1946, p. 52, elizabetharthur.org; The Mystery Writers of America.

Ascot, Rita

Actress Rita Ascot is credited with scripting at least one series during radio's Golden Age, *Meet Your Navy* (1943).

Source: *Variety* July 14, 1943, p. 82.

Ashkenazy, Irwin (also Irvin, Ashkenazie)

Irwin Ashkenazy (December 31, 1910–December 19, 1982) was born in New York City but claimed to have spent some of his childhood in Florida where he played football and even took up boxing which paid his way through college. In the early 1930s he reportedly fought a heavyweight bout at New York's Madison Square Garden. Ashkenazy worked as an actor as well as writer, his scripts appearing on radio as early as 1934 on broadcasts featuring Phil Harris. After some time with the J. Walter Thompson agency Ashkenzay took a job on WLW's continuity staff. Some of his later script writing credits include *Curtain Time* (1947), *The First Nighter Program* (1948), *Hopalong Cassidy* (1949), and *Night Beat* (1950–1952). Though he did some television writing in the early 1950s, Ashkenazy spent the rest of his show business career as an actor.

Other Radio: *The Saint*; *Your Movietown Radio Theatre*.

Sources: Barer; *Variety* June 19, 1934, p. 58, September 25, 1934, p. 42.

Ashman, Jane

Jane Ashman's earliest known years in radio were spent writing *Women in the Making of America* and *Gallant American Women* (1939–1940) for the WPA and U.S. Office of Education with Eva Hansl. She's credited with another network broadcast, "Americans All, Immigrants All" in 1939. Later, during World War II Ashman wrote a number of episodes for a government-sponsored program called *Consumer Time* (1942–1943) which included episodes on topics such as "Shoes," "Food Conservation," and "School Lunches."

Through the 1940s Ashman worked for the NBC and Mutual networks before moving into television at the end of the decade. She attempted some freelance writing for *Good Neighbors* (1948) and *Stand by for Crime* (1949), the latter of which was described as having "stilted lines" and an "implausible murder solution." In 1949 Ashman teamed up with Ralph Ferrin to create Ashman-Ferrin Productions, a Chicago-based television production company that did not leave much of an imprint on the burgeoning industry.

Radio: *Du Barry Success Magazine* (ca. 1945).
Plays: *Congo Square* (1947, with Joy Scott and Tom Scott)
Sources: Hyatt, p. 10; Rouse; Westkaemper; *Billboard* June 4, 1949, p. 14; *Variety* February 28, 1945, p. 36, March 9, 1949.

Atkins, Violet

The obscure writer Violet Atkins is primarily known for his scripts contributed to *Treasury Star Parade*, broadcast in support of the war effort. He is known to have produced some works with Margaret Lee under the pseudonym Lee Atkins.

Books: *If This Be My Harvest* (1949).
Television: *Cataline Swim* (1956, with Lee Perenchio).
Film: Was involved in Howard Hawks' *Battle Cry* that was ultimately axed before it got too far into production.
Sources: McCarthy p. 353–357; Wertheim p. 190.

Auerbach, Arnold

Arnold M. Auerbach (May 23, 1912–October 19, 1988) started writing while a student at Columbia University and early on met **Herman Wouk** with whom he would collaborate on a number of projects. To earn some money early in his writing career, Auerbach and Wouk worked for **David Freedman**, a radio comedian writer. This experience led them to submit material to **Fred Allen**, one of the premier radio comedians in the late 1930s. Allen liked their comedy and hired the pair to write for his weekly program from 1936 to 1941.

The outbreak of war led Auerbach to leave Allen's show and enlist in the armed forces where he continued to write material produced to entertain the troops. He spent the years immediately after the war working on some Broadway musical revues, including *Call Me Mister, Inside U.S.A.,* and *Bless You All.* Initially popular, the revue genre was declining by 1950 so Auerbach turned his attention to television.

During his years in television Auerbach wrote for some of the premier entertainers in the field including Milton Berle, Al Jolson, Frank Sinatra, and Phil Silvers. His broadcasting career was capped with a 1956 Emmy Award for Best Comedy Writing on *The Phil Silvers Show*.

Looking back on writing for radio, especially comedy, Auerbach commented that "freshness and enthusiasm inevitably wane; formulas resurface; set patterns emerge." The amount of jokes and humorous material required for a weekly show—especially an hour-long program as in Allen's case—was monumental.

Books: *Funny Men Don't Laugh* (1965, memoir); *Is That Your Best Offer?* (1971).
Sources: Adir p. 44–45; Allen *Treadmill* p. 70–71; Auerbach; Havig p. 86; Nachman; Taylor p. 256–260; *Broadcasting-Telecasting* March 26, 1956, p. 111; *Radio Mirror* November 1938 p. 64; *Variety* January 2, 1946, p. 42, April 17, 1946, p. 69, April 28, 1948, p. 59; emmys.com.

Ayers, Stuart

Stuart Ayers was a New York writer who dabbled in radio in the late 1920s and increasingly found more work in the industry through the 1930s, first on serials such as *Stella Dallas* (1937–1938) but later on more serious programming such as *The American School of the Air* (1938–1940).

Sources: *Broadcasting* January 15, 1940, p. 56; *Variety* January 25, 1939, p. 26.

Bacher, William A.

Known primarily in radio for his work as one of the field's highest paid producers, Bacher did some writing upon entering broadcasting in the very early 1930s. His writing credits include *The Maltine Story Hour* (1930–1931), *Melody Lane* (1931), *Radio Minstrel Tales* (1931), and *Showboat* (ca. 1932).

Source: Barbas p. 186.

Backus, Georgia

Remembered more for her radio acting and role in *Citizen Kane*, Georgia Backus (October 13, 1901–September 7, 1983) did some writing early in her career. Originally a stage actress, Backus would do some writing to pay the bills and this led to a position with WABC of the CBS chain in 1930. She started off as a continuity writer and was soon given the opportunity to write, direct, and perform in a number of dramatic programs. Backus' writing responsibilities in these early days included *Dusty Pages* (1930), *Romantic Ancestors* (1930), *Ward Tip Top Club* (1930), and *Joe Palooka* (1932).

Around 1932 Backus left CBS to pursue freelance opportunities including starting Radio Events, Inc., with Joseph Koehler, a company that provided a number of services to radio stations, including scripts. Backus married **Hi Alexander**, a fellow radio writer, in 1935. In the 1940s Backus moved into motion pictures but her performing career fizzled when she was forced to appear as a hostile witness before the House Un-American Activities Committee.

Radio: *Mardi Gras* (1930); *Nocturnes* (1932); *Manhattan Matinee* (1935); "Lefty Peroni" (1938), radio play for the Federal Theatre Project; *This Is My Story* (ca. 1943).

Theater: *Absolutely Free* (1934, with Gladys Shaw Erskine); *Laughing Moon* (1934); *Speak of the Devil* (1934, with Hi Alexander).

Sources: *Broadcasting* July 5, 1940, p. 56; *Radio Digest* March 1930, p. 60; *Radio Mirror* March 1936 p. 79; *Radio Revue* February 1930 p. 37; *What's on the Air?* April 1930 p. 20; July 1930 p. 34.

Bagni (Dubov), Gwen

Gwen Bagni (January 24, 1913–May 13, 2001) had a fifty-year career writing for radio, television, and film. Dubov grew up in a family of vaudeville performers and she herself entered the writing end of show business in the late 1930s in Hollywood. A decade later she transitioned to radio where, with husband **John Bagni**, she co-wrote scripts for *Escape, Family Theatre, Night Beat, The Silent Men,* and *Suspense*. She moved to writing for television in 1950 (while continuing to collaborate on screenplays), still with her husband, a medium for which she would write until 1987. Bagni even returned to radio briefly in the early 1970s on *Hollywood Radio Theatre*, one of a few new drama programs developed to take advantage of the radio nostalgia boom that lasted through the mid–1970s. Notable television series that used her stories included *Leave It to Beaver, The Brady Bunch*, and *Eight Is Enough*. In 1953 she and her husband received the Screen Writers Guild award for Best Written Teleplay with their script "The Last Voyage." With subsequent remarriages she was also known as Gwen Bagni Gielgud and Gwen Bagni Dubov.

Film: *Captain China* (1950, with Lewis R. Foster); *Untamed Frontier* (1952, with John Bagni and Gerald Drayson Adams); *The Last Wagon* (1956, with James Edward Grant and Delmer Daves).

Sources: Gwen Bagni Papers; *Broadcasting-Telecasting* February 22, 1954, p. 86; *Film Bulletin* December 17, 1956, p. 2; *Motion Picture Daily* July 18, 1952, February 26, 1954, p. 2; *Showmen's Trade Review* November 5, 1949, p. 23.

Bagni, John

John Bagni (born December 24, 1910) was a career actor, appearing in dozens of motion pictures and serials from the mid–1930s to 1950. At the end of the 1940s Bagni tried his hand at writing radio scripts and with his wife **Gwen Bagni** wrote for some of the era's most prominent dramas including *Escape, Family Theatre, Night Beat, The Silent Men* and *Suspense*. Bagni moved smoothly into television beginning in 1950 where he and his wife won the first Best Written Teleplay award given by the Screen Writers Guild in 1953 for their piece "The Last Voyage." Bagni died on February 13, 1954, at the age of 43 from a heart attack.

Television: *Fireside Theatre; Four Star Playhouse; Hollywood Half Hour.*

Sources: *Broadcasting-Telecasting* February 22, 1954, p. 86; *Motion Picture Daily* February 26, 1954, p. 2.

Bailey, Harry

Harry Bailey's earliest known writing work was the serial *What's in a Name?* on which he replaced **Milton Geiger** and he also wrote for Ben Bernie during the early 1940s. During the war Bailey joined the radio division of the Office of War Information in Washington in the summer of 1943 and soon after provided scripts for *Men at Sea* (NBC). Additional war-time work included a program that promoted the Third War Loan with **Arch Oboler**, **Don Quinn**, and **Carroll Carroll**. After the war Bailey joined **Fred Allen**'s writing staff.

Radio: *Double Or Nothing*.
Sources: Everitt p. 209; *Broadcasting* September 6, 1943, p. 14; *Variety* October 22, 1941, July 7, 1943, p. 38, July 21, 1943, p. 34, October 8, 1947, p. 25.

Ballard, Aline

Aline Ballard's most active writing period seems to have been the mid-to-late 1930s. Her work in radio was with serials and these included *Kay Fairchild, Stepmother* (1938–1942), *The Trouble With Marriage*, and *Grandma Beale's Story*. *Trouble* was a daily soap opera that debuted on July 31, 1939, sponsored by Procter & Gamble for their Oxydol cleaning product. The cast included Mary Patton, Stanley Harris, Frances Dale, Janet Logan, and Burton Wright. *Grandma Beale* (ca. 1939) may have been the same series as *Grandma Travels* (ca. 1939), another show for which Ballard wrote. Ballard also is known to have published stories in pulp magazines such as *Love Story Magazine* and in various newspapers.

Theater: *Travel Is So Broadening* (1937).
Television: *Heroines of the Santa Fe* (1963).
Sources: Street & Smith Papers; Cox *A to Z* p. 120; *Motion Picture Daily* July 18, 1939, p. 8; *Variety* May 10, 1939, p. 37, November 1, 1939; *Abilene Reporter-News* September 10, 1939, p. 9; *Boston Daily Globe* April 10, 1936, p. 37.

Balzer, George

George Balzer (September 1, 1915–September 28, 2006) cemented his spot in radio history as one of Jack Benny's primary writers for a quarter of a century on both radio and television. His father moved the family to California somewhat on a whim in 1920. As a young man Balzer fell ill and lying in bed for an extended time forced him to listen to radio to an extent he'd never done before. Just for fun, he wrote a couple scripts for Jack Benny's program.

Balzer later broke into radio writing for Bob Burn's spot on *Kraft Music Hall* featuring Bing Crosby and followed that with a stint on *The Burns & Allen Show* (ca. 1941) during which he was teamed with his mentor, **Sam Perrin**. During the summer of 1942 Balzer and Perrin worked on *Tommy Riggs and Betty Lou*, a summer replacement series for *The Burns & Allen Show*.

In September 1943 Balzer went to work on Jack Benny's writing team. Recalling the 25 years for which he wrote for Benny, Balzer simply said "They weren't long enough." Balzer only took one notable hiatus from Benny's program when he and Perrin (also then working for Benny) wrote the book for the Broadway musical *Are You With It?* that ran from 1945–1946. After that point, Balzer worked strictly for Benny. Balzer's work was recognized in 1959 when he won an Emmy for Outstanding Writing Achievement in Comedy for *The Jack Benny Program*; he received five additional nominations for his work on the same show. Balzer's post–Benny television credits included writing for Red Skelton and Lucile Ball.

Sources: Fein p. 192; Mott p. 101; Wertheim p. 314; Young; *Broadcasting* September 20, 1943, p. 36; *Variety* September 17, 1941, p. 44, June 24, 1942, p. 28, Interview excerpts; emmys.com.

Bannister, Albert

Writer Albert Bannister took over scripting duties on *Mary Noble, Backstage Wife* in 1942. In 1951 he was charged with writing the television series *Mickey Finn*.

Sources: *Broadcasting* July 9, 1951, p. 67; *Variety* December 2, 1942, p. 33, April 4, 1945, p. 26.

Barker, Al (Albert)

Al Barker began writing for the stage and radio about the same time, around 1933. His earliest efforts appear to be freelance scripts used on *Story Behind the Story* (1933) and *Grand Hotel* (1934–1935). In 1935 Barker was hired by NBC's Chicago outlet WENR as a continuity writer and subsequently created a serial, *Shoestring Castle* (ca. 1935), and *Hector in Hollywood* (ca. 1936) with Gayle Gitterman.

Beginning in 1937 Barker brought the juvenile serial *Don Winslow of the Navy*, based on Frank Martinek's comic strip, to the airwaves along with Martinek. He was behind at least one other NBC-Blue feature, *1001 Wives* (1939). After five years with NBC Barker resigned in 1940 to write for New York–based Transamerican Broadcasting & Television Corp. There he continued to write *Don Winslow* and also added *Little Orphan Annie* and *Terry and the Pirates* to his weekly duties.

In the summer of 1942 while his three juvenile shows were on hiatus, Barker took over as script supervisor for the Transamerican-produced *Famous Jury Trials*. That summer he also took over writing responsibilities for *Kitty Foyle* with **Doris Halman**. Later in September he created *Commandos* with George Harmon Coxe, a show of "pure adventure" but that "lacked a pervading theme." *Commandos* was Barker's last series with Transamerican; he quit soon after to try a freelance career. Transamerican desperately wanted him to stay, and even offered a raise so he would continue to write *Don Winslow of the Navy*, but after five years Barker was done with that show.

When Transamerican colleague Pete Jaeger quit and went to work for the NBC-Blue network in early 1943, he took *Terry and the Pirates* with him, having brokered the original deal gaining rights from the Tribune syndicate for a radio version. Barker, having written the serial for some time, quickly agreed to follow Jaeger. Later that year he agreed to begin scripting *Mystery Time*.

The next year, 1944, Barker began to focus more on his own creations. While maintaining steady income writing *Terry and the Pirates*, he dropped *Kitty Foyle* to develop two original series, *King's Row* and *It Could Happen to You*. *King's Row* was based on Henry Bellaman's novel of the same name and both spec series were developed with Harry Hoff. The partners planned to offer both series in either 15-minute daily episodes or 30-minute single episode formats.

Radio: *NBC Minstrels of 1938.*
Theater: *The Dark Goes Mad* (1933); *Finesse* (1934); *Portrait by Proxy* (1934); *Ladies in Linen* (1935); *American Holiday* (1936) produced by the Federal Popular Priced Theater in New York; *Overnight* (1940).
Sources: Cox *A to Z* p. 122; Vermazen p. 276; *Broadcasting* February 15, 1935, p. 20, September 1, 1935, p. 36, January 1, 1936, p. 18, March 1, 1936, p. 22, May 15, 1939, p. 32, February 1, 1940, p. 54, March 1, 1940, p. 50, January 11, 1943, p. 20; *Variety* April 15, 1942, p. 28, May 27, 1942, p. 27, September 23, 1942, p. 25, September 30, 1942, p. 38, January 13, 1943, p. 31, May 12, 1943, p. 40, June 30, 1943, p. 32, February 2, 1944, p. 30.

Barley, Ann

Ann Barley was originally from Detroit but a writing career took her around the United States and to war-torn Europe. One of her first jobs was reporting for the *The Daily News* (Miami, FL) and then later for *Time* magazine. Her supervisors at *Time* called her back from Madrid in 1935 to begin writing broadcasts for their *March of Time* series. Barley soon began writing radio scripts as a freelancer and had two of them aired on the prestigious *Cavalcade of America* program (1935–1936).

By 1940 Barley was writing regularly for the serial *Pursuit of Happiness*. The next year, 1941, she was hired by Transamerica to co-write another soap opera, *As the Twig Is Bent*, with **Don Becker** and she stayed with the series even after it transitioned to *We Love and Learn*. Barley contributed regularly to *Armstrong Theatre of Today* (1942) and concurrently served on the Eastern Regional Council of the Radio Writers' Guild. When the United States entered World War II Barley joined the War Department in the public relations branch of the industrial production division where she produced *Women Shoulder Arms*, a series of interviews between female war workers and soldiers. She won a Distinguished Service Medal for her war programming direction.

After the war Barley adopted two French children and raised them as a single mother in the Washington area and later wrote a book about the experience, *Patrick Calls Me Mother*.

Radio: *We the People.*
Sources: *The Radio Annual* 1942 p. 959; *Radio and Television Mirror* June 1942 p. 12; *Variety* July 17, 1935,

p. 67, March 12, 1941, p. 33, May 20, 1942, p. 30, September 2, 1942, p. 36; *Lewiston Daily Sun* April 19, 1946, p. 3; *New York Herald Tribune* November 2, 1944, p. 5, April 12, 1948, p. 15.

Barnes, Beth

A University of Alabama graduate, Beth Barnes joined the continuity staff of WSB, Atlanta, in 1942. There she immediately jumped into producing programming to support the growing war effort. Barnes wrote and produced *You Wanna Fight? Here's How*, a show illustrating how citizens can support the war effort. She was also responsible for *United We Fight! United We Give!*. In 1943 Barnes' title at WSB was Director of War Programs and the next year she had advanced to Production Manager. While at WSB Barnes was also responsible for *The Quartermaster Quarter-Hour*, which was based on material from the War Department. She also created original dramas while in Atlanta including *Foster's Corner*, a melodrama about a small-town judge.

In early 1944 Barnes resigned from WSB to go to work for **Arch Oboler** where she assisted with *Everything for the Boys*. Later that same year she was hired by CBS' Hollywood continuity office at KNX along with **E. Jack Neuman**. Over the next few years Barnes wrote for a number of West Coast series including *The City* on CBS' Pacific network (1947), *The Whistler* (1948), and *Family Theatre* (1948, 1949). For several years Barnes was one of the writers with **Karl Schlichter** for *California Caravan*, a West-Coast anthology series (1947–1950).

Sources: *Broadcasting* July 13, 1942, p. 41, August 10, 1942, p. 28, February 14, 1944, p. 46, July 17, 1944, p. 44; *Broadcasting-Telecasting* February 20, 1950, p. 47; *The Radio Annual* 1943 p. 392, 1944 p. 399; *Radio Life* March 30, 1947, p. 10; *Variety* January 6, 1943, p. 102, September 8, 1943, p. 28, December 8, 1943, p. 28.

Barnes, Forrest

Forrest Barnes entered radio as early as 1932 when he started working as writer and announcer for *Famous Operas* over KMPC in Beverly Hills. A program he started as a sustainer on KMPC, *American Paradise*, moved in 1934 to KFWB under the sponsorship of the Alberta Food Co. By 1936 Barnes had moved to KFI-KECA as the continuity editor and there he began dabbling in motion pictures with some shorts for Warner Bros.

Barnes debuted his *Great Gunns* series over KFI in mid–1936, the story of a fictional theater family named the Gunns. This series would find success over several years, being bought for Australian distribution in 1939 and later appearing on the Mutual network starting in the summer of 1941. This Chicago-based version featured such classic performers as Bret Morrison and Barbara Luddy.

Other 1936 writing credits included his series *The Barnstormers* and some scripts for *The First Nighter Program*, a series that solicited freelance stories. Barnes had at least two new programs in 1937, *Streamlined Shakespeare* (a NBC-Blue summer series starring John Barrymore) and *Thrills*, a 30-minute show for Union Oil Co. That year he also joined Principal Productions' Radio Dept. along with *Rise of the Goldbergs*' creator **Gertrude Berg**.

As an American Radio Features staff writer in 1938 Barnes wrote *That's Life*, a dramatic transcribed series, and he also started a writing partnership with Robert Lewis of the H. N. Swanson agency. At the end of the decade Barnes became heavily involved in the Western division of the Radio Writers Guild, a writers union that broke away from the American Federation of Radio Artists. He was elected region president in 1939 and then national president in 1940.

Barnes scripted a number of series through the 1940s including *Once Upon a Midnight*, a series of Edgar Allen Poe adaptations for KECA (1940), and *Promoting Priscilla*, a summer replacement series for Jergens Co., featuring Jim Ameche and Gale Page (1940). After **Ted Maxwell** left the West Coast for Chicago, Barnes took over writing duties for *Hawthorne House* in 1940 and then originated another program, *Alias John Freedom*, in 1942. The show was initially carried over San Francisco's KPO, the station to which Barnes was transferred when NBC split the Red and Blue networks. *Alias John Freedom* was criticized in the media for being overly violent.

During World War II Barnes wrote for *The Man Behind the Gun* (1942–1944) as well as some *Treasury Salute* broadcasts. After the war he went to work collaborating with **True Boardman** and **Artie Philips** writing *The Adventures of Maisie* scripts.

Radio: *The Silver Theatre* (1938); *Texaco Star Theatre* (1938); *Suspense* (1951).

Film: *Western Gold* (1937)

Sources: *Broadcasting* November 15, 1934, p. 22, April 15, 1936, p. 44, November 1, 1936, p. 72, December 1, 1936, p. 28 July 1, 1937, p. 36, May 15, 1938, p. 36, April 1, 1939, p. 57, April 1, 1940, p. 75, July 1, 1940, p. 17, February 2, 1942, p. 50, February 9, 1942, p. 54; *Broadcasting-Telecasting* December 10, 1945, p. 95; *Motion Picture Daily* April 13, 1937, p. 12, May 21, 1937, p. 9; *Variety* February 13, 1934, p. 37, February 12, 1936, p. 50, May 25, 1938, p. 34, September 11, 1940, p. 26, April 29, 1942, p. 37.

Barnes, Howard McKent

Howard McKent Barnes was born in Baltimore in the mid–1880s and was a busy actor until a spine injury forced him to turn to writing. He wrote and saw many of his plays produced during the 19-teens and 1920s and in 1929 moved to Chicago. In the late 1930s Barnes tried his hand penning a few radio scripts for series such as *Curtain Time* (ca. 1937), *Way Down Home* (1937–1938, also called *Back Home*) dramatizing the life of James Whitcomb Riley, and *Wings of Dawn* (1937). He was working on a religious program, *Club Time*, sponsored by Club Aluminum Products Co. but the 61-year-old Barnes died of a heart attack October 19, 1945, before his first script for the series ever aired.

Sources: *Variety* September 29, 1937, p. 39, October 24, 1945, p. 45; *The Washington Post* September 26, 1937, p. A5.

Barnett, Sanford (Sandy)

Sanford Barnett had a long run in radio as an employee of the J. Walter Thompson Co., nearly twenty years. Almost all of that time was devoted to *Lux Radio Theater*, one of the most revered programs in the Golden Age of radio. From its premier in the mid–1930s Barnett worked as the director for the show's weekly adaptations of Broadway productions early in its run and then Hollywood films for most of its duration.

With his directing responsibilities Barnett also frequently wrote the interview portion of each episode involving the week's big name movie stars. At the end of 1943 the series' primary adaptor, **George Wells**, left to write screenplays for MGM. Barnett was removed from the director's position and assigned to be the new adaptor, a job he held until the end of the show's radio run in 1955. When *Lux Video Theatre* was created for television Barnett also took on those writing duties.

Barnett's only other identified radio writing was for *The Fleischmann's Yeast Hour* (ca. 1935) and then a later Fleischmann's 1937 summer program.

Sources: *Broadcasting* October 15, 1938, p. 56, December 27, 1943, p. 40; *Broadcasting-Telecasting* October 24, 1955, p. 36; *Motion Picture Daily* April 9, 1937, p. 14; *Radio Mirror* June 1939 p. 43; *Variety* July 7, 1937, p. 35.

Barnouw, Erik

Erik Barnouw (June 23, 1908–July 19, 2001) graduated from Princeton in 1930 and, with no other stronger job prospects, moved into radio after a trip abroad. This first position was with the Erwin, Wasey Agency working with the Camel Cigarettes account as a radio program director. Production and direction work kept Barnouw busy for the next several years, during which time he was connected with such programs as *Bobby Benson of the H-Bar-O Ranch*, *Camel Quarter Hour*, *Forum of Liberty*, and *True Story's Court of Human Relations*. Between 1939 and 1940 Barnouw wrote for *The Pursuit of Happiness* one of **Norman Corwin's** early directing efforts, a celebration of American heritage.

Throughout the 1940s Barnouw did a considerable amount of freelance writing and his work appeared on numerous episodes of *Cavalcade of America*, *The Radio Edition of the Bible* (1945–1946), *Theatre Guild on the Air* (1946–1953), and *VD Radio Project* (1948). From 1942 to 1944 Barnouw worked as a script editor for NBC and then moved to working with the Armed Forces Radio Service from 1944–1946. In 1946 he became a professor at Columbia University where he had been teaching radio writing courses since the 1930s.

Despite a notable career in radio, Barnouw is most widely remembered among radio enthusiasts today for his three-volume work detailing the history of radio and early television. Published between 1966 and 1970, *A History of Broadcasting in the United States* was one of the first comprehensive histories of the medium and continues to serve as one of the foundational references in the field fifty years after the publication of the first volume.

Sources: *Variety* February 9, 1944, p. 39, February 23, 1944, p. 28, May 30, 1945, p. 31, 34, 38.

Barry, Peter

Peter Barry was an actor in his younger days in New York with little success. Tired of lending Barry money, Martin Gabel suggested he try writing, which Barry did. One of his earliest known assignments was none other than *The Shadow*, which he co-wrote with **Sidney Slon** during the 1941–1942 season. Soon after, he contributed a number of scripts to *Suspense* between 1942 and 1944.

Barry wrote for a number of series throughout the 1940s, none of them particularly popular then or now. Among these programs was *The Gertrude Lawrence Theatre* (1943), *The Eddie Garr Revue* (1944, with Dave Schwartz), *Listen Carefully* (1946), *Love Story Theatre* with Jim Ameche, *Scotland Yard* (1947), *The Falcon* (ca. 1947), and *Exploring the Unknown* (ca. 1947). *Listen Carefully* had a unique concept, presenting different short mysteries over the course of a single program that studio audience members were then called upon to help solve.

While Barry continued to contribute the occasional script to *The Shadow* in the mid–1940s, he returned with much more regularity in 1947 through the 1950 season. One of his primary assignments during the late 1940s was *Call the Police*, a series which served as a summer replacement for *Amos 'n' Andy* and *Fibber McGee & Molly* for three seasons from 1947 to 1949. It never moved beyond a summer series, however, leaving Barry free to write for other series during the regular program season.

In the early 1950s Barry was behind two private investigator series, *The Big Guy* (1950) and "the uninspired" *Charlie Wild, Private Detective* (1950). The latter took over the air time of *The Adventures of Sam Spade*, a series that eventually left the air because of alleged associations between Spade creator Dashiell Hammett and leading actor Howard Duff and Communist organizations. Barry had at least one other radio foray in 1954 with a new series called *Decision!* over ABC.

Barry successfully transitioned into television beginning in the late 1940s with such series as Procter & Gamble's *Fireside Theatre*. Radio's *Charlie Wild, Private Detective* also appeared on the small screen in 1951.

Theater: *Lamp This* (1938, musical comedy with Hume Cronyn).

Sources: Cox *Crime Fighters* p. 47, 65; Grams *Shadow* p. 171–173; *Billboard* August 9, 1947, p. 14, 15, January 6, 1951, p. 6; *Broadcasting-Telecasting* January 18, 1954, p. 16; *Variety* December 7, 1938, p. 53, September 15, 1943, p. 34; June 21, 1944, p. 34, September 11, 1946, p. 37, October 2, 1946, p. 40, March 19, 1947, p. 36, June 11, 1947, p. 38, March 30, 1949, p. 26.

Barth, Ruth

Ruth Barth was one of several radio professionals to develop at Kansas City's KMBC and move on to bigger radio opportunities. Barth, who eventually married fellow KMBC alum **Paul Henning**, did more acting than writing but nevertheless earned credit writing for some of radio's most recognizable series.

While employed as a continuity writer for NBC in the late 1930s Barth contributed to *The March of Time* and *Cavalcade of America*. Barth's *Cavalcade* script was chosen by Norman Weiser as one of the top ten scripts of the year and republished in book form. Other shows for which Barth wrote in the 1940s were *The Bell Telephone Hour* (ca. 1942), *We, the People, at War* (ca. 1944), *I Know the Enemy* (ca. 1945), and a United States Treasury Department series in 1946.

Sources: *Broadcasting* January 15, 1939, November 10, 1941, p. 32 p. 48; *Variety* October 27, 1937, p. 54, May 13, 1942, p. 37, April 19, 1944, p. 23, March 21, 1945, p. 31, May 22, 1946, p. 23.

Bassett, John

John Bassett has three confirmed radio writing credits to his name, all dating from 1942–1943. His work appeared on *Murder Clinic* (1942–1943), *Stories America Loves* (ca. 1942), and the serial *Kitty Foyle* until July 1943.

Sources: *Billboard* February 20, 1943, p. 6; *Variety* March 18, 1942, p. 34, June 30, 1943, p. 32

Bates (Gunderson), Barbara

Not to be confused with the film actress of the same name, Barbara Bates (March 28, 1917–July 29, 2007) the writer left her job as a journalist with the *Yankee Press & Dakotan* to write continuity for Yankton, SD's WNAX. There she wrote the continuity for *Ma Brown* sponsored by Occident Flour. She also worked at Omaha's WOW and Rapid City, SD's KOTA. Around 1940 Bates took a job as a radio copywriter for Kansas City's R. J. Potts-Calkins-Holden agency. Bates was a writer for the Hummert's Air Features, where she wrote for *Just Plain Bill* and *Mr. Keen, Tracer of Lost Persons*. After her husband, Robert Gunderson, returned from the service in 1946 Bates stepped away from radio but continued to write articles and even a couple books over the subsequent years. Western Dakota Technical Institute in Rapid City, SD, bears a scholarship named after Bates.

Sources: Cox *Mr. Keen* p. 59; *Broadcasting* May 1, 1939, p. 42, *The Radio Annual* 1944 p. 825; *WOW News Tower* December 1, 1943, p. 3, January 1, 1946, p. 5.

Battle, John Tucker

Texas-native John Battle (October 1, 1902–October 30, 1962) was a busy radio writer and actor in the early 1930s when he wrote and appeared on *Triple Bar X Days and Nights* (ca. 1933), *Roses and Drums* (ca. 1933), and *Tydol Jubilee* (c. 1933). In one interview Battle stated he preferred writing over acting but didn't find a lot of satisfaction in either because even a masterpiece was forgotten soon after it broadcast, never to be heard again. Battle wrote *H-Bar-O Rangers* from 1934 to 1935, one of a number of titles under which the Bobby Benson Western series aired. Battle contributed to Rudy Vallee's program (ca. 1936) and in 1937 he penned *Follow the Moon* for Andrew Jergens' lotions.

Battle was still active in radio in the early 1940s, writing *Napoleon was Right* (1942, Blue network), contributing to *Hello, Americans* (1942–1943) and acting on a number of series. Battle wrote a number of screenplays in the 1940s and 1950s and then some television scripts in the late 1950s up until his death in 1962.

Radio: "All God's Children" (1940, CBS, with **John Whedon**); *Forecast* (ca. 1940); *The Mercury Summer Theatre on the Air* (1946).

Sources: Eva Jessye Collection; Orson Welles Materials; Cox *A to Z* p. 82; French & Siegel p. 24; *Broadcasting* August 1, 1940, p. 58, November 9, 1942, p. 43; *Radio Fanfare* July-August 1933, p. 24, 49–50; *Variety* May 29, 1935, p. 38, March 4, 1936, p. 57, September 9, 1942, p. 28.

Baumer, Marie

Marie Baumer (July 6, 1904–July 31, 1977) was a playwright in the 1920s before signing with Paramount in 1930 to do a couple of screenplays. She entered radio writing serials for Frank and Ann Hummert. Baumer was the author of *Young Widder Brown*, *Our Gal Sunday*, *Mary Noble, Backstage Wife*, and *Second Husband* before being assigned to *Stella Dallas*. By 1941 she left *Stella* to replace **Carl Buss** as writer for *Woman of Courage* in October. Baumer moved on from that series in March 1942 and onto other serials such as *Romance of Evelyn Winters* (1945), *Mr. Chameleon* (1948–1951), and *Mr. Keen, Tracer of Lost Persons* (1944–1954). After radio she penned a number of television episodes through the 1950s into the very early 1960s.

Theater: *The Blind Spot* (1929, with George Abbott); *Penny Arcade* (1930).

Film: *Sinners Holiday* (1931).

Sources: Cox *Mr. Keen*; *Variety* October 8, 1941, p. 25, March 18, 1942, p. 30, April 4, 1945, p. 27, July 23, 1948, p. 84; jfredmacdonald.com.

Bearson, Lawrence (Larry)

After writing for the WPA during the Great Depression, Larry Bearson's first known radio scripts were for CBS' *Men Against Death* (1938). He subsequently wrote for *Grand Central Station* and *Theatre of Today* before moving on to the Hummert feature *Young Widder Brown* (1940). During the early 1940s Bearson scripted *Into the Light* (1941–1942) and worked with Elinor Abbey to create *Home Fires* (1942).

Theater: *The Ivory Tower* (1946, with George Wolf).

Film: *No Sense of Guilt* (1949, with George Wolf).

Sources: Cox *A to Z*; *The Columbia Program Book 1938* p. 35; *Billboard* June 20, 1942, p. 7; *Los Angeles Times* October 26, 1949, p. 23; *New York Herald Tribune* January 28, 1946, p. 13A; *Variety Radio Directory* 1940–1941.

Beasley, Irene

Known on radio as the "The Girl From Dixie" as early as 1925, Irene Beasley (1904–1980) was a singer/songwriter originally from Tennessee but who spent much of her childhood in Amarillo and Mississippi. She wrote and performed on a children's series, *Aunt Zelena*, done in black voice from New York between 1932–1933. She is often credited with writing the musical quiz program *Grand Slam* (1946–1953), but it was, in fact, written by **Lillian Schoen**.

Sources: Irene Beasley Papers; *Radio Digest* November 21, 1925, p. 13; *Variety* October 2, 1946, p. 35.

Beattie, Dan (Daniel C.)

Daniel Beattie was in the radio business by the early 1940s as a script editor for Furness-Beattie Radio Productions in Washington, D.C. Among his series for that company was the six-days-weekly *Helen Holden, Government Girl*, part of the Mutual network's midday serial block in 1941. Beattie was contacted at that time by WXYZ's **Fran Striker** who wanted to gauge Beattie's interest in coming to write for the Detroit station. Beattie turned him down and in 1942 moved into an executive position with the U.S. Recording Co. in Washington.

After a trip to Detroit to talk with WXYZ executives Beattie later decided to give them a shot and relocated to begin writing for some of their titles. In 1943 he completed his first *Green Hornet* script and would go on to complete 164 more for the series into the early 1950s. As might be expected, Beattie was put to work writing for all of WXYZ's big three shows, contributing scripts to *The Lone Ranger* as of 1944 and *The Challenge of the Yukon* as of 1945 into the mid–1950s.

With the demise of radio drama Beattie moved into copy editing and worked for some time with Detroit's Ross Roy Inc. before moving to New York's Geyer, Morey, Madden & Ballard Inc.

Theater: *Oh Say! Can't You See?* (1933); *Down to Rio* (1948).

Sources: Grams *Green Hornet*; Levering p. 88; *Broadcasting* November 30, 1942, p. 31; *Broadcasting-Telecasting* January 26, 1959, p. 84; *The Radio Annual*, 1941 p. 657; *Variety* December 3, 1941, p. 42.

Becker, Bob

Bob Becker's formal schooling did not point to a future career in radio; he simply fell into the line of work as so many did in that time. A 1912 graduate of Beloit College, one of Becker's first jobs was with the Field Museum in Chicago. With this institution he made several trips to South America and in the 1920s he began writing about these travels for *The Chicago Tribune*. Becker supplemented these tales with other general stories of outdoor life.

This newspaper work led to appearances on the paper's sister station WGN as early as 1931 in which he adapted his written accounts for the air. The series *To the Land of the Takatu* was filled with tales of strange animals, vegetation, and tribesmen. A year later he aired some of his sports stories and then on October 3, 1932, debuted his first radio serial, *The Devil Bird*. Using his experiences traveling in South America, Becker's adventure program focused on three Boy Scouts and their leader, Grant Dailey, in a search for the mysterious Devil Bird artifact. During the series' initial run most of the parts were played by Paul Fogarty, actor and writer for WGN.

The Devil Bird reached its pinnacle of popularity in 1933. Not only did the station establish a fan club for the program, but it was aired over a small network of regional stations which included WCCO (Minneapolis), KMBC (Kansas City), KMOX (St. Louis), WHAS (Louisville), and KFAB (Lincoln, NE). Additionally, the cast was expanded so that Fogarty was not responsible for all the performing. Success was short-lived, however, and the program left the air in mid–1933.

Later in the decade Becker returned to the air with a radio version of his *Tribune* column about dogs. Known first as *Dog Club of the Air* and later as *Dog Chats*, Becker kept listeners' attention for a number of years in the 1930s and early 1940s with his canine-centered program.

Source: Ellett "From Jungles to Dog Shows."

Becker, Don

Don Becker (d. October 18, 1991) developed his writing skills at Cincinnati's WLW where he had numerous responsibilities, including writing continuity and weekly shows by 1929. Chief among those programs was *Weak-end Satires*, a zany series of sketches that premiered in 1928 over WSAI and often incorporated Becker's ukulele playing. He briefly moved to the NBC network in 1931 but returned to WLW and started writing *Ken-Rad Unsolved Mysteries* in 1933.

Becker provided continuity for any number of WLW features in the mid–1930s including a 1935 musical program sponsored by Headlight and Crown Mfg. Co. and *Famous Jury Trials*, dramatizations of famous historical cases (ca. 1936). Other shows that kept him busy by 1936 were *Little Mother Mag*, *The Life of Mary Sothern*, *Waterfront Wayside*, *For Men Only*, *Smoke Dreams*, *Give 'em the Heat*, and *Loves of Southern Seas*.

In late 1936 Becker left WLW a second time, this time for good. He went to work for Transamerican Radio Corp. writing and producing various series. Among these was *The Life of Mary Sothern*, a series he had been writing since its debut in 1934. In 1938 Becker and co-writer **Carl Bixby** premiered *Life Can Be Beautiful*, a daily serial they would write together until 1954. While with Transamerican he also wrote scripts for *This Day Is Ours* (1938–1940), *The Man I Married* (1939–1942), *Beyond These Valleys* (ca. 1940), and *As the Twig Is Bent* with **Ann Barley** (ca. 1941). For a time Becker added the Biblical drama *Light of the World* to his workload when its original writer **Katharine Seymour** did not renew her contract with Transamerican. Becker departed Transamerican in 1944 when he created his own production company.

Radio: *We Love and Learn*.

Sources: *Broadcasting* January 15, 1933, p. 18; *Radio Digest* October 1929, p. 44; *Radio Mirror* December 1936, p. 68, November 1940 p. 50; *Variety* August 7, 1935, p. 46, April 8, 1936, p. 40, August 12, 1936, p. 43, 44, March 12, 1941, p. 33, March 4, 1942, p. 30, April 15, 1942, p. 28, December 6, 1944, p. 23; *What's on the Air?* June 1931, p. 8.

Beckmark, Peggy

Peggy Beckmark was the writer and lead actress in *Teena and Tim* (also *Tena and Tim* and *Tina and Tim*), comedy skits that were airing locally in Minneapolis as early as 1932 over WCCO. After going off the air for some time, Beckmark revived the series in 1941 on transcription retitled *Life with Tena*. In yet another incarnation *Tena and Tim* was aired over CBS from 1944–1946 as a daily quarter-hour serial.

Sources: *Broadcasting* August 18, 1941, p. 46; *Variety* November 21, 1933, p. 46, August 16, 1944, p. 34.

Beloin, Ed (Edmund)

Ed Beloin (April 1, 1910–May 26, 1992) spent seven years writing for Jack Benny's popular radio program alongside **Bill Morrow** (1936–1943). Beloin was scheduled to be inducted into the Army in 1943 but was rejected on medical grounds. Instead of returning to Benny Beloin moved into motion pictures, an industry he'd been exposed to when contributing material to Jack Benny's films. After writing a number of pictures in the 1940s and 1950s Beloin began authoring teleplays in the 1960s for such shows as *The Lucy Show* and *My Three Sons*. Beloin also got more involved in the production side of television including with the small screen version of the *Thin Man*, based on Dashiell Hammett's Nick and Nora Charles who appeared in just about every media format of the time.

Source: *Variety* June 9, 1943, p. 3.

Benet, Stephen Vincent

Awarded Pulitzer Prizes in 1929 and 1944 (posthumously) and elected a Fellow in the American Academy of Arts and sciences in 1931, Stephen Vincent Benet (July 22, 1898–March 13, 1943) was an accomplished writer who contributed a few scripts to some of radio's prestigious series before passing away at the age of 44. Benet's radio work included stories for *The Columbia Workshop* (1937–1940), *Cavalcade of America*, *The Free Company* (1941), a collaborative effort by a group of writers to counter foreign propaganda, *This Is War!* (1942), aired simultaneously on all four networks, and *Dear Adolph* (1942).

Radio: "Listen to the People" (July 4, 1941).
Source: Grams *Cavalcade*.

Bennett (Shapiro), Jay

Jay Bennett (December 24, 1912–June 27, 2009) had a long writing career that started in radio around 1940 with contributions to *Grand Central Station*. Bennett said later that he wrote over two dozen scripts before his first one was bought. By 1944 he had contributed scripts to more than a dozen different series including *Blue Theatre, Bulldog Drummond, The Falcon, Freedom's Workshop, Green Valley, U.S.A., The Kate Smith Program, Listeners' Playhouse, Manhattan at Midnight, Men, Machines, Victory, Molle Mystery Theatre,* and *National Radio Forum.*

Bennett's most notable accomplishments came as a mystery writer in the 1970s and 1980s, especially in the area of juvenile literature where he won back-to-back Edgar Allen Poe Awards for Best Juvenile Mystery Fiction in 1974 and 1975.

Theater: *Lions After Slumber* (1948).
Television: *The Mono-Drama Theater* (1953); *One Man's Story* (1953).
Sources: Cox *Crime Fighters* p. 32; Drew P. 35–38; *The Radio Annual*, 1944 p. 824; *Billboard* February 14, 1953, p. 11; *Variety* November 27, 1940, p. 29; TheEdgars.com.

Benoff, Mac

Mac Benoff's (Sept. 21, 1915–November 16, 1972) first notable writing job was *Honolulu Bound* with Phil Baker in 1939. From there he soon moved on to writing for Ed Gardner's *Duffy's Tavern* (1941–1943). In 1943 Benoff was writing for Fanny Brice and then beginning in 1946 for *The Mel Blanc Show* (1946–1947). Benoff's most singular work was the story of Luigi Basco on *Life With Luigi* that he scripted from 1948 until 1953 and that he directed as well later in its run. When the television version was created in 1952 Benoff was tabbed to write the scripts.

Radio: *Baby Snooks* (1948); *Sam Pilgrim's Progress* (1949).
Sources: Mac Benoff Papers; *Broadcasting* September 13, 1943, p. 14; *Broadcasting-Telecasting* April 7, 1952, p. 78; *Variety* April 23, 1941, p. 23, March 14, 1945, p. 55.

Bercovici, Leonardo (Leonard)

Leonard Bercovici (January 4, 1908–November 22, 1995) entered radio writing the serial *Billy and Betty* for a short time in 1939 and then co-wrote an early version of *The Life of Riley* with **Bob Sloan** in 1941. Bercovici created and wrote his own series, *Helpmate*, in 1941 and from that show he spun off *Classroom for Democracy* in 1942. Bercovici lost control of *Help Mate* toward the end of 1942 after one year on the air when he refused to modify the content to suit the sponsor's wishes. Bercovici's later years were spent writing screenplays, including Cary Grant's *The Bishop's Wife* (1947) and television programs. His association with the Blacklist derailed a promising Hollywood writing career.

Radio: *Forecast* (1941); *Carnival* (1943); *The Commandos* (1943, with **Sid Slon**).
Theater: *Royal Welcome* (1943).
Sources: *CBS Program Book* 1941 p. 23; *Variety* April 26, 1939, p. 19, July 23, 1941, p. 46, January 7, 1942, p. 120, September 2, 1940, p. 40, October 21, 1942, p. 86, October 28, 1942, p. 31, March 3, 1943, p. 32, April 14, 1943.

Berg, Gertrude

Gertrude (Tillie) Edelstein (October 3, 1898, or 1899–September 14, 1966) was born in Harlem, NY, and had a relatively uneventful early life. She married Lewis Berg when she was 19 and settled into her quiet role as wife and mother. In her freetime she began writing skits that reflected the life of a middle class Jewish woman married to a n'er-do-well. Berg was given the opportunity to appear on New York's WMCA reading a commercial in Yiddish. Building on this, Berg approached CBS with a skit she entitled *Effie and Laura*. They gave it one broadcast then canceled.

Encouraged, Berg wrote a new sketch about a Jewish family and called it *The Rise of the Goldbergs*. It focused on the economic struggles of Jake Goldberg and his family, scratching out an existence in a Bronx tenement. Himan Brown, still an up-and-coming radio personality at the time, claims to have been responsible for getting NBC interested in the series. The network offered Berg a one-month contract and $75 per week. The year was 1929, the United States was entering the Great Depression, and Berg's creation struck a chord with listeners, quickly becoming one of the highest rated shows by 1932. Berg had complete control of the show, directing even seemingly minute details. She knew her characters so well that she reportedly could crank out a script in 30 minutes and even did so in eight minutes when a cast member failed to show up at the broadcasting studio.

The Rise of the Goldbergs went on a hiatus in 1934 so the cast could make personal appearances but Berg returned to the air in 1935 with a new program called *House of Glass*, again using her Jewish childhood as inspiration. Her father had operated a hotel as did the lead character in the serial and that gave Berg plenty of character and story ideas for the fictional hotel. *House of Glass* proved less endearing than the Goldberg family so it was cancelled later in 1935 and Berg brought her original series back to the air in January 1936 as *The Goldbergs*.

At the same time she penned a premier script for *The Ziegfield Follies of the Air* with **Dave Freedman** but while the show went on for a short time, Berg did not continue with the show as writing duties were taken over entirely by the advertising agency. *The Goldbergs* was on the air until 1937 when Berg went to work for Principle Productions writing a screenplay. *The Goldbergs* returned yet again in 1938 and aired until 1945 when the series finally ran out of gas for good. It was briefly revived for radio between 1949 and 1950, largely due to its popularity on television around the same time.

Rise of the Goldbergs was a successful television program, airing 1949–1951. It returned as *Molly* for the 1952–1953 season on NBC, followed by a season on the DuMont network, and then a final season filmed in 1955 and aired in syndication. Berg won the Emmy Award for Best Actress in 1951 for her role on the series. She was later nominated for the 1962 Emmy for Outstanding Continued Performance by an Actress in a Series (Lead) on *The Gertrude Berg Show*.

Radio: *Mama Talks* (1936); *The Fifth Wheel* (1939)

Sources: *Broadcasting* March 31, 1941, p. 30; *Radio Mirror* July 1935, p. 83, April 1936, p. 90; *Radio and Television Mirror* June 1941, p. 10; *Variety* February 19, 1936, p. 51, February 26, 1936, p. 51, January 7, 1942, p. 120; emmys.com.

Berger, Hal

Hal Berger was a West Coast writer, busy in motion pictures and radio by 1933. His first original radio series may have been *The In-Laws*, aired over Hollywood's KFAC beginning in 1933 and his second, *Forge of Freedom*, followed in 1934. *The In-Laws* switched between stations through the 1930s before being picked up by CBS' West Coast chain in 1937. In 1938 Berger tested the waters of the transcription market when he wrote and produced 39 episodes of a series entitled *Sunny Side Up* for 20th Century Radio Productions and later that year his successful *The In-Laws* was distributed via transcription as well. His *Shafter Parker and His Circus* was carried nationwide by Mutual in 1941 after some time of local broadcasting (1939–1941).

During and after the war Berger spent more time acting and producing and less on his writing endeavors. He also continued his baseball recreations that he'd started doing in the 1930s.

Sources: *Broadcasting* July 1, 1938, p. 38, October 15, 1938, p. 52; *Motion Picture Daily* January 7, 1938, p. 7; *Variety* June 13, 1933, p. 37, February 27, 1934, p. 38, February 26, 1941, p. 32.

Berger (Redman), Sylvia

Sylvia Berger joined CBS' script staff after a stint as a copywriter with the network's sales department in 1941. She worked on a number of CBS series through the 1940s including *Armstrong Theatre of the Air*, *CBS Is There*, *Columbia Workshop*, *Theatre of Romance*, and *You Are There*. When **Norman Corwin** followed up his *An American in England* series with *An American in Russia* (1943), Corwin enlisted Sylvia Berger to help bring the short-lived series to the air. Berger also did some non-network freelance work on *Cavalcade of America*, *The Eternal Light* (1948–1963), and *Ford Theatre*, and *Inside New York* (1951).

Radio: *Generation* (1943); 7th War Loan Drive (1945)

Sources: *Billboard* December 15, 1951, p. 11; *Variety* July 16, 1941, p. 26, May 26, 1943, p. 30, June 13, 1945, p. 4, August 27, 1947, June 2, 1948, p. 24.

Bester, Alfred

A law school dropout, Alfred Best (December 18, 1913–September 30, 1987) started publishing science fiction stories in 1939 and after a couple years selling short stories moved to writing for DC Comics on some of the company's biggest names, including Superman and Green Lantern. During World War II Bester wrote the newspaper strips *The Phantom* and *Mandrake the Magician* while their creator Lee Falk served in the armed forces.

Bester's radio work came about towards the end of the war when his wife mentioned that *Nick Carter, Master Detective* was accepting script submissions. He specialized in writing mystery-adventures programs during his time in radio through the late 1940s. Among the most recognizable series for which he wrote were the aforementioned *Nick Carter, Master Detective*, *The Shadow*, *The New Adventures of Nero Wolfe*, and the last *Charlie Chan* broadcast run from 1947 to 1948. Bester wrote a couple lesser-known mystery programs, *Mystery of the Week* (1946) and *Mystery Without Murder* (1947). Bester also contributed a few scripts to the premier old-time radio revival program of the 1970s, *The CBS Radio Mystery Theatre*.

Bester is considered one of the legends of science fiction, recognized as the Science Fiction Writers of America's ninth Grand Master and being inducted posthumously into the Science Fiction and Fantasy Hall of Fame in 2001. In 1953 he won the first Hugo Award for Best Novel for his 1951 *The Demolished Man* and was nominated in 1954, 1959, and 1975 for Best Short Story, 1960 for Best Short Fiction, and 1975 for Best Novel.

Radio: *Harvest of Stars*.
Sources: Grams *Shadow* p. 251–255; *Variety* August 21, 1946, p. 38, April 2, 1947, p. 35, July 9, 1947, p. 72; TheHugoAwards.com.

Bierstadt, Edward Hale

Edward Hale Bierstadt had a varied writing career including plays, essays, articles, and books before spending some time in the radio industry. Bierstadt was hired on to NBC's continuity department in the late 1920s and was subsequently responsible for authoring at least some of the *Empire Builders* episodes during the 1928–1929 season as well as *Westinghouse Salute* ca. 1929. Bierstadt was developing a reputation as something of an amateur criminologist, reflected in another of his series, *Historic Trials* (1929). He was credited with dramatizing Warden Lawes' *Twenty Thousand Years in Sing Sing* for the air in 1933 as well as co-authoring the premier episode of *The Shadow* in 1937.

Books: *Dunsany the Dramatist* (1920); *Curious Trials & Criminal Cases, From Socrates to Scopes* (1928).
Sources: Grams *Shadow*; *Radio Digest* March 1933 p. 4; *Radio Review* December 1929 p. 23; *New York Herald Tribune* June 30, 1929, pg. G2; *Washington Post* July 11, 1929, p. 9.

Bigelow, Joe

A contributor to *Variety* magazine in the 1930s, Joe Bigelow went to work for motion pictures studios for a short time in the late 1930s before joining J. Walter Thompson Co. as a writer. By 1939 he was on the scripting team for *The Rudy Vallee Show* before moving back to the West Coast to write for *Kraft Music Hall* on which he would write regularly for the next couple of years. After the Rudy Vallee program Bigelow was assigned to write *The Chase & Sanborn Show* (ca. 1941) starring Edgar Bergen and Charlie McCarthy where he stayed for two years, finally becoming head of the show's writing team. Thompson Co. shifted Bigelow in 1943 to *What's New?* and then to *Bakers of America Program* in 1944. Later in the decade Bigelow moved up to the rank of vice-president and in the 1950s was associated with a number of minor television programs.

Sources: *Broadcasting* October 1, 1939, p. 50, February 3, 1941, p. 33, March 31, 1941, p. 16; August 16, 1943, p. 28; *Variety* May 24, 1939, p. 27, August 9, 1939, p. 33 June 7, 1944, p. 34.

Bingham, Harrison Y.

Harrison Y. Bingham, active in Chicago radio in the late 1940s, is known to have contributed to at least two series, *Terry and the Pirates* and *Those Sensational Years*, both in 1947. He is also credited with one *Dr. Christian* script in 1948. In the 1950s Bingham was a writer for the television serial *The Secret Storm*.

Sources: *Variety* January 21, 1948, p. 34; welovesoaps.net.

Bixby, Carl

Carl Bixby (May 4, 1895–June 29, 1978) was a high school dropout but forged a very successful writing career nonetheless. In the 1920s he worked in the New York advertising world and by the end of the decade headed the Writers Bureau, Inc., essentially serving as an agent connecting non-fiction writers with businesses that needed odd jobs done, such as brochure copy.

From there he moved into radio and in 1934 was involved in a notable project, the adaption of a radio serial into a novel, the opposite of the usual route of serializing a novel. The program, penned by Bixby, was called *Dangerous Paradise* over NBC. In 1935 he was tabbed to write the scripts for a Grace Moore radio program, possibly called *Love Ahoy*.

It was writing for *Life Can Be Beautiful* with **Don Becker** that proved to be one of Bixby's biggest successes; the daily show aired from 1938 until 1954. Just a few weeks after its premier, Bixby and Becker were assigned a second serial, *This Day Is Ours* (1938–1940), based on the initial positive response to *Life Can Be Beautiful*. The duo of Bixby and Becker premiered yet another serial, *The Man I Married,* in 1939 and it ran until 1942 with a few months off the air in 1941. Bixby penned the soap opera *Kitty Foyle* that debuted in the summer of 1942 and then *Mrs. Minivera* upon its premier over CBS at the end of 1943.

Though still plenty busy in radio, Bixby eased into television in 1948 with *Try and Do It* on NBC and returned to his bread and butter, serials, writing dialog for television's *Edge of Night* (ca. 1959) and *The Secret Storm* when it moved to 30 minutes in 1962.

Radio: *Big Sister*; *Second Husband*; *Reader's Digest — Radio Edition* (1946).
Television: *Studio One* (ca. 1950), *Theatre Time* (ca. 1950).
Sources: *Sponsor* March 18, 1963, p. 32; *Variety* October 30, 1929, p. 76, March 20, 1934, p. 37, September 4, 1935, p. 36, September 11, 1935, p. 38, October 5, 1938, p. 28, July 9, 1941, p. 24, April 15, 1942, p. 28, May 20, 1942, p. 35, November 17, 1943, p. 32, January 16, 1946, p. 28, May 19, 1948, p. 24.

Blake, Howard

Howard Blake worked as a writer, producer, and director during his years in radio. He wrote for **Fred Allen** in the mid–1930s and in 1938 collaborated on two projects. The first was a comedy series co-written with Ed Cashman and the second was a variety show called *Let's Get Together* that starred Jack Berch and was co-written with Fred Kress.

Some of Blake's writing credits during the 1940s were *Mayor of the Town* (1942–1948), *Scramby Amby* (intermittently between 1941 and 1947) a word scramble quiz show on which he also served as producer, and a 1945 summer series with Frances Langford and Spike Jones. Later in the decade Blake worked on *That's Life* starring Jay Flippen (1946–1947) on which he again wrote and produced, *Meet the Missus* (1944–1949), and *Carnation Family Party* (1949) over CBS' Pacific Coast network. Though Blake started writing for television as early as 1952 on *Al Pearce and His Gang* over CBS-TV, he stayed busy in radio throughout the 1950s as a writer on *The Bob Hope Show* (ca. 1953) and with his own program, *The Bill Goodwin Show*, in 1957.

Sources: *Broadcasting* October 10, 1949, p. 70; *Broadcasting-Telecasting* February 11, 1952, p. 56, January 19, 1953, p. 14; *Motion Picture Daily* February 3, 1938, p. 8; *Radio Showmanship* January 1949 p. 4; *Variety* August 3, 1938, p. 36, *Variety* July 19, 1944, p. 24, June 20, 1945, p. 28, May 8 1946 p. 38.

Blake, Peggy

Peggy Blake wrote for a number of soap operas in the mid–1940s including *Barry Cameron* (1945–1946), *Just Plain Bill* (ca. 1944), and *Rose of My Dreams* (ca. 1946–1947). She also contributed scripts to anthology series such as *The First Nighter Program* (1944–1952), *Grand Central Station* (ca. 1944), and *Stars Over Hollywood* (ca. 1945).

Radio: *David Harum*; *Strange Romance of Evelyn Winters*.
Sources: *Cox Soap Operas* p. 44; *Radio Mirror* April 1945 p. 25; *Variety* March 8, 1944, p. 34, July 12, 1944, p. 26, December 4, 1946, p. 30, WeLoveSoaps.net.

Block, Hal

Hal Block, a graduate of the University of Chicago, arrived in New York in 1935 and soon landed a job writing for Abbott and Costello before joining the writing team for *The Phil Baker*

Show with **Sam Perrin** and **Arthur Phillips**. In 1938 he was hired to lead the writing staff for the new *Texaco Star Theatre*, then in 1940 he went to work penning scripts for *The Burns & Allen Show*.

While employed as NBC's West Coast director of publicity, Blok wrote for many wartime programs. Among these were *Millions for Defense* (1941), *Stage Door Canteen, Treasury Hour*, and *Treasury Star Parade*, as well as dialog for entertainers such as Jean Arthur who toured military posts. In 1943 Block spent some time on a special assignment with the British Broadcasting Corp. where he helped with *Tommy Get Your Fun* among other projects.

Block provided routines for Bob Hope on his 1943 USO tour while also working on *Yankee Doodle Doo*. For a time in 1944 he was a writer for Ed Wynn's *Happy Island* but had to leave that series when he signed a contract making him exclusive to Phil Baker's *Take It Or Leave It* show and Milton Berle's *Let Yourself Go*. For the two programs Block reportedly made $2,150 per week, making him one of the highest paid writers on radio at the time.

For a few years Block was a panelist on the popular TV program *What's My Line*. After being fired in 1953 he briefly had a late-night television show in Miami and eventually left show business by the end of the decade.

Songs: "Buy a Bond Today" (1944 with Milton Berle); "The U.S.A. By Day and the R.A.F. By Night" (1944); "Those Senator McCarthy Blues" (1954).

Other Radio: *Christmas Roundup* (1944); *Philco-Variety Radio Hall of Fame* (1944).

Sources: *Broadcasting* August 23, 1943, p. 20, October 1, 1938, p. 60, March 15, 1939, p. 26, July 1, 1940, p. 36; February 2, 1942, p. 55; *The Film Daily* November 3, 1944, p. 29; *Radio Mirror* July 1937, p. 67; *Variety* May 6, 1936, p. 42, July 16, 1941, p. 32, May 27, 1942, p. 4, August 5, 1942, p. 44, April 28, 1943, p. 55, August 18, 1943, p. 33, January 19, 1944, p. 46, April 19, 1944, p. 23, September 20, 1944, p. 33, January 24, 1945, p. 31.

Blocki, Fritz

Fritz Blocki is credited with writing the serial *Mary Noble, Backstage Wife* in the late 1930s, *In Care of Maggie Horn* (ca. 1941), and for *Chick Carter, Boy Detective* (1943–45).

Other Radio: *Bond Wagon; The Callahans*.

Sources: *Variety* January 25, 1939, p. 26; *The Radio Annual*, 1945 p. 825.

Boardman, True Eames

The son of two actors, True Boardman and Virgina True Boardman, it is no surprise that True Eames Boardman (October 25, 1909–July 28, 2003) ended up in show business. A child actor in the 19-teens, Boardman moved into radio in the early 1930s primarily as an announcer and actor for KFI before joining the producing and writing staff at KHJ, Los Angeles. One of Boardman's earliest ongoing writing efforts was *I Want a Divorce* (1940) before writing for *Forecast* (1940) and beginning a long run as the main author for *The Silver Theatre*, the latter a series for which he'd been narrator since 1937.

After spending time in the Armed Forces Radio Services during the war, in the mid–1940s Boardman expanded his writing to *Skippy Hollywood Theatre* (ca. 1944), *The Adventures of Maisie* (1945–1946), *This Is My Best* (1945), and Rexall shows including 1947's *Dan Carson*, a summer replacement for *The Jimmy Durante–Garry Moore Show*. Though Boardman had many narrator and announcing roles, he continued to write throughout the late 1940s and into the early 1950s on *Radio City Playhouse* (1949), *Family Theatre* (1949–1952), and *Presenting Charles Boyer* (1950).

Boardman contributed to a handful of screenplays during the 1940s but as radio waned he turned his focus primarily to television where he wrote for series such as *Perry Mason* and *The Virginian* through the early 1970s.

Other Radio: *Hollywood Hotel* (ca. 1936 with Happy Cronman), *This Is Our America* (ca. 1942); *For Services Rendered* (1945); *And Sudden Death* (1946); *Chevrolet on Broadway* (1948).

Television: *My Three Sons* (1962); *Bonanza* (1971).

Sources: *Broadcasting* March 15, 1935, p. 37, March 16, 1942, p. 34; *Broadcasting-Telecasting* December 10, 1945, p. 95; *Motion Picture Daily* October 29, 1936, p. 2; *Variety* October 25, 1939, p. 55, November 7, 1945, p. 42, February 27, 1946, p. 39, November 10, 1948, p. 35.

Boasberg, Al

Al Boasberg (December 5, 1892–June 18, 1937) spent the 1920s writing over 100 vaudeville comedy routines and material for numerous motion pictures, developing a reputation as one of the industry's best gagmen. A long time writer for George Burns and Gracie Allen on vaudeville, he wrote their broadcast material for some time before leaving in 1932, claiming the pay wasn't sufficient.

While he earned the same 10 percent commission he earned from the pair's stage work, radio constantly required fresh material every week, thus the same percentage wasn't enough. Renegotiations brought him back for a 13-week stint on the show later in 1932. Boasberg was also credited that year with being one of the first gagmen to get on-air credit for his work before signing an exclusive contract with Blackett-Sample-Hummert. Boasberg's biggest writing achievement came in the mid-1930s when Jack Benny hired him to write for his radio show.

Boasberg had supplied Benny material in his vaudeville days and the pair was now reunited as Jack began his rise to the top of the radio ratings. While Boasberg may never have been a prolific radio writer because the money was so much better in movies, the industry lost a considerable talent when he died of a heart attack at the age of 44.

Sources: *Exhibitors Herald-World* October 25, 1930, p. 46; *Hollywood Filmograph* June 15, 1929, p. 32; *Variety* May 10, 1932, p. 55, August 16, 1932, p. 41, August 30, 1932, p. 51, October 4, 1932, p. 48.

Bogert, Vincent (Vin, Vinnie)

Vincent Bogert's (July 27, 1914–November 28, 1978) radio writing career was capped by an extended run on *Duffy's Tavern* from 1946 to 1950, moving in 1951 to writing for a short time for *The Eddie Cantor Show*. Bogert was awarded the 1956 Emmy for Best Comedy Writing for his work on *The Phil Silvers Show* and he then wrote for several years on *The Garry Moore Show* in the 1960s.

Sources: Vincent Bogert Papers; emmys.com.

Borden, Ruth

Ruth Borden was one of the Hummert's writers on their many serials. Her assignments in the late 1930s included *Alias Jimmy Valentine* (after it moved to a once-a-week schedule), *Our Gal Sunday*, *Second Husband*, and *Valiant Lady*. Other credits include *Front Page Farrell*, *The Helping Hand*, and *John's Other Wife* in 1941 with a return to *Second Husband* in 1942. Borden went on to pen *Mary Noble, Backstage Wife* (ca. 1942), *Perry Mason* (ca. 1943–1945), *A Brighter Tomorrow* (1947), *Hearthstone of the Death Squad* (1948) and *The Romance of Helen Trent* (ca. 1949, 1955).

Sources: *Billboard* April 19, 1947, p. 7, December 17, 1949, p. 10; *Broadcasting* October 13, 1941, p. 66; *Motion Picture Daily* June 7, 1939, p. 8; *TV Radio Mirror* April 1955 p. 76; *Variety* January 25, 1939, p. 26, October 8, 1941, p. 25, December 24, 1941, p. 34, June 24, 1942, p. 39, September 2, 1942, p. 36, October 20, 1943, p. 39.

Bostic, Joe

Joe Bostic (d. 1988) was the host, director, and writer of a number of African-American-oriented programs from the 1930s to the 1970s. Among his credits were *The Negro Business Hour* (1932–1935), *Harlem on Parade* (1935–1936), *Man About Harlem* (1936), and *Tales from Harlem* (1937–1939).

Sources: Ellett *Black Radio*; McNeil p. 46–47.

Boucher, Anthony

Anthony Boucher (pen name of William Anthony Parker White, August 21, 1911–April 29, 1968) wrote for a number of mystery series in the mid- to late 1940s. He entered radio in 1944 when he took over co-writing tasks with **Manfred Lee** on *The Adventures of Ellery Queen*, the radio feature starring the famed detective created by Lee and his cousin **Frederic Dannay**, who left the show in 1944.

When working on *The New Adventures of Sherlock Holmes* series (1944–1948) Boucher made a good teammate for **Denis Green**. Boucher, a strong admirer of Holmes' writer Arthur Conan Doyle, laid out the plot while Green focused on polishing the dialog. Boucher also contributed scripts for *The Casebook of Gregory Hood*, written with partner Denis Green, a 1946 summer replacement series for *Sherlock Holmes*. Boucher was based in San Francisco while Green worked in Los Angeles. After just a few years of scripting radio Boucher left the field to open up more time for his other writing projects.

Boucher was a respected reviewer and critic of mystery literature for *The San Francisco Chronicle, Chicago Sun Times, New York Herald Tribune,* and *New York Times Book Review.* He was also editor for *The Magazine of Fantasy & Science Fiction* (1949–1958), *Best from Fantasy and Science Fiction* (1952–1959), and *True Crime Detective.* Boucher wrote many stories for the era's leading pulp magazines and supervised a number of lines of mystery books as well.

Boucher was a founding member of the Mystery Writers of America, a member of its Board of Directors beginning in 1948, and its president beginning in 1951. He was a winner of Edgar Awards in 1946, 1950, and 1953 for Outstanding Mystery Criticism with an additional nomination in 1951.

Other Radio: *Molle Mystery Theatre* (1945).
Books: *The Case of the Seven of Calvary* (1937); Various collections of reviews, commentaries, and short stories.
Sources: *Variety* September 15, 1937, p. 31, September 5, 1945, p. 26, February 23, 1948, p. 53; mysterynet.com; theedgars.com.

Boulette, Leo

After a few years as a continuity writer for Chicago's WLS in the late 1930s and early 1940s, Leo Boulette moved to program director and head of the artists' bureau with Danville's WDAN in 1940. He subsequently moved to WIZE in Springfield, OH, and then to his own Leo Boulette Agency in 1941. After a short time later Boulette relocated his agency to Three Rivers, MI.

While heading his radio advertising agency, Boulette started writing for WXYZ in 1943, providing scripts for *The Green Hornet* and *The Lone Ranger* on a freelance basis. He was hired by the King-Trendle Broadcasting Corporation later that year. He provided scripts only until 1945, tendering his resignation with the complaint that expectations were too high for the compensation provided.

Songs: "Our Candlelight Dreams" (1939).
Sources: Grams *Green Hornet* p. 194–195; *Broadcasting* March 15, 1938, p. 46, June 1, 1939, p. 46, March 1, 1940, p. 51, October 1, 1940, p. 54, January 20, 1941, p. 47, November 3, 1941, p. 46.

Boyle, Betty (Elizabeth M.)

In 1943 Betty Boyle (d. January 19, 1998) was identified as the first woman to graduate from NBC's Hollywood sound effects training program, a result of the male talent drain due to the World War. She was immediately assigned to *Eyes Aloft*. Her most prominent radio writing assignment was on *Lum 'n' Abner* in the late 1940s with head writer **Roswell Rogers**. In 1949 she was one of the writers assigned to the KTTV dedication broadcast. Beginning in the 1950s Boyle engaged in a number of business ventures in the Las Vegas area where she passed away many years later.

Other Radio: *Free World Theatre* (1943).
Sources: Hollis p. 136, 138; *Broadcasting* February 1, 1943, p. 47; *Variety* March 16, 1949, p. 32; *Las Vegas Sun* obituary January 21, 1998.

Braun, J. Gilbert

Gilbert Braun was a production and public relations man for a number of radio talent agencies in the late 1930s and 1940s. In 1946 Braun made his first stab at writing a radio series, *The Avenger*, with his wife **Ruth Braun**. Later that year Braun and his wife once again teamed up to write a series, *Adventures of Frank Merriwell*, based on the dime novels by Burt L. Standish, pseudonym for Gilbert S. Patton. The Brauns had a third series, *Horatio Alger's Stories*, produced by Charles Michelson Inc. in 1951. Braun did some solo writing as well, including *Mark Trail* (1950) and *Tom Corbett, Space Cadet* (1952).

Sources: *Broadcasting-Telecasting* April 23, 1951, p. 69; *Variety* January 2, 1946, p. 24, October 9, 1946, p. 53.

Braun, Ruth

Ruth Braun was part of a husband-wife radio team, with husband **Gilbert Braun**, with whom she wrote *The Avenger* (ca. 1946), *The Adventures of Frank Merriwell* (ca. 1946), and *Horatio Alger's Stories* (ca. 1951).

Sources: *Broadcasting-Telecasting* April 23, 1951, p. 69; *Variety* January 2, 1946, p. 24, October 9, 1946, p. 53.

Brecher, Irving

Irving Brecher (January 17, 1914–November 17, 2008) was a prominent screenwriter during

Hollywood's Golden Age, working on Marx Brothers pictures, *The Wizard of Oz*, and winning an Oscar for his screenplay *Meet Me in St. Louis*. However, Brecher also left his mark in radio.

Brecher debuted on the air with *Folies de Paris* featuring Willie and Eugene Howard (1935) then became the head writer for Milton Berle's *Community Sing*, a 1936–1937 series and in 1938 for the *MGM Good News Hour*. His most memorable radio work, however, was the creation of *Life of Riley* that ran from 1944 to 1951. Brecher packaged the entire production and was the writer initially, though he eventually turned that task over to others. The 1949 film based on the show was written by the veteran screenwriter as well.

Other Radio: *Radio Screen Actors Guild* (ca. 1939).
Theater: *Moustache by Jonathan* (1952, with Jo Swerling).
Sources: Young; *The Film Daily* September 2, 1936, p. 3; *Radio Mirror* November 1938 p. 40; *Variety* January 11, 1939, p. 35.

Brecher, Jack

Jack Brecher, brother of **Irving Brecher**, worked on the writing team for *The Life of Riley* (1946–1948).

Source: *Billboard* September 11, 1948, p. 12.

Breen, Richard (Dick)

Richard Breen (June 26, 1918–February 1, 1967) wrote scripts for Jack Webb's early radio shows including *Are These Our Children* (1946), the comedy *The Jack Webb Show* (1946) and early detective programs *Pat Novak, For Hire* (1947), described as "sassy, brassy," and *Johnny Modero: Pier 23* (1947), the latter of which he created. *Johnny Modero* is widely considered a repackaging of *Pat Novak* by another name, since *Novak* was still on the air and being written by **Gil Doud**.

Breen's fame came writing screenplays and his talent was acknowledged with the 1954 Academy Award for Writing (Story and Screenplay) for his work on *Titanic*. He adapted Webb's properties onto film and television as well.

Film: *Niagara* (1953); *Dragnet* (1954); *Pete Kelly's Blues* (1955).
Television: *Dragnet* (1967, 1969).
Sources: *Variety* October 2, 1946, p. 34; oscars.org.

Brenner, Ray

Ray Brenner (October 21, 1927–June 5, 1995) was one of the writers for *The Phil Harris–Alice Faye Show*, a popular spin-off of the top-rated *Jack Benny Show*. Brenner's work in radio during the early 1950s was relatively short but he had a long career in television, writing from the early 1960s into the early 1980s. Brenner wrote teleplays for such classic series as *The Andy Griffith Show*, *Gomer Pyle: USMC*, and *Charlie's Angels*. The quality of his work was recognized with two nominations for Writers Guild of America awards for Episodic Comedy and Episodic Drama in 1968 and 1976 respectively.

Television: *The Dinah Shore Chevy Show* (1958–1959); *McHale's Navy* (1964–1965); *Fantasy Island* (1980).
Source: Dunning.

Breslin, Howard

Howard Breslin (December 23, 1912–May 30, 1964) was a regular radio play writer through the 1940s. He was an ongoing contributor to such series as *Aunt Jenny* (ca. 1941) with frequent collaborator Knowles Entrikin and *Mayor of the Town* (mid–1940s). On the latter series Breslin alternated weekly scripts with **Charles Tazewell** by 1945. One of his last series was Parker Fennelly's *Lawyer Tucker* written with **David Howard** (1947) and produced by Knowles Entrikin. Breslin also contributed to magazines including *Collier's*, *This Week*, and *Saturday Evening Post* before focusing more on novels in his later years.

Other Radio: *The Columbia Workshop* (1940); *The Funeral of General Von Blatz* (1942 with David Howard); *Hallmark Playhouse* (1952).
Theatre: *Off the Record* (1942, with Knowles Entrikin), later *Off the Air* (1946).
Books: *The Tamarack Tree* (1947), more than a dozen others.
Sources: Tucker p. 49; *Billboard* April 12, 1947, p. 5; *Broadcasting* May 11, 1942, p. 20, July 19, 1943, p. 40; *Variety* November 19, 1941, p. 38, June 18, 1947, p. 26.

Brooks, Margo

Margo Brooks was one of a number of writers for *The Romance of Helen Trent* during its long run from 1933–1960.

Source: Dunning

Brooks, Matt

A vaudeville comedian before entering radio, Matt Brooks was hired by Eddie Cantor to write material for his run on *The Chase & Sanborn Hour* ca. 1933 and *CBS Texaco Town* ca. 1937. He was scheduled to pen Joe Penner's *Tip Top Show* in 1940 with frequent collaborator **Eddie Davis**.

Movies: *Duffy's Tavern* (1945, contributed sketches).
Theater: *George White's Scandals of 1939* (1939, with **Eddie Davis** and George White); *Hold on to Your Hats* (1940 with Guy Bolton and Eddie Davis).
Sources: Grams "Duffy's Tavern"; *Broadcasting* December 15, 1937, p. 76, January 1, 1940, p. 44; *Variety* May 9, 1933, p. 38.

Brooks (Flippen), Ruth

After studying radio writing at Northwestern University, Ruth Brooks (September 14, 1921– July 9, 1981) wrote radio plays for about three years before moving into motion pictures. She began as a scriptwriter for NBC in the early 1940s working on shows such as *The Adventures of Maisie*, *The Billie Burke Show*, and *This Is My Best*. Brooks joined New York's Compton Advertising as a copywriter in 1944 and added *Words at War* (1944), and *Here's Babe Ruth* (1944) to her radio accomplishments.

Soon after, Brooks left for the West Coast where she signed as a writer with Warner Bros. and wrote the screenplays for a number of films in the 1950s and 1960s including for the *Gidget* franchise. During the 1960s and 1970s Brooks contributed scripts to a number of television series such as *Bewitched*, *The Brady Bunch* and *Gidget*. In 1968 she was nominated for an Emmy for Outstanding Writing Achievement in Comedy for her work on *That Girl* and in 1975 for a Daytime Emmy for Outstanding Writing for a Daytime Special Program.

Sources: *Broadcasting* August 28, 1944, p. 114; *Variety* July 12, 1944, p. 30; *The Hartford Courant* September 13, 1946, p. 13; emmys.com.

Brown, George Frame

George Frame Brown (March 1, 1896–November 19, 1979) was a struggling New York actor when he appeared in a broadcast on WRNY. This led to an ongoing series on WABC, *The Music and Musings of Dr. Mu* in 1927 and subsequently on *Main Street Sketches* in January 1928. He left within a few months and created a nearly identical show, *Real Folks*, on NBC that he both wrote and voiced the main characters.

Real Folks aired until 1931 when Brown retired from radio for a time before returning with a new 1935 series, *Tony and Gus*. Reusing some of the dialects he'd used in *Real Folks*, Brown's new series focusing on two immigrants only lasted a few months. Brown was basically done with radio after *Tony and Gus* and though he continued to write sporadically over the years, Brown lost his small fortune in bad investments and scraped by in his last years on a series of manual labor jobs.

Source: Ellett "George Frame Brown and His *Real Folks*."

Bublick, David

David Bublick (d. December 30, 1955) studied law and was even admitted to the New York bar but never worked professionally as an attorney. Instead, he focused on writing for radio and, later, television. Throughout the 1940s he wrote several episodes of *Fashions of the Times*. Other 1940s era programs with which Bublick is credited are *Exploring the Unknown* (1946), Agatha Christie's *Hercule Poirot* (ca. 1946), and the *Fred Allen Show* from which he departed in 1947 so he could collaborate with his wife **Judith Bublick** on a Gabriel Heatter program over Mutual.

Bublick is most widely remembered for co-scripting many *Shadow* episodes with his wife during the series' final two years. Other series during the 1950s to which he contributed scripts were *2000 Plus* (1950), *The Search That Never Ends* (1953), and *Keep Healthy* (1955).

Other Radio: *The Adventures of Charlie Chan*.
Theater: *Destination Unknown* (1936, with Judith Bublick).
Sources: Grams *Shadow* p. 427; *Broadcasting* November 28, 1955, p. 94; *The Ellensburg Capital* (WA) August 22, 1947.

Bublick, Judith

Judith Bublick co-wrote many radio scripts with her husband **David Bublick**, most prominent among them *The Shadow* during its final two years and *The Adventures of Charlie Chan*. She continued writing after her husband's death on *By the People* (1955–1956) and later on television.

Television: *High Adventure* (1957).
Sources: Grams *Shadow* p. 427; *Billboard* November 18, 1957, p. 14.

Buck, Ashley

Ashley Buck was a writer and actor on *Pioneers of Science*, produced by the Federal Theatre's Radio Division in 1937. He continued in radio, penning the rarely remembered serial *We Are Always Young* (1941), a six-per-week series co-written with Nicholas Cosentino. Buck was called in to adapt *Flashgun Casey* (later *Casey, Crime Photographer*) to the airwaves in 1943 from its original incarnations in the pulps and on screen. He later was credited with *Adventure Comes to Mr. Timothy* (ca. 1947), *This Is Adventure* (1948) and *Sleep No More* (1951), a series that was offered by its production company in both radio and TV versions.

Books: *Beyond Laughter*.
Sources: *Billboard* January 31, 1942, p. 7; *Broadcasting* May 7, 1951, p. 80; *Variety* September 15, 1937, p. 31; February 19, 1941, p. 30, July 14, 1943, p. 46, October 8, 1947, p. 30, January 28, 1948, p. 36.

Buffum, Ray

Ray Buffum's (August 8, 1904–December 13, 1980) radio career started in earnest in Nebraska editing *Watts News* in 1935, the in-house publication for stations owned by the Union Holding Co. in Lincoln and Omaha. He soon transferred to Nashville's WROL where he became a continuity writer and a year after that, 1936, was hired by Hollywood's KFWB. While with the station Buffum wrote an original play, "The Dreamer," that Al Jolson included in one of his 1937 broadcasts.

From KFWB Buffum jumped to the Robert S. Taplinger Inc. agency where he worked as a continuity writer for the Ruthrauff & Ryan radio shows that included Jolson, Joe Penner, and Milton Berle. After writing both *Big Town* and the *Al Jolson Show* in the late 1930s, Buffum returned to the Midwest by 1940 but was soon on to the East Coast in 1941 when he joined Ted Bates Inc. as a script editor and writer where his first assignment was *City Desk*.

A year later and back on the West Coast Buffum wrote *Smarty Party* for NBC and later in 1942 he was assigned to work with Don Thompson on *Hawthorne House*. Buffum moved up the executive chain at San Francisco's KPO until 1944 when he briefly started writing screenplays before returning to Hollywood radio on KNX in 1945. Over the next few years Buffum proceeded to write for such notable series as *Rogue's Gallery* (ca. 1945), *A Man Named Jordan* (1945), *Twelve Players* (1945), and *The Casebook of Gregory Hood* (ca. 1947).

Through the late 1950s and early 1960s Buffum wrote for a number of Western television programs as well as a handful of motion picture screenplays.

Other Radio: *Big Town* (ca. 1938); *The Whistler* (1945); *The Buddy Rogers Show* (audition, 1947); *Prowl Car* (1949); *Those Young Bryans* (1956, audition).
Television: *The Adventures of Wild Bill Hickok* (1958); *Death Valley Days* (1961); *Laramie* (1963).
Sources: *Broadcasting* October 15, 1936, p. 52, September 1, 1937, p. 80, November 1, 1938, p. 54, September 15, 1940, p. 52, April 28, 1941, p. 38, August 3, 1942, p. 46, August 31, 1942, p. 34, September 18, 1944, p. 46; *Motion Picture Daily* June 15, 1937, p. 8, August 9, 1937, p. 8; *Variety* September 4, 1935, p. 41, November 2, 1938, p. 36, December 28, 1938, p. 21, September 24, 1947, p. 2.

Burch, Bill

Bill Burch did a lot of directing and producing work in radio through the 1940s and 1950s but his most notable writing assignment was as head writer for *Truth or Consequences* beginning in 1945.
Source: *Broadcasting* August 20, 1945, p. 54.

Burnett, Murray

Murray Burnett (December 28, 1910–September 23, 1997) famously co-wrote an unproduced play with Joan Alison entitled *Everybody Comes to Rick's* that was the inspiration for *Casablanca*. His forays into radio writing included *I Was a Convict* (1946), *True Detective Mysteries* (ca. 1947), and *Theatre Five* (1965). During the radio drama revival of the 1970s Burnett was hired to write several stories for *CBS Radio Mystery Theatre* between 1974 and 1982.

Television: *Mr. Tutt Goes West* (1956).
Sources: *Broadcasting* November 12, 1956, p. 12; *Variety* September 25, 1946.

Burns, Willie

William Burns (March 12, 1902–January 20, 1966), George Burns' brother, started working on the *Burns & Allen* scripts as early as 1935. He worked with the act for 25 years on both radio and television. He also worked as a script consultant for television's *Mr. Ed* from 1961 to 1966.
Sources: *Variety* October 2, 1935, p. 45, October 6, 1948, p. 30.

Burrows, Abe

Abe Burrows (December 18, 1910–May 17, 1985) started writing for radio in the late 1930s and in 1938 was penning Eddie Garr's NBC series with **Frank Galen**. He moved to Hollywood in 1939 and started writing for *The Texaco Star Theater* and then moved to Rudy Vallee's *Sealtest Theatre*. In 1941 Ed Gardner hired him to lead the writing team for his new feature *Duffy's Tavern* after working together on Gardner's *This Is New York*.

Originally scheduled to write for *The Danny Kaye Show*, Burrows backed out so he could pursue some of his own projects that came to fruition in the next couple years. Burrows created and wrote a serial, *Holiday and Company* (CBS, February–April 1946) and when that folded went to work writing *The Ford Show* starring Dinah Shore later in 1946. The Ford assignment lasted into 1947 and soon after he joined the writing staff of *The Joan Davis Show* while handling writing chores for his own series, *The Abe Burrows Show*, that started that year. His show eventually transitioned into *Breakfast with Burrows* around 1950.

Though a highly respected radio writer, Burrows' greatest fame came in the musical theater where he wrote the book for *Guys and Dolls* as well as *How to Succeed in Business Without Really Trying*. Burrows was awarded the 1962 Pulitzer Prize for Drama with Frank Loesser for *How to Succeed* as well as that year's Tony Awards for Musical Author, Musical Director, and Musical. His *Guys and Dolls* earlier won the 1951 Tony for Best Musical.
Other Radio: *Philco Radio Time* (1949).
Sources: Abe Burrows Papers; *Broadcasting* October 1, 1939, p. 50, February 3, 1941, p. 10. *Variety* January 12, 1938, p. 40, September 11, 1946, p. 42, September 25, 1946; Grams personal communication.

Burt, Frank

Frank Burt's writing career was relatively short but very prolific. From the late 1940s to mid-1950s Burt wrote scripts for a number of radio series including *The City* (1947), *The Whistler* (1947), *The Unexpected* (1947–1948), *The Man Called X* (1950), *Hollywood Star Playhouse* (1950–1953), *This Is Your FBI* (1952), and *Hallmark Hall of Fame* (1954). Burt's most famous radio work was the Jimmy Stewart western *The Six-Shooter* that ran from 1953 to 1954, for which Burt penned all but one story.

On television Frank Burt wrote many scripts for Jack Webb's *Dragnet* series during the 1950s. He stayed busy authoring many dozen other teleplays during the decade as well as receiving credit for numerous screenplays, including Stewart's *The Man from Laramie* (1954). Burt died of a heart attack in 1958 at the age of 38.
Television: *I Led 3 Lives* (1953); *The Restless Gun* (1957–1959).
Sources: Hayde & Morgan; *Variety* April 7, 1948, p. 30.

Burton, Laverne

Laverne Burton has at least two radio writing credits, *Treasury Salute* (1945) and *I Was There*.
Source: Dunning p. 340.

Burtt, Bob (Robert)

Bob Burtt called on his time as a World War I pilot in creating the series *The Air Adventures of Jimmie Allen* with fellow veteran **Wilfred G. "Bill" Moore** in 1933. The daily serial found success for several years in the mid-1930s but was dropped by its sponsor, Skelly Oil, in 1937 whereupon the company began working with Burtt and Moore to create yet another airborne adventure, this one called *Captain Midnight*. In between these two efforts Burtt was responsible for the creation of a separate aviation thriller, *Ann of the Airlanes* in 1938.

Debuting in October 1939 over WGN, *Captain Midnight* went on a ten-year broadcasting streak and became one of the most memorable old-time radio programs of all time, thanks in part to its premiums. Captain Midnight was a legendary World War I fighter pilot who worked with the Flight Patrol (later the Secret Squadron) to track down the menacing Ivan Shark. Captain Midnight patrolled the airways until 1949.

Burtt and Moore have been credited with two more popular aviation-themed radio series, though their connections to both are somewhat unclear and supported by little documentary evidence. Burtt's authorship of *Sky King* is questioned by Maggie Thompson in *Radio on the Range* and his work on *Hop Harrigan* could not be confirmed by any primary sources. Moore died of a heart attack in 1939 and could not have been involved in the later projects. Possibly Burtt was involved directly or indirectly on both series, or perhaps his work on *Jimmie Allen* and *Captain Midnight* has been confused with other flying heroes as memories faded over ensuing decades.

More episodes of *Jimmie Allen* were authored in an attempt to reboot the series after World War II, but Jimmie's time had passed and the new version did not meet with much success.

Film: *The Sky Parade* (1936).
Sources: French & Siegel p. 170; Harmon *Radio Mystery*; Kallis, Jr.; Cagle 2006; *Broadcasting* March 1, 1933, p. 33; *Film Daily Year Book, 1938* p. 531; *Radio Daily* February 2, 1938, p. 8.

Buss, Carl A.

Carl Buss was a screenwriter for Paramount before picking up some work in radio with Blackett—Sample—Hummert of Chicago. In 1936 he was authoring *Judy and Jane* under the sponsorship of Folgers coffee and later that year Buss' own show, *A Modern Girls' Romance*, was bought by Hearst Radio. He was responsible for the scripts of *Woman of Courage* in the late 1930s before being replaced by **Marie Baumer** in 1941. Buss in turn replaced **Doris Halman** on the Hummert show *Mr. Keen, Tracer of Lost Persons*. Buss wrote for at least a couple different series in the mid–1940s including *The High Places* (ca. 1945) and *The Sparrow and the Hawk* (1945–1946).

Sources: Cox *Mr. Keen*; *Broadcasting* March 15, 1936, p. 14; *Variety* July 22, 1936, p. 36; October 8, 1941, p. 25, March 25, 1942, p. 30, February 14, 1945, p. 26.

Byrne, Brian J.

Brian J. Byrne had a handful of writing credits in a half-dozen years writing radio drama. His earliest work was *Slums Cost You Money* (1938–1939) for the Federal Theatre Radio Division followed soon with several scripts for *The Shadow* (1939–1940), *The Columbia Workshop* (1939), and *Lincoln Highway*. Byrne wrote for *The Shadow* as late as 1944 and *The CBS Workshop* in 1946.

Sources: Grams *Shadow*; *Billboard* March 23, 1946, p. 13.

Byron, Ed (Edward)

Ed Byron (October 20, 1905–November 21, 1964) was reputed to be the creator of WLW's *Moon River*, a program that, because of the station's huge national reach beyond Cincinnati, had relatively outsized fame. A director and producer for much of his career, Byron was responsible for some writing assignments over the years. One of the first was *What's My Name?*, a 1939 summer replacement program for Fred Allen's *Town Hall Tonight*. Bryon also served as director and retained ownership of the series.

Byron was scripting a series in the late 1930s called *Prosecuting Attorney* but it never found a sponsor and when he signed to work on *Mr. District Attorney* for Phillips H. Lord, Bryon had to shelve his own program. Frequently cited as writer of the series, contemporary accounts indicate that Bryon's primary responsibilities were directing and, later, producing, and that he was most likely no more than a co-writer. Both Byron and Lord claimed credit for creating the long running and profitable series, and it may never be possible to tease out exactly who was responsible for what portion of *Mr. District Attorney*. Regardless, Byron obtained control of the series during the early 1940s before entering the service with the Army in 1943.

A huge fan of true crime, Byron supposedly spent time in disreputable locales to stay up-to-date on street mannerisms and lingo. *Mr. District*

Attorney was a perennially popular show with modest costs, thus proving to be a very profitable property for Byron over many years.
  Other Radio: *Music by Gershwin* (1934).
  Television: *Mr. District Attorney* (1955).
  Sources: Rimler p. 72; *Broadcasting* February 8, 1943, p. 33; November 13, 1940, p. 27; *Variety* June 21, 1939, p. 27, April 15, 1942, p. 34.

Cady, Jerry (Jerome)

Jerry Cady (August 15, 1903–November 7, 1948) entered radio in 1932 with Los Angeles' KECA-KFI after working as a reporter for *The Los Angeles Record*. One of his programs for the station was *Tapestries of Life* (1932), a variety show featuring a pre–*Jack Benny Show* Don Wilson. The next year Cady scripted *Makers of History* dramatizing events in American history. Later in 1933 he wrote and produced another historical series, *Lives of the Great*, that was distributed on transcription.

Cady moved to New York in 1935 to pursue more writing opportunities there with the Fletcher & Ellis agency. He was soon writing a program for Buddy Rogers and Jeannie Lang and directing a series featuring Babe Ruth. By the next year Cady was scripting a series for Mary Pickford back on the West Coast as well as *Dalt & Zumba* for Radio Recorders Inc. and later in 1936 he signed with 20th Century Fox to write screenplays.

From 1936 on Cady grew into a prolific screenwriter beginning with B films including entries to the *Mr. Moto* and *Charlie Chan* series and moving up to major features including *Guadalcanal Diary* and *Call Northside 777*. Cady's talent was recognized in 1945 with an Academy Award nomination for Best Original Screenplay for *Wing and a Prayer*.

Cady did keep his radio contacts and occasionally contributed his skills to the airwaves including filling in for **Phil Rapp** in 1942 on NBC's *Post Toasties Time*. That same year he is credited with writing Major Hoople's *Our Boarding House*, a sitcom based on Gene Ahern's comic strip of the same name.
  Sources: *Broadcasting* June 15, 1932, p. 22, July 1, 1936, p. 99, August 24, 1942, p. 56; *The Film Daily* August 5, 1936, p. 2, August 7, 1936, p. 4; *Hollywood Filmograph* February 25, 1933, p. 11; *Radio Mirror* February 1935 p. 41; *Variety* September 13, 1932, p. 78, November 21, 1933, p. 41, September 11, 1935, p. 41, February 26, 1936, p. 43.

Calmer, Ned (Edgar)

Originally a newspaper reporter, Ned Calmer (July 16, 1907–March 9, 1986) wrote scripts for *Mary Noble, Backstage Wife* in the late 1930s according to James Thurber. Calmer earned his fame not writing soap operas but as one of the Morrow Boys on CBS radio during World War II and working as a newscaster into the late 1960s. He remained, however, a writer of fiction on the side, publishing a number of novels over the years.
  Books: *Beyond the Street* (1934); *The Strange Land* (1950); *The Anchorman* (1970); *The Winds of Montauk* (1980).
  Sources: Cox *Radio Journalism* p. 177; *Radio and Television Mirror* December 1950 p. 35; easyace.blogspot.com.

Campbell, Kane

Kane Campbell worked in advertising over 20 years but only one of his radio writing assignments is known by name, *Gasoline Alley*, the 1941 adaptation of Frank King's comic strip. Campbell stayed true to the strip, basically working the week's strips into daily episodes. In 1943 Campbell moved to Chicago where he joined WGN as a continuity writer and two years later in 1945 he was named head copywriter for Grace & Bement in Detroit and credited with writing various musical and variety radio programs. By the 1950s Campbell had moved into the production side of radio and television.
  Sources: *Broadcasting* February 17, 1941, p. 39, August 16, 1943, p. 38, January 29, 1945, p. 52.

Carlton, Sam

Sam Carlton was writing George Jessel's radio material as early as 1934 and continued to do so throughout the 1930s, serving as head writer for Jessel's Radio Enterprises at the end of the decade. Some of these programs included *Thirty Minutes in Hollywood* (1938) and *George Jessel's Jamboree* (1939). During the 1940s Carlton pursued other writing opportunities including *The Danny Kaye Show* (1945) on radio and *The*

Texaco Star Theatre (1948) on television but returned to Jessel who developed his own television show in 1953.

Sources: *Broadcasting* February 1, 1938, p. 58, April 1, 1939, p. 67, November 30, 1953, p. 16; *Variety* January 2, 1934, p. 79, April 11, 1945, p. 30, October 27, 1948, p. 27.

Carmer, Carl

Carl Carmer (October 16, 1893–September 11, 1976) was a university professor during the 19-teens and 1920s and had begun developing a reputation for his observations on American life before entering radio in 1937 with a CBS program exploring the flavor of different regions of the country in *Your Neck of the Woods*. He returned to the medium as a consultant on *Cavalcade of America* in 1939 and was a writer for *The Pursuit of Happiness* (1939–1940). During the war Carmer contributed original stories to *News from Home*, a transcribed series broadcast to U.S. troops and *The World and America* (1943–1944) retelling historical tales. The latter series was sponsored by *Time* magazine, also behind the more famous *March of Time* series, perhaps explaining why Carmer is sometimes cited as an author for that series. After World War II Carmer provided some scripts to *Columbia Workshop* (1946–1947).

Books: *Stars Fell on Alabama* (1934).
Sources: *Broadcasting* December 15, 1939, p. 22, December 15, 1940, p. 48, June 1, 1942, p. 39, June 14, 1943, p. 12; *Radio Mirror* September 1937 p. 7.

Carr, John Dickson

John Dickson Carr (November 30, 1906–February 27, 1977) was a prominent American mystery writer though many of his classic writings in the 1930s and 1940s were written while he lived in England. Carr is most closely associated with *Suspense*, for which he penned many scripts as well as adapting stories of others and even serving as host on occasion.

Carr's 1943 *Suspense* story "Cabin B-13" was spun-off to its own series called *Cabin B-13* in 1948 that lasted for a few months. Carr recycled a number of his *Suspense* scripts for the series in order to make his weekly writing deadlines.

Source: *Variety* July 7, 1948, p. 22.

Carrington, Elaine Sterne

Elaine Carrington (June 14, 1891–May 4, 1958) began her writing career in the early 1920s and wrote dozens of screenplays and plays by 1930 as well as numerous short stories and even a handful of novels and story collections. In 1932 Carrington was convinced to try her hand at radio and she managed to get some sample scripts into the hands of NBC executives who saw promise in her work.

Carrington's first aural creation was *Red Adams* that ran three times per week for a few months from 1932 to 1933 and again under sponsorship from 1933–1935 as *Red Davis*. When the sponsor changed, the series changed names once again, becoming *Pepper Young's Family*. In 1939 Carrington debuted *When a Girl Marries* that ran until 1957 and then in 1944 *Rosemary* premiered, broadcasting until 1955. Unlike the Hummerts who hired a stable of writers for the day-to-day scripting of their shows, Carrington wrote her three series, estimated at nearly 40,000 words per week at one point.

Carrington had other radio credits including a 13-episode series called *When a Man Marries* developed specifically for Burgess Meredith and his wife and *Trouble House* (1936–1937) that was a portion of *The Heinz Magazine of the Air*, a variety show of interviews, music and guest features. After World War II Carrington developed a series called *Elaine Carrington Playhouse* in 1946 and then the short-lived serial *Marriage for Two* in 1948.

Sources: Elaine Carrington Papers; *Broadcasting* August 9, 1943, p. 28, May 12, 1958, p. 68; *Radio Mirror* May 1946 p. 6; *Variety* August 4, 1937, p. 31, October 4, 1944, p. 22, 24, March 3 1948 p. 32.

Carroll, Bob, Jr.

Bob Carroll, Jr., (August 12, 1918–January 27, 2007) won a radio script contest in 1940, initiating what would be a long and successful writing career in radio and television. He joined CBS' writing staff at their Hollywood outlet in 1943 and was initially assigned to research a program called *Don't You Believe It*. Through the 1940s Carroll worked on *Potluck Party* (1944), *The Bill Thompson Show* (1946) and *It's a Great*

Life (1948) before joining the writing team for Lucille Ball's *My Favorite Husband* (1948–1950), her radio show that preceded her iconic television program *I Love Lucy*.

Sources: *Broadcasting* May 31, 1943, p. 33, March 13, 1944, p. 36; *Variety* January 12, 1949, p. 22.

Carroll, Carroll

Born Carroll Weinschenk (April 11, 1902–February 5, 1991) and known professionally as Carroll Carroll, Carroll dropped out of high school and wrote for a number of magazines and newspapers before entering radio in 1932 with the J. Walter Thompson Agency. Recognized for his quick wit, Carroll's show credits include a virtual who's-who of the era's comedians.

One of his first assignments with Thompson was writing for the *Burns & Allen* program in the early 1930s and also Eddie Cantor's program until 1934. He subsequently served as the writer and producer of Al Jolson's *Shell Chateau* from 1935 to 1936 and that same year he was credited with writing *NTG and His Girls* (1935–1936), a musical variety series featuring Nils Thor Granlund.

By 1937 Carroll was the main writer for *Kraft Music Hall* starring Bing Crosby and is credited with developing much of Crosby's on-air aura. He stayed with Crosby's show many years, departing in 1944. Other shows for which Carroll wrote during his years at Thompson include *The Gene Autry Melody Ranch* (ca. 1940), *The Edgar Bergen & Charlie McCarthy Show* (ca. 1942), *The Frank Sinatra Show* (1942–1945), the first edition of that program, *Over Here* (1942–1943), and *The Old Gold Show* with Bob Crosby (ca. 1943). Other credits were a 1945 Tommy Dorsey summer series for Fitch and various Elgin Watch holiday specials in the mid–1940s.

Not all of Carroll's efforts were highly regarded, however. He was one of the writers for the trainwreck of a talk show called *The Circle*. Sponsored by Kellogg's, big name stars such as Ronald Coleman and the Marx Brothers were brought together to discuss issues of the day. He recalled that since the star hosts were given the power to control their portion of the broadcast, the creators—including the writing staff—were hamstrung in their efforts to create a lively and entertaining show.

After fourteen years with J. Walter Thompson Carroll left in 1946 to join the Ward Wheelock agency. There he wrote and supervised such programs as *Club Fifteen* (1947–1953), a musical series with Bob Crosby, *Meet Corliss Archer* (ca. 1947), and *Double Or Nothing*, a long-running quiz show.

Carroll continued writing for radio even as it declined in the face of television's ascension. His later writing was featured on *The Ford Road Show* in 1957 and some 1960s Edgar Bergen specials. Familiar with Bergen from his time writing for *Bergen and McCarthy* during its radio run, they reunited in the 1960s to create some anniversary shows for Chase & Sanborn which had sponsored Bergen's radio show for many years. Using old transcription records Carroll put together specials for 1964, 1965, and 1966 to which Bergen then added narration linking the clips together.

Sources: *Broadcasting* January 1, 1940, p. 24; *Radio Mirror* April 1937 p. 83; *Sponsor* November 23, 1957, p. 82; *Variety* December 13, 1932, p. 33, June 16, 1943, p. 36, July 10, 1946, p. 33, April 16, 1947, p. 26, August 4, 1948, p. 24.

Carroll, Jean

Jean Carroll wrote for a number of the Hummert serials in the post-war era, from the mid–1940s to the late 1950s including *Our Gal Sunday, Mr. Keen, Tracer of Lost Persons, Mr. Chameleon*, and *Young Widder Brown*. While Carroll is sometimes said to be the stand-up comic of the same name from the 1950s, no direct evidence could be found to support this conclusion. Nor does it seem likely that a successful stage comedienne would write soap operas on the side for the middling wages offered by the industry.

Other Radio: *It Takes a Woman* (ca. 1945).

Sources: *Cox Same Time* (1996); *Variety* October 31, 1945, p. 36.

Carroll, Richard

Richard Carroll (October 27 1898–March 11, 1959) was a busy screenwriter who is only known to have contributed to a couple radio series, both in the 1940s. The first was *The Hallmark Charlotte Greenwood Show* (1944–1946) for which he seems to have only contributed a very few scripts. Carroll's most notable radio work was 1948's *Shorty Bell*, a big-budget series starring Mickey Rooney that ended up a flop.

Film: *Love Time* (1934); *Two Yanks in Trinidad* (1942); *Back from Eternity* (1956).
Source: *Variety* March 31, 1948, p. 23.

Carson, Lee

Lee Carson, not to be confused with the news correspondent of the same name, wrote for at least three radio programs in the early 1950s, *The New Beulah Show* (1953–1954), *My Little Margie* (1952–1955), and *Meet Corliss Archer*.
Source: *Broadcasting-Telecasting* December 14, 1953, p. 36.

Castellaw, Chet

Chet Castellaw spent the 1940s writing for some of radio's top comedy programs including *Kraft Music Hall* (1944), Bob Hope's *The Pepsodent Show* (1945–1948), *Joan Davis Time* (1948), and *The Martin and Lewis Show* (1949). Later Castellaw became a reverend and writer in the Church of Religious Science.
Sources: *Broadcasting* August 21, 1944, p. 63; *Variety* April 2, 1947, p. 35.

Cenedella, Robert

Robert Cenedella (October 8, 1911–September 28, 2002) is a relatively unknown name among radio historians yet was a prolific author in the medium nonetheless. He was writing for radio as early as 1939 on *The Chase & Sanborn Hour* and stayed very busy through the 1940s providing stories and adaptations for numerous shows including *The Sammy Kaye Show* (ca. 1943), *The Textron Theatre* with Helen Hayes (1945), *The Theatre Guild on the Air* (1946, 1947) on which he also served as script editor, *Cavalcade of America* (1946, 1948), *Hollywood Players* (1946), *House of Mystery* (1946), *Radio Reader's Digest* (1946–1948), and *The Electric Theater* (1948–1949).

Cenedella's radio work continued unabated into the early 1950s on *You Are There* (1950), *Up for Parole* (1950), *All-American Sports Show* (1953), *Best Plays* (1953), *NBC Star Playhouse* (1953), *Rocky Fortune* (1953), and *Best Music* (1954).

His career was sidelined in the 1950s with the Blacklist but he managed to reemerge on some late radio broadcasts into the late 1960s including *Suspense* (1961) and *Theatre Five* (1964–1965). Cenedella finished his career developing and writing network soaps on television in the 1960s and very early 1970s.
Television: *Guiding Light* (1952); *Another World* (1969–1971); *Secret Storm*; *Return to Peyton Place*; *Somerset*.
Sources: Adcock; *Billboard* December 29, 1945, p. 11; *Broadcasting* August 16, 1943, p. 28, *Variety* May 15, 1946, p. 28, June 12, 1946, p. 28, September 11, 1946, p. 34, September 18, 1946, p. 26, October 6, 1948; *The Free Lance-Star* (VA) June 18, 1979, p. 11; ambulance-brother.wordpress.com.

Chapin, Martha

March Chapin was one of a handful of writers who penned scripts for *The Adventures of Bill Lance*, a 1944–1945 detective series.
Source: Cox *Crime Fighters*.

Charlot, Harry Engman

Harry Charlot (d. October 3, 1935) was a short story writer who turned to radio in the late 1920s, writing stories for the Judson Radio Program Corporation's *True Detective* radio show. For that series Charlot created a mysterious narrator he dubbed The Shadow. He died under somewhat suspicious circumstances not fully known to this day.
Source: Grams *Shadow*.

Charteris, Leslie

Leslie Charteris (actually Leslie Charles Bowyer-Yin, May 12, 1907–April 15, 1993) was a busy writer turning out short stories and novels, many based on his famous creation, Simon Templar, The Saint. In the early 1930s Charteris wrote a few screenplays and turned to radio for just a short time, taking over scripting *The Adventures of Sherlock Holmes* in 1944. Though *The Saint* was a long-running radio series, Charteris was generally not involved in writing the episodes though he was credited at times with some editing responsibilities.

Sources: *Broadcasting* January 8, 1945, p. 50; *International Photographer* July 1933 p. 30; *Variety* July 26, 1944, p. 24.

Chase, Kay

Kay Chase took over writing the WGN serial *Painted Dreams* in 1932 after creator **Irna Phillips** left the station in a dispute, and that same year started acting on the show as well. She is credited with writing *The Romance of Helen Trent* in 1937 and in 1938, less than a year after *Valiant Lady* debuted, Chase and her husband Tom Goodrich were writing those scripts as well. Chase was still active in radio in the early 1950s, penning *The Singing Marshal* during its 1950–1951 run.

Sources: French & Siegel p. 166; *Chicago Sunday Tribune* February 19, 1939, p. 4W, November 30, 1941, p. 9W; *Motion Picture Daily* March 23, 1937, p. 10, November 10, 1938, p. 2.

Chevigny (Chivigny), Hector

The earliest known radio series written by Montana-born Hector Chevigny (June 28, 1904–April 20, 1965) was *Pioneers*, aired over Seattle's KOMO in the early 1930s before he moved to the city's KOL as continuity director in 1935. That job was short-lived as Chevigny moved to Hollywood before the end of the year to work first with Radioaids, Inc., and then for KNX as continuity director.

After working into 1937 as a writer for *Hollywood Hotel* and *Black Chapel*, Chevigny moved again to Young & Rubicam Inc. where he was soon added to the writing staff of the *Charlie Chan* series produced by Irving Fogel Radio Productions as well as authoring 100 episodes of a transcribed series, *Lady of Millions*. In 1938 Chevigny replaced John Slott scripting CBS Pacific's *White Fires*, the dramatizations of famous lives.

The 1940s was a very busy decade for Chevigny during which time he wrote hundreds of scripts for over a dozen identified series: *Woodbury's Hollywood Playhouse* (1939–1940), *Klondike* (1940), the story of Alaska in 1898, *Big Town* (1940), *Keystone of Hollywood* (1940), *Red Ryder* (1942), *Gulf Screen Guild Theatre* (1941), *Cavalcade of America* (1942), *Portia Faces Life* (1940–1951), *Creeps by Night* (1944), *Treasury Salute* (1945), Morton Downey's program in 1945 sponsored by Coca Cola, *A Brighter Tomorrow* (1947), *Plays by Ear* (1947), *We the People* (1947–1949), and *Mr. and Mrs. North* (1948–1950).

If Chevigny didn't write for as many series in the 1950s it's only because the daily serials to which he was committed required so much time and because he was serving in an elected capacity for the Writers Guild. Nevertheless, he worked on a number of different series through the decade right up until 1962 when the final primetime dramatic network radio shows left the air. These programs included *The Halls of Ivy* (1950), *Valiant Lady* (1951–1952), *The Second Mrs. Burton* (ca. 1952–1959), *CBS Radio Workshop* (1956), and *Suspense* (1962).

Chevigny lost his sight in 1943 and moved to New York for several surgeries that were ultimately unsuccessful. Thereafter he had to rely on stenographers to write his words for him.

Other Radio: *Inner Sanctum*

Books: *Lost Empire* (1937); *The Czar Is Far Away* (1942).

Sources: Hector Chevigny Scripts; *Broadcasting* January 1, 1935, p. 22, October 1, 1935, p. 34, October 1, 1936, p. 44, July 15, 1937, p. 70, August 1, 1937, p. 66, October 1, 1938, April 15, 1940, p. 66, February 2, 1942, p. 39, *Radio Mirror* December 1945 p. 53; *Sponsor* July 1947 p. 53; *Variety* November 14, 1945, p. 39.

Chevillat, Dick

Dick Chevillat (December 31, 1905–May 10, 1984) started writing for Sealtest around 1940 and was assigned to a number of shows during his years with the ice cream producer. He was writing for *The Rudy Vallee Show* with **Bill Demling** in 1942 and by 1944 on *The Joan Davis–Jack Haley Show* (also *The Sealtest Village Store*) with Sy Wills and **Ray Singer**. After Davis left and Haley remained as the solo host, Chevillat stayed with the program (ca. 1947). Chevillat and Singer stayed together in 1947 when they signed to work on the writing team for *The Phil Harris–Alice Faye Show*, an outgrowth of the husband and wife team's appearances on the *Fitch Bandwagon*. Considered one of the era's best programs by radio enthusiasts, Chevillat wrote for Harris-Faye into the 1950s.

After radio Chevillat stayed busy writing for television from the mid–1950s to 1970, most notably on *The Frank Sinatra Show* (1957–1958) and *Green Acres* (1965–1971).
Sources: *Broadcasting* October 12, 1942, p. 36; *Variety* September 6, 1944, April 24, 1946, p. 44, April 2, 1947, p. 35, August 20, 1947, p. 25.

Christy, Floyd

Floyd Christy (d. May 21, 1962) was the co-writer with **Jimmy Scribner** for *The Johnson Family* (1934–1950), the story of the African-American village Chickazola voiced entirely by Scribner.
Source: *Radio Life* May 26, 1946, p. 32.

Clark, Marian

Marian Clark (d. February 26, 1963) joined Los Angeles' KNX in 1943 as a junior writer after graduating from the station's ten-week workshop for female staff. She worked in the news department for some time and later, after befriending writer **Kathleen Hite**, penned dozens of Western radio broadcasts in the final years of the medium's Golden Age, between 1957 and 1961. Her work was primarily featured on *Gunsmoke* and *Have Gun, Will Travel*. Clark died at the relatively young age of 50 after a brief illness.
Sources: Wright "Gunsmoke's Unknown Writer"; *Broadcasting* February 22, 1943, p. 50, March 11, 1963, p. 91.

Cole, Alonzo Deen

Alonzo Deen Cole (February 22, 1897–March 31, 1971) left his mark in radio as the definitive author of two widely remembered programs, *The Witch's Tale* and *Flashgun Casey, Crime Photographer*. *The Witch's Tale* debuted over New York's WOR in 1931 and Cole wrote the series for seven years. Along the way he reused some of the *Witch's* scripts while penning stories for the 1932–1933 season of *The Shadow*.

After leaving *The Witch's Tale* in 1938 Cole wrote more episodes for *The Shadow* (1938–1939) and went to work for Phillips H. Lord as script editor and writer for some of Lord's series. The relationship lasted two years but ended in an ugly lawsuit that dragged on into the early 1940s when Cole accused Lord of stealing an idea that was turned into the wildly successful *Mr. District Attorney*.

In 1943 *Flashgun Casey, Crime Photographer* arrived on the air, the radio adaptation of George Harmon Coxe's popular crime fighter. The series ran into the mid–1950s under a few different titles and Cole scripted nearly all of the approximately 400 episodes.
Other Radio: *Darling and Dearie* (1938 audition); *Star Spangled Theatre* (1941).
Sources: Cox & Siegel; Grams *Shadow*; *Broadcasting* October 1, 1938, p. A7; *Motion Picture Daily* June 23, 1941, p. 4.

Cole, Beatrice

Beatrice Cole co-wrote *It's Always Albert* for transcription in 1948 with **Jacqueline Susann**. In 1951 she wrote Susann's television program, *Jacqueline Susann's Open Door*.
Theater: *Lovely Me* (1946 with Jacqueline Susann, originally *The Temporary Mrs. Smith*).
Sources: *Billboard* June 2, 1951, p. 6; *Variety* May 26, 1948, p. 23.

Coles, Stedman

Stedman Coles was most active as a radio writer during the 1940s, penning *Roger Kilgore, Public Defender* (1948), *Crime Cases* (1946), *The Shadow* (1943–1946), *Crime Club* (1948), *Nick Carter, Master Detective* (1948), and *Secret Missions* (1949). Coles is also credited on *Famous Jury Trials*, *Mr. Keen, Tracer of Lost Persons*, and *Top Secrets of the FBI*.
Film: *Follies Girl* (1943)
Sources: Grams *Shadow*; *Variety* December 4, 1946, p. 36, April 7, 1948, p. 30.

Colwell, Bob (Robert)

A gifted gag writer, Bob Colwell was an early radio writer of comedy material, scripting for *The Eddie Cantor Show* (ca. 1931 or 1932) and George Jessell's sketches on *The Chase & Sanborn Hour* (ca. 1932). His talent landed him a position with the J. Walter Thompson Agency in the early 1930s where he oversaw the writing of numerous programs over many years including a Kraft-Phenix Cheese program (1936) and Kellogg's *The Circle* (1939), on which he was called to resuscitate after it got off to a rough start. During World War II Colwell worked for the Office of War Information while on leave from Thompson.

Colwell left J. Walter Thompson in 1946 to co-found a new agency, Sullivan, Stauffer, Colwell, & Bayles where he spent ten years before returning to Thompson in a creative position with fewer executive duties in 1956. During this time, Colwell's radio responsibilities faded as he focused more on other responsibilities in other mediums.

Other Radio: *The Rudy Vallee Show.*
Sources: *Broadcasting* May 1, 1932, p. 16, March 15, 1936, p. 40; *Broadcasting-Telecasting* May 14, 1956, p. 35; *Motion Picture Daily* March 7, 1939, p. 16; *Variety* March 14, 1933, p. 34, March 8 1939 p. 41, December 6, 1944, p. 25, August 7, 1946.

Conkle, E. P. (Ellsworth Prouty)

E. P. Conkle (July 10, 1899–February 18, 1994) was a playwright of the 1930s and a longtime professor at the University of Texas. He wrote one radio series, CBS' *Honest Abe*, that aired for 36 episodes between 1940 and 1941.

Sources: E. P. Conkle Papers; *Variety* July 10, 1940, p. 25.

Conlon, Paul

Paul Conlon (February 20, 1900–February 26, 1980) performed "George and Rufus" sketches over New York's WMCA before joining Long Beach, CA's KFOX as a continuity writer in 1932. Later in the decade by 1937 he was scripting for Ed Wynn and in 1940 he was the author of NBC's *Signal Carnival*. In 1943 Conlon joined the *Judy Canova Show*, added *Louisiana Hayride* in 1944, then in 1946 started to work on *The Abbott & Costello Show* where he wrote until 1949.

Sources: *The Film Daily* July 6, 1937, p. 7; *The Radio Annual, 1940* p. 792; *Variety* September 15, 1932, p. 18, August 11, 1943, p. 34, February 16, 1944, p. 28, January 9 1946 p. 97.

Conn, Harry

Harry Conn (b. December 1, 1892) started in radio supplying material to George Burns and Gracie Allen. Burns recommended Conn to his friend, Jack Benny, and Conn earned his place in radio lore helping adapt Benny's vaudeville characteristics into a perennial radio fan-favorite. He was reportedly making a hefty $1,500 per week with Benny—who was far from cheap in reality—but Conn's compensation demands finally grew too large and he left the show in 1936. The split was acrimonious and Conn eventually sued for $65,000, insisting that he was instrumental to the success of Benny's show.

Conn went to write for former radio headliner Joe Penner who made a name for himself a few years earlier with a handful of catchphrases that swept the nation and then quickly grew stale. Penner hired the proven writer for his radio comeback in 1936 with *The Joe Penner Show* but there was no magic in the pairing and Conn left after a few months, replaced by **Don Prindle**.

In January 1937 Conn wrote two scripts for Al Jolson's program and that summer wrote for Walter O'Keefe on *Town Hall Tonight*. At the very end of 1937 Conn returned to the air with his own series, *Earaches of 1938*. The effort fell flat and by the spring of 1938 Conn was penning material for Eddie Cantor's show and later that summer scripting an audition disc for Milton Berle. Conn joined yet another program in the fall of 1938, *The Jack Haley Variety Show* that he wrote with **Hal Fimberg** until November before resigning. Conn faded from radio's limelight after this point though he occasionally reemerged in the following years, even writing some material for the duo Smith & Dale when they appeared on television's *Steve Allen Show* in 1956.

Film: *Broadway Melody of 1936.*
Sources: Allen *Treadmill* p. 12; *Broadcasting* October 1, 1938, p. A6, November 15, 1938, p. 41; *Motion Picture Daily* December 14, 1936, p. 4, January 28, 1937, p 8, July 2, 1937, p. 13, August 15, 1956, p. 4; *Radio Mirror* February 1938 p. 42; *Variety* August 14, 1935, p. 31, April 6, 1938, p. 26, June 29, 1938, p. 27.

Connelly, Joe

A writer for the J. Walter Thompson agency, Joe Connelly (August 22, 1917–February 13, 2003) was one of the premier comedy writers of the 1940s, working on scripts for some of the biggest names on the air. In 1942 he was sent to the agency's Hollywood office to collaborate with **Carroll Carroll** on Victor Borge's Kraft program and the next year he worked with **Joe Bigelow** on *The Chase & Sanborn Hour* with **Bob Mosher** replacing Bigelow for the 1943–1944 season. Connelly was moved to Edgar Bergen's show in 1944 with Mosher and then *Maxwell House Iced Coffee Time* with **Leonard Levinson**.

During the mid–1940s Connelly wrote on *The Frank Morgan Show* (1945) and *The Fitch Bandwagon* (1946–1947 with Bob Mosher) after it assumed a sitcom format with Phil Harris and Alice Faye. Connelly's longest writing assignment began in 1947 when he joined the writing team for *The Amos 'n' Andy Show*, where he wrote until the early 1960s even as the once-great comedy had devolved into the DJ program *Amos 'n' Andy Music Hall*.

Despite this success in the radio industry, Connelly's real fame came in television where he created *Leave It to Beaver* in 1957 with long-time collaborator Mosher and *The Munsters* in 1964. He was also behind **Freeman Gosden** and **Charles Correll**'s animated television series *Calvin and the Colonel* (1961–1962). Connelly was nominated for an Oscar for Best Writing (Motion Picture Story) in 1956 for *The Private War of Major Benson*.

Other Radio: *The Harry Von Zell Show* (1946, audition); *Meet Mr. McNutley* (1954, co-created with Bob Mosher)

Sources: *Broadcasting* January 11, 1943, p. 32, August 16, 1943, p. 20, 28; *Variety* April 1, 1942, p. 28, April 19, 1944, p. 23, June 21, 1944, p. 34, June 18, 1947, p. 28.

Connor, Herbert R. (Herb)

Herb Connor was a West Coast writer who wrote for *House Undivided*, a Don Lee serial (1937), *The Hermit's Cave* (early 1940s), and *The Whistler* (1942).

Source: *Broadcasting* August 15, 1937, p. 36.

Cook, Dwight

Dwight Cook wrote for *The March of Time* in the mid–1930s before going to work for the J. Walter Thompson agency in 1937 where he worked on *The Chase & Sanborn Show*.

Source: *Motion Picture Daily* April 26, 1937, p. 15.

Cook, Virginia (sometimes Cooke)

Virgina Cook was identified as the writer of *Speed Gibson of the International Secret Police*, a transcribed series produced from 1937 to 1940 and later as co-writer with William Thompson of the 1939 transcribed series *My Prayer Was Answered*. After working as a freelance writer, Cook was hired by Walter K. Neill Inc.'s radio division in 1941. In 1944 Cook was pegged to write *The Gallant Heart*, a serial that premiered that year and the next year she wrote for *The Billie Burke Show*. Between 1950 and 1953 Cook adapted several episodes of *Family Theatre*.

Other Radio: *Lives of Harry Lime*; *Today's Children*.

Sources: *Broadcasting* June 15, 1939, p. 51, June 9, 1941, p. 34; *Variety* April 4, 1945, p. 39.

Cool, Gool

Gomer Cool (April 20, 1908–March 4, 2012) started working at Kansas City's KMBC in the late 1920s performing a variety of tasks including writing, singing, and acting. By 1932 he settled into what would be his primary role for the station as writer and violinist for the Texas Rangers, one of the station's house bands. In 1934 he and **Paul Henning** wrote a local series, *The A–G Musical Grocers*, and then in 1935 Cool penned 65 episodes of the musical-drama serial *Life on the Red Horse Ranch*, a transcribed program that found modest success on plains and interior West radio stations.

In 1939 the Texas Rangers were relocated to southern California with the hope that there would be more opportunities to establish themselves on the national scene than was possible in Kansas City and Cool wrote various test scripts for Rangers programs. The band struggled as World War II broke out and Cool quit KMBC to write full-time for CBS. Among his series with the network were a word game series for *Sweetheart Soap* (ca. 1943), *Hawk Larabee* (1947), *Rocky Jordan* (1948–1950), more Texas Rangers broadcasts throughout the decade, *A Memo from Molly* (1950), and some episodes of *The Whistler* (1952).

Cool left the radio business in the mid–1950s and opened a candy store that he ran for many years. He passed away peacefully at the age of 103.

Sources: Ellett *Texas Rangers*; *Broadcasting* April 26, 1943, p. 117; *Broadcasting-Telecasting* November 6 1950 p. 72; *Variety* May 8 1934 p. 43, February 2, 1949, p. 24.

Cooper, Courtney Ryley (Riley)

Courtney Ryley Cooper (October 31, 1886–September 29, 1940) was a colorful character who worked with circuses and newspapers before turning to writing for different mediums in the 1920s. He authored hundreds of short stories, a few of which were adapted into motion pictures before he had a chance at radio. Evidence from 1957, thirty years after the fact, suggests that Cooper adapted one of his plays ("Yellow") for radio transcription as early as 1927. His first verified radio scripting was for *The Gibson Family*, an expensive Proctor & Gamble show that attempted to bring an original musical to the air every week beginning the fall of 1934. His writing contribution to the show was the libretto while Howard Dietz and Arthur Schwartz wrote the songs and lyrics. *The Gibson Family* was revamped in May of 1935 without Cooper in an effort to boost ratings and cut costs.

Late in 1937 Cooper was engaged to write a proposed Edward G. Robinson series in which he was cast as a newspaper editor. Originally called *Today*, it sounds like a precursor to *Big Town* that debuted a few weeks later without Cooper's involvement. Cooper died in 1940 under somewhat suspect circumstances. He was found hung in a hotel room but FBI memos hinted he might have been murdered.

Books: *Memories of Buffalo Bill* (1919); *Annie Oakley, Woman at Arms* (1922); *Ten Thousand Public Enemies* (1935).

Sources: Courtney Ryley Cooper—Missouri Valley Special Collections; *Broadcasting-Telecasting* February 4, 1957, p. 22, March 4, 1957, p. 16; *Variety* May 29, 1935, p. 43; October 6, 1937, p. 29.

Cooper, Wyllis (Willis)

Wyllis Cooper (January 26, 1899–June 22, 1955) got his radio start on Chicago's WBBM where he wrote *The Lost Legion* in 1932, based on the French Foreign Legion and later renamed *Tales of the Foreign Legion* in 1933. He also scripted a series about Catholics through American history while with WBBM. After switching from CBS to NBC in 1933 to become a continuity chief, Cooper created, directed, and wrote *Lights Out!* that debuted in 1934. He also scripted a daily juvenile thriller called *Flying Time* (1935) before resigning from NBC in 1935 to write freelance. Soon thereafter Cooper added the serial *Betty and Bob* to his scripting duties.

Cooper left radio and Chicago in 1936 to pursue opportunities in screenwriting, where he wrote such films as *Son of Frankenstein* and installments in the *Mr. Moto* film series. A career in motion picture career never took off, however, and he returned to radio within a year.

In 1937 Cooper was back on the air with some scripts for *Hollywood Hotel* and by 1940 with scripts for a number of series including Campbell Soup's *A Short Short Story*, *Charlie and Jessie*, and the second incarnation of *The Campbell Playhouse* (1940–1941). 1941 proved to be just as busy with writing assignments for *Spirit of '41*, *Good Neighbor*, and the serial *The Story of Bess Johnson*. With the United States' entry into World War II Cooper was brought in to write *The Army Hour*, during which he called on his experience as a veteran of the First World War. His goal was to write a show that was "100 percent authentic" whether that was "good, bad, or indifferent." Cooper scripted at least two additional series during the war, *Great Americans* (ca. 1942) and *Arthur Hopkins Presents* (1944).

In the summer of 1946 some of Cooper's old *Lights Out!* scripts were recycled when the radio series was brought back as a summer replacement and also when a televised version was aired on NBC. Much to Cooper's irritation, he was credited in both instances despite having no connection with either effort and not even being made aware his scripts were being used.

Some of Cooper's later radio series included *Crime Club* (1947), and a return to his spine-tingling roots with a new program, *Quiet, Please!*. It aired until 1949 when he took over writing for *We the People* and also saw his first television effort, *Volume One, Numbers One to Six*, broadcast on ABC TV in 1949. His last major series was *Whitehall 1212* (1951–1952) before passing away at 56.

Sources: *Broadcasting* July 1, 1935, p. 98, November 15, 1935, p. 36, October 27, 1941, p. 33, February 14, 1949; *Broadcasting and Telecasting* April 25, 1949, p. 64; *Motion Picture Daily* May 22, 1941, p. 8; *Radio and Television Mirror* April 1940 p. 45; *Radio Digest* April 1932 p. 64; *Variety* January 31, 1933, p. 38, 62, July 18, 1933, p. 59, October 22, 1941, May 20, 1942, p. 39, March 1, 1944, p. 32, July 3, 1946, p. 31; *Chicago Tribune* August 29, 1935, p. 23.

Corcoran, Robert (Bob)

Robert Corcoran left his mark on a number of radio and television series during the 1950s, though only *Suspense*, for which he wrote some episodes at the end of its run from 1961–1962, is widely remembered. His other programs were *The Rayburn and Finch Show* (1951), *Stagestruck* (1953–1954), *Peter Lind Hayes* (1954), and *Indictment* (1956–1959).

Television: *Jimmy Hughes, Rookie Cop* (1953); *Modern Romances* (1954); *Patti Page Show* (1956 summer replacement for *Perry Como Show*).

Sources: Hyatt p. 46; *Billboard* August 18, 1951, p. 9, June 19, 1954, p. 50; *Broadcasting* February 13, 1956, p. 18, June 25, 1956, p. 14; WeLoveSoaps.net.

Correll, Charles

Charles Correll (February 2, 1890–September 26, 1972) earned his broadcasting fame by co-creating the enduringly popular but controversial *Amos 'n' Andy* program. He met longtime partner **Freeman Gosden** as a young man working with the Joe Bren Producing Company. They started on radio in the mid–1920s as song-and-patter performers but added writing to their list of aural duties when they created a series for WGN entitled *Sam 'n' Henry*, a broadcast answer to the popular newspaper serial comic strips. The program focused on two rural black men who move from the South to Chicago and inevitably got involved in typical rube-in-the-city trouble.

After two years on WGN, Correll and Gosden—dissatisfied with their contract—moved their program to intra-city rival WMAQ, renamed it *Amos 'n' Andy*, and started a meteoric rise to fame. By 1931 *Amos 'n' Andy* had become a national fad; apocryphal stories indicate commerce would come to a stop for ten minutes while the show aired. Amos and Andy were on radio until 1960 in various formats, a tenure that spanned the entire length of radio's Golden Age and that few other performers could match.

Loved by many for his portrayal of Andrew H. Brown, Correll's writing prowess is often overlooked. For the two years of *Sam 'n' Henry* and then for the first several years of *Amos 'n' Andy* Correll co-wrote six scripts every week. When the show was revamped in 1943 and turned into a traditional sitcom, writing duties were turned over to a talented team of comedy writers.

Correll's skill as an actor is indisputable as is attested by the program's popularity for so long. However, without engaging characters and storylines, *Amos 'n' Andy* would be among the countless forgotten dialect characters of the era. Correll is deserving of accolades as a top-rate writer for creating material that, at its height, pulled in over half of all radio listeners.

Source: McLeod.

Corwin, Norman

Norman Corwin (May 3, 1910–October 18, 2011) was one of the most critically acclaimed writers of radio scripts during the medium's Golden Age. Because he lived to be 101 and remained active teaching and staying in contact with the broadcasting history community until his passing, Corwin has also developed somewhat of an outsized popularity in comparison to his writing peers from the 1930s and 1940s.

The Boston-born Corwin recalled writing his first story at age seven, an escape from the poverty of his childhood surroundings, but it was a high school teacher who pushed him to hone his writing and consider pursuing it after graduation. Eschewing college to his parents' dismay, a seventeen-year-old Corwin took his first job as a writer for the Greenfield (Mass.) *Recorder*. He subsequently took his brother's former position with the Springfield (Mass.) *Republican* and soon after published his first book, a volume of quotations divided by themes.

Like so many radio professionals of the time, Corwin ended up on the air by happenstance. Springfield's WBZA asked him to interview a local hero on the air, a one-time event which led to his appointment as the *Republican*'s radio editor. With a pianist friend he created *Rhymes and Cadences*, interludes of poetry readings and music. Getting restless in Springfield, Corwin jumped at the chance to audition for Cincinnati's giant WLW that held tryouts in New York in 1935 for new talent. Thrilled when he was hired, Corwin's stay with Powel Crosley, Jr.'s station lasted just a few weeks. Questioning the station's ban on publicizing any labor difficulty, he was promptly informed that his position was being eliminated. Pink slip in hand, Corwin quietly landed back in Massachusetts and rejoined WBZA as an editor. During this time he took to the air with *Norman Corwin's Journal* over another Springfield station, WMAS.

Corwin got a position with 20th Century Fox studios in Manhattan through his brother Emil, who was leaving the company. There Corwin created publicity for their films and then with New York's WQXR where he founded *Poetic License* that featured contemporary poets and their work. His work with WQXR—and some help again from his brother Emil—brought Corwin to the attention of the networks. First, NBC hired him to contribute to their variety show *The Magic Key of RCA*. Unimpressed, NBC didn't ask him for further scripts. Not long after, however, W. B. Lewis, a CBS vice-president, subsequently hired him in April 1938.

Corwin cut his network teeth on CBS' *Living History* and *Americans at Work*, before he was called on to produce episodes of CBS' experimental *The Columbia Workshop*. Thrilled at such a huge opportunity so soon after getting into radio, Corwin quickly realized he was somewhat over his head, with no experience handling professional performing talent and working at the high technical standards expected by the network. He toiled away, honing his radio writing skills, and within three years he became synonymous with the series, having 26 weeks of the show's schedule at his complete disposal.

In addition to his work with *The Columbia Workshop*, Corwin spent several months writing *Words Without Music* and was pleasantly surprised when Lewis offered to preface the series title with Corwin's name, a nearly unheard of honor. *Words Without Music* ran for six months between 1938 and 1939 and attracted some critical praise, including the attention of Edward R. Murrow. With the outbreak of war gripping Europe, Corwin focused several broadcasts on illuminating the evil of the continent's fascist governments. The series included two of his earliest classic stories, "The Plot to Overthrow Christmas" and "They Fly Through the Air With the Greatest of Ease."

With the conclusion of *Words Without Music* in the summer of 1939, Corwin had a subsequent run of programs including *So This Is Radio*, *Pursuit of Happiness*, and *Twenty-Six by Corwin*. He was thrust further into the national spotlight with the December 15, 1941, broadcast of *We Hold These Truths*, an hour-long celebration of the 150th anniversary of the Bill of Rights that was carried on all four networks. The cast included luminaries such as Jimmy Stewart, Edward G. Robinson, and Orson Welles, the music of the New York Philharmonic, and an address by president Franklin Roosevelt. Aired just a week after the Japanese attack on Pearl Harbor, *We Hold These Truths* took on added gravitas and it's estimated that half of the nation tuned in to listen. As war loomed, Corwin also contributed to *The Free Company* (1941), a collaborative effort by a group of writers to counter foreign propaganda. Soon after, Corwin was assigned to write six of the thirteen episodes of *This Is War!*, a series carried in early 1942 on all four networks as the United States turned its national attention to conducting war in Europe and the Pacific.

For four months in 1942 CBS sent Corwin to the warfront in England where he wrote about the tribulations of a nation facing the dire threat of Nazi Germany. He wrote stories reflecting the common man and woman in the street and about their place in the larger war effort. The program, *An American in England*, faced numerous technical obstacles that hampered Corwin's natural drive to push the limits of radio.

This series was followed quickly by *Passport for Adams* and *An American in Russia*, both broadcast in 1943. *Passport for Adams* focused on a country newspaperman and was Corwin's response to the Office of War Information that had asked him to create a program that would contribute to goodwill with allied nations. Then, in 1944, Corwin was given *Columbia Presents Corwin*, a series that allowed him a near free hand in creating plays for the air. Upon its conclusion in the late summer of that year, Corwin wrote an hour-long "documentary" of FDR that aired the night before election day. It was so biased toward Roosevelt over his opponent, New York governor Thomas E. Dewey, that the networks refused to allow such works in the future that might sway election results.

A few months later Corwin wrote yet another piece of radio propaganda, this one in celebration of the end of the war in Europe. *On a Note of Triumph*, broadcast May 8, 1945, was narrated by Martin Gabel and proved so popular that it was repeated on May 13. That summer *Columbia Presents Corwin* was reprised for two months.

In the late 1940s Corwin's influence at CBS began to wane, with network head William Paley suggesting that more commercially popular fare from the writer would be welcome. One of Corwin's last notable works with the network was *One World Flight* in 1947, a series he proposed in response to his winning the One World Award commemorating Wendell Willkie. Corwin's prize was a round-the-world trip, during which he recorded over 100 hours of interviews and interactions with a variety of international men and women. In 1948 Corwin left CBS after a decade with the network and went to work for United Nations Radio after a brief courtship with NBC. The position with U.N. Radio led to his writing of *Document A/777*, a program in favor of an international Bill of Human Rights that received radio's Peabody Award. Other U.N. series included *Citizen of the World*, *Could Be*, and *The Pursuit of Peace*.

Corwin was caught up in the post-war Communist scare when he was included on an FBI list of suspected communist sympathizer (according to Confidential Informant ND 336). He even came under personal attack in the United States Congress by Nevada Senator Pat McCarran and in 1950 was listed in the infamous *Red Channels: The Report of Communist Influence in Radio and Television*. The Red Scare waned as did the popularity of radio drama and Corwin wrapped up a distinguished career writing for the medium with a BBC play on October 4, 1955.

After radio Corwin continued to write, keeping busy with stage, television, and book projects. He briefly returned to his radio roots in 1979, scripting a story for *Sears Radio Theatre*, one of a handful of radio drama revival programs during the era. He also wrote six holiday shows for National Public Radio in 1983 and *More by Corwin* for NPR in the late 1990s. He began teaching college courses in the 1960s and continued to do so until his death, most notably at UCLA and USC.

Other Radio: Corwin contributed stories to numerous anthology series, many fondly remembered by old-time radio enthusiasts including *The Gulf Screen Guild Theatre* (1940, 1941), *Cavalcade of America* (1940, 1944), *The Silver Theatre* (1944), *The Lady Esther Screen Guild Theatre* (1946).

Television: *FDR* (1963); *Inside the Movie Kingdom* (1964); *Seven Seas* (1970); *Norman Corwin Presents* (1972–1973); *Judgement: The Court Martial of the Tiger of Malaya* (1974).

Theater: *The Rivalry* (1959); *The World of Carl Sandburg* (1960); *The Odyssey of Runyon Jones* (1972); *Cervantes* (1973); *Together Tonight! Jefferson, Hamilton, and Burr* (1976).

Film: *The Blue Veil* (1951); *Scandal at Scourie* (1953); *Lust for Life* (1956, nominated for an Academy Award); *Moby Dick* (1956); *No Place to Hide* (1956); *The Naked Maja* (1958); *The Story of Ruth* (1961); *Madison Avenue* (1962).

Books: Numerous books of Corwin scripts including *Thirteen by Corwin* (1942) and *More by Corwin* (1944). *Overkill and Megalove* (1963); *Holes in a Stained Glass Window* (1978); *Greater than the Bomb* (1981); *Trivializing America* (1983); *Norman Corwin's Letters* (1994); *One World Flight: The Lost Journal of Radio's Greatest Writer* (2009); *New Millennium: The Final Radio Plays of Norman Corwin* (2012, published posthumously).

Others: Musical cantata called *Yes Speak Out Yes* (1968).

Sources: Bannerman; www.normancorwin.com.

Cosentino, Nicholas (Nicolas, Nick)

Playwright Nicholas Cosentino is credited with two radio series, the serial *We Are Always Young* (1941) and *Theatre Five* (1965).

Theater: *Moon Over Mulberry Street* (1935); *They Live in Brooklyn* (1944); *A Kiss for Peter* (1946).

Television: *Leave It to Papa* (1951).

Sources: *Billboard* January 27, 1951, p. 9; *Variety* July 30, 1941, p. 30.

Cowgill, Rome

Rome Cowgill was a script editor at WHY, the University of Wisconsin, and the Voice of America. He authored the influential *Fundamentals of Writing for Radio* in 1949.

Source: *Broadcasting* July 4, 1949, p. 66.

Crandall, Perry

Perry Crandall is most closely associated with two syndicated programs, *The Misadventures of Si and Elmer* (1933) and *Magic Island* (1936) for which he served as author, producer, and announcer. In the mid-1930s Crandall was on the staff of San Diego's KGB before he resigned to join the Atlas Radio Corp. in Hollywood in 1937. He authored KGB series *Life of Edison*, *Sycamore Street*, *Tales of the Tuna Clippers*, and *True Air Adventures*. In 1938 he joined C. P. MacGregor where he wrote *Crimson Trail*.

Sources: *Broadcasting* September 1, 1938, p. 46; *Motion Picture Daily* August 16, 1937, p. 18; *Variety* September 1, 1937, p. 80.

Crane, Harry

Comedian Harry Crane (born Harry Kravitsky, April 23, 1914–September 13, 1999) started his humor career in standup and was performing professionally by 19. Beginning in the late 1930s Crane started to pen comedy scripts for radio, first on *Texaco Star Theater* (1939) and then for dozens of other programs. Until the early 1950s Crane was often working on multiple shows at a time, authoring jokes for Edgar Bergen, Abbott and Costello, Joan Davis, and Jimmy Durante among many.

Among the notable series for which Crane wrote during the 1940s were *Al Pearce and His Gang* (1940), *The Chase & Sanborn Program* (1941–1942), *Abbott & Costello* (1942–1944), *Blue Ribbon Town* (1943–1944), *The Jack Carson Show* (1944–1945, 1948–1949), *The Jack Kirkwood Show* (1945–1946), *The Borden Show* (1946), *The Abe Burrows Show* (1947–1950), *Adventures of Ozzie & Harriet* (1947–1948), *Arthur's Place* (1947), *The Bickersons* (1947), *The Jimmy Durante–Gerry Moore Show* (1945–1947), *The Jimmy Durante Show* (1947–1948), *The Joan Davis Show* (1945–1947), *The Danny Thomas Show* (1948), *Joan Davis Time* (1947–1948), and *Leave It to Joan* (1949).

During this prolific decade Crane also co-wrote a number of screenplays for MGM before finding success in television in the 1950s. He worked with Jackie Gleason on *Cavalcade of Stars* and subsequently helped develop *The Honeymooners*. Crane was one of Gleason's most trusted writers throughout the 1950s on a number of his series. He also worked closely with Dean Martin for many years as well as scripting awards programs for the Academy Awards, the Golden Globes, and the Emmys.

Other Radio: *Amos 'n' Andy*; *Command Performance*; *Duffy's Tavern*; *Meet Millie*.

Sources: Harry Crane Papers; *Variety* April 19, 1944, p. 23.

Crosby, Leigh (Lee)

Leigh Crosby was Blackett-Sample-Hummert's radio account executive for General Mills in the 1930s before working for a succession of radio advertising agencies including Arthur Kudner, Inc., Leon Livingston, Gardner, Lord & Thomas, and Barton A. Stebbins. With wife **Virginia Crosby** he is credited with co-writing *Aunt Mary* and *Bob and Victoria*.

Sources: *Broadcasting-Telecasting* April 4, 1949, p. 104; *Variety* May 6, 1936, p. 49.

Crosby, Virginia

Virginia Crosby, wife of **Leigh Crosby**, learned the radio writing craft under **Irna Phillips** on serials such as *The Guiding Light*, *Road of Life*, and *Today's Children*. With husband Leigh she created *Aunt Mary* in 1944 on the West Coast and wrote the program for its duration. She is also credited with writing *Bob and Victoria* (1947) and *Dr. Paul* (1949).

Sources: *Broadcasting* April 4, 1949, p. 104; *Variety* January 26, 1949, p. 30.

Cross, Joe

Joe Cross adapted the *Buck Rogers of the 25th Century* comic strip to the air and followed that up with the adaptation of another King Feature, *Mandrake the Magician* in 1935. In 1936 Cross scripted a third King Features comic for radio, *Tim Tyler's Luck*, and *What's My Name?* from

1938–1941. Cross created television's *I Challenge You* for Dumont in 1945 and attempted to revive *What's My Name?* in 1946.

Sources: *Broadcasting* April 15, 1936, p. 62, April 23, 1945, p. 14; *Variety* December 4, 1935, p. 33, November 22, 1939, p. 40, July 9, 1941, p. 26.

Crossen, Kendall

Kendall Foster Crossen (July 25, 1910–November 29, 1981) held a variety of jobs before beginning a writing career in earnest with the Works Progress Administration and then as editor of *Detective Fiction Weekly*. In succeeding years Foster worked for *Munsey's Magazine* and authored numerous pulp stories and novels under a variety of names including Bennett Barley, M. E. Chaber, Richard Foster, Christopher Monig, and Clay Richards.

As Ken Crossen he is credited with scripting for *Kate Smith, Molle Mystery Theatre, Famous Jury Trials* (all pre–1945) and *Suspense* (1948–1949). Under the Richard Foster pseudonym he co-wrote the scripts for *The Green Lama*. Crossen also contributed stories to *Bold Venture, The Saint,* and *Escape*.

He published a series of novels as M. E. Chaber starring Milo March, an insurance investigator and one of the stories was adapted as the film *The Man Inside* (1958). He made a brief stab at television with a 1959 episode of *77 Sunset Strip* and an episode of *The Man from Blackhawk* (1959–1960).

Short Stories: *Baffling Detective Mysteries* (1943); *Banner Mysteries* (1945); *Double Detective* (1940–1941, 1971); *Popular Detective* (1952–1953); *Rare Detective Cases* (1942); *Startling Stories* (1952); *Thrilling Wonder Stories* (1953).

Sources: The Kendall Foster Crossen Collection; Grams *Suspense; Motion Picture Daily* December 17, 1958, p. 1; *The Radio Annual* 1945 p. 826; *Variety* June 7, 1939, p. 44; thrilling detective.com.

Crump, Irving

Irving Crump (December 6, 1887–July 3, 1979) was the managing editor of *Boys' Life* for many years between 1915 and 1952 and author of a number of juvenile science fiction novels featuring Og, a Neanderthal. Among several different commercial outlets, Og's adventures were turned into a radio series (1934–1935) written by Crump entitled *Og, Son of Fire*. In 1941 he adapted *Treasure Island* to a 39-week 3-episodes-per-week serial. Crump claimed he wrote over 1,000 scripts in his time, among them many episodes of *Jack Armstrong, All-American Boy*. This last claim has so far not been independently verified.

Sources: Wylie p. 271; Hopkinson *Og; Broadcasting* April 28, 1941, p. 20; *Variety* September 25, 1935, p. 50; sf-encyclopedia.com.

Crusinberry, Jane

Jane Crusinberry (born Harriet Jane McConnell, October 3, 1892–February 1984) wrote one series during her radio career but it was quite a successful one. She created and wrote *The Story of Mary Marlin* beginning in 1934 from the soap opera capital of Chicago. Other than vacations when a substitute took over, Crusinberry wrote every episode herself during the show's eleven year run from 1934 to 1945. Even when she sold her ownership of the serial Crusinberry continued on as a contract author. *The Story of Mary Marlin* appeared briefly on television, 1951–1952.

Sources: *Radio Varieties* April 1940 p. 10; *Variety* September 29, 1943, p. 32.

Crutcher, Jack

Jack Crutcher was active in radio in the early 1950s before he moved to film and television. Among his radio work were the series *The Sweeney and March Show* (1946–1951, intermittent), *Much Ado About Doolittle* (1950), and *The Penny Singleton Show* (1950).

Other Radio: *My Favorite Husband*.
Television: *The Jonathan Winters Show* (1956).
Film: *Jalopy* (1953).
Sources: Adir p. 231; *Radio Life* March 30, 1947, p. 4.

Crutcher, Robert Riley

Robert Riley Crutcher (August 20, 1911–August 10, 1974) wrote for a number of comedy series during the era's heyday including Fanny Brice's *Good News of 1939* and *Good News of 1940* (for Maxwell House) and for Edgar Bergen and Charlie McCarthy on *The Chase & Sanborn Hour* (ca. 1939). In 1940 Crutcher contracted to write *The Silver Theatre*, alternating scripts with **True Boardman**. Crutcher wrote the first five episodes of *The Eddie Bracken Show* in 1945 before parting ways with the producers over a contract disagreement. He also did some writing for *This Is My Best* that year and in 1946 agreed to write Frank Morgan's *The Fabulous Dr. Tweedy* for an impressive $3,000 per week.

Crutcher was contracted to write a number of screenplays during the 1940s, very few of which apparently were produced. With the decline of primetime radio comedy Crutcher made a name for himself in television, most notably with the popular *Bewitched* in the late 1960s.

Theater: *The Lady Dances* (1936).
Television: *The Thin Man* (1958–1959); *Hazel* (1961–1966); *Bewitched* (1966–1968).
Film: *Between You and Me* (1941); *Girl Trouble* (1942).
Sources: *Broadcasting* October 15 1940 p. 80; *Variety* December 17, 1944, p .21, March 7, 1945, p. 31, April 3, 1946, p. 31.

Crutchfield, Les

Les Crutchfield (January 25, 1916–October 6, 1966) was a very busy writer in the post–War era until the demise of the art form. His background was unusual for a network writer, stumbling into the field after meeting director Norm Macdonnell while working as an engineer at Cal Tech. Crutchfield's graduate studies included physical chemistry and mathematics which led him for a time into the mining industry as a foreman and explosives expert.

Crutchfield reportedly wrote his first script for a 1946 episode of CBS' experimental program *The Columbia Workshop* before finding work on several more traditional dramas of the late 1940s including *The Man Called X* (1947–1948, 1950–1951), *Escape* (1947–1951, 1953) and *The Story of Dr. Kildare* (1949–1950). His 1950s work demonstrates the range of his writing skills as he provided scripts for *I Fly Anything* (1950–1951), *The Modern Adventures of Casanova* (1952), an Errol Flynn-driven transcription series, *Rogers of the Gazette* (1953–1954), *Romance* (1950, 1952, 1954–1957), *Yours Truly, Johnny Dollar* (1953–1956), *Fort Laramie* (1956), and *Suspense* (1948, 1959–1960). His most popular work might be the 81 scripts he wrote for the beloved *Gunsmoke*. Crutchfield wrote for numerous television programs during the 1950s but his most notable work was on *Gunsmoke*, with which he was well acquainted.

Other Radio: *Breakdown* (1947); *T-Man* (1950); *The Bakers' Theatre of Stars* (1953); *The Chase* (1953); *The Six-Shooter* (1953).
Sources: Barabas & Barabas p. 36; *Broadcasting* August 1, 1955, p. 66; *Variety* January 8, 1947, p. 114.

Curtin, Tom

Tom Curtin was a Harvard-educated war correspondent during World War I and his first radio program in 1931, *Thrillers* (NBC), dramatized some of his adventures sneaking behind enemy lines. In 1932 Curtin wrote police dramas for *The Lucky Strikes Hour*, also over NBC, and in 1933 he authored Charlie Chan scripts for *Five Star Theatre*. Curtin's most widely documented series was 1935's *The Black Chamber*, a thrice-weekly program on which he collaborated with Herbert O. Yardley.

Sources: *The Many Lives of Herbert O. Yardley*; *Radio Digest* December 1931 p. 13, Summer 1932 p. 31, March 1933 p. 11; *Boston Globe* April 7, 1935, p. 50.

Curtis, Nathaniel

Primarily a screenwriter in the 1940s, Nathaniel Curtis (September 21, 1909–April 6, 1983) was hired to write *You Can't Take It With You* in 1944 when it was adapted for a new radio series. He later wrote a number of television episodes from the early 1950s into the 1960s.

Source: *Billboard* August 19, 1944.

Dahm, Frank

Frank Dahm's radio career started on Chicago's WGN in 1926 as announcer alongside Bill Hay and Quin Ryan and also broadcasting the Chicago Bears NFL games. By 1928 he was the station's program director as well as a writer of considerable continuity and forgotten series such as *Old Time Prize Fights*. Dahm moved to San Francisco's KPO in 1930 to work as program director but within a year he went to work writing for Blackett-Sample-Hummert where he scripted *Little Orphan Annie* in the early 1930s and later *Ma Perkins*.

Dahm sold his own creation in 1937, the serial *Pretty Kitty Kelly*, that aired until 1940. He took over writing responsibilities for *City Desk* from **Frank Gould** in 1941 and for *Sea Hound* in 1943. In 1946 he was assigned to scripting *Married for Life*.

Sources: *Broadcasting* December 28, 1942, p. 50; *Motion Picture Daily* February 17, 1937, p. 8; *Radio Digest* October 1927 p. 10, October 1928 p. 118, December 1930; *Sponsor* April 1949 p. 29; *Variety* February 5, 1941, p. 34, April 14, 1943, p. 34, October 23, 1946, p. 30; *Chicago Tribune* March 20, 1932, p. 6N.

Dana, Richard

Richard Dana recalled starting in radio in 1934 after graduating from Princeton. He was contacted by Phillips H. Lord who needed a junior writer and Dana was hired despite only having minimal play writing experience and subsequently worked on *Gang Busters* among other Lord productions. Dana later moved from the Biow Co. to the Young & Rubicam script staff in 1938 where he worked on *We, The People*. He wrote for *Manhattan at Midnight* in 1940 and then *The March of Time* before joining the radio branch of the Office of War Information in 1942.

Dana scripted *Treasury Salute* (1945–1946), *Your Hit Parade* (1946–1947), and *Exploring the Unknown* (1946–1947) after the war and then worked as the chief of Roy de Groot Consultants script department in the late 1940s. For a time he also wrote *Memo from Lake Success* for United Nations radio, *Experience Speaks* for Mutual, and *Mr. President*. By the end of the decade Dana was focusing more on television, first with Hendreick Booraem's Holland Productions and then with Young & Rubicam in 1950.

Other Radio: *Appointment with Life*; *Kollege of Musical Knowledge*.

Sources: *Broadcasting* August 1, 1938, p. 46, November 13, 1950, p. 13; *Motion Picture Daily* March 25, 1949, p. 6; *The Radio Annual* 1945 p. 826, 1948 p. 745; *Variety* August 14, 1940, p. 28, June 24, 1942, p. 37, March 21, 1945, p. 31, February 16, 1949; Interview, December 1970, WTIC.

Danch, Bill

Bill Danch focused mainly on comedy during his time authoring radio scripts. In 1942 he left Edgar Bergen's *Chase & Sanborn Hour* to write on the *Fibber McGee & Molly* show, where he wrote until entering the Army in 1943 to work for the Armed Forces Radio Service. When the show went on summer hiatus that year, Danch joined the writing staff for *Tommy Riggs and Betty Lou*, a summer replacement for *Burns & Allen*.

After Danch finished his service with the Army he worked with Jack Douglas to prepare another audition record for **Tommy Riggs** in 1945. He wrote for Fanny Brice's *Baby Snooks* program for a time but was removed from that series at the end of the 1945–1946 season. Danch is also credited with scripting *Front and Center* (1947), *Sealtest Variety Theatre* (1949), *The Harold Peary Show* (1950–1951), and again *Fibber McGee & Molly* (1953–1954).

Other Radio: *The Adventures of Sterling Holloway* (1948, audition).

Sources: *Broadcasting* March 8, 1943, p. 32; *Variety* February 11, 1942, p. 30, June 24, 1942, p. 28, November 28, 1945, p. 38, June 12, 1946, p. 25.

Dann, Sam

Sam Dann wrote for a handful of radio series during the era's Golden Age including *Grand Marquee* (1947), *Chandu the Magician* (1949–1950), and *The American Jewish Caravan of Stars* (1953). He is most widely remembered, however, for writing over 300 episodes of *CBS Radio Mystery Theater*, a revival of the dramatic radio genre that aired between 1974 and 1982.

Source: Payton & Grams.

Dannay, Frederic

Frederic Dannay's (born Daniel Nathan, October 20, 1905–September 3, 1982) most famous creation was Ellery Queen, a mystery icon whose name is still familiar to audiences today. Dannay and cousin **Manfred Lee**, the story goes, created Ellery Queen while dining out for lunch in 1928. The pair found success with Queen in many media formats including novels, film, and television. The character also had intermittent runs on radio that lasted nearly a decade.

Dannay and Lee were approached in 1938 by George Zachary, a CBS executive who was looking to put a good mystery program on the chain.

After reading some Queen novels he believed the format employed by Dannay and Lee to challenge the reader was a match for his radio idea. While the initial compensation was modest, radio offered the potential to reach a vast new number of fans. The pair agreed to Zachary's deal and set about learning to write for a new medium.

In preparation for the new Ellery Queen radio series, Dannay scripted some episodes of *Alias Jimmy Valentine*, a production of the Hummerts. More notably, they contributed scripts to *The Shadow*'s 1938–1939 season. Shortly before Ellery Queen arrived on the airwaves yet another Dannay and Lee program debuted, *Author! Author!* (1939–1940). Listeners presented seemingly impossible mystery starts that panelists were then required to finish.

Ellery Queen debuted in 1939 for a series of hour-long broadcasts but this proved unsustainable and after several weeks the show was cut back to thirty minutes. Dannay stayed with the show for five years before leaving due to the writing pressures of writing for radio and print mediums. He was replaced by **Anthony Boucher** in 1944.

Dannay continued to write and edit *Ellery Queen's Mystery Magazine* but the death of two wives from cancer slowly sapped his energy over the ensuing decades. With his third wife came a short revival and he re-involved himself in a number of Queen projects, especially for television. However, his age eventually caught up with him and Dannay's health steadily deteriorated after 1980 until his death in 1982.

Other Radio: *The Ford Theatre* (1948, with Manfred Lee).
Sources: Grams *Shadow*; Nevins & Grams.

Davenport, William (Bill)

Bill Davenport was long-time writer for *The Adventures of Ozzie and Harriet*, a program that ran from 1944 to 1954. Other radio credits include scripts for *A Day in the Life of Dennis Day* and *Sweeney and March* (1946–1951, intermittent). With **Frank Fox**, Davenport was the initial writer for Lucille Ball's *My Favorite Husband* in 1948 but he had to leave that series when *Ozzie and Harriet* returned from summer hiatus. He followed the Nelsons into television, writing the small screen adaptation of their radio series as well as the *Fibber McGee & Molly* television show (1959–1960) and *The Bill Bendix Show* (1962).

Sources: *Broadcasting* May 21, 1951, p. 80, March 23, 1959, p. 105, February 19, 1962, p. 117; *Variety* October 6, 1948, p. 25, January 5, 1949.

David, Marvin

Marvin David has been identified as a contributing writer to at least two programs, *Grand Marquee* (1946) and *Faces in the Window* (1953). He spent most of his broadcasting career involved with Chicago programming.

Sources: *Chicago Tribune* obituary April 24, 2003.

Davidson, David

David Davidson (May 11, 1908–November 1, 1985) was born in New York City and stayed near home, graduating from City College and then the Columbia School of Journalism. After working for the *New York Evening Post* for three years beginning in 1933, Davidson began to write serials. His first program was *Just Plain Bill* (1936-ca. 1939) followed by *Second Husband* (1938–1942), *Society Girl* (1939), and *Mr. Keen, Tracer of Lost Persons* (ca. 1941–1942). In 1942 Davidson joined the Office of War Information and briefly returned to *Mr. Keen* in 1943 when it became a weekly broadcast.

Davidson scripted dozens of teleplays from *The Ford Theatre Hour* in 1951 to *Judd for the Defense* in 1967. Because of his disenchantment with the quality of some television writing, Davidson began writing under the name Albert Sanders.

Books: *The Steeper Cliff* (1947).
Sources: Cox *Mr. Keen*; *Motion Picture Daily* September 27, 1939, p. 10; *Variety* January 25, 1939, p. 26, March 18, 1942, p. 34 April 29, 1942, p. 36, June 24 1942 p. 39, December 8, 1943, p. 30; *New York Times* obituary, November 3, 1985.

Davis, Eddie

Eddie Davis worked as a cab driver before getting into writing radio gags for comics including Al Jolson (1935), Eddie Cantor (1932–1937), Joe Penner (1936), Jack Haley (1938 on *Log*

Cabin Jamboree), and Abbott and Costello (1941 on *The Chase & Sanborn Hour*). During the 1941–1942 season Davis signed with co-writer Dave Schwartz to pen a series for Schaefer beer starring comics Harry Savoy and Russ Brown and in the fall of 1942 Davis was called in to punch up Al Jolson's CBS show. Davis slowly transitioned into Broadway musicals by the end of the 1940s, leaving radio behind. His theater works included the books for *Follow the Girls* (1944–1946) and *Ankles Aweigh* (1955).

Sources: *Broadcasting* August 1, 1937, April 21, 1941, p. 32 p. 60; *Motion Picture Daily* June 17, 1935, p. 8; *Radio Mirror* April 1938 p. 87; *Variety* September 17, 1941, p. 31, October 21, 1942, p. 3; *The Pittsburgh Press* July 3, 1936, p. 8.

Davis, Mac

Mac Davis is credited with scripting Bill Sterns' popular *Colgate Sports Newsreel*, but he also had his own script writing company, Mac Davis Features. Among his script series were *Across the Sport Page of the World*, *Diamond Dust*, *Football Fables*, *Heartbeats in Sport Headlines*, *That's Baseball*, *There Were Such Moments in Sport*, *Jax Cavalcade of Sports*, *Once in a Lifetime*, and *The Thrill Quiz*. Davis also had his own syndicated sports column "Heartbeats in Sport Headlines."

Sources: *Radio Annual* 1946 p. 802; *Radio Showmanship* April 1942 p. 140, September 1942 p. 307.

Davis, Owen

Owen Davis took over writing the continuity for *The Gibson Family*, an ambitious weekly radio program written in the style of a Broadway musical when original writer **Courtney Ryley Cooper** decided he'd had enough.

Source: *Radio Mirror* February 1935 p. 38.

Davis, Phil

Phil Davis was a continuity writer for Pittsburg's WCAE in the early 1940s before signing on with the popular *Truth or Consequences* ca. 1943. During his time in the Army Davis scripted the recruiting show *Week-End Pass* (1944) before returning to the *Consequences* quiz show for the rest of the 1940s.

Sources: *Broadcasting* March 1, 1943, p. 35; *Variety* August 26, 1942, p. 55, December 27, 1944, p. 27.

Dawson, John (see E. Jack Neuman)

John Dawson was a pseudonym of prolific writer **E. Jack Neuman** when writing *Yours Truly, Johnny Dollar* from 1955–1957 and adapting scripts for television's *Have Gun, Will Travel* to radio.

Source: Wright "Produce it Again."

Dawson, Ronald

Primarily an actor and director, Ronald Dawson did a bit of writing during his decades in radio. In 1932 while at Washington's WOL he adapted films into radio plays for the station's stock company and in 1941 Dawson served as WCHS' continuity chief in Charleston, WV. Much of Dawson's writing was freelance for The Script Library, a service that provided scripts to stations without the staff to write their own. He joined the cast of *The Romance of Helen Trent* in 1942 where he is credited with both acting and writing for the long-running serial. After scripting *It's Maritime* in 1945 Dawson started the Lend-Lease Library in 1947, a service similar to The Script Library that provided one-shot radio scripts (rather than series) to stations without a writing staff.

Other Radio: *The Jubilaires*; *Wilderness Road*.

Sources: *Broadcasting* November 15, 1932, p. 30, November 17, 1941, p. 32, July 13, 1942, p. 41; *The Radio Annual* 1945 p. 827; *Variety* October 1, 1947, p. 30.

de Graffe, Richard

Richard de Graffe scripted *The Adventures of Michael Shayne* in the mid–1940s. Shayne, created by Brett Halliday, was the star of multiple film series.

Source: *Radio Life* August 19, 1945, p. 4–5.

Demling, Bill (also Doemling)

Bill Demling (November 11, 1909–August 1974) was a comedy writer who started in radio after graduating from Detroit's Wayne University (now Wayne St.) and finding work in 1931 with a local station. From there he moved to Chicago's NBC outlet and then to the West Coast where he got work writing comedy films. With a solid reputation for humor he returned to radio by 1934 where he scripted such series as *Comedy Capers* (1934–1935), *Nonsense and Melody* (1935), and *Shell Chateau* (1935). In 1937 he resigned from Hollywood's KFWB to work at Young & Rubicam writing *The Packard Hour*. In 1938 he was assigned to the *Joe E. Brown Show*, for Joe Penner in 1939, then in 1942 Demling took a position on the writing staff for *The Rudy Vallee Show*. Other writing credits include *Blue Ribbon Town* (1944), *The Judy Canova Show* (1945), and *The Jack Kirkwood Show* (1946).

Television: *Hank McCune Show* (1949).

Sources: *Billboard* October 29, 1949, p. 9; *Broadcasting* September 1, 1937, p. 32, December 15, 1938, p. 47, April 6, 1942, p. 32, January 17, 1944, p. 44, January 16, 1945, p. 72; *Radio Varieties* April 1941 p. 15; *Variety* January 9, 1946, p. 162; *The Pittsburgh Press* September 8, 1939, p. 41.

Denison, Merrill

Though born in Detroit, Merrill Denison (June 23, 1893–June 13, 1975) was raised in Canada where he trained as an architect and began writing plays in the 1920s. Denison was offered work by United States sponsors after hearing his scripts for Canadian National Railways' *The Romance of Canada* in the early 1930s. The financial opportunities in the States surpassed anything available in his native Canada and his U.S. radio credits include *Democracy in Action* (1939), *True Stories from Britain* (1941), *The Prudential Hour* (1942–1943), and *A Woman of America* (1943). In later years he wrote a number of books on business histories focusing on tractor-maker Massey-Harris (1949), the Molson Brewing Company (1955), and the Bank of Montreal (1966–1967).

Books: *Klondike Mike, an Alaskan Odyssey* (1943).

Sources: *Broadcasting* May 26, 1941, p. 25, March 22, 1943, p. 42; *Variety* December 27, 1932, p. 32, June 28, 1939, p. 38, June 3, 1942, p. 36.

Denker, Henry

Trained as a lawyer, Henry Denker (November 25, 1912–May 15, 2012) wrote a few episodes of CBS' experimental program *The Columbia Workshop* in 1942 and also contributed scripts to *Suspense* (1944), *Cavalcade of America* (1946, 1947), and *Radio Reader's Digest* (1946). His signature work was *The Greatest Story Ever Told* (1947–1956), dramatized stories from the Bible for which he served as director and writer for many years. Denker also published dozens of plays, novels, and screenplays from the 1950s into the 2000s.

Sources: *Variety* July 29, 1942, p. 27, September 15, 1948, p. 40.

Derman, Lou

Lou Derman (September 27, 1914–February 15, 1976) wrote for numerous radio series before successfully moving into television. He scripted a steady succession of radio programs, primarily comedies, through the 1940s including Ed Wynn's *Happy Island* (1944–1945), *Let Yourself Go* with Milton Berle (1945), *The Eddie Cantor Show* (1945, 1947), *Kiss and Make Up* hosted by Milton Berle (1946), *The Mighty Casey* (1947), *Robert Q. Lewis's Little Show* (1947), *That's Rich* (1947), and *The Jim Backus Show* (1948).

Derman's longest tenure was on the writing team of *Life With Luigi* from 1948 until 1954. Other 1950s-era programs for which Derman wrote were *The Phil Harris–Alice Faye Show* (1953) and *Our Miss Brooks* (1953–1955).

The series for which Derman wrote on television is even more impressive. Among the dozens of shows for which he contributed teleplays, Derman was co-creator and head writer for *Mr. Ed* (1961–1966), a writer on *Here's Lucy* (1970–1971), and a writer and producer for *All in the Family* (1973–1975).

Source: Lou Derman Papers.

Devine, Jerry

A former child actor in the early 1920s, Jerry Devine (November 11, 1908–May 20, 1994) was a busy radio writer in the 1930s and early 1940s before opening his own production company after World War II where he focused on putting together program packages more than just writing. Among his writing credits were *Kate Smith Variety Hour* (ca. 1938), *Tommy Riggs* (1939), *The Shadow* (1938–1941), *Reg'lar Fellers* (1938), *Mr. District Attorney* with **Ed Byron** (1942–1944), and *Radio Hall of Fame* (1945). Devine was most closely involved with *This Is Your FBI*, a series for which he wrote, directed, and produced between 1945 and 1953. Devine was still writing into the 1990s and even wrote a radio adaptation of his play *Children of the Wind* that was broadcast by California Artists Radio in 1993.

Other Radio: *Big Town*; *The Pursuit of Happiness*.

Sources: Jerry Devine Papers; Grams *Shadow*; *Radio-Television Mirror* August 1941 p. 41; *Variety* November 29, 1939, p. 28, July 8, 1942, p. 37; *Los Angeles Times* September 13, 1992, p. F88.

DeWitt, John

John DeWitt (d. June 20, 1984) was a writer for Blackett-Sample-Hummert serials in the 1930s including *Our Gal Sunday* (1937) and *David Harum* (1942). When he entered the Naval Reserve in 1942 his wife Johanna took over scripting *David Harum*.

Other Radio: *Appointment with Life*.

Sources: *Broadcasting* November 30, 1942, p. 45; *The Radio Annual* 1945 p. 827; *Variety* December 15, 1937, p. 30, January 21, 1942, p. 35, October 28, 1942, p. 34.

Diamond, Selma

Selma Diamond (August 6, 1920–May 13, 1985) recalled cutting school to watch vaudeville comics as a child and even started to supply them with gags in return for candy. She advanced to selling jokes to cartoonists and even wrote her own strip for a time, *Jeannie*. As a young woman she made her way to California with just twenty dollars and the name of an agent and in short order found herself writing for some of the era's greatest comedians. Among them were Grouch Marx on *Blue Ribbon Town* (1944), Garry Moore (1944–1945), Rudy Vallee on *The Drene Show* (1945–1946), Kenny Baker on *Glamour Manor* (1946–1947), Phil Silvers (1947), and Arnold Stang (1947). Diamond was one of **Goodman Ace**'s writing staff charged with turning *The Big Show* (1951–1952) into a ratings dynamo against both the upstart television industry and network competitor CBS, a task that failed.

Diamond moved into television writing for *Texaco Star Theatre* (1953–1954) with Ace, and Perry Como's *Kraft Music Hall* in the early 1960s. Despite being one of the premier female comedy writers of the time, she is now largely remembered for her work as an actress on such shows as *Too Close for Comfort* (1980–1984) and especially *Night Court* (1984–1985).

Sources: *The Radio Annual* 1944 p. 730; *TV Radio Mirror* April 1961 p. 11, 40–41; *Variety* January 3, 1945, p. 107, September 3, 1945, p. 26, October 2, 1946, p. 35, August 13, 1947, p. 34, December 10, 1947, p. 28.

Dickson, Sam

Sam Dickson was a West Coast radio man, writing for KYA by the late 1920s and working in various capacities including producer as early as 1932. His first identified writing assignments were *Winning the West* and *Hawthorne House*, both ca. 1935 on KPO and KFI respectively. Dickson's next known series were on KGO, *Saunders of the Circle X* (1941–1942) and the 1942 series *Thunder Adams*, a series that featured John Cuthbertson, Earl Lee, Henry Shumer, Jack Edwards, Lu Tobin, and Gilbert Morgan. In 1942 Dickson began writing *This Is Your Home*, stories about San Francisco, a show that ran for several years and for which Dickson is credited with writing more than 300 episodes. Dickson was a writer and producer for San Francisco's KNBC at the end of the 1940s and was working on *Rickey's San Francisco Hour* when he retired in 1954.

Sources: *Broadcasting* June 15, 1935, p. 17, November 14, 1949, p. 74; *Broadcasting-Telecasting* February 15, 1954, p. 98; *Motion Picture Daily* May 27, 1938, p. 8; *Radio Mirror* August 1935 p. 43; *Radio Showmanship* May 1947 p. 166, *Variety* October 17, 1932, p. 49, November 6, 1935, p. 43; bayarearadio.org.

Dinelli, Mel

Mel Dinelli (October 6, 1912–November 28, 1991) specialized in suspense stories and contributed a number of scripts to *Suspense* over a number of years (1944–1949, 1956, 1959). Additionally, Dinelli was on the writing team for *The Adventures of Philip Marlowe* from 1948 to 1949.

Film: *The Spiral Staircase* (1945); *House by the River* (1950); *Step Down to Terror* (1958).

Source: Cox *Crime Fighters* p. 21.

Disque, Brice, Jr.

Brice Disque (June 21, 1904–January 1959) served in various capacities during radio's Golden Age including as producer of *Movie Pilot* on

WEAF (1937). In 1939 Disque left his writing position with King Features where he penned *King Features Presents* to work as a scripter for Phillips H. Lord's programs including *By Kathleen Norris*, which he directed as well, and *Gang Busters*. At the same time he continued to pen *Romance of Oil*. Disque left Lord in 1942 to pursue freelance work including his new series *For Valor* but soon after took a job as script editor with NBC. Later that summer he resigned to join the Army Air Force. After the war Disque went back to work writing for various advertising agencies including Compton and Marschalk & Pratt and submitting freelance scripts to programs such as *Cavalcade of America*.

Other Radio: *March of Time*; *Radio News Week*; *Living-1948*.

Sources: Brice P. Disque, Jr., papers; *Broadcasting* January 1, 1940, p. 36, May 11, 1942, p. 122; *Motion Picture Daily* August 6, 1937, p. 6, June 29, 1942, p. 8, August 20, 1942, p. 15; *Radio and Television Mirror* January 1940 p. 45; *Variety* April 26, 1939, p. 19, December 20, 1939, p. 26, October 1, 1947, p. 25.

Dixon, David

David Dixon stepped in to write some episodes of *Bobby Benson and the B-Bar-B Riders* during the 1949 to 1955 run when his father, **Peter Dixon**, became too ill to continue scripting for the series. The younger Dixon was a veteran of the series, having acted on an earlier version of the program in 1935 when his father was again the scriptwriter.

Sources: French & Siegel p. 24, 26; *Variety* September 11, 1935, p. 38.

Dixon, Peter

Peter Dixon authored the radio series, *Cub Reporter*, ca. 1930 and soon after he added *Raising Junior* (1930–1933), an early sitcom that reportedly introduced Walter Tetley to the airwaves. Dixon next wrote for *Bobby Benson* (1932–1936, entitled *R–Bar–O Ranger* early on) and was the primary writer of the 1935 *Robinson Crusoe, Jr.* juvenile series. Other 1935 series scripted by Dixon were *The Story of a Thousand Dollars*, *The House Detective*, and the serial *Home Town*. Other Dixon-penned programs were *Comic Page of the Air* (1936), *Gateway to Hollywood* (1939), *Gene Autry's Melody Ranch* (1940), and later in the 1940s a revival of *Bobby Benson and the B-Bar-B Riders* (1949–1955).

Books: *Radio Writing* (1931); *Radio Sketches* (1936).

Sources: *Broadcasting* January 15, 1935, p. 20, March 1, 1935, p. 8, November 1, 1935, p. 64, September 15, 1936, p. 46, January 15, 1940, p. 24; *Radio Digest* September 1931 p. 71; *Variety* April 23, 1930, p. 71, September 11, 1935, p. 44, February 1, 1939, p. 26.

Donavan, Hobart

Henry Hobart Donavan (August 25, 1905–December 2, 1976) was active first in Milwaukee radio and then in Chicago as a continuity writer in the 1930s. Among the series for which he was known to have written were *Sound-O* (1943), *Beat the Band* (1943), *Alias John Freedom* (1943), *Ed McConnell and the Buster Brown Gang* (1944–1945), *Life of Riley* (1945), and *Lassie* (1947–1950). During the 1950s Donavan is credited with a handful of episodes over several radio series.

Other Radio: *Fantasy* (1947, audition).

Television: *The Loretta Young Show* (1955).

Sources: *Broadcasting* December 1, 1938, p. 42, December 27, 1943, p. 38, July 23, 1945, p. 66; *Variety* June 2, 1943, p. 34, July 14, 1943, p. 48, September 13, 1944, p. 34.

Dorfman, Sid

Sid Dorfman (September 16, 1917–October 1988), a busy broadcast writer in the late 1940s, scripted a number of comedy programs. Among them were *Duffy's Tavern* (1946), *The Joan Davis Show* (1947), *The Jack Paar Show* (1947), *Sealtest Village Store* with Jack Carson (1947–1948), *The Sweeney and March Show* (1948), *The Ammident Show* (1950), *The Baby Snooks Show* (1951), and *The Burns & Allen Show* which he joined in 1949 and stayed with into television during the early 1950s.

Television: *The Burns & Allen Show* (1950–1955); *M*A*S*H* (1973–1977).

Sources: *Broadcasting* August 15, 1949, p. 52; *Variety* June 26, 1946, p. 38, April 2, 1947, p. 35, June 4, 1947, p. 29, August 13, 1947, p. 34.

Doud, Gil (Giles)

Gil Doud (March 1, 1914–December 17, 1957) was behind a number of West Coast action and adventure programs in the post-war period. A sound effects artist for KHJ and writer for *Calling All Cars* before working as a welder then as an enlisted man during World War II, Doud later scripted for some of radio's most memorable series. In 1947 Doud took over **Jo Eisinger**'s co-writing duties on *The Adventures of Sam Spade* and worked with **Bob Tallman** on the series until June 1949. During that same span he and Tallman also wrote *The Voyage of the Scarlet Queen* (1947–1948) and then Doud moved to *Yours Truly, Johnny Dollar*, for which he wrote until 1952.

Doud contributed numerous scripts to other radio series even as he was beginning to establish himself in television and motion pictures. His further aural credits include *Steve Canyon* (1948), *Escape* (1950), *Pursuit* (1950), *Log of the Black Parrot* (1950, audition), *The Lineup* (1954), *I Cover the Waterfront* (1955), *Fort Laramie* (1956), *Gunsmoke* (1956), and *Suspense* (1951–1958). Doud passed away at the age of 43, cutting off a very promising writing career.

Television: *Suspense* (1951); *Gunsmoke* (1956–1957).
Film: *Thunder Bay* (1953); *Walk the Proud Land* (1956).
Sources: Abbott "Writers on Radio"; *Broadcasting* August 17, 1942, p. 53; *Broadcasting-Telecasting* November 29, 1954, p. 14; *Variety* February 23, 1949, p. 30.

Dougall, Bernard

Bernard Dougall (1908–1972) was a major contributor to the *Maxwell House Showboat* in the mid–1930s and to *Mary Small's Junior Revue* in 1937. During the early 1940s Dougall worked as a continuity writer and producer for the William Esty Company on a show called *Eyes and Ears of the Air Force* (1942) and then by 1944 as a writer for the Blue Network on such programs as *Connee Boswell Presents* (1944), and *Paul Whiteman Club* (1947).

Dougall wrote for numerous other series as a freelance author, some of the most memorable being *Front Page Drama* (1942–1948), *The Adventures of Jungle Jim* (1943–1946), *The Falcon* (1943–1953), and *Mr. President* (1947–1953). He also penned episodes for other shorter-lived programs including *Hannibal Cobb* (1949, 1950–1951), *Family Circle* (1951), *Newsstand Theater* (1951), and *The American Music Hall* (1954).

Sources: Bernard Dougall scripts; Cox *A to Z* p. 95; Cox *Crime Fighters* p. 32; *Billboard* June 26, 1943, p. 7, May 19, 1951, p. 10; *Broadcasting* April 24, 1944, p. 50; *The Radio Annual* 1940 p. 124; *Variety* October 28, 1942, p. 26, March 8, 1944, p. 34, July 2, 1947, p. 27.

Dougall, Tom

Tom Dougall, graduate of the University of Michigan, was a long-time writer at Detroit's WXYZ beginning in 1934. He started with programs such as *Ann Worth, Housewife* but sold the series' rights for $10 and some job security with the station. It was reported in 1938 that the station's ace writer **Fran Striker** recruited Dougall to work on the station's big series *The Green Hornet* and *The Lone Ranger*, though historian Martin Grams suggests that Dougall's contributions to *The Green Hornet* were modest. Soon after, Dougall created *Challenge of the Yukon* (later *Sgt. Preston of the Yukon*).

Dougall wrote for the WXYZ series into the 1950s breaking only for a stint in the Army during World War II. After the war he added non–WXYZ series to his workload including *Buck Rogers* (1946) and *Adventures of Col. Flack* (1947).

Sources: Grams *Green Hornet*; *Variety* August 21, 1935, p. 49, May 4, 1938, p. 29, October 2, 1946, p. 35, June 11, 1947, p. 40.

Douglas, Jack

Jack Douglas (born Douglas Linley Crickard, July 17, 1909–January 31, 1989) was a gag writer for Bob Hope on *The Pepsodent Program* (1938–1941), *Sunbrite Smile Parade* (1939), *Gulf Screen Guild Theatre* (1939–1942), and *Silver Theatre* (1940–1941) in the late 1930s and early 1940s. In 1941 Douglas left to write for Red Skelton and was subsequently sued by Hope who claimed Douglas was under exclusive contract to write for his show. Resolved amicably, Douglas went on to write for Skelton on both radio and television for nearly fifteen years.

Douglas wrote for numerous series throughout the 1940s, primarily comedies, such as *Over Here* (1942), *Tommy Riggs and Betty Lou* (1942), *Campbell's Soups Show* (with Jack Carson, 1944–1945), *Kay Kyser's Kollege of Musical Knowledge* (1945), *The Adventures of Ozzie and Harriet*

(1944–1945), *The Jimmy Durante–Garry Moore Show* (1946), *The Jack Paar Program* (1947), *The Sealtest Village Store* (1947–1948), *The Jack Carson Show* (1948–1949), *The Martin & Lewis Show* (1949), and *The Phil Harris–Alice Faye Show* (1953–1954).

Douglas's venture into television was highly successful, lasting into the late 1970s writing for comedy programs including *Rowan & Martin's Laugh-In* (1969–1970) and *Jack Paar Tonite* (1973).

Television: *Ed Wynn Show* (1950); *Peter Lind Hayes and Mary Healy Show* (1950–1951); *Beatrice Lillie Show* (1951); *George Gobel Show* (1954–1955).

Sources: Jack Douglas Papers; *Broadcasting* November 3, 1941, p. 40; *Variety* June 24, 1942, p. 28.

Drake, Elliot

Elliot Drake is credited with writing two series from radio's Golden Age, *John Steele, Adventurer* (1949–1951) and *High Adventure* (1950, 1953). Drake frequently served as director on both programs as well.

Source: martinggrams.blogspot.com

Driscoll, David

David Driscoll, not to be confused with the long-time WOR figure of the same name, was a speech professor at Brooklyn College when Himan Brown hired him to write his scripts in the 1930s. Brown and Driscoll collaborated on *Marie, the Little French Princess* (1930s), *Green Valley, U.S.A.* (1944), *Passed by the Censor* (1944), *Inner Sanctum* (1945), and *Affairs of Dr. Gentry* (1957).

Other Radio: *Joyce Jordan, M.D.; Young Dr. Malone.*

Sources: *Cox A to Z; Skutch* p. 14–15; *Broadcasting-Telecasting* January 21, 1957, p. 10; *Variety* January 12, 1944, p. 36, March 1, 1944, p. 42; *Brooklyn Daily Eagle* June 7, 2010.

Driscoll, John

John Driscoll began as a continuity writer with the Batten, Barton, Durstine & Osborn agency for *March of Time* in the 1930s. Driscoll became one of the primary writers for *Cavalcade of America* during its first four years, 1938–1941.

Sources: Bird p. 115; Grams *Cavalcade; The Radio Annual*, 1939 p. 751.

Drummond, David

Starting on Portland radio in the early 1930s, David Drummond wrote up to three scripts a week between 1931 and 1935 for KGW and KEX. Some of his series while scripting in the Pacific Northwest were *Homicide Squad* (1932–1935), *The Price of Glory* (1934), and *Sports Views, Reviews, and Interviews* (1935). Drummond moved to NBC in San Francisco in 1936 and wrote for *Tenth Row Center* (1939), the serial *Hawthorne House* (ca. 1940), and *City of St. Francis* (1940). Drummond is also known to have been writer-director for *Hero of the Week* (1943) on NBC Blue's Pacific stations.

Sources: *Broadcasting* August 15, 1935, p. 42, January 1, 1936, p. 34, October 15, 1939, p. 67, October 15, 1940, p. 66, September 6, 1943, p. 46; *Variety* March 20, 1934, p. 40, March 27, 1934, p. 42, December 11, 1935, p. 40.

Dudley, Paul

An announcer on Boston-area radio in the early 1930s, Paul Dudley (November 26, 1912–May 18, 1959) headed West in 1936 where he focused more on writing work at KHJ. His work with the station included *Blazing Travel Trails* (1937) before he took a position with the Lord & Thomas Agency as a continuity writer for *The Passing Parade* (1938) and his own series *Courage for Love* (1938), that he sold to Warner Bros. Studios. Other pre–War Dudley programs included *Grand Central Station* (1939), *Pot O' Gold* (1939–1941), *Treasure Chest* (1940–1941), and *Treasury Hour* (1941).

During the war Dudley was active writing for Coca Cola's *Spotlight Bands* from 1941 until 1943 when he took a professional hiatus and enlisted. Immediately after returning to civilian life Dudley was right back writing, directing, and producing. One of his first post–War projects was a revival of *Pot O' Gold* (1946–1947) that did not match the popularity of the original run. His next project was Frank Sinatra's *Lucky Strike Hit Parade* (1947).

Dudley's most memorable series was *Yours Truly, Johnny Dollar*, written with **Gil Doud** from its debut in 1948 until 1952. The adventures of an insurance investigator, it was a bit of a turn for Dudley from the musical and audience shows he'd

focused on for much of the decade. Having written for Sinatra and episodes of *Martin Kane* for television, Dudley was starting to break into motion pictures as well when he died at 46 in 1959.
Other Radio: *Steven Canyon* (1948, audition).
Television: *The Frank Sinatra Show* (1951); *Martin Kane* (1952–1953); *The New Adventures of Martin Kane* (1957).
Film: *Solomon and Sheba* (1959).
Sources: *Broadcasting* September 15, 1936, p. 40, May 1, 1938, p. 30, 56, December 15, 1939, p. 40, August 24, 1942, p. 16; *Motion Picture Daily* April 9, 1937, p. 14; *Variety* June 28, 1939, p. 30, November 5, 1941, p. 34, September 10, 1947, p. 28.

Duffield, Brainerd

Brainerd Duffield (January 16, 1917–April 5, 1979) is credited with writing episodes of *The Ford Theater* (1947–1949), *NBC University Theatre* (1949–1950), and the 1970s revival program *Sears Radio Theatre* (1979). Duffield is more widely remembered for his more than fifty stage plays, most notably a one-act adaptation of Shirley Jackson's *The Lottery*. In addition, he wrote for Hollywood studios for many years and some television in the 1950s.
Television: *Studio One* (1952–1953); *Front Row Center* (1955).
Film: *Treasure of Last Canyon* (1952).
Sources: Parker p. 482; TV.com.

Dunkel, John

John Dunkel (February 21, 1915–February 22, 2001) worked for McMann Advertising Service in the 1930s before working his way up to continuity director for CBS West Coast on such shows as *Raffles* (1942–1943), *The Romance of the Ranchos* (1941–1942), and *The Whistler* (1944–1945, 1951). Around 1945 Dunkel tried to write as a freelancer and scripted *Harvest of Stars* among others before returning to KNX in 1947 where he again climbed the CBS corporate ladder to become the West Coast executive director in 1949.

Dunkel is credited with writing for many fondly-remembered CBS series, especially Westerns. From the late-1940s through the 1950s Dunkel scripted *Suspense* (approximately six episodes between 1945 and 1959); *Escape* (1947–1950, 1954), *Dimension X* (1950), *Rocky Jordan* (1950), *Romance* (1950, 1954–1955), *Gunsmoke* (1955–1959), *Fort Laramie* (1956), and *Have Gun, Will Travel* (1958–1959).
Other Radio: *I Was There.*
Sources: John Dunkel Radio Scripts; Grams *Suspense*; *Broadcasting* July 19, 1943, p. 40, September 17, 1945, p. 60; *Variety* October 10, 1945, p. 31.

Durham, Richard

Raised in a poor household on Chicago's Southside, Richard Durham (September 6, 1917–April 27, 1984) managed to talk himself into a job with the Illinois Writers Project (IWP), a federal work program for out-of-work writers in 1939. Durham's first radio script aired June 23, 1940, on *Legends of Illinois* about Joseph Smith's attempt to establish a Mormon settlement in Illinois.

Durham's script writing improved with practice and his work appeared on other series including WGN's *Great Artists* (1941). After the IWP closed down he received notice that NBC's WMAQ had bought a script and he contributed more to the station's series *Art for Our Sake* in 1942. In 1943 Durham later recalled selling freelance scripts to the popular juvenile program *The Lone Ranger*. After graduating from NBC and Northwestern University's radio institute that year, Durham claimed he landed some writing assignments for the serial *Ma Perkins* and anthology series *Suspense*, though the latter claim is discrepant from published *Suspense* references.

Unable to make a living writing scripts, Durham worked as a reporter for the *Chicago Defender*. Initially involved in the development of 1946's *Democracy USA* series sponsored by the *Defender*, Durham was fired by the paper and thus, briefly, from the radio show. Recognizing his radio experience, he was brought back on to the project later in 1946. To supplement the regular but modest income from the show, Durham got work fleshing out script ideas for **Irna Phillips**' serials. Using that background Durham created his own serial, *Here Comes Tomorrow*, focusing on the African-American family the Redmonds. The program debuted in September 1947 and ran about a year, outlasting *Democracy USA* that ended in early 1948.

In the summer of 1948 Durham's trademark series *Destination Freedom* premiered on NBC. Working around the station's strict boundaries imposed due to sensitivity to racial issues, Durham dramatized the lives of figures such as Harriet Tubman and Denmark Vesey. Praised by critics, Durham brought *Destination Freedom* to an end in 1950 due to constant clashes with executives about his vision for the series. With a one-year-old at home it was time to put aside the series' stress and mediocre pay to pursue other opportunities.

Nevertheless, Durham was livid when NBC resurrected *Destination Freedom* as a tribute to white historical heroes and entered into litigation to assert his ownership of the series. This, and possibly his association with left-wing organizations, seemed to end his career path on radio even though he was eventually recognized as the legal owner of the program.

Durham subsequently went to work writing for the United Packinghouse Workers of America until 1957 and then as editor of the Nation of Islam's *Muhammad Speaks*. Among his later projects was a black television soap opera on Chicago's WTTW, *Bird of the Iron Feather* (1970), and *The Greatest* (1975), a memoir written with Muhammad Ali.

Sources: Ellett *Black Radio*; Williams.

Dutton, Myron

Myron Dutton was a busy producer and director in radio starting in the late 1930s but he also had some writing assignments during his career. Among the series on which Dutton had some writing credits were *This Is Judy Jones* (1941), *Hello Americans* (1942–1943), *Your Blind Date* (1942), *The Ginny Simms Show* (1943), and *Revere All-Star Revue* (1948).

Sources: Orson Welles Materials; *Motion Picture Daily* May 13, 1943, p. 11; *Variety* March 17, 1948, p. 29.

Easton, Harvey

Harvey Easton wrote for two law enforcement programs, *The Line-Up* (1951) and *Richard Diamond, Private Detective* (1953).

Source: Wright "The Line-Up."

Edgley, Leslie (Les, Leo)

Leslie Edgley joined Chicago's NBC offices as a continuity writer in 1936 and worked there four years on shows including *There Was a Woman* before leaving in 1940 to pursue freelance work. He returned to the job two years later where some of his projects included writing for *The Story of Sandra Martin* (1945), *Suspense* (1945), and *The Whistler* (1945–1948).

Television: *Mr. & Mrs. North* (1953).
Film: *The Thirteenth Hour* (1947, originally *The Hunter Is a Fugitive* in the Whistler series).
Books: *No Birds Sing* (1940).
Theater: *Wonder Child* (1939).
Sources: Cox *Crime Fighters* p. 242–243; *Broadcasting* December 1, 1936, p. 46, March 15, 1940, p. 48, October 23, 1944, p. 46; *Motion Picture Daily* April 2, 1946, p. 5; *Radio Daily* November 16, 1937, p. 8; *Variety* August 21, 1940, p. 29.

Edwards, Blake (William Blake Crump)

When Blake Edwards' (July 26, 1922–December 15, 2010) mother remarried, a young Edwards was introduced to early Hollywood where both his step-father and step-grandfather worked in directing and producing. Edwards chose a career in motion pictures and worked as an actor for a short time in the early 1940s before turning to writing for film in the mid–1940s and radio at the end of the decade. In 1949 Edwards was signed to write his first radio program, Dick Powell's new private eye program *Richard Diamond, Private Detective*. The next year Edwards added a second series to his writing duties, the police drama *The Line-Up* (1950–1953). He reportedly rode along with police officers and viewed many line-up procedures to make the show as realistic as possible. *Yours Truly, Johnny Dollar*, following the adventures of an insurance investigator, was penned for a few episodes by Edwards between 1951 and 1953.

In the early 1950s Edwards began writing for television with Powell's *Singer Four Star Playhouse* in 1952. Among his most prominent television credits were *The Mickey Rooney Show* (1954–1955), *Mr. Lucky* (1959–1960), a small screen adaptation of his radio creation *Richard Diamond, Private Detective* (1957–1960), *Peter Gunn* (1958–

1961), and *The Pink Panther* (1969). Edwards' most famous motion pictures screenplays were for the Pink Panther franchise over three decades.

In addition to acting and writing, Edwards directed and produced numerous films, highlighted by 1961's classic *Breakfast at Tiffany's*. In 1983 he was nominated for an Oscar for his screenplay for *Victor Victoria* and in 2004 he received an honorary Oscar recognizing his body of work in the film industry. He was married to actress Julie Andrews for 41 years.

Film: *Panhandle* (1948); *Stampede* (1949).

Sources: *Broadcasting* July 30, 1951, p. 73; *Motion Picture Daily* December 9, 1952, p. 5; *Variety* April 13, 1949, p. 32.

Ehrlich, Max

Max Ehrlich (October 10, 1909–February 11, 1983) started his writing career while a student at the University of Michigan. He was a correspondent for Albany, New York's *Knickerbocker Press and Evening News* then, after graduating, for his hometown Springfield, MA, *Republican and Daily News*. In the late 1930s Ehrlich entered radio with WSPR as head writer of the station's script division where he wrote for programs such as *Sunday Barnstormers*.

Between 1939 and 1941 Ehrlich wrote scripts for the American Jewish Committee while doing the occasional network piece like NBC's *Echoes of History* (1941). He also began selling freelance scripts to commercial series including Edward G. Robinson's *Big Town* in 1941 to which he would eventually contribute over a dozen stories. From 1941–1945 he wrote for the American Red Cross' script division on such series as *That They Might Live*, *Service Unlimited*, and *Voice of the Red Cross*. His freelance scripts from this era include episodes of *The Shadow* and *Counterspy*.

After World War II Ehrlich began penning more stories for a number of bigger-name network programs including *The Aldrich Family* (1945), *House of Mystery* (ca. 1946), and *The Crime Cases of Warden Lawes* (1946–1947), dramatizations based on Lewis E. Lawes' time as warden at New York's Sing Sing prison. Ehrlich also joined the writing team for *Murder at Midnight* (1946–1947) lead by **Robert Newman** at this time.

Ehrlich's writing assignments during the later years of the decade were focused more on mystery, crime, and detective fare with *Nick Carter, Master Detective* (1947), *The Shadow* (1947–1948), *Sherlock Holmes* (1948–1949), and *The Big Story* (1948), joining the latter's writing team of **Allan Sloane** and **Arnold Perl**. However, he continued to demonstrate his versatility while providing scripts to *CBS Is There* (1947–1948) and, much later, *By the People* (1955–1956).

In the late 1940s Ehrlich turned his attention to television where he wrote many dozens of teleplays through the 1950s. Among his television series work was *Barney Blake—Police Reporter* (1948), *The Big Story* (1950–1955), *Suspense* (1950–1952), *Treasury Men in Action* (1950–1953), *Assignment Foreign Legion* (1956–1957), and *The Defenders* (1961–1962). Later in his writing career Ehrlich wrote a number of novels that included *The Reincarnation of Peter Proud* (1973), *Reincarnation in Venice* (1979), and *Shaitan* (1981).

Other Radio: *Words at War* (1944); *We Came This Way* (1945); *Crisis in War Town* (1945).

Sources: Max Simon Ehrlich Papers; Grams *Shadow*; *Broadcasting* February 1, 1938, p. 76; *Motion Picture Daily* January 30, 1956, p.10; *Variety* February 5, 1941, p. 42, February 19, 1941, p. 30, November 24, 1943, p. 38, May 8, 1946, p. 27, May 29, 1946, p. 43, November 27, 1946, p. 42, May 5, 1948, p. 32.

Einstein, Harry

Harry Einstein (May 6, 1904–November 23, 1958) was a Boston-born comic who achieved nationwide fame with a Greek character Nick Parkyakarkus that he began to develop as a child. Einstein first appeared on Boston radio in the late 1920s performing some comedy routines but quit after a few months, deciding there was no money in it. He then started as the advertising director for Boston's Kane Furniture Co. and was quite content for a few years before trying his hand at a whole new series of radio sketches in 1932, co-written with his friend Joe Hines. This second aural effort was a success and Einstein immediately picked up a sponsor for his nighttime work, though he did not quit his day job with Kane Furniture.

After hearing Einstein at a social banquet where Eddie Cantor was the featured speaker, Cantor wired requesting a meeting with Einstein about the possibility of bringing the Greek character to Cantor's New York program. Parkyakarkus was a hit with Cantor's listeners and became a regular during the spring of 1934. Cantor topped Einstein's salary with Kane and hired him full-time for the 1934–1935 season as well as the two following seasons. **Phil Rapp** was Cantor's head writer so it's not clear what influence Einstein had on the script. That year Einstein's Parkyakarkus character earned the first of several film roles that would be produced over the subsequent decade.

Around 1939 Al Jolson added Einstein's Parkyakarkas to his radio show but Einstein was no longer credited with any of the writing duties. After a short stint of trying to turn Parkyakarkus into a stage show Einstein brought him back to the airwaves in 1945 with *Meet Me at Parky's* which he co-wrote with **Hal Fimberg**. *Parky's* ran until 1948 after which Einstein semi-retired from radio.

In 1958 Einstein suffered a heart attack in the middle of a Friar's roast for Lucille Ball and Desi Arnaz from which he did not recover. Two of his sons, Albert Brooks and Robert Einstein, became comedic actors in their own right.

Sources: *Radio Mirror* April 1935 p. 28–29, 63–64, June 1949 p. 34–35, p. 86–88; *Variety* January 11, 1939, p. 23, September 18, 1946, p. 26.

Eisinger, Jo (Joe, Joseph)

Jo Eisinger (July 24, 1909–January 1991), with **Bob Tallman**, was hired to adapt Dashiell Hammett's private eye Sam Spade for radio and to ensure he stood out from the throng of air detectives. Writing as Jason James due to his contract with Columbia Pictures, Eisinger co-wrote *The Adventures of Sam Spade* with Tallman for the series' first nine months before he decided to pursue other opportunities in the spring of 1947. His other known radio work includes *The Cases of Mr. Ace* (1947), a radio adaptation of George Raft's 1946 film *Mr. Ace*, two episodes of *Suspense* (1948), and Jack Webb's *Pete Kelly's Blues* (1951).

Eisinger wrote a number of screenplays, television movies, and television episodes through the 1950s and 1960s, the most prominent of them being *Gilda* (1946) with Glenn Ford and Rita Hayworth. Some other earlier films included noir titles *Night and the City* and *The Sleeping City* (both 1950), and he later wrote several episodes for the 1959–1960 crime drama *The Lawless Years*. As late as 1983–1984 Eisinger was still drawing on these noir crime roots when he penned two scripts for a television revival series *Philip Marlowe, Private Eye*.

Television: *The Cases of Eddie Drake* (1948, as Jason James, based on *Mr. Ace* radio series).
Theater: *A Point of Honor* (1936); *America's Grandma* (1937); *What Big Ears* (1942, with Judson O'Donnell)
Sources: *Sponsor* May 1947 p. 8; *Variety* April 23, 1947, p. 36.

Elinson, Irving (Izzy)

Irving Elinson (April 8, 1907–December 28, 1967) was a longtime writer for Eddie Cantor's radio programs between the late 1930s and mid–1940s. He had joined Cantor's writing team by 1937 on *Texaco Town* and followed when Cantor relocated to the West Coast in 1942. Elinson remained after Cantor's head writer, **Phil Rapp**, departed and continued to pen gags for Cantor's 1940s series *Time to Smile*, *The Eddie Cantor Show*, and *The Pabst Blue Ribbon Show*.

Elinson made a career apart from Cantor in 1960s television on various comedies including *The Real McCoys* (1958–1963), *Make Room for Daddy* (1957–1964), *The Joey Bishop Show* (1962–1964), and *The Lucy Show* (1963–1966). Though not a regular writer, Elinson contributed scripts to such fondly remembered programs as *Mr. Ed*, *My Favorite Martian*, and *Bewitched* as well.

Sources: *Broadcasting* December 15, 1937, p. 50; *Variety* November 4, 1942, p. 30, October 4, 1944, p. 24.

Eller, Herman

Herman Eller has a handful of writing credits including the series *Guess It and Win It* (1944–1945) and for performers Jack Gleason (ca. 1945) and Groucho Marx (ca. 1945).

Television: *Varsity Varieties* (Hollywood, 1949).
Sources: *Billboard* July 23, 1949, p. 14; *The Radio Annual* 1945 p. 827.

Ellington, Richard

Mystery writer Richard "Duke" Ellington (1914–1980) was the main writer for *The Fat Man* (1946–1951) and the shorter series *The Top Guy* (1951–1953). Ellington also published five novels featuring private eye Steve Drake between 1948 and 1953 and a few short stories in mystery digests in the 1950s and 1960s. He later gave up the writing field and ran a small hotel in the U.S. Virgin Islands until the 1970s.

Sources: Cox *Crime Fighters* p. 260–261; Mystery-file.com.

Elliott, Geraldine

Geraldine Elliott was a writer for Detroit's WJR noted for writing and producing an early creep show, *The Hermit's Cave*. During her years at the station Elliott held various titles including continuity writer, dramatic director, and education director.

Sources: *Broadcasting* March 1, 1939, p. 62; *Variety* September 22, 1937, p. 33.

Elliotte, John

John Elliotte's (February 6, 1902–June 20, 1986) first notable radio credits date from 1945 with two series, *The Nebbs* and *A Date with Judy*. He is best remembered for a long run on perennially popular *The Great Gildersleeve* (1947–1955). In the 1950s Elliotte followed *Gildersleeve* to television and wrote several episodes for the short-lived series. He went on to write for a variety of television programs through the 1960s including *Dennis the Menace*, *Father Knows Best*, and *Gentle Ben*.

Other Radio: *Star Performance* (1944)

Sources: Wright "A Date With Judy"; *Billboard* September 22, 1951, p. 9; *Variety* September 15, 1948, p. 31.

Ellis, Antony

Antony Ellis (March 1, 1920–September 26, 1967) was a British-born writer who was a prolific radio scripter throughout the 1950s. A talented author, Ellis started in show business as a summer-stock actor before moving to Hollywood to find parts in motion pictures. Ellis found more success as a writer and became a regular contributor to several series throughout the 1950s, primarily *Pursuit* (1950–1952), *Escape* (1950–1953), *Romance* (1950–1956), *Suspense* (1950–1960), and *Gunsmoke* (1952–1953). He contributed scripts to other prominent programs including *Crime Classics* (1953), *Hallmark Hall of Fame* (1954–1955), and *CBS Radio Workshop* (1956).

Ellis showed himself a man of many talents, proving to be just as adept at acting, directing, and producing, thus leading to the culmination of his radio career, *Frontier Gentleman* (1958). One of several adult Westerns appearing during the final days of network radio drama, Ellis wrote, directed and produced the series. Despite being "a lovely piece of radio" by noted radio historian John Dunning, the series lasted less than one year.

Television proved fruitful ground for Ellis where he's known to have written scripts for nearly two dozen programs, including *The Man from U.N.C.L.E.* and *Gunsmoke*. As producer he worked on *Black Saddle* (1959–1960) and *Michael Shayne* (1961).

Other Radio: *The Log of the Black Parrot* (1950, audition with **Gil Doud**); *On Stage* (1953); *The Bakers' Theatre of Stars* (1953); *Adventure of Captain Courage* (1955, audition); *O'Hara* (1956); *Theatre of Romance*.

Sources: French & Siegel; Grams *Suspense*.

Ellis, Caroline

Caroline Crockett Ellis (July 19, 1877–May 17, 1963) spent her first decades in rural Kansas, eventually marrying a farmer and helping to keep up the farmstead. In the 1910s or early 1920s Ellis started writing in her free time and some of her work began appearing in *Kansas City Post* columns and then *The Denver Post*.

Ellis was widowed in 1923 and, unable to keep up the farm on her own, entered the retail industry in Detroit where she had some family. By the late 1920s Ellis had returned to Kansas City working for different department stores and in 1932 she got her first crack at radio. She began preparing a program for a local retailer that premiered in 1933 on KMBC, *Joanne Taylor's Fashion Flashes*.

After three years writing and acting on *Flashes* Ellis developed a new transcribed series for Montgomery Ward entitled *The Travels of Mary*

Ward. Airing one year, Ellis moved on to another opportunity when General Mills enlisted her to create a program advertising their wares, *Caroline's Golden Store*. After a six-month test run over Des Moines' WHO the show was moved to Chicago and broadcast over the NBC Red network.

General Mills soured on *Caroline's Golden Store* after two years and Ellis returned to Kansas City where she began authoring and hosting *The Happy Homemaker* (also *The Happy Home*) and later sketches for *Radio Schoolhouse* through the 1940s and early 1950s. Ellis retired from broadcasting around 1953 when KMBC's ownership changed hands.

Sources: Ellett "Caroline Ellis"; Caroline Ellis family papers.

Ellis, David

Primarily an actor, David Ellis took his turn writing a few radio scripts. Some are obscure such as *Twelve Players* (1948) and *Make Believe Town* (1949) while others were much more popular both by audiences then and by old-time radio enthusiasts now. These programs include *Escape* (1950), *Yours Truly, Johnny Dollar* (1950, with **Gil Doud**), *Suspense* (approximately one dozen between 1949 and 1959), *Night Beat* (1951–1952), and *Gunsmoke* (1952).

Sources: Grams *Suspense*; *Variety* February 11, 1948, p. 34.

Ellis, Herb

Herb Ellis (b. January 17, 1921) began as an announcer and became a busy West Coast radio actor during the latter 1940s and 1950s. In the midst of his roles, however, he took the opportunity with **Cleve Hermann** to pen a few episodes of the adventure program *Jason and the Golden Fleece*, a series that ran from 1952 to 1953. Ellis was a working actor, appearing on television into the mid–1970s.

Sources: *Broadcasting-Telecasting* November 10, 1952, p. 111; radiospirits.info.

Epstein, Jerome

Jerome Epstein (January 17, 1922–November 16, 1991) specialized in scripting mystery and private investigator shows. Among his writing credits are *Manhattan at Midnight* (1942), *Mr. & Mrs. North* (1943–1944), *Hollywood Mystery Time* (1944), *Tonight in Hollywood* (ca. 1945), *Michael Shayne, Private Detective* (1946), *The Falcon* (1948, 1950–1951), and *Adventures of the Saint* (1950). After radio Epstein found work in televison, first as a writer in the 1950s then as a producer in the 1960s and early 1970s.

Other Radio: *Mulligan's Travels* (1947, audition).
Sources: Barer; *Broadcasting* October 16, 1944, p. 58; *The Radio Annual* 1945 p. 828; *Radio & Television Mirror* September 1942 p. 32; *Variety* January 13, 1943, p. 35.

Eric, Elspeth

Elspeth Eric (September 15, 1907–1993), a graduate of Wellesley College, worked as a sales clerk, copywriter, model, and tutor before getting her acting break. Eric was a character actress who appeared in hundreds of programs across a successful career. At the tail end of the era of dramatic radio Elspeth had her chance to script two episodes of *Suspense* in 1962. She also contributed scripts to post–Golden Age shows *Theatre Five* (1965) and over 100 to *CBS Radio Mystery Theatre* (1974–1977). On television she is credited with writing for the soap opera *Another World* (1969–1970).

Sources: Grams *Suspense*; *Radio Mirror* August 1938 p. 43; cbsrmt.com.

Erthein, James

James Erthein worked as a scriptwriter on at least two old-time radio programs, *The Adventures of Charlie Chan* (ca. 1944) and *The Shadow* (1952).

Source: *Variety* July 12, 1944, p. 30.

Ettinger, Ed (Edward)

Ed Ettinger (July 23, 1893–December 1, 1980) wrote for Al Jolson in the early 1930s while working for the J. Walter Thompson agency when the vaudeville star was making the move into radio. Years later while in the employ of the Ruthrauff & Ryan agency he returned to Jolson's team on a new aural series in 1937. With Al Lerner in 1943–1944 Ettinger scripted Sammy Kaye's program *The Old Gold Show* that after a few months was known as *Everybody's Inn* before being reassigned to *Broadway Matinee* in early 1944. Ettinger had the challenging task in 1945 of creating an air show based on the Broadway column of Earl Wilson and shortly afterward he was assigned to *Hobby Lobby* (1945–1946). Ettinger's long and varied radio career also included stints scripting for *What Makes You Tick?* (1948–1951), *Dancing Party* (1955), and *Police Blotter* (1957).

Film: *The Man Who Wouldn't Talk* (1940).
Theater: *A Present Is a Present* (1956).
Sources: *Broadcasting* January 3, 1944, p. 18; *The Film Daily* January 23, 1940, p. 5; *Motion Picture Daily* March 12, 1937, p. 14, April 16, 1937, p. 14; *Variety* January 13, 1943, p. 28, February 23, 1944, p. 28, January 10, 1945, p. 32, September 5, 1945, p. 26, February 27, 1946, p. 30; mareotr.org.

Everitt, Arva

Arva Everitt is known to have written episodes for the Phillips H. Lord series *Counterspy* that aired intermittently from 1942 to 1957.

Sources: Cox *Crime Fighters* p. 84; *The Radio Annual* 1945 p. 828.

Farber, Les

Les Farber entered radio in 1931 and gradually worked his way to Hollywood's KNX where he scripted *Romance of the Ranchos* (1948) and *Second Cup of Coffee* and *Command Theatre* ca. 1952. Years later he contributed three teleplays to *Lassie* (1960–1961).

Sources: *Billboard* November 20, 1948, p. 6; *Broadcasting-Telecasting* January 7, 1952, p. 20.

Farr, Finis (Phinus)

Finis Farr established himself as a mystery and crime writer on NBC in the late 1920s and early 1930s. Two of his earliest hits were *Mystery House* (1930) with detective Ransome Renwick and *Thurlow Wade* (1930). Within two years he was contributing scripts to programs on multiple stations including *Without Warning* over Cincinnati's WLW in 1932 and *Seeing It Through* over New York's WEAF that same year. A third 1932 series was *The Phantom of Crestwood* (1932) that was also a motion picture.

Among Farr's other writing projects in the 1930s was the radio show *Bar X Days and Night* (1934) featuring an early hillbilly act with Carson Robison and John and Bill Mitchell. He is credited with another musical program during that same time, this one starring George Gershwin and guest musicians in *Music by Gershwin*. Farr went to work for *Time* in 1936 and wrote pieces for numerous periodicals such as *Esquire, Cosmopolitan, Town and Country, Pictorial Review,* and *The Ladies Home Journal*. For a short time Farr worked as a continuity writer for the Pedlar & Ryan, Inc. agency before taking over as writer for the popular *Mr. District Attorney* on a freelance basis in 1940. By 1942 Farr had moved to *March of Time* and was subsequently assigned to WQXR when *Time* became a major stockholder in the station.

Farr enlisted during World War II and was assigned in 1943 to the Radio Section of the War Department's Bureau of Public Relations where he worked on *The Army Hour*. For his service he received a Bronze Star Medal for "handling a series of recorded programs in the field under difficult technical and living conditions."

After the end of the war one of Farr's first writing jobs was for *Time for Women* (1946) before being hired as script editor for Mutual Broadcasting beginning in October 1947. One of his last radio series was *The Gentleman Adventurer* (also known as *Special Agent*) in 1948. Farr is credited with scripting two television episodes for *Martin Kane* (1950) and *Appointment with Adventure* (1956). In the 1960s Farr turned to writing biographies with volumes focused on boxer Jack Johnson (1964), Margaret Mitchell (1965), and Westbrook Pegler (1975).

Books: *The Elephant Valley* (1967).
Sources: *Broadcasting* January 15, 1932, p. 18, March 15, 1936, p. 40, August 1, 1940, p. 108, July 12, 1943, p. 40, August 30, 1945, p. 30; *The Film Daily* August 26, 1932, p. 2; *Radio Digest* February 1930; *Radio Mirror* December 1934 p. 44–45, 87–88; *Variety* February 25, 1948, p. 22, March 11, 1942, p. 36, September 9, 1942, p. 26, January 9, 1946, p. 192, October 1, 1947, p. 28, March 31 1948 p. 28; *What's on the Air?* September 1930 p. 19; *Daily Boston Globe* June 22, 1941, p. D8; *The Hartford Courant* September 19, 1929, p. 14; *New York Herald Tribune* October 30, 1932, p. F8.

Faulkner, George

George Faulkner spent the first several years of his radio writing career working for J. Walter

Thompson on Rudy Vallee's program from 1930 to 1938. With **Carroll Carroll** Faulkner created *The Circle* (originally *The Kellogg Hour*, 1938–1939) on which he worked for about a year before returning to Vallee's show. In 1939 Faulkner wrote for **Norman Corwin**'s *The Pursuit of Happiness* (1939) for a few months before taking a leave due to an extended illness.

Faulkner left J. Walter Thompson in 1940 to go to work for the CBS production staff. There he worked on *Forecast* (1940) and then several War-era programs including *This Is War!* with Andre Kostelantez (1942), *Over Here* (1942–1943), *Camel Caravan* (1943), and *Uncle Sam* (1943). Faulkner demonstrated his writing prowess during the following years penning various comedy and anthology programs such as *The Jimmy Durante–Gerry Moore Show* (1943), *The Radio Hall of Fame* (1943), *It Pays to Be Ignorant* (1944), and *The Prudential Hour* (1944).

After the war Faulkner's assignments trended toward more serious material with two years for Ford Motor Co. on *Ford Festival of American Music* (1946) and *The Ford Theatre* (1947–1948). Later he added *Cavalcade of America* (1949–1953), *American Portraits* (1951) and *Stroke of Fate* (1953) to his credits.

Sources: Taylor *Capitalism* p. 63; *Broadcasting* May 1, 1936, p. 48, December 15, 1938, p. 26, March 15, 1939, p. 76, December 1, 1939, April 1, 1940, p. 101, February 16, 1942, p. 32; *Variety* April 15, 1936, p. 36; July 14, 1937, p. 35, July 17, 1940, p. 26, February 3, 1943, p. 30, February 17, 1943, p. 25, October 13, 1943, p. 26, April 19, 1944, p. 23, October 4, 1944, p. 24.

Faust, Gil

Gil Faust was an actor, director, and producer of various programs during the 1940s and occasionally took on writing duties. His known scripting credits include *Aunt Mary* in the mid–1940s and **Carlton Morse**'s *Woman in My House* in the late 1940s.

Source: Cox *Soap Operas* p. 130.

Ferro, Mathilde

Mathilde Ferro (May 6, 1906–November 26, 1990), with her husband **Theodore Ferro**, was responsible for writing the Hummert serial *Lorenzo Jones* for many years during its 1937–1955 run. She had at least one other radio credit with her husband, four episodes of *The Eternal Light* in 1958–1959. Ferro wrote for numerous television series over a 30-year period on such shows as *Matinee Theatre* (1955), *Wagon Train* (1961), and *Peyton Place* (1964–1965).

Other Radio: *Jed Snowden* (1939, audition).
Books: *Fear Is the Parent* (1948).
Sources: *Radio News Tower* June 1, 1937, p. 2; *Variety* May 4, 1938, p. 29, April 2, 1947, p. 35.

Ferro, Theodore

Theodore Ferro (March 25, 1924–November 15, 2003) wrote for the serial *Lorenzo Jones* for many years (ca. 1938–1949) with his wife **Mathilde Ferro**. Later Ferro wrote for a wide variety of television programs from *Robert Montgomery Presents* (1955–1956) to *Bonanza* (1961) to *Leave It to Beaver* (1959–1963) to *General Hospital* (1983).

Other Radio: *Jed Snowden* (1939, audition); *The Eternal Light* (1958–1959).
Theater: *Those Esmonds* (1933, with Mathilde Ferro); *Fear Is the Parent* (1948).
Sources: *Radio News Tower* June 1, 1937, p. 2; *Variety* May 4, 1938, p. 29, April 2, 1947, p. 35.

Fields, Sidney

Sidney Fields (February 5, 1898–September 28, 1975) was a theater straight man when he was hired as performer and writer with Eddie Cantor's radio program in 1935. He worked with Cantor on the air and in stage routines until 1940 when he left to script Rudy Vallee's radio show. Not long after, Fields joined the writing team and left that job in 1942. He spent the next two years writing and appearing on Johnny Morgan's *Rhythm Road* (1943) and then Morgan's follow-up *Broadway Showtime* (1944).

In 1944 Fields became part of the writing team for *The Abbot & Costello Show*, a job that lasted through 1952 after the duo had received their own television show. Fields continued to act after his writing days wound down and appeared in several episodes of *Jackie Gleason: American Scene Magazine* in the mid–1960s.

Other Radio: *The Comedy Writers Show* (1948, with Eddie Cantor).
Theater: *Green as Grass* (1942, musical revue).
Sources: *Broadcasting* February 15, 1940, p. 54, October 2, 1944, p. 50, August 18, 1952, p. 36; *Variety*

September 25, 1935, p. 4, January 7, 1942, p. 114, July 21, 1943, p. 34, March 1, 1944, p. 30; allmovie.com.

Fifield, William

William Fifield, a 1937 graduate of Whitman College in Washington, began working in radio soon after finishing school. Starting his career as an announcer, first with KUJ, Walla Walla, and then WBBM, Chicago, Fifield also assumed some continuity tasks. Fifield arrived in California in 1940 with wife Mercedes McCambridge, a busy radio actress. After a short time with CBS' New York outlet, in 1943 Fifield joined the staff of Hollywood's KNX and wrote for such shows as *The Whistler*, *Rocky Jordan*, and *Suspense*. In November 1949 Fifield was named writer of CBS' *Jeff Regan, Investigator* series with **William Froug** but departed in 1950.

Fifield wrote numerous works of fiction and non-fiction over the years including short stories, essays, and novels as well as interviews for *The Paris Review* with such historical figures as Pablo Picasso and Jean Cocteau. His writing was regarded highly enough to earn Fifield an O'Henry Prize in 1943 for his short story "The Fisherman of Patzcuaro." In 1950 Fifield left radio entirely and moved to Europe for forty years where he wrote full time.

Books: *The Devil's Marchioness* (1957); *Modigliani: The Biography* (1976).
Sources: William Fifield Papers; Grams *Suspense*; *Broadcasting* July 1, 1937, p. 54, June 15, 1940, p. 54, October 26, 1942, p. 38, December 13, 1943, p. 38, November 4, 1949, p. 74, June 19, 1950, p. 38; theparisreview.com.

Fimberg, Hal

Hal Fimberg (February 26, 1907–April 6, 1974) was one of Jack Haley's lead writers, co-writing *Log Cabin Jamboree* (1937–1938) with **Eddie Davis** and then Haley's *Jack Haley Variety Show* (1938). During that period Fimberg is also credited with penning a series of Eddie Durham transcriptions (1937). Fimberg joined Joe Penner's writing team for *Tip Top Show* (1939) before starting a screenwriting career in Hollywood in 1940. Unable to find solid footing in films, Fimberg continued in radio with the *Al Pearce Show* in 1941. In 1944 Fimberg joined **Sidney Fields** writing *The Abbott & Costello Show* as well as some of their big screen work. His last known radio series was *Which Is Which* (1945).

Fimberg wrote a number of screenplays in the 1940s including Abbot and Costello's *The Naughty Nineties*. In the 1950s he primarily scripted for television including *My Favorite Husband* (1953) and *The Donald O'Connor Show* (1954–1955). He later co-wrote the Derek Flint spy-spoof films of the 1960s.
Other Radio: *This Is My Story* (1943).
Sources: Kanter p. 9–10; *Broadcasting* October 1, 1938, p. A6, September 15, 1939, p. 44, August 11, 1941, p. 34, January 17, 1944, p. 44, March 19, 1945, p. 50, September 19, 1955, p. 208; *Motion Picture Daily* February 20, 1937, p. 4.

Fine, Morton

Morton Fine (December 24, 1916–March 7, 1991) was a struggling magazine writer before turning to radio scripting in the late 1940s where he found his talents in steady demand. Fine didn't attempt a writing career until about age 30 when he finished a master's degree in English at the University of Pittsburgh. After winning a Doubleday Award and selling five articles to a magazine that subsequently went under without publishing a single issue, Fine moved to California. Perhaps this rocky freelance start combined with his earlier years working for an advertising agency, an aircraft manufacturer, and a bookshop followed by a stint in World War II as a roving reporter led him to seek a new start on the West Coast.

Some editors of *Look* magazine suggested Fine try his hand at radio scripting and soon after he met **David Friedkin** and the two became one of the legendary writing teams of radio's Golden Age. Fine's earliest known radio work was providing continuity for the transcribed *Here's Looking at You* in early 1948. Some of his earliest work with Friedkin appeared on the series *Johnny Fletcher* and *Front Page* with Dick Powell (both 1948), the latter adapted from the play by **Ben Hecht** and Charles MacArthur. Fine is credited with scripts on *Let George Do It* (1948), *Philip Morris Playhouse* (1949), and *Gunsmoke* (1949) before finding his niche with Friedkin authoring crime and mystery programs.

Though broadcast from California for most of its run, *Broadway Is My Beat* (1949–1954) reflected the gritty underbelly of New York and was the first major series on which Fine left his indelible print with Friedkin. That same year the pair began providing scripts to *Pursuit* and *Escape* as well. While providing near-weekly stories for *Broadway*, in 1950 Fine and Friedkin debuted on *The Line-Up*, contributing regularly, and the anthology program *Suspense*, for which they wrote nearly three dozen shows up until 1958.

Fine is closely associated with three additional series from the early 1950s, all co-authored with Friedkin. From 1950 to 1951 they penned *Bold Venture* starring motion picture stars Humphrey Bogart and Lauren Bacall, a transcribed adventure series set in Cuba. Then between 1952 and 1954 the duo provided numerous scripts for *On Stage*, an anthology series created by Elliott and Cathy Lewis, one of the most influential couples in radio drama, as well as *Crime Classics*, stories of historic crimes.

With radio ceding popularity to television as the 1950s rolled on, Fine soon found himself busy writing for the small screen, though not before writing for radio's *Hallmark Hall of Fame* (1954–1955) and *Romance* (1954). Fine was a regular contributor to television's *Frontier* (1955–1956), *Bold Venture* (1959), and *I Spy* (1965–1968) but saw his work produced into the early 1980s.

Other Radio: *Police Line-Up* (1950, audition); *Sara's Private Caper* (1950); *The Adventures of Robin Hood* (1951, audition); *The McCoy* (1951, audition).

Sources: *Variety* May 12, 1948, p. 28, June 16, 1948, p. 26; *The Sherbrooke Telegram* June 15, 1950, p. 14.

Fine, Sylvia

Sylvia Fine (August 29, 1913–October 28, 1991) was a music major from Brooklyn College and then a busy writer of small-time stage musicals and revues when she met Danny Kaye at an audition for *Sunday Night Revue*. It wasn't, it turns out, the first time they'd met. Fine and Kaye grew up on the same street and attended the same high school in Brooklyn; Kaye had even worked for Fine's father, a dentist, for a short time. But the two never got to know each other until that fateful audition.

There was a chemistry between the two and Fine and her writing partner Max Liebman agreed to start writing material for Kaye who had been struggling for years to establish himself in show business. The first collaborative work between the three was *The Straw Hat Revue* (1939), a production that did not earn any of them much fame, though soon after they got married in Florida.

Fine and Kaye made an early radio appearance on an episode of CBS' *Forecast* in 1940 but he didn't get a regular spot until 1945 on a Saturday night program sponsored by Pabst Beer. That fall he got his own series, *The Danny Kaye Show*, written by Fine and one of CBS's premier writers, **Goodman Ace**. The series ran for just a year but Kaye made numerous guest appearances on various programs over subsequent years, presumably with material written by Fine.

Later Fine wrote television material for Kaye's broadcast specials and other specials, notably some for PBS in the 1970s and 1980s. She continued to be a prolific composer with dozens of songs in numerous television and motion picture productions through the 1950s and 1960s. Despite varying claims about Fine's marriage to Kaye, the couple stayed together until his death in 1987.

Sources: *Modern Screen* January 1945 p. 32–33, 79–82; *People* October 1, 1979; *Screenland* April 1944 p. 84; *Swing* August 1945 p. 53–54; *Variety* July 24, 1940, p. 26, March 21, 1945, p. 38, October 3, 1945, p. 36; www.dannykaye.net.

Finger, Len

Len Finger worked as a program manager for Texas stations KTAT and KFDM in the late 1930s before joining NBC's Blue network in 1942. There he scripted *Metropolitan Auditions of the Air*, *Where Do We Stand* (both 1943) and *World of Song* and *Dunninger* (both 1944) before resigning in 1944 to work freelance. Among his post–Blue series were *Luncheon with Lopez* (1945) featuring Vincent Lopez, *Exploring the Unknown* (1947), and *Warriors of Peace* (1947).

Other Radio: *Famous Jury Trials*.

Sources: *Broadcasting* September 28, 1942, p. 36, February 22, 1943, p. 34; *Radio Daily* April 7, 1937, p. 8; *Variety* December 29, 1943, p. 21, January 5, 1944, p. 135, April 19, 1944, p. 23.

Finke, Jack (or Jacques)

Jacques Finke attended Cornell University with the goal of becoming a professional writer. While there he got some experience writing for *Aeropagus*, the campus literary magazine, school musicals, and for a college radio group. His career took a detour to Columbia where he studied accounting to please his father, though he spent more time reading and honing his writing than sitting in class.

Finke's father eventually lost his patience and Finke talked himself into a job at CBS as an apprentice writer. Max Wylie heard some of Finke's material and invited him to join the scripting department where he later claimed to have written continuity for every program on the chain. During these early years with CBS he scripted five episodes of *The Columbia Workshop* (ca. 1942).

After three years Finke left to script *Your Hit Parade* and *The Cities Service Program* for an agency and then decided to try freelancing and his work was used on *Radio Readers' Digest, Report to the Nation, Romance* (all ca. 1942–1943), and *Suspense* (one half-dozen episodes between 1942 and 1947). In 1943 Finke was inducted into the Armed Forces where he was assigned to write *Voice of the Army* (1943–1945).

Finke contributed scripts to a number of radio dramas near and after war's end including *The Whistler* (1945), *The Doctor Fights* (1945, 2nd series), *The Adventures of Sam Spade* (1947), *The Chase* (1953), and hundreds of episodes of *The FBI in Peace and War* (1947–1955) with **Louis Pelletier**. Finke is credited with a handful of teleplays in the 1950s.

Sources: *Broadcasting* July 2, 1945, p. 10; *Radio Mirror* May 1945 p. 50; *Variety* April 2, 1947, p. 35, August 27, 1947, p. 31.

Finn, Herb (Herbert)

Herb Finn (July 28, 1912–May 28, 2002) dreamed of being an actor but got his break in show business as a writer for radio's *Amos 'n' Andy* and then for another program with an African American lead, both the third and fourth series of *Beulah* that ran from 1947–1953 and then 1953–1954. He was later on the scripting team for *Duffy's Tavern* (ca. 1947), a program that was described as a perfect preparation for his time on television's classic show *The Honeymooners* (1955–1956) followed by *The Jackie Gleason Show*. Finn is most widely known for his television legacy that also included episodes of such sixties series as *Dennis the Menace* (1962), *The Flintstones* (1962–1966), and *Gilligan's Island* (1964–1967).

Sources: *Motion Picture Daily* April 16, 1956, p. 9; *TV Radio Mirror* December 1958 p. 22-23; *Variety* October 8, 1947, p. 26; July 17, 2002.

Fischer, Marvin (Marv, Fisher)

Marvin Fischer's first identified series writing for radio was *Hall of Fun*, a 1938 variety show on NBC that featured Tom, Dick, and Harry among other entertainers. The following year he was signed to write for *Signal Carnival* until 1941, first with **Paul Conlon** and later with Stanley Davis. In 1941 Fischer penned some motion pictures for Columbia and then that fall went to work on *Al Pearce and His Gang* (1941–1942, along with Davis who was previously his partner for *Signal Carnival* as well as with **Hal Fimberg**.

In the Army during World War II Fischer was assigned to write for *Yank*, a troop publication, then upon leaving the service he immediately joined the staff of the *Chase & Sanborn Show* in 1945. Not long after, Fischer was added to *The Jack Carson Show* (1945–1947, later *The Sealtest Village Store*). By 1948 Fischer had joined the staff of rapid-fire comic Bob Hope, with whom he stayed for several years into the early 1950s before writing for *The Phil Harris–Alice Faye Show* between 1953 and 1954. Fischer tried his hand at television in the early 1950s and is credited with several episodes of *The Colgate Comedy Hour* and later the *NBC Comedy Hour*.

Sources: *Broadcasting* September 15, 1939, p. 42, September 8, 1941, p. 32, September 29, 1941, p. 38, August 27, 1945, p. 30, December 10, 1945, p. 68, January 16, 1956, p. 14; *Variety* May 11, 1938, p. 26, March 26, 1941, p. 4, September 22, 1948, p. 24.

Fisher, Robert

Robert Fisher (September 21, 1922–September 19, 2008) is first known to have written for radio on *Amos 'n' Andy* (1946–1947) after it had changed to a 30-minute sitcom format. In early

1949 he started writing for the *Alan Young Show* and later in the year he was named writer for *Baby Snooks* with **Arthur Stander** in 1949, where he wrote until 1951.

Fisher had a long career in television, writing for dozens of series between 1952 and 1986. From early programs such as *Doc Corkle* (1953) with Eddie Mayehoff and *The People's Choice* (1959) with Jackie Cooper, to *Leave It to Beaver* (1960), *I Dream of Jeannie* (1965) and *Alice* (1977–1981).

Theater: *The Impossible Years* (1965); *Happiness Is Just a Little Thing Called a Rolls Royce* (1968); *Minnie's Boys* (1970).

Sources: *Broadcasting* March 21, 1949, p. 66, November 7, 1949, p. 69; *Sponsor* January 24, 1959, p. 28–29; *Telecasting* March 2, 1953, p. 70; *Variety* October 9, 1946, p. 53, October 8, 1947, p. 24.

Flynn, Bess

Bess Flynn got her start in Chicago radio as an actress during the early 1930s, first on *The Gumps* and later on the pioneering serial *Painted Dreams*, created by **Irna Phillips**. When Phillips left *Painted Dreams* in a dispute over the show's sponsorship the writing duties were handed over to others, one of them being Bess Flynn for a time. Having gained confidence as a writer, Flynn created two serials of her own in 1935, *Bachelor's Children* and *We Are Four*, the latter of which was sponsored by Libby's. She gave up writing *Painted Dreams* in order to keep up with her two own programs though she continued to act in it.

By 1940 Flynn was writing *Life Begins*, a show that in September of that year was retitled *Martha Webster* and starred Flynn in the lead. She scripted *Webster* at least until 1941 and in 1942 she took over writing chores on another soap opera, *We Love and Learn*, when writer **Don Becker** went on leave due to illness. Though not credited as the writer, Flynn was the advisor on yet another serial, *We, The Abbotts* (1940–1942). *Bachelor's Children* carried on for eleven years until 1946 even as her other programs gradually left the air. At the time *Bachelor's Children* left the air Flynn was reported to be developing another show, *Tomorrow's Children*, with Margaret Culkin Banning though it isn't known to have aired.

Sources: *Motion Picture Daily* February 25, 1937, p. 15; *Radio Daily* July 7, 1937, p. 4, September 22, 1937, p. 1, 3; *Variety* September 4, 1940, p. 37, September 11, 1940, p. 28, July 9, 1941, p. 24, November 5, 1941, p. 38, July 1, 1942, p. 32; *Chicago Tribune* March 24, 1935, p. 6W, September 8, 1935, p. 4NW, August 10, 1946, p. 20.

Folliott, Doria

Doria Folliott (1906–1974), an English-born writer, made her first known foray into radio in 1941 when her serial *The Promised Land* was recorded in an attempt to find a sponsor. This experience allowed her to step in as a substitute scripter for **Jane Crusinberry** on *The Story of Mary Marlin* when Crusinberry took her annual summer vacations in 1942 and 1943. The following year she wrote *Open Door* (1944) for a time while **Sandra Michael** was under doctor's orders to take some leave. Over a decade later she wrote many episodes for television's *Robert Montgomery Presents* (1954–1957).

Other Radio: *Pepper Young's Family*; *A Woman of America*.

Books: *Signpost to Murder* (1964).

Sources: *The Radio Annual 1945* p. 828; *Variety* November 19, 1941, p. 40, June 24, 1942, p. 29, April 19, 1944, p. 30.

Fontaine, Leo

A drama critic for the *New York Morning Telegraph* and subsequent scripter for Transradio Press and the networks, Leo Fontaine is now remembered primarily as a writer and continuity director for the Radio Division of the Works Progress Administration in the late 1930s. Among his assignments was adapting two contemporary novels for the air, James Truslow Adams' *Epic of America* and Mary Roberts Rinehart's *Tish*. Both authors had donated radio rights for the projects. Fontaine co-wrote *Epic of America* with Joel Hammil and wrote *Tish* independently.

Fontaine also polished the final scripts for special broadcasts such as the 1937 coronation of King George VI of England. In 1938 Fontaine was responsible for writing *Slums Cost You Money*, produced by the Radio Division in conjunction with the Federal Housing Administration. He was assigned more dramatic fare in 1939 when the Division received rights to adapt Detective O'Malley stories from *Collier's Magazine*, the first two of which were Fontaine's responsibilities. Fontaine was still contributing radio scripts many years later for commercial series including *Gang Busters* (1943) and *Nick Carter, Master Detective* (1950).

Other Radio: *The Women of the Day* (WPA).
Sources: *Billboard* February 20, 1943, p. 6; *Broadcasting* October 15, 1937, p. 65, June 1, 1938, p. 32; *The Radio Annual* 1938 p. 520; *Variety* May 12, 1937, p. 38, January 18, 1939, p. 27, May 31, 1939, p. 23.

Foreman, Carl

After graduating from the University of Illinois, Chicago-born Carl Foreman (July 23, 1914–June 26, 1984) moved to California where he joined the writing team for Eddie Cantor's radio program in 1942 as he was attempting to establish himself as a screenwriter. After a stint in the service Foreman returned to the film industry where he wrote *High Noon* (1952), *The Bridge on the River Kwai* (1957), and *The Guns of Navarone* (1963). Despite being Blacklisted for membership in the American Communist Party years before, Foreman posthumously won an Academy Award for Adapted Screenplay for *Kwai* and was nominated for five more (1950, 1951, 1953, 1962, and 1973).

Source: *Billboard* October 10, 1942, p. 6.

Forman, Ed

Ed Forman was a writer for *Stage Door Canteen* (1943) before debuting on *The Abbott & Costello Show* around 1944, a show for which he is credited later with becoming the head writer. In 1947 Forman and Lou Costello got their pet project, *The Abbott & Costello Kid Show*, on ABC in an effort to fight juvenile delinquency. Forman continued with the comedy duo through the 1940s and into television.

Other Radio: *Forecast* (1940).
Sources: *Radio and Television Mirror* July 1948 p. 76; *Variety* July 14, 1943, p. 82, April 19, 1944, p. 23.

Foster, George

George Foster was a writer on **Goodman Ace**'s staff for a number of radio and television programs. How the two became associated professionally is unknown but in 1949 Foster assisted in writing the *Easy Aces* television series produced by Ziv Television.

Between 1950 and 1952 Foster and Ace's other writers were charged with turning NBC's *The Big Show* into a ratings smash to both fend off an emerging television industry and regain listeners lost to network competitor CBS. Despite access to an endless array of top talent, the program failed to live up to the network's hopes.

Foster had many years of writing still ahead of him, however, primarily on television. Most notably, with Ace and staff he wrote for Perry Como's television series between 1955 and 1959. The show's writers were nominated for Primetime Emmy Awards in 1957 and 1959.

Sources: Macfarlane & Crossland; *Broadcasting* December 19, 1949, p. 62.

Foster, Richard (See Kendall Crossen)

Foster, Royal

Royal Foster was a long-time writing partner with Ken Murray, teaming together on numerous projects from early 1930s into the 1950s. On radio Foster scripted *The Ken Murray-Oswald Show* (1937), then *Hollywood Hotel* (1937) after Murray switched programs, and back to *The Ken Murray Show* in 1939. In 1940 Foster worked on *Texaco Star Theatre* with **Fred Allen** (under the same sponsor as the Murray programs) followed by a Ken Murray transcription series, *Parade of Stars* (1941) co-written with **Keith Fowler** and **Frank Galen**.

Foster began writing for Edgar Bergen in the early 1940s both on his film *Here We Go Again* (1942) and his popular radio series *The Edgar Bergen & Charlie McCarthy Show* (1944–1948). He had at least on other radio credit, the short-lived show *Stop and Go* (1943).

Television: *Ken Murray Show* (1952).
Theater: *Earl Carroll's Sketch Book* (1935); *Blackouts of 1949* (1949, with Ken Murray).
Sources: *Broadcasting* September 1, 1937, p. 80, May 1, 1940, p. 60, March 22, 1943, p. 32; *The Film Daily* August 28, 1942, p. 93; *Radio-Television Mirror* June 1951 p. 88; *Sponsor* January 1948 p. 48; *Variety* November 5, 1941, p. 34.

Fowler, Keith

Keith Fowler (August 6, 1906–April 3, 1973) debuted as a radio author as early as 1935 on *Atlantic Family*, a rare show that broadcast from Philadelphia. Co-written with Henry Weiner, the pair teamed up on *The Frank Parker Show* later that year. For the latter half of the 1930s Fowler was a member of Rudy Vallee's writing team often tasked with penning material for program guests. These shows included *Fleischmann's Yeast Hour* (1936), *The Royal Gelatin Hour* (1936–1937), *The Royal Desserts Hour* (1938), and *The Rudy Vallee Hour* (1938). Interspersed with his Vallee assignments was the job of providing W. C. Fields' material for *The Chase & Sanborn Hour* in 1937. During his time with Vallee Fowler started writing with **Frank Galen** and the two became long-time collaborators.

Between 1939 and 1941 Fowler scripted for two series, **Fred Allen**'s *Texaco Star Theatre* (1939–1940) and Ken Murray's *Parade of Stars* (1941). For the 1941–1942 season Fowler signed to write for *The Burns & Allen Show* and he would spend the rest of the decade writing for the comedy couple. Between 1941 and 1949 he left the show only for an approximately eighteen-month stint in the Army (1944–1945) where he wrote *The Fighting AAF*. Toward the end of his radio writing days Fowler moved to *Fibber McGee & Molly* (1951–1953), spending two years with the venerable show during its twilight years.

With radio comedians abandoning ship for television during the early 1950s Fowler went with them and rejoined his old friends George Burns and Gracie Allen on their small screen series from 1953 to 1958. He later wrote for *Dennis the Menace* (1961–1963) and *The Addams Family* (1964–1965) among many television series into the late 1960s.

Other Radio: *Forecast* (1940–1941); *Gulf Screen Guild Theatre* (1942); *A Day in the Life of Dennis Day* (1950); *Silver Theater*.

Theater: *Three Blind Mice* (1936).

Sources: *Broadcasting* October 1, 1939, p. 51; *Radio Daily* August 31, 1937, p. 4; *Variety* September 18, 1935, p. 60, September 25, 1935, p. 44; October 7, 1936, p. 37, September 1, 1937, p. 34, April 4, 1945, p. 39.

Fox, Frank

A writer for Bob Hope in the 1940s, Frank Fox turned to sitcoms during the post-war era and was quite successful, scripting for *A Day in the Life of Dennis Day* (1946), *The Adventures of Ozzie and Harriet* (1947–1949), and the initial episodes of Lucille Ball's *My Favorite Husband* (1948) when it debuted as a summer replacement for *Ozzie and Harriet*. On all three shows he teamed with **Bill Davenport** among others. Fox also earned credit as a writer for Sweeney and March during their intermittent broadcasts from 1946 to 1951).

Fox was increasingly focused on television after 1950, the year in which he scripted *The Ed Wynn Show* for the medium along with new collaborator **Jess Goldstein**, though the duo created and wrote one last radio series together, *It's Always Sunday* (1951). Though Fox would write for television until 1970, his most famous work was *My Little Margie* that he created and then wrote from 1952 to 1955. The program was simultaneously produced over radio as well, a characteristic of several series during the mid–1950s

Sources: *Broadcasting* May 8, 1950, p. 62; *Variety* October 9, 1946, p. 53, July 14, 1948, p. 30, October 6, 1948, p. 25; jackraymondradio.com.

Fox, Fred

Fred Fox (August 26, 1902–August 27, 1981) joined the writing staff for *The Judy Canova Show* in early 1945 where he stayed until at least 1950 and there are numerous claims that he provided gags to Groucho Marx as well. An unusual credit for Fox was writing and drawing for numerous newspaper comic strips. Among them were *Good Time Guy* (1929), *Freckles and His Friends* (over 30 years before its 1971 demise), *Ella Cinders* (1940–1961), and *Odd Bodkins* (1941).

Sources: *Variety* January 17, 1945, p. 32; lambiek.net.

Fox, Gibson Scott

Gibson Fox was a sound effects artist at Detroit's WXYZ before he began writing scripts for two of their series, *Secret Agent* and *The Lone Ranger* (both ca. 1938). He was still writing for the masked man over a decade later after the Lone Ranger became a television hero (1949–1960). He also wrote for non–WXYZ programs including *The Shadow* (1946–1947, 1948), *Hopalong Cassidy* (1950–1951), *The Clyde Beatty Show* (1950), and *The Silver Eagle, Jim West of the Mounties* (1952). Fox contributed several scripts to *Hawaiian Eye* (1960–1962).

Other Radio: *True Story Theatre* (ca. 1942).

Sources: Grams *Shadow*; Harmon *Radio Mystery* p. 122–124; *Billboard* February 25, 1950, p. 62; *Radio Mirror* January 1943, p. 9; *Variety* July 27, 1938, p. 36, December 7, 1938, p. 22.

Fox, S. Fred

Working his way up from merchandising to production at San Francisco's KYA, Fred Fox (July 26, 1915–October 23, 2005) joined the station's continuity staff in 1939 though he continued to have production responsibilities in subsequent years. After joining KFSO in 1941 Fox spent two years as a writer with the station before joining the Overseas Branch of the OWI in 1943. After one year Fox rejoined the commercial ranks as writer on Bing Crosby's *Kraft Music Hall* (1944) on a team headed by Dave Gregory but jumped to *The Bob Hope Show* shortly thereafter. It was the beginning of a long partnership; Fox would write for Hope for more than 45 years, until 1990.

Fox's work with Hope was a springboard to television where he wrote prolifically for decades. Among his most famous series were *The Real McCoys* (1959–1963), *The Andy Griffith Show* (1961–1967), *The Red Skelton Hour* (1968–1970), and *The Love Boat* (1978–1985). Through the 1980s he wrote numerous televised Bob Hope specials.

Other Radio: *The Doris Day Show* (1953); Credited with writing radio material for George Burns and Gracie Allen, Jack Carson, and Spike Jones.

Sources: *Broadcasting* May 1, 1939, p. 42, October 1, 1939, p. 50, March 10, 1941, p. 50, October 20, 1941, p. 41, March 8, 1943, p. 30, August 21, 1944, p. 63, September 11, 1944, p. 60; *Variety* October 29, 1941, p. 38; *Variety* obituary.

Franchey, William

William Franchey worked for a few different agencies in the 1940s including Wm. Esty & Co., Ros S. M. Durstine Inc., Russel M. Seeds Co., and McCann-Erickson handling writing and other creative work. He was a member of the writing team for **John Guedel**'s *People Are Funny* ca. 1944 then provided scripts for *World News Parade* (later *World Parade*) 1944–1945.

Sources: *Broadcasting* September 27, 1943, p. 54, January 16, 1945, p. 46; *Variety* April 19, 1944, p. 23, April 4, 1945, p. 27.

Frank, Melvin

Melvin Frank (August 13, 1913–October 13, 1988) was a Chicago native who met his longtime writing partner **Norman Panama** while studying at the University of Chicago. After graduating they briefly wrote for Milton Berle before getting jobs writing for Bob Hope on *The Pepsodent Show* (1938–1939) who also gave them a shot in motion pictures when they scripted Hope's 1942 film *My Favorite Blonde*. Before abandoning radio Frank spent time writing for *The Rudy Vallee Show* (1940–1941) and *Command Performance* (1942).

This short radio career was followed by a long and successful film career, first as a screenwriter then as director and producer. Among his most famous screenplays are *Mr. Blandings Builds His Dream House* (1948), *White Christmas* (1954), and two of the Bob Hope-Bing Crosby *Road* films. He was nominated for four Oscars for Best Writing, the first three of them with Norman Panama, in 1947, 1955, 1961, and 1974.

Sources: *Broadcasting* March 15, 1940, p. 51, October 12, 1942, p. 56; *New York Times* obituary.

Frankel, Doris

By 1930 the New York City–born Doris Frankel (1909–1994) had published a book of poetry, *The Sun Beats Down*, and started writing and producing *Poetry Recital* on New York's WPCH. At that same time she began writing screenplays for Universal and Warner Bros. studios as well. A playwright through most of the 1930s, Frankel focused more on radio during the 1940s and then television after the demise of dramatic radio.

Among the radio programs for which she wrote were *The Brighter Day* (that she followed to television in 1954), *Cavalcade of America* (1946–1950), *Harvest of Stars*, *The Listening Post*,

Sky Blazers, Theater of Today, and *Young Widder Jones* (1938). During the television era she scripted for *The Colgate Hour, Playhouse 90,* and *Suspense* and then later in her career on the soap operas *Search for Tomorrow* and *All My Children,* the latter of which she earned a Daytime Emmy in 1978.

Theater: *Don't Throw Glass Houses* (1938); *Love Me Long* (1949).

Sources: Frankel Papers; *Broadcasting-Telecasting* January 11, 1954, p. 14; *Variety* January 25, 1939, p. 26.

Franklin, Paul

Paul Franklin (May 30, 1899–May 15, 1980) was a busy West Coast writer, churning out nearly three dozen screenplays between 1936 and 1949—almost all of them Westerns—and authoring a number of radio series in between film projects. His earliest radio shows included *Hollywood Hotel* (1934), *Your Hollywood Parade* (1938), *Cavalcade of America* (1941, 1944), and *King Size Weekly* (1941).

Franklin's longest tenure was with *Red Ryder* on which he served as both writer and director between 1942 and 1949. He briefly scripted *The Roy Rogers Show* in 1943 and then *Amos 'n' Andy* until 1945, leaving the legendary sitcom so he could try more directing. As a scriptwriter Franklin also contributed to *The Zane Grey Show* (1947–1948, also director), *Story of Dr. Kildare* (1950), and *Yours Truly, Johnny Dollar* (1957). Throughout the 1950s Franklin wrote many television scripts, especially for Westerns, but did not work for a notable length of time on any one series.

Other Radio: *Wings to Victory* (1943).

Sources: *Broadcasting* March 1, 1938, p. 35, December 22, 1941, p. 37, April 20, 1942, p. 34; *Hollywood Filmograph* October 27, 1934, p. 2, *Variety* December 15, 1943, p. 30, January 17, 1945, p. 30, October 1, 1947, p. 25.

Fraser, Ferrin

Ferrin Fraser (May 11, 1903–April 1, 1969), a Columbia University graduate, entered radio in the early 1930s, writing for such series as *Red Book Dramas* (1932) before being hired as CBS' continuity director for a time in 1933. He stayed in this position less than one year but continued writing for *Triple Bar X*. Fraser's next radio series featured Frank Buck, an animal collector, and then in 1935 he took over writing *Little Orphan Annie* for several years. Years later Fraser scripted several episodes of *Nick Carter, Master Detective* (1951–1952).

Books: *Fang and Claw* (1935); *Tim Thompson in the Jungle* (1935); *On Jungle Trails* (1936); *All in a Lifetime* (1941); *Jungle Animals* (1945), all with Frank Buck.

Sources: *Broadcasting* February 1, 1933, p. 20; *Variety* October 10, 1933, p. 32; *Variety Radio Directory* 1938–1939 p. 359; *Chicago Tribune* November 25, 1935, p. 16; *Los Angeles Times* August 14, 1933, p. 14; otrsite.com.

Freedman, Benedict

Benedict Freedman (December 19, 1919–February 24, 2012) followed his father, **David Freedman**, into radio writing; At 18 he earned a job on Al Jolson's Lifebuoy program (1938). The following year he started scripting for *Texaco Star Theatre* with **Fred Allen** and for *Melody Madness* during the summer replacement season. By 1942 Freedman had joined Red Skelton's writing team, a professional relationship that would last over a decade on radio and several years beyond that on television. Freedman scripted numerous comedy programs on television including *The Mickey Rooney Show* (1954), *The Red Skelton Hour* (1951–1956), and *My Favorite Martian* (1964–1965). Over 50 years old in 1970, Freedman earned his Ph.D. in mathematics from UCLA and started a second career as college professor.

Other Radio: *Lux Radio Theatre* (1950).

Books: *Mrs. Mike* (1947); *Lootville* (1957).

Sources: David Freedman Papers; *Broadcasting* April 1, 1939, p. 57, June 15, 1939, p. 46; *Variety* September 14, 1938, p. 24, September 23, 1942, p. 32; *New York Times* obituary, 2012.

Freedman, Bill

Bill Freedman wrote for at least a couple shows during the Golden Age of radio, including *Duffy's Tavern* (ca. 1947–1948) and *Beulah* (1953–1954) when Amanda Randolph took over permanently in the title role. Freedman was busy on television scripting for series such as *The Gale Storm Show* (1956–1960), *My Favorite Martian* (1964–1965), and *The Brady Bunch* (1969–1974).

Source: *Variety* April 2, 1947, p. 35.

Freedman, David

Romanian-born David Freedman (April 26, 1898–December 8, 1936) was Eddie Cantor's chief gag writer for vaudeville and motion pictures in the late 1920s and continued in that role as Cantor established himself on radio in the early 1930s. His talent was so highly regarded that he became one of the first credited scripters on the air.

Freedman was involved in the creation of Fanny Brice's Baby Snooks character in 1934 as a part of the stage production *Ziegfeld Follies* and by 1935 he was rumored to be earning $500 per radio script for Cantor. During the early 1930s Freedman also wrote for Al Jolson (*Kraft Music Hall*), George Givot, Helen Menken, Tom Howard & George Shelton, and Block & Sully and throughout the 1930s Freedman penned a number of mostly forgotten film shorts.

A rift developed between the long-time collaborators in 1934 and Freedman sued Cantor in 1935 for $250,000, claiming he was owed 10 percent of Cantor's earnings over the past few years. After that break Freedman moved to Rudy Vallee's *Fleischmann Yeast Program* for the 1935–1936 season and then to Milton Berle's writing team in 1936. That year he also contributed jokes to NBC's *Jumbo* program with Jimmy Durante to the tune of $650 per week though the Texaco-sponsored show was judged a failure after a short run. On top of the comedy writing world, Freedman died suddenly in his sleep in 1936 at the age of 38. His son, **Benedict** (Ben) **Freedman** carried on in radio but Freedman's suit against Cantor was subsequently dismissed due to his passing.

Other Radio: *Bob Crosby Show*; *The Red Skelton Show*.

Books: *Yoo-Hoo, Prosperity! The Eddie Cantor Five-Year Plan* (1931, with Cantor).

Sources: *The Film Daily* April 4, 1935, p. 3; *Radio Mirror* May 1935 p. 60; *Variety* October 16, 1932, p. 51, October 31, 1933, p. 41, January 9, 1934, p. 44, February 12, 1935, p. 56, February 27, 1935, p. 47, October 16, 1935, p. 50, February 26, 1936, p. 58, March 25, 1936, p. 19.

Freedman, Hy

An employee of John Guedel Radio Productions, Hy Freedman (April 10, 1914–March 31, 1986) wrote several years for the series *You Bet Your Life* (1947–1960) both on radio and then television. Though much of the show was ad-libbed by host Groucho Marx, Freedman and others created a basic structure for the episodes and supplied gags that could be inserted or altered where needed.

Television: *His and Hers* (1956, pilot).

Sources: *Billboard* December 22, 1956, p. 3; *Variety* October 29, 1947, p. 28; davidpietrusza.com.

Freedman, Morris

Morris Freedman (October 6, 1920–April 27, 2015) wrote steadily in the post–War years, his most prominent radio work coming on *Duffy's Tavern* (1946–1949) and *The Jimmy Durante Show* (1950). He continued in television writing for *The Ray Milland Show* (1954–1955), *Meet Millie* (1955–1956), *Professional Father* (1955), and *How to Marry a Millionaire* (1957–1958).

Other Radio: *That's Rich* (1954)

Sources: Morris Freedman Collection; *Variety* April 2, 1947, p. 35.

Freeman, Ben Peter

A University of Chicago graduate, Ben Peter Freeman (October 17, 1901–December 11, 1992) subsequently moved to New York where he got work reporting for the *New York Times*. He published some baseball stories and other freelance work and in the mid–1940s was hired to script *The Adventures of Superman* (1946–1948). Freeman followed that up with scripts for other adventures series including *The Adventures of Babe Ruth* (1949), *Mark Trail* (1950), and *Tom Corbett, Space Cadet* (1952). He is also known to have scripted a few episodes of television's *Adventures of Superman* between 1952 and 1953. Freeman gave up writing in 1953 and went to work for his brother's Chicago-area construction company.

Sources: *The Radio Annual* 1946 p. 817; *Variety* November 12, 1947, p. 44; *Variety* obituary February 3, 1993.

Freeman, Everett

Everett Freeman (February 2, 1911–January 24, 1991) was a regular writer for the *Saturday Evening Post* in the early 1930s when he started dabbling in radio, writing an early sketch with **David Freedman**. This experience led to his writing for various Philip Morris-sponsored programs in the mid–1930s.

After a few of his *Post* stories were adapted for motion pictures, Freeman began to focus his writing on the movie studios during the latter half of the decade. Even as his screenwriting career took off, Freeman continued to earn radio credits on programs such as *Gulf Screen Guild Theatre* (1939) and *The Eddie Cantor Show* and writing sketches for Fanny Brice's Baby Snooks.

Freeman's screen writing included dialog for Jack Benny's *Buck Benny Rides Again* (1940) and 1947's *The Secret Life of Walter Mitty*. In the 1950s he got busier with television, scripting both dramas and comedies, notably several episodes of *Bachelor Father* (1959–1962).

Sources: *The Film Daily* April 2, 1935, p. 2; *Variety* October 31, 1933, p. 41; *New York Times* obituary January 26, 1991.

Frey, Helen

Helen Frey is most noted for her contributions to children's broadcasting on WHA, University of Wisconsin. She wrote the radio play "Wilbur, the Sleepy Little Ghost" that was aired a number of times on *The Story Lady* and won an award from the Institute for Education by Radio. During World War II Frey served in the Women's Army Corps where she wrote scripts for radio and bond rallies. After her service Frey was awarded the H. V. Kaltenborn radio scholarship for 1948–1949 to the University of Wisconsin.

Sources: Cowgill p. 160–161; Davidson p. 142; *The Milwaukee Sentinel* October 25, 1948, p. 13.

Friedkin, David

After studying violin at Julliard, David Friedkin (March 8, 1912–October 15, 1976) set his sights on becoming an actor but ended up finding success as a scriptwriter instead. One of his first radio assignments was Burl Ives' *Philco Radio Show* in 1947 but soon after he met **Morton Fine**, with whom he would collaborate on countless scripts. Two of their earliest programs together were an adaptation of **Ben Hecht**'s and Charles MacArthur's play *The Front Page* and *The Philip Morris Playhouse*.

In 1949 Friedkin was signed with Fine to author a new *Dick Tracy* series supervised by Rudy Vallee, though it remains unclear whether the program was ever aired. The weekly series was to be augmented by a quarter-hour television series written by Ron Davidson. That same year the duo premiered on what may be their most famous show, *Broadway Is My Beat* (1949–1954), featuring gritty detective Danny Clover. The following year they added a second series, *The Line-Up*, to their regular workload for a short time.

Long reluctant to commit himself to a radio series, Humphrey Bogart was convinced to take the lead in *Bold Venture* (1951–1952) because a transcribed series would provide the flexibility his professional schedule required. Scripted by Friedkin and Fine, the Frederic W. Ziv-produced series co-starred Bogart's wife Lauren Bacall and was set in exotic Havana.

Friedkin, often with Fine, was closely linked with producer/director Elliott Lewis for many of his years in radio. From *Broadway* and *The Line-Up* during his early scripting years, Friedkin also dramatized infamous historical crimes on Elliott's *Crime Classics* (1953–1954), and later wrote multiple episodes of *Suspense* and *On Stage* (1952–1954) under Elliott's direction

As Friedkin established himself in the industry he gradually branched into directing and producing, responsibilities he undertook in the television industry as well, though he never stopped writing. Among his television scripting credits are *Bold Venture*, *The Virginian*, and *I Spy*.

Other Radio: *Guest Star* (1949, 1951); *Gunsmoke* (1949, audition); *Pursuit* (1949); *Escape* (over one dozen episodes, 1949–1954); *Police Line-Up* (1950, audition); *Sara's Private Caper* (1950, audition); *The Adventures of Robin Hood* (1951, possible audition); *The McCoy* (1951, audition); *Think* (1953); *Hallmark Hall of Fame* (1954); *San Francisco Final* (1954); *Romance* (1954).

Sources: *Broadcasting* April 9, 1951, p. 72; *Variety* February 26, 1947, p. 34, April 27, 1949, p. 23.

Froug, William (Bill)

William Froug (May 26, 1922–August 25, 2013) started writing after his service in World

War II and his earliest scripts may have been episodes of *Favorite Story* in 1946. He joined CBS' West Coast network in 1948 and immediately started writing for a variety of programs. He worked with author Richard Foster (**Kendall Crossen**) to bring Foster's hero of several novels, *The Green Lama*, to radio in a series that lasted just three months in 1949. His next assignments were scripting for *Rocky Jordan* and *Jeff Regan, Investigator* (both 1949–1950), the latter featuring Jack Webb of future *Dragnet* fame. After authoring *Memo from Molly* (1950–1951) Froug began moving into more supervisory roles such as overseeing program writing, though he continued in on-air directing of *The Hallmark Hall of Fame* from 1953–1954 and writing for *Romance* (1952–1956).

William Froug was a significant force behind the revival of *The CBS Radio Workshop* (earlier known as *The Columbia Workshop*) in 1956. As a CBS vice-president Froug felt there was still some demand for cutting-edge, experimental radio drama, even though the medium was quickly losing ground to television. Froug got the green light from network executives and scripted the opening episodes himself, a two-part adaptation of Aldous Huxley's *Brave New World*.

Television was the real peak of Froug's career where, though he continued to script teleplays, he produced such series as *The Twilight Zone* (1963–1964), *Gilligan's Island* (1964–1965), and *Bewitched* (1966–1967). He earned a Primetime Emmy nomination in 1967 for his work on *Bewitched*. By the 1970s Froug turned to teaching, eventually becoming a popular professor in UCLA's screenwriting program. Always honest about the slim chances of making a career in motion pictures, Froug's books and courses on writing were nonetheless highly regarded. Froug made a brief return to his radio writing roots in 1979 with an episode of the revival series *Sears Radio Theatre*.

Other Radio: *Make-Believe Town* (1949); *The Whistler* (1949); *Madison, That's Me* (1952); *The Judge* (1952); *Escape* (1952); *Sunday Playhouse* (1955); *Suspense* (1955).

Sources: William Froug Papers; Grams *Twilight Zone*; *Broadcasting* January 15, 1951, p. 48; *Motion Picture Daily* April 30, 1952, p. 9.

Fulton, Lou

Lou Fulton entered radio in 1928 where he held various positions by 1943 when he earned the opportunity to write for *The Jack Carson Show* with **Len Levinson**, featuring the popular Hollywood actor. In 1944 he was hired for a very different type of show, *Melody Roundup* with Andy Devine and the Sons of the Pioneers. The following year Fulton penned the scripts for another musical program, *The Fitch Bandwagon* with Cass Daily, a show that he took over as producer in 1945.

Fulton served as the script supervisor for Kay Kyser's *Comedy of Errors* show in 1947 and was reunited with Devine later that year as writer for *The Andy Devine Show*. His last known radio authoring was featured on *The Rex Allen Show* in 1952.

Sources: French & Siegel p. 18–19; *Broadcasting* April 2, 1945, p. 52; *Sponsor* March 9, 1953, p. 80; *Variety* June 2, 1943, p. 38, May 31, 1944, p. 40, March 28, 1945, p. 32, June 18, 1947, p. 28.

Funt, Julian

Julian Funt (March 24, 1906–April 8, 1980) was a busy writer of daytime serials from the late 1930s to the early 1950s. Some of his earliest works were *Hilda Hope, M.D.* (1939) and *Joyce Jordan, M.D.* which he co-created with Himan Brown (1938–1942). In 1942 Funt started a run as author of *Big Sister* (ca. 1942–1950) as well as Himan Brown's *Littletown, U.S.A.*, that very possibly was revamped as the more widely remembered *Green Valley, U.S.A.* just a few weeks later. Funt later moved on to *A Woman's Life* (1945), originally known as *Bright Horizon*, *This Is Nora Drake* (1947–1948), and *Young Dr. Malone* (1950). Funt reportedly lost his job on *Malone* due to the era's Blacklist but managed to resume his career on television.

Television: *City Hospital* (1953); *Search for Tomorrow* (1963–1965).

Theater: *The Dancer* (1946).

Sources: *Radio Varieties* September 1940 p. 11; *Variety* June 1, 1938, p. 34, August 30, 1939, p. 28, January 14, 1942, p. 28, June 24, 1942, p. 36, July 8, 1942, p. 36, December 5, 1945, p. 27, November 5, 1947, p. 34; soapoperanetwork.com.

Futran, Herb

Herb Futran was a Chicago writer with a long but uncelebrated career in radio. He was writing

Then and Now with **Bess Flynn** and *Sunbrite Junior Nurse Corps.* by 1936 and in 1937 the transcribed *Boots and Saddles*, a horseracing-themed show created by George W. Davis. Futran was the author for *The Adventures of Omar* (1943–1944) and recognized in 1945 as the only Midwest scripter for two daily serials including **Irna Phillips**' *Woman in White* (1945–1947). In 1946 Futran joined an exodus of Chicago talent relocating to the West Coast as radio drama in the Windy City continued its gradual decline. Out West he continued to write for serials until at least 1950.

Other Radio: *Escape* (1949).

Sources: *Broadcasting* August 23, 1943, p. 20; *Radio Daily* March 29, 1937, p. 6, December 1, 1937, p. 4; *Variety* January 24, 1945, p. 28, April 4, 1945, p. 27; *Chicago Tribune* September 8, 1936, p. 20.

Gabrielson, Frank

Frank Gabrielson (March 13, 1910–January 24, 1980) wrote for all the major performing arts mediums from the 1930s to the 1950s. From stage productions such as *Fiddlesticks* (1936) and *The Wizard of Oz* (1942) to a handful of motion pictures in the 1940s including *Something for the Boys* (1944) and *It Shouldn't Happen to a Dog* (1946), Gabrielson worked in a variety of genres. His radio work, however, was confined to more serious fare on prestige programs like *Cavalcade of America* (1943–1951) and *The Theatre Guild on the Air* (1947–1948). Gabrielson's later television credits reflected his skill at authoring across categories; He provided teleplays for *Suspense* (1949), *The United States Steel Hour* (1955), and *Leave It to Beaver* (1960) among numerous series.

Other Radio: *I Remember Mama* (1948, audition).

Sources: *Variety* April 11, 1948, p. 31; July 14, 1948, p. 23.

Galen, Frank

Frank Galen broke into big-time radio scripting pieces for Eddie Garr on Rudy Vallee's *Fleischmann Yeast Show* around 1937 and continued to co-write Garr's radio material with **Abe Burrows** until 1939 when both joined **Fred Allen**'s *Texaco Star Theatre* (1939–1941). Galen next scripted gags for *The Burns & Allen Show* (1941–1943) before his military service during World War II.

After the war Galen was signed as head of the writing team in 1946 for *A Day in the Life of Dennis Day*, the tenor's solo program spun off from *The Jack Benny Show*. He wrote for Day until at least 1949 and between 1951 and 1954 Galen penned *Meet Millie*. By 1951 Galen was supplementing and even replacing some of his radio assignments with television work including CBS' *The Alan Young Show*. Some of Galen's other television projects included *My Friend Irma* (1952) and *Meet Millie* (1952–1957).

Other Radio: *Forecast* (1941); *Gulf Screen Guild Theatre* (1942).

Sources: *Broadcasting* October 1, 1939, p. 51, January 17, 1944, October 22, 1951, p. 57; *Radio Daily* December 23, 1937, p. 15; *Swing* October 1952 p. 450; *Variety* October 15, 1941, p. 26, August 14, 1946, p. 30.

Garson, Henry

Henry Garson (March 31, 1912–May 29, 2003) was signed to the writing team of Paul Whiteman's radio program sponsored by Chesterfield in 1937 but his career is not very well documented until the post–War era. From 1946 to 1947 Garson scripted *Kay Kyser's Kollege of Musical Knowledge* and then later in 1947 joined *The Bill Goodwin Show*. He briefly worked on *Meet Me in St. Louis* (1948) before beginning on his signature aural series, *Junior Miss* (1948–1954), which he also directed. One of Garson's final radio series before settling into television was *The Cobbs* (1954).

By 1955 Garson had found his first long-term writing assignment for the small screen, *Make Room for Daddy* (1955–1957), and then *The Danny Thomas Show* (1956–1957). Comedy remained Garson's specialty, highlighted by authoring teleplays through the 1960s for series such as *The Lucy Show* (1965–1966) and *Family Affair* (1966–1971).

Other Radio: *The Burns & Allen Show*.

Sources: Henry Garson Collection; *Radio Daily* December 22, 1937, p. 2.

Gebhart, Lee

Before joining WLW in the early 1930s Lee Gebhart was the South American correspondent for United Press. In 1935 he moved to Philadelphia's WCAU as a continuity writer where he wrote *Dramalogues* (1935) and *Trade Winds* (1936), but *Ma Perkins* (1936) was by far his most popular series. By 1939 he was scripting *Donna Curtis* for the CBS network.

Sources: *Motion Picture Daily* June 6, 1939, p. 8; *Variety* August 14, 1935, p. 31, August 28, 1935, p. 41.

Geiger, Milton E. M.

Milton Geiger (December 29, 1907–September 28, 1971) was a rare find for the radio networks; a skilled radio author with no prior writing training or experience. A 1929 graduate of Cleveland's Western Reserve University and practicing pharmacist in Cleveland, Ohio, when he sold his first radio script in 1935, "One Special for Doc," aired at least twice on the *Royal Desserts Hour* (1936) and the *Chase & Sanborn Hour* (1938). Geiger's raw talent was spotted by CBS' Writing Division almost immediately. After producing another of his early works on their prestigious *Columbia Workshop*, CBS discovered Geiger was a complete novice and encouraged him to write more. Max Wylie, head of CBS' Writing Division later said Geiger was the only "find" he'd encountered during all his years on radio, a writer with such innate talent for broadcasts.

When not working on prestigious works like *The Columbia Workshop* Geiger contributed to such programs as *County Seat*, a daily serial which ran from 1938 to 1939 and was directed by **Norman Corwin**, himself one of radio's most renowned writers, and the romance serial *Joan and Kermit* (1938). Geiger wrote a number of dramatic sketches for Rudy Vallee's program (1938–1940) and *The Texaco Star Theatre* (1938), and full scripts for *The Story of Terry Reagan, Attorney at Law* (1938).

Not all of Geiger's stories were hits, however. After penning *Who Knows* (1940–1941) he was assigned in 1941 to Vick Chemical's *What's in a Name*, a program promptly declared a dud by *Variety*. He was replaced by **Harry Bailey** after only two episodes, demonstrating that even the most skilled writers fell flat at times. During 1942 Geiger authored an early program promoting the War effort, *Keep 'Em Rolling*, and the next year regularly wrote for *Treasury Star Parade*. One of his first on-going dramatic series was the anthology *Philip Morris Playhouse* (1943), followed by *The Philco Radio Hall of Fame* (1944–1946), *The Doctor Fights* (1944, 1945), *We Who Dream* (summer 1944), *The Ginny Simms Show* (1944), and *Radio Proudly Presents* (1945).

Geiger's late-1940s works included both anthology and single-character programs such as *Hollywood Star Time* (1946), *The Adventures of Philip Marlowe* (1947), *The Hallmark Playhouse* (ca. 1948, later *The Hallmark Hall of Fame*), *Four Star Playhouse* (1949), *Screen Director's Playhouse* (1949–1951), and *Hollywood Star Playhouse* (1949–1952) where he adapted stories from *Cosmopolitan*. Among his short-term projects during this time were *Shorty Bell* (1948), based on the novels by Frederick Hazlitt Brennan, and *The Croupier* (1949). Interestingly, even at the height of his writing during these years he claimed to still practice pharmacy part-time at his brother's drug store.

Geiger contributed more scripts to *Hallmark Hall of Fame* around 1953 and continued to write for radio via the Armed Forces Radio and Television Service well into the 1960s and for the Salvation Army's post–Golden Age series *Heartbeat Theatre* (1966). He wrote a number of scripts for television during the 1950s for series including *Lassie* (1955), *Perry Mason* (1957), and *Laramie* (1960–1961) but he never wrote extensively for any single program.

Other Radio: *The Circle* (1939); *Inner Sanctum* (1941); *Knickerbocker Playhouse* (1941); *Broadway Matinee* (1943); *Men at Sea* (1944); *The Doctor Fights* (1945); *Molle Mystery Theatre* (1945); *Her Honor, The Judge* (1948, audition); *NBC Theatre* (1949); *Lux Radio Theatre* (1954).

Sources: Milton Geiger Papers; Wylie p. 90–91; *Broadcasting* November 1, 1943, p. 28, April 2, 1945, p. 64, March 14, 1949, p. 14, 63; *Radio Mirror* September 1938 p. 46, February 1939 p. 43; *Variety* September 13, 1939, p. 22, October 8, 1941, p. 28, October 22, 1941, January 19, 1944, p. 45 June 14, 1944, p. 26, September 13, 1944, p. 22, October 18, 1944, p. 30, June 25, 1947, p. 27, May 12, 1948, p. 29.

Gelbart, Larry

Larry Gelbart (February 25, 1928–September 11, 2009) mastered every writing form he attempted, from radio to television and from Broadway to Hollywood. He began by honing his comedy craft as a teenager, his first sketch for Danny Thomas appearing on the air in 1944 when he was sixteen. Soon after, Gelbart was writing for *Duffy's Tavern* in 1946 before providing scripts to *The Joan Davis Show* in the spring of 1947 and then to *The Jack Paar Show* during the summer of that year. The Paar job lasted just a few weeks as the entire writing team was dismissed in July after ongoing creative differences with Paar. Gelbart next scripted for Jack Carson's *Sealtest Village Store* (1948) but found his niche when he was hired on to Bob Hope's writing staff for the 1948–1949 season. He stayed with Hope until at least 1952 and then began taking advantage of television opportunities.

Gelbart's greatest television achievement was his role in the creation and development of the hit series *M*A*S*H* with which he was involved from 1972 until 1976. He earned both an Emmy and a Peabody Award for his work with the show. He was no less successful in the motion picture industry, earning Oscar nominations for his screenplays for *Oh, God!* (1977) and *Tootsie* (1982). Gelbart even conquered the challenge of live theater, winning two Tony Awards for his musical books *A Funny Thing Happened on the Way to the Forum* (1962, with Burt Shevelove and Stephen Sondheim) and *City of Angels* (1990).

Other Radio: *Command Performance*; *The Eddie Cantor Show*.

Sources: Young; *Variety* October 9, 1946, p. 52, April 2, 1947, p. 35, June 4, 1947, p. 29, July 30, 1947, p. 31, September 1, 1948, p. 36.

Gendot, Adrian

Adrian Gendot (January 21, 1914–March 17, 1981) joined San Francisco's KYA in 1936 where he had both continuity and production responsibilities. Some of his earliest jobs were hosting an amateur playwright program (1936) and producing *Frivolities* (1937). In 1940 he wrote and produced *Swap Shop* where callers offered unwanted items for trade and also *Honeymoon Cottage* after he moved to KFRC. Later in 1940 Gendot joined the writing team for Jack Kirkwood's *KFRC Breakfast Club*. His radio work was put on hold in 1942 when he enlisted in the service.

By the post–War period Gendot had worked himself into a position with CBS' West Coast chain writing for a number of its second-tier adventure programs such as *The Private Practice of Dr. Dana* (1947–1948), *Rocky Jordan* (1949–1951), *Jeff Regan, Investigator* (1949), and *Crime Correspondent* (1949). Gendot stayed busy scripting for such programs into the 1950s, adding *Dangerous Assignment* (1950–1953), *Adventures of Philip Marlow* (1951), and *Tales of the Texas Rangers* (1951) to his resume early in the decade. Over a ten-year span Gendot provided many scripts to *The Whistler* (1946–1955), a show that relied primarily on freelance talent. One source claims that Gendot wrote several additional episodes of *The Whistler* under the pseudonym "Steve Hampton." Rounding out his radio career was a short stint on *Yours Truly, Johnny Dollar* (1956), one of the last prime-time radio dramas.

Gendot had a moderately successful television career during the 1950s, scripting dozens of episodes of *Dangerous Assignment* (1952) while he was writing the radio version at the same time, and over a dozen teleplays for *The Whistler* (1954–1955), which he was also still occasionally writing for on radio. His career seems to have fizzled out by the 1960s after he wrote three programs for the 1961–1962 season of *Perry Mason*.

Film: *Pathways to Yesterday* (1957, for Illinois Bell); *White Magic* (1957, for Morton Salt).

Sources: Berard & Englund; Froug p. 43; *Broadcasting* February 15, 1936, p. 29, May 15, 1940, p. 68, December 15, 1940, p. 58; *The Radio Annual* 1940 p. 856; *Radio Daily* October 25, 1949, p. 3; *Variety* November 18, 1936, p. 49, February 10, 1937, p. 38.

Gershman, Ben

Ben Gershman (February 5, 1907–February 1, 1995) was born in England but had a very successful career writing for American radio and television. He spent almost a decade working on *The Adventures of Ozzie and Harriet* both on radio and television in the late 1940s to mid–1950s. Gershman contributed scripts to many of the era's most beloved TV shows including

Leave It to Beaver (1957–1958), *The Andy Griffith Show* (1961–1962), and *The Brady Bunch* (1970–1974).

Sources: Cox *Sitcoms*; *Variety* January 5, 1949, p. 98.

Gerson, Sidney

Sidney Gerson was a freelance writer whose worked appeared on *Americans at the Ramparts* (1942), *Meet Your Navy* (1944), *Treasury Salute* (1945–1946), and *NBC's Short Story* (1951).

Sources: *Variety* April 19, 1944, p. 23; *Chicago Tribune* April 6, 1942, p. 16.

Gibson, Pauline

Pauline Gibson, a CBS writer beginning in the late 1930s, is first known to have scripted *The Ghost of Benjamin Sweet* (1938), a spin-off of a *Columbia Workshop* episode. Co-written with Frederick Gilsdorf, *Sweet* starred Carl Swenson in the title role. The original *Workshop* broadcast proved so popular it was re-aired in 1939. She was also responsible that year for a 26-episode run of *Wings for the Martins*, written in conjunction with the U.S. Office of Education and the National Congress of Parents and Teachers. Gibson created a new children's serial, *Chimney House*, in 1939 that set popular children's literary characters in new adventures. Gibson is also documented as writing quarter-hour shows *Trial of Harry Morley* and *Tom Dixon Meets the Enemy* in 1942 under the auspices of the Office of Civilian Defense.

Sources: *Broadcasting* January 15, 1939, p. 66; *Radio and Television Mirror* September 1939 p. 50; *Variety* June 22, 1938, p. 29, November 2, 1933, p. 29, September 23, 1942, p. 24.

Gibson, Walter B.

Starting as an insurance agent in the 1920s, Walter Gibson (September 12, 1897–December 6, 1985) decided a career as a professional magician had more to offer him and Gibson left behind a staid life in insurance and attempted to make a name in show business. This too was short-lived and he next turned to reporting which led to his ghost writing magic-themed articles for numerous publications in the mid–1920s.

In the early 1930s Gibson was hired by Street & Smith to write pulp stories for their Shadow character under the pseudonym Maxwell Grant. Its success was nearly instantaneous and beyond the expectations of all involved, including Gibson. He proved too busy, however, to script the radio series, so the task was left to others with some input by Gibson.

It wasn't until the 1940s that Gibson made time to write some radio scripts, first for *Nick Carter, Master Detective* (1943), a pulp hero like the Shadow, and then *Chick Carter, Boy Detective* (1943–1945), the adopted son of master detective Nick. During the mid–1940s Gibson was involved with *The Avenger* (1945–1946), a blatant copycat of the Shadow who didn't last beyond a 26-episode transcribed series. Though credited with writing the program, **Gilbert and Ruth Braun** were the true authors with Gibson perhaps providing suggestions and guidance.

Gibson returned to his love of magic in the late 1940s when he wrote *Blackstone, the Magic Detective* (1948–1950), inspired by real-life magician Harry Blackstone, Sr. His last work with radio was *Strange* (1955), a series of broadcasts he narrated but didn't author that featured tales of the supernatural. Gibson continued to write works of both fiction and non-fiction well into the 1960s and even 1970s.

Sources: Grams *The Shadow*; *Broadcasting* April 12, 1943, p. 14.

Gilbert, Doris

Doris Gilbert, niece of producer Ed Wolf, was the head of the continuity department for World Broadcasting in the mid–1930s before resigning in 1937 to work in motion pictures. A film career didn't take off right away so she continued writing for radio on *Omar the Swingmaker* (1937–1939) and in 1938 her sketches appeared on both *The Rudy Vallee Hour* and a drama show hosted by theater producer William A. Brady. She returned full time to radio by 1939 when she was signed to co-script *True Story Time*, a replacement for *Mary and Bob*, with Laurence Hammand and Ruth Lovaire. By 1941 she was a regular scripter for *Gene Autry Melody Ranch* and she also worked on a radio version of *Gone* with the Wind, a project that is not known to have come to fruition.

Gilbert rejoined the J. Walter Thompson agency in 1942 and was subsequently charged with adapting a series of *New Yorker* stories by Sally Benson into the series *Junior Miss* featuring Shirley Temple and produced by Ed Wolf Associates. Unfortunately, creative differences led to both Benson and Gilbert withdrawing from the project but Gilbert went on to pursue opportunities in Hollywood.

Her screenplays started appearing on the big screen in 1944; *Ladies Courageous* and *Storm Over Lisbon* were among her first but she had at least one more job in radio writing *The Penny Singleton Show* in 1950. By the 1950s Gilbert began writing for television. She was a versatile writer, providing teleplays for programs such as *The Adventures of Superman* (1952), *Science Fiction Theatre* (1955–1956), and *Bourbon Street Beat* (1960).

Sources: Ansboro p. 182; *Broadcasting* July 28, 1941, p. 37, February 16, 1942, p. 10; *The Film Daily* October 3, 1944, p. 10 p. 12; *Radio Daily* December 16, 1937, p. 4; *Variety* October 12, 1938, p. 31, May 24, 1939, p. 21, March 26, 1941, p. 37, January 14, 1942, p. 3.

Gillis, Jackson

A native of Washington, Jackson Gillis (August 21, 1916–August 19, 2010) started writing for radio after completing his military service during World War II. For about five years Jackson wrote for West Coast dramatic series like *The Whistler* (1947–1948), *Jeff Regan, Investigator* (1948), *Rocky Jordan* (1949), and *Let George Do It* (1949–1954).

Beginning in 1952 Gillis focused more on television and wrote well over one hundred teleplays through the 1980s. He contributed to numerous instantly recognizable series including *The Adventures of Superman* (1953–1956), *Lost in Space* (1965–1968), *Wonder Woman* (1978–1979), and *Murder, She Wrote* (1985–1986).

Books: *The Killers of Starfish* (1977); *Chainsaw* (1988).

Sources: Jackson Gillis Collection; Cox *Radio Crime Fighters* p. 145; *New York Times* obituary, August 28, 2010.

Glickman, Will

Will Glickman (March 7, 1910–March 11, 1983) was one of Eddie Cantor's primary writers on his early 1940s show and Glickman sometimes contributed to Cantor's summer replacement series like *The Alan Young Show* (1944). For a short time in late 1944 and early 1945 he served as head writer for Ed Wynn before taking over *Gaslight Gaieties*. Glickman scripted Jackie Kelk's *Continental Celebrity Club* in 1946 and Hildegarde's *The Campbell Room* for the 1946–1947 season.

Some of his final radio assignments were *The Big Talent Hunt* (1948) emceed by Jim Backus and *The Ethel Merman Show* (1949). Glickman also began testing the television waters in 1949, scripting *School House* and *The Henry Morgan Show* that year. He found work in television until the 1960s with credits on *Car 54, Where Are You?* (1961–1962) and *The Jimmy Dean Show* (1963–1964).

Theater: *Mrs. Gibbons' Boys* (1949, with **Joe Stein**).

Sources: Will Glickman Papers; *Broadcasting* September 25, 1944, p. 30; *Variety* January 10, 1945, p. 30, February 28, 1945, p. 24, April 17, 1946, p. 34, October 9, 1946, p. 53, March 24, 1948, p. 34, January 26, 1949, p. 36, February 16, 1949, p. 28.

Goff, Norris

Norris Goff (May 30, 1906–June 7, 1978) teamed with partner **Chester Lauck** to create one of radio's most enduring and beloved programs, *Lum 'n' Abner*. Originally from Cover, AR, Goff worked in the family's grocery store then attended The University of Arkansas before transferring to the University of Oklahoma. A college education was in stark contrast to the country simpleton he portrayed, Abner Peabody.

Like Lauck, Goff returned to and settled down in Arkansas after college and developed a reputation in the area for his blackface work with Lauck, a type of act that was still acceptable at the time, following the popularity of radio's *Amos 'n' Andy*. When Hot Springs, AR, station KTHS held a flood relief benefit broadcast the station invited the duo to perform. Goff and Lauck switched their routine after arriving at the station because of the numerous other blackface Amos and Andy imitators on the bill. They quickly renamed their skit *Lum 'n' Abner* and radio history was made.

Lum 'n' Abner was a hit with listeners and KTHS asked them to come back a number of times as listener interest grew. Thinking this might be their chance to make it in radio, in July 1931 the pair relocated to Chicago, a radio mecca second only to New York at the time. They auditioned for NBC, were offered $150 but negotiated for $350, and interested a sponsor, Quaker Oats, in their program. With the stars aligning, *Lum 'n' Abner* started a run of more than two decades on the air. The show aired five to six days per week for a quarter hour until 1941. Goff co-wrote each script with Lauck. Additional writers were gradually brought in and the format changed from intimate character and story development to a more traditional sitcom format with an orchestra and live studio audience.

Source: Hall.

Goldsmith, Clifford

Clifford Goldsmith's (March 29, 1899–July 11, 1971) professional writing career started inauspiciously enough with a play entitled *What a Life* that took place in a high school office and included a relatively minor character named Henry. It was a more serious piece and a producer named George Abbott suggested Goldsmith lighten it up. Nevertheless, Goldsmith had little faith in the play and considered a half interest in it for a winter coat. Encouraged by Rudy Vallee who saw the play and asked him to work the material into some short radio sketches during 1938, Goldsmith hit on a winning idea.

Henry was turned into the lead character (voiced by Ezra Stone who also had the part on stage) and the concept was tested in a few standalone broadcasts. The popularity of these shorts led to Goldsmith's being contracted to write fresh Aldrich sketches for *The Kate Smith Hour* during the 1938–1939 season. Riding its popularity from Smith's program, Goldsmith hooked NBC on giving his characters their own series as a summer replacement for comedy king Jack Benny. *The Aldrich Family*, that followed the exploits of bumbling but well-meaning teen Henry Aldrich and his long-suffering family, quickly rose to the top ten in ratings whereupon Goldsmith soon found himself one of the highest paid writers in radio, pulling down a reported $3,000 per week.

Goldsmith penned a set of *Aldrich Family* television scripts in 1949 but handed over regular writing duties to others during the show's run (1949–1953). After the radio version left the air for good in 1953, Goldsmith made a foray into television where he wrote a number of episodes for a variety of comedy programs, primarily in the 1960s. Among them were *Leave It to Beaver* (1957), *The Donna Reed Show* (1960–1966), *Petticoat Junction* (1966), and *The Flying Nun* (1969).

Film: *Life With Henry* (1940).

Sources: *Radio & Television Mirror* April 1941 p. 4; *Radio Daily* December 14, 1949, p. 2; *Variety* August 3, 1938, p. 25, September 21, 1938, p. 27.

Goldstein, Jess

Jesse Goldstein (October 31, 1915–May 14, 1959) was a premier writer of comedy material both on radio and television and worked with many of the industry's biggest names during a career that was cut short at the age of 44. Some of his earliest radio scripting was for *The Victor Borge Show* with Benny Goodman (1946–1947), *The Danny Kaye Show* (1946) and *The Eddie Albert Show* (1947). Goldstein was added to *The Eddie Cantor Pabst Blue Ribbon Show* with partner **Jay Sommers** for the 1947–1948 and 1948–1949 seasons.

Goldstein's television work was just as impressive, writing for *The Ed Wynn Show* (1950), *The George Burns & Gracie Allen Show* (1951–1953), *I Married Joan* (1953–1955), and *The Red Skelton Show* from 1955 until Goldstein's death in 1959.

Other Radio: *It's Always Sunday* (1951, audition with **Frank Fox**).

Sources: *Broadcasting* May 8, 1950, p. 62; *Variety* August 7, 1946, p. 42, May 28, 1947, p. 28, June 18, 1947, p. 28.

Goll, Ralph

Ralph Goll authored adventures stories for WXYZ's *The Green Hornet* (1943) and *The Lone Ranger* (1947–1956) for many years. Several of his radio scripts were adapted into television episodes of *The Lone Ranger* between 1950 and 1955.

Source: strykerahc.org.

Goodman, Hal (Harold)

Hal Goodman (May 9, 1915–September 3, 1997) is remembered for his contributions to at least three radio series, *The Bob Hope Show* (1947), *The Sweeney and March Show* (1948) and *The Martin and Lewis Show* (1949–1950). Goodman's biggest success came on the small screen where he earned eight Emmy Award nominations and one win in 1971 on *The Flip Wilson Show*.

Other Radio: *Rochester* (1950, audition).
Source: Hal Goodman Papers; *Variety* April 2, 1947, p. 35; *Los Angeles Times* obituary September 5, 1997.

Gordon, Jack

A scriptwriter for *CBS Workshop* before his service in World War II, Jack Gordon turned to the theater in 1945 right after his time in the military came to an end. He did have at least one more radio credit with *Cloak and Dagger* (1950), one of several secret service shows that were popular during the post-war years. This series focused on the covert activities of the Office of Strategic Services during World War II.

Theater: *Sweet City* (1945).
Source: *Variety* June 20, 1945, p. 24.

Gordon, Shirley

Shirley Gordon's first significant broadcast credits writing for dramatic programs were earned on *Suspense* (1950–1951), *The Whistler* (1952), and *On Stage* (1953–1954). With television on the rise, Gordon contributed to series such as *The Bob Cummings Show* (1955–1958) and *My Three Sons* (1961–1962). Gordon returned to dramatic radio in the 1970s when the art form experienced a brief period of revival. *Hollywood Radio Theatre* (1973) and *Sears Radio Theatre* (1979) produced some of Gordon's scripts. In addition to radio and television Gordon spent much of her freelancing writing for magazines, political campaigns, and children's books.

Source: oakpark.com.

Gosch, Martin

Primarily a director and producer, Martin Gosch (June 25, 1911–October 20, 1973) did handle some writing chores, often uncredited. In 1941 Gosch and Howard Harris created an audition adaptation of *Mr. and Mrs. North*, a project they first tried to sell under a different title, *The Amazing Mr. Smith*. The duo switched gears in 1942, signing on to write a summer-replacement show starring Edna Mae Oliver, *The Remarkable Miss Tuttle* (later *The Remarkable Miss Crandall*). Gosch was hired as the producer for *The Abbott & Costello Show* in 1942 and he stayed with the comedy series until approximately 1945, also working on the show's writing team.

After 1945 Gosch focused his energies on other areas, creating a film production firm with Melvyn Douglas in 1946, a Broadway play, *Gentleman from Athens*, in 1947 and producing television's *Tonight on Broadway* in 1948. He wasn't entirely done with radio, however, penning *Electric Hour* in 1947.

Other Radio: *Keep 'em Rolling* (1942); *Mayor of the Town* (1942).
Film: *Hula Honeymoon* (1941, with Howard Harris).
Books: *The Last Testament of Lucky Luciano* (1975, with Richard Hammer).
Sources: Martin A. Gosch Papers; *Broadcasting* August 15, 1939, p. 42, March 17, 1941, p. 36, June 22, 1942, p. 58, September 7, 1942, p. 9, 48; *Variety* October 8, 1941, p. 25, April 29, 1942, p. 36, July 16, 1947.

Gosden, Freeman

Freeman Gosden (May 5, 1899–December 10, 1982), with **Charles Correll**, was one half of the legendary radio duo *Amos 'n' Andy*. As a young man Gosden sold automobiles and tobacco, then learned radio operation in the Navy during the first World War. Gosden got into show business and soon met Correll who would become his career-long partner while working with the Joe Bren Producing Company. The pair happened into radio, performing on small Chicago stations for sometimes nothing more than their next meal.

The beginning of their success was 1926 when they went on the air with *Sam 'n' Henry*, a six-times-per week serial centered on two black men who move from the rural South to the urban North in search of new opportunities. During two years on WGN Gosden and Correll's series grew in popularity and they eventually realized that their contract–$300 per week—was inadequate compared to the revenue they were generating for the station. When the station refused to let them record their shows and sell them to other stations, a pioneering syndication effort, the duo finished their contract and angrily moved to another Chicago powerhouse station, WMAQ. There, the names were changed to Amos Jones and Andrew H. Brown but the rest of the show—renamed *Amos 'n' Andy*—pretty much went on as before and became a national smash by 1931 when it pulled in over half of all radio listeners during its broadcast.

During *Amos 'n' Andy*'s early years Gosden and Correll continued to write each daily script. Reportedly Gosden would pace around the room absentmindedly playing with a coin and dictating stories while Correll used his stenographer's training to jot down the script that he would then pound out on a typewriter. Eventually they gave up writing chores and fully engrossed themselves in their acting responsibilities; after the show's 1943 revamp a full team of writers was brought in to produce a weekly thirty-minute sitcom-style script.

While Gosden is widely remembered because of his work portraying Amos Jones and later Kingfish Stevens who essentially supplanted Amos on the show, his writing talent is generally overlooked. This is a curious development considering the tremendous popularity of *Amos 'n' Andy* in its heyday and its continued appreciation in old-time radio circles today. One explanation for this oversight is the relative rarity of extant recordings of the program's early years when Gosden was in charge of the daily scripts. His ongoing reputation is based far more on his recorded acting performances than on the lost broadcasts that more prominently featured his writing. Even though *Amos 'n' Andy* was on radio until 1960 and then on television as a short-lived series, Gosden was never again responsible for writing duties after the series' initial run.

Source: McLeod.

Gould, Frank

Frank Gould was a Brooklyn native and graduate of Columbia University's School of Journalism. He worked as a newspaper reporter for many years before writing his first radio scripts in the late 1930s. Gould's first network broadcasts were for *The Columbia Workshop* (1939, 1942). In 1941 he drew on his life experiences to script *City Desk*, about the adventures of newspaper reporters Jack Matthews and Linda Collins. Gould is credited with writing for *The Phil Harris–Alice Faye Show* more than a decade later in 1953.

Theater: *The Scene of the Crime* (1940); *Tenting Tonight* (1947).

Sources: *The Christian Science Monitor* November 28, 1939, p. 13; *Boston Daily Globe* January 2, 1941, p. 4; *The Washington Post* January 5, 1941, p. 11.

Green, Bob

Little is known about Bob Green other than he scripted some episodes of *Challenge of the Yukon* in 1945 and many episodes of *The Lone Ranger* between 1944 and 1947.

Source: radiogoldindex.com

Green, Denis

Originally an actor, Denis Green (April 11, 1905–November 6, 1954) gravitated toward scriptwriting by the early 1940s. He is most well-known for his run on *The New Adventures of Sherlock Holmes* (1944–1949), co-written briefly with Bruce Taylor and **Leslie Charteris**, but **Anthony Boucher** soon settled in as his long-time partner. Green's responsibility was to flesh out Boucher's plot outlines and complete the dialog. Since Green was not a big fan of Holmes, some historians feel he was able to give the iconic detective a fresh and distinctive voice.

In the midst of their *Holmes* run Green and Boucher created *The Casebook of Gregory Hood* as a summer replacement series for Holmes though it continued past its original summer season. A number of prominent actors appeared as Hood during the series' intermittent run including Gale Gordon, Elliott Lewis, and Jackson Beck. Writing duties for *Hood* were assumed by **Ray Buffum** in 1947.

Other Radio: *The Adventures of the Thin Man*.

Sources: *Broadcasting* September 11, 1944, p. 44; *Variety* July 26, 1944, p. 24, May 15, 1946, p. 46.

Green, Paul

Paul Eliot Green (March 17, 1894–May 4, 1981) was a playwright during the first decades of the 20th century who won the Pulitzer Prize for Drama for his 1926 work *In Abraham's Bosom*. During the 1930s Green strayed into more experimental theater and by 1940 made a tentative foray into radio with a script for American history anthology series *Cavalcade of America*, a show for which he would write once more in 1948. He contributed one story, "A Start in Life," to *The Free Company* (1941), a collaborative effort by a group of writers to counter foreign propaganda. That same year Green also scripted one episode for CBS' *The Columbia Workshop* (1941).

Sources: Paul Green Papers; *Variety* January 29, 1941, p. 40.

Greene, John L.

John Greene (November 10, 1912–October 4, 1995) got his start in radio scripting children's shows in New York before relocating to Hollywood in the late 1930s where he scripted such shows as *Attorney at Law*, *Dick Tracy*, and *Texaco Star Theatre*. With **Albert G. Miller** and Leonard Holton Greene authored *Meet Mr. Meek* ca. 1941 and by 1942 had taken over writing duties for *Blondie*, based on Chic Young's newspaper strip, a program for which he wrote until at least 1947. Greene spent the final years of the decade on the writing team for *The Adventures of Ozzie and Harriet*.

After radio Greene became a prolific television writer. His early work was for series adapted from radio including *My Friend Irma* (1952–1953), *Our Miss Brooks* (1955), and *Blondie* (1957). The pinnacle of Greene's scripting career came in the 1960s during which he wrote dozens of teleplays for *The Real McCoys* (1958–1963), *The Andy Griffith Show* (1962–1966), and *Bewitched* (1964–1971). Greene was central to the creation of the mid–60s sitcom *My Favorite Martian* and is credited with writing or advising on all the stories.

Sources: *Billboard* September 13, 1947, p. 19; *Broadcasting* May 1, 1939, p. 52; *Variety* March 12, 1941, p. 24, March 25, 1942, p. 37, obituary October 9, 1995.

Gregory, David

Little is known of the writer David Gregory other than his credits on three radio programs, *The Doris Day Show* (1952), *The Bill Goodwin Show* (1957), and *Club Fifteen* (1947–1953), a musical program.

Sources: Dunning; radiogoldindex.com.

Griffin, Frank

Frank Griffin's (d. 1945) documented radio writing career is short but highly noteworthy, nonetheless. After writing for *Native Sons* and *Freiheit* in the early 1940s, he was hired to script *Labor for Victory* over NBC in 1943. At the time the trade magazine *Variety* claimed it was the first time an African-American was known to have written a network series. Griffin died just two years later at the age of 37.

Sources: Ellett *Black Radio*; *Variety* September 22, 1943, p. 30.

Gross, Milt

Milt Gross (March 4, 1895–November 29, 1953) was a professional cartoonist who wrote and illustrated a number of strips during the first half of the 20th century. When he went to work for the Hearst chain in 1931 Gross had his first opportunity in radio, writing sketches for *Club Car Special* (1934), sponsored by Hearst. None of his strips have much name recognition now, decades after his death, but at the time one was popular enough to be adapted to a radio series overseen by Gross, *That's My Pop* (1945).

Sources: Milt Gross Papers; toonopedia.com.

Gruskin, Edward

Edward Gruskin's (June 16, 1914–November 15, 2005) first known writing assignments were adapting Street & Smith characters for the airwaves on *Doc Savage* (1943), *Nick Carter, Master Detective* (1943, with **Walter Gibson**), and *Chick Carter, Boy Detective* (1943–45). He was involved with at least one post–War series, *Rendezvous in Paris* (1948). Years later Gruskin is credited with some television work, including *Flash Gordon* (1954–1955) and *Lassie* (1961).

Sources: Grams *Shadow* p. 226; *Variety* March 10, 1943, p. 30, October 15, 1947, p. 35.

Guedel, John

John Guedel (October 9, 1913–December 15, 2001) earned paychecks a number of ways early in life, working as a ditch digger and traveling salesman before moving into the entertainment industry. He really wanted to be a writer but the closest he got initially was writing for Hal Roach on film shorts, some featuring comedian team Stan Laurel and Oliver Hardy and the Little Rascals.

By 1936 Guedel found himself working in radio as a continuity writer for the Dan B. Miner Co. in Los Angeles and in 1938 he took over the agency's entire radio department. That same year he produced an audition record in 1938 for a modest $30. Originally called *Pull Over, Neighbor* and starring Art Baker, the show ran for more than three years. In 1941 Southern Pacific replaced Wilshire Oil as the sponsor and the series was renamed *All Aboard*, still starring Baker with Guedel writing and producing.

Guedel once again revamped his show in 1942, reportedly after watching an audience listening to a boring dinner speaker. He had the idea to create a platform for individuals to be put up to stunts that would reveal the humorous side of human nature. Reading one day of a program cancellation, Guedel called on the ad agency and pitched them this latest idea, *People Are Funny*. The agency was intrigued and got it placed on NBC under the sponsorship of Brown & Williamson Tobacco Co. Art Baker, soon joined by Art Linkletter as co–M.C., continued as the host and the program was a hit.

Art Linkletter took over after eighteen months and became a legend, much to the chagrin of Baker. Early in the run Guedel served as primary writer, though his father **Walter Guedel** helped. He later ceded writing chores to others to focus on directing and producing. Formal scripts waned, however, as Linkletter preferred to ad-lib his work. Guedel didn't completely give up writing, penning a 1943 novel, *Tornado*, that was adapted into a motion picture.

In 1945 Guedel and Linkletter put their brains together and created *House Party*, another Linkletter-hosted feature that took more of a human interest angle. Guedel did not write for *House Party*, by this time choosing to focus on producing various projects. Guedel's creations were wildly successful; *People Are Funny* ran from 1942 to 1960 and *House Party* aired from 1945 to 1967.

Film: *General Spanky* (1936).
Sources: *Broadcasting* August 1, 1938, p. 46, December 1, 1940, p. 20, March 31, 1941, p. 21, April 27, 1942, p. 46; *The Radio Annual* 1938 p. 715; *Variety* August 19, 1936, p. 7.

Guedel, Walter

Walter Guedel worked as a manufacturing executive before turning later in life to writing detective fiction. By 1940 the senior Guedel was writing continuity for the Dan B. Miner Co. on shows such as *Radio Charades* (1940–1941) and *They Say Today* (1941). In 1943 he was hired by his son **John Guedel** to write jokes for the younger's radio shows *People Are Funny* and *House Party*. Both *People Are Funny* and *House Party* were eventually entirely hosted by Art Linkletter who preferred not to work from scripts so writing chores for the programs became minor jobs, though Walter Guedel continued to be credited with writing *House Party* into the 1950s.

Sources: *Broadcasting* January 1, 1941, p. 46, May 26, 1941, p. 30, April 5, 1943, p. 40; *The Radio Annual* 1940 p. 224, 1950 p. 765.

Gussman, Charles

Charles Gussman (June 29, 1913–October 18, 2000) began writing for radio on Cincinnati's WLW before moving to Detroit's WWJ in 1937. Upon relocating to Chicago Gussman penned the new air adaptation of *Li'l Abner* from the comic strips beginning in 1939 as well as adaptations for *Author's Playhouse* (1941). In 1942 he returned to Detroit and assumed some announcing duties in addition to scripting programs including *Major V* (1942). Within a year he advanced to network writing and penned for such series as *Second Husband* and *Battle Stations* (both ca. 1943).

In 1945 Gussman wrote a script for Roi Ottley's African-American program *New World A'Coming* and at the end of the year took over writing *Sparrow and the Hawk*. During the latter years of the 1940s Gussman wrote for a variety of series including *Out of This World*, *Romance*, *Silver Theatre* (all 1947), and *Doctor Standish, Medical Examiner* (1948). Evidence suggests that Gussman found a niche in the serials around 1950 and wrote for *The Right to Happiness*, *The Road of Life*, and *Young Dr. Malone*. Gussman found steady work in television with soap operas and penned stories for *Search for Tomorrow*, *The Road of Life*, and *Days of Our Lives*.

Sources: *Broadcasting* December 1, 1939, February 16, 1942, p. 37; *Radio-TV Mirror* August 1952 p. 78; *Variety* August 25, 1937, p. 38, December 16, 1942, p. 30, July 14, 1943, p. 82, August 11, 1943, p. 32; December 5, 1945, p. 36, July 7, 1948, p. 23; *New York Times* obituary October 28, 2000.

Hagen, Harry

Harry Strand-Hagen wrote and hosted a radio spelling bee for one year before revamping his show as an audience participation program, *True or False*, in 1938. Hagen served as creator, writer, and host for the series' first five years, after which he auditioned other ideas while maintaining ownership of the quiz show. One of Hagen's follow-up shows was *Cover Girl* (1944), co-created with Harry Conover.

Sources: *Variety* December 29, 1937, p. 28; November 15, 1944, p. 23.

Haggart, John

During the 1930s and 1940s John Haggart wrote a number of plays before he eventually drifted into radio. His broadcasting niche was writing soap operas, notably *The Brighter Day*, before being lured to television serials in the early 1950s.

Theater: *Mackeral Skies* (1934); *Reno* (1937); *Salt of the Earth* (1944).
Television: *A Woman to Remember* (1949); *The Family Doctor* (ca. 1950).
Sources: Cox *Soap Operas*; *Billboard* December 16, 1950, p. 6; *New York Herald Tribune* November 17, 1944, p. 14.

Hall, Wilbur

Wilbur Hall was a specialist in the Western format, penning at least two series in the genre in the mid–1930s. According to Max Wylie, Hall was an expert in the world of cowboys and cattle and was working as a rancher when he wrote his first radio play. That script became the premier episode of his first series, *Six-Gun Justice* (1935). The original 26-week run was so popular that the network was forced to add thirteen more episodes to their schedule. This program was followed in 1937 with the Western serial *Gun Smoke Law* (1937). The next year Hall veered from his proven writing formula to write and emcee a *Wedding Ring Party*, a give-away show featuring engaged couples.

Sources: Cox *Crime Fighters*; Wylie p. 105–106; *Motion Picture Daily* April 20, 1938, p. 8; *Radio Daily* August 3, 1937, p. 4; *Variety* April 13, 1938, p. 28.

Halman, Doris

Doris Halman (October 28, 1895–May 1984) was a scenarist for the American Play Company and Fox in the early 1930s and later moved into radio. She is credited with scripting for *Alias Jimmy Valentine* (1938), *Mr. Keen, Tracer of Lost Persons* (ca. 1942), *The Old and the New* (1943), and *Song of the Stranger* (1947–1948). Halman later authored a number of teleplays in the 1950s.

Sources: Cox *A to Z*, *Mr. Keen*; *Motion Picture Herald* April 23, 1932, p. 12; *Variety* January 25, 1939, p. 26, March 18, 1942, p. 34, August 18, 1943, p. 30.

Hammond, Lawrence

Lawrence (Larry) Hammond worked as a director and writer for Blackett-Sample-Hummert in the late 1930s. Among the various serials for which he wrote were *Mary Noble, Backstage Wife*, *John's Other Wife*, *Our Gal Sunday*, and *Young Widder Jones*. Hammond later moved on to freelance work in the 1940s.

Sources: *Variety* May 4, 1938, p. 29, January 25, 1939, p. 26.

Hampton, Bill

Bill Hampton made his debut in radio writing lyrics and patter for the Kings Jesters circa 1937, and the work soon led to a new job with Kay Kyser. Hampton stayed with *Kay Kyser's Kollege of Musical Knowledge* until 1941 when he discovered a talent for more dramatic writing. His first scripts were for *The Gulf Screen Guild Theater* (1941–1943, later *The Lady Esther Screen Guild Theatre*) and *Silver Theatre* (1941).

With the armed services requiring many radio writers to put their professional work on hold, Hampton left the *Screen Guild Theatre* to pick up some plum assignments as a freelance author. In 1944 he took charge of writing *The Cass Daily–Frank Morgan Show* for a few months then in 1946 was hired for a dramatic program sponsored by Camay as well as *This Is Hollywood*. Other later 1940s series for which Hampton provided scripts were *Proudly We Hail* (1947), *The Anacin Hollywood Star Theatre* (1948), and *Family Theatre* (1949).

Sources: *Broadcasting* July 28, 1941, p. 37, June 7, 1943, p. 34; *Radio Daily* February 16, 1937, p. 6, March 15, 1937, p. 6; *Variety* January 28, 1942, p. 30, July 26, 1944, p. 39, July 31, 1946, p. 34.

Hanna, David

A long-time assistant editor for the *Hollywood Reporter* and drama critic for *The Los Angeles Daily News*, David Hanna penned the series *Tapestries of Life* during the mid–1940s. It was a biographical broadcast, revamped by its sponsor Forest Lawn Memorial Park from a program originally aired in the early 1930s. Hanna was a prolific author throughout his career, writing many articles and books.

Books: *Come Up and See Me Sometime: An Uncensored Biography of Mae West* (1976); *James Dean: His Tragedy, His Life, His Films* (1989).

Sources: *Billboard* May 24, 1947, p. 13; *Broadcasting* September 15, 1932, p. 21, July 10, 1944, p. 49; *Radio Life* April 28, 1946, p. 8; *Variety* obituary July 12, 1993.

Hansen, Albert

Albert Hansen was a writer for the Young & Rubicam agency in the 1940s. Among his assignments was scripting the musical program *The Carnation Contented Hour* in the late 1940s until at least 1951.

Sources: *Billboard* September 29, 1951, p. 11; *Broadcasting* June 22, 1942, p. 46.

Harmon, David

David Harmon (September 3, 1918–August 28, 2001) worked as a staff writer for CBS beginning in the early 1940s. Some of his earliest scripts were used on *America in the Air, Cavalcade of America, Man Behind the Gun, Only Yesterday, Salute to Youth,* and *Treasury Star Parade* (all 1943). After a six-month stint with the J. Walter Thompson agency from 1943–1944 he was given a 4F classification by the Army and subsequently returned to radio as a freelance writer.

Among his war-time work were scripts for *Soldiers of the Press* (1944), *Chesterfield Supper Club* (1944–1945), *We Came This Way* (1945), and *University of the Air* (1945). During the post–War era Harmon wrote for a variety of programs including *Exploring the Unknown* (1947), *Adventures of Superman* (1949), *Rivers of America* (1949), and *Confidentially Yours—Jack Lait* (1950). He revisited the early war years with *Now Hear This* (1951), set against a naval backdrop and *Cloak and Dagger* (1950), that followed the adventures of the Office of Strategic Services. Before turning to television Harmon completed stories for *Armstrong Theatre of Today* (1953) and *Big Story* (1954).

Harmon easily found steady work in television as early as 1953 writing for *Danger* (1953–1954) and *The Man Behind the Badge* (1955). Much of his writing appeared on drama and adventure programs including *The Rifleman* (1962) and *Star Trek* (1967–1968) though he ventured into other genres with scripts for shows such as *Gilligan's Island* (1965) and *The Brady Bunch* (1970–1972). He was still active in the field until the early 1980s.

Other Radio: *Radio Reader's Digest* (1945); *Magazine Theatre* (1951); *Highway U.S.A.* (1953); *Men in Black* (audition, 1953).

Theater: *I Ain't Talking* (1944).

Sources: David Harmon Papers; *Variety* February 17, 1943, p. 30, March 24, 1943, p. 34, August 11, 1943, p. 32, February 9, 1944, p. 32.

Harris, Howard

Howard Harris' (February 15, 1912–March 22, 1986) earliest documented radio work was sketches written for Tallulah Bankhead's appearances on Rudy Vallee's show in 1938, the success of which led to a contract on *The Phil Baker Show* by 1939. In 1941 Harris co-wrote with **Martin Gosch** an audition episode for a show called *The Amazing Mr. Smith*, an adaptation of *Mr. and Mrs. North*, heroes of numerous novels and a Broadway play. The series finally hit the airwaves later in the year under the property's original name *Mr. and Mrs. North*. Just weeks later the duo took over writing chores on *The Nichols—Family of Five* (originally called *Living Diary*).

In 1942 Harris worked on a number of different shows including *The Abbott & Costello Show*, *Keep 'em Rolling*, and *Private Life of Josephine Tuttle* (later *Remarkable Miss Crandall*). He and Gosch also collaborated on the initial episodes of *Mayor of the Town* with its head writer **Jean Holloway**.

Harris contributed to the scripts of *The Abbott & Costello Show* for a year before accepting an assignment with *The Bob Burns Show* in 1943–1944 along with Burns' summer replacement *Blue Ribbon Town*. Later that same Harris moved to yet another program, *Big Town*, and by year's end, *The Jimmy Durante–Garry Moore Show* (1943–1944).

Harris continued team comedy writing with **Sid Zelinka** after the end of the war on Dinah Shore's *Birdseye Open House* (1945–1946), *The Amos 'n' Andy Show*, *The Joan Davis Show* (1947), and *Meet Me at Parky's* (1947). When Hollywood star Jack Carson received his own program Harris joined the team of *The Jack Carson Show* (1948) followed by *The Sealtest Variety Theatre* (1948–1949).

While Harris continued to script for radio into the 1950s on such minor series as *That's Rich* (1954) and *Meet Mr. McNutley* (1954), his attention turned to television. There he wrote for comedies including *The Jackie Gleason Show* (1953), *You Bet Your Life* (1954–1955), *Gilligan's Island* (1962), and *Petticoat Junction* (1965–1966).

Other Radio: *The Judy Holliday Show* (1948, audition).

Theater: *Hula Honeymoon* (1941, with Martin Gosch).

Sources: *Broadcasting* March 17, 1941, p. 36, September 1, 1941, p. 41, December 1, 1941, p. 48, June 29, 1942, p. 13, September 7, 1942, p. 9, January 18, 1943, p. 30; *The Film Daily* June 23, 1938, p. 4; *Motion Picture Daily* March 22, 1939, p. 8; *Variety* July 14, 1943, p. 48, October 27, 1943, p. 28, December 29, 1943, p. 22, March 5, 1947, p. 28, October 13, 1948, p. 27.

Harrison, Paul

Paul Harrison was a producer for NBC in the 1940s but he added writing to his job duties for a 1948 series featuring Jack Pearl and Cliff Hall. Three years later in 1951 he produced, directed, and wrote the series *It's Higgins, Sir* (1951), though he handed over scripting chores to others early in the series' run. The show was the basis for Harrison's 1962–1963 television program *Our Man Higgins*.

Sources: Leszcazk p. 147; *Variety* June 16, 1948, p. 26.

Hart, Elizabeth

Elizabeth Hart, with husband **James Hart**, was part of a husband and wife writing team active from the late 1930s through the 1940s. One of their first aired scripts was used on *The Columbia Workshop* in 1938 and they would provide a number of additional stories to the series through 1946. After writing numerous scripts for *March of Time* they were then credited in 1941 with two series, *Gold If You Find It* and later in the year the *Big Sister* spin-off (1941–1942). With the United States fighting in World War II the Harts went to work on two war-themed programs, *Treasury Star Parade* (1942) and *This Is Our Enemy* (1943).

During the post-war years James and Elizabeth were credited on *The Molle Mystery Theatre* (1946) and *Great Scenes from Great Plays* (1949). In 1948 they were signed to develop scripts for a series based on attorney Herbert L. Maris who won freedom for hundreds of wrongly incarcerated prisoners, but it's not clear if the series was ever aired.

Theater: *Reasonable Facsimile* (1947, with James Hart).

Sources: *Sponsor* February 26, 1951, p. 58; *Variety* April 23, 1941, p. 34, April 15, 1942, p. 29, May 29, 1946, p. 46, March 31, 1948, p. 41.

Hart, Evelyn

Evelyn Hart started writing radio scripts while on staff at WFIN in Findlay, OH, and in 1944 joined the script department at WABC before moving to Mutual in 1945. Hart also wrote scripts for The Play's The Thing, Inc., a venture to broadcast updated version of Shakespeare plays beginning in 1945 and sold scripts to the *Dr. Christian* series in 1946.

Other Radio: *Just Plain Bill*.

Sources: *Broadcasting* February 7, 1944, p. 40; *Variety* April 18, 1945, p. 36, November 21, 1945, p. 36.

Hart, James

James Hart, with his wife **Elizabeth Hart**, penned episodes of *The Columbia Workshop*, *March of Time*, and *Bright Horizon* among other programs in the years immediately preceding the United States' entry into World War II. With war underway Hart took a job writing and editing material for the Red Cross in 1942 and continued there until 1946 when he returned to CBS' Writing Division in New York.

After war's end Hart worked with his wife on shows such as *Molle Mystery Theatre* but also scripted separately on programs including *Woman's Club* (1946), *American School of the Air* (1947), and *Born in a Merry Hour* (1947). Hart was also starting to do some production work at that time on *Joe Powers of Oakville* among other shows. As CBS moved much of their sustaining program production to the West Coast at the end of the 1940s, Hart was one of those relieved of scripting duties.

Sources: *Sponsor* February 26, 1951, p. 58; *Variety* April 23, 1941, p. 34, April 15, 1942, p. 29, April 3, 1946, p. 29, May 15, 1946, p. 34, May 29, 1946, p. 46, September 11, 1946, p. 44, March 31, 1948, p. 41.

Hartogensis, Harold

Harold Hartogensis scripted a number of episodes of the Works Progress Administration New York radio series *Experiments in Symphonic Drama*, *Men Against Death*, and *Elizabethan Radio*, all in 1938.

Source: WPA Radio Scripts.

Harvey, Helen Gould

Helen Harvey's early radio career developed at KSFO as a home economist and commentator on a show called *Hollywood Silhouettes* in 1935. By 1938 Harvey had earned herself a place on the writing staff of *The Burns & Allen Show*.

Sources: *Broadcasting* June 1, 1935, p. 30, August 15, 1935, p. 42; *The Radio Annual* 1938 p. 617.

Harvey, Jack

Jack Harvey, manager for Jimmy Durante, joined Milton Raison around 1933 to write all the material for the comedian's radio, stage, and motion picture engagements. The next years of his career are a mystery but during the 1940s Harvey is known to have worked on a number of network programs, mainly comedies. Among his most notable series credits are *Hap Hazard* (1941), *Wings Over the World* (1943), and *The Danny Kaye Show* (1945). During the second half the 1940s Harvey scripted a succession of Joan Davis shows from *Joanie's Tea Room* (1945–1947) to *Leave It to Joan* (1949).

During the 1950s while still contributing to radio programs *Granby's Green Acres* (1950) and *My Little Margie* (1954–1955) Harvey increasingly turned to television and by the end of the 1950s he wrote exclusively for the small screen. His television credits include *Damon Runyon Theatre* (1955–1956), *Home Run Derby* (1960), and *The Donna Reed Show* (1965–1966).

Other Radio: *The Henn House* (1950, audition).
Television: *The Peter and Mary Show* (1950); *Al Pearce and His Gang* (1952).
Sources: *Billboard* July 16, 1949, p. 10; *Broadcasting* December 29, 1941, p. 29, August 27, 1945, p. 74, December 4, 1950, p. 22, February 11, 1952, p. 56; *Variety* April 11, 1933, p. 2.

Hasty, John Eugene (Jack)

Born in the last years of the 19th century, Jack Hasty moved to San Diego from Lafayette, IN, at the age of 16 and during World War I did publicity for the Marine Corps. He got started in the radio industry around 1927 on the West Coast and began writing "Ed and Zeb" sketches for Al Pearce as early as 1932. He would go on to write for Pearce on numerous projects over the subsequent dozen years. In 1935 Hasty penned scripts for the C.P. MacGregor production of *The Shadow* that led, by the late 1930s, to a job as producer, director, and writer for the McCann-Erickson agency.

Among Hasty's documented writing assignments for the agency were scripts for a National Biscuit-sponsored program, Jean Hersholt's *Dr. Christian* (for which he wrote until at least 1942), and Gruen watch-sponsored *A Time for Love* in 1937. In 1939 Hasty penned more "Eb and Zeb" sketches that appeared on the weekly *Al Pearce and His Gang* program, *The Ford Summer Show*, as well as some experimental television broadcasts for NBC scheduled for the World's Fair.

During the early 1940s Hasty moved to the J. Walter Thompson agency where he worked on programs including *We, the Abbotts* (1940), *Lincoln Highway* (1940–1942), and *Al Pearce & His Gang in Fun Valley* (1943). He then continued his writing partnership with Pearce on the 1944 series *Here Comes Elmer* and was assigned to *The Charlotte Greenwood Show* for the 1944–1945 season.

By the end of the 1940s Hasty had migrated to film and television, working for Jerry Fairbanks' production company and the J. Walter Thompson agency at different times.

Other Radio: *The Dinglebenders* (1932); *Benny Rubin's Whirligig* (1936); *On Broadway* (1938); *Death Valley Days*.

Sources: Grams *The Shadow*; *Broadcasting* June 1, 1932, p. 19, September 27, 1943, p. 63; *Motion Picture Daily* February 10, 1939, p. 8; *Radio Daily* September 14, 1937, p. 4, November 3, 1937, p. 1, February 4, 1938, p. 5; *Radio Mirror* September 1935 p. 66, May 1939 p. 45; *Variety* June 9, 1937, p. 39, July 19, 1939, p. 28, October 2, 1940, p. 26, November 1, 1944.

Hawkins, Ruth

Ruth Hawkins, writer for the Young & Rubicam agency, is known for her work scripting *The Adventures of the Thin Man*, an adaptation of Dashiell Hammett's Nick and Nora Charles stories. In the 1950s Hawkins wrote for television as well, both for Young & Rubicam and the Fred Wittner Advertising agency.

Sources: *Broadcasting* February 18, 1957, p. 38; *Variety* August 13, 1947, p. 31.

Hawkins, Stuart

Stuart Hawkins was involved professionally in radio almost from the medium's commercial advent. A graduate of Annapolis, Hawkins worked for WJZ as publicity director between 1923 and 1925 and then as a radio critic until 1929 for *The New York Herald Tribune*. For the next few years he worked in the radio department of the N. W. Ayer & Son agency before deciding to quit and focus on his writing, during which time he published some novels.

Hawkins returned to radio in 1935 with NBC's New York outlet and subsequently wrote scripts for a number of series over the next decade. These included *The Columbia Workshop* (1938), *City Desk* (1941), *Bright Horizon* (1944), a spin-off of the *Big Sister* serial, and several episodes of *Cavalcade of America* (1942–1947). Hawkins reportedly wrote the serial *Myrt & Marge* for a number of years in the late 1930s and returned to pen the program in 1942. Later in the 1940s Hawkins turned to freelance writing assignments.

Books: *No Man Is Single* (1934).

Sources: *Broadcasting* December 15, 1925, p. 34; *Variety* October 9, 1935, p. 36, August 27, 1941, p. 30.

Hayes, John Michael

John Michael Hayes (May 11, 1919–November 19, 2008) began writing as a boy and after high school he paid his way through Massachusetts State College with scripting jobs for local radio stations. Before spending time in the Army during World War II Hayes worked on various Proctor & Gamble serials.

After the war and an illness that forced him to postpone his writing career, Hayes found work writing for numerous West Coast radio series, including many among the most fondly remembered by old-time radio enthusiasts. His scripts were used on *The Whistler* (1945), *Suspense* (1947, 1950–1951, 1957), *Twelve Players* (1945, 1948), and *Rocky Jordan* (1949) during the 1940s. Hayes was no less prolific in the 1950s, scripting for *Escape* (1950), *Yours Truly, Johnny Dollar* (1950), *The Adventures of Sam Spade* (1950–1951), *Night Beat* (1950–1951), *The Story of Dr. Kildare* (1950, 1951), and *Richard Diamond, Private Detective* (1951).

Hayes quickly became an in-demand screenwriter in the early 1950s and wrote a quartet of pictures for Alfred Hitchcock, including the classics *Rear Window* (1954) and *To Catch a Thief* (1955), the former earning him an Academy Award nomination. He earned a second nomination for 1957's *Peyton Place* and Hayes' scripts continued to appear in motion pictures and television into the 1970s.

Other Radio: *Alias John Doe*; *Amos 'n' Andy*; *My Favorite Husband*; *Sweeney and March* (1946–1951, intermittent).

Sources: DeRosa; Grams *Suspense*; *Broadcasting* November 9, 1959, p. 92; *Los Angeles Times* obituary November 27, 2008.

Hays, Larry

Larry Hays worked as a station manager KSRO in Vallejo, CA, and freelance writer in San Francisco before enlisting in the United States Marine Corp. during World War II. As a lieutenant in the Marines Hays wrote, narrated, and produced *Halls of Montezuma* (1942–1943) over Mutual while on duty. He later worked to create teams to record and document military maneuvers and assaults.

In 1945 after Hays' discharge from the armed forces he went to work as a scriptwriter for the Don Lee Network in Hollywood. Over the next several years he is credited with scripting for *Club Hollywood* (1946), the 1946 season of *The Cisco Kid*, *The Lone Wolf* (1948), and *Wild Bill Hickok* (1952–1954). Hays also assumed some directing duties for programs such as *California Caravan* (1947–1952).

Sources: Cox *Radio Crime Fighters*; *Broadcasting* October 19, 1942, p. 38, May 10, 1943, p. 35, December 4, 1944, p. 32, November 19, 1945, p. 60; *Radio Life* June 23, 1946, p. 34–35; *Variety* February 11, 1948, p. 32.

Hecht, Ben

Ben Hecht (February 28, 1894–April 18, 1964) was one of the premier screenwriters during Hollywood's Golden Age, though he considered himself at heart a playwright who simply wrote films for the money. He dabbled a few times in radio as well, primarily in the 1940s. Hecht is often credited with scripting *The Jumbo Fire Chief Program* with Charles MacArthur, a series that ran from 1935–1936 under the sponsorship of Texaco. However, as was made clear in a legal dispute that lasted long after the program left the air, while Hecht and MacArthur penned the original musical theatre production on which the broadcasts were based, they were not involved in creating the radio scripts. In fact, it appears that **David Freedman** filled in the original stage script with gags and humorous sketches to create the radio version of *Jumbo*.

Among Hecht's confirmed radio scripts are *The American Comedy of the Air* (1943) and a story called "Miracle in the Pullman" used as part of the sixth War Loan Drive in 1944. The latter effort led to discussions with the Blue Network about an ongoing Hecht-authored series, discussions that aren't known to have come to fruition. Hecht wrote two episodes of the long-running *Suspense* (1944, 1947) and material for *The Ford Theatre* (1948) as well. Hecht had a brief television career with *The Ben Hecht Television Show* that ran for a few months in 1958–1959.

Nominated for six Academy Awards between 1929 and 1947 Hecht won twice, for *Underworld* (1929) and *The Scoundrel* (1936, with Charles MacArthur). During a prolific writing career that was still going strong at the time of his death, Hecht is credited with approximately 70 screenplays as well as numerous additional television projects.

Sources: Ben Hecht Papers; Grams *Suspense*; *Broadcasting* December 1, 1935, p. 42; *Variety* October 23, 1935, p. 62, March 18, 1936, p. 39, March 25, 1936, p. 19, November 22, 1914, p. 30, November 29, 1944, p. 2.

Hediger, Ted

After his college years that took Ted Hediger to St. Paul, San Francisco, and St. Louis, Hediger settled into the fledgling radio industry by 1928. He worked for WRHM (Minneapolis), KWK (St. Louis), KTM (Los Angeles), and KGB (San Diego) before arriving in Chicago as an NBC announcer in 1930. Just a few years later Hediger was back in Minneapolis on WCCO acting and performing.

Finally in 1937 Hediger took a position with NBC's outlet in Hollywood producing various programming. His first known writing projects came in 1940 with *Spotlight on Youth* and *Hollywood Tomorrow*. On leave from NBC, Hediger began doing some work for J. Walter Thompson in 1941 writing the *Kraft Music Hall* and *The Rudy Vallee Show* in 1942.

At this time Hediger went to work for the agency full time producing and writing for Xavier Cugat's *Your Dubonnet Date* in 1943–1944 (and later Cugat's *Casa Cugat* ca. 1946). The last half of the decade Hediger focused on private eye shows including *I Deal in Crime* (1946–1947), the follow-up sustainer *Ross Dolan, Detective* (1948), and *Martin Kane, Private Eye*

(1949–1950). Though not the primary writer, Hediger gets occasional credit for writing contributions to Alan Ladd's *Box 13* (1947–1948).

Sources: *Broadcasting* September 15, 1937, p. 40, September 1, 1940, p. 84, February 2, 1942, p. 34; *Radio Digest* March 1928 p. 126, December 1930 p. 74; *Variety* January 1, 1935, p. 90, September 25, 1940, p. 27, July 30, 1941, p. 27, June 2, 1948, p. 24; *St. Petersburg Times* July 16, 1950, p. 31.

Heider, Fred

Fred Heider (April 9, 1915–May 17, 1992) was a junior NBC staff writer in the early 1940s who also did freelance work such as scripting *Story Shop* over WEVD. He left to author for the Red Cross in 1942 and returned to network writing in 1944 on the Blue network. Heider's later work included *The Johnny Thompson Show* (1946) and *Chesterfield Supper Club* (ca. 1947–1948).

Heider's television work focused more on directing and producing such programs as *Club Embassy* (1952–1953) with Bob Elliott and Ray Goulding, and the *Bell Telephone Hour* (1961–1962), though he did receive credit for scripting *The Martha Wright Show* (1954).

Sources: Hyatt p. 42, 59; *Broadcasting* July 17, 1944, p. 44; *Radio and Television Mirror* November 1948; p. 57; *Variety* July 1, 1942, p. 35, September 11, 1946, p. 42, February 26, 1947, p. 34.

Heisch, Glanville

Glanville Heisch, editor of the *Pelican* while a student at the University of California, is believed to have entered radio around 1933 on the continuity staff of KFI in Los Angeles. He immediately started scripting *Fun Factory* and within three years he was promoted to production manager.

Heisch is most well known as the writer behind *The Cinnamon Bear*, a juvenile Christmas series that has an outsized reputation among old-time radio enthusiasts in relation to its original radio run. Debuting in 1937, the story of the Cinnamon Bear, the Barton children, and the Crazy Quilt Dragon continues to be annual listening for fans of radio's Golden Age.

Much of Heisch's subsequent work was directing and producing, yet he did take periodical writing jobs, both for the station and on a freelance basis, one of them being *Mickey Mouse Theatre of the Air* (1938). In 1942 Heisch resigned his position with KFI to join the San Francisco office of the Office of War Information and returned to private industry in 1944 with KNX.

Heisch soon moved into an executive position with McCann-Erickson where he stayed for many years. Eventually he became a busy television producer, most prominently for *Mr. Magoo* (1960) and *Dick Tracy* (1961).

Sources: *Broadcasting* March 1, 1933, p. 19, January 1, 1938, p. 24, August 31, 1942, p. 34; *Radio Daily* June 10, 1937, p. 6.

Helm, Harvey

Harvey Helm was a long-time writer for George Burns and Gracie Allen, from their days in vaudeville, across various iterations of their radio show, until the end of their television show. During the course of a nearly thirty-year writing partnership with the two, Helm is only known to have had a handful of jobs separate from them. Among those few scripting assignments were *Al Pearce & His Gang* (1940), *Your Dubonnet Date* (1943), *The Adventures of Ozzie and Harriet* (1944), and *The Red Skelton Show* (1948). He didn't miss a beat when George and Gracie transitioned to television and wrote for their televised broadcasts until 1958, and scripted episodes for just a handful of other shows before passing away in 1966.

Other Radio: *Amos 'n' Andy*.

Sources: Epstein p. 130; *Broadcasting* August 15, 1938, p. 79, August 1, 1940, p. 84, September 6, 1943, p. 8; *Radio Mirror* March 1936 p. 68; *Variety* July 5, 1944, p. 39.

Henning, Paul

Paul Henning (September 16, 1911–March 25, 2005) was one of a number of radio writers and performers who honed their craft at Kansas City's KMBC before moving on to network productions. After several years writing and producing for KMBC, Henning relocated to Chicago in 1937 to work with Don Quinn on *Fibber McGee & Molly* while employed by Needham, Louis & Brorby Inc. In 1939, by which time he was credited with writing assistance on the popular program, Henning married **Ruth Barth**, a fellow writer originally from Kansas City.

Henning joined the writing staff of *The Rudy Vallee Show* for two years (1940–1942) before beginning a long run writing for *The Burns & Allen Show* during the 1942–1943 season. In 1952 after a short time splitting his time between *Burns & Allen* and *The Alan Young Show*, Henning left *Young* to work exclusively for *Burns & Allen* until the mid–1950s when he started a multi-year run on *The Bob Cummings Show* (1955–1959).

Television proved to be fertile ground for Henning's humor, where he created and wrote the classic rural-themed comedies *The Beverly Hillbillies* (1962–1971), and *Petticoat Junction* (1963–1970). Henning's screenplay credits are thin but impressive nonetheless, earning an Academy Award nomination in 1962 for Best Screenplay (with Stanley Shapiro) for *Lover Come Back*.

Other Radio: *Dan Dunn, Secret Operative*; *The Joe E. Brown Show*; *Melody and Madness*.

Sources: Young; *Broadcasting* December 15, 1937, p. 82, January 15, 1939, p. 48, March 15, 1940, p. 50, October 12, 1942, p. 49, October 22, 1951, p. 57; *Los Angeles Times* obituary March 26, 2005.

Herbert, F. Hugh

Frederick Hugh Herbert (May 29, 1897–May 17, 1958) was a prolific screenwriter and playwright during the 1920s and 1930s who made a single but memorable foray into radio. In 1943 *Meet Corliss Archer*, based on a teenager introduced in his play *Kiss and Tell*, made its air debut. The series ran until 1956 but by 1948 Herbert had passed off the writing duties to others, though he continued to receive a healthy royalty for his creation. Herbert's Archer characters spawned a small franchise that, in addition to theater and radio, spanned into motion pictures, comic books, and television.

Sources: *Broadcasting* August 23, 1943, p. 38; *Variety* April 24, 1946, p. 39, June 23, 1948, p. 26.

Hermann, Cleve

Cleve (sometimes Cleave) Hermann has only one known radio credit, the short-lived West Coast series *Jason and the Golden Fleece* (1952–1953), co-written with **Herb Ellis**. Hermann also has at least one television credit, an unnamed 1951 show featuring Jeanne Cagney. There was an L.A.-area sports broadcaster by the same name but no evidence suggests these are the same person. Possibly the name is a pseudonym for another radio performer or writer, not an uncommon practice at the time.

Sources: *Broadcasting* November 10, 1952, p. 111; *Los Angeles Times* May 14, 1951, p. 30.

Hermann, Harry

Originally a freelance writer and producer, Harry Hermann (b. ca. 1908) wrote *Mother and Dad* (1943) before taking a job with J. Walter Thompson Co. in 1943. By 1947 he had been promoted to one of the agency's chief script men. During his time in television Hermann was more involved in production than writing.

Other Radio: *Mr. District Attorney*.

Sources: *Broadcasting* March 1, 1943, p. 30; *Radio Mirror* June 1943 p. 43; *Variety* November 12, 1947, p. 30.

Herzinger, Carl

Carl Herzinger had a long and productive writing career that included radio, film, and television. His work remains largely unknown but among his identified writing were scripts for *Hollywood Mardi Gras* (1937), *Man About Town* (1940), *The Al Pearce Show* (ca. 1941), *Signal Carnival* (1941–1942), *Memoirs of Mischa, the Magnificent* (1942), and *Lum 'n' Abner* (1953). Herzinger's television scripts were used on *Make Me Laugh* (1949) and *Father Knows Best* (1956, 1960).

Motion Pictures: *Lum and Abner Abroad* (1956).

Sources: *Billboard* July 11, 1942, p. 6; *Broadcasting* November 10, 1941, p. 37; *The Radio Annual* 1941 p. 68; *Radio Daily* September 8, 1937, p. 1, 3; *Variety* April 27, 1949, p. 41.

Hewson, Isabel Manning

Isabel Manning Hewson (Kirkland), a reported Philadelphia socialite, wrote advertising copy for N. W. Ayers before starting a home economics program on the radio in 1932 that eventually was called *Petticoat of the Air*. Originally on the Mutual network, by 1943 she had moved to the Blue network with a broadcast entitled *Morning Market Basket*. Hewson's first known fiction effort, the children's serial *The Land of* the Lost, premiered over Blue in 1943 (later moving to Mutual). The series proved popular enough to lead to two books, *Land of the Lost* (1945) and *Adventures in the Land of the Lost* (1946), and a comic book series published by Educational Comics (1946). The program left the air in 1948 but some animated shorts were released in 1951.

Sources: French "Land of the Lost"; *Broadcasting* October 18, 1943, p. 42; *Radio Daily* March 16, 1937, p. 5; *Radio Mirror* November 1943 p. 80; *Variety* April 8, 1936, p. 38, June 12, 1946, p. 61.

Higley, Philo

Philo Higley began his writing career with some New York newspapers including the *Herald Tribune* and *Morning Telegraph*. In 1932 Higley wrote his first play, *Excursion*, the first of several that would be produced during the decade, some of which were adapted to film. Higley moved on to do publicity for a couple West Coast movie studios in 1933 and several years later in 1941 signed a contract with the Columbia film studio. During this same time he scripted what is believed to be his first radio series, *The Helen Hayes Theatre* (1941).

Less than a year into the screenplay contract Higley was appointed chief of the Film and Radio section in the Office of Price Administration in 1942. Late in the war he was assigned writing duties on *The Navy Hour* (1945). Higley returned to radio scripting after the war with at least one identified series, *World Service* (1947). However, evidence suggests that Higley came under suspicion during the Hollywood Blacklist era and had trouble finding work for several years. When the BBC series *Horatio Hornblower* was brought to the United States in 1952 Higley was called on to write the scripts adapted to an American audience.

Television: *Sure as Fate*, or *Studio One* (1951).

Sources: *Billboard* June 21, 1952, p. 4; *Broadcasting* July 2, 1945, p. 65; *The Film Daily* June 22, 1932, p. 2, June 28, 1933, p. 11; *Motion Picture Herald* August 22, 1942, p. 68; *Variety* July 9, 1947, p. 38; *New York Herald Tribune* December 5, 1947, p. 21; *The Tryon Daily Bulletin* December 22, 1941, p. 4.

Hiken, Nat

Gag writer Nat Hiken (June 23, 1914–December 7, 1968) cut his teeth on *The Grouch Club* (1938–1940), a West Coast program before being hired for **Fred Allen**'s *Texaco Star Theatre* in 1940 where he stayed until 1947 while adding *The Milton Berle Show* to his work schedule in 1946. By 1947 Hiken felt that it was time to look for other opportunities that might include some level of ownership in a series, though some speculated that his additional work on Berle's program had strained Hiken's relationship with Allen.

One of Hiken's first packaging efforts was *The Arnold Stang Show*, co-created with **Goodman Ace** in the spring of 1948. The series didn't go anywhere but when Berle returned to the air in 1948 he and Hiken were responsible for packaging the new series. After one final radio series, *The Magnificent Montague* (1950–1951), Hiken jumped into television where he built on his radio success. Hiken's fame rests on his creation and writing of *The Phil Silvers Show* (1955–1959) and *Car 54, Where Are You?* (1961–1963).

Sources: Nat Hiken Papers; *Broadcasting* September 15, 1940, p. 54; *Radio and Television Mirror* November 1939 p. 7; *Variety* December 4, 1946, p. 27, June 25, 1947, p. 23, March 10, 1948, p. 30.

Hite, Kathleen

Kathleen Hite (June 17, 1917–February 18, 1989) was one of the most prolific writers in the latter years of radio's Golden Age and she went on to a very successful television career as well. After attending university in Wichita, KS, and working for a local station there until 1943, Hite moved to California where, in short order, she was hired as a secretary and soon promoted by CBS' Pacific chain as their first female writers.

Hite's early work for CBS included scripts for *The City*, *Fact or Fantasy*, *The Ghost Walks* (1946–1947), *One for the Book*, *The People Next Door*, and *The Private Practice of Dr. Dana*. Recognizing her story telling prowess, Hite was elevated in 1950 to the position of script editor for *The Whistler* and *The Adventures of Philip Marlowe* until approximately the end of the year. At that time she decided to leave CBS to work as a freelance writer, a job that was less secure but potentially more lucrative.

The gamble paid off and Hite went on to contribute to many esteemed dramas and westerns of the era. Among them were *Suspense* (1951), *Night Beat* (1952), *Escape* (1952–1954), *Gunsmoke* (1953–1960), *Rogers of the Gazette* (1953–1954), *Romance* (1952–1957), *Hallmark Hall of Fame* (1953), *Lux Summer Theatre* (1953), and *Fort Laramie* (1956). Hite's television scripting increased during the 1950s and eventually culminated in long runs with *Gunsmoke* (1957–1965) and *The Waltons* (1974–1981).

Sources: Kathleen Hite Scripts; Grams *Suspense*; Wright "Kathleen Hite"; *Broadcasting* June 19, 1950, p. 38.

Hodapp, William

William Hodapp entered the radio industry after serving on the faculty of the Indiana University extension school teaching acting, drama, and writing. In 1937 he joined NBC's Chicago outlet as a continuity writer where he scripted *Empires of the Moon, 1001 Wives* (ca. 1939), *Jane Arden*, and *How Do You Know?* (1940). Hodapp contributed scripts to a number of series after World War II including *The Adventures of Sinbad* (1946), *The Author Meets the Critic* (1947), *Tales of the Foreign Service* (1947), *NBC University Theatre* (1948), and the post–**Richard Durham** *Destination Freedom* (1950–1951).

Sources: Phyllis Merrill Papers; *Billboard* June 14, 1947, p. 14; *Broadcasting* May 15, 1939, p. 32, October 1, 1939, p. 82; *Radio Daily* July 28, 1937, p. 7, March 30, 1938, p. 4.

Holland, Gerald

Over a period of three years Gerald Holland scripted *The Land We Live In* for KMOX, a 30-minute dramatization of St. Louis history aired from 1937–1939. In 1939 Holland took a job with NBC in New York as a staff writer where he immediately started scripting *Magic Waves* (later *Radio Waves*, 1939–1940) and later *Canadian Holiday* (1940). While with NBC Holland also authored *Great Plays* (1941), *Swop Night* and *Cab Calloway's Quizzicale* (both ca. 1942), and *This Nation at War* (1943).

After a brief time pursuing freelance work Holland returned to NBC and later wrote for Mutual. Other series for which he wrote during the 1940s were *Words at War* (1943–1945), *The Sportsmen's Club* (1944–1945), *Arthur Hopkins Presents* (1944), *Teentimers Club* (1945), *Cavalcade of America* (1945, 1951), *Scattergood Baines* (1949), and *Mister Feathers* (1949–1950).

Sources: Terrace *Program Openings*; *Broadcasting* November 15, 1938, p. 62, September 15, 1939, p. 52, October 1, 1939, p. 60, September 15, 1940, p. 52, September 20, 1943, p. 36; *Radio and Television Today* May 1940 p. 13; *Variety* April 8, 1942, p. 32.

Holloway, Jean

Jean Holloway (Gratia Jean Casey, April 16, 1917–November 11, 1989) broke into network radio in the late 1930s as a 21-year-old former student from San Jose State Teachers College (now San Jose State University) who traveled to New York hoping to land a Broadway acting role. Instead, she was discovered by Ted Collins, Kate Smith's manager, who hired her to write original sketches and adapt other works for *The Kate Smith Hour* (1940–1942, 1943). CBS quickly put her to work scripting the serial *My Son and I* in addition to Smith's program.

Holloway was a prolific writer and her scripts were used on dozens of radio programs during the 1940s. Those documented programs include *Cavalcade of America* (1941), *Mayor of the Town* (1942–1948), *Dangerously Yours* (1944), *The Matinee Theatre* (1944–1945), and *Romance* (also *Theatre of Romance*, 1943–1946). Among her post–War work were stories for *Encore Theatre* (1946), *Maxwell House Coffee Time* (1947, summer replacement), *Mr. President* (1948–1950), *The Hallmark Playhouse* (1948–1953, later *The Hallmark Hall of Fame*), *Hollywood Showcase* (1948), *The Railroad Hour* (1948–1952), and *Story of Dr. Kildare* (1949–1950).

Though she did a bit of motion picture work in the 1940s, Holloway never got a lot of traction there and instead focused on television as the 1950s unfolded. She wrote numerous TV movies and individual episodes but her first big assignment for the small screen was an adaptation of *Mayor of the Town* (1954–1955). Holloway wrote many episodes for *Wagon Train* (1959–1961) and *The Ghost and Mrs. Muir*

(1968–1970), the latter of which she also helped develop. Nearly 45 years after starting in radio Holloway still contributed to programs such as *Fantasy Island* (1983).

Other Radio: *Forecast* (1941); *Portraits* (1941, audition); *Don Ameche Show* (1946, auditions); *Sealtest Variety Theatre* (1948).

Film: *Till the Clouds Roll By* (1946); *Words and Music* (1948); *Summer Holiday* (1948).

Sources: *Broadcasting* November 1, 1940, p. 91, October 5, 1942, p. 38, January 17, 1949, p. 71; *Radio Daily* December 12, 1949, p. 5; *Variety* June 26, 1946, p. 38.

Holt, Felix

A newspaper cartoonist for *Stars and Stripes* during World War I and then in Chicago before starting in radio, Felix Holt (December 20, 1898–June 2, 1954) joined Detroit's WJBK in 1931. He then became the publicity and news director for WXYZ from the mid–1930s to mid–1940s during which time he contributed stories for the station's big three programs, *Challenge of the Yukon*, *The Green Hornet*, and *The Lone Ranger*. After leaving the station in 1945 to script for CBS in New York, Holt wrote for some other series including the juvenile Western serial *Cimarron Tavern* (1945–1946) and *Doctor Standish, Medical Examiner* (1948).

Novels: *The Gabriel Horn* (1951); *Daniel Boone Kissed Me* (1954).

Sources: French & Siegel p. 33–34; Grams *Green Hornet*; Kleber p. 437–438; *Broadcasting* April 2, 1945, p. 28; *Radio Romances* September 1945 p. 6; jacksonpurchasehistory.org.

Hoople, Henry

Henry Hoople was a Chicago comedian who played the character Elmer the Swede, a dialect act, both on vaudeville and on radio in the 1930s. By 1941 Hoople was writing as well as performing, starring in *Lightning Jim* and writing *The Blue Frolics* ca. 1944. Later in 1944 he started writing *The Judy Canova Show* with **Fred Fox**, a program they wrote until 1949 while contributing dialog to Canova's 1945 film *Hit the Hay*.

Sources: *Broadcasting* October 13, 1941, p. 48; *Radio Mirror* November 1936 p. 75; *Variety* February 23, 1944, p. 26, December 20, 1944, p. 25.

Hope, George

George Hope, Bob Hope's younger brother, had a respectable career in radio and television, first as a writer and later as a producer, despite being overshadowed by his sibling. As early as 1938 Hope was writing for *Give Me a Sentence* on WHN and during the war was involved with programs such as *Stockton Field Army Show* (1942). Hope spent time with at least two top comedy programs, those of Bob Hope (1943) and Jack Benny (1944) then after the war he teamed with Eddie Bracken for *The Eddie Bracken Show* (1946–1947). During the television era Hope was involved with brother Bob's series and specials.

Sources: *Broadcasting* December 6, 1943, p. 32, April 22, 1963, p. 58; *Variety* June 8, 1938, p. 28.

Hopkins, Neal

Neal Hopkins' first identified radio stories were written for the CBS series *Sisters of the Skillet* and *Your Unseen Friend* (ca. 1937) before he began writing continuity for Lang-Worth Feature Programs, Inc. from 1939 to 1941. In 1941 Hopkins signed with NBC to write *Spin & Win with Jimmy Flynn* in addition to a variety of special programming. Among his NBC assignments were *WJZ Takes the Cake* (1941), *For Distinguished Service* (1942), *Frankly Mr. Feebish* (1942), *Joe and Mabel* (1942), *Treasury Star Parade* (1942), and *Words at War* (1943–1945). Hopkins resigned from NBC in 1944 to pursue freelance opportunities that included *This Is Helen Hayes* (1945).

Other Radio: *Two on a Shoestring*.

Sources: *Broadcasting* July 14, 1941, p. 32, November 30, 1942, p. 27, February 26, 1945, p. 62; *Motion Picture Daily* April 9, 1942, p. 8; *Radio Daily* February 16, 1937, p. 4, April 9, 1937, p. 3; *Variety* July 2, 1941, p. 28, October 8, 1941, p. 26, April 22, 1942, p. 30.

Hopkins, Pauline

Born into a theatrical family, Pauline Hopkins was a playwright in the early 1930s but by 1933 she had migrated to radio where she authored *Tony and Baby* over Omaha's KOIL (later over WOW). Sometime before 1936 Hopkins moved to New York and by that year was scripting the sponsored *While the City Sleeps* over WEAF. The next year, having earned credits on *The First*

Nighter Program and *Grand Hotel*, she moved again to Cincinnati's WLW where she wrote the serial *The Mad Hatterfields* (1937–1939). Later that year Hopkins co-wrote a second serial, *We Live Again*, with Nancy Palmer and in 1938 Hopkins added a third serial, *Midstream* (1938–1941) to her workload.

Hopkins and husband Owen Vinson left Cincinnati in 1939 to join Chicago's Carl Wester & Co. where Vinson would assume production responsibilities while Hopkins continued authoring her serials. The couple opened their own Chicago office in 1941, by which time Hopkins was scripting *That Brewster Boy* in addition to *Midstream*. Together they edited *Knickerbocker Playhouse* scripts that Hopkins occasionally wrote. Hopkins and Vinson moved yet again, this time to Los Angeles, in 1945. Some of her later scripts were used on *Let George Do It* (ca. 1947) and *Curtain Time* (ca. 1948).

Other Radio: *It's a Woman's World* (1943).
Sources: *Broadcasting* February 15, 1933, p. 24, September 1, 1939, p. 50, September 22, 1941, p. 69; *Radio Mirror* February 1938 p. 4, 80; *Radio Showmanship* March 1943 p. 103; *Variety* March 18, 1936, p. 44, August 4, 1937, p. 43, June 1, 1938, p. 27, April 2, 1947, p. 35.

Hotchkiss Posener, Barbara

Barbara Hotchkiss (January 1918–November 25, 2013), a graduate of the Merdith School of New Hampshire and later Columbia University, was a news editor for Washington's WRC before a promotion gave her the opportunity to write scripts. In 1948 she is credited with writing *Meet Mrs. America* and as late as 1953 she is known to have been writing copy for Paris & Peart Advertising. In her later years Hotchkiss worked with numerous volunteer organizations and worked on local television productions on Long Island.

Other Radio: *The Eddie Cantor Show*
Television: *The Big Payoff; Glamour Manor; Strike It Rich.*
Sources: *Broadcasting* March 27, 1944, p. 46, April 13, 1953, p. 90; *Variety* July 21, 1948, p. 26; 27east.com

Howard, Cy

An amateur play writer and actor while a graduate student at the University of Wisconsin in 1939, Cy Howard (born Seymour Horowitz, September 27, 1915–April 29, 1993) spent the next three years attempting to get a break acting on Broadway. Finding only moderate success, he decided to try radio at Houston's KTRH followed by a job with WBBM's (Chicago) sales staff in 1942. Howard left the following year to sign with the writing staff of *The Jack Benny Show* that included other newcomers **Milt Josefsberg**, John Pickerberry, and **George Balzer**. Howard stayed just a few weeks before resigning to take the lead in a **Maxwell Anderson** play.

For a few months in early 1944 Howard had some comedy roles and emcee duties on the air but soon he was back behind the typewriter writing material for *Palmolive Party*. However, he wasn't ready to commit to radio and spent the latter half of 1944 and 1945 rewriting the book for Broadway's *Glad* and taking responsibility for some staging duties.

In 1946 Howard returned to radio as a writer-director-producer for CBS and soon brought Milton Berle's summer series *Kiss and Make Up* to the air. Howard juggled over a dozen program ideas during his early months at the network and in early 1947 *My Friend Irma* auditioned on the air. Initially a sustaining program, CBS invested a lot of resources in the program and it paid off with a seven year run on radio with adaptations to film and television as well. Originally conceived and auditioned as *Little Immigrant* (1948), Cy Howard's *Life with Luigi*, his second big hit, premiered about eighteen months after *Irma* and aired from 1948 to 1953.

After ushering his two main creations to television in the early 1950s, Howard wrote for the small screen into the mid–1960s where he created various properties, most notably *Harrigan and Son* (1960–1961).

Sources: *Broadcasting* September 28, 1942, p. 35, September 20, 1943, p. 36, November 22, 1943, p. 42; *Motion Picture Daily* January 16, 1946, p. 6; *Variety* May 3, 1939, p. 50, May 3, 1944, p. 32, November 29, 1944, p. 43, July 3, 1946, p. 26, April 21, 1948, p. 23, September 29, 1948, p. 47; *New York Times* obituary April 30, 1993.

Howard, David

David Howard teamed with **Howard Breslin** to write for at least two series, *Author's Playhouse* (1942) and *Lawyer Tucker* (1947).

Source: *Variety* February 11, 1942, p. 25.

Howell, Bob

Bob Howell created and wrote the unconventional quiz show *It Pays to Be Ignorant* (1942–1951) while working at WNLC (New London, CT) in the late 1930s and then WELI (New Haven, CT). He created the program around 1941 with future wife **Ruth Howard Howell**. Originally entitled *Crazy Quiz*, the couple was at first happy just to collect some royalties from it before they eventually decided to explore the show's potential and moved to WKNY in New York in 1943. Howell passed away soon after, around 1944.

Sources: *Broadcasting* October 15, 1938, p. 26, July 15, 1939, p. 42, August 30, 1943, p. 69; *Radio Mirror* May 1947 p. 62; *Variety* March 1, 1944, p. 43.

Howell, Ruth Howard

Born to parents who earned their living in vaudeville, Ruth Howard entered the business early, briefly stopping to get some formal schooling in Philadelphia. She originally started writing homemaking scripts, despite knowing next to nothing about being a housewife and parlayed that into a respectable writing and acting career in Utica, NY, Chicago, New Haven, CT, and eventually New York.

She co-created *It Pays to Be Ignorant* around 1941 (originally *Crazy Quiz*) over WELI with future husband **Bob Howell**. With her father's connections the couple got the program on New York radio where it ran until 1951. Howard carried on as head writer after her husband passed away in 1944.

Sources: *Broadcasting* October 15, 1938, p. 26, July 15, 1939, p. 42, April 21, 1941, p. 32, August 30, 1943, p. 69; *Motion Picture Daily* April 6, 1937, p. 6; *Radio Mirror* May 1947 p. 62; *Variety* March 1, 1944, p. 43; *The Pittsburgh Press* July 29, 1945, p. 28.

Howlett, Eric

Eric Howlett had both writing and production duties for a WJR (Detroit) serial in 1935 and then on their famous *The Hermit's Cave* ca. 1937. He was also involved with other WJR programs including *This Is My Story* (1937).

Sources: *Variety* August 21, 1935, p. 48, September 22, 1937, p. 33, October 20, 1937, p. 41.

Hubbard, Tom

Tom Hubbard is credited with writing two series in the later years of the radio's Golden Age, *Captain Starr of Space* (1953) and *Mike Malloy, Private Cop* (co-creator, 1953–1954).

Source: *Broadcasting* July 30, 1956, p. 26.

Hughes, Don

Don Hughes scripted the early 1950s juvenile science fiction program *Tom Corbett, Space Cadet* (1952).

Source: radiogoldindex.com

Hughes, Russell

Reportedly authoring scripts as early as 1929, Russell Hughes (January 15, 1910–April 16, 1958) was a continuity writer for WLW until 1936 when he resigned to pursue freelance opportunities. One of these jobs was assisting with the writing for *The Uncrowned King*, a 1937 Transamerican Broadcasting series. That same year he joined a Hollywood station, KFWB, as a writer-producer where among his series was *Experimental Theatre*. In 1938 Hughes briefly worked for Radio Transcription Co. of America but returned to producing for KFWB in 1939 where he worked until joining the Army in 1942.

After his time in the service Hughes spent several years writing for a number of radio series including *Cavalcade of America* (1944–1951), *The Whistler* (1946, 1951), and *Cresta Blanca Hollywood Players* (1946). Hughes wrote two well-preserved programs for Mayfair Productions at the end of the 1940s, *Box 13* (1948–1949) and *The Damon Runyan Theatre* (1948–1949). *Box 13* featured Alan Ladd who, nearly fifteen years earlier, worked for Hughes in some of Ladd's first radio work. Some of Hughes' final radio work before moving into motion pictures and television was scripts for *Richard Diamond, Private Detective* (1950), *Night Beat* (1950), *Tales of the Texas Rangers* (1950–1951), and *The Chase* (1953).

Television: *The Ford Television Theatre* (1956–1957); *Perry Mason* (1957).

Sources: *Broadcasting* May 1, 1938, p. 55, July 15, 1939, p. 54, March 30, 1942, p. 38; *Motion Picture Daily*

November 13, 1936, p. 7; *Radio Daily* May 17, 1937, p. 7, November 15, 1937, p. 12, November 22, 1937, p. 6; *Sponsor* October 1948 p. 13; *Variety* September 25, 1935, p. 52, February 13, 1946, p. 30.

Huntley, Lester

Lester Huntley is credited with scripting two serials in the years just before the United States entered World War II, *Kitty Keene, Incorporated* (during its 1937–1941 run) and *This Small Town* (1940), and then *Ma Perkins* after the war (1946).

Sources: Cox *Crime Fighters* p. 153; *Radio Annual* 1946 p. 818; *Variety* October 9, 1940, p. 31

Hursley, Doris and Frank

Doris Hursley (September 29, 1898–May 5, 1984) was a practicing lawyer who decided to try writing for radio, giving up a spot on the Industrial Commission of Wisconsin to do so. Meanwhile, her eventual husband Frank Hursley (November 21, 1902–February 3, 1989) was an associate professor of English at the University of Wisconsin's Milwaukee campus who took a leave from his position to write for radio.

In the early 1940s the couple turned their full attention to creating radio fiction. Among their first known work are scripts for *Aunt Jenny's True Life Stories* and two serials, *Life Is What You Make It* (1941) and *Helpmate* (1942). During the war Doris and Frank scripted *American Women* (1942–1945) and *Service to the Front* (1944–1946) while immediately after the war they wrote for *Those Websters* (1946–1948) and *The Light of the World* (1946).

Little of their later radio work involved serials, the genre in which the Hursley's made their initial mark and would later find their lasting fame. Among their shows were *Sealtest Variety Theatre* (1948), *Prudential Show* (1948), *The Truitts* (1950–1951), *My Little Margie* (1952), *Cousin Willie* (1953), *That's Rich* (1954), and *Have Gun, Will Travel* (1959).

The Hursleys' biggest impact came in television where they wrote *Search for Tomorrow* for many years (ca. 1957–1964) and subsequently created and authored the long running *General Hospital* beginning in 1963. The family's personal life was not unlike the many serials they authored over the years. Both Frank and Doris were married with children when they met and the divorces that led to their eventual marriage led to decades of strained relationships.

Sources: Frank and Doris Hursley Papers; *Broadcasting* October 18, 1942, p. 16; *Radio Mirror* June 1946 p. 11–12; *Variety* October 28, 1942, p. 31, November 15, 1944, p. 26, October 6, 1948, p. 24; umich.edu.

Huston, Lou

Lou Huston started his radio career on California stations, the earliest known being Long Beach's KFOX. There he wrote *Small Town Hotel* (1937), *Hal Nichols and His School Kids* (ca. 1937), for which he is credited with writing over 1,000 episodes by 1937, and *Burning Questions* (1938). For a time in 1938 Huston worked as a gag writer for Jack Pearl. In 1941 Huston joined KMPC as continuity editor where he co-authored the station's version of *The Hermit's Cave* until late 1942 when he joined the Army. After the war Huston went on to pen stories for *The Whistler* (1946), *Suspense* (1949, 1957), and finally a long run on *Space Patrol* (1952–1955).

Huston was a steady writer for television from the late 1950s to late 1960s. While his work appeared in a variety of genres from *Science Fiction Theatre* (1955–1957) to *Highway Patrol* (1957–1959), he was most prolific in comedies including *The Addams Family* (1964–1965), *Gilligan's Island* (1965), and dozens of episodes of *Petticoat Junction* (1965–1966).

Sources: Bassior; *Broadcasting* February 10, 1941, p. 34, November 9, 1942, p. 40; *Radio Daily* May 19, 1937, p. 8, June 2, 1937, p. 4, January 14, 1938, p. 3, March 16, 1938, p. 4.

Ingram, Gail

Gail (Austrian) Ingram (July 3, 1924–April 13, 2007) was a freelance writer who worked for a time as assistant to her husband Harry Ingram (d. March 17, 1952), an NBC producer and director in the late 1940s. Among her early works were scripts for *Molle Mystery Theatre* and later in the decade she penned monthly stories for *The Big Story* (1947–1948) and *Tales of Fatima* (1949). Ingram also wrote a few episodes for *The Shadow* (1950–1951) and possibly *Casey, Crime Photographer* (1948) with her husband.

After Harry died suddenly of a heart attack at the age of 40, Gail continued to write for television through the 1950s and 1960s, most notably on *The Big Story* (1954–1957), *The Millionaire* (1958–1959), and *My Three Sons* (1963–1967). She eventually retired to San Diego to concentrate on raising a family.

Sources: Cox & Siegel; Grams *The Shadow*; *Variety* November 26, 1947, p. 31, January 12, 1949, p. 22; classictvhistory.wordpress.com.

Irving, Peter

Peter Irving is known to have been writing for radio as early as 1944 when he was named assistant radio director of the Office of Price Administration where he was responsible for writing, directing, and producing programs. Some of Irving's work included *Somerset Maugham Radio Theatre* (1946), *Squad Room* (1954), *True Detective Mysteries* (ca. 1957–1958, writer-producer-director), and *Exploring Tomorrow* (1958). Irving was still providing scripts for radio even after the commonly recognized end of the Golden Age, earning credit on *Theatre Five* in 1964. Irving dabbled in television, writing some stories for *For All Time* that may or may not have aired.

Sources: *The Film Daily* July 19, 1946, p. 3; *Radio-TV Mirror* December 1957 p. 52; *Variety* October 18, 1944, p. 30, July 31, 1946, p. 36.

Isaacs, Charlie

Canada-born Charlie Isaacs (September 17, 1914–December 13, 2002) began writing for radio indirectly in the 1930s; he claimed that jokes he submitted to Minneapolis-area newspapers were clipped and used by comedians broadcasting from New York. After getting some encouragement from **Fred Allen**, Isaacs took the bold step of relocating to New York without any job lined up. Despite meeting Allen and some agency men, nothing came through so Isaacs returned to Minnesota for a year before taking a try on the West Coast.

Some of Issacs' first gigs for radio were writing for *The Jack Haley Show* and *Al Pearce & His Gang*. As early as 1937 Issacs was tagged to script an air adaptation of the popular *Looney Tunes* cartoon series and soon after was hired to script for Edgar Bergen on *The Chase & Sanborn Hour* until 1938. By 1940 he was head of the writing staff for Radio Productions Inc. on features such as *Egad—the Gadsbys*.

In 1942 Isaacs was added to *The Ransom Sherman Show* on CBS and then the *Camel Caravan* before joining the Coast Guard toward the end of the year. During his time in the service Isaacs assisted **Jess Oppenheimer** in writing various programs for the government's war effort including *Command Performance*, *G.I. Journal*, and *Jubilee* in 1945. The post-war years were a busy time for Isaacs where he earned writing jobs on *Vox Pop* in 1945, *The Bob Burns Show*, *Radio's Biggest Show*, and *Sad Sack* in 1946, and *The Fabulous Doctor Tweedy* and Al Jolson's *Kraft Music Hall* in 1947. Before moving into television in the 1950s Isaacs was a member of the writing team for *The Martin and Lewis Show* ca. 1949 and is credited with co-writing the 1950 auditions for *The Rochester Show*.

Isaacs' most memorable assignments on the small screen were comedies, among them *The Jimmy Durante Show* (1952), *Hey, Jeannie!* (1956–1958), and *Alice* (1978–1981).

Other Radio: *The Rudy Vallee Show* (1941); *The Milton Berle Show* (1942); *The Ford Show* (1947); *Amos 'n' Andy*; *Baby Snooks Show*; *Johnny Mercer's Music Shop*; *Kraft Music Hall* with Bing Crosby; *Texaco Star Theater*.

Sources: Charles Isaacs Papers; Young; *Broadcasting* February 15, 1940, p. 71, February 23, 1942, p. 36, November 30, 1942, p. 33, April 12, 1943, p. 33; *Variety* November 17, 1937, p. 41, June 19, 1946, p. 26, October 2, 1946, p. 34, August 20, 1947, p. 24; *Los Angeles Times* obituary.

Jacobs, Morris

Morris Jacobs was on the writing staff of the Benton & Bowles agency until 1936 when he went to work for the Democratic National Committee's radio division. Subsequent years were spent penning serials for Blackett-Sample-Hummert (including *Young Widder Jones*) and patriotic scripts for the Radio Branch of the Bureau of Public Relations during World War II.

Sources: *Broadcasting* May 12, 1941, p. 22; *Variety* August 12, 1936, p. 44.

Jacobs, Seaman

A Broadway press agent before World War II, after his release from the service Seaman Jacobs

(February 25, 1912–April 8, 2008) spent several years writing scripts for radio comedies. Among his credits are writing gags for **Fred Allen** and Henry Morgan in addition to scripts for *The Johnny Morgan Show* (1946), *The Wynn Show* (1947), *The Jack Paar Show* (1947), and *The New Beulah Show* (1953).

Jacobs' best days came in television, however, where he wrote for various comedies from *The Ed Wynn Show* (1949–1950) to *The Love Boat* (1978–1985). In between were such classics as *Petticoat Junction, Diff'rent Strokes*, and *The Andy Griffith Show*. He contributed to dozens of television specials featuring the likes of Bob Hope and George Burns up until the early 1990s.

Sources: Seaman Jacobs Scripts; *Variety* July 24, 1946, p. 36, February 12, 1947, p. 26, October 8, 1947, p. 25; *Variety* obituary.

Jacoby, Coleman

Coleman Jacoby (April 16, 1915–October 20, 2010) started on the bottom rung of the entertainment ladder as a doorman and painter in a nightclub, and slowly started to write more and more gags for stage performers. In 1943 Jacoby had the opportunity to head to California to script for Bob Hope's show where he remained until joining **Fred Allen**'s staff in early 1944. Later that year Jacoby wrote for Sammy Kaye's *Tangee Varieties* until 1945, subsequently moving to *The Beatrice Kay Show* (1945–1946). At the end of the decade Jacoby signed to co-write Milton Berle's *The Texaco Star Theatre* (1948–1949).

After a few years in radio Jacoby successfully wrote for a number of television series, highlighted by three consecutive Emmys (1956–1958) for Best Comedy Writing while with *The Phil Silvers Show*. He was nominated for three additional Emmys between 1959 and 1971.

Film: New narration for dozens of old Mack Sennett silent films (1947).
Sources: *Variety* November 24, 1943, p. 2, March 1, 1944, p. 32, September 6, 1944, p. 30, December 8, 1948, p. 45; *New York Times* Obituary.

James, Ed

Ed James (June 5, 1908–March 6, 1995) wrote a number of forgotten motion pictures between 1938 and 1943 before doing freelance radio writing for several years. In 1949 James' show *Father Knows Best* premiered, running until 1953 on radio and until 1960 on television. James is also credited with writing for *The Phil Harris–Alice Faye Show* in 1953.

Source: *Los Angeles Times* obituary.

Jampel, Morton Carl

Carl Jampel started in radio on Michigan stations WSOO (Sault Ste. Marie, MI) as a production manager ca. 1941, followed by a stop at WFDF (Flint) as an announcer. He jumped to the network level in 1942 when he joined NBC's publicity department and within a year found himself writing promotional scripts. Jampel worked on the *Truth or Consequences* staff in 1943 and during the second half of the 1940s scripted a number of radio programs. The most popular was *The Adventures of Archie Andrews* (1946–1951) but others included *Detect and Collect* (1945), *Club Zero* (1948), and the *Slapsie Maxie Show* (1948). During the 1950s and 1960s Jampel directed and produced television programs and even opened his own production company.

Other Radio: *Your Three Wishes* (1947, audition); *Suzie* (1948, audition).
Sources: *Broadcasting* September 8, 1941, p. 19, August 23, 1943, p. 40; *Variety* July 15, 1942, p. 32, June 23, 1943, p. 45, June 20, 1945, p. 30, February 19, 1947, p. 24, March 24, 1948, p. 36, May 19, 1948, p. 38, August 4, 1948, p. 24.

Jessup, Richard

Richard Jessup (January 2, 1925–October 22, 1982) is known to have written some episodes of the *Tom Corbett, Space Cadet* series in 1952 that may have been adaptations of the scripts written for the television show that ran concurrently.

Source: solarguard.com.

Johansen, Al

Al Johansen was one of a number of writers who worked on scripts for *Duffy's Tavern* (ca. 1947).

Source: *Variety* April 2, 1947, p. 35.

Johnson, Doug

Doug Johnson was a Chicago-area writer for both radio and television in the late 1940s and 1950s. He is credited with *Lights Out!* and *A Life in Your Hands* (1952) on radio and the successful early serial *Hawkins Falls, Pop. 6200* on television (1951). He later joined the New York office of McCann Erickson as an advertising executive.

Source: *Chicago Tribune* August 3, 1960, p. 16.

Johnston, Johanna

Formerly Johanna DeWitt, Johnston took over scripting *David Harum* for her then-husband **John DeWitt** when he enlisted in the Naval Reserve in 1942. In 1944 Johnston was involved in preparing a daily serial based on Thornton Wilder's *Our Town* before joining the CBS writing staff in 1946. Her 1950s work included stints writing for *Let's Pretend* (1952–1954), *Autumn in New York* (1956), *CBS Radio Workshop* (1956), and the serial *The Second Mrs. Burton* (late 1950s).

Other Radio: *Counselor-at-Large* (1947, audition); *Sing It Again* (ca. 1948).

Sources: *Broadcasting* August 7, 1944, p. 52; *Variety* October 28, 1942, p. 34, July 24, 1946, p. 42, January 1, 1947, p. 26, March 10, 1948, p. 42.

Johnston, Joseph

A writer for the *New York Daily News* and then the Pathe News dialog department, Joseph Johnston earned a spot on the airwaves scripting *The American Radio Newsreel* (1939), one of radio's first syndicated news programs produced by Ayers-Prescott.

Sources: *Broadcasting* December 1, 1939, p. 57; *Variety* September 8, 1937, p. 6, November 29, 1939, p. 22.

Johnstone, Jack

Jack (born Earl Ransom) Johnstone (1906–November 16, 1991) was a busy producer and director of radio programs during radio's Golden Age but he earned some writing credits during the years as well. After studying abnormal psychology in college Johnstone jumped at the chance to work in radio in 1939. Some of the earlier shows on which he added writing duties to his directing responsibilities were *Johnny Presents* (1939), *Buck Rogers* (1939), and *The Adventures of Superman*. Johnstone's scripts have been preserved in dozens of episodes of *Yours Truly, Johnny Dollar* during dramatic radio's waning years, 1956–1962.

Book: *Who Knows?* (1942).

Sources: Wright "Produce It Again, Sam!"; *Motion Picture Daily* March 1, 1939, p. 7; *Radio and Television Mirror* October 1939 p. 50; deadreckoning1.wordpress.com;

Jones, Arthur

A little-known writer for the airwaves during the 1940s, Arthur Jones' most memorable program was *The King's Men* (1949), a summer replacement for the top-rated *Fibber McGee & Molly* featuring their singing quartet.

Sources: *Broadcasting* August 30, 1943, p. 44, July 18, 1949, p. 58.

Jones, Grover

Grover Jones (November 15, 1893–September 24, 1940) was a prolific screenwriter up until 1940 when he died at the age of 46. During his twenty years in motion pictures Jones wrote over 100 screenplays and numerous short stories in addition. Between 1937 and 1939 Jones scripted a handful of episodes of *Silver Theater* (1937–1939), a highbrow dramatic program. His radio plays were primarily air adaptations of his short stories.

Sources: *Motion Picture Daily* November 12, 1937, p. 18; *Variety* September 29, 1937, p. 29.

Jones, Venzuella

A graduate of Pittsburgh's Kings School of Dramatic Arts, Venzuella Jones acted, directed, and wrote wherever she could find work. On radio Jones authored two programs that aired for just a few months, *Muddy Waters* and *A Harlem Family* (both 1935).

Source: Ellett *Black Radio*.

Josefsberg, Milt

After working for a time as a Broadway press agent, Milt Josefsberg (June 29, 1911–December 14, 1987) went on to write for two of radio's biggest comedians at the height of radio's Golden Age. He spent at least five years with *The Bob Hope Show* (1938–1943) and more than a decade as a member of the writing team for *The Jack Benny Show* (1943–1955).

While Josefsberg will forever be linked to Benny's program, considered by many to be the best radio series of all time, he did write for a handful of other shows as well over the years. Among them were Cass Daley's *Bandwagon* broadcasts (1945) and *The Bill Goodwin Show* (1945). Josefsberg also served as an advisor to *The Jack Paar Show* on a rotating basis with Benny co-writers **Sam Perrin**, **George Balzer**, and **John Tackaberry**.

Josefsberg's television career is no less revered than his years in radio. Some of his earliest work in the medium was on *The Milton Berle Show* (1958–1959) and later included *The Jack Benny Program* (up until 1961), *The Lucy Show* and *Here's Lucy* (1964–1971), and *All in the Family* (1975–1979). In addition, he served as a consultant on early 1980s classics *Mork & Mindy*, *Laverne & Shirley*, and *Happy Days*.

Sources: *Variety* August 22, 1945, p. 40, December 12, 1945, p. 32; *Los Angeles Times* obituary; **Mel Shavelson** interview emmytvlegends.org.

Joyce, Betty

Betty Joyce was writing for WHOM in New York/New Jersey when she expressed interest in writing for George Trendle and WXYZ. After scripting for KDKA, WMBS (Uniontown, PA), and WHOM, in early 1943 Joyce submitted a sample script for Trendle's review. While he and **Fran Striker** at first considered Joyce on a trial basis, a sudden opening at the station allowed her the opportunity to step right in writing for WXYZ's program, including their big three, though the bulk of her scripts were for *Challenge of the Yukon* and *The Lone Ranger*. Joyce's work was used on both series well into the 1950s.

Source: Grams *The Green Hornet*.

Julian, Arthur

Arthur Julian (March 7, 1923–January 30, 1995) spent just a few short years learning the writing craft in radio on *Suspense* (1947) and most notably *Beulah* (1951–1954) before transitioning to a long career in television. Julian's small screen credits range from *The Red Skelton Hour* (1953–1954) to *Hogan's Heroes* (1965–1971) to *Amen* (1987–1990).

Sources: Grams *Suspense*; *Variety* November 5, 1947, p. 28.

Junkin, Harry W.

Harry Junkin (January 5, 1916–April 1, 1978) was a Canadian-born writer who began making a name for himself in dramatic radio just after the end of World War II. Junking wrote for numerous series, among them *Sunday Serenade* (1946), *Popular Playhouse* (1947), *Radio City Playhouse* (1948–1950, that he also directed and hosted at times), *Top Secret* (1950), *Mr. I. A. Moto* (1951), *Big Town* (1951), *The Chase* (1952), and *Mr. District Attorney* (1953). Junkin began writing teleplays as early as 1949 and during his career provided scripts to *Lux Video Theatre* (1951–1953), *Wagon Train* (1958), and *The Saint* (1963–1969).

Sources: *Variety* February 20, 1946, p. 26, January 1, 1947, p. 30, April 30, 1949, p. 34.

Jurist, Edward

After studying theater at the University of Michigan and graduating in the late 1930s, Edward Jurist (April 8, 1916–March 12, 1993) soon embarked on a radio and television writing career that lasted more than four decades, proving himself to be one of the most capable comedy writers in the business. Jurist spent over a decade as one of the chief authors for *The Aldrich Family* (1940–1952) but also provided stories and jokes to a variety of genre programs such as *The Columbia Workshop* (1941), *Manhattan at Midnight* (1941–1943), *The Kate Smith Show* (1943), *Mr. Keen, Tracer of Lost Persons* (1944–1945), *Words at War* (1944–1945), *The Sportsmen's Club* (1945), *The Great Gildersleeve* (1946), *Our Miss Brooks* (1948), and *The Jonathan Winters Show* (1956–1957).

Jurist's time penning for television was no less impressive and included time spent on *Leave It to Beaver* (1957–1959), *Bewitched* (1964–1971), *M*A*S*H* (1971–1973), and *Diff'rent Strokes* (1979–1985).

Sources: Edward Jurist Papers; *Variety* October 6, 1943, p. 26; *New York Times* obituary.

Kane, Frank

Brooklyn native Frank Kane (July 19, 1912–November 29, 1968) left law school to support his wife and newborn child as a writer for various New York City newspapers. After World War II Kane began writing freelance scripts for radio among other jobs. Some of the most popular series on which Kane's work appeared were *Gang Busters, The Fat Man, Nick Carter, Master Detective,* and *The Shadow* (1945–1949). His stories were also used on *You Have to Go Out* (1947), *Barrie Craig, Confidential Investigator* (1951), *Counter Spy, Casey, Crime Photographer, Mr. Keen, Tracer of Lost Persons* (1945), and the *Lawless Twenties*. Sources have claimed that he created both *Call the Police* (1947) and *Jim Rogers, Claims Agent* (1946).

During the 1950s Kane wrote at least two dozen episodes of television's *Mike Hammer*. Before his death in 1968 Kane published dozens of novels, many in the private eye genre, and many more for detective magazines.

Sources: Cox *Mr. Keen;* Cox & Siegel; Grams *Shadow; Variety* May 16, 1945, p. 39, July 31, 1946, p. 26, June 11, 1947, p. 38; thrillingdetective.com.

Kane, Henry

Henry Kane (1918–1988) was a lawyer by training but authored dozens of private investigator novels and short stories over a quarter-century from approximately 1947 to 1972. He is credited with just one radio series, *Crime and Peter Chambers* (1954) for which he was creator, producer, and writer. The program was based on a character who he'd originally used in many novels. Kane also wrote a handful of motion picture screenplays and some television episodes of various drama and private eye shows.

Sources: *Broadcasting* June 9, 1958, p. 18; *Harrison's Reports* November 1, 1958, p. 174; thrillingdetective.com.

Kane, Joseph

Joseph Kane (January 23, 1899–September 22, 2002) was a renowned writer of reference books and trivia publications that numbered several dozen. An endless font of facts and curious tidbits, Kane had his own program, *Famous First Facts* (1938–1939), and another show in 1944, the title for which has not yet been uncovered. He subsequently provided much of the quiz material for *Break the Bank* (ca. 1948) and other shows later on television.

Sources: *Variety* August 3, 1938, p. 23, October 4, 1944, p. 22, February 26, 1947, p. 34, November 10, 1948, p. 28.

Kanter, Hal

A native of Savannah, GA, Hal Kanter (December 18, 1918–November 6, 2011) moved to California when he was 17 and soon after arriving in Hollywood procured himself a very short-lived job writing jokes for Howard Snyder and **Hugh Wedlock, Jr.,** who were writing both Eddie Cantor's radio program and *The Camel College* every week. Kanter got his first official radio writing job in 1936 as a junior writer at $50 a week for Jack Haley's *Log Cabin Jamboree.* This job, too, was extremely short-lived.

Ghost writing provided a reasonable income for a newcomer like Kanter and over the next two years he relocated between the coasts a couple times for new writing jobs, including providing jokes for *The Joe Penner Show,* material for W. C. Fields on *The Lucky Strike Hit Parade,* and entire scripts with **Eddie Davis** for the vaudeville duo Olsen and Johnson who were then appearing on Kate Smith's radio program. Olsen and Johnson liked Kanter's jokes and hired him at $50 per week to write jokes for their Broadway revue during its 1939 run. Dismissed from that gig, Kanter turned to earning small money writing scripts for *Lincoln Highway, Star Spangled Theater,* and more *Grand Central Station.*

In 1941 Kanter was inducted into the United States Army and a few months later married Doris Prouder on September 5, 1941. After basic training he was assigned to the Public Relations office in Lowery Field, CO, where he wrote regular pieces for the PR office, local newspapers, a comic strip, humor column, and 45 episodes of a KOA series called *Private Hal Kanter of Lowry Field,* sometimes known as *The Lowry Field Theatre of the Air.* Kanter appeared on air as well, hosting a disc jockey series and two weekly series, *Canteen Quiz* and *The Bookworm* on KOA. Eventually he was transferred to the

Pacific where he helped establish WXLE on a tiny rock in the middle of the ocean to counter the propaganda of Tokyo Rose. The station was moved to Guam as WXLI.

After the war Kanter got a job writing on **Goodman Ace**'s team for *The Danny Kaye Show*, along with **Arthur Alsberg**, **Herbert Baker**, and **Arnold Auerbach**, until the program's end in 1946. He quickly moved on to Don Ameche's *Drene Time* that fall, but it was cancelled at year's end. Kanter quickly moved to writing for Ozzie Nelson's show but didn't care for the style so got hired onto *Amos 'n' Andy*. He joined the Radio Writers Guild and was later elected president of the West Coast branch. In 1947 Kanter started writing for Bing Crosby's *Kraft Music Hall*, a job that lasted through the end of the decade. His reputation was such that he worked on multiple radio series; during the summer of 1947 Kanter wrote scripts for *The Jack Paar Show*, Jack Benny's summer replacement. Kanter's demands to remain with Paar after it was picked up for a longer run were rejected, however, and they parted ways.

Besides *The Kraft Music Hall*, one of Kanter's last radio jobs was writing for *Beulah* (1947–1949), a fifteen-minute daily show starring Hattie McDaniel at the time. Alternating writing a week's worth of episodes opposite **Arthur Phillips**, Kanter in turn hired **Howard Leeds** and **Arthur Julian** to assist him with the scripts.

In 1948 Kanter took the job as head writer for Ed Wynn's new CBS television show. However, with television still considered a risky venture, he continued his work with Bing Crosby's radio series. While Wynn's show did not last too long, it signaled the beginning of a half-century-long television career for Kanter. Some highlights of Kanter's television work included writing for *The George Gobel Show* (1954–1956), *Valentine's Day* (1964–1965), *Julia* (1968–1971), and *The Jimmy Stewart Show* (1971–1972). He was highly regarded within the Hollywood community, regularly working on the Academy Awards annual broadcast from the 1980s into the 2000s, near the end of his life. Kanter earned three Emmy Awards over the length of his career, in 1955, 1991, and 1992.

Kanter also had his hand in a number of screenplays, most notably the next-to-last Bob Hope and Bing Crosby Road film, *Road to Bali* (1952).

Other Radio: *Fun in Swing Time*; *The Borden Show* (1946); *Red Cross Show* (1945); *Star Spangled Theater* (1940, 1941).

Television: *All in the Family* (1971–1979).

Sources: Hal Kanter Papers; Buxton & Owens p. 6, 28, 94; Corliss p. 45; Kanter; Ohmart *Don Ameche* p. 128–129; Paar p. 78; Young; *Broadcasting* September 15, 1941, p. 32, October 13, 1941, p. 55; *Variety* November 20, 1946, p. 40, July 7, 1948, p. 20, July 14, 1948; Interview with Chuck Schaden October 23, 1999.

Keene, Day

Born in Chicago as Gunnar Hjerstedt, Day Keene (March 28, 1904–January 9, 1969) was a prolific author who penned several dozen novels and short stories, primarily in the private eye and mystery genres during the 1940s and 1950s. On radio Keen's scripts appeared on *Kitty Keene, Incorporated* (ca. 1937), and reportedly on *Little Orphan Annie*. A few of Keen's works were used on film and television.

Sources: Harmon *Radio Mystery*; *Radio Daily* August 31, 1937, p. 6; thrillingdetective.com.

Kelley, Welbourn

Writer Welbourn (sometimes Welbourne) Kelley is a little-documented author whose earliest known radio work was with Transradio Press before he joined the NBC press department in 1936, transferring within a year to continuity work. During this time he scripted numerous news broadcasts such as *The New York Times Goes to Press* (1937), *Ninety Years of News* (1938), and review shows such as *Headlines of 1936*, *The Ten Biggest News Stories of 1939*, and *Headlines of 1940*.

By 1940 Kelley was also penning dramatic fare and even had one of his own programs (*Linda Dale*, co-created with Elizabeth Coe Todd) on the air. His other credits during the time included *The ABC of NBC* (1937), *Radio Guild on the Air* (1940), *Chamber Music Society of Lower Basin Street* (1941–1942), and *Words at War* (1945). After World War II Kelley went to work for Radio Free Munich in Munich for a year before returning to New York where he continued freelance radio writing. Kelley's later work was used on *The MGM Theatre of the Air* (1949), *If Fight We Must* (1951), *King's Row* (1951–1952), and *The Big Show* (1952).

Sources: NBC Records; *Billboard* October 22, 1949, p. 9; *Broadcasting* April 15, 1936, p. 44, February 1, 1954, p. 76; *Radio Daily* January 14, 1937, p. 14; *Variety* November 6, 1940, p. 30; martingrams.blogspot.

Kelsey, John (Jack)

Jack Kelsey was a CBS staff writer in the mid–1940s and his scripts appeared on such shows as *My Best Girls* (1944–1945), *Destiny Trails* (1945, for NBC) that included 39-chapter adaptations of Fenimore Cooper's novels *The Deerslayer* and *The Last of the Mohicans*, *Joe Powers of Oakville* (1946), *The Whistler* (1946–1951), and *The First Nighter Program* (ca. 1947).

Other Radio: *Just Plain Bill*.

Sources: Cox *Soap Operas*; *Variety* November 28, 1945, p. 30, September 11, 1946, p. 33, October 8, 1947, p. 24.

Kent, Mona

Born Ramona Hunt in Iowa, Mona Kent (1909–1990) had a healthy career writing radio and television soap operas, most notably *Portia Faces Life* from 1940 to 1951 and then until 1954 when the series transitioned to television. Evidence suggests Kent got her broadcasting start scripting some soap operas entitled *Roads to Adventure* and *The Barrett Outfit* over Denver stations. In 1943 while *Portia* was running strong on NBC, Kent created *Woman of America*, another serial that had a short broadcast life.

After *Portia* left the television airwaves Kent premiered *Woman with a Past*, a CBS serial that lasted just a few months. Some of her other television work was used on *Captain Video and His Video Rangers* (1949) and numerous other one-shot productions.

Other Radio: *The Carters of Elm Street* (1939, serial); *On Guard America* (1941, for the Treasury Defense Savings Program).

Novels: *Mirror, Mirror on the Wall* (1949).

Sources: Mona Kent Papers; *Broadcasting* December 8, 1941, p. 51; *Variety* October 2, 1940, p. 26, June 9, 1943, p. 23.

Kent, Priscilla

After doing publicity writing for Constance Hope Associates and serving on the editorial staff of the *New York Herald-Tribune*, Priscilla Kent joined NBC's script division in 1942. One of her first series was a religious program, *We Believe*. In 1943 Kent was assigned to *The March of Mercy* and *The Parker Family* and in 1944 she contributed to *Words at War* and *Now Is the Time*. Kent was also a primary writer for *Home Is What You Make It* (1944–1945) and some of her later scripts appeared on *Those Websters* (1945) and *Cavalcade of America* (1945–1948). Kent is also identified as one of the writers for the serial *The Second Mrs. Burton* during its time on the air.

Theater: *Strange Bedfellows* (1944); *The Star and the Sword* (1946).

Sources: NBC Records; Cox *Soap Operas*; *Billboard* February 17, 1945, p. 4; *Broadcasting* March 30, 1942, p. 39 March 6, 1944, p. 62; *Variety* June 3, 1942, p. 25, May 5, 1943, p. 36, April 2, 1947, p. 35.

Kibbee, Roland

Roland Kibbee (February 15, 1914–August 5, 1984) started his show business career writing for radio in Los Angeles, most notably for *The Grouch Club* during the 1930s. Around 1940 he joined the writing staff of the *Fred Allen Show* with his partner **Nat Hiken** and is also credited with writing for Groucho Marx and Fanny Brice before moving into a successful career in motion pictures and television.

After a decade writing screenplays including the Marx Brothers' *A Night in Casablanca*, Kibbee wrote regularly for television until the early 1980s on series such as *The Bob Newhart Show* (1961–1962), *It Takes a Thief* (1968–1970) which he created, and *Barney Miller* (1977–1981). Kibbee's writing career was capped by two Emmy awards in 1974 and 1982, and three additional nominations between 1962 and 1977.

Sources: Everitt; Havig p. 82; *Broadcasting* October 1, 1940, p. 54; *New York Times* obituary August 10, 1984.

Kinoy, Ernest

Ernest Kinoy (April 1, 1925–November 10, 2014) was a prolific writer in the post–World War II years of radio drama and widely remembered by modern old-time radio fans because so much of his work survives via show recordings.

Kinoy's university studies at Columbia were put on hold when he left to serve in the Army during the war. He was captured and became a prisoner of war, surviving time at the Stalag IX-B camp and later Berga, a camp for slave labor. Upon returning to the United States after his service Kinoy returned to his studies and Columbia University and resumed his involvement with its radio station. Soon after, Kinoy began writing radio scripts by 1946 and by 1948 he had been hired as a staff writer for NBC.

Kinoy likely wrote thousands of scripts during his years with NBC and while it is impossible to chronicle every one, several series for which he wrote several stories are documented. They include *NBC University Theater* (1948–1951) and its sequel *The New Theater* (1951), *Dimension X* (1950–1951), *Hollywood Love Story* (1951–1953), *NBC Presents: Short Story* (1951–1952), *My Secret Story* (1952–1954), *Best Plays* (1952), *The Big Story* (1952), *The Marriage* (1953–1954), *NBC Star Playhouse* (1953–1954), *Rocky Fortune* (1953–1954), *Woman in Love* (1953–1955), *Dr. Sixgun* (1954–1955), *X Minus One* (1955–1958), and *Five-Star Theatre* (1956–1958).

During his decades as a professional scriptwriter Kinoy earned a reputation as a fine dramatic writer and was awarded two Emmys for his work on *The Defenders* (1964) and the miniseries *Roots* (1977). He was nominated three additional times between 1977 and 1982.

Other Radio: *New World A'Coming* (1948); *Radio City Playhouse* (1948); *Eternal Light* (1949); *Production Five* (1955–1956).

Theater: *Golden Rainbow*; *It's About Time*; *Jacob and the Indians*.

Sources: Ernest Kinoy Papers; *Variety* September 25, 1946, p. 44; *New York Herald Tribune* June 23, 1945, p. 15; Archive of American Television interview.

Klee, Lawrence

Lawrence Klee was a busy writer during the late 1930s, through the 1940s and into the early 1950s, authoring a number of series produced by the Hummerts. Before the war Klee scripted *Hearts in Harmony* (1941) and *Chaplain Jim* (ca. 1943–1944), and then during the war he volunteered his writing talent to the Victory Players of the American Theatre Wing, an organization of professional performers that wrote and acted in patriotic material. Immediately following World War II Klee created and wrote *The Clock* (1946–1948), an anthology series of suspense stories. This was followed by stints on *The Fat Man* (1946–1950), a Dashiell Hammett creation, and *Mr. Keen, Tracer of Lost Persons* (1947–1950, 1954). Two more of Klee's creations reached the airwaves, *Man Against Crime* (1949–1954) and *The Chase* (1952–53), an anthology program. Klee's *The Clock* was adapted for television in 1949 as was his *Man Against Crime* that aired from 1952 until 1954 and again briefly in 1956.

Other Radio: *Mary Noble, Backstage Wife*; *Front Page Farrell*; *Mr. & Mrs. North*; *Mr. Chameleon*; *Valiant Lady*.

Sources: Lawrence Klee Papers; Cox *Mr. Keen*; *Variety* January 26, 1944, p. 35, July 25, 1945, p. 10, November 10, 1946, p. 26, August 27, 1947, p. 24; thrillingdetective.com.

Klein, Larry

Larry Klein was a premier writer for radio comedy programs after World War II and then for decades into the television era. Highlights of his radio work include *The Pepsodent Show* with Bob Hope (1946), *Village Store* with Eve Arden (1947), Eddie Cantor's *Pabst Blue Ribbon Show* (1948), *The Burns & Allen Show* (1950), *Sara's Private Caper* (1950 with Ken Starr), and *The Bob Hope Show* again (1951–1952). Klein's television credits include *The Milton Berle Show* (1958–1959), *The Carol Burnett Show* (1969–1970), and *The Tonight Show* (1977–1988). He earned an Emmy for his work on *The Flip Wilson Show* in 1971.

Other Radio: *The Edgar Bergen Show*; *The Martin and Lewis Show*.

Sources: The Larry Klein Collection; *Billboard* August 2, 1947, p. 13; *Broadcasting* June 26, 1950, p. 44.

Klinker, Zeno

Born in the Los Angeles area around 1900, Zeno Klinker tried various means of making a living before finding his way into radio. He performed with a number of bands during the 1920s before the Great Depression caused the demise of many musical careers. In the early 1930s he wrote some successful gag Christmas cards and then a series of joke books, the former of which continued to provide royalties for many years.

Edgar Bergen met Klinker at a film show where Klinker was lecturing. He introduced himself and invited Klinker to join his writing team. Thereafter he became a writer for *The Edgar Bergen & Charlie McCarthy Show* in 1937 and scripted Bergen's jokes for much of the rest of their careers, including nearly two decades on radio. He claimed to write about 500 jokes per week, with less than 100 used on a broadcast. Klinker provided the material to Bergen who would then read through and select what he considered the best that Klinker then crafted into a program. Bergen's Effie Klinker dummy was reportedly named after the writer.

Sources: Erickson p. 127; *Broadcasting* October 10, 1955, p. 16; *Variety* September 17, 1941, p. 9; *Los Angeles Times* July 28, 1946, p. C1, 2, November 11, 1971, p. E1.

Knight, Raymond

Raymond Knight (February 12, 1899–February 12, 1953) was a wildly successful writer, actor, and director for NBC early in the network's history in the late 1920s. Originally from Salem, MA, Knight attended Boston University where he studied law and later passed the bar. Not content to settle into a quiet life as a lawyer, Knight returned to Harvard and studied acting and writing and pursued further studies at Yale under George Pierce Baker. Knight's writing prowess was recognized in 1927 when he received the Drama League's prize for best one-act play of the year. He subsequently directed an experimental theater group in Boston and then moved to New York where he wrote the book for a musical revue called *See America First* in 1928.

During an illness in 1928 Knight decided maybe he'd try a career in radio though he didn't have any professional experience in the field. He talked himself into a job with NBC where he went to work writing commercials and continuity. He wrote for *Triadors* (1928) and also did some directing on shows such as *Empire Builders* and *Real Folks*. Other series on which Knight worked were *Embarrassing Moments in History*, *The Gold Spot Pals*, and *Hello, Mars!* When a programmer approached Knight to come up with some sort of comedy show to fill empty airtime on the company's Blue network, Knight created *The Cuckoo Hour* that debuted in 1930.

Knight wrote the show and performed the main voices as well. His wit gained an appreciative audience, something he attributed to his actual lack of vaudeville background. So many of his competitors from the vaudeville circuits used jokes and routines that had been circulating for years while his material was more fresh.

The Cuckoo Hour ran through the mid–1930s and Knight created a number of other programs during this time including *The Hickock Program* (1930), *Making the Movies* (1932), *Raising Junior* (1930–1932, an early sitcom that introduced Walter Tetley), *Wheatenaville Sketches* (1932–1934), and *Billy Bachelor Sketches* (1934–1935). Later in 1932 Knight was named president of Beacon Syndicate, a company that marketed scripts to stations and agencies.

In 1935 Knight revived his own hour-long program called *Ray Knight's Cuckoo Clock* but it was short-lived and he soon turned to writing plays, among them *At Home Abroad*. He briefly dabbled in film, releasing two one-reelers, *Life's Little Problems* and *Cuckoo Newsreel*, in 1937. Knight eventually made his way back into radio in the 1940s working as a director and executive at NBC though he managed to do some writing including *A House in the Country* (1941–1942), a serial he created.

From 1943–1944 Knight served as the Blue Network's production manager before joining Young & Rubicam as a producer for Ed Wynn's 1944 series *Happy Island*. At the time of his death Knight was reportedly a writer for the Bob and Ray program.

Sources: *Broadcasting* June 15, 1932, p. 23, September 15, 1932, p. 14, June 1, 1933, p. 26, May 1, 1935, p. 36, August 14, 1944, p. 53; *Movie Makers* November 1937 p. 569; *Radio Mirror* October 34 p. 61, September 1935 p. 55; *Television Digest* February 14, 1953, p. 8; *What's on the Air?* December 1929 p. 40, May 1930 p. 18, June 1930 p. 6; *Variety* January 23, 1934, p. 36.

Knight, Ruth Adams

Ruth Adams Knight (October 5, 1894–1974) studied writing at Toledo University around

1915 and when the first World War claimed many writers from the *Toledo Times*, she joined the paper in 1918. After a decade of working as a journalist in Toledo, Knight's writing ambitions took her to New York in 1929 where she migrated into radio in the early 1930s.

Knight's earliest known radio scripts were for a series called *Copy* (1932) set against a newspaper backdrop. Among the series for which she wrote in the late 1930s and early 1940s were *Cavalcade of America* (1937–1939), *Aunt Jenny's Real Life Stories* (1938), *Death Valley Days* (1938–1941), *Dr. Christian* (1938–1942), *On Guard America* (1941) for the Treasury Department Savings Program, *Theatre of Today* (1941–1943), *Brave Tomorrow* (1943–1944 NBC serial), and *Those We Love* (1944), another serial.

Knight also published some non-fiction works including *Stand by for the Ladies: The Distaff Side of Radio Announcing* and *Lady Editor: Careers for Women in Publishing* (1941, with Muriel Fuller and Marjorie Shuler). Additionally, she wrote fiction novels and numerous short stories that were published in *Collier's*, *Cosmopolitan*, and similar magazines.

Sources: Ruth Adams Knight Papers; *Broadcasting* November 1, 1932, p. 31, December 8, 1941, p. 51; *Radio Annual* 1941 p. 211; *Variety* September 20, 1939, p. 34, November 17, 1943, p. 37, June 28 1944 p. 32.

Knight, Vick

Originally a continuity editor for Cleveland's WGAR then WBK in the early 1930s writing programs such as *I.O.U.*, Vick (sometimes Vic) Knight (August 5, 1908–May 17, 1984) joined CBS in 1934 in a production role for a year before opening his own production office. Knight wrote "Cartwheel," a script rerun on CBS a number of times, including on the network's *The Columbia Workshop* in 1936 as well as some guest dialog for *The Rudy Vallee Show* (1937). However, much of his career was spent as a director and producer for the likes of Eddie Cantor, **Fred Allen** (for whom Knight was credited as a member of the writing) and Milton Berle.

During World War II Knight first did work for the War Department before taking a job as radio manger for first the Biow Agency and then Foote, Cone & Belding. He did return to scripting after World War II on programs including *Jonathan Trimble, Esq.* (1946) as well as a USO promotional series (1948). Knight had a musical streak as well and wrote or co-wrote a number of songs during his career, the most famous of which was "I Love Coffee, I Love Tea" (1943).

Sources: *Broadcasting* April 26, 194 p. 134; *Radio Digest* May 1932, p. 40; *Radio Daily* March 9, 1937, p. 4, March 25, 1942, p. 7; *Variety* July 12, 1932, p. 42, November 20, 1934, p. 36; November 13, 1935, p. 38, August 5, 1936, p. 34, October 1, 1941, p. 47, July 17, 1946, p. 36.

Koch, Howard

Howard Koch (December 12, 1901–August 17, 1995) is most famous for his screenplays, for which he received an Academy Award nomination in 1942 (*Sergeant York*) and an Oscar in 1944 as co-writer of *Casablanca*. After authoring several plays in the late 1920s and 1930s, Koch left his mark on radio, however, as scripter for *Mercury Theater of the Air*, Orson Welles' series. There he wrote possibly the most infamous radio broadcast of all time, 1938's "The War of the Worlds," based on the novel by H. G. Wells. Though Koch went on to write well over a dozen screenplays and numerous television episodes, *Casablanca* and "War of the Worlds" were his legacy, the inspiration for many telecasts, books, and short stories he produced over a long career.

Sources: *New York Times* obituary August 18, 1995; bard.edu.

Kogan, David

David Kogan (December 22, 1916–2009) was a highly regarded author of radio mysteries along with partner **Robert Arthur**. In over a decade of collaboration the pair earned two Edgar Awards (1950, 1953) and two additional nominations (1949, 1951) presented by the Mystery Writers of America, for their radio dramas.

Kogan's first broadcasts were WOR's *Dark Destiny* (1942–1943) soon followed by their long-running *The Mysterious Traveler* (1943–1952), a show still popular with old-time radio enthusiasts, on which Kogan also worked as producer and director. Through the 1940s Kogan built his reputation with additional scripting on shows that ranged from straight-laced mystery to tales that delved into the weird and supernatural.

Among Kogan's known credits are *Nick Carter, Master Detective*, *Men at Sea* (1944), *Strange Dr. Weird* (1944–1945), *The Shadow* (1944), *The Road Ahead* (1945), *The Sealed Book* (1945), the musical-mystery *A Voice in the Night* (1946), and *Murder by Experts* (1949–1950).

Sources: *Variety* August 26, 1942, p. 36, December 8, 1943, p. 30, August 2, 1944, p. 28, May 9, 1945, p. 26, May 15, 1946, p. 34; theedgars.com.

Kraft, Hy

Hyman Kraft (1899–1975), a playwright in the 1920s and 1930s with some screenplay credits during the 1930s and 1940s, most notably for Lena Horne's and Cab Calloway's *Stormy Weather* (1943), is remembered among radio historians for one series. From 1948 until it left the air in 1953, Kraft was on the writing team of *Life With Luigi* along with **Arthur Stander** and creator **Cy Howard**.

Source: *Variety* September 29, 1948, p. 47.

Kramer, Milton J.

Milton Kramer's documented radio work dates from the late 1940s when he scripted for *Famous Jury Trials* (1945–1947), *Attorney for the Defense* (1946), and *Casey, Crime Photographer* (1947). He is also credited with authoring *Counterspy* and *Nick Carter, Master Detective* during their runs. On television Kramer's work appeared on *The Chevrolet Tele-Theatre* (1949) and *Plainclothesman* (1951).

Sources: Cox *Crime Fighters*; *Billboard* July 7, 1951, p. 6; *Variety* June 12, 1946, p. 28.

Kronman, Harry

Harry Kronman (June 22, 1901–June 10, 1979) was a go-to writer for director **William Bacher** and Kronman wrote countless scripts for Bacher over many years during the 1930s and 1940s. Kronman's earliest documented work was *The Maxwell House Show* that he scripted with Bob Andrews circa 1937. Soon after, he moved to *Texaco Star Theater* (1938–1939) while also writing for *Big Town* (1939) and *The Kate Smith Hour* (1939). Kronman's early 1940s credits included *Hollywood Premier* (ca. 1941), *Shirley Temple Time* (1941, with **Jess Oppenhiemer**), and *Junior Miss* (1942).

In 1943 Kronman started authoring scripts for *The Screen Guild Theater*, an assignment that lasted a decade until 1953. During that time he also wrote *The Dick Haymes Show* (1946–1947) and *Hollywood Soundstage* (1951–1952) that he also directed. After radio Kronman had a lengthy career in television until the early 1970s and wrote for a number of popular programs including *The Rifleman* (1959–1960), *The Untouchables* (1960–1963), and *Gunsmoke* (1965–1973).

Other Radio: Louella Parsons' material for *Hollywood Hotel*.

Sources: Screen Guild Players Recordings Collection; *Broadcasting* October 1, 1938, p. 60, November 1, 1939, p. 24 March 10, 1941, p. 10, April 14, 1941, p. 39, November 10, 1941, p. 34; *Radio Mirror* October 1939 p. 4; *Variety* November 24, 1937, p. 26, April 29, 1942, p. 34, September 18, 1946, p. 20.

Krum, Fayette

During the 1920s Fayette Krum (January 13, 1903–February 18, 1952) worked as a reporter for *The Chicago Daily News* and *The Chicago Herald-Examiner*, which is where she may have met her future husband James W. Mulroy, a 1925 Pulitzer Prize winner. In the early 1930s Krum began to get more regular work in radio where she eventually became the head writer of *Girl Alone* (1935–1941), a daily serial that she wrote for six years. In 1939 Krum was on the writing team of *1001 Wives*, a sustaining show on NBC-Blue. After *Girl Alone* left the air in 1941 Krum worked as a freelancer for two years before taking a scripting job in 1943 with CBS. She is known to have authored at least one other show, the serial *The High Places*, for a short time in 1944 before joining the Compton Advertising Agency in 1945.

Sources: *Broadcasting* August 1, 1935, p. 30, May 15, 1939, p. 32, July 10, 1944, p. 44, November 5, 1945, p. 54; *Variety* October 11, 1944, p. 27; *Chicago Tribune* February 20 1952 p. 6F.

Kurtzman, Samuel

In the late 1930s Samuel Kurtzman (December 11, 1910–January 14, 1998) started providing gags for Eddie Cantor's radio show and in 1939 was hired to *The Bob Hope Show* staff. Kurtzman, a Russian immigrant, was a dentist by training and evidence suggests that by 1940 he had had enough of writing jokes professionally and returned to dentistry. His son, Joel Kurtzman, was a prominent American economist.

Sources: *Broadcasting* January 15, 1939, p. 48; *Variety* December 1, 1937, p. 35, September 11, 1940.

Lachman, Morton

Morton Lachman (March 20, 1918–March 17, 2009, sometimes spelled Lachmann) started in radio on a whim after studying journalism at the University of Washington and serving in the army during World War II. In 1947 Lachman noticed a call for scripts by Hope's agent and submitted some work. This led to a 27-year professional relationship that spanned radio and television. His other radio credits include *The Martin and Lewis Show* (1949, 1951) and *Mr. and Mrs. Blandings* (1951), based on the film *Mr. Blandings Builds His Dream House*.

Lachman was highly successful in television as well, first as a writer and then as a producer. He authored several episodes of *All in the Family* (1976–1979) and then was one of the primary scripters of *Gimme a Break!* that he co-created and produced. Lachman earned two Emmy awards during his illustrious career, in 1974 and 1978, neither for writing, however.

Sources: *Broadcasting* January 19, 1953, p. 15; *Sunday Times* April 12, 2009, p. 12; emmys.com.

Ladd, Hank

Primarily recognized as part of a highly-regarded comedy team with Bert Wheeler, Hank Ladd (December 12, 1908–June 9, 1982) is also recognized for some radio script writing. One of his earliest efforts was *The Judy Canova Show* (ca. 1937), to which he returned years later in 1945.

Sources: *Broadcasting* October 29, 1945, p. 64; *Radio Daily* March 26, 1937, p. 4.

Langworthy, Yolande (Yolanda)

Yolande Langworthy (real name Frances Reade), a graduate of Toronto's Haverdill Musical Conservatory, was a writer for some of CBS' early children's shows including *Mountainville True Life Sketches*, *Adventures of Helen and Mary*, and *Land o' Make-Believe* (all ca. 1930), the latter transitioning into *Let's Pretend* in the early 1930s. She was also the scripter for *Arabesque* (1929–1930), modern retellings of stories from *Arabian Nights* and one of the network's most popular series. The show's popularity was used to attract audiences to a particular timeslot before being moved to establish another timeslot on CBS' broadcast schedule. In 1937 Langworthy left CBS to write exclusively for Radio Events, Inc.

Book: *Poems from Arabesque* (1930).

Sources: *Motion Picture Daily* September 24, 1937, p. 30; *Radio Digest* June 1930 p. 108, September 1930 p. 102; *What's on the Air?* February 1930 p. 16, May 1930 p. 32, June 1930s p. 16.

Lansworth, Lew

Lew Lansworth was a writer and producer for Eddie Cantor and Jimmy Durante in the early 1930s before opening his own radio consulting business in 1935. The effort was short-lived as he joined San Francisco's KFRC later that year as a continuity writer and producer. As a writer for the Lord & Thomas agency in 1940, Lansworth created and authored the mystery quiz program *Whodunit?* Lansworth's other radio credits include authoring *The Main Line* (1943) and *Murder Will Out* (1945–1946).

Other Radio: *The Saint* (1947).

Sources: Barer p. 248; *Broadcasting* May 1, 1935, p. 30, December 15, 1935, p. 40; *Variety* October 30, 1940, p. 40, November 8, 1943, p. 67.

Lauck, Chester

Chester Lauck (February 9, 1902–February 21, 1980) with collaborator **Norris Goff** brought to the airwaves one of radio's most popular comedy programs, *Lum 'n' Abner*. A native of Alleene, AR, Lauck attended The University of Arkansas before pursuing further studies at the Academy of Fine Arts in Chicago (from which he did not graduate). His formal education belied the country-bumpkin characterizations of his fictional Lum Edwards.

As young adults Lauck and Goff earned a local reputation for their blackface act, still popular at the time. When invited to perform over Hot Springs, AR, station KTHS for a flood relief benefit, they switched their routine at the last minute because of the glut of other blackface Amos and Andy impersonators lined up to perform. On the spot they renamed themselves Lum and Abner and subsequently became a staple of old-time radio.

Lum and Abner were called back to the station a few times as listener interest grew and in July 1931, the duo decided to move to Chicago, then a center for live dramatic radio. They auditioned for NBC, negotiated for $350 after an initial offer of $150, and quickly found a sponsor, Quaker Oats. Unbeknownst to all involved, this deal was just the beginning of a program that would air over two decades. Lauck was responsible for scripting the daily quarter-hour shows with Goff until 1941 when other writers were gradually brought on board.

Source: Hall.

Lauferty, Lillian

Lillian Lauferty, daughter of a prominent family in Boston, was a newspaper writer and short story writer in the early 1920s whose work was serialized in such columns as "Advice to the Lovelorn" and "When a Girl Marries." Her work often appeared under the name Beatrice Fairfax, a penname created and also used years before by Marie Manning on her pioneering love advice column at the turn of the century. Manning resumed writing the column after the Great Depression wiped out much of her savings. In the 1930s Lauferty began authoring for radio and in 1936 her serial *Big Sister* debuted and in 1938 her second program, *Your Family and Mine*, made its premier.

Sources: Cox *Radio Soap Operas*; *The American Hebrew* January 13, 1922, p. 267; *The Moving Picture World* July 31, 1920, p. 612; *The Motion Picture Magazine* April 1924 p. 111; *The Pittsburgh Press* November 29, 1945, p. 2; *Radio Daily* March 24, 1938, p. 1; *Variety* October 7, 1936, p. 43, June 30, 1937, p. 38.

Laurents, Arthur

Arthur Laurents (July 14, 1917–May 5, 2011) started his writing career in radio before earning a place as one of Broadway's premier authors and directors. As a student at Cornell University Laurents recalled writing and producing numerous radio plays, but this experience did not lead to professional work after he graduated. In 1939 he signed up for a class at Columbia taught by CBS producer **Bill Robson** where he wrote a script, "Now Playing Tomorrow," that Robson subsequently submitted for broadcast on CBS. This led to regular work for the network on series including *Cavalcade of America*, *Lux Radio Theatre*, *Man Behind the Gun*, *Mr. District Attorney*, and *Thin Man*. During Laurents' time in the Army (approximately 1941–1945) Laurents authored *Assignment Home* (1944–1945), a highly regarded program focusing on issues involving returning veterans.

In late 1945 Laurents' first Broadway play, *Home of the Brave*, debuted and he began to develop a career in the legitimate theater. He wrote the book for classic musicals *West Side Story* (1957) and *Gypsy* (1959) though his Tony Award came in 1968 for *Hallelujah, Baby!* Laurents had two further Tony nominations (1975 and 2008) and one additional win (1984) as a director. Though not as prominent in motion pictures, he nevertheless received two Oscar nominations for Best Picture and Best Original Screenplay for *Turning Point*.

Other Radio: *This Is Your FBI* (ca. 1945).
Sources: Laurents; *Radio Mirror* June 1945 p. 49; *Variety* December 13, 1944, p. 34, June 20, 1945, p. 25.

Laven, Paul

Paul Laven (d. May 1, 1950) was a gag writer on Bob Hope's radio program from at least 1944 until his death at age 43 in 1950.

Sources: *Broadcasting* September 11, 1944, p. 60, May 8, 1950, p. 46.

Lawrence, Jerome (Jerry)

Jerome Lawrence (July 14, 1915–February 29, 2004) was one half of a writing team (with partner **Robert E. Lee**) that authored hundreds of radio scripts through the 1940s before turning to the theatre in the 1950s. After graduating from Ohio State University and UCLA in the late 1930s Lawrence worked for various small newspapers then started writing radio plays for KMPC in Los Angeles in 1938.

Among Lawrence's earliest known works were scripts for *Saturday Morning Party* (1939) and a variety of musical broadcasts and remotes. Between 1939 and 1941 more of his scripts began appearing over the CBS network on programs including *Man About Hollywood* (1940), *Meet Mr. Music* (1940), *Martha Mears* (1940–1941), and *Skipper Storm* (1940–1941). At this time Lawrence also began dabbling in more dramatic fare including an episode of *The Columbia Workshop* (1942) and *They Live Forever* (1942), co-written with **Howard Teichmann**. Other credits before he began scripting for The Armed Forces Radio Service (AFRS) are Lady Esther's *Album of the Week* (1942), *A Date with Judy* (1942), and *Personal Album* (1942–1943).

Lawrence's writing began to focus on war-related matters in earnest in 1942, approximately the same time when he started teaming up with Robert E. Lee. Between 1942 and 1945 Lawrence co-wrote numerous scripts with Lee for the AFRS and they authored *Mail Call, Song Sheet, The World We're Fighting For,* and *Yarns for Yanks* as well as dozens of special event scripts. Other war-time scripts were used on *Free World Theatre* (1943), a show for which Lawrence was recruited by **Arch Oboler** to co-script with Budd Schulberg, and *Everything for the Boys* (1944).

Early in the post-war era Lawrence was assigned to *Request Performance* (1945–1946), a version of *Command Performance* broadcast for American listeners. In 1946 Lawrence and Lee brought *Favorite Story* (1946–1949) to the air, dramatizations of stories from classic literature. Lawrence continued to return to his scripting roots with musical programs such as *Songs by Sinatra* (1947) and the next year's *Call for Music* (1948) with Dinah Shore, Johnny Mercer, and Harry James.

By the end of the decade Lawrence and Lee stayed busy with more dramatic stories presented regularly on *The Railroad Hour* (1948–1954), a musical drama anthology series, and *The Hallmark Playhouse* (later *The Hallmark Hall of Fame*, 1950–1953). Still, he demonstrated diversity by scripting for *Presenting Charles Boyer* (1950) and the **Don Quinn**-created *Halls of Ivy* (1950–1952), a Ronald Colman–led comedy set on the campus of a small college.

Lawrence made a foray into television in the early 1950s writing for *The Unexpected* (1951–1952), *Favorite Story* (1952–1954), and *West Point* (1956–1957), but his post-radio reputation is built on decades as a playwright with co-writer Lee of dozens of produced plays and musicals. The musical *Mame*, an adaptation of their play *Auntie Mamie*, for which they wrote the book was nominated for several Tony Awards including best musical.

Other Radio: *Columbia String Trio* (1939); *Under Western Skies* (1939); *Jean O'Neill Show* (1939–1940); *Stars Over Hollywood* (1943); *Nightcap Yarns* (1951).

Sources: Jerome Lawrence-Robert E. Lee Collection; Lawrence and Lee papers; *Broadcasting* May 25, 1942, p. 37, June 29, 1942, p. 24; *Variety* June 3, 1942, p. 26.

Lawrence, Jim

Jim Lawrence was one of many writers that contributed scripts to the popular juvenile programs produced by Detroit's WXYZ. Between 1949 and 1950 Lawrence wrote two stories for *The Green Hornet* and many for *Challenge of the Yukon*.

Source: Grams *The Green Hornet*.

Lay, John Hunter

John Lay was the writer for *Famous Jury Trials* before leaving the job to work in public relations for the Army Air Corps. in 1942.

Film: *Slightly Honorable* (1939).

Sources: *Variety* April 15, 1942, p. 28, May 27, 1942, p. 27.

Lazarus, Erna

A busy screenwriter in an era when female writers were few and far between, Erna Lazarus (June 16, 1903–February 19, 2006) left her mark not only in motion pictures but radio and television as well. Before America's entry into World War II she scripted for Lippe & Lazarus Productions ca. 1941 and soon after was authoring *Mayor of the Town*. She is also credited with the quiz show for servicemen, *Stop or Go* (1944–1945).

Motion Pictures: *Atlantic Flight* (1937); *Blonde from Brooklyn* (1945); *Secrets of Beauty* (1951).
Television: *Racket Squad* (1952); *The Donna Reed Show* (1963–1966).
Source: *The Radio Annual* 1941 p. 661.

Leaf, Margaret

Writing with partner **Helen Walpole**, Margaret Leaf impressed NBC editor Lewis Titterton with a script about Mark Twain. Their prospective script eventually became *Adventures in Reading*, one of many network educational series that appeared on the air in the 1930s and 1940s.
Sources: *Broadcasting* January 1, 1940, p. 36; *NBC Presents* May 1939 p. 7.

Lear, Norman

Norman Lear (b. July 27, 1922) briefly worked in radio before moving on to an illustrious career in television. His notable radio credit was co-scripting *The Martin and Lewis Show* on radio and television with **Ed Simmons**, for which they were named gag writers of the year in 1952 by the National Association of Gag Writers. Lear's writing television writing credits stretch back to *The Colgate Comedy Hour* in 1950 but are highlighted by *Sanford and Son*, *All in the Family*, and *The Jeffersons*, all of which he created and developed.
Source: *Broadcasting* February 18 1952 p. 92.

Lee, Leonard

Leonard Lee (September 4, 1903–August 24, 1964) was a busy studio screenwriter in the 1930s and early 1940s before serving in the armed forces during World War II. He returned to motion pictures after the war into the early 1950s when he moved to television, writing dozens of teleplays through the 1950s. In the late 1940s Lee, who had authored some Sherlock Holmes stories for the big screen, scripted Holmes' radio program for a short time.
Source: audio-classics.com.

Lee, Manfred

Manfred Lee (January 11, 1905–April 3, 1971), born Manford Lepofsky but registered as Emanuel Benjamin Lepofsky on his birth certificate) was one half of the writing team—with cousin **Frederic Dannay**—that created the famous sleuth Ellery Queen, whose fame for solving mysteries may be second only to the legendary Sherlock Holmes.

Before Queen's creation Lee earned a living writing promotional material for the Pathé studio. Created while the cousins shared a meal in 1928 to talk about submitting a story to a writing contest, the character was a hit in almost every entertainment medium of the era; books, motion pictures, radio, and eventually television.

After appearing in books, stories, and films for a decade, Lee and Dannay started to develop Queen's program around 1938. They quickly learned to craft radio scripts, most notably episodes of *The Shadow* from 1938 to 1939 before creating the weekly mysteries for a reported $350 per week. The producers of the radio program insisted on an unusual format in which the mystery would be paused at its climax to allow guests to try and offer the correct solution. This concept met with mixed success depending on the guests but found adequate audiences to ensure an intermittent run for ten years, between 1939 and 1948 across all the major networks.

Lee stayed with *The Adventures of Ellery Queen* during its entire run on radio, pounding out scripts with Tom Everitt who replaced Dannay for a few months upon Dannay's departure in 1944. Dannay's permanent replacement, however, was **Anthony Boucher**, himself a well-known mystery author and reviewer.

Ellery Queen's popularity was such that during the first year of *The Adventures of Ellery Queen* Dannay and Lee participated in *Author, Author* as their fictional character. Using listener-submitted ideas, Dannay and Lee would compete with a panel of guests to concoct interesting stories from the chosen premises.

Lee continued to co-write Queen novels with Dannay up until the early 1960s when he stepped aside to be replaced with various writers. His health declined and Lee died of a heart attack on April 2, 1971.
Sources: Grams *The Shadow*; Nevins & Grams.

Lee, Robert E. (Bob)

Robert Edwin Lee (October 15, 1918–July 8, 1994, not to be confused with the Young & Rubicam producer of the same name) was one half of a prolific writing team with **Jerome Lawrence** that left its mark in both radio and the theater. One of Lee's earliest known air works was *Flashback*, a WGAR (Cleveland) show reenacting historical moments.

Lee met and began writing with Lawrence in 1942 and some of their earliest work was programming for the Armed Forces Radio Service including *Mail Call, Personal Album, Song Sheet, The World We're Fighting For*, and *Yarns for Yanks*. During the war years Lee wrote a number of scripts for military training and entertaining purposes.

After the end of the war Lee and Lawrence immediately scripted *Request Performance* (1945–1946), a civilian edition of *Command Performance*. They soon started producing some dramatic scripts for *Favorite Story* (1946–1949), *The Railroad Hour* (1948–1954), *Young Love* (1949–1950), and *Hallmark Playhouse* (1950–1953) in addition to their traditional musical fare (*The Frank Sinatra Show*, 1947). *The Halls of Ivy*, a series created by *Fibber McGee & Molly's* **Don Quinn**, represented a turn toward light comedy writing by Lee and Lawrence.

By the 1950s Lee had turned his focus to writing plays and musicals for the theater with partner Lawrence. Together they turned out more than three dozen works, the most famous being *Mame* (1966), a musical adaptation of their play *Auntie Mame*, that received several Tony Award nominations.

Other Radio: *Ceiling Unlimited* (1946); *Escape* (1953); *Mr. and Mrs. Blandings* (1950); *The Saint; Suspense* (1947).

Sources: Jerome Lawrence—Robert E. Lee Collection; Lawrence and Lee Papers; *Broadcasting* October 15, 1940, p. 76.

Leeds, Howard

Howard Leeds started a life in show business as a child actor in a few films during the 1930s. His writing career began in the late 1940s scripting for *Suspense* in 1947 and soon after that the comedy *Beulah* (1948–1954), a spin-off from *Fibber McGee & Molly*. In the early 1950s Leeds found more work in television where he went on to write over four decades. During his long career Leeds wrote for *The Red Skelton Hour* (1953–1954), *My Three Sons* (1962–1963), and *Diff'rent Strokes* (1979–1984). He was also responsible for developing or creating the hit 1980s series *Silver Spoons* and *The Facts of Life*.

Sources: Hattie and Sam McDaniel Papers; *Variety* November 5, 1947, p. 28; interview with Connie Martinson.

Leeson, David

David Leeson (June 14, 1930–February 25, 1971) appears to have had a short career writing for radio, his only known credit being *Young Dr. Malone* that he was authoring in 1960 when the program left the air during the final days of the radio's Golden Age of drama.

Source: Cox "Young Doctor Malone."

Lefferts, George

George Lefferts (b. 1921) edited various school newspapers as a youth and studied English at the University of Michigan before being called away to war. After four years in the armed services Lefferts returned home without any imminent job prospects and chose to find work writing since, as a married man, he didn't have time to pursue his first love, medicine. He was soon hired by NBC where he had the opportunity to hone his craft under the guidance of **Ernest Kinoy**.

Lefferts' earliest writing credits are *Lucky Stars* (1946), *Believe It Or Not* (1947–1948), *NBC University Theater* (1948–1951), and *Radio City Playhouse* (1949) while his 1950s credits include *Dimension X* (1950–1951), *NBC Presents: Short Story* (1951–1952), *Best Plays* (1952), and *Dr. Sixgun* (1954–1955). Lefferts was called on to script *Rocky Fortune* (1953–1954), a dramatic show featuring Frank Sinatra, after the decline of Sinatra's 1940s singing popularity. As radio drama faded from the airwaves in the 1950s Lefferts migrated to television but still provided scripts for the class science-fiction series *X Minus One* (1955–1958) and the anthology program *NBC Radio Theater* (1956).

Lefferts' earliest television work may have been for *Lights Out!*, originally a radio horror show. He wrote episodes for numerous series and tele-films over a writing and producing career that lasted into the early 1980s. He earned two Emmy Awards (1969 and 1975) with three additional nominations.

Other Radio: *The All-American Sports Show* (1953); *Inheritance* (1954).

Sources: *Variety* July 17, 1946, p. 26; airlockalpha.com; nj.com.

Leslie, Aleen

Aleen Leslie (born Aleen Wetstein, February 5, 1908–February 2, 2010) studied play writing at Ohio State University but was unable to complete her studies due to the financial hardships of the Depression. Leslie found work as a columnist for most of the 1930s and used her connections to work herself into a screenwriting job by the end of the decade. She earned over a dozen screen credits by the 1950s.

Leslie's most enduring creation was *A Date With Judy*, one of the era's several adolescent-centered shows. Originally intended as a showcase for her friend Helen Mack, Mack ended up producing instead of performing in the series for a time. The series started initially as a summer replacement for three years (1941, 1942, and 1943) before finally earning full-time status from 1943 to 1950. *Judy* later spawned a movie and television series.

Novels: *The Scent of Roses* (1963); *The Windfall* (1970).

Film: Four Henry Aldrich motion pictures (1943–1944).

Sources: Aleen Leslie Papers; *Broadcasting* June 7, 1943, p. 40; *Los Angeles Times* obituary February 9, 2010.

Leslie, Leonard

Leonard Leslie, an obscure writer from radio's Golden Age, is credited with authoring the radio version of *Bulldog Drummond*, a crime-solver who appeared in various media.

Source: Cox *Radio Crime Fighters*.

Leslie, Phil

Phil Leslie's (March 11, 1909–September 23, 1988) introduction to the world of show business started inauspiciously as a bookkeeper for the St. Louis Amusement Co. in the early 1930s and then as an assistant manager at a local theater. He began to write on the side and by 1939 earned the opportunity to work on the West Coast as a gag writer for Al Pearce. When the job dissolved a few months later he spent the next two years working in a Lockheed plant and then looking for writing work. He managed to sell some material to *Major Hoople* (1942–1943), a sitcom based on Gene Ahern's *Our Boarding House*, that helped catch the eye of **Don Quinn** who invited him to become his new assistant co-writing *Fibber McGee & Molly*. A masterful joke writer, Quinn needed Leslie to focus on developing a story for each week's episode.

Leslie eventually worked up to writing half of each week's show while Quinn wrote the other half. Their partnership clicked and together they scripted one of radio's premier comedies until 1951 when Quinn left and **Keith Fowler** took his place. Leslie's partners would change in subsequent years but he stayed with Fibber and Molly until the series finally came to an end in 1956. He did not follow Jim and Marian Jordan when they continued their characters in short sketches on NBC's *Monitor* program in subsequent years.

Aside from *Fibber McGee & Molly* Leslie also scripted *The Charlotte Greenwood Show*, a summer replacement series in 1944 for Bob Hope's program. During the 1945 summer season when Al Pearce went on summer hiatus Leslie was assigned to write *The Marlin Hurt and Beulah Show*, featuring the white actor Marlin Hurt as Fibber McGee and Molly's black female domestic servant Beulah. When Hurt died suddenly of a heart attack less than one year into the series' run, Beulah's program left the air in 1946. It returned one year later with another white man, Bob Corley, taking the lead role but without Leslie as the writer. Yet another summer series authored by Leslie was *The King's Men*.

Leslie provided scripts for numerous television comedies, primarily during the 1960s, even though he later claimed it was not a medium he enjoyed as much as radio. Among his small-screen credits are *Leave It to Beaver* (1957–

1958), *Hazel* (1962–1965), and *The Addams Family* (1964–1966).

Other Radio: *Johnny Mercer's Music Shop; Kraft Music Theatre; Roy Rogers Show* (with Don Quinn).

Sources: *The Film Daily* December 12, 1934, p. 5; *Variety* March 22, 1939, p. 61, June 21, 1944, p. 34, May 9, 1945, p. 29; Interview with Chuck Schaden, 1973.

Lesser, Julian "Bud"

Julian Lesser (January 18, 1915–March 22, 2005) was born into show business, the son of producer Sol Lesser. After a premier education at Stanford and Harvard, Lesser returned to California to start his career working in publicity for his father in 1934 before moving up to assistant director and production executive later in the decade.

After the end of World War II Lesser formed his own film production company and eventually produced a number of low-budget pictures for various companies. Lesser's radio work dates to the early 1950s and it's not clear how he got involved with broadcasting. His most well-known scripting credit was the transcribed series *Tarzan* (1950–1951), a character with which Lesser was familiar from earlier motion picture responsibilities. After some production work in television during the 1950s Lesser explored other opportunities including real estate investments, though he always maintained his Hollywood connections.

Other Radio: *Stars Over Hollywood* (1953); *Big Jim McClain* (1953, audition).

Source: *The Film Daily* April 15, 1948, p. 5.

Levinson, Leonard L.

Leonard Levinson (1904–1974) wrote for a variety of comedy programs during a career that was in full swing by the late 1930s when he was signed by the William Esty Co. for a Camel cigarette program. Joe Penner's *Tip Top Show* (1939) is one of the earliest known programs for which Levinson scripted. This led to an assistant position with **Don Quinn** on *Fibber McGee & Molly* in 1940 and the next year he left to author *The Great Gildersleeve* (1941–1942), a spin-off of *Fibber McGee*.

Levinson stayed one year with *Gildersleeve* and resigned in 1942 to take a position with the Office of War Information. After his service Levinson spent some time on *The Al Jolson–Monty Woolley Show* (1943), *The Jack Carson Show* (1943–1947), *The Stu Erwin Show* (1945), and *Family Theatre* (1947).

In the late 1940s Levinson began branching out into other areas including stage productions and motion pictures. He co-founded Impossible Pictures, a producer of cartoons, and wrote the book for *Mr. Strauss Goes to Boston* (1945). Levinson returned briefly to *Fibber McGee & Molly* in the 1950s.

Other Radio: *Just Outside Hollywood* (1948, audition).

Sources: Stumpf & Ohmart; *Broadcasting* September 15, 1939, p. 44, February 1, 1940, p. 54, August 3, 1942, p. 39, May 24, 1943, p. 33; *Radio Daily* August 3, 1937, p. 6; *New York Times* obituary February 2, 1974.

Levitt, Gene

Eugene Levitt (May 28, 1920–November 15, 1999), a graduate of the University of Wyoming, started as a journalist before World War II and entered dramatic radio after war's end. Though Levitt is mostly remembered for writing, directing, and producing in television from the 1950s to 1970s, his radio career lasted a few years and included work for a number of West Coast programs that are still enjoyed by many old-time radio enthusiasts. Among them are *The Whistler* (1947), *The Adventures of Philip Marlowe* (1948–1950), *The Line-Up* (1950–1951), and *Rocky Jordan* (1951). Among his long list of television credits the most prominent is the creation of *Fantasy Island* (1977–1984).

Source: *New York Times* obituary November 24, 1999.

Levy, Parke

Parke Levy (April 19, 1908, or July 15, 1908–March 8, 1993) attempted college as a young man and took advantage of writing opportunities at Temple University, writing for *The Owl* (that he claimed to found) and authoring some stage musicals for the theater department. Levy finally decided he was too busy cranking out pulp magazine stories so he decided to give up on earning a degree.

Comedy, however, was where Levy found his calling, initially providing jokes for early radio comedian sensation Jack Pearl who he met after a performance in Philadelphia. After being cut in 1933 for budgetary reasons, Pearl continued to use his work periodically. By 1934 Levy had found a position on the writing staff of Joe Penner's broadcast as well as scripting various motion picture shorts such as *Rah! Rah! Rhythm* for Fox-Educational (1936). Levy moved again in 1937 to the series of another popular comedian of the era, Ben Bernie, and added Ed Wynn's broadcasts to his writing load for the next couple years. With **Alan Lipscott**, Levy's long-time co-writer, Levy also began scripting regularly for Lew Lehr in 1938.

Levy's time with *Duffy's Tavern* around 1942 represented a break from his work for gag-oriented shows to a more story-oriented series. His run on Duffy's was followed with work on *The Abbott & Costello Show* that he claimed only lasted a couple weeks due to creative differences, though he is credited on the show from 1946 to 1948. Parke's subsequent writing for *My Friend Irma* (1947–1953) and *December Bride* (1952–1953) was much more substantial.

Outside of radio Levy authored a half-dozen screenplays, some based on his hit radio show *My Friend Irma*. He also scripted for a few television shows from the mid–1950s to mid–1960s including his radio creation *December Bride* (1954–1959). Tired of creative strife involving his television work, Levy retired in the mid–1960s having obtained adequate financial security.

Theater: *Right This Way* (1938); *Three After Three* (1939); *Johnny on a Spot* (1942).
Other Radio: *Professor and Mrs. O'Reilly* (1949 audition with **Cy Howard**).
Sources: Young; *Radio Annual* 1940 p. 700; *Radio Daily* December 10, 1937, p. 2, February 7, 1938, p. 10, December 19, 1949, p. 8; *Radio Mirror* June 1934 p. 68; Variety February 21, 1933, p. 62, November 18, 1936, p. 12, March 18, 1942, p. 34; *New York Times* obituary March 13, 1993.

Lewerth, Margaret

Margaret Lewerth worked for New York station's WMCA and WABC in the mid-to-late 1930s in various capacities, including director of Phil Cook's *Morning Almanac* program on WABC (1937) as well as hosting her own show.

Around 1937 Lewerth was hired as a CBS scriptwriter and was soon assigned to *Americans at Work* (1938–1940). Lewerth scripted a variety of programs on CBS through the 1940s including *Cavalcade of America* (1940, 1942), *Gay 90s*, *Story of Bess Johnson*, *Eyes and Ears of the Air Force*, and *Hour of Charm* (all ca. 1941–1942). She had two different stretches authoring *Great Moments of Music* (1942 and 1944) and also contributed to *The Columbia Workshop* (1938, 1946, 1949), the serial *Helpmate* (1941–1944), and *Highways in Melody* (1946). Lewerth had at least two television credits in the 1950s and 1960s.

Sources: *Broadcasting* January 1, 1940, p. 36; *Radio Daily* June 16, 1937, p. 5, September 15, 1937, p. 2; *Variety* October 20, 1937, p. 42, June 18, 1941, p. 30, November 25, 1942, p. 88, February 27, 1946, p. 30.

Lewi, Jack

Little is known about Jack Lewi, but he was active in radio at least in the early 1940s. A continuity writer for The Joseph Katz Company ca. 1940, both series on which he scripted were musical programs including Frank Parker's *Squib Show* (1942) and *Calling America*, a short-lived 1943 series that focused on human interest stories of America's armed forces.

Sources: *Broadcasting* June 7, 1943, p. 44; *The Radio Annual* 1940 p. 219; *Variety* November 18, 1942, p. 34.

Lewin, Al (Albert)

Albert Lewin (July 29, 1916–April 23, 1996), not to be confused with the contemporary film director of the same name, started his comedy career doing cartoons for various magazines including *Colliers*. His first writing assignment for radio was providing gag's for CBS's *Billy House's Wrigley Laughliner* in 1938. Other pre-war radio projects were *Avalon Time* and *Musical Cookbook* (both 1938) and *Voice from Nowhere* (1939). After serving about six months in European duty during World War II, Lewin was moved to the Armed Forces Radio Service where he scripted comedy material for various comedians.

Upon returning to civilian life Lewin contributed to many more comedy shows through the 1940s such as *Tommy Riggs and Betty Lou*

(1942), a summer replacement for *Burns & Allen*, *Kraft Music Hall* (1942), *The Ransom Sherman Show* (1942), *The Chase & Sanborn Program* (1942–1943), and *Blood and Fire* (1943–1944).

Lewin was even more prolific in television, writing regularly from the mid–1950s until the early 1980s. Some notable television credits include *The Eddie Cantor Show* (1955), *My Favorite Martian* (1964–1966), *The Odd Couple* (1970–1972), and *Diff'rent Strokes* (1978–1983).

Other Radio: *The Eddie Cantor Show*; *Scattergood Baines*.

Source: Albert Lewin Papers.

Lewis, Al

Al Lewis (October 25, 1912–February 3, 2002) started his performing arts career as an actor but found success only after developing his writing and comedic style on programs such as **Fred Allen**'s *Texaco Star Theatre* (ca. 1942), *Only Yesterday* (1943), *The Camel Program* (1944), *Command Performance* (1944–1945), *The Danny Kaye Show* (1945–1946), and *Sweeney and March* (1946–1948). At this time Lewis created the enduring *Our Miss Brooks* (1948–1957), the story of a high school teaching staff that proved just as successful for many years on television as on radio in the 1950s and was even adapted into a 1956 motion picture.

Other Radio: *G.I. Journal*; *Jubilee*; *Mail Call*; *Philco Radio Time*; *Request Performance*.

Source: Al Lewis Radio and Television Scripts.

Lewis, Milton

Milton Lewis was a busy writer in the late 1940s, most notably on a radio adaptation of Dashiell Hammett's *Thin Man* mystery, *The Adventures of the Thin Man* (1945–1948), and Himan Brown's thriller program *Inner Sanctum* (1945–1951). Lewis took over scripting the serial *This Is Nora Drake* (1948) from frequent collaborator **Julian Funt** and is also credited with authoring *Murder by Experts* (1950).

Theater: *The Dancer* (1946, with Julian Funt).

Sources: *Life* October 23, 1944, p. 110; *Variety* December 3, 1947, p. 32, July 21, 1948, p. 31.

Lewis, Mort

Mort Lewis was an early radio gag writer who managed to evolve with the medium and stay relevant as a writer into at least the late 1940s. His writing is documented as early as 1933 for Willie and Eugene Howard sketches on *The Studebaker Show* and the following year (1934) for sketches used on *The Paul Whiteman Show*. Lewis scripted spots for Frank Fay's appearances on *The Rudy Vallee Show* (1936) and, that same year, spots for *Pipe Smoking Time*. In 1936 Lewis started a professional association with Pick Malone and Pat Padgett, a blackface minstrel pair, and wrote their material until 1938 when he decided to pursue some other opportunities.

Lewis explored other writing outlets, signing with Educational in 1936 to write shorts for one year and in the fall of 1937 signing to author sketches for the *Ziegfeld Follies* theater show. For a short time his radio material was heard only overseas, used by Ben Lyon and Bebe Daniels on their European radio show in 1938.

By 1939 Lewis returned to network radio and subsequently wrote a number of programs that demonstrated his proficiency beyond the gags and patter for which he was previously renowned. His series from this era included *If I Had the Chance* (1939), *Behind the Mike* (1940–1942), *Celebrity Theatre* (1942), *Nothing but the Truth*, later *This Is the Truth* (1942), and *Horror Inc.* (1943).

Pick and Pat convinced Lewis to return as their gag writer around 1942 and he stayed with them for several years, even as dialect humor faded in popularity, while also scripting Paul Whiteman's *Radio Hall of Fame* (1944), Billie Burke's *Carton of Cheer* (1945), *Jonathan Thimble, Esq.* (1946), *Truth or Consequences* (ca. 1948), *Topical Times* (1948), and *Stroke of Fate* (1953).

Other Radio: Material for Burns & Allen, Ben Bernie, Ed Wynn; *Little Orvie with Skippy* or *Tomorrow the World* (audition, 1943).

Sources: *Broadcasting* September 1, 1939, p. 70, January 25, 1943, p. 25; *Radio Daily* August 27, 1937, p. 3; *Radio Mirror* April 1936 p. 90, November 1938 p. 64; *Variety* October 3, 1933, p. 41, May 1, 1934, p. 36, January 13, 1937, p. 44, April 1, 1942, p. 30, April 18, 1945, p. 34, April 17, 1946, p. 34, April 7, 1948, p. 24.

Libbott, Robert

Little is currently known of writer Robert Libbott but he was a steady West Coast author for at least a decade from the mid–1940s to mid–1950s. His work appeared on *The Whistler* (1944–1946), *The City* (1947), *The Unexpected* (1947–1948), *Rocky Jordan* (1948), *The Man Called X* (1950–1951), *Hollywood Star Playhouse* (1950–1953), and *Hallmark Hall of Fame* (1954–1955).

Source: RadioGoldIndex.com.

Lipscott, Alan

Alan Lipscott (born Abe Lipschutz, July 9, 1894–November 20, 1961) entered show business as a gag writer in vaudeville and then radio, frequently teaming with **Parke Levy** by the late 1930s. Lipscott was writing for Ed Wynn ca. 1937 and Lew Lehr's broadcasts for the next three years (1938–1940). At the turn of the decade Lipscott authored Ben Bernie's radio material (ca. 1939) as well as a number of theater productions. Lipscott's comedy matured with the medium as demonstrated by his work on Gary Moore's *Camel Caravan* and Ed Gardner's *Duffy's Tavern* (both ca. 1943). The highlight of Lipscott's radio career came writing *The Life of Riley* (1944–1951), a popular program that eventually moved to television.

With his jump to television via *The Life of Riley*, Lipscott left radio behind to successfully script for numerous small screen programs right up to the time of his death. Among the shows were *Willy* (1954–1955), *The People's Choice* (1955–1957), and *Bachelor Father* (1959–1961).

Theater: *Three After Three* (1939, with Levy); *Man in Dress Clothes* (1939, with Levy); *Off the Record* (1940 with Levy); *Zanities of 1943* (1942); *Johnny on a Spot* (1942).

Sources: *The Radio Annual* 1940 p. 700; *Variety* January 11, 1939, p. 27, November 22, 1939, p. 50, March 10, 1943, p. 28.

Liss, Joseph

Joseph Liss was a script writer and editor for much of the 1940s, first for the federal government and then as a freelancer. His earliest work was for *The Columbia Workshop* (1939, 1942, 1946) but then beginning around 1941 as a member of The Library of Congress Radio Project with Alan Lomax and **Archibald MacLeish**. During this time he contributed to both *Report to the Nation* and *Human Adventure*. After war broke out Liss served with the script division of the Office of War Information (ca. 1943) and from there to the Office of Inter-American Affairs until 1946. During this time he worked on the scripts for *The Doctor Fights* (1944–1945).

After 1946 Liss left the government sector to earn a living doing freelance writing and editing. One of his first jobs was co-writing *Fighting Senator* on CBS (1946). Later he scripted for *Eternal Light* (1945, 1947), *CBS Is There* (1947–1948), and *You Are There* (1948–1950). Liss wrote various dramatic television scripts during 1950s and 1960s.

Sources: Segal; *The Radio Annual* 1941 p. 973, 1943 p. 119; *Variety* November 19, 1941, p. 1, July 29, 1942, p. 27, March 28, 1945, p. 32, June 20, 1945, p. 25, July 25, 1945, p. 36, April 10, 1946, p. 41, July 31, 1946, p. 26.

Little, Herbert, Jr.

Herbert Little, Jr., was a prolific radio author throughout the 1940s, primarily with partner **David Victor**. He got his foot in the door of network radio with *Her Honor, Nancy James*, a serial that ran from 1938 to 1939. Over the next three years Little scripted a number of shows with Victor including *Your Happy Birthday, Wheatana Playhouse* (1940–1942), and at least three other series in 1941, *Hilltop House, Danger Is My Business*, and *My Man Godfrey*. In 1941 they also filled in on *The O'Neills* while the regular author was ill and eventually took over the job full time in 1942.

The next few years were marked by steady work both with comedy and mystery formats. Little's scripts appeared on *Cohen the Detective* (1943), *Alias the Deacon* (1945, audition), and *The Mary Small Show, Hollywood Mystery Time*, and *Matinee Theatre* (all 1945). Between 1945 and 1947 the duo wrote *Joanie's Tea Room* (featuring Joan Davis) while also scripting *The Mel Blanc Show* (1946). Little's longest writing tenure was on the hard-boiled detective program *Let George Do It* (1948–1952) with some side work on *Adventure, Inc.* (1948).

After radio Little found considerable success scripting television Western shows throughout the 1950s. His work was used on *Gunsmoke* (1956), *Rawhide* (1959), and *The Rifleman* (1958–1960) among others.
Television: *Jackson and Jill* (1949, with Victor).
Sources: Tucker *Joan Davis*; *Variety* January 25, 1939, p. 34, November 20, 1940, p. 25, January 1, 1941, p. 29, April 23, 1941, p. 24, October 29, 1941, p. 38, September 1, 1943, p. 34, June 6, 1945, p. 30, 36, June 20, 1945, p. 35, July 30, 1947, p. 36.

Lowther, George

George Lowther (April 9, 1913–April 28, 1975) was a versatile talent in the radio business, starting as a NBC pageboy and eventually becoming production manager for the network's electrical transcription by 1937. Within a year Lowther started writing for *Dick Tracy* and *Terry and the Pirates* and in 1939 his scripts were used on *The Shadow*. By the early 1940s Lowther was back with NBC directing various programs but also narrating and scripting *Superman*, taking over directing duties as well around 1942. Lowther became so involved with the show that he left NBC to go to work for Superman, Inc. in 1943. While continuing as writer, narrator, and director of *Superman*, Lowther also took over producing *Hop Harrigan* and *Highway Patrol* on a freelance basis.

Though Lowther earned at least two more writing credits during the era's Golden Age on *The Tom Mix Ralston Straight Shooters* (ca. 1944–1950) and *Theatre Five* (1964), he started working on television productions right after the end of World War II. Much of the rest of his career was spent in executive positions. Decades later during dramatic radio's brief revival in the 1970s Lowther wrote dozens of scripts for Himan Brown's *CBS Radio Mystery Theater* (1974–1975).
Sources: Grams *Shadow*; Harmon *Radio Mystery*; *Broadcasting* April 5, 1943, p. 32, May 17, 1943, p. 36; *Motion Picture Daily* August 14, 1937, p. 4; *Variety* September 9, 1942, p. 29.

Luke, Fred

Fred Luke has only one known writing credit in the dramatic radio genre, *Hashknife Hartley* (1950–1951), a radio series based on Wilbur C. Tuttle's western novels.
Sources: French and Siegel; *St. Petersburg Times* July 2, 1950, p. 43.

Lynch, Peg

Peg Lynch (born Margaret Frances Lynch, November 25, 1916–July 24, 2015) is inseparable from the radio series that she authored and also in which she acted for over a decade, *The Private Lives of Ethel and Albert*, also broadcast at times as *The Couple Next Door*.

Lynch got her start in radio as a young teenager on a station owned by a friend's father. She began writing copy and had the opportunity to interview countless celebrities who came through town on visits to the Mayo Clinic. She reportedly sold her first script to Minneapolis' WCCO before studying English at the University of Minnesota. While writing for a small Minnesota station Lynch created the characters of Ethel and Albert in the late 1930s for a short spot on her radio show. Recognizing their advertising potential, Lynch never sold the rights to the show and focused on developing the couple as a radio property at stops at a number of stations in the following years.

In 1944 *Ethel and Albert* found a regular sponsor, hired Alan Bunce as Albert, and subsequently aired in quarter- and half-hour slots (both on radio and then television) until 1960 with occasional interruptions. Lynch later revived the characters for a series of short sketches on NBC's *Monitor* between 1963 and 1964, and then again on *The Little Things in Life* from 1975–1976 when dramatic radio was experiencing a minor revival.
Sources: Peg Lynch Papers; peglynch.com; *Variety* obituary July 27, 2015.

Lynne, Virginia Safford

Virginia Safford Lynne is not a well-known writer from radio's heyday but nevertheless she was a busy writer who was featured on juvenile, drama, and comedy series. Over a documented twenty-year scripting career Lynne authored *Tommy Parker, G-Scout* (1937), *The Wayside Theatre* (1938), *Grand Central Station* (1941), *Manhattan at Midnight* (1943), *This Is My Story* (1943), *The Great Gildersleeve* (1943), *Grand*

Hotel (1944–1945), *Grand Marquee* (1946–1947), *The First Nighter Program* (1947–1949), *Guest Star* (1951), *Stars Over Hollywood* (1952–1953), and the final season of *Great Gildersleeve* (1956–1957).

Other Radio: *His and Hers* (1953, audition).

Sources: Stump & Ohmart; *Radio Daily* March 30, 1937, p. 8; *Variety* July 14, 1943, p. 44, October 8, 1947, p. 24.

Lyon, Peter

Peter Lyon (born Robert Crawford Lyon) had a distinguished career as a freelance writer, not known to have worked directly for the any of the networks. From his first identified series, *March of Time* (1939), Lyon would go on to write for a wide variety of dramatic radio genres. Representative of his work was scripts for *Cavalcade of America* (1941–1946), *Are You a Missing Heir* (ca. 1942), *Have a Thrill* (1942), *Labor for Victory* (1942–1944), *Theatre Guild on the Air* (1945), *Eternal Light* (1948–1951), *Broadway Is My Beat* (1949), *You Are There* (1950), and *Medicine U.S.A.* (1952). For a short time in 1942 Lyon partnered with **Robert Richards** and **Robert Tallman** to form a production firm, Playwright Producers, that subsequently created *For Us the Living* (1942). In the early 1950s Lyon found himself Blacklisted by radio producers due to his work with the Writers Guild that came under investigation by Senator Joe McCarthy.

Sources: Peter Lyon Papers; *Broadcasting* May 25, 1942, p. 39, June 29, 1942, p. 62; *Motion Picture Daily* September 1, 1939, p. 2; *Variety* June 3, 1942, p. 26; *New York Times* obituary October 20, 1996.

Mabley, Edward

Edward Mabley (March 7, 1906–December 16, 1984), better known for his plays, made his mark in radio writing *The American School of the Air* (1944–1945). He scripted episodes for various television anthology series during the 1950s.

Theater: *Temper the Wind* (1946); *Glad Tidings* (1951).

Sources: Edward Mabley Papers; *New York Times* obituary December 19, 1984.

MacDougall, Ranald

Ranald MacDougall (March 10, 1915–December 12, 1973) got his foot in the radio industry's door as a page for NBC. He began submitting scripts and was eventually hired as a staff writer for the network after working for a time in the mimeograph department. MacDougall's scripts were broadcast as early as 1937, prompting his promotion within the company. His earliest known story was 1937's "Whimsy at Large" and within two years was writing *There Was a Woman* (1938), *Ideas That Came True* (1939), and *Radio Guild* (1939–1940).

MacDougall scripted a variety of dramatic programs during the early 1940s including *Listener's Playhouse* (1940), *Defense for America* (1941), *The World's Best* (1941), *Great Plays* (1940–1941), *Ted Steele* (1942), and *This Is War* (1942). After several years with NBC MacDougall resigned to join CBS where he would earn credit on some war-oriented programming. He is most remembered for his work on *The Man Behind the Gun* (1942–1944), created with director **William N. Robson**, a program that won a Peabody in 1942. Another project with Robson was the show *The 22nd Letter* (1942). The next year MacDougall wrote some episodes of **Norman Corwin**'s *Passport for Adams* (1943), a series produced at the request of the Office of War.

MacDougall had some screenwriting opportunities arise after World War II and he began writing more for motion pictures and less for radio. Some of his final radio works were for *Suspense* (1945, 1950) and *Romance* (1948). MacDougall would eventually see close to two dozen scripts used in film and television, as well as a number of teleplays in the 1950s and 1960s. The critical high point of MacDougall's writing career was an Oscar nomination for his *Mildred Pierce* screenplay in 1945.

Sources: *Broadcasting* August 16, 1943, p. 20; *Motion Picture Daily* September 17, 1937, p. 10; *Radio Daily* October 7, 1937, p. 8; *Variety* May 21, 1941, p. 26, August 6, 1941, p. 27, February 4, 1942, p. 33, July 29, 1942, p. 24.

MacGillan, Dan

Dan MacGillan worked as a gag writer for *Mortimer Gooch* (1936–1937), the story of a chewing gum salesman.

Source: *Radio Daily* March 3, 1937, p. 4.

Mack, Dick

As a continuity writer for the J. Walter Thompson agency in the late 1930s, Dick Mack was a writer and script editor for *The Chase & Sanborn Hour* featuring Edgar Bergen and Charlie McCarthy as early as 1938. In 1939 he also contributed to Joe Penner's *Tip Top Show* and eventually ascended to the head of Bergen's writing team in 1940.

Mack succeeded Ed Gardner as producer and writer of Rudy Vallee's *Sealtest Show* in 1941 and gradually relinquished scripting duties to concentrate on directing and producing. Well into the 1950s Mack continued to direct and produce a number of radio comedies.

Sources: *Broadcasting* September 15, 1939, p. 44, April 15, 1940, p. 71; *The Radio Annual* 1938 p. 709; *Radio Mirror* February 1938 p. 30; *Variety* February 12, 1941, p. 28.

Mack, Nila

Born in Arkansas City, Kansas, to a railroad engineer, Nila Mack (October 24, 1891–January 20, 1953) made a career in vaudeville, early film in Chicago, and on Broadway stages before moving into radio in the late 1920s at a small Kansas station. In 1930 CBS convinced her to return to the network and work on *The Adventures of Helen and Mary*, a children's show that was struggling to find an audience.

With a vision to incorporate more fairy tales, Mack gradually transformed *Helen and Mary* into the long-running *Let's Pretend* (possibly dubbed *Children's Theatre of the Air* for a time) by 1934. It took nearly a decade but CBS' William Paley finally prevailed upon Mack to accept a sponsor, Cream of Wheat. Mack oversaw all aspects of *Let's Pretend*, serving as director and producer as well as contributing her share of writing content. Beyond this series Mack primarily worked as a director, credited on such shows as *You Decide* and *Let Freedom Ring*. Mack was closely involved with *Let's Pretend* until she passed away from a heart attack in 1953.

Other Radio: *Night Club Romances*.
Sources: Nila Mack Papers; *Variety* December 21, 1927, p. 54, February 20, 1934, p. 31; shemadeit.org.

MacLane, Roland

Roland MacLane (February 21, 1903–February 26, 1984), a successful television comedy writer in the 1950s and 1960s on shows such as *The Life of Riley* (1954–1958), *Leave It to Beaver* (1958–1963), and *Gilligan's Island* (1964–1967), honed his craft writing radio gags for *The Edgar Bergen & Charlie McCarthy Show* and *The Charlie Ruggles Show* (1945) followed by situational comedies *My Friend Irma* (1948–1951) and *Meet Millie* (1951).

Sources: *Variety* June 20, 1945, p 28, September 1, 1948, p. 30.

MacLeish, Archibald

Archibald MacLeish (May 7, 1892–April 20, 1982), a Pulitzer Prize-winning poet, created a number of radio scripts in the late 1930s and early 1940s, often focusing on the pending war in Europe and the war effort in the United States after 1941. His famous radio play "The Fall of the City" for *The Columbia Workshop* aired April 11, 1937. MacLeish was a contributor to *The Free Company* (1941), a collaborative effort by a group of writers to counter foreign propaganda, as well as special scripts aired during World War II.

Sources: *Motion Picture Daily* January 31, 1941, p. 8; *Radio Daily* April 13, 1937, p. 8; *Variety* October 26, 1938, p. 34.

MacQuarrie, Haven

Haven MacQuarrie, a Hollywood producer and vaudeville performer, had a few radio shows of his own for which he performed writing duties, the first being *Do You Want to Be an Actor?* aired ca. 1937. This was followed by *Your Marriage Club* (1941) and *Noah Webster Says* (1942–1943), where he was host, creator, writer, producer, and director. In the mid–1940s MacQuarrie operated his own radio production company, Haven MacQuarrie Ideas.

Sources: *Broadcasting* April 14, 1941, p. 44, March 23, 1942, p. 28; *The Radio Annual* 1945 p. 699; *Radio Mirror* March 1937 p. 58.

Maguire, Arnold

Arnold Maguire, a 1919 graduate of St. Matthews College in San Mateo, CA, tried his hand at a number of jobs including photographer, reporter for the *San Francisco Chronicle*, and actor before arriving early to radio, performing on the air beginning in 1930. He joined San Francisco's KFRC that year to handle writing and directing duties for *Blue Monday Jamboree* and *Hodge Podge Lodge*. Maguire added to his writing experience as the station's chief continuity writer in 1935 and subsequently joined NBC in 1936.

Maguire's work with NBC included *Carefree Carnival, Mission Trails* (1942) and *Tune Out Time* (1942). In the early 1940s he joined the Foote, Cone & Belding agency to work as a producer during the mid–1940s before immersing himself in television after war's end. Maguire passed away suddenly in 1949.

Sources: *Broadcasting* September 15, 1935, p. 31, January 12, 1942, p. 22, February 21, 1949, p. 10, 84; *Radio Daily* December 20, 1949, p. 4; *Radio Mirror* November 1934 p. 42, June 1936 p. 106; *Variety* January 19, 1932, p. 46, January 24, 1933, p. 53.

Malone, Joel

Joel Malone (1916–1993) sold numerous scripts to film companies in the early 1940s, though it's not clear how many were adapted into motion pictures. He also produced a steady stream of scripts that were primarily used on dramatic programs, especially in the mystery and suspense genres. Malone's radio credits include *Nightcap Yarns* (1941), *Suspense* (1944, 1948), *Theatre of Romance* (1945), *The Opie Cates Show* (1947), and *The Whistler* (1946–1952), the last frequently penned with **Harold Swanton**. Malone produced a number of teleplays in the 1950s and 1960s, many of them for television's version of *The Whistler*.

Sources: Grams *Suspense; Broadcasting* May 12, 1941, p. 91.

Malone, Ted

Ted Malone (born Frank Alden Russell, May 18, 1908–October 20, 1989), started in radio in the mid–1920s on a small Kansas City station that would later become CBS-affiliate KMBC. His first assignments as a high school student were broadcasting football and basketball games. As was common in those primitive days on the airwaves, Malone did a little bit of everything when he went to work full time in the industry, including acting, singing, and producing.

From the late 1920s into the early 1930s Malone proved to be one of the station's most prolific writers and was responsible for two of the most important series aired over KMBC. In 1929 he created *Happy Hollow*, a daily (except Sundays) quarter-hour program that chronicled life in a rural village and featured a plethora of characters, played by nearly every employee on the station's payroll. *Happy Hollow* was extremely successful in the Kansas City region, running into the mid–1930s and found moderate success elsewhere when it was picked up by CBS's West Coast network and carried on the network's stations west of Kansas City a couple times in the early 1930s. *Happy Hollow* was one of several rural sketch serials that arrived on the air at the turn of the decade, none more popular and long-lasting than *Lum 'n' Abner*. Malone's creation was one of the earliest and, considering the few large stations in the nation's central region at the time, likely very influential to many competitors over succeeding years.

Malone made yet another historic contribution to radio writing in 1931 when his *Phenomenon* series hit the airwaves in November. *Phenomenon*, that ran until the summer of 1932 as a six-times-per-week series, was arguably one of the first science fiction programs on radio. It featured the adventures of time-traveling Jerry Powers who visited many historic eras via the Anacraphone, a device invented by Dr. Light. KMBC made many efforts to sell the series, both the scripts and potential recordings to stations and sponsors, during Malone's time with the station but with very little success.

Interestingly, when Malone left KMBC around 1936 because of differences with ownership about payments, he gave all rights to *Phenomenon* to the station because he wanted to be done with the relationship and move on. The syndicated series, that currently survives in audio format only in a university archive, used rewritten scripts based on Malone's original material.

Despite these two significant contributions to two different radio genres, Malone's biggest success was with the human interest broadcasts that he punctuated with poetry readings and other snippets of literature that he found interesting. His most famous series are *Between the Bookends*, that ran from 1929 until the 1950s, *Pilgrimage of Poetry*, that aired from 1939 to 1940, and *American Pilgrimage*, that was broadcast from 1940 to 1941. While much of these programs' content was recitation of verse, short stories, and anecdotes, Malone wrote all the commentary and patter into which this content was interspersed.

Malone's style was strikingly popular and his recorded shows were on the air well into the 1980s with programs that, while shorter than during radio's Golden Age, were not significantly different in tone and content. He was such a master of his craft that even by the 1960s he rarely worked from full scripts, often going before the microphone with nothing more than pieces of literature to be read and a few notes and thoughts scribbled on a sheet of paper.

Sources: Arthur B. Church Papers; Ted Malone Papers.

Manhoff, Bill

William "Bill" Manhoff (June 25, 1919–June 19, 1974) contributed to a number of highly regarded radio comedies in the 1940s and early 1950s before turning to television and motion pictures. By 1944 Manhoff had earned a spot on the *Duffy's Tavern* writing team where he worked until ca. 1946 then in 1947 took the helm of scripting *Arthur's Place* and *The Tony Martin Show*. After a stint with the Jack Benny spin-off *A Day in the Life of Dennis Day* (1950) Manhoff was appointed head writer of *Meet Millie* in 1951.

This radio experience led to a two-decade career authoring television broadcasts until his untimely death at age 54. Manhoff's credits range from *Texaco Star Theatre* (1954–1955) featuring Jimmy Durante and Donald O'Connor on a rotating basis, *The Real McCoys* (1957–1959), and *All in the Family* (1972).

Other Radio: *Hollywood Showcase*.
Theater: *The Owl and the Pussycat* (1964).
Sources: *Broadcasting* November 12, 1951, p. 65; *Variety* September 20, 1944, p. 34; July 9, 1947, p. 76, October 1, 1947, p. 26.

Manley, William Ford

William Ford Manley and fellow New York University faculty member Henry Flake Carleton debuted their radio show *Soconyland Sketches* (originally *Socony Hour*) in 1928. At the same time Manley created a series of broadcasts based on stories from the Bible called *Bible Dramas* (1928–1929) then teamed again with Carleton to author *Great Moments in History* ca. 1930. Between 1929 and 1930 the pair also scripted *Gus and Louie* and *Jo and Vi* (sometimes known as *Mr. and Mrs.*).

In the early 1930s Manley contributed numerous scripts to CBS' *American School of the Air* while also premiering "The Snow Village Sketches," stories that he started to include in *Soconyland Sketches* in the early 1930s. Recognizing his stature in broadcasting, during the early 1930s Manhoff and frequent collaborator Carlton were at the forefront of the effort to allow writers to keep all but one-time broadcast rights to their material.

By 1936 the "Snow Village" material was transitioned into its own program due to a change in sponsors. *Snow Village* returned to the air in 1942, still penned by Manhoff, in a quarter-hour serial format sponsored by Procter & Gamble and later as a weekly half-hour program. Manhoff brought *Snow Village* back to the air yet again in 1946 for a short run, though critics regarded the effort as little more than a tired rehash of small-town New England stories and characters.

Theater: *Wild Waves* (1932, set against a broadcasting background and eventually the premise for the film *Big Broadcast*).
Sources: NBC Records; *Broadcasting* September 15, 1936, p. 22, March 15, 1932, p. 17, December 7, 1942, p. 10; *Radio Broadcast Advertiser* September 1928 p. 304; *Radio Digest* March 1930 p. 58, December 1932 p. 26; *Variety* February 29, 1928, p. 57, April 19, 1939, p. 35, January 16, 1946, p. 28; *Boston Globe* July 20, 1930, p. 44.

Marcin, Max

Poland (then Germany)-born Max Marcin (May 5, 1879–March 30, 1948) started a writing career as a reporter for *The New York World* and *The New York Press* in the early 20th century before moving on to write dozens of films stretching from the silent era of the mid–1910s to the dawn of the sound era in the late 1920s. He also scripted more than an additional dozen Broadway plays during these years before he started turning out radio scripts in 1938. First his work was featured on Philip Morris' *Johnny Presents* followed by *Guess Where?* in 1939. Beginning in 1940 Marcin created then worked as both writer and producer of *Crime Doctor*, a series with a healthy run from 1940 to 1947. The main character, Dr. Benjamin Ordway, caught Hollywood's attention and a number of *Crime Doctor* films were produced during the 1940s.

Sources: *Broadcasting* December 15, 1938, p. 16; *Variety* March 29, 1939, p. 22; *New York Herald Tribune* obituary April 20, 1948.

Marcus, Lawrence (Larry)

Larry Marcus (July 19, 1917–August 28, 2001) started writing radio scripts while in the service during World War II. His early works were used on *Grand Hotel*, *Inner Sanctum*, *The Whistler* (all ca. 1944), and *The Pay-Off* and *Suspense* (both 1945). After the war Marcus wrote regularly for *Dark Venture* (1945–1947), *New Adventures of Michael Shayne* (1948), *Final Edition* (1948), additional *Suspense* stories (1948–1958), and *Night Beat* (1949–1951). Marcus wrote dozens of teleplays and screenplays from the 1950s to the 1980s, earning an Oscar nomination in 1981 for his co-adaptation for the screenplay of *The Stuntman*.

Television: *Impulse* (1952).

Sources: Grams *Suspense*; *Broadcasting* December 18, 1944, p. 68; *Sponsor* November 1948 p. 75; *Variety* March 23, 1945, p. 36 July 14, 1948, p. 30, October 20, 1948, p. 22; *New York Times* obituary September 1, 2001.

Margolis, Herbert

Television and screenwriter Herb Margolis made a brief stop in radio early in his career penning Jack Webb's *Johnny Modero: Pier 23* in 1947.

Source: *Variety* April 30, 1947, p. 37.

Marion, Charles

Charles R. Marion (November 12, 1914–September 29, 1980) began writing for the *New York Post* before moving to Los Angeles in 1939 where he entered radio. Some of his earliest scripts were heard on the programs of Bob Burns and Charlie Ruggles. Marion worked as a writer for Associated Releases in the early 1940s and in 1942 was added to Eddie Cantor's writing staff on *Time to Smile*. The following year Marion joined *The Abbott & Costello Show*. He is also credited with authoring radio's *Miss Pinkerton, Inc.* (1946). The bulk of Marion's career is represented by dozens of screenplays during the 1940s and 1950s and many more television scripts through the 1960s, including *The Addams Family* (1964–1965).

Sources: *Broadcasting* October 5, 1942, p. 41, November 22, 1943, p. 42; *The Radio Annual* 1942 p. 675; *Los Angeles Times* obituary October 6, 1980.

Marion, Ira

A writer for the Federal Theater Project and then a freelance scripter in the early 1940s, Ira Marion joined the Blue Network's scriptwriting division in 1942. One of his first assignments was *African Trek* (1942). Marion wrote for the children's *Little Blue Playhouse* (1943–1944) and numerous broadcasts in support of the war effort including *Army Nurse* (1945). In addition to *Best Sellers* (1945), *New World A'Coming* (1946), *The Court of Missing Heirs* (1947), *Mr. President* (1948), and *Modern Romances* (1949) for ABC, Marion also scripted some syndicated series including *Crime Does Not Pay* (1949–1951) and *The Black Museum* (1952). Marion is also credited with scriptwriting duties on *Metropolitan Opera Auditions of the Air* in 1958.

Sources: *Broadcasting* April 27, 1942, p. 35, July 12, 1943, p. 23; *Variety* June 10, 1942, p. 31, February 28, 1943, p. 32, April 13, 1949, p. 34.

Marks, Laurence (Larry)

Larry Marks (August 23, 1915–January 1, 1993) was one of many comedy writers during radio's Golden Age who moved from program to program, supplying new jokes and material to a medium that required voluminous amounts of fresh gags to keep listeners tuning in. Marks is first identified as a contributor to Gracie Fields' program on the Blue Network in 1944 and subsequently turned up on the writing team for *Duffy's Tavern* in 1945.

After *Duffy's Tavern* Marks wrote gags for *The Alan Young Show* (1946), then in 1947 he was hired to script for *The Dick Haymes Show* followed by *The Jack Paar Show* that same year. A brief stint on *Joan Davis Time* (1948) was followed by many years providing material for Bob Hope, who needed a large writing staff due to his style of fast delivery. Marks is credited on Hope's radio broadcasts at least through 1954 when Hope began transitioning fully to television along with many other radio personalities. Radio prepared Marks for two successful decades in television, highlighted by significant contributions to *Hogan's Heroes* (1965–1968) and *M*A*S*H* (1972–1978).

Other Radio: *Fred Allen Show*
Sources: Larry Gelbart Papers; *Broadcasting* October 23, 1944, p. 16, November 19, 1945, p. 60, *Variety* April 17, 1946, p. 40, June 4, 1947, p. 29, October 1, 1947, p. 21; *Los Angeles Times* obituary January 7, 1993.

Marquis, Arnold

Arnold Marquis earned a living as a news writer and then for different Midwestern radio stations before finding a position with NBC's production staff in San Francisco in 1936. Marquis was a versatile radio professional and by 1939 was getting experience scripting *Oh, Mr. Dinwiddie* in 1939. During the 1940s Marquis' most notable writing tasks were *Unlimited Horizons* (1940–1943 intermittent) on which he was also producer and researcher, *Pacific Story* (1943–1947), and *The Fifth Horseman* (1946). He is also credited with authoring some episodes of *Suspense* (1948) and *The Thirteenth Juror* (1949). Capitalizing on years of direction and production experience, Marquis opened his own production company in the late 1940s.

Sources: *Broadcasting* September 15, 1936, p. 40, November 12, 1945, p. 68, January 17, 1949, p. 75; *Variety* September 27, 1939, p. 34, July 10, 1946, p. 32.

Marshall, Sidney

Sidney Marshal is credited with authoring stories for *The First Nighter Program*, *Knickerbocker Playhouse*, and *Grand Central Station* in the late 1930s and early 1940s. He authored other drama programs until the 1950s when the turned to television. Among them were *The Man Called X* (1947–1948, 1950–1952), *I Love Adventure* (1948), *Family Theatre* (1949–1950), *The Adventure of the Saint* (1950), *Somebody Knows* (1950), *The Line-Up* (1952), *Suspense* (1953), *Yours Truly, Johnny Dollar* (1953), and *Romance* (1954).

Source: *Variety* September 24, 1941, p. 32.

Martini, Roland

Roland Martini (March 31, 1903–September 20, 1966), writer of over 500 pulp stories before being lured into radio, started as an author for Blackett-Sample-Hummert where he was credited in the early 1930s with turning out over 30,000 words per week across 20 series. These documented series included *Secret Three*, *Inspector Stevens & Son*, *Penrod and Sam*, and *Skippy*. Around 1933 he accepted a position with the Gardner Advertising Agency where he oversaw radio affairs for two decades.

Other Radio: *Little Orphan Annie*; *The Tom Mix Ralston Straight Shooters* (ca. 1933).
Sources: Cox *Radio Factory*; French & Siegel; *Radio Fanfare* October 1933 p. 3; *Sponsor* March 1947 p. 50; *Variety* February 14, 1933, p. 34; *The Hartford Courant* September 24, 1966, p. 4.

Masters, Monty

Monty Masters (born Monty Mohn, January 28, 1912–December 5, 1969) was a San Francisco radio writer on *Spotlight Playhouse* (1946), *Monty Masters Variety Show* (1949), and scriptwriter and co-host of *The Mad Masters* (1946–1947), featuring his wife Natalie. Masters is remembered for serving as producer, director, and writer on the series *Candy Matson, YUkon 2-8209*, one of the few detective programs of the era featuring a female. The program found enough audience for a two-year run between 1949 and 1951. His show business career struggled after *Matson* left the air, though he is credited with authoring at least one story for *Family Theatre* (1953).

Sources: French *Private Eyelashes* p. 211–227; *Broadcasting* October 24, 1949, p. 21.

Maxwell, Ted

Oakland, CA, native Ted Maxwell was a pioneering broadcaster, writing, acting, and producing material on San Francisco's NBC station around 1928. One of his earliest series identified by historians is *Life of the Reillys* (no relation to the later *Life of Riley*) that ran (1932–1933) and *Memory Lane*, the latter running over seven years.

Maxwell left for Chicago in 1934 but returned to the coast two years later when he took over authoring the serial *Hawthorn House*, revived *Memory Lane* (1937), and debuted his new show *Death at Midnight* (1937). In 1938 he debuted *Toast to the Town* before relocating yet again to Chicago where he was immersed in the world of serials starting with *Woman in White* in 1941 and then *The Story of Mary Marlin*.

In 1942 Maxwell moved on to scripting chores for *We Love and Learn* and *Light of the World*, followed by *Bright Horizon*, a spin-off of *Big Sister* serial. His late 1940s credits include *Out of the Deep* (1945–1946), *The World and David Lee* (1947), *The Story of Holly Sloan* (1947–1948), based on Rupert Hughes' novel *Static*, and *Family Theatre* (1947–1948). Maxwell died at the height of his career in 1948 at the age of 49.

Sources: *Broadcasting* November 15, 1932, p. 22, September 1, 1936, p. 37, July 1, 1937, p. 72; *Radio Daily* September 20, 1937, p. 8; *Radio Digest* December 1929 p. 66, February 1930 p. 98; *Variety* August 1, 1933, p. 56, June 8, 1938, p. 39, February 26, 1941, p. 32, April 15, 1942, p. 28, December 12, 1945, p. 38, December 15, 1948, p. 63.

Maypole, Roy

Roy Maypole, Jr., (February 26, 1914–July 4, 1976) had a long and winding career in broadcasting that took him to numerous stations during his early years before finally settling in Los Angeles. In the late 1930s Maypole worked at WHBF (Rock Island, IL), WCFL (Chicago), WWJ (Detroit), WARD (Brooklyn), WOV, and WABC (both New York), in various capacities including producer, announcer, researcher, program director, and writer. Frequently identified as a continuity writer, his only known series was the serial *Kay Fairchild, Stepmother* ca. 1939.

Maypole joined the Marine Corps. in 1943 as a combat correspondent and was widely recognized for recording the Marine landing on Bougainville island. After the war Maypole focused more on producing new programming and by the early 1950s was hosting local television shows in the Los Angeles area.

Sources: Cox *A to Z* p. 120; *Broadcasting* February 3, 1941, p. 33, May 19, 1943, p. 42; *Radio Daily* October 18, 1937, p. 6; *Milwaukee Journal* January 17, 1944, p. 2; paleycenter.org.

McCarthy, Steve

Steve McCarthy joined Detroit's WXYZ around 1947 scripting *The Lone Ranger*, a series for which he'd write into the mid–1950s. McCarthy began writing scripts for another WXYZ program, *The Green Hornet*, in 1948 and wrote over 150 episodes during the next few years. He is also credited with authoring stories for *Challenge of the Yukon*, the station's third big show.

Sources: Cox *Crime Fighters*; Grams *Green Hornet*.

McClain, John

John McClain, a former New York reporter, was signed to script *Hollywood Hotel* during the 1938–1939 season before moving on to writing a number of screenplays in the early 1940s.

Source: *Broadcasting* August 15, 1938, p. 38.

McConnor, Vincent

A playwright and freelance radio writer in the early 1940s, Vincent McConnor (November 8, 1907–July 6, 1997) joined the CBS script department in 1943. His credits over a decade of radio include *It's Maritime* (1945), *Studio One* (1947–1948), *Ford Theatre* (1949), *NBC University Theatre* (1950), and *NBC Presents: Short Story* (1951–1952). McConnor wrote across numerous media, including the theater during the 1940s, television in the 1950s and early 1960s, and several novels into the 1980s.

Sources: *Broadcasting* April 24, 1944, p. 50; *Variety* February 2, 1949, p. 24.

McCracken, Chester

While a scriptwriter for the Benton & Bowles agency's Hollywood office, Chester McCracken authored *Kate Hopkins, Angel of Mercy* ca. 1940–1941.

Source: *Broadcasting* August 18, 1941, p. 40.

McDonagh, Richard

Richard McDonagh (February 12, 1908–February 2, 1975) reportedly worked his way into an NBC continuity writer position in 1937 after submitting some scripts while working as an elevator operator for the network. Some of his earliest stories were used on *America's March on Crime* (1938), *Magic Key*, and *The Lady Esther Show* (both 1939). Other 1940s programs included *Wings Over America* (1940), *The Catholic Hour* (1941), *Down Mexico Way* (later *Pan American Holiday*, 1942), and *The March of Mercy* (1943). One of McDonagh's best preserved series is *Words at War* (1943–1945) and toward the end of its run McDonagh was named head of NBC's script department. He remained busy as a writer, editor, and supervisor in television until at least 1970.

Sources: NBC Company Records; *Broadcasting* August 1, 1938, p. 42; *Radio Daily* March 19, 1937, p. 5; *Variety* June 14, 1939, p. 32; *Washington Post* April 20, 1941, p. L5.

McGaughey, Dudley Dean

Dudley Dean McGaughey (1906–October 3, 1986) was a freelance writer who published under various pseudonyms. His time in radio seems to span most of the 1940s, much of that time spent as a continuity writer for the Keystone Broadcasting System (as Dean Owen) before he entered the Army in 1943. After the war McGaughey returned to his typewriter, penning stories, scripts, and magazine pieces, including reviews for *Billboard*.

McGaughey specialized in Westerns but he freelanced in whatever genre he could get assignments. His identified radio credits include *Adventures of Michael Shayne*, *All-Star Western Theatre*, and *The Whistler* (all 1946) as well as the short-lived *Hawk Durango* (1946) which became *Hawk Larabee* in 1947.

Other Radio: *The City*; *Glamour Manor*; *Hopalong Cassidy*.

Sources: Dudley Dean McGaughey Collection; French & Siegel p. 96; *The Radio Annual* 1942 p. 320; *Variety* March 3, 1943, p. 26, May 14, 1947, p. 34; mysteryfile.com.

McGill, Jerry

Edmund Robert "Jerry" McGill (August 18, 1905–1980), the son of stage actors, earned a degree from the University of Florida and was later a Rhodes Scholar at Oxford. After school McGill worked as a newspaper reporter for a time before his writing interests turned to radio. One of his earliest known series was *Bambi* (1936) with Helen Hayes and he is also thought to have provided some stories to *Cavalcade of America* as well during the late 1930s. McGill was an author for *Mother o' Mine* (1941), *Mr. District Attorney* (1942), *Dick Tracy* (1943), *Famous Jury Trials* (1943, also director), and *Appointment With Crime* (1943–1944) before joining the staff of *Big Town* as director and periodic writer for much of the rest of its run into the early 1950s. Originally scheduled to script for *The Shadow* during the 1942–1943 season, historian Martin Grams has verified McGill's scripts were not used on the legendary series until the final seasons between 1950 and 1954.

Other Radio: *Growing Pains* (1940, audition).

Sources: Grams *The Shadow*; *The Radio Annual* 1947 p. 883; *Radio Daily* August 16, 1937, p. 8; *Variety* March 26, 1941, p. 37, March 11, 1942, p. 36, March 17, 1943, p. 30.

McGreevey, John

John McGreevey (1922–2010) started writing radio plays while a student at Indiana University. He spent many years in the industry in Arizona throughout the 1940s where he wrote for KTAR and also wrote and directed his own show, *Arizona Adventure* (1948–1954). Before getting into television in the 1950s, McGreevey had stories used on *Armstrong's Theatre of Today*, *Cavalcade of America*, *Dr. Christian*, *Nick Carter, Master Detective*, and *Suspense*. Between 1964 and 1977 McGreevey won an Emmy Award and received four further nominations.

Sources: McGreevey Papers; Cox *Radio Crime Fighters*; emmys.com.

McKay, Ted

Pittsburgh native Ted McKay built a comedic reputation writing for *The Bob Hope Show* as well as programs for Milton Berle, Red Skelton, and Henry Morgan in the late 1940s before passing away at 50 or 55 (sources vary) in 1973.

Sources: *Pittsburgh Post-Gazette* November 9, 1973, p. 11; *Pittsburgh Press* November 9, 1973, p. 14.

McKean, Eddy

Eddy McKean has been identified as the joke writer for the final season (1946–1947) of the quiz show *Darts for Dough*.

Source: *Variety* February 26, 1947, p. 34.

McKee, Bob

An announcer as early as the 1930s, Bob McKee was later heard on such programs as *Jack Armstrong* (1946) and *The World's Great Novels* (1947). During many years in broadcasting McKee took turns as a writer on series such as *Pierre the Trapper* (1938), *A Life in Your Hands* (1949–1952), *Destination Freedom* (1951), and an early CBS news broadcast in 1946.

Sources: *Variety* June 2, 1937, p. 43, September 21, 1938, p. 38, June 26, 1946, p. 35.

McKnight, Tom

A booker, producer, and writer for the Keith-Albee vaudeville circuit before radio, Tom McKnight (February 4, 1901–April 22, 1963) was a busy agency writer and producer by the 1930s. He assisted with the scripts for the Marx Bros. early show *Flywheel, Shyster, and Flywheel* (1932–1933), *Uncle Charlie's Tent Show* (1935), *Broadway Merry-Go-Round* (1937), *The Phil Baker Show* (1939), *The Shadow* (1939), and *The Don Ameche Show* (1940). McKnight left writing for full-time production work during World War II and soon transitioned to overseeing motion pictures and then eventually television programming in the 1950s and early 1960s.

Theater: *Ziegfield Follies* (1937).

Sources: *Broadcasting* April 1, 1940, p. 26; *Radio Daily* February 16, 1937, p. 2; *Variety* May 17, 1939, p. 26, October 4, 1944, p. 43.

McLeod, Victor

Vic McLeod (August 2, 1904–December 12, 1972) wrote well over 100 film shorts during the 1930s and another dozen screenplays in the early 1940s before spending most of the rest of the decade as a comedy writer for the airwaves. His resume includes stops at *Kraft Music Hall* (1943), *Stop or Go* (1944–1945) a quiz show for servicemen, *The Chase & Sanborn Show* as Bergen & McCarthy's head writer (1944), *The Bob Burns Show* (1945–1946, 1947), *The Tommy Dorsey Show* (1946), and *Jeffers the Butler* (ca. 1947). McLeod did some writing for television on *The Woody Woodpecker Show* (1957) and *The Lucy Show* (1964, 1967) among others while also doing a good amount of production work.

Sources: *Broadcasting* August 16, 1943, p. 28, September 4, 1944, p. 60; *Variety* April 19, 1944, p. 23, July 3, 1946, p. 30.

McNeill, Don

A native of Galena, IL, Don McNeill (December 23, 1907–May 7, 1996) virtually invented the morning radio show during his long tenure on the air. Originally planning on a career as a cartoonist, McNeill considered the potential of radio and after graduating from Marquette University went to work for Milwaukee's WISN in 1928 where he announced and edited scripts. The next year he moved to WTMJ, associated with the *Milwaukee Journal*, and the year after that to WHAS, the *Louisville Courier-Journal*'s radio station. Teaming with Van Fleming, the pair formed a performing duo and headed West, eventually landing in San Francisco.

By 1933 McNeill's decision to pursue radio was not looking wise. He had split with Fleming, failed in a bid to find broadcasting work in New York, and returned to Milwaukee with few job prospects. Applying to NBC in June 1933, he received encouragement to travel to Chicago for an audition. The opening was for an 8:00 a.m. slot, a graveyard for radio professionals, with few listeners and, thus, a nearly non-existent budget. McNeill imagined how he could revamp the moribund *The Pepper Pot* morning program and sufficiently impressed NBC executives that he won the spot over two competitors.

McNeill's radio writing career lasted just a few months more as he pounded out his own scripts, incorporating all the stories, jokes, and anecdotes he could squeeze from newspapers and joke books. As his *Breakfast Club of the Air* gained listeners, they began submitting their own jokes and stories by the hundreds and McNeill decided it would be a whole lot easier to let the listeners craft the show while he just improvised his way through the time.

Laying aside his scripting chores was a risk but one that turned out for the best. The resulting unpredictability of the show added to its charm and McNeill could focus his energies on other aspects of the show. *The Breakfast Club* was McNeill's career; when it left the air after more than three decades in 1968, he retired and lived his remaining years out of the public view.

Sources: Donald T. McNeill Collection; *Radio Digest* September 1930 p. 66; *Variety* February 2, 1932, p. 52, May 8, 1934, p. 42.

Meadow, Herb

Herb (Herman) Meadow's (May 27, 1911–March 1, 1995) first radio work was announcing on a small Brooklyn station that also purchased his first scripts ca. 1933. This propelled him to Hollywood where he authored approximately a dozen screenplays before immersing himself in television. Meadow dabbled in radio, scripting about half a dozen episodes of *Suspense* between 1948 and 1955. With Sam Rolfe Meadow created the adult western *Have Gun, Will Travel* that debuted on CBS television in 1957. In an unusual twist, the show was then adapted to radio (1958–1960). The bulk of his career, however, was spent writing for television where he contributed episodes to dozens of series between the 1950s and 1970s.

Source: *Los Angeles Times* obituary March 6, 1995.

Meadow, Leon

A writer for Blackett-Sample-Hummert in the late 1930s and early 1940s, Leon Meadow left his mark on such shows as *The Hallmark Charlotte Greenwood Show* (1945), *The Molle Mystery Theatre* (1946), and *Murder by Midnight* (1946) after World War II.

Source: *Broadcasting* June 29, 1942, p. 43.

Medbury, John P.

A humorist during the 1910s and 1920s who appeared on stage and wrote newspaper columns, John Medbury (November 9, 1893–June 29, 1947) began appearing on radio with his monologs in 1930. Critics noted his material did not adapt well to radio in the early days, especially on Fred Waring's Old Gold program in 1933, when radio still expected more gags and less of Medbury's style of subtle humor.

Attitudes had changed by 1937, however, and Medbury found a place writing for George Burns and Gracie Allen. His tenure with Burns and Allen lasted about five years before he struck out to pursue other projects. Among them were *Captain Flagg and Sergeant Quirt* (1941-1942), a short-lived effort about two Marines that drew some criticism from the Marine Corps.

Quirt was followed by a partial-season substitution on Baby Snooks' Post Toasties program in 1942 when writer **Phil Rapp** took a sabbatical. Medbury subsequently moved on to *Pabst Blue Ribbon Town* (1943), *Adventures of Ozzie and Harriet* (1945), and *Amos 'n' Andy* (1946).

Film: *Travelaugh* series of Columbia shorts (1930–1931); Dialog for approximately one dozen films in the 1930s and early 1940s.

Sources: Bradley; *Broadcasting* March 8, 1943, p. 30; *Radio Daily* October 21, 1937, p. 5; *Radio Fanfare* June 1933 p. 3; *Variety* October 22, 1930, p. 74, August 12, 1942, p. 42, October 9, 1946, p. 53; *The Baltimore Sun* October 29, 1922, p. 5.

Meiser, Edith

Edith Meiser (May 9, 1898–September 26, 1993) started performing in the legitimate theater in the 1920s and took a stab at vaudeville with a solo show in the late 1920s before finding her place as a writer and actor in radio. Meiser, wife of writer-producer **Tom McKnight** and sister of writer **Ruth Borden**, debuted as an aural scripter with her series *The Adventures of Polly Preston* (1929–1931). Meiser was a big fan of Sherlock Holmes, falling in love with Conan Doyle's character while on a long sea voyage as a youngster. As an adult she was so convinced of Holme's radio potential that she wrote two scripts based on Doyle's stories and pitched them to NBC. An executive was intrigued by the scripts but chose not to pursue it any further since there was no sponsor on the horizon. Convinced of the character's broadcasting potential, Meiser took it on her self to find a sponsor, which she did.

Meiser's first Sherlock Holmes program premiered in 1930, and she served as both author and actress on it. Holmes initially aired until the mid–1930s but when Meiser was not working on the series she had numerous other programs to write. They included *Alias Edward Taylor* (1930), *Barbara Wayne* (1931), *Island Boat Club* (1932), *Rudyard Kipling Stories* (1932), *O. Henry Stories* (1932), *Mysteries in Paris* (1932–1933), *20 Years in Sing Sing* (1933), and *The Helen Hayes Theater* also called *The New Penny* (1935–1936).

During the second half of the decade Meiser showed no signs of slowing down and penned many more scripts for a number of series. Among them were *City Desk* (1936), *Welcome Valley* (1936–1937), *The Adventures of Big Bill Baker* (1937), *Fortune Stories* or *A Case for Mr. Fortune* (1937–1938) that was adaptations of the stories of H. C. Bailey's detective Reginald Fortune, *The Life and Love of Dr. Susan* (1939), *What Would You Have Done?* (1939), *Hellinger Stories* (1940), Don Ameche's *Old Gold Program* (1940), *Luncheon at the Waldorf* (1940–1941), *Another Case for Quest* (1941), and *My Sister Eileen* (1944).

For much of the 1930s Meiser was connected with *The Shadow*, primarily as a script editor though she is also identified as writing many scripts for the show early in its run. She continued to script for various incarnations of Sherlock Holmes on the airwaves, eventually adapting all the original Doyle stories and creating new adventures for the master detective. Using Doyle's characters and stories as starting points for the fresh material, Meiser proved so adept that reportedly even Doyle's family was impressed with her work.

One of Meiser's last radio credits was for a different sleuthing show, *Nick Carter, Master Detective* (1945–1946). During the latter half of the 1940s Meiser migrated back to her acting roots and began to take more performing opportunities and wound down her writing responsibilities.

Sources: Edith Mesier Papers; Meiser Collection; Grams *Shadow*: *Broadcasting* June 1, 1936, p. 11, December 1, 1939, p. 61; *Motion Picture Daily* September 16, 1937, p. 11, February 3, 1939, p. 12; *Radio Digest* December 1931 p. 77; *Radio Mirror* November 1935 p. 8; *Variety* February 8, 1928, p. 36, February 14, 1933, p. 34, March 28, 1945, p. 30; *New York Times* obituary September 27, 1995.

Meltzer, Louis (Lew)

Louis Meltzer was a 1940s screenwriter as well as radio author, working on series including *Duffy's Tavern*, *Secret Life of Walter Mitty* (1948), and *The Morey Amsterdam Show* (1949).

Television: *The Show Goes On* (1950).
Sources: *Billboard* April 24, 1948, p. 5, January 28, 1950, p. 10.

Menkin, Larry

Lawrence Menken enters the historical radio record in 1936 when he was hired as a scriptwriter for WXYZ, a position he left within a month for a job with WMCA. One of his efforts in 1938 was the creation of an experimental program for which he sought a sponsor but the next year he was involved with a much more mainstream Chesterfield show featuring Fred Waring. Menken left for NBC in 1944 and soon began writing for *Words at War* (1944) then in 1945 Menken took leave from his job for a spot with the Armed Forces Radio Service. Among Menken's post-war works were *The Sparrow and the Hawk* (1945–1946), *The Molle Mystery Theatre* (1946), and *Rooftops of the City* (1947).

Television: *Inside Detective* (1950).
Sources: *Billboard* May 6, 1944, p. 6; *Broadcasting* July 30, 1945, p. 81; *Variety* February 19, 1936, p. 57, May 18, 1938, p. 28, June 7, 1939, p. 13, July 9, 1947, p. 72; *The Baltimore Sun* July 16, 1950, p. F11.

Merlin, Barbara

West Coast native Barbara Merlin (1917–July 24, 1997) got her radio start on KFRC before moving to KHJ. Merlin was a busy writer for the airwaves for over a decade, often with her husband **Milton Merlin**. She earned author credits on *The Ginny Simms Show* (1943–1945), *Everything for the Boys* (1944), *Boston Blackie* (1944), *The Man Called X* (1944–1946), *The Adventures of Bill Lance* (1947), and *Mr. President* (1947–1948). From 1950 to 1952 the couple assumed writing duties on *Hall of Ivy*, a series created by *Fibber McGee & Molly* writer **Don Quinn**. Before moving to television she also scripted *Presenting Charles Boyer* (1950) and *Family Theatre* (1950). After working in television for much of the 1950s and 1960s, Merlin went to work for United Artists from 1968–1971 before beginning more than two decades with *The National Enquirer*.

Sources: Milton and Barbara Merlin Collection; *Los Angeles Times* obituary July 31, 1997.

Merlin, Milton

Milton Merlin (March 12, 1905–October 29, 1996) spent the 1930s working in motion pictures, first with Paramount from 1933–1936 and then MGM until 1940. Milton would later insist he had little respect for Hollywood filmmaking. After directing and producing pictures with a young Judy Garland and Mickey Rooney, Merlin started writing screenplays in the late 1930s and that segued into radio scriptwriting for most of the 1940s.

Merlin teamed with wife **Barbara Merlin** for much his radio work and together they scripted *The Ginny Simms Show* (1943–1945), *Everything for the Boys* (1944), *Boston Blackie* (1944), *The Man Called X* (1944–1946), *The Adventures of Bill Lance* (1947), *Mr. President* (1947–1948), and *Halls of Ivy*, perhaps their most prominent air show. After the original writing team of **Jerome Lawrence** and **Robert Lee** departed Merlin and Merlin penned the weekly episodes from 1950 to 1952. Merlin's latter radio credits included *Presenting Charles Boyer* (1950) and *Family Theatre* (1950) before his career came to a screeching halt with Hollywood's Blacklist.

It would be at least five years before Merlin once again was authoring under his own name, this time on television. One of his first assignments was adapting *Halls of Ivy* to the visual medium but he would later pen episodes of *Bonanza* and *I Spy*.

Sources: Milton and Barbara Merlin Collection; Milton Merlin Papers; *Los Angeles Times* obituary November 1, 1996.

Merrick, William

Little is known of the author William Merrick, who served as a correspondent for the Associated Press before a minor radio career. Merrick was one of several writers who discovered their knack for radio plays courtesy of the producers of *The Columbia Workshop* in the late 1930s. Two other series on which Merrick worked have so far been identified, *Men, Machines, and Victory* (1942), an 8-week defense series and *March of Time*, both before he went to serve in World War II.

Sources: *Broadcasting* August 20, 1945, p. 82; *Radio Mirror* September 1939 p. 50; *Variety* June 10, 1942, p. 34.

Merrill, Howard

Howard Merrill (March 27, 1916–April 20, 2002) was practically raised in show business, acting at the age of 3 thanks to his mother's association with **Gertrude Berg**. Merrill was a prolific child actor, appearing in some 58 silent pictures and then on radio programs by age 10 at the very beginning of the network age, in 1926. His air appearances include series such as *Penrod*, NBC's adaptation of **Booth Tarkington**'s books, and *Mountainville True Life Sketches* (both 1930). In 1937, with a reported 3,000 broadcasts already under his belt as well as a syndicated newspaper column, Merrill heard his first script aired on the Blue network's *On Broadway* show while he was also attending Columbia University.

From the late 1930s through the 1940s Merrill was assigned to a variety of broadcasts, at times working for networks and sometimes for agencies like Pelar & Ryan. His air author credits include *Archie Andrews* (1943), *The Adventures of Leonidas Witherall* (1944–1945), *The Beatrice Kay Show* (1946) a musical spin-off of another musical program, *The Gay Nineties Revue*, *Leave It to Mike* (1946), *Secret Missions* (1948–1949) an adaptation of book by Rear Admiral Ellis M. Zacharias, *You Are There* (1948), *Sherlock Holmes* (1948–1949), and *The Adventures of the Abbotts*, adapted stories from the series of novels by Frances Crane. Merrill subsequently wrote for television for over a quarter century.

Sources: *Exhibitor's Trade Review* March 8, 1924, p. 22; *Radio Daily* November 18, 1937, p. 2, March 3, 1938, p. 3; *What's on the Air?* March 1930 p. 16, April 1930 p. 32; *Variety* June 23, 1943, p. 46, June 7, 1944, p. 34; *New York Times* obituary May 10, 2002.

Merrill, Mildred

Mildred "Mickey" Merrill has left behind little documentation of authoring for the airwaves outside of a long run with WXYZ's *Challenge of the Yukon* (1945–1952, later *Sgt. Preston of the Yukon*).

Source: *Challenge of the Yukon* log by Terry Salomonson.

Meston, John

A native of Pueblo, CO, it is appropriate perhaps that John Meston (July 30, 1914–March 24, 1979) is best remembered for his contributions to the influential Western show *Gunsmoke*. Though educated at Dartmouth with some time spent in Paris, Meston never lost his sense of the West. Meston eventually landed a job as an editor with the CBS network where he began collaborating with director Norman Macdonnell.

The pair started authoring scripts for series such as *Escape* and *Romance* before creating their lasting legacy, *Gunsmoke*, in 1952. Meston found himself so busy with the series that he left his job with CBS to work as a freelance writer for the series. He ended up contributing almost 200 scripts to the radio show and nearly the same number for the television version.

Sources: Barabas & Barabas; Wright "*Gunsmoke's* Unknown Writer."

Michael, Sandra

Denmark-born Sandra Michael made a significant name for herself in the world of radio soap operas during the 1940s, though she was far from a fan of the genre's typical forms. Michael's family moved the United States in the 1910s or 1920s where they ended up in Montana for a few years en route to California. As a young woman Michael settled in the Milwaukee area where she did various on-air work to earn her salary including announcing fashion shows, writing advertising copy, and assisting with a children's hour.

Finding little success with these jobs, Michael tried freelance writing and that eventually led her to Hollywood where she briefly provided some dialog for Jean Hersholt and Francis Lederer among others. Back in Wisconsin Michael's first programs began appearing on regional radio networks in the mid–1930s but had enough commercial potential to be transcribed by the Columbia Phonograph Co. for wider distribution through the Cramer-Krassett Co. of Milwaukee.

Michael's earliest serials were *The Monticello Party Line* (1935–1938), *Welcome, Neighbor* (1936), and *Magnificent Lady* (1937), before moving to more widely heard network programs. While still in Milwaukee Michael married John Gibbs (born J. Ed Giebisch), a Cramer-Krassett Co. director, who went on to a long and successful career producing and packaging shows, eventually with his own company.

The pre–War years were a prolific time for Michael as evidenced by the credits she earned authoring *Valiant Lady* (1938), *The Affairs of Anthony* (1938–1940), *1001 Wives*, a sustaining NBC-Blue feature (ca. 1939), *The Story of Mary Marlin* (1939), and *Lone Journey* a serial that originally aired from 1940 to 1943 but was revived repeatedly and over different networks until 1952. Michael also penned a handful of non-serial dramatic plays, one of which was included on a broadcast of *The Kate Smith Hour* in 1942.

As other profiles of Michael have noted and as was even recognized by critics of her own time, Michael had little interest in the clichéd plot devices used by most of the era's soap operas including the use of cliffhangers and well-tread, formulaic storylines. Her disdain for these practices was epitomized by *Against the Storm* that debuted soon after the outbreak of World War II. The *New York Times* described it as in a whole different league than its broadcast competitors, with well-developed characters who held unique world views philosophies. Michael was known to fill entire episode scripts with speeches, monologs, ballads, and readings of such authors as Walt Whitman and Edgar Lee Masters.

Despite rave critical reviews that included a 1941 Peabody Award for Outstanding Entertainment in Drama, *Against the Storm* left the airwaves after three years. Despite respectable ratings, what Michael later suggested she really wanted was a full half-hour every day, a demand to which her sponsor would not acquiesce. Finally, Michael walked away to pursue other projects though the series made a brief return in 1949.

Michael's longest-running program may have been *Lone Journey*, a series that debuted in 1940 and ran intermittently until 1952. She was aided in the authoring duties by her brother Gunnar Mickelson (using the penname Peter Michaels), and was sometimes described as having novelesque qualities. In fact, Michael even set about adapting the series into a novel, though the resulting work is not known to have ever been published.

The mid–1940s saw Michael work on at least two additional series. She created another original program, *The Open Door* (1943–1944), that had a fairly short run and attempted to uphold the standards laid out by *Against the Storm*. She also had a stint penning *Woman in White* when the serial's author had to step away for a time. The latter years of Michael's career are still a mystery, though she is known to have scripted some episodes of television's *Robert Montgomery Presents* in the mid–1950s.

Sources: French & Siegel; *Broadcasting* August 15, 1935, p. 44, July 1, 1936, p. 66, May 15, 1939, p. 32, February 15, 1938, p. 63, May 15, 1939, p. 32; *Radio and Television Mirror* June 1940 p. 50, September 1940 p. 37; *Radio Daily* December 20, 1937, p. 4; *Variety* April 23, 1941, p. 35, October 21, 1942, p. 22, July 14, 1948, p. 24; *New York Herald Tribune* July 13, 1941, p. E8.

Miller, Albert G.

Albert Miller (December 28, 1905–1982) was educated at the University of Pennsylvania and soon after graduating joined the N. W. Ayer & Son agency until 1933 when he decided to attempt freelance writing. His freelance credits include *Frank Hawks* (1936), **Fred Allen**'s *Town Hall Tonight*, Walter O'Keefe's show, and *Pontiac Varsity Show* (all 1937), *Ben Bernie and all the Lads* (1938–1939), *Information Please* (1939–1940), George Jessel's show (1939–1940), *Maudie's Diary* (1941–1942), and *Michael and Kitty* (ca. 1941) before World War II.

After the war Miller is credited with *Those Websters* (1946), *Official Detective* (1956), and *Theatre Five* (1964–1965), over a span of two decades. Much of his later work focused on children's material, primarily books, though he made a few forays into television.

Other Radio: *Buck Rogers of the 25th Century*; *Eno Crime Club*.
Theater: *The Sellout* (1933); *The Shaggy Dog* (1947).
Television: *The Cheaters* (1961–1962).
Sources: Cox Crime Fighters; *Broadcasting* May 26, 1941, p. 22; *Variety* December 31, 1941, p. 26; *Variety Annual 1940–1941* p. 1000; *New York Times* obituary June 29, 1982.

Miller, Arthur

Arthur Miller (October 17, 1915–February 10, 2005), one of the mid–20th centuries most prominent playwrights, authored a handful of radio scripts in the late 1930s and early 1940s. His work primarily appeared on CBS' experimental *Columbia Workshop* (1939) and the prestige series featuring stories from United States history, *Cavalcade of America*. Broadcast historian **Erik Barnouw** noted that Miller could be counted on to come in and beat a deadline when necessary. While a Peabody, radio's most prestigious award, eluded Miller, it was one of the few awards Miller did not receive during his accomplished career. The awards he did receive included a Primetime Emmy, Pulitzer Prize, and Tony Award.

Theater: *Death of a Salesman* (1949); *The Crucible* (1953).
Source: *Variety* March 24, 1943, p. 34.

Miller, Peg

Peg Miller was a member of CBS' highly regarded news team, scripting the network's *Report to the Nation* ca. 1943.
Source: *Variety* January 13, 1943, p. 28

Miller, Sigmund

Sigmund Miller (August 10, 1910–August 5, 1998) sharpened his writing craft during the 1940s, authoring countless radio plays, most notably in the suspense and mystery genres. Some of his documented programs include *Inner Sanctum* (1941–1946), *Zero Hour* (1943, with Jack Sher), *Murder at Midnight* (1946), *Cavalcade of America* (1946), *Suspense* (10 episodes, 1943–1950), *CBS Is There* (1947), *Lest We Forget* (1948), *Stories to Remember* (1948), *The Eternal Light* (1948–1949), *You Are There* (1949), and *The New Frontier* (1950).

Miller's true passion was the theater and as early as 1943 some of his works were being staged. That year he was involved with a number of other writers in creating a series of *Lunchtime Follies*, productions intended to entertain war plant workers over their lunch break. Miller's writing career was upended during the McCarthy era and he was forced to move to London and write under a pseudonym to make a living throughout the 1950s.

Theater: *Albert the First* (1950); *One Bright Day* (1950, 1952); *Masquerade* (1959).

Books: *The Snow Leopard* (1959); *That's the Way Money Goes* (1962).

Sources: Grams *Suspense*; Segal; *Radio Mirror* March 1943 p. 8; *Variety* May 8, 1946, p. 27, May 22, 1946, p. 45, December 31, 1947, p. 22, November 10, 1948, p. 39; *New York Herald Tribune* January 30, 1943, p. 8; *New York Times* obituary August 17, 1998.

Milton, Paul

Paul R. Milton, a playwright and screenwriter for Paramount in the early and mid–1930s, approached radio later in the decade and worked steadily in the industry through the 1940s. Milton even scripted for television as early as 1941 on NBC's *Soldier Town* series. Martin was called on to author a variety of programming as evidenced by a list of his credited works that includes *The March of Time* (1942–1946), *I Know the Enemy* (1945), *Exploring the Unknown* (1946), *Spotlight on America* (1946), *True Confessions* (1946), commentator Gabriel Heatter (1947), *Mr. and Mrs. North* (1947), *Mr. President* (1947–1948), *Great Scenes from Great Plays* (1948), *Under Arrest* (1949–1950), *Counterspy* (1949–1951), *Crime Fighters* (1950), and *Treasury Agent* (1958).

In the early 1950s Milton provided anti–Communist testimony during the House Un–America Activities Committee hearings and was also involved in the creation of AWARE, an anti–Communist group active in the entertainment industry.

Film: *Search for Beauty* (1934).

Sources: *Film Daily* October 16, 1941, p. 6; *Film Daily Year Book* 1935 p. 187; *Variety* August 23, 1943, p. 35, March 21, 1945, p. 31, July 2, 1947, p. 36, November 9, 1947, p. 28.

Mitchell, Robert (Bob)

Robert Mitchell (April 27, 1918–October 13, 1992) was a graduate of the University of Wyoming where he was heavily involved in theater and radio productions. After his time in World War II Mitchell moved to Hollywood where he spent several years developing a writing career in radio, most notably on *The Whistler* (1947), *The Adventures of Philip Marlowe* (1948–1950), *Box 13* (1949), *The Line-Up* (1950), *Rocky Jordan* (1951), and *Gunsmoke* (1957–1958). Television beckoned and Mitchel and frequent collaborator **Gene Levitt** moved to New York to join Steve Allen's writing staff. When that job ended Mitchell returned to California and, with his wife Esther Mitchell, continued scripting episodes for a variety of television adventure shows until the 1970s.

Other Radio: *The Dinah Shore Show*; *Make-Believe Town*; *Murder by Experts*; *The Spirit*.

Television: *Front Page Detective* (1951–1952); *Perry Mason* (1961–1964); *Charlie's Angels* (1978–1979).

Sources: Bob & Esther Mitchell Collection; Cox *Crime Fighters*; *Los Angeles Times* obituary October 22, 1992.

Mole, John

John Mole has been identified as the writer for two dramatic radio series, *Gang Busters* (ca. 1943) and then *Armstrong Theatre* (1945) upon joining the Batten, Barton, Durstine & Osborn agency.

Sources: Grams *Gangbusters*; *Billboard* February 20, 1943, p. 6; *Broadcasting* April 23, 1945, p. 52.

Monroe, Charles

Charles Monroe, a graduate of the University of Michigan and Yale, is a little-known author who worked in theater with the Connecticut Players and Pinon Players before joining Air Features, Inc. to write a number of serials as well as episodes *Columbia Workshop* (1940) and *Lux Radio Theatre* (ca. 1941). In 1942 Monroe moved to CBS where he authored a number of programs including *Good Listening* (1943), *Raymond Scott Show* (1943), *June Moon* (1947), *Romance* (1948–1949), *Doctor Standish, Medical Examiner* (1948), *Cabin B-13* (1948), *Report Card* (1948), *Main Street Music Hall* (1950), *The Peggy Lee Show* (1952), and *The Mindy Carson Show* (1952). After advancing to director of CBS' writing division in 1949, Monroe was elevated to an executive-level position shortly before his death in 1960.

Other Radio: *Cimarron Tavern*; *Edge of Night*; *Full Circle*; *The Sparrow and the Hawk*.

Sources: *Variety* August 25, 1937, p. 60, February 5, 1941, p. 42, January 20, 1943, p. 35, December 15, 1943, p. 32, March 31, 1948, p. 28; *New York Herald Tribune* December 28, 1960, p. 17.

Monroe, Robert

Robert Monroe (October 30, 1915–March 17, 1995), graduated from Ohio State University in 1937 before getting a job with Cleveland's WHK and then Cincinnati's WLW as a writer and director. Monroe subsequently moved to New York where he has been identified as the scriptwriter for *Air Youth for Defense* (1942) and *Screen Test* (1944).

Later in the decade he formed Robert Monroe Productions, a company that was responsible for producing more than two dozen radio programs at its height. Though often credited as a producer, sources indicate Monroe may have continued to have a hand in authoring episodes for some of the series including *High Adventure* (1947–1949), *There's Always a Woman* (1948), *Manhattan Playhouse* (1949), *John Steele, Adventurer* (1949–1956), and *Scramble* (1942–1943).

During the 1950s Monroe was an executive with the Mutual Broadcasting System before his production company began acquiring radio stations in the mid–Atlantic region. Increasingly, Monroe turned his attention to researching altered states of consciousness, or out-of-body experiences, and founded the Monroe Institute to conduct more formal investigation into the phenomena.

Books: *Journeys Out of the Body* (1971); *Far Journeys* (1985); *Ultimate Journey* (1994).
Sources: *Motion Picture Herald* June 17, 1944, p. 34; *Variety* July 27, 1938, p. 36, January 14, 1942, p. 34; monroeinstitute.org.

Moore, Carroll, Jr.

Carroll Moore (May 4, 1913–February 5, 1977) came to radio late, just before television began making significant inroads to the medium's listenership. His plays were used on *Carrington Playhouse* (ca. 1946), *Guest Star* (1947), and *The Henry Morgan Show* (1948). Moore's writing skill was recognized years later with three primetime Emmy nominations in 1966, 1971, and 1975.

Television: Herb Shriner's *Two for the Money* (1953).
Sources: *Variety* June 12, 1946, p. 26, March 26, 1947, p. 44, February 4, 1948, p. 31.

Moore, Nancy

Nancy Moore worked as a writer for serial producers Frank and Anne Hummert then later as a CBS scribe and subsequently as a freelancer. Her various radio series over the years included *Bright Horizon* (1945), *Hollywood Story* (1947), *The Ford Theatre* (1947–1949), and two programs from the era of 1970s drama revival, *CBS Radio Mystery Theater* (1974–1975) and *Vanity Fair* (1975). Moore's most notable television work was a Claymation series called *Davey and Goliath* produced by the Lutheran Church in America during the 1960s and 1970s.

Other Radio: *Mary Noble, Backstage Wife; Second Husband.*
Sources: Heilbut p. 251; *Variety* March 28, 1945, p. 27, January 8, 1947, p. 113, September 3, 1947, p. 23.

Moore, Sam

Sam Moore (d. September 13, 1989) was one of the initial writers of the beloved *Great Gildersleeve*, one of radio's first spin-off programs in 1942. His career in show business has been only lightly documented and what little has been written about Moore's life seems to be somewhat confused. In an unlikely circumstance, there were two Sam Moores active in radio in California in the 1930s, and their work has been mistakenly overlapped. While there was a Sam Moore in the Bay area who performed—and apparently even wrote—for radio during the 1930s after years in vaudeville, this was not the same Sam Moore who would become a successful network writer.

The Great Gildersleeve's Moore was a producer and lead continuity writer for the top-tier J. Walter Thompson agency in the early 1930s, first in New York and then in Los Angeles and Hollywood as of 1934. There he worked on Mary Pickford's program for Royal Gelatin and *One Man's Family* before taking over as the director of the William Esty agency's radio division in 1936. There he oversaw *Camel Caravan*, a program that featured Jack Oakie for at least one season, before resigning to work freelance radio and as a contract writer for 20th Century Fox then MGM.

Moore's major radio job during the late 1930s was co-scripting Maxwell House's *Good News* program of 1937, 1938, 1939, and 1940 with **Phil Rapp**. His other pre–1942 series include the summer replacement program *Meredith Wilson's Musical Review* (1940), *Three Ring Time* featuring Milton Berle with Ed Rice and *Tommy Riggs and Betty Lou* (both 1941), and then at the end of 1941 he moved from Bergen and McCarthy's *Chase & Sanborn Hour* to *The Old Gold Program*.

With **John Whedon** Moore wrote *The Great Gildersleeve* from 1942 until 1947, after which he is credited with being one of the five writers (including director **William N. Robson** on the hour-long variety show *Did They Ask You?* (1947). Other post–Gildersleeve work included *The Danny Thomas Show* (1948) and *The Ford Theatre* (1948).

Moore is credited with being involved with the formation of the Radio Writers Guild in 1937 and served as president in the mid–1940s. In 1946 he was elected 2nd vice-chair of the Hollywood Writers Mobilization and also was an active member of the Hollywood Community Radio Group, one of four organizations applying for an open AM frequency. Both of these connections got him in trouble with post-war Communist hunters. California state senator Jack Tenney opposed the Radio Group's bid charging it was dominated by Communist sympathizers.

A few years later Moore was summoned to testify before the House Un-American Activities Committee about his membership with the Mobilization group that was accused of being a Communist front organization. Moore refused to answer questions pertaining to an alleged membership in the Communist Party despite the Committee's insistence that they had a copy of his Party card number. Little is known about Moore after his run-in with the government over his political leanings. He does not appear to have done much television work, at least under his own name, though evidence has been found of scriptwriting for the *Ford Show* in 1961.

Television: *Hogan's Daughter* (1949), Moore had directing and writing duties, the latter shared with old collaborator John Whedon.
Film: *The Merry Merriweathers* (1941, MGM).
Musicals: *Texas Lil' Darling* book written with John Whedon, music by Robert Emmet Dolan, lyrics by Johnny Mercer. The show was titled *Hell Bent for Election* and *A Day in the Country* during its development and received a poor critical reception.
Other: Three sets of Great Gildersleeve records released by Capitol between 1944 and 1947. Co-written with John Whedon.
Sources: Smoodin & Martin p. 119; Stumpf & Ohmart p. 73–74; Sies p. 98, 111, 166, 268; *Billboard* December 28, 1946, p. 8; *Broadcasting* December 1, 1935, p. 56, September 1, 1941, p. 36, July 1, 1940, p. 51; *Business Screen Magazine* no. 6, 1961 p. 38; *Radio Digest* September 1931 p. 49; *Radio & Television Mirror* December 1939 p. 48; *Variety* November 6, 1934, p. 45, September 3, 1941, p. 34, December 24, 1941, p. 27, March 25, 1936, p. 35.

Moore, Wilfred (Bill, William) G.

Wilfred Moore served as a fighter pilot in the First World War I and a commercial test pilot in the 1920s when he co-created the radio program *The Air Adventures of Jimmie Allen* with veteran **Bob Burtt**. The Skelly oil company was quick to sign on as sponsor and the program originally ran for four years, from 1933 until 1937. Upon its cancellation Skelly demonstrated it was not disillusioned with the creative talent of Moore and Burtt by working with the pair to create a new radio aviator, *Captain Midnight*. In between these two series both Moore and Burtt created individual aviation-themed programs with shorter runs, Moore's entitled *Howie Wing* (1937–1938) and *Angels in Blue* (1938, possible audition only).

As popular as *Jimmie Allen* was, Moore and co-writer Burtt topped themselves with the creation of *Captain Midnight*, another ace pilot who debuted on Chicago's WGN in October 1939. The series ran a full decade and attracted a huge audience of young listeners with its premiums and club novelties. Ivan Shark was the object of many of Captain Midnight's adventures, as were the Nazis during the World War II years.

Moore has been credited over the years with writing additional aviation programs, *Hop Harrigan* (1942–1948) and *Sky King*, but this is not possible as he died of a heart attack in 1939 after a game of tennis.

Film: *The Sky Parade* (1936).
Sources: Cagle 2006; French & Siegel p. 170; Harmon *Radio Mystery*; Kallis, Jr.; *Broadcasting* March 1,

1933, p. 33; *Film Daily Year Book, 1938* p. 531; *Radio Daily* January 17, 1938, p. 1, 8; *Variety* December 22, 1937, p. 27, October 11, 1939, p. 40.

Moore, William

William Moore, a West Coast manager for William Esty & Co., is credited with authoring scripts for the agency's *Blondie* (ca. 1941), based on the comic strip by Chic Young.
Source: *Broadcasting* January 13, 1941, p. 58.

Morgan, Helen

Helen Morgan was the creator and author of Mutual's *Lady Be Beautiful* (1946), a women's fashion and beauty-oriented program.
Source: *Variety* May 1, 1946, p. 42.

Morheim, Louis

Lou Morheim (March 25, 1922–September 8, 2013) was a working writer, penning numerous screenplays during the 1940s and dozens of television episodes through the 1950s and 1960s but never breaking out with a blockbuster film or series. His single known radio credit is the Jack Webb program *Johnny Modero: Pier 23* that aired in 1947.
Source: *Variety* April 30, 1947, p. 37.

Morrow, William (Bill) S.

Bill Morrow (August 16, 1907–February 5, 1971) helped boost *The Jack Benny Show* to the top of the ratings when he took on scripting duties with **Ed Beloin** in 1936. After seven years Morrow left to enter the service in 1943. Upon Morrow's return to civilian life he soon partnered with Bing Crosby and became the singer's lead scriptwriter for nearly the next quarter-century. Beginning in 1946 Morrow joined Crosby's *Kraft Music Hall* and later that year followed Crosby to *Philco Radio Time* where he worked as the producer-writer as he did on the follow-up *Bing Crosby Show* beginning in 1949.

Morrow took a break penning for Crosby in the late 1950s when he signed on as Frank Sinatra's television writer in 1957. Three years later Morrow was back at Crosby's side, scripting radio's new *Bing Crosby–Rosemary Clooney Show*. Throughout the 1960s Morrow authored scripts for Crosby television series and specials.

Sources: *Broadcasting* January 25, 1960, p. 90; *TV Radio Mirror* October 1957 p. 6; *Variety* February 13, 1946, p. 30.

Morse, Carlton E.

Born in Jennings, LA, Carlton Morse (June 4, 1901–May 24, 1993) would become one of the premier creators and writers of radio properties during the medium's Golden Age. His family relocated to Oregon while Morse was still a boy and his upbringing on a fruit and dairy ranch provided material he would use in his future programs. As the First World War wound down Morse enrolled for studies at the San Francisco campus of the University of California. One of his jobs was with a newspaper and in the 1920s he met and married Patricia DeBall.

Morse moved into radio in 1929, taking a job with NBC just three years after the network's creation. There at KGO he cut his teeth writing and producing a number of programs including *Chinatown Squad, The Cross-Eyed Parrot, House of Myths, Jack and Ethel, Let's Get Associated, Phantoms at Sea,* and *Split-Second Tales*. In the early 1930s Morse began formulating a family saga, inspired by John Galsworthy's *The Forsythe Saga,* and *One Man's Family* premiered in 1932.

Morse received permission for an on-air try-out from the network's Don Gilman to write three chapters (the series would be written in chapters throughout its run) that could be wrapped up if the decision was made to discontinue the series. That Gilman's son would have a role perhaps helped the effort reach the airwaves. *One Man's Family* debuted for San Francisco listeners on April 29, 1932, and didn't leave the air for twenty-seven years. Morse wrote *One Man's Family* for much of its early run, letting other writers come on board only later.

Even more famous than *One Man's Family* among radio enthusiasts was Morse's legendary *I Love a Mystery* (1939–1944), still a favorite of many to this day. While scripting his two most famous creations concurrently, at one point Morse had a regular routine, writing *One Man's Family* on Monday and Tuesday and spending the rest of the week on *I Love a Mystery*. His writing guides were a globe and some reference volumes. In the mid–1940s he created another show, this one syndicated, called *Adventures by Morse* that followed the exploits of San Francisco detective Capt. Bart Friday. Just a couple years later in 1948 Morse attempted to rekindle the excitement of *I Love a Mystery* by reuniting the show's heroes for a new set of adventures in *I Love Adventure*. Instead, the program sputtered and limped off the air after thirteen weeks.

Though well-known for the above four programs, it's sometimes forgotten that Morse authored numerous other series during a long career, many of them dramatic serials in the tradition of *Family*. Among these lesser-known works are *His Honor, The Barber* (1945–1946) the story of a down-home philosopher judge, *The Upper Room* (1947), *Family Skeleton* (1953–1954), *The Woman in My House* (1951–1957), and *It's the Berries* (1954).

Radio: *An American Family Saga* (1944, audition); *The Bennetts* (1946); *Tell Me a Story* (1946, audition); *Family Theatre* (1949); *Behold a Woman* (1950); *Uncle Judge Ben* (1951, audition).

Sources: Carlton Morse Copyright Collection; *Radio Digest* August 30, 1930, p. 88; bayarearadio.com.

Morwood, William

William Morwood was a British actor, director, and playwright who dabbled in radio in the late 1940s. Unable to earn a living entirely on his writing, Morwood taught at various schools and theaters in New York and on the West Coast. His earlier radio credits were *Inner Sanctum* and *Bulldog Drummond* and he later wrote for *Murder at Midnight* (1946-1947), *The Shadow* (1946-1947), and *You Are There* (1948).

Other Radio: *Road of Life*; *The March of Mercy* (1943); *Mr. Keen, Tracer of Lost Persons* (1946).

Sources: NBC Records; Cox *Mr. Keen*; Grams *Shadow* p. 384–385.

Moser, James Edward

James E. Moser (March 10, 1921–March 17, 1993) worked as a reporter for the *San Francisco Examiner* in the mid–1940s, before being hired on to ABC's news staff in 1945. One of his first known series was *One Out of Seven* (1945–1946) and he wrote for other dramas such as *The Story of Doctor Kildare* (1949) before working with creator Jack Webb to put together the audition episode of *Dragnet*, one of the most popular police procedural series of all time, on both radio and television. Moser authored scripts for *Dragnet* during its long run from 1949–1957 and received an Edgar Award in 1951 for his writing on the series. Moser's other radio credits include *Pete Kelly's Blues* (1951) and *Suspense* (1952).

Moser was a successful television scriptwriter into the 1970s with primetime dramatic programs, and even had telefilms aired in the early 1980s. Despite some experience with screenplays, Moser did not leave much of a mark in motion pictures.

Television: *Dragnet* (1951–1958); *Ben Casey* (1961–1966, creator); *Doctor's Hospital* (1975–1976, creator).

Film: *Wings of the Hawk* (1953).

Sources: *Broadcasting* May 7, 1951, p. 85; *Motion Picture Daily* September 29, 1953, p. 8; *Variety* October 31, 1945, p. 42.

Mosher, Bob

A New York–based writer for the J. Walter Thompson agency in the early 1940s, a move to the West Coast in 1942 springboarded Bob Mosher's (January 18, 1915–December 15, 1972) writing career into one of the most illustrious in radio and television. In California Mosher joined the writing staff of *The Edgar Bergen & Charlie McCarthy Show* (1942–1944, with **Joe Bigelow** and **Joe Connelly**), followed by stints on *The Chesterfield Music Shop* with Johnny Mercer (1944), *The Frank Morgan Show* (1945), *The Ginny Simms Show* (1946), and *The Fitch Bandwagon* (1946–1947, with Joe Connelly) after it assumed a sitcom format with Phil Harris and Alice Faye.

By far Mosher's most significant radio legacy is over a decade of scripting *The Amos 'n' Andy Show* (later *The Amos 'n' Andy Music Hall*) between 1946 and 1960, including the first season of its brief television run. In the midst of this Mosher was also responsible for the scripts of the widely panned *Meet Mr. McNutley* (1953–1954).

On television Mosher co-created *Leave It to Beaver* (1957–1963) and *The Munsters* (1964–1966) with long-time writing partner Joe Connelly and later scripted for *Mayberry R.F.D.* from

1968 until the time of his death in 1971. His achievements were recognized with nominations for both an Oscar (1956) and a primetime Emmy (1958). Described as a quiet prankster by those who knew him best, Mosher also understood the value of his work and partner Connelly noted that they retained ownership of a portion of their television creations which provided healthy financial returns over their lifetimes.

Other Radio: *Barnaby* (1945, audition); *The Harry Von Zell Show* (1946, audition).

Sources: Cox *The Munsters*; *Broadcasting* February 16, 1942, p. 34, August 16, 1943, p. 20, December 31, 1951, p. 60; *Variety* July 26, 1941, p. 24, February 27, 1946, p. 36.

Moss, Carlton

Newark, NJ, native Carlton Moss (February 14, 1909–August 10, 1997) may be the most under-appreciated African-American author in the annals of dramatic radio. On the air as early as 1930 on WEVD's *The Negro Art Group Hour*, Moss had his own series by the fall of that year on NBC. The series, *Careless Love*, is the first known dramatic program written by a black writer and featuring black performers that aired on a regular schedule. The show left the air in 1933 and Moss followed it with *Folks from Dixie*, a comedy that Moss undertook half-heartedly because it was the style desired by the network. His third black-centric series was *Meetin' House* (1934–1936), the story of a Southern circuit preacher.

By 1940 Moss had grown disillusioned with radio and the fact that his shows could not attract commercial sponsors. He relocated to Hollywood and became involved in motion pictures, his most famous credit in this area on Frank Capra's *The Negro Soldier* during World War II. Moss gradually moved into industrial films where he had more control over his product and later in life taught at Fisk University and University of California-Irvine.

Source: Ellett *Black Radio*.

Mullen, Virginia

Also an actor during the 1940s and 1950s, Virginia Mullen (March 11, 1906–January 30, 1988) co-wrote the radio series *Doorway to Life* (1947–1948) and *Tell Your Story* (1947).

Source: *Variety* February 26, 1947, p. 82.

Mundy, Talbot

Talbot Mundy (April 23, 1879–August 1940), a popular pulp writer and novelist who had previously authored the million-selling *King of the Khyber Rifles*, was one of the first scripters for the Blackett-Sample-Hummert show *Jack Armstrong, All-American Boy*, taking over the series in 1936 until his death in 1940.

Sources: Taves; *Broadcasting* July 5, 1939, p. 82, August 2, 1943, p. 38; *Radio Daily* September 1, 1937, p. 2.

Murcott, Joel

Joel Murcott (March 28, 1915–February 16, 1978) joined the Blue network's publicity staff in 1945 but was fired just a few months later; Murcott claimed it was due to his union organizing activities while ABC claimed he had been hired on a temporary basis. He pursued freelance scripting opportunities while also becoming the radio editor for *The Hollywood Reporter*. Murcott reported on industry news until 1949 when he took a new position with the transcription company Bruce Eels & Assoc.

Murcott's radio credits were numerous and attest to his proficiency crafting tales across various dramatic genres. Among them were *Suspense* (1947, 1950), *Family Theatre* (1947), *Sealtest Variety Theatre* (1948), *Hallmark Playhouse* (1949, 1953), *The Whistler* (1949), *The Adventures of Frank Race* (1949–1950, writer and director), *Escape* (1950), *Story of Doctor Kildare* (1950, 1951), *Tales of the Texas Rangers* (1950–1952), *Defense Attorney* (1951), *The Big Show* (1951–1952), *The Silent Men* (1951–1952), *Gunsmoke* (1952), *The Scarlet Pimpernel* (1952–1955, adapted from the book by Baroness Emmuska Orczy), and *Yours Truly, Johnny Dollar* (1953). Murcott's television career spanned two decades and featured contributions to *Alfred Hitchcock Presents* (1957–1962) and *Bonanza* (1967–1973).

Sources: *Billboard* February 5, 1949, p. 7, November 3, 1945, p. 32; *Broadcasting* May 28, 1945, p. 42, January 24, 1949, p. 77; *The Radio Annual* 1948 p. 245; martingrams.blogspot.com.

Murphy, Nan

Nan Murphy scripted for a number of agencies in the late 1930s including Blackett-Sample-Hummert, Morse, International, Inc., and N. W. Ayer & Son on shows such as *Young Widder Brown*.

Sources: *Broadcasting* May 1, 1935, p. 34; *Radio Annual* 1938 p. 706.

Murray, Dave

Dave Murray wrote gags for two of classic radio's biggest comedians, Edgar Bergen on *The Chase & Sanborn Hour* (ca. 1941) and Bob Hope. He was also part of the staff of the *Fibber McGee & Molly* spin-off *Beulah* (1946).

Sources: *Broadcasting* September 29, 1941, p. 45; *Variety* January 23, 1946, p. 32.

Murray, John

John Fenton Murray (February 19, 1917–July 24, 1996), born in Lincoln, NE, was exposed to the stars when his family moved to Los Angeles in 1930 and he got a job working at the Ambassador Hotel. After studying writing at the City College of Los Angeles, Murray served in the Navy during World War II then joined the writing staff for Red Skelton's program (ca. 1943–1955) after returning to civilian life. After nearly a dozen years with Skelton, including the transition to television in 1951, Murray joined *The Jimmy Durante Show*. Later, Murray received credit for writing for *McHale's Navy* (1964–1966), *Gilligan's Island* (1966–1967), and *Operation Petticoat* (1977–1978).

Sources: *Broadcasting* May 29, 1944, p. 46, October 8, 1951, p. 74; *Sarasota Herald-Tribune* July 29, 1996, p. 6B.

Neiman, Irving Gaynor

Irving Neiman (April 25, 1916–August 25, 1996) sold NBC his first script in the early 1940s after graduating from New York's City College and before being drafted into the service. While in the Army, Neiman wrote part of *Army Play-by-Play* a 1943 Broadway production written by military personnel. *Joe and Mabel*, originally aired 1941 to 1942 before Neiman's drafting, remains his only known radio work at this time, though he resumed the show for a short time after the war was done. Nevertheless, he carved out a quarter-century scripting career on television, writing for series and a number of TV movies.

Sources: *Variety* December 19, 1945, p. 28; *New York Times* obituary August 31, 1996.

Nelson, Ozzie

Ozzie Nelson, born Oswald George Nelson (March 20, 1906–June 3, 1975), came to national prominence as an orchestra leader in the 1930s and his success was such that he would likely be remembered today for this portion of his career alone. Various radio work in the late 1930s and early 1940s prompted him to create his own program, a fictional sitcom based on his real-life family which included wife Harriet and sons David and Eric (Ricky).

Though not a smash hit, *The Adventures of Ozzie and Harriet* was successful, airing from 1944 until 1954. The television version was just as successful, lasting from 1952 until 1966. Though a number of writers were employed on the radio show during its decade-long existence, Nelson provided a significant amount of material week in and week out.

Sources: *Variety* September 4, 1946, p. 34; museum.tv.

Neuman, Ernest Jack

E. Jack Neuman (February 27, 1921–January 15, 1998) was a workhorse writer, scripting for many of the most popular West Coast dramatic radio programs after serving in World War II. Neuman began developing as a writer while covering sports for the *Denver Post* before attending the University of Missouri where he studied English and journalism.

After college Neuman spent fours year with the Marine Corps during which time he sold his first works for radio and even motion pictures. Upon leaving the military Neuman joined CBS' writing staff where he scripted for *Suspense* (1943, 1947, 1949–1960), *Meet Miss Sherlock* (1946), *The Whistler* (1947, 1948), *The City* (1947), *Hawk Larabee* (1947), *Jeff Regan, Investigator* (1948–1950), *Box 13* (1948), *Rocky Jordan* (1949), *Escape* (1950, 1952–1954), *Yours*

Truly, Johnny Dollar (1950, 1952–1953, 1955), *The Adventures of Sam Spade* (1950), *The Story of Doctor Kildare* (1950–1951), *Night Beat* (1950–1951), *Richard Diamond, Private Detective* (1951), and *The Line-Up* (1951–1952).

Much of this work was finished while Neuman worked on his law degree, with which he graduated in 1951 as part of UCLA law school's first class. During the early 1950s Neuman wrote more and more for television, overlapping with his continued output on radio with stories for *On Stage* (1953–1954), *Rogers of the Gazette* (1953–1954), *Hallmark Hall of Fame* (1953–1954), *Romance* (1954–1957), *Fort Laramie* (1956), and *Pursuit* (1949–1952).

Neuman's television work reflected that of his years in radio, dramatic stories in various genres including Westerns and crime-detective. More than just a reliable script writer, Neuman created some series that reached the airwaves including *Sam Benedict and Mr. Novak*.

On radio Neuman used at least two different pseudonyms, **John Dawson** and Jack Dawson. Under the former he wrote dozens of scripts for *Yours Truly, Johnny Dollar* (1955–1957) and *Have Gun, Will Travel* (1958–1959), one of the rare shows that debuted on television before arriving on radio.

Other Radio: *Alias Jane Doe*.
Sources: E. Jack Neuman Papers; *Variety* obituary January 22, 1998.

Newman, Robert

For a scriptwriter with a career as extensive as Robert Newman's, little is known of his background at this time. Newman is remembered primarily for works of drama and suspense but as his list of credits demonstrates, was also comfortable with comedy and serials as well.

Series that so far have been linked to Newman include *The Fleischmann's Yeast Hour* (1935–1936), *Hawks Sky Patrol* (1936), *The Chase & Sanborn Hour* (1941), *Inner Sanctum* (1941–1946), *News from Home* (1942), *Major North, Army Intelligence* (1945), *Mystery in the Air* (1945), *Murder at Midnight* (1946–1947), *The Rudy Vallee Show* (1947), *Big Sister* (1949–1950 with **Julian Funt**), *Rogers of the Gazette* (1953–1954), and *Theatre Five* (1964–1965). Newman's scripts were also used during the brief 1970s revival of dramatic radio on the *CBS Radio Mystery Theater* (1974, 1977) and the *CBS Radio Adventure Theater* (1977).

Other Radio: *The Adventures of the Thin Man; The Man from G-2*.
Sources: *The Film Daily* January 19, 1937, p. 11; *Variety* May 20, 1942, p. 33, April 25, 1945, p. 30, July 11, 1945, p. 32.

Newman, Walter Brown

Walter Newman (February 11, 1916–October 14, 1993) entered radio after the end of World War II during which he served as a navigator and instructor. His first scripts appeared on CBS's experimental *The Columbia Workshop* (1946) but his work would eventually be used across the network's evening broadcast schedule. While providing scripts for dramatic programs such as *Family Theatre* (1947) and *The Molle Mystery Theatre* (1947), one his first regular assignments was the comedy series *The Joan Davis Show* (1947).

Newman's list of credits reflects his ability to write across different genres, from Mickey Rooney's *Shorty Bell* (1948), to **Don Quinn**'s comedy *Halls of Ivy* (1949–1951), Cary Grant's *Mr. and Mrs. Blandings* (1951), *Romance* (1953), the premier of *Gunsmoke* (1952), *Suspense* (1948, 1949, 1951) and *Escape* (1949, 1954).

The bulk of Newman's work after 1950 was for television and motion pictures as demand for his scripts increased. He created TV's *The Beachcomber* and was nominated for three Academy Awards (1952, 1966, 1979) and a primetime Emmy. Interestingly, two of his most famous screenplays, *The Magnificent Seven* (1960) and *The Great Escape* (1963) didn't even bear Newman's name due to behind-the-scenes differences with the producers.

An unquestionably talented writer, colleague **William Froug** later recalled that Newman was a quiet and very private man who was both a perfectionist and highly protective of his work. He also was very lax with deadlines, a particular irritant in industries where expensive projects are highly dependent on timely completion schedules.

Other Radio: *Crusade for Children* (1948); *On Stage* (1953).
Film: *The Big Carnival* (1951, also *Ace in the Hole*); *Cat Ballou* (1965); *Bloodbrothers* (1978).
Sources: Froug; *Broadcasting* February 5, 1951, p. 26; *Radio Daily* December 9, 1949, p. 2; *Variety* December 18, 1946, p. 41, March 26, 1947, p. 29.

Nichols, Anne

Anne Nichols (November 26, 1891–September 15, 1966) wrote numerous plays and acted in some silent films but she is most remembered for *Abie's Irish Rose*, her play that was turned into two motion pictures as well as a radio series that aired from 1942 to 1944. She was involved in writing the radio scripts with Alfred "Rip" van Ronkel and may have served as more an overseer later in the show's run.
Sources: Ann Nichols papers; *Motion Picture Daily* March 25, 1943, p. 10.

Niss, Stanley

Raised in St. Louis, Stanley Niss (June 16, 1916–July 22, 1969) entered the newspaper industry as a young man, writing for St. Louis and then Dallas papers as early as 1935. After working as a publicist for a time, Niss relocated to New York to once again write for a newspaper in 1943. Fate intervened one day while Niss was working for a story disguised as a vagrant and he met Phillips H. Lord, a successful radio producer.

Almost immediately Lord offered Niss a job writing scripts for twice what he was making with the paper. Niss demonstrated a keen eye for a good script, authoring over one thousand by his own account over years of writing and editing, and supervising countless more as Lord entrusted him with more responsibility. Niss' premier credits include several years working on *Gang Busters* (1946–1953) and subsequently *21st Precinct* (1953–1956).

In 1949, with television's emergence, Niss took a job with CBS that would eventually allow him to step into that medium. Throughout the 1950s and 1960s Niss wrote and produced many different television programs, initially for CBS and then for Desilu Productions. His specialty was crime and law enforcement themes, most notably *Hawaiian Eye* (1959–1961) which he is also credited with creating.
Other Radio: *Counterspy*; *CBS Radio Workshop* (1956).
Sources: Grams *Gang Busters*; *Motion Picture Daily* June 22, 1954, p. 5; *Baltimore Sun* August 29, 1954, p. L11; *Newsday* July 23, 1969, p. 58.

Norman, Wallace K.

Wally Norman created and co-wrote *Kitty Keene, Incorporated* (1937–1941) and has been credited with authoring *Little Orphan Annie* and *Deadline Mystery* (1947).
Sources: Cox *Crime Fighters*; mysteryfile.com.

Norris, Kathleen

Kathleen Norris (July 16, 1880–January 18, 1966) was a best-selling novel and serial author during the first decades of the 20th century, penning nearly 100 books that popularized themes that would be widely used on radio serials. Norris broached radio in 1945 scripting the soap opera *Bright Horizon*, a spin-off of *Big Sister*. The serial was renamed *A Woman's Life* later in the year and despite the initial burst of publicity brought by hiring such a famous author, Norris was removed from the show at the end of 1945. She made at least one other foray into radio with *Movie Matinee* (1946). An early radio program, *By Kathleen Norris* (1939–1941), a serialization of some of her novels produced by Phillips H. Lord, is not known to have involved Norris directly.
Sources: *Broadcasting* March 26, 1945, p. 33; *Variety* September 20, 1939, p. 31, August 22, 1945, p. 40, December 11, 1946, p. 32.

Nosserman, Dick

Dick Nosserman remains an obscure author, credited with only one known radio series, *The Smiths of Hollywood* (1946–1947).
Source: Dunning p. 621–622.

Oboler, Arch

Arch Oboler (December 7, 1909–March 19, 1987) is recognized as one of the most gifted writers of radio's Golden Age, highlighted by his scripts of horror and macabre stories early in his career. As a teenager in Chicago he began submitting scripts to the city's NBC studio and developed a thick skin to rejection; he reportedly wrote 50 plays before his first, "Futuristics," was finally accepted by a NBC production chief and put on the air.

The script was used in conjunction with the opening of NBC's famed Radio City in New York in 1934 and for it Oboler received $50, a decent paycheck for the time but less than he was hoping for. To add a few dollars to the payment he did some voice work for the broadcast.

Oboler's first steady radio work was a series of short sketches for *Grand Hotel* (1934–1935) and *The Rudy Vallee Hour*. Soon after, Don Ameche, also on the rise on Chicago radio, signed him to a one-year contract to write material for him for *The Chase & Sanborn Hour* (1937–1938). It was during this stint that Oboler authored one of the more notorious broadcasts of the era, Mae West's "Adam and Eve" play. The December 12, 1937, broadcast resulted in West's banishment from radio for over a dozen years and some strong-arming on the part of the Federal Communications Commission toward stations that had aired the show.

Oboler is not known to have suffered much backlash from writing the script; indeed, it was a fairly innocent piece between Eve and the snake in the Biblical Eden. West, however, managed to take the benign sketch, infuse it with her oozing sexuality, and raise the moral outrage of listeners, the press, and even politicians.

From these early light comedy assignments Oboler moved on to *Lights Out!* (1936–1939, 1942–1945), one of the most renowned spook shows of the era. He was charged with following the program's creator, **Wyllis Cooper**, who moved west to Hollywood for other opportunities. In 1938 he agreed to co-write scripts for the big-budget *Your Hollywood Parade*.

It wasn't long, however, before Oboler moved to more artistic ventures, among them a script about the world's ugliest man. Wanting to ensure it was produced exactly as he imagined it in his head, Oboler sunk most of his money into the studio and talent to record the script. NBC's Lewis Titterton liked what he heard and gave Oboler his own series, *Arch Oboler's Plays*, in 1939. *Plays* was an anthology series that allowed Oboler to explore the wide expanses of his creative imagination, not having to pin himself down to a narrow genre. The series only lasted one year and it couldn't find a sponsor in that time.

When *Plays* left the air in March 1940, Oboler went to work on other series not of his own creation, including *Everyman's Theater*, *Everything for the Boys*, *Plays for Americans*, and *The Treasury Star Parade*. *Everyman's Theater* (1940–1941) used many Oboler scripts, several of which he recycled from his earlier programs. A short-lived Oboler effort was *Free World Theater*, an anthology series he created after discussions with Office of War Information official William Lewis. Conceptualized as the dramatization of the ideas of world leaders for American citizens, Oboler wrote the premier incorporating some thoughts by Henry Wallace. *Plays for Americans* (1942) was yet another war-related project undertaken by Oboler.

In 1944 Oboler was put in charge of a new series, *Everything for the Boys*, that was to star screen actor Ronald Colman. It was Colman's first dramatic radio work and did not provide the radio fame he was hoping for. That the two had little tolerance for each other, on both personal and professional levels, did not get the production off on the right foot. With *Everything* off the air, Oboler managed to bring his *Plays* anthology back to the air in 1945 but its run was even shorter this time, lasting just six months.

Oboler directed and wrote briefly for *The James and Pamela Mason Show*, a short-lived 1949 series featuring the British film star and his wife. Their collegial relationship quickly soured, however, and Oboler only wrote three episodes before leaving.

Recognized as one of the most talented writers in the radio business, motion picture studios inevitably came calling for Oboler and he is credited with more than a half-dozen screenplays. Unlike Orson Welles, however, with whom Oboler was sometimes compared at the time, Oboler's films did not find much commercial or critical success. Oboler predicted, correctly, that television would overtake radio and bring about the end of dramatic radio as it was known at the time. Despite briefly having his own comedy program in 1949 and contributing teleplays to a number of dramatic anthology programs during the 1950s and 1960s, Oboler's fame now rests entirely on his body of radio work.

Other Radio: *The First Nighter Program* (1935); *Irene Rich* (1936–1937, serial); *Portraits for Americans* (1943).

Films: *Escape* (1940); *Gangway for Tomorrow* (1943).

Book: *Everything Happened to Him* (1936).

Sources: *Broadcasting* January 25, 1943, p. 39; *Radio Daily* April 2, 1937, p. 4; *Radio Mirror* April 1938 p. 19; *Variety* March 11, 1936, p. 43; *Chicago Tribune* September 20, 1935, p. 16; parallax-view.org.

O'Brien, Robert (Bob)

Robert O'Brien (May 8, 1918–November 7, 2005) scripted jokes and scenarios first for Jack Benny (1943) and then for *The Eddie Cantor Show* (1945–1946) as the comedian attempted to stay relevant in an evolving and maturing radio industry. At the same time, O'Brien's first screenplay *Lady on a Train* (1945, co-written with **Ed Beloin**) was released, to be followed by about a half-dozen more films before he turned full-time to television scripting. O'Brien proved adept at creating humor for the small screen and worked for nearly a decade on Lucille Ball's series during the 1960s and 1970s. He also made significant contributions to *Mr. Ed* (1958–1963).

Sources: *Broadcasting* September 13, 1943, p. 38; *Motion Picture Daily* August 9, 1945, p. 3; *Variety* October 3, 1945, p. 36.

O'Flaherty, Maggie

Maggie O'Flaherty served as a producer and writer for *Quiz Kids* in the early and mid–1940s while also editing an unofficial publication of jokes and puns called *Grimy Gazette* (ca. 1943) that was sent to servicemen overseas. In 1948 she moved from Chicago to New York to take over scripting duties on Tommy Dorsey's broadcast.

Sources: *Variety* March 10, 1948, p. 30; *Spartanburg Herald-Journal* March 28, 1943, p. 4; otrsite.com.

Oldham, Vera

Originally a secretary for the Earnshaw-Young agency, Vera Oldham's writing samples convinced the producers of *Chandu the Magician* to hire her as the primary writer for the children's adventure serial from 1932–1936. The program premiered in Los Angeles and was added to stations up the West Coast before finally being added to the Mutual network in the mid–1930s. *Chandu*'s popularity prompted its spread to stations in the Midwest and eventually on the East Coast. Upon the completion of the program's original run in 1936, *Chandu*'s sponsor showed its appreciation for Oldham's work by awarding her a year-long vacation in East Asia and then a brand new Studebaker automobile when she returned.

During Oldham's last year on *Chandu the Magician* she was signed to write another Don Lee serial, *Drums* (1935–1937), and then after *Chandu*'s conclusion she joined Maxwell House's *Showboat* in 1937. In 1939 Oldham scripted both *Parker Family* and *The Story of Ellen Randolph* (1939–1941) but dropped the first when the sponsor balked at her writing two similar shows. Oldham joined the WAVES, the women's naval reserves and stepped away from radio.

Though it's not clear when Oldham returned to scribing for the airwaves, in 1948 she was called in to redo her old *Chandu* scripts for a fresh new run through 1950. During that job she also signed with ABC television in 1949 though her work continued to appear on the air in following years on shows including *Newsstand Theater of the Air* (1951).

Other Radio: *Those Websters*.

Sources: *Billboard* April 14, 1951, p. 8; *Broadcasting* June 15, 1936, p. 32, July 15, 1937, p. 46, January 2, 1950, p. 62; *Radio Daily* November 10, 1949, p. 6, December 21, 1949, p. 5; *Variety* July 12, 1939, p. 26, October 18, 1939, p. 22.

Oliver, Edith

As a special program writer for the Biow Agency in the 1940s, Edith Oliver researched material for writer Charles Martin on *The Philip Morris Playhouse* (1943) and had the same responsibility on Phil Baker's quiz show *Take It Or Leave It* (1940–1952), for which she also wrote the questions.

Sources: *Broadcasting* January 31, 1949, p. 27; *Variety* March 30, 1943, p. 30, July 14, 1943, p. 37.

Oppenheimer, George

George Oppenheimer (February 7, 1900–August 14, 1977) had a long and varied writing career that seemed to touch on just about every medium utilizing the written word. Oppenheimer worked in the book industry (co-founding Viking Press), motion pictures (most notably with MGM), and television as it came of age in the 1950s. Oppenheimer penned plays, newspaper columns during World War II, several books on the theater, and worked as the drama critic for *Newsday* for the last two decades of his life.

Amidst this, Oppenheimer found time to contribute to the scripts for The Marx Brothers' 1932–1933 series *Flywheel, Shyster, and Flywheel*. This would not be his only assignment penning for the comedy team, later working on the screenplays for *A Night at the Opera* (1935) and *A Day at the Races* (1937).

Sources: George Oppenheimer writings; *Variety* December 13, 1932, p. 33; *New York Times* obituary August 16, 1977.

Oppenheimer, Jess

Jessurun "Jess" Oppenheimer (November 11, 1913–December 27, 1988) developed his comedy writing over a decade and a half on radio, penning jokes for some of the era's biggest stars. While still a student at Stanford University in the early 1930s he started hanging around KFRC and was immediately taken with the medium. One of Oppenheimer's first writing jobs was for *The Twin Star Show* (1937) followed soon after by Packard's *Hollywood Mardi Gras* with Fred Astaire for the Young & Rubicam agency (1937). Oppenheimer's following shows included *The Jack Benny Show*, *The Chase & Sanborn Hour*, *Gulf Screen Theatre Guild* (1939), and *The Rudy Vallee Show* (1941).

While serving in the Coast Guard during World War II Oppenheimer met the son-in-law of Fanny Brice and after his time in the service was finished accepted a position writing for *The Baby Snooks Show*. He stayed with Brice for six years and in 1948 was chosen to script a series for Lucille Ball, *My Favorite Husband*.

Oppenheimer cemented his place in show business history when he was tagged in 1950 to head the creation of a television show for Ball. The result was the smash hit *I Love Lucy* on which he worked for five years. He subsequently stayed active in television through the 1960s, most often in production and executive positions.

Sources: Oppenheimer & Oppenheimer; *Broadcasting* November 15, 1939, p. 80, June 30, 1941, p. 40; *Radio Daily* August 10, 1937, p. 5; *Variety* March 17, 1937, p. 37, August 21, 1946, p. 42; *New York Times* obituary December 30, 1988.

Orloff, Arthur E.

Arthur E. Orloff (November 25, 1908–September 16, 1994) remains a little-known scriptwriter of more than a dozen screenplays during the late 1940s—early 1950s as well as of numerous teleplays in the 1960s. Orloff's primary radio credit was the adult Western series *Hawk Larabee* (1947–1948).

Sources: *Showmen's Trade Review* December 6, 1947, p. 14; *The Screen Writer* December 1947 p. 55.

Osborne, Innes

Innes Osborne remains an obscure author responsible for little-known mystery program *The Orange Lantern* (1932) set in East Asia.

Source: *Radio and Amusement Guide* September 4–10 p. 2.

Owen, Dean (see Dudley Dean McGaughy)

Panama, Norman

Norman Panama (April 21, 1914–January 13, 2003) joined with **Melvin Frank**, a friend whom he met while studying at the University of Chicago, to create a potent comedy scripting duo that found success in both radio and motion pictures. Panama helped Bob Hope get his radio career off the ground by co-authoring the first season of his *Pepsodent Show* (1938–1939). The next year he joined the writing team for Phil Baker in 1939 and then after another year signed with Rudy Vallee's Sealtest program.

In the early 1940s Panama increasingly wrote for films but took a hiatus in 1942 when he was assigned to the War Department's Radio Department. Panama's subsequent resume in motion pictures is impressive and includes *Mr. Blandings Builds His Dream House* (1948), *White Christmas* (1954), and some of the Bob Hope/Bing Crosby *Road* films.

Other Radio: *Command Performance.*

Sources: Young; *Broadcasting* February 15, 1940, p. 54; *The Film Daily* June 9, 1942, p. 8; *Motion Picture Daily* June 22, 1939, p. 8; *Los Angeles Times* obituary January 25, 2003.

Paul, Norman

Norman Paul (November 22, 1913–July 1, 1979) was a comedy writer on radio and television for nearly four decades. On the airwaves Paul wrote for *Fun With Dunn* (1943), *The Alan Young Show* (1945–1946), Eddie Cantor's *Pabst Show* (1946–1947), *The Tony Martin Show* (1947–1948), *The Danny Thomas Show* (1948), and *The Edgar Bergen Show* (1951–1954). Paul's television credits include beloved comedies *The George Burns & Gracie Allen Show* (1955–1958), *Gomer Pyle: USMC* (1967–1969), and *Good Times* (1974–1978).

Sources: *Billboard* October 23, 1943, p. 10; *Variety* July 24, 1946, p. 42, October 1, 1947, p. 26, April 21, 1948, p. 24.

Pearson, Ben

Ben Pearson, writer for CBS' Pacific network at station KNX in the early 1940s, joined the J. Walter Thompson agency in 1942 to work as an assistant under George Welles who was writing *Lux Radio Theatre* at the time. Some of his other premier radio scripting duties included *The First Nighter Program* (1944) and *Stop or Go* (1943–1945), a quiz show for servicemen.

In 1946 Pearson left the West Coast for New York to head the radio operations of the Lyons agency. One of his later radio credits was *The Player* (1948). In the late 1940s Pearson also took on some television duties and focused more on production work than writing.

Other Radio: *Justice* (1946, audition); *The Wonderful Wileys* (audition).

Sources: *Billboard* November 3, 1951, p. 60; *Broadcasting* September 28, 1942, p. 39, June 14, 1943, p. 36; *Motion Picture Daily* June 12, 1942, p. 8; *Variety* August 14, 1946, p. 26.

Pelletier, Louis (Lou)

Louis Pelletier (March 7, 1906–February 11, 2000), a Pittsburg native who graduated from the Barnard School for Boys and Dartmouth, held a variety of jobs before the age of 30 when he was introduced to the world of show business by actor-friend Bob Sloan. The pair started to write some plays on a whim and their first, *Howdy Stranger!* (1937), made its way to Broadway and was later turned into a Dick Powell movie. This was followed by a couple more plays that didn't find similar success but inspired Pelletier to try radio.

His first scripts were bought by the J. Walter Thompson agency for Rudy Vallee's program and this led to some script work on a friend's serial. Pelletier freelanced on shows including *Are You a Genius?*, *Commandos*, *Man Behind the Gun*, *Romance*, and *Suspense*, before being hired by the CBS script department in 1942 where he was promptly put on the writing staff for *Kay Thompson & Co.* Later that same year Pelletier was inducted into the Army and assigned to *The Voice of the Army.*

Pelletier continued to author radio plays during his free time then returned to scripting full-time after the war for programs such as *The Doctor Fights* (1945), *The Whistler* (1945), *Molle Mystery Theatre* (1946), *Adventures of Sam Spade* (1947), and *The FBI in Peace and War* (1944–1955), for which he contributed over 500 episodes. Pelletier later was a successful screenwriter in the 1960s with *Big Red*, *Follow Me Boys*, *Horse in the Gray Flannel Suit*, *Smith*, and *Those Calloways.*

Sources: Cox "Drama! Thrills! Action!"; *Broadcasting* February 2, 1942, p. 34; *Motion Picture Daily* January 29, 1942, p. 12; *Radio Romances* May 1945 p. 51; *Variety* August 20, 1947, p. 24.

Perkins, Kenneth

Born to American parents in India, Kenneth Perkins (May 16, 1890–June 7, 1951) graduated with an English degree from the University of California–Berkeley and eventually found his niche writing Western fiction. Many of his stories were adapted to motion pictures dating to the silent era, as early as 1922. Perkins briefly experimented with radio and signed to author some stories for *Hawk Durango* (1946). Evidence suggests Perkins was also landing the occasional acting role, perhaps to supplement declining writing income. Many of his stories were adapted for television in the 1950s, years after his passing.

Sources: *Exhibitor's Herald* July 22, 1922, p. 53; *Variety* July 17, 1946, p. 26; martingrams.blogspot.com.

Perl, Arnold

After growing up in New York, Arnold Perl (April 14, 1914–December 11, 1971) started his career writing copy and editing for a literary agency. After a period working on documentary films he started to script freelance in radio. Some of his first stories were sold to *Bulldog Drummond*, *Grand Central Station*, and *Inner Sanctum*. Perl spent his spare time creating audition shows, authoring magazine pieces, and selling ideas for motion pictures.

When war came Perl took a job with the United Nations Information Office and worked on series such as *Uncle Sam* (1943) and also had consulting work with the War Department. After his induction in 1943 Perl was initially assigned to the Medical Corps. but was subsequently reassigned to the Army Service Forces Productions Unit where he worked on scripts for *Weapons for Victory* (1945).

Perl earned a reputation for writing quality and timely documentary scripts on such topics as race relations and the post-war baby black market. But he also held his own on drama programs such as *Fighting Senator* (1946), *Assignment Home* (1945–1946), *American Portrait* (1946), *The Eternal Light* (1947), *The Amazing Mr. Tutt* (1948), *The Big Story* (1948, 1949), *Great Scenes from Great Plays* (1949), *Up for Parole* (1950), and *I Fly Anything* (1951). Perl wrote steadily for television until his death in 1971.

Two of Perl's greatest achievements came in other fields, Broadway and motion pictures. In the 1950s he wrote some plays based on the short stories of Sholom Aleichem and other Jewish writers that vividly portrayed Jewish life in Tsarist Russia in the early 20th century. This material would later be worked into the smash musical *Fiddler on the Roof*. A decade later Perl penned a documentary about Malcolm X based on Alex Haley's biography, and this picture would later provide inspiration for Spike Lee's 1992 biopic of Malcolm X.

Other Radio: *American School of the Air* (1948).

Sources: *Radio Mirror* May 1945 p. 49; *Variety* February 24, 1943, p. 30, August 7, 1946, p. 33, April 14, 1948, p. 22.

Perrin, Nat

Nat Perrin (March 15, 1905–May 9, 1998) was a busy comedy screenwriter, penning material for the Marx Brothers, Gracie Allen, and Abbott and Costello on the big screen. His primary radio achievement was the scripting of the Marx Bros. near-legendary series *Flywheel, Shyster, and Flywheel* (1932–1933).

Source: *The Hollywood Reporter* February 27, 1933, p. 4.

Perrin, Sam

Sam Perrin (August 15, 1901–January 8, 1998) began his network writing career co-scripting *The Phil Baker Show* (1934–1938) with **Arthur Phillips** for the Gulf Oil Co. After stepping in to write some material for Jack Benny in 1936 while **Harry Conn** was in a dispute with Benny and refused to write it himself, Perrin briefly rejoined Benny's writing team in 1938. When Gulf Oil started sponsoring *The Gulf Screen Guild Theatre* in 1939, Perrin again teamed with Phillips until 1941 to author the series' scripts.

Perrin changed programs again in 1941 to pen *The Burns & Allen Show* and during the 1942 summer season authored the replacement show *Over Here* featuring **Tommy Riggs** and Betty Lou. Perrin once again signed to write for Jack Benny in 1943 and became one of a team of four scriptwriters during *The Jack Benny Show*'s heyday where he stayed until it left the air.

Occasionally Perrin took on other tasks, including serving as an advisor to *The Jack Paar* show on a rotating basis with co–Benny writers **George Balzer**, **John Tackaberry**, and **Milt Josefsberg**. But Perrin and Benny developed a tight bond and Perrin wrote for the legendary comedian after he transitioned to television and worked on Benny's television specials until almost 1970.

Television: *Here's Lucy* (1969–1972); *Archie Bunker's Place* (1979).

Sources: *Broadcasting* October 15, 1938, p. 42, November 15, 1939, p. 80, August 25, 1941, p. 38, November 22, 1943, p. 42; *Radio Mirror* September 1937 p. 78.

Peterson, Jean

Jean Peterson has been identified as a writer for the children's series *Our Barn* and *Coast to Coast on a Bus* in the late 1930s.

Source: Dunning.

Phares, Frank H.

Frank Phares (February 13, 1913–December 24, 1968) was a working writer, first in radio during the 1940s and then on television through the 1950s. His aural credits include *Cheers from the Camps* (1942), *Foreign Assignment* (1943–1944), *Texaco Star Theatre* (1944–1945), and *This Is Your FBI* (1945–1947).

Sources: *Variety* June 24, 1942, p. 39, September 1, 1943, p. 36, October 4, 1944, p. 24.

Phillips, Arthur

Arthur Phillips was a busy screenwriter through the 1930s and 1940s while also authoring a steady succession of comedy programs over two decades. With **Sam Perrin** he co-wrote *The Phil Baker Show* from 1934 to 1938 and then after the war joined the staffs of *The Rudy Vallee Show* (1945), *The Judy Canova Show* (1948), *The Adventures of Maisie* (1949–1950), and *The Martin and Lewis Show* (1953). Phillips spent another 25 years penning for television including ten years on *The Red Skelton Show* (1961–1971) and numerous Dean Martin specials during the 1970s. He earned two Emmy nominations for his work on Skelton's program.

Sources: Hayde "Martin & Lewis"; *Broadcasting* February 23, 1953, p. 93; *Radio Mirror* September 1937 p. 78, May 1949 p. 59.

Phillips, Irna

A native of Chicago and one of ten siblings, Irna Phillips' (July 1, 1901–December 23, 1973) father died when she was young and she later claimed not to have had a very pleasant childhood. After high school Phillips first attended Northwestern University, then the University of Illinois in Champaign–Urbana, and finally the University of Wisconsin. She earned her teaching certificate and taught for four years in Ohio at Dayton's Teachers College before discovering radio in 1929.

While home on summer break one year Phillips visited a Chicago radio station and found herself unexpectedly asked to read some lines on the air. She spent the rest of the summer kicking around that station and then quit her teaching job in the fall after she had an argument with her then-boyfriend. Returning to Chicago she quickly found work on the air with WGN.

Phillips' first scripting opportunity came when the station manager asked her to create a special for Memorial Day. She did, it was well-received, and she was subsequently asked to create a serious daily story. Initially Phillips' work was heard on a program with Ireene Wicker, known as the Singing Story Lady, and soon after that she was offered $50 a week to take charge of a new serial, *Painted Dreams*. The show was widely recognized as one of the first radio soap operas and Phillips—with her focus on two keys to success in soaps, cliffhanger endings and thoughtful character development—eventually found herself one of the biggest creators in the genre next to Frank and Anne Hummert. In her prime Phillips outlined and scripted five serials, dictating an estimated two million words a year to secretaries.

Phillips had a falling out with WGN in 1932 when she claimed ownership and rights to *Painted Dreams*, a highly unusual claim at the time, though one that was being pursued by more authors as the medium matured. While she filed a lawsuit to settle the affair with WGN, Phillips continued to create and write new material even as the suit wound through the courts for eight years (eventually resulting in a decision against her).

That year she introduced *Today's Children* to audiences, basically a reworking of her *Painted Dreams* formula. NBC liked it and put it on the air over their outlet WMAQ. By 1935 the network had added the daily *Welcome Valley* to her workload and the next year the weekly *Masquerade*.

1937 proved to be a big year for Phillips with the introduction of two legendary soaps. Her longest-lasting creation, *The Guiding Light*, debuted that year and with only minor interruptions ran on radio until 1956 and then on television until 2009, an astounding 72-year broadcasting run. That same year Phillips premiered another serial, *Road of Life*, that was no small success in its own right, airing until 1958. Phillips tried to introduce yet another series that year, *The Hand of Man*, but it failed to find the traction of her other works.

Even when series were going well, as was *Today's Children*, Phillips was not against bringing it to an end. When she decided there wasn't anything left to do with her characters on *Today's Children* without getting into the melodrama she claimed to distain at the time, she wrapped up the storyline in 1938. This decision was probably also related to the death of her mother, the inspiration for the broadcast's main character. The program was quickly replaced with her *Woman in White* (1938–1942), focusing on the story of a nurse.

An offshoot of *The Guiding Light*, *The Right to Happiness* debuted in 1939 and went on to an impressive 21-year run. Phillips wrote the serial at first and then handed it off to Art Gladd until 1942, when she sold the property to Proctor & Gamble who promptly moved the show from Chicago to New York and assigned **John M. Young** as writer.

Phillips introduced more programs during the 1940s, though none proved as durable as her first creations. *Lonely Women* arrived on the airwaves in 1942 but the title was changed to the previously-used *Today's Children* because she did not like the original name. In 1946 Phillips developed another property again using a prior title, *Masquerade* (1946–1947), so she could sell an hour-long block of soaps to General Mills. With four consecutive shows on the air, Phillips liked connecting them together, purposefully having characters show up between the different programs.

Among Phillips' later works was *The Brighter Day*, a spin-off of *Joyce Jordan, M.D.*, which ran from 1948 to 1956. Later in her career Phillips would be almost entirely in charge of her productions, finding her own sponsors, paying the casts and crew, and placing it on the networks. For all her effort Phillips earned an estimated $5,000 per week at her peak.

As early as 1949 Phillips was jumping into television soap opera with *These Are My Children* and then overseeing some of her other series' transitions to the visual format. Her contributions to television soaps are no less impressive, creating *As the World Turns* and *Another World* and working closely on *Days of Our Lives* and *Peyton Place* among many others.

Sources: Irna Phillips Papers; *Broadcasting* December 6, 1943, p. 28, December 10, 1945, p. 75; *Radio Daily* April 2, 1937, p. 4, July 12, 1937, p. 6; *Radio Mirror* January 1936 p. 74, February 1938 p.4, November 1939 p. 40, 68–69; *Variety* December 29, 1931, p. 116, September 27, 1932, p. 56, March 27, 1935, p. 39, June 10, 1942, p. 38.

Phillips, Paul

Paul Phillips spent about a decade authoring radio scripts, first as the continuity director for New York's WMCA and then, after a move in 1936, for KMOX in St. Louis. There he is known to have penned *All Hands on Deck* and *St. Louis Blues* before returning to New York in 1939 to join CBS as a continuity writer where he wrote *Flow Gently, Sweet Rhythm*, a musical program featuring African-American performers.

Phillips departed CBS in 1941 to script *The Golden Treasury of Song* but returned to network writing with NBC and their series *Chamber Music Society of Lower Basin Street* and *Strictly from Dixie*. It was not long before Phillips switched employers again, this time landing with the Lord & Thomas agency where he began to get his feet wet producing as well as writing on programs such as *Hit Parade* and *Information Please*. He spent much of the rest of the decade in the role of producer, leaving the writing to others.

Sources: *Broadcasting* August 1, 1939, p. 44, December 1, 1940, p. 47; *Variety* April 22, 1936, p. 43, August 9, 1939, p. 35, March 5, 1941, p. 28, July 23, 1941, p. 35, November 5, 1941, p. 29.

Pickard, John

Australia-born John Pickard (b. April 6, 1910) arrived in the United States in the mid-1930s after having worked as a continuity writer with the National Broadcasting Commission in Australia from 1932–1935. In his new position with NBC's San Francisco outlet Pickard was assigned to write and perform in an adaptation of *Three Musketeers* (1935) and then *Along Life's Highway* (1936). Pickard is credited with creating, writing, and directing *Young Dr. Malone* with collaborator **Frank Provo** before taking leave to serve in the Office of Public Relations of the Quartermaster Replacement Training Center in 1942. After the war Pickard spent many years co-scripting *Wendy Warren and the News* between 1947 and 1958. Pickard started his career as an actor and he continued to perform on the air even during his years of authoring stories.

Other Radio: *The Doctors; The Love of Life; The Nurses.*

Sources: John Pickard—Frank Provo Collection; Heilbut p. 242; *Broadcasting* October 15, 1935, p. 35, July 20, 1942, p. 32; *Variety* September 9, 1936, p. 33.

Porter, Garrett

Garrett Porter, formerly a reporter for the United Press, was one of the writers for *Time* magazine's *March of Time* ca. 1935 and was still with the program in 1942. He is also credited with penning several episodes of *Cavalcade of America* (1940–1941, 1947).

Sources: *Broadcasting* September 1, 1935, p. 10, September 14, 1942, p. 36.

Posner, Henry

Henry Posner was a member of the writing team for the popular *The Life of Riley* series in the late 1940s.

Source: *Variety* April 2, 1947, p. 35.

Powell, Dick

The writer Dick Powell was a well-regarded scripter for network shows in the 1940s and early 1950s but, unfortunately, sharing a name with a prominent actor at the same time has made chronicling his career a challenge for radio historians. He is known to have authored for *Life of Riley* (1944–1951), *The Man from Homicide* (1951), *Mr. Aladdin* (1951), and *The Saint* (1950). Powell served as the first (and only) president of the fledgling Television Writers of America union that was soon crushed by the networks when they refused to abide by the anti–Communist oath of loyalty agreements then popular in broadcasting.

Sources: Buhle & Wagner p. 58–59; Cox *Crime Fighters; Variety* January 19, 1949, p. 35.

Pray, Rupert

Originally in sales for KTSB and then traffic manager for the Northern California Broadcast System, Rupert Pray (May 9, 1912–February 5, 1973) had the opportunity to start scripting radio shows in the late 1930s. His first identified program was *Tales from an Antique Shop* on the Don Lee network in 1938 followed in 1939 by *Thrills of the Highway Patrol*. In the 1940s Rupert is known to have written *Electric Hour* (ca. 1944), *Forever Ernest* (1946), and *The Ozzie and Harriet Show* (1947).

Sources: *Broadcasting* February 1, 1939, p. 60, September 25, 1944, p. 22; *Radio Daily* January 27, 1938, p. 7; *Variety* May 1, 1946, p. 38.

Presnell, Robert, Jr.

Born to motion picture writer and executive Robert Presnell, Sr., Presnell Jr. (July 21, 1914–June 14, 1986) followed his father's footsteps into the world of show business. After a stint as a newspaper reporter in Milwaukee Presnell started writing, directing, and producing for radio in the 1930s in New York. He is credited with authoring *The Smiths of Hollywood* (1946), originally dubbed *The Smiths of San Fernando*, and directing *I Love a Mystery* and *The Orson Welles Show* on the radio. Presnell's television career spanned three decades and included writing dozens of teleplays.

Theater: *The Urgent Air* (1946).

Sources: *Variety* September 26, 1945, p. 46; *Los Angeles Times* obituary June 17, 1986.

Price, Roger

Roger Price (March 6, 1918–October 31, 1990) was a comedian whose work appeared in all manner of media across a span of nearly half a century. Price was born in West Virginia and as a young man attended the Greenbrier Military Academy. An appointment to West Point was derailed by his poor eyesight so he attended the University of Michigan for two years instead. This was followed by two years at Chicago's Academy of Art, paid for by working on NBC's continuity department.

By 1944 Price had joined Bob Hope's writing team, penning gags for his *The Pepsodent Show* (1944–1948) and touring across the globe with Hope. He also made authoring stops on *The Bill Goodwin Show* (1947), *The Comedy Writers Show* (1948), and *The Martin and Lewis Show* (1949) while also acting when the opportunity presented itself. On the side Price honed his jokes by performing in nightclubs.

Price earned minor roles in numerous television episodes over several decades, moderated the quiz show *How To*, served as a panelist on *Name's the Same*, and even provided commentary on the 1956 presidential campaign. He published the newspaper feature *Droodles*, was involved in the creation of the Mad Libs party game, and co-founded the publishing firm Price, Stern, Sloan.

Books: *In One Head and Out the Other.*
Sources: *Variety* December 24, 1941, p. 34, September 20, 1944, p. 34; *Hartford Courant* November 3, 1990, p. E8; *Lewiston Evening Journal* February 18, 1956, p. 5A.

Prindle, Don

After pursuing a career in acting that culminated in roles on a small Midwestern circuit, James Donald Prindle (August 22, 1904–October 25, 1968) gravitated to the airwaves. Prindle was promoted to studio manager of Seattle's KOL in 1935, and then spent a short time with WLS before joining KNX in Hollywood in 1936. This return to the West Coast led to Prindle's job on Joe Penner's writing staff, which also included Penner's film efforts, until 1939.

Prindle moved to *The Al Pearce Show* ca. 1941, *The Abbott & Costello Show* in 1942, *The Al Jolson–Monty Woolley Show* in 1943, and then the summer replacement *Judy Canova Show* in 1943. In order to focus on his own series, *Ice Box Follies*, Prindle left as head writer for *Abbott & Costello* in 1945. Prindle also scripted *The Kay Kyser Show* (1947) before making a foray into television with *Make Me Laugh* in 1949.

Other Radio: *Heidt Time for Hires* (1944).
Sources: *Broadcasting* December 15, 1935, p. 40, October 15, 1936, p. 53, September 7, 1942, p. 48, May 24, 1943, p. 33, June 21, 1943, p. 14; *Motion Picture Daily* December 14, 1936, p. 4; *The Radio Annual* 1941 p. 68; *Radio Daily* September 17, 1937, p. 5; *Variety* February 21, 1945, p. 32.

Provo, Frank

Frank Provo (November 16, 1913–November 20, 1975), born in North Carolina but raised in San Francisco, started to perform as a teenager. He won a Shakespeare contest while in high school in Burlingame, CA, that brought him a two-year scholarship to the Pasadena Community Playhouse where he earned some juvenile leads. His long broadcasting career started at eighteen as an actor on such West Coast shows as *Death Valley Days*, *Hawthorne House*, *Night Editor*, and *Winning the West*. In his off time Provo would write, a practice that resulted in air plays as early as 1932 (*Shoe Leather Sonata*) and led to future radio work on *My Son and I* (1938–1941), a daily serial, *Young Dr. Malone* (ca. 1941, with **John Pickard**), and *Wendy Warren and the News* (1947–1958). In 1969 Provo began teaching dramatic writing at Simon's Rock, part of Bard College in Great Barrington, MA, and eventually became head of the dramatic arts program.

Television: *Concerning Miss Marlowe* (1954–1955, with John Pickard); *From These Roots* (1958–1960, with John Pickard).
Theater: *Dagmar*; *The Education of Emily Adams.*
Sources: John Pickard & Frank Provo Collection; *Radio Mirror* June 1936 p. 68; *Variety* October 26, 1938, p. 24, July 2, 1941, p. 23, June 25, 1947, p. 27; *Los Angeles Times* September 7, 1932, p. 14; *New York Times* obituary November 22, 1975.

Pugh, Madelyn

Madelyn Pugh (March 15, 1921–April 20, 2011), a 1942 graduate of Indiana University, wrote short pieces for WIRE before moving to California where she got a job in continuity with NBC and then CBS. With **Bob Carroll, Jr.,** she is credited with scripting nearly 1,000 radio and television episodes. Her future career trajectory was put in place when she joined with Carroll to write Lucille Ball's *My Favorite Husband* (1948–1951). When the radio show evolved into the television smash *I Love Lucy* Pugh remained at the center of the writing team. She wrote for Ball during the entirety of the comedian's career.

Other Radio: *That's a Good Idea* (1945); *Columbia Workshop* (1946); *It's a Great Life* (1948).

Sources: *Variety* November 13, 1946, p. 36, January 12, 1949, p. 22; *New York Times* obituary April 21, 2011.

Purdum, Herb

Herb Purdum (August 4, 1921–April 16, 1993) started his career near the end of dramatic radio's heyday authoring *Richard Diamond, Private Detective* (1949), *Hopalong Cassidy* (1950–1951), *Escape* (1951, 1952), *Romance* (July 1952), and *Gunsmoke* (1952) before spending three decades scripting television, especially dramatic programs such as *Boston Blackie* (1951–1953) and *Death Valley Days* (1966–1970).

Sources: Death Valley Days Collection; Cox *Crime Fighters*; *Broadcasting* November 5, 1951, p. 28.

Quillan, Joe

Joe Quillan (August 31, 1916–April 6, 1961) joined Eddie Cantor's radio show in 1937 but also penned Cantor's motion picture and stage performances as well. Quillan's work with Cantor continued even he while served in World War II as a scriptwriter for the armed forces on programs including *Flight to the Pacific* (1945). After the war Quillan continued on *The Eddie Cantor Show* until 1949, joined the *Joan Davis Show* (1946–1947), and then *Our Miss Brooks* (1950–1953) where he stayed as the series moved to television (1952–1956).

Other Radio: *A Day in the Life of Dennis Day* (1946, 1950); *A Date with Judy* (1948).

Theater: *Banjo Eyes* (1941); *Nellie Bly* (1946).

Sources: Joe Quillan Papers; *Broadcasting* July 30, 1945, p. 54; *Radio Daily* November 26, 1937, p. 7; *Variety* August 20, 1941, p. 3, October 9, 1946, p. 53.

Quinn, Don

Don Quinn (November 18, 1900–December 30, 1967), a quick wit despite leaving school after tenth grade so he could serve in World War I, was a professional cartoonist and gag writer from Grand Rapids, MI. He found moderate success selling material to the vaudeville duo of Olsen and Johnson among others before watching assignments dry up after the 1929 stock market crash. Nevertheless, for some time Quinn continued to send cartoons to various magazines that would subsequently toss his pictures but run the gags.

In the early 1930s Quinn moved to Chicago with the hope of landing work in radio, an industry that was demonstrating considerable commercial growth despite the ongoing Depression. Initially he didn't find any more success in radio than he had with magazines. In fact, most employees around the stations treated him "like a leper."

It was a fateful day in 1931 when Quinn happened to run into a harried Jim Jordan at WENR. Jordan had heard that Quinn wrote jokes so paid him to write some material for broadcasts he and wife Marian were doing called *The Farmer Rusk Hour*. While the ten dollars Quinn received for his jokes was nice, more important in the long run was the partnership that developed between Quinn and the Jordans.

Their first collaborative effort was *Smackout—The Crossroads of the Air*, a daily fifteen-minute program that debuted Monday, March 2, 1931, on WMAQ. The series focused on Uncle Luke Gray, the proprietor of a country store who was consistently "smack out" of everything. The Jordans received $200 a week for the program of which they paid Quinn $40. In return he created a world of characters, including Perky McSnark, Squire Lovejoy, Carnivorous Morton, Jorp Cankle. In all, he penned 948 scripts for the series before it went off the air August 3, 1935, a healthy run of 4½ years.

Smackout, however, was just a tune-up. In 1934 John Jeffry Louis, head of his own advertising company that counted S. C. Johnson & Son as a client, heard *Smackout* on his car radio. For some time he'd been wanting to find a new vehicle to advertise Johnson's products, preferable a comedy. Louis paid Quinn $75 for a sample script. The effort was apparently satisfactory and on April 16, 1935 (with *Smackout* still on the air), *Fibber McGee & Molly* arrived on the airwaves. Response was underwhelming but station executives were patient and Quinn and the Jordans slowly molded their creation into one of the most beloved old-time radio programs of all time.

Quinn created an inimitable world around the home located at 79 Wistful Vista. While the Jordans worked with Quinn on crafting the weekly scripts, the brilliance of the program is ultimately ascribed to him. From characters such as Wallace Wimple, Throckmorton P. Gildersleeve, and Mayor LaTrivia to the commercials seamlessly integrated into the storyline to Fibber's frequent tongue twisters, Quinn's boundlessly creative mind cranked out a fresh script week after week, year after year.

Unlike most top-ranked comedies of the era, the Jordan's didn't have a writing team; they had Quinn who was all they needed. In 1938 he took on an assistant, Winsor "Win" Anderson, about whom little is known. Five years later Quinn finally ceded some writing chores to a second writer, **Phil Leslie**. Leslie was a master writer himself and his contributions kept the program clicking on all cylinders.

The CBS network made some so-called "talent raids" in 1947 and signed some of NBC's biggest talent including **Charles Correll** and **Freeman Gosden** (*Amos 'n' Andy*) and Jack Benny. The Jordans stayed loyal to NBC but sold all rights to the program for a significant sum. Quinn was part of the deal and signed an exclusive seven-year contract with the network. Quinn's talents were recognized by the Jordans and they made sure he was the highest paid writer in radio at the peak of his career, pulling down $3,000 per week. That the show had one main writer kept costs low compared to other top comedies and contributed to his generous paychecks. Quinn's motto "Be fair in all things; don't offend people; don't hurt their feelings, Keep it clean—and keep it friendly—and it will keep you" certainly served him well over a three-decade career.

In 1949 Quinn announced his intention to depart *Fibber McGee & Molly* at the end of the season. He was developing a new program, *Halls of Ivy* (1950–1952), but agreed to stay on as writer and consultant for the 1950–1951 season of *Fibber*. *Halls of Ivy* featured Ronald Colman and wife Benita Hume as William and Vicky Hall, president and wife of Ivy College, a nondescript institution of higher education. The series debuted in January of 1950 and ran for 2½ years on radio and lasted on television until 1955. Quinn didn't write many of the scripts himself but served as supervisor and contributed ideas and suggestions. The series won a prestigious Peabody broadcasting award and is still enjoyed by modern listeners. Years after the series left the air Quinn insisted *Halls of Ivy* was one of the best comedy's in radio's short history and that his time on that program was some of the best of his life.

In 1953 Quinn signed on to serve as supervisor of comedy shows produced by Young & Rubicam, Inc. Among his television projects during the 1960s Quinn served as a script consultant for *Petticoat Junction*, the creation of **Paul Henning**, one of Quinn's former protégés. Later—essentially during his retirement years—Quinn ran a commercial production company, an industry he complained was rife with kickbacks and under the table deals.

Other Radio: Ole Olsen & Chic Johnson *Swift Reviews* (1933–1934); *Cavalcade for Victory* (1943); *Lady Esther Screen Guild Theatre* (1947, with Fibber and Molly McGee); *The Prudential Family Hour of Stars* (1949).

Television: *Yancy Derringer* theme song (1958–1959).

Films: *This Way Please* (1937), *Look Who's Laughing* (1941), *Here We Go Again* (1942), contributed the material used by the Jordans for all three; *Heavenly Days* (1944), co-scripted with Howard Estabrook; *Public Pigeon No. 1* (1957) with Larry Berns; *My Son, the Chimp* (1965) with Henry Sharp.

Theater: *The Ballad of Will Rogers* (1961, co-authored with **Arnold Marquis**); Titled *Will* during pre-production.

Other: Three-record set *Fibber McGee & Molly with Teeny on the Night Before Christmas* on Capitol Records (1945); Speech-writer for James Wilson, gubernatorial candidate in California, 1950.

Sources: Baughman p. 15, 19; Hickerson p. 193; Jackson & Abbott p. 154; Stumpf & Price; *American Magazine* vol. 133, p. 76; *Broadcasting* April 1, 1963, p. 136; *Liberty* Winter 1972 p. 70–71 (reprinted from *Liberty* April 18, 1942); *Radio News* July 1941 vol. 19 p. 91; *Radio-TV Mirror* 1952 p. 40–41, 98–100; *Readers Digest* 1945; *Screen World* Vol. 9, 1958; *Los Angeles Times* December 3, 1951, p. 30, March 12, 1953, p. 26, March 29, 1963, p. D16.

Quinn, Stanley

Stanley Quinn started in radio in 1936 and soon found work at the J. Walter Thompson agency where he would work with just a couple interruptions into the television age of the early 1950s. His first dated radio scriptwriting was for Edgar Bergen and Charlie McCarthy on *The Chase & Sanborn Hour* ca. 1939. In 1940 he was relocated by the agency to Australia to oversee their radio productions there until the latter years of World War II when he joined the Mutual Broadcasting System as a correspondent in the Pacific. After the end of the war Quinn returned to J. Walter Thompson where he was involved in the production of various early television broadcasts.

Other Radio: *The Kraft Music Hall* (occasional substitute writer); *The Rudy Vallee Show*.
Sources: *Broadcasting* September 15, 1939, p. 67, November 15, 1940, p. 85, September 3, 1945, p. 28; WTIC interview.

Radcliffe, Virginia

Virginia Radcliffe has been connected with a number of dramatic radio programs over a nearly three-decade span. Among them are *Charlie Chan* (1937), *Suspense* (1944), *Theatre Guild of the Air* (1948), *Cavalcade of America* (1948–1950), and *Theatre Five* (1964).

Sources: *Radio Daily* July 27, 1937, p. 7; *Variety* September 8, 1948, p. 33.

Ragaway, Martin

Martin Ragaway (January 29, 1923–April 20, 1989) spent just a very few years in radio scripting *County Fair* (1946), *The Milton Berle Show* (1946), Phil Harris and Alice Faye's *Fitch Bandwagon Show* (1948), and *The Abbott & Costello Show* (1948–1949) before commencing an Emmy-winning career in television and motion pictures.

Other Radio: *The Dinah Shore Ford Show*; *The Phil Baker Show*; *The Guess Who Show*.
Sources: *The Radio Annual* 1946 p. 820, 1948 p. 920; *Los Angeles Times* obituary April 22, 1989.

Randon, Lee

Lee Randon wrote a number of scripts in the late 1940s for WXYZ's trio of adventure shows, *The Green Hornet*, *The Lone Ranger*, and *Challenge of the Yukon*.

Source: Grams *Green Hornet*.

Rapp, John

John Rapp was associated with Eddie Cantor for at least a decade, writing for his broadcast series as early as 1938 and as late as 1949.

Sources: *Variety* October 5, 1938, p. 34; paleycenter.org.

Rapp, Phil

Phil Rapp (March 26, 1907–January 23, 1996) entered radio in 1931 selling gags to performers including Beatrice Lillie and George Burns and Gracie Allen, and by 1932 was scripting programs for Georgie Price. Rapp's first significant radio assignment was as Eddie Cantor's writer in the mid 1930s. He worked with Cantor for several years, also contributing to Cantor's screen work of the era.

After penning for *The Twin Stars Show* (1937) and the Betty Lou routines for *The Rudy Vallee Show* (1937), Rapp connected with Fanny Brice and her Baby Snooks character in 1938 and wrote for her *Metro Good News Show* (later *Maxwell House Coffee Time* until 1943. Following a disagreement between Rapp and Brice, Rapp —by then the show's director as well as writer— resigned in 1943. A short time later Frank Morgan, who had also become a regular on Brice's show, also opted out of his contract and reunited with Rapp for a new program proposal that didn't get off the ground.

Rapp spent a year out of radio, working on a musical and penning a screenplay, before returning to *Coffee Time* in an advisor position in late 1944. In 1946 Rapp took over the writing of Don Ameche's *Drene Program* that also featured Frances Langford, marking the beginning of a string of collaborations between the three that lasted several years and brought the *The Bickersons* to the airwaves (1946–1951). Rapp spent a couple seasons on the staff of *The Charlie McCarthy Show* (1947–1948) as well.

Sources: *Broadcasting* September 1, 1941, p. 14, September 20, 1943, p. 26; *Radio Daily* March 19, 1937, p. 1, 3, November 16, 1937, p. 6; *Radio Mirror* November 1938 p. 64, December 1938 p. 19; *Variety* August 23, 1932, p. 42, November 10, 1943, p. 3, December 20, 1944, p. 29, November 20, 1946, p. 40, October 6, 1948, p. 24.

Ravetch, Irving

A native of New Jersey, Irving Ravetch (November 14, 1920–September 19, 2010) went to live in California as a boy for health reasons and eventually graduated from UCLA. An aspiring playwright, Ravetch joined CBS' Hollywood radio outlet in 1943 where he worked on some of the network's most admired dramatic programs including *Escape* (1947–1950) and *Suspense* (1948).

Ravetch made his name in motion pictures, however, as part of a dynamic writing team with his wife, Harriet Frank, Jr. He penned nearly two dozen screenplays over a long career that earned him two Academy Award nominations in 1963 and 1979.

Sources: *Broadcasting* February 22, 1943, p. 34; *New York Times* obituary September 21, 2010.

Redd, Robert L.

Robert Redd (d. July 8, 1983) started his radio career in Portland, OR, before moving down the coast to San Francisco and then to Hollywood. By 1935 he was a writer and producer for NBC until resigning to sign with the William Esty & Co. agency in 1936. While also working regularly as a producer, Redd wrote numerous shows during the late 1930s and early 1940s.

Among Redd's scripting credits are *Cavalcade of American Aviation* (1938, also producer) to promote the Paramount film *Men With Wings*, *Little Old Hollywood* (1939–1940, also called *Little Ol' Hollywood*) on which he penned the "Two Happy People" sketches, *All Aboard* (1940), *Secret Legion* (1942, with James Fonda), *The Hedda Hopper Show* (1942), *The Sealtest Village Store* with Jack Haley and Joan Davis (1944, 1947–1948, producer during the latter years), *Hollywood Star Time* (1946, 1949, also producer), and *Point Sublime* (1940–1948, intermittently).

Redd's *Eyes Aloft* (1942–1943) series was a World War II–era program that sought to increase participation in the West Coast's Aircraft Warning System. He reportedly traveled more than 25,000 of coastal roadway to prepare for the program. After the war Redd increasingly focused on the production side of broadcasting, notably working on *The Jack Haley Show* (1947) and *The Martin and Lewis Show* (1949) as producer. By the early 1950s Redd had his own production company and later worked for an advertising agency as a time buyer.

Sources: *Broadcasting* November 1, 1935, p. 42, June 15, 1938, p. 14, December 1, 1939, p. 63, June 1, 1940, p. 71, April 6, 1942, p. 37; *The Radio Annual and Television Yearbook* 1956 p. 170; *Variety* December 18, 1940, p. 23, April 8, 1942, p. 3; UPI obituary July 15, 1983.

Reeves, Mary Watkins

A romance writer for periodicals in the early 1930s, Mary Watkins Reeves (ca. 1913–1999) spent a number of years in the late 1930s and early 1940s penning various daytime serials including *Romance of Helen Trent* and *Stella Dallas*.

Sources: *Variety* January 25, 1939, p. 26, December 24, 1941, p. 34; *New York Times* obituary February 19, 1999.

Resnick, Sidney (also Sid Reznick)

Sidney Resnick (July 29, 1919–July 24, 2012) scripted a steady stream of second-tier network comedy programs through the 1940s before landing on television in the following decade. Resnick's credits include *The Durante–Moore Show* with Jimmy Durante and Gerry Moore (1943–1945), Ed Wynn's *Happy Island* (1944), *Gaslight Gaities* (1945, with **Will Glickman**), *The Jack Kirkwood Show* (1946), *The Phil Silvers Show* (1947, also producer), *The Wrigley Show* (1948), *The Great Talent Hunt* (1948), and *The Martin and Lewis Show* (1949). Resnick's television career is highlighted by time on *The Tonight Show* (1969–1970).

Other Radio: *Young Mr. Gabriel* (1947, audition).
Books: *How to Write Jokes* (1954).
Sources: National Broadcasting Company Records; *Billboard* July 5, 1947, p. 14, April 3, 1948, p. 10; *Variety* September 13, 1944, p. 22, April 11, 1945, p. 32, October 6, 1948, p. 30; *The Hartford Courant* February 11, 1970, p. 31.

Reynolds, Ed

Ed Reynolds was one of a great number of comedy writers who was hired by Ed Gardner to write for his program *Duffy's Tavern*.

Source: *Bridgeport Sunday Herald* August 27, 1950, p. 46.

Rhine, Larry

Larry Rhine (May 26, 1910–October 27, 2000) attended UCLA where he majored in English, competed for debate team, and wrote columns for the school paper. This background led to his hiring as both an announcer and writer in San Francisco, reportedly replacing Art Linkletter.

After relocating to New York Rhine went to work scripting *The Log Cabin Show* with Jack Haley (1937) and *The Ben Bernie Show*, the latter for seven years until Bernie's death in 1943. Bernie helped Rhine get a job with the motion picture studios and worked on screenplays while mailing his scripts to Bernie in New York until World War II. During the war Rhine was assigned to the Office of War Information where he broadcast propaganda to Japan. Upon returning to civilian life Rhine returned to radio as a freelance writer, eventually signing with Ed Gardner's *Duffy's Tavern* (1948–1951). Around 1950 Rhine entered television where he contributed scripts to dozens of series over more than thirty years and earned two Emmy nominations in 1963 and 1978.

Other Radio: *Life of Riley.*
Television: *Mr. Ed* (1962–1966); *The Brady Bunch* (1972–1974); *All in the Family* (1975–1979).
Sources: *Motion Picture Daily* July 29, 1937, p. 11; *Radio Daily* October 21, 1937, p. 5; *Variety* October 13, 1948, p. 26; *Los Angeles Times* obituary November 2, 2000; Rhine interview emmys.com.

Rhymer, Paul

Widely recognized by his contemporaries as a great American wit, Paul Rhymer (1905–October 26, 1964) created one of radio's most enduring series, *Vic and Sade*. After attending Illinois Wesleyan (without graduating) in the mid–1920s, by 1929 Rhymer worked himself into a position as continuity writer with NBC based on some short stories and articles he'd published.

Rhymer's first series with the network was *Keystone Chronicles* (1929–1931), set around a small-town newspaper. His work also appeared on *The Busyman Program*, *The Three Doctors*, and *Smokey Rogers: Fire Chief*. *Vic and Sade* was auditioned for NBC executives on March 28, 1932, and debuted June 30, 1932. It was a minimalist show featuring just two performers, Art Van Harvey and Bernadine Flynn. As a daily broadcast *Vic and Sade* was confined to broadcast periods filled with melodramatic soap operas, but it found an appreciative audience nonetheless and aired for twelve years until September 24, 1944. Rhymer's creation proved so popular its sponsor even aired it on two networks during a three-year span. *Vic and Sade* was reincarnated for brief runs in 1945 and again in 1946 and then attempted to find new life on television in 1949.

Rhymer continued to write after *Vic and Sade* left the air, though he never duplicated the success of his original creation. Much of his work appeared in the form of articles and reviews but between 1950 and 1952 Rhymer authored *The Public Life of Cliff Norton*, a series of five-minute television sketches.

Sources: Paul Rhymer Papers; Hetherington.

Rice, Craig (Georgiana Ann Randolph)

Craig Rice (born Georgiana Ann Randolph, June 5, 1908–1957) was a popular author of mystery stories and novels in the mid–20th century. After some time writing for *The Milwaukee Journal* and *The Chicago American* Rice went to work for radio station WCLO ca. 1930 or 1931 as a writer, performer, and time seller. In 1931 Rice joined the Beacon Syndicate where she cranked out continuity scripts while she continued to write for WCLO on the station's *WCLO Syndicate Serials* (1933). On that show she introduced one of her first fictional characters, Professor Silvernail.

A string of novels in the 1940s introduced John J. Malone, a lawyer who was later adapted to the air with the program *Murder and Mr. Malone* (1947–1949). The series was broadcast under numerous titles including *The Amazing Mr. Malone*, *John J. Malone for the Defense*, *Attorney John J. Malone*, in addition to *Murder and Mr. Malone*, making it difficult for fans to stay tuned in.

Sources: Marks; *Broadcasting* November 1, 1931, p. 19, January 15, 1932, p. 9, March 1, 1933, p. 29; *Variety* November 20, 1946, p. 40, January 1, 1947, p. 21.

Rice, Gerald

Gerald Rice has been identified as an author of *Double or Nothing* ca. 1946.
Source: *Variety* February 27, 1946, p. 30.

Richards, Robert (Bob)

Robert Richards graduated from Harvard and harbored a dream of becoming a pilot before finally joining the writing staff of *The March of Time* radio show in the late 1930s, eventually ascending to the position of director of radio productions there. In 1939 he moved to the *March of Time* film division to write screenplays. While doing freelance scripting for *Cavalcade of America* (1941–1944) Richards founded a production company with fellow writers **Peter Lyon** and **Robert Tallman** in 1942 called Playwright Producers, the first of their offerings being *For Us the Living*. Richards wrote a number of screenplays and over fifty episodes of *Suspense* during the 1940s and 1950s. He came under scrutiny in the early 1950s for alleged left-wing sympathies and he saw writing opportunities dry up and his career faltered, even while using various pseudonyms. As late as 1960 he was one of several authors suing for damages as a result of the Blacklist.
Sources: Grams *Suspense*; Living Films; *Broadcasting* June 29, 1942, p. 62; *Motion Picture Daily* September 1, 1939, p. 2; *Hartford Courant* December 31, 1960, p. 8; *Los Angeles Times* September 21, 1951, p. 1.

Richards, Silvia (also Sylvia)

Silvia Richards wrote steadily for radio through the 1940s, most notably for *Cavalcade of America* (1944), *The Adventures of Bill Lance* (1944), *Suspense* (1943–1959), *The Phillip Morris Playhouse* (1949), *Escape* (1950), and *The Hallmark Hall of Fame* (1955). Her marriage to **Robert L. Richards** ended as a result of the studio Blacklist in the 1950s.
Source: Grams *Suspense*.

Richton, Addy

Sometimes writing as Adelaide Marston (with **Lynn Stone**), Addy Richton (1912–March 31, 1995) teamed with Stone to script the serial *Hilltop House* (1937–1941) until taking over writing chores on *Woman of Courage* and the new *Keeping Up With Rosemary* in 1942. A former teacher, Richton spent at least a decade writing for radio soaps, often with Stone, including *This Life Is Mine* (1943–1945), *Valiant Lady* (ca. 1945), and *The Best Things in Life* (1947).
Other Radio: *Five Star Jones* (1936); *Cavalcade of America* (1942); *Theatre Five* (1965).
Sources: *Broadcasting* May 10 1943 p. 47; *Radio Daily* October 28, 1937, p. 12; *Variety* March 18, 1942, p. 30, June 3, 1942, p. 30; *St. Petersburg Times* October 10, 1943, p. 23; *Washington Post* May 15, 1947, p. 8.

Ridgeway, Agnes

Agnes Ridgeway proved herself an adaptable scriptwriter, penning for diverse programming such as *The Rudy Vallee Show* (1936–1938), *The Chase & Sanborn Hour* (1939), *Those We Love* (1939–1941, 1942, serial), and *The First Nighter Program* (1944).
Sources: *Radio Daily* June 1, 1937, p. 6; *Atlanta Constitution* August 23, 1944, p. 8; *Los Angeles Times* June 3, 1937, p. 10; *Milwaukee Journal* June 11, 1942, p. 2.

Riggs, Tommy

Tommy Riggs (October 21, 1908–May 21, 1967) was born with a condition called "bi-vocalism" by some doctors, a trait that allowed him to effortlessly switch the pitch of his voice from that of a typical male to that of a young girl. Riggs used this trick to great effect as a young man to startle those around him and to entertain in social situations.

After some odd jobs after graduating from college, Riggs got work in a Pittsburg vaudeville house and then eventually a radio spot on Pittsburgh's WCAE in 1931. Riggs' "act" introduced listeners to Betty Lou, the moniker for his alternate voice, and this led to a succession of jobs with KDKA, Cleveland's WTAM, and Cincinnati's WLW. Riggs had his big break in 1937 when he earned nearly 50 guest appearances on Rudy Vallee's program, leading to his own show written entirely by Riggs.

The appeal of Riggs and Betty Lou was fleeting. Despite some guest appearances on *The Kate Smith Show* and even his own summer replacement series in 1942 written by a professional group of scripters audiences lost interest, augmented by Rigg's absence from the air due to service in the Navy during World War II.
Source: Vitty "Tommy Riggs."

Robinson, Jack

Jack Robinson started writing plays with collaborator **Gene Stone** in the late 1930s as part of the Federal Theatre Project before testing the waters in broadcasting during the 1940s. Perhaps his first radio assignment was the *Pabst Blue Ribbon Town* with Groucho Marx ca. 1943–1944 followed by a couple seasons on Rudy Vallee's *Drene Show* (1945–1946). As a freelance writer some of his other script writing jobs included *The Great Gildersleeve* (1947–1949), *The Halls of Ivy* (1950), and *Honest Harold* (1950–1951).

Theater: *Ready! Aim! Fire* (1937); *Two a Day* (1938); *Hit and Run* (1939).

Sources: *Broadcasting* March 8, 1943, p. 30, September 8, 1950, p. 70; *Variety* January 9, 1946, p. 144.

Robinson, Ken

A graduate of the Chicago Central School of Commerce, Ken Robinson went to work as a reporter and announcer in the early 1930s for Hearst Radio Inc. and its newspaper *The Chicago American*. Part of Robinson's duties was creating scripts that were heard on the airwaves as early as 1933 when he authored a series of shows called *Inside the Rackets*, exposing Chicago's gang scene. Two years later he was called on to adapt stories from Hearst's magazines for broadcasts over its radio network and in 1936 he started writing the serial *Dan Harding's Wife* (1936–1939).

Robinson joined NBC in 1936 as an assistant continuity editor and is credited with authoring *The Adventures of Dari Dan* in 1937, the same year he became the network's Midwestern continuity chief. In 1940 Robinson resigned to take the position of program director with the Neisser-Meyerhoff agency though he still did some writing at times for shows such as *Island Venture* (1945).

Sources: *Broadcasting* June 1, 1933, p. 21, June 1, 1936, p. 56, August 15, 1940, p. 74; *Radio Daily* March 9, 1937, p. 6; *Variety* September 25, 1935, p. 51, December 16, 1936, p. 44.

Robison, David

Trained as a musicologist at the University of Vienna and Columbia University, David Victor Robison (d. November 30, 1978) taught music history at Columbia and Fisk University in Nashville. Upon relocating to the West Coast Robison took a job with RKO Pictures in the 1940s and made at least two forays into radio scripting *Presenting Charles Boyer* (1950) and *Stars Over Hollywood* (1952). Robison was a victim of the Blacklist in 1953 and for many years wrote for television under the name Paul David. Some of his final works were stage plays written and produced in the 1960s and 1970s.

Theater: *Promenade, All* (1971);

Sources: Horne; *Los Angeles Times* obituary December 4, 1978, p. F16; *New York Times* obituary December 5, 1978.

Robson, William N.

William N. Robson (October 8, 1906–April 10, 1995), a graduate of Yale, started in show business as a screenwriter in the mid–1930s before moving to the CBS network's West Coast chain where he stayed for over a decade in a long and distinguished career. While directing was the area in which he built his legacy, Robson did his share of writing over the years as well. One of his earliest writing projects was *Calling All Cars* (1933–1939), on which he served as director as well. Other series to which Robson contributed scripts were *Beyond Reasonable Doubt* (1939), *Four for the Fifth* (1944), *Hawk Larabee* (1946), *Escape* (1947), *Fort Laramie* (1956), *Have Gun, Will Travel* (1960), and *Suspense* during its latter days (1955–1962). His scripts appear more frequently as radio's Golden Age wound down, a time when networks had trouble finding talented writers for their broadcasts. Though Robson found work in television, the Blacklist crippled his prospects and he never attained the stature in the visual medium that he held in radio.

Other Radio: *Romance*.

Sources: Grams *Suspense*; *Los Angeles Times* obituary April 17, 1995.

Roddy, Lee

Lee Roddy (b. August 22, 1921), a 1945 graduate of the Los Angeles City College, had his first writing success selling stories to an Oakland newspaper when he was just 14 years old. Roddy wrote for Hollywood's KMPC before joining

The Mayers Co. Roddy scripted the anthology series *California Caravan* before deciding radio scripting didn't pay enough. He wrote radio ad copy for several years before turning his focus to managing radio stations. Roddy went on to author dozens of books, both fiction and nonfiction, that sold millions of copies.

Sources: *Broadcasting* July 2, 1945, October 8, 1945, p. 52; modestoradiomuseum.org.

Rodman, Howard

Howard Rodman (February 18, 1920–December 5, 1985) made his network scripting debut with an episode of *Columbia Workshop* in 1946. He went on to contribute to a number of series including *American Portrait* (1946), *NBC Presents* (1951), *Dimension X* (1951), and *The U.N. Story* (1951) but much of his radio work was for documentaries and other special broadcasts.

Rodman was a skilled writer of teleplays, authoring hundreds over a 35-year career in the medium. Highlights include writing for *Studio One* (1954–1959), *Naked City* (1961–1963), and *Route 66* (1960–1963). Rodman created at least two shows, *The Man and the City* (1971–1972) and *Harry O* (1974–1976), and writing as Henri Simoun he authored *The Six Million Dollar Man* television film in 1973.

Other Radio: *The Human Angle* (1948, audition); *The American School of the Air*.
Sources: *Variety* April 17, 1946, p. 34; *Hartford Courant* April 16, 1952, p. 13; *Los Angeles Times* obituary December 8, 1985, p. B4.

Roeburt, John

John Roeburt (March 15, 1909–May 22, 1972) was a widely published author of primarily crime and detective fiction. His work appeared not only on radio but as short stories, novels, television broadcasts, and motion pictures. On the air Roeburt was most active for about a decade spanning 1943–1953, with his work featured on *The Adventures of the Falcon* (1943–1945), *Counterspy* (1944), *Wide Horizons* (1944), *Bulldog Drummond* (1944–1955), *It's Murder* (1944–1945), *House of Mystery* (1945), *Inner Sanctum* (1947–1951), *The Brighter Day* (1949), *Tales of Fatima* (1949), *International Airport* (1949–1951), *The Affairs of Peter Salem* (1950–1951), *Barrie Craig, Confidential Investigator* (1951–1955), *Private Files of Matthew Bell* (1952), *By the People* (1956–1957), and *Suspense* (1961–1962). Roeburt wrote some television stories through the 1950s as well as a number of novels, a few of which were based on his Jigger Moran character.

Theater: *Second Breakfast* (1944).
Books: *Jigger Moran* (1944); *Seneca, U.S.A.* (1947).
Screenplays: *Dark Memory* (1946); *The Queen's Mark* (1951); *The Long Count* (1955).
Sources: John Roeburt Collection; *Broadcasting* May 23, 1949, p. 72; *Variety* March 8, 1944, p. 51.

Rogers, "Roz" Roswell B.

A graduate of the National School of Broadcasting in the mid–1930s, Roswell Rogers (October 8, 1910–August 6, 1998) took a job on the continuity staff of KMTR followed by a similar position with KNX in 1937. Near the end of that year he started writing for Jack Haley's *Log Cabin Jamboree*. In 1940 Rogers signed a two-year deal with Joe Penner and when that was done in 1940 worked on the *Don Ameche Show*.

Rogers soon moved to the *Al Pearce Show* until 1941 and that year started a long association with *Lum 'n' Abner*, a job he would have into the 1950s including some screenplays for the duo as well. He found time for a season of *The Opie Cates Show* (1947–1948) during his time with *Lum 'n' Abner* but Rogers' greatest fame would come as a primary script writer for *Father Knows Best*, first on radio (1952–1954) then later on television (1954–1960). The TV version also earned Rogers three Emmy nominations in 1958 and 1959.

Television: *Window on Main Street* (1961–1962, creator);
Sources: Hollis; *Broadcasting* December 15, 1937, p. 50, April 15, 1938, p. 50, June 15, 1940, p. 56, October 27, 1941, p. 32; *Motion Picture Daily* February 11, 1937, p. 10; *Los Angeles Times* June 30, 1935, p. A8, March 9, 1949, p. A1.

Roman, Lawrence (Larry)

Larry Roman (May 30, 1921–May 18, 2008) was a freelance writer during the 1940s and is credited with scripting for a number of West Coast dramatic programs including *Suspense* (1943), *I Was There* (1945), *The Whistler* (1945), *The*

Electric Hour (1945), *The Nelson Eddy Show* (1946), *Jeff Regan, Investigator* (1948), *Adventures of the Saint* (1951), *Night Beat* (1952), *Escape* (1953), and *The Modern Adventures of Casanova* (1952), the latter featuring a declining Errol Flynn. Roman's longest run came on *Rocky Jordan* (1948–1951), co-written with **Gomer Cool**, using the U.S. Army's Pocket Guide to Egypt to make the show more authentic. After radio, Roman wrote screenplays and television films that were aired from the 1950s into the early 2000s.

Sources: Cox *Radio Crime Fighters*; *Variety* September 19, 1945, p. 29, February 27, 1946, p. 30.

Rose, Jack

Jack Rose (November 4, 1911–October 21, 1995) wrote gags for Milton Berle and then scripts for Bob Hope's *The Pepsodent Show* in the early 1940s before focusing on screenplays until the early 1980s. Rose received three Oscar nominations (1955, 1958, 1973).

Source: *Los Angeles Times* obituary October 24, 1995.

Rose, Ralph

A fairly unknown writer during radio's Golden Age, Ralph Rose has been credited with episodes for numerous dramatic programs including *The Whistler* (1944), *The Rise Stevens Show* (1945), *The Theater of Famous Radio Players* (1945–1946), *Tell It Again* (1948–1949), *Suspense* (1949), *Hollywood Star Playhouse* (1952), and *The Roy Rogers Show* (1953–1954). He also served as director on Rogers' program near the end of the series' run.

Other Radio: *The Young at Heart* (1947, audition)
Sources: *Radio Mirror* December 1943 p. 24; *Variety* July 4, 1945, p. 26.

Rose, Si (also Sy)

Si Rose (January 15, 1896–May 11, 1976) penned gags for some of the biggest comedians on radio at the tail end of the medium's Golden Age. Among them were *The Bob Hope Show* (1947), *The Martin and Lewis Show* (1949), and *Edgar Bergen and Charlie McCarthy* (1951–1956). Rose's television career stretched well into the 1970s.

Sources: *Variety* April 2, 1947, p. 35.

Ross, Bob

Bob Ross (June 26, 1908–1970) attended Cornell University before getting his writing break with the Marx Brothers. He subsequently wrote for *Texaco Star Theatre* ca. 1938–1940 for hosts Eddie Cantor followed by **Fred Allen** before becoming one of the first outside writers that **Charles Correll** and **Freeman Gosden** brought in to assist in scripting *Amos 'n' Andy*. He was closely involved in its 1943 format change that gave the show a more traditional radio sitcom feel and eventually took over as the head of the shows expanded writing staff. Ross wrote for the ill-fated *Amos 'n' Andy* television adaptation then later scripted for Correll and Gosden's animated series *Calvin and the Colonel* (1962). Ross contributed to the classic shows *Leave It to Beaver* (1958–1962) and *The Andy Griffith Show* 1964–1968) before creating *Mayberry R.F.D.* (1968–1970), a *Griffith Show* spin-off.

Source: *Broadcasting* October 1, 1939, p. 51, July 15, 1940, p. 49; *Radio Mirror* June 1949 p. 23; *Variety* August 25, 1943, p. 29, April 13, 1938; *New York Times* obituary August 19, 1970.

Ross, Claris A.

Claris Ann Ross graduated from Northwestern University's School of Speech with the help of the Edgar Bergen Scholarship Fund and in 1945 signed to write for *The Chase & Sanborn Show*. Ross worked as a staff writer for several years scripting *NBC University Theater* (1948–1951), *Dimension X* (1950), *NBC Symphony Orchestra* (1951), *NBC Presents: Short Story* (1951–952), and *Best Plays* (1952–1953).

Sources: National Broadcasting Records; *Broadcasting* August 20, 1945, p. 76.

Ross, Jerome D.

Jerome Ross (February 10, 1911–February 11, 2012) was a freelance writer and director during radio's Golden Age who also found work in early television. Among his writing credits for radio are *Mr. Keen, Tracer of Lost Persons* (1939), *Children of Divorce* (1948), *The Casebook of Gregory Hood* (1949), *Palmolive Revue, Society Girl, Stella Dallas,* and *Mrs. Wiggs of the Cabbage Patch*.

Ross' television career spanned into the 1970s and include authoring for programs including *The Untouchables* (1959–1960), *The Outer Limits* (1963), and *Marcus Welby, M.D.* (1969–1976).

Sources: *Broadcasting* April 7, 1941, p. 10; *Variety* September 29, 1948, p. 43; *New York Times* obituary.

Rosten, Norman

An award-winning poet and playwright in his later years, Norman Rosten (January 1, 1913–March 7, 1995) spent a few years during and just after World War II scripting radio plays. Among the series for which he wrote were *The Star-Spangled Theatre* (1941), *Cavalcade of America* (1941–1943), *The Bell Telephone Hour* (1943, 1947), *The Doctor Fights* (1944), *Radio Almanac* (1944), *Theatre Guild on the Air* (1945), and *A Brighter Tomorrow* (1946). Rosten was proclaimed Brooklyn's poet laureate in 1979.

Other Radio: *Treasury Star Parade.*
Books: *Under the Boardwalk* (1968); Seven books of poetry.
Theater: *First Stop to Heaven* (1941).
Sources: *Variety* July 28, 1943, p. 33, June 14, 1944, p. 26, November 13, 1946, p. 34; *New York Times* obituary March 9, 1995.

Ruben, Aaron J.

Aaron Ruben (March 1, 1914–January 30, 2010) is remembered for his directorial work on television classics such as *The Andy Griffith Show*, *Gomer Pyle U.S.M.C*, and *Sanford and Sons*. Like many in television from that era, however, Ruben got his start in radio, scripting a number of comedy programs. **Nat Hiken**, a relative by marriage, encouraged Ruben to write material on spec and submit it to some agencies.

This led to writing material in 1943 for Wally Brown on *The Dinah Shore Show* and soon after, *The Burns & Allen Show*. After two years Hiken again contacted Ruben and encouraged him to leave Hollywood to come join the staff of **Fred Allen**'s show in New York, which he did in 1945. At the end of the decade Ruben wrote on the staffs of *The Milton Berle Show* (1947–1948) and then in 1949 *The Frank Morgan Show*. By 1951 Ruben had moved to television where he received three Emmy nominations in 1972 and 1973. Later in his life Ruben volunteered as a staunch court-appointed advocate for abandoned and abused children.

Sources: *Broadcasting* September 11, 1944, p. 44; *Variety* April 2, 1947, p. 35, April 6, 1949, p. 32; Ruben interview, emmytvlegends.org.

Rubin, Jack

Jack Rubin (1910–October 10, 1952) was a skilled author of both dramatic and comedy scripts for the airwaves. During his decade in radio Rubin's work appeared on *NBC Comedy Theatre* (1944), *The Rudy Vallee Show* (1945), *This Is Hollywood* (1947), *The Hallmark Playhouse* (1948–1950), *Screen Director's Playhouse* (1950–1952), *The Hardy Family* (1949–1953), and *Defense Attorney* (1952). Rubin was responsible for a number of screenplays during these years as well but his early death at 42 cut short a promising career.

Other Radio: *Dark Venture* (1952).
Sources: Jack Rubin Papers; *Broadcasting* October 20, 1952, p. 85.

Ruscoll, Joseph

Joseph Ruscoll (November 2, 1906–November 19, 1956) worked as a freelance scriptwriter in the early 1940s before joining the CBS writing staff in mid–1943. Among his earlier credits are *The Columbia Workshop* (1942, 1946–1947), *Treasury Star Parade* (1942), *Camel Caravan* "Our Town" sketches (1942–1943), *The Cavalcade of America* (1943), and *Eyes of the Air Force* (1943).

Later in 1943 Ruscoll joined the Army and received a medical discharge early in 1945. He immediately resumed his network writing on programs such as *Theatre of Romance* (1945), *Fighting Senator* (1946), *The Molle Mystery Theater* (1946–1947), *Murder at Midnight* (1946–1947), *Suspense* (1948–1949), *Broadway Is My Beat* (1949), and *Murder by Experts* (1949). Ruscoll focused more on television in the 1950s, especially crime and suspense shows, before dying at age 50 in 1956.

Sources: Grams *Suspense*; *The Radio Annual 1945* p. 832; *Variety* October 21, 1942, p. 41, November 11, 1942, p. 30, July 21, 1943, p. 34, July 31, 1946, p. 26.

Russell, Joseph

Little-recognized author Joseph Russell is remembered for stories penned for *Cavalcade of America* and *Silver Theater*.

Source: Dunning.

Ryf, Robert (Bob)

Despite earning a Ph.D. in Education, Robert Ryf wrote for many of the shows that originated from Hollywood's KNX in the 1940s and 1950s. On his long list of broadcast credits are episodes of *The Whistler* (1945–1946, 1949), *The Private Practice of Dr. Dana* (1947–1948), *New Adventures of Michael Shayne* (1948, based on the series of detective novels written by Brett Halliday), *Final Edition* (1948), *Escape* (1948–1949), *Dangerous Assignment* (1949–1953), *Tales of the Texas Rangers* (1951), *The Silent Men* (1951), *Romance* (1954), and *Yours Truly, Johnny Dollar* (1955–1958). In the early 1950s Ryf scripted for Donlevy Development Company, Inc. for a televised version of *Dangerous Assignment*.

After nearly two decades writing for radio and television Ryf decided to utilize his doctorate and returned to academia. He joined the faculty of his alma mater, Occidental College in Los Angeles, where he developed and reinstituted an honors program in 1959. By the mid–1970s Ryf had ascended to the position of Dean of Faculty.

Other Radio: *A Man Named Jordan*; *Dragnet*; *Hallmark Hall of Fame*; *Jeff Regan, Investigator*; *Rocky Jordan*.

Sources: Froug; *Broadcasting* November 26, 1945, p. 58; *Production Encyclopedia* 1952 p. 659; *Variety* September 29, 1948, p. 47; oxy.edu.

St. Clair, Gordon

Veedersburg, IN, native Gordon St. Clair is recognized for authoring at least one radio series, NBC's *A Tale of Today* (1933–1939).

Sources: *Radio Mirror* June 1938 p. 58; *The Pittsburg Press* June 24, 1934, p. 5.

St. Clair, Leonard

Leonard St. Clair (April 5, 1916–February 10, 1986) was a busy writer during radio's heyday and his work was featured on many shows, primarily dramatic in content. His credits include *Manhattan at Midnight* (1943), *Suspense* (1943, 1946), *Results, Inc.* (1944), *Michael Shayne* (1946), *Mayor of the Town* (ca. 1946–1947), *Presenting Charles Boyer* (1950), *Halls of Ivy* (1950), *Hallmark Playhouse* (1950–1953), *Hollywood Star Playhouse* (1951), *Hallmark Hall of Fame* (1953–1954), *Stars Over Hollywood* (1953), *Meet Mr. McNutley* (1954), *Romance* (1954, 1957), *Suspense* (1954), *Lux Radio Theatre* (1954–1955), *CBS Radio Workshop* (1956), and *ABC Mystery Time* (1957).

Books: *The Emerald Trap; Fortune and Death; The Seadon Fortune.*

Sources: *Variety* June 16, 1943, p. 30, September 11, 1946, p. 36; *Los Angeles Times* obituary February 13, 1986.

Saks, Sol

Sol Saks (December 13, 1910–April 16, 2011) dreamed of being a writer so he planned on a career in newspapers as had many aspiring writers of the time before him. But with the rise of radio there was a new outlet for authors and while writing for the *Northwestern Daily* his first scripts were used on *Non-Royalty Radio Plays* in 1939. Soon after Saks got his first jobs scripting for *Thunder and Lightning* and *Wings of Destiny*, both broadcast out of Chicago. Another of his Chicago series was *Uncle Walter's Doghouse* (1942).

In 1943 Saks moved to Los Angeles where he became a sought-after writer, often for comedy programs. He briefly took the continuity writing spot for *Philco Hall of Fame* with Paul Whiteman (1945) but didn't find the job particularly challenging. Within a short time Saks left for a multi-year stint authoring *The Adventures of Ozzie and Harriet*. Saks' work appeared on many other beloved comedies including *Baby Snooks*, *Duffy's Tavern*, Dinah Shore's *Birdseye Open House*, and *Beulah* (ca. 1951).

Saks' big break would come in television, however. After entering the medium penning *My Favorite Husband*, he went on to write for *Alcoa Theatre*, *I Married Joan*, and *Mr. Adams and Eve*. In 1964 Saks created and wrote the pilot for *Bewitched*, from which he went on to earn a small fortune. Active well into his 90s, Saks' later years were spent writing plays that were produced in community theaters.

Film: *Walk, Don't Run* (1966, Cary Grant's final movie).
Other Radio: *Bullet Trenton, C.D.*; *The Danny Kaye Show*; *The First Nighter Program*; *Grand Central Station*; *The Red Skelton Show*; *While America Sleeps*.
Sources: Young; *Variety* May 13, 1942, p. 32, February 28, 1945, p. 25, July 4, 1945, p. 30; *Los Angeles Times* obituary April 21, 2011.

Sangster, Margaret

Margaret Elizabeth Sangster (1894–1981) was the granddaughter of the poet of the same name and a prolific writer in her own right. Sangster was hired to the editorial staff of *The Christian Herald* at fifteen, thus beginning a long career in the publishing industry. During World War I she was sent overseas by the *Herald* to serve as the publication's war correspondent and through the 1920s worked as editor for various publications.

By the mid–1930s radio had become a financially viable career path so Sangster started authoring daytime serials, some of her first being *Hope Alden's Romance* and *Living Dramas of the Bible*, both of which debuted in 1937. These efforts were soon followed by *Arnold Grimm's Daughter*, a Frank and Anne Hummert production. Loathe to credit their writers, Sangster was one of the few of the Hummert's small army of writers to earn individual recognition while penning the serial.

These early works were followed by numerous other programs oriented to female listeners including *The Story of Ellen Randolph* (1939–1941), *House on Q Street* (1943), *Dick and Jeannie* (1946–1947), *Joyce Jordan, M.D.* (1948–1949), *My True Story* (1947–1960, based on content from *True Story* magazine), and *Whispering Streets* (1952–1960). Over the course of her active years Sangster wrote numerous articles, poems, and short stories for newspapers and magazines, sometimes using her own name but frequently using a number of pseudonyms.

Other Radio: *On Guard America* (1941).
Sources: Margaret E. Sangster, Jr. Collection; *Broadcasting* June 1, 1940, p. 60; *Motion Picture Daily* January 11, 1937, p. 4, April 21, 1937, p. 7; *Radio Mirror* September 1937 p. 40, April 1950 p. 28–29, 103; *Radio Showmanship* January 1946 p. 33; *Variety* November 3, 1943, p. 30, November 10, 1948, p. 30.

Saroyan, William

Pulitzer Prize and Academy Award-winning playwright and novelist William Saroyan (August 31, 1908–May 18, 1981) made a few forays into radio while acknowledging it was a very different writing format than stage plays. Saroyan contributed scripts to *The Columbia Workshop* (1939, 1940), *The Free Company* (1941), and *The Pursuit of Happiness*.

Sources: Balakian; *Broadcasting* June 15, 1939, p. 64; *Variety* February 26, 1941, p. 29; xroads.virginia.edu.

Savage, Courtenay

Courtenay Savage has been identified as one of the writers for the comedy-drama serial *Aunt Mary* ca. 1944.

Source: *Broadcasting* February 14, 1944, p. 46.

Schiller, Bob

An economics graduate from UCLA, Bob Schiller (b. November 8, 1915) turned his resume of *Stars and Stripes* articles into a short audition run on *Duffy's Tavern* (ca. 1947–1948) that, in turn, led to a multi-year on-and-off again run with the series. Producers liked his material and Schiller eventually moved on to write for *Abbott & Costello* (ca. 1946), the *Mel Blanc Show*, *The Adventures of Ozzie and Harriet*, and *The Jimmy Durante Show* before exiting for a highly successful television career.

On the small screen Schiller was one of the primary writers for the early smash *I Love Lucy* (1955–1957) followed by *The Lucy-Desi Comedy Hour* (1957–1960) and *The Lucy Show* (1962–1968). Schiller also penned dozens of episodes for *The Carol Burnett Show*, *Flip*, and *All in the Family*.

Other Radio: *December Bride*; *Sweeney and March*.
Sources: Young; *Variety* November 6, 1946, p. 34, October 13, 1948, p. 26.

Schlichter, Karl

Karl Schlichter was one of the writers for the West Coast anthology show *California Caravan* in the late 1940s.

Other Radio: *The Unseen Enemy*.
Sources: *Broadcasting* February 20, 1950, p. 47; *The Screenwriter* March 1946 p. 21.

Schoen, Lillian

After graduating from the University of Chicago Lillian Schoen worked for a number of radio stations in the Pittsburgh region as a continuity editor. She then proceeded to work for several broadcasting agencies including Compton Adv. and Kermit-Raymond Radio Productions. Among her writing credits during the late 1940s were *Raising a Husband* (1945), *Hollywood's Open House* (1946), *Grand Slam* (1946–1953), *The Paul Whiteman Show* (1947), *School Teacher* (1947), *The Lee Sweetland Show* (1947), and *Modern Romances* (1949).

Other Radio: *Ford Theatre* (1947); *Junior Partners* (1948, audition).

Sources: *Broadcasting* August 18, 1941, p. 33; *Variety* December 26, 1943, p. 30, March 6, 1946, p. 38, October 16, 1946, p. 63, May 28, 1947, p. 30, April 13, 1949, p. 34.

Schoenfeld, Bernard

A playwright during the 1930s, Bernard Schoenfeld (August 17, 1907–April 25, 1990) was responsible for the debut episode of *Brave New World*, an idea supported by both the Works Progress Administration (WPA) and CBS network, from 1937 to 1938. In an era of rising global tensions between the Communist Soviet Union, Fascist Germany, and Western democracies, the series sought to grow relationships between the United States and its neighbors. Schoenfeld's government scripting continued with *The World Is Yours* (1938) and by 1941 he had gone to work for the Office of the Interior as a scriptwriter.

Over the next two years Schoenfeld moved between different federal agencies including the Office of Production Management, the Office of Emergency Management, and finally the Office of War Information where he served as a director of radio services with the United States entering World War II. While working in Washington, D.C. Schoenfeld scripted *Keep 'Em Rolling* (1942) and *This Our Enemy* (1942–1943) among others.

After his time with the government Schoenfeld went to work writing commercial fare including *The Adventures of Christopher London* (1950) and a few screenplays in the 1940s and early 1950s. He penned dozens of teleplays over twenty years for dramas such as *Alfred Hitchcock Presents* (1956–1960) and *The Twilight Zone* (1964).

Sources: Lee p. 121–122; *Broadcasting* January 12, 1942, p. 48; *Motion Picture Daily* May 1, 1941, p. 8.

Schofield, John Paul

John Paul Schofield started writing for films during the silent era in the early 1920s and only moved into radio much later. While working for John A. Clements Associates in the mid–1940s John Paul Schofield was responsible for *Meet the Folks* (1947), based on dramas from the Hearst Sunday supplements. The next year he was tapped to author scripts for *I Love Adventure* (1948), a short-lived **Carlton Morse** series which couldn't recapture the audience of Morse's earlier *I Love a Mystery*.

Sources: *Motion Picture Daily* August 14, 1945, p. 8; *Variety* June 11, 1947, p. 34.

Schuffman, Dan

Dan Schuffman's time in the radio business was spent penning stories for *The Fat Man*, *The First Nighter Program*, and *Perry Mason* in the 1940s. By 1949 Schuffman had started writing for ABC's television network; he would go on to serve in various capacities in Chicago-area television until the early 1970s.

Sources: Cox *A to Z*; *Billboard* October 22, 1949, p. 9.

Schwartz, Albert "Al"

While attending law school Al Schwartz (November 29, 1910–March 25, 1988) realized he wanted to write comedy instead and in the early 1930s started writing jokes for Walter Winchell's newspaper columns and then for Milton Berle. After finishing his law degree Schwartz went to work for Berle then joined *The Pepsodent Show* with Bob Hope during its first season, 1938–1939, and stayed through 1946. After several years with Hope, Schwartz signed with his brother **Sherwood Schwartz** to script *The Alan Young Show* (1946–1947) and *The Danny Thomas Show* (1947–1948). These were followed by stints on Jack Kirkwood's *The New Swan Show* (1948–1949), *The Phil Harris–Alice Faye Show* (1953), and *That's Rich* (1954).

Schwartz was no less successful in television than on radio and penned scripts for Jackie Gleason, Milton Berle, and sitcoms such as *The Brady Bunch* and *Gilligan's Island*. His humor was recognized and rewarded with an Emmy award for his work on *The Red Skelton Show* in 1961.

Other Radio: *The Adventures of Ozzie and Harriet*.
Sources: *Broadcasting* October 15, 1938, p. 44; *Variety* April 4, 1933, p. 30, August 14, 1946, p. 21, December 3, 1947, p. 26; *Los Angeles Times* obituary March 29, 1988.

Schwartz, Sherwood

Like his brother **Al Schwartz**, Sherwood Schwartz (November 14, 1916–July 12, 2011) didn't dream of writing comedy as a youngster, but while studying in Southern California to become a physician the opportunity arose. Al got Schwartz a job writing for Bob Hope during the 1939–1940 season where he stayed for a few seasons before joining the war effort and scripting a number of series for the Armed Forces Radio Service including *Jubilee*, *Mail Call*, and *Command Performance*.

After the war Schwartz continued authoring scripts for sitcoms such as *The Adventures of Ozzie and Harriet*, *The Alan Young Show*, and *The Beulah Show*. Schwartz moved into television with *I Married Joan*, won an Emmy for his writing on *The Red Skelton Show*, and created two of the 1960s most venerable television shows, *Gilligan's Island* and *The Brady Bunch*.

Other Radio: *The Danny Thomas Show*.
Sources: Young; *Variety* November 4, 1942, p. 30, July 24, 1946, p. 42, May 12, 1948, p. 29; *Los Angeles Times* obituary July 13, 2011.

Scofield, Louis (Lew, Lou)

Louis Scofield's early radio experience came with Crosley's Cincinnati station WLW in the late 1930s before he moved to Chicago in 1939. There Scofield started freelance scripting on shows including *This Is the Underground* (1943) and became a news writer for WCFL ca. 1945. Employed for a period by the Owen Vinson & Co. agency, Scofield continued to freelance and his scripts were used on *Incredible but True* (1945), *Captain Midnight* (1947), *Nick Carter, Master Detective* (1948), and *Curtain Time* (1948).

Sources: Gotfried p. 230–232; *Broadcasting* September 20, 1943, p. 36, February 5, 1945, p. 46; *Radio Showmanship* January 1946 p. 32; *Variety* April 2, 1947, p. 35.

Scott, Ashmead

Active in radio as early as the mid-1930s as writer, director, and producer, Ashmead Scott (November 27, 1893–February 3, 1965) spent several years writing for CBS. Among his aural scripting credits are *Your Witness* (1937–1938), *Jack Oakie's College* (1938), *Texaco Star Theatre* (1938), *Blondie* (1939–1940), *Bob Burns Show* (1941–1942), *Life of Riley* (1944–1946), and *The Baby Snooks Show* (1947–1948). Scott found only moderate success in film and television.

Sources: *Broadcasting* November 1, 1937, p. 52, August 18, 1941, p. 38; *Radio Mirror* January 1938 p. 36, May 1938 p. 56, November 1939 p. 45; *Variety* August 27, 1947, p. 24.

Scribner, Jimmy

Jimmy Scribner was one of numerous white radio actors who assumed the roles of various black characters. He played all the roles in *The Johnson Family* (1934–1950), a show that focused on a small African American town, Chickazola. He was also the primary writer of the series, with assistance from Floyd Christy.

Source: *Radio Daily* November 23, 1937, p. 8.

Seldes, Gilbert

An essayist and cultural critic and commentator, Gilbert Seldes (January 3, 1893–September 29, 1970) spent a few years with CBS during the pre-War years as Director of Programming and writing for series such as *Americans All, Immigrants All* (1938–1939) and *The Pause That Refreshes on the Air* (1940–1944), a musical variety featuring Andre Kostelanetz. Seldes later served as a dean of the Annenberg School of Communication at the University of Pennsylvania.

Other Radio: *Ford Theatre* (1948).
Sources: Gilbert Seldes Papers; wnyc.org.

Seymour, Adele

Adele Seymour joined her sister **Katharine Seymour** in 1942 as co-writer for *The Light of the World*, a program that serialized Biblical dramas. The show ran until the mid–1940s before it started reusing the Seymour's scripts. Seymour also assisted her sister with writing *Thus We Live* during the same period.

Sources: *Variety* June 24, 1942, p. 29, September 2, 1942, p. 36.

Seymour, Katharine

A native of Hampton, VA, and a 1925 graduate of Barnard College, Katharine Seymour was one of radio's early writers, joining WEAF as a continuity editor in 1925. For a decade she edited and scripted for the NBC outlet on series such as *Famous Loves* and *The Family Goes Abroad*. Seymour turned to freelance work in 1935 and authored and edited material for producers including Transamerica. Here most notable writing assignment was for *The Light of the World*, dramatizations of Biblical stories that aired from 1940 to 1945. She took a brief hiatus from the show in 1942 due to contractual conflicts but returned as head writer until the mid–1940s. Seymour's sister, **Adele Seymour**, joined the show in 1942. Seymour never fully recovered from a surgery in 1944 and passed away in 1945.

Other Radio: *On Guard America* (1941); *Thus We Live* (ca. 1942).

Books: *How to Write for Radio* (1931); *Practical Radio Writing* (1938).

Sources: *Radio Revue* December 1929 p. 39; *Variety* November 29, 1939, p. 28, February 14, 1945, p. 25.

Shavelson, Mel (Melville)

Mel Shavelson (April 1, 1917–August 8, 2007) spent five years in radio writing for Bob Hope's *The Pepsodent Show* (1938–1943). Shavelson went to author dozens of screenplays over a forty-year career that included two Oscar nominations in 1955 and 1958.

Sources: Mel Shavelson Collection; *New York Times* obituary August 11, 2007.

Shaw, Irwin

Playwright and short story writer Irwin Shaw (February 27, 1913–May 16, 1984) produced scripts for *The Gumps* and *Dick Tracy* in the 1930s to supplement his income from his publications and stage works at the time. Shaw also contributed scripts to the experimental *Columbia Workshop* (1937–1938). Over many years Shaw wrote a number of novels that would eventually sell more than 14 million copies, his most popular being 1948's *The Young Lions*.

Other Radio: *The Rudy Vallee Show*.

Sources: Shnayerson; *Motion Picture Daily* April 29, 1937, p. 10; *Variety* April 22, 1936, p. 44; *New York Times* obituary May 17, 1984.

Shaw, Robert

After studying at the University of Wisconsin and writing a gossip column for the school paper, Robert Shaw (November 11, 1917–March 30, 1996)—not to be confused with either the film actor or musical conductor of the same period—joined NBC's publicity department. After a time he left the network and began making a name for himself as scriptwriter in the early 1940s on *Front Page Farrell* and *David Harum* (ca. 1942) for Blackett-Sample-Hummert.

Through much of the 1940s Shaw penned *Mr. District Attorney*, created by **Ed Byron** and in 1947 he brought another Bryon creation, *The Adventures of Christopher Wells*, to the airwaves. In a turn of events that could have come straight out of one of Shaw's stories, at the age of 30 he received a multi-million dollar inheritance from his father. Shaw continued to write, however, since he would not receive the money for another fifteen years.

Shaw seamlessly moved to television in the 1950s and contributed to numerous soap operas over several decades. His writing career reached its apex in 1980 when he wrote the "Who Shot J.R.?" storyline for the primetime drama *Dallas*.

Other Radio: *Gang Busters*; *The Guiding Light*; *Mr. Keen, Tracer of Lost Persons*; *Philo Vance*; *Search for Tomorrow*; *Stella Dallas*.

Sources: Cox *Mr. Keen*; *Broadcasting* October 12, 1942, p. 35; *Variety* October 7, 1942, p. 26, May 7, 1947, p. 44, July 16, 1947, p. 31, September 10, 1947, p. 1; *Lakeland Ledger* April 24, 1996, p. B4; *Los Angeles Times* obituary April 20, 1996.

Shayon, Robert Lewis

Robert Shayon (August 15, 1912–June 28, 2008) originally hoped to make a living as an actor but after lean years in the mid–1930s found more success by submitting program ideas and scripts as a freelance writer. Shayon joined his brother's firm, Fanchon & Marco, as a writer and his first series *Twenty Years Ago-and Today* was picked up by New York's WOR in 1937. The following year Shayon joined WOR as an assistant producer but got experience in all facets of radio, including directing and announcing in addition to producing and scripting programs such as *Once Upon a Time* (1938), *Author! Author!* (1939), and *WOR Summer Theatre* (1942).

In 1942 Shayon moved from WOR to CBS where he had primarily executive duties. Still, he had opportunities to display his writing talent, most notably on *The Man Behind the Gun* (1942–1944) and *CBS Is There* (1947–1949, later *You Are There*). As radio declined Shayon was lured into television and later worked as a television critic for *Christian Science Monitor* and *Saturday Review*. Shayon also earned the title of Professor Emeritus at the University of Pennsylvania's Annenberg School for Communication.

Sources: *Motion Picture Daily* August 26, 1937, p. 17, May 23, 1938, p. 10; *The Radio Annual* 1940 790; *Variety* November 30, 1938, p. 26; *New York Times* obituary July 16, 2008.

Shean, Jim

Jim Shean's scripts were used on juvenile shows in the latter years of dramatic radio's Golden Age. The best example of his work is *Bobby Benson and the B-Bar-B Riders* (1949–1955). In the mid–1950s Shean joined Buena Vista Film Distribution Co. as a copywriter.

Sources: Siegel & French; *Motion Picture Daily* December 12, 1955, p. 3.

Sheekman, Arthur

A humorist who started his writing career in newspapers during the 1920s, Arthur Sheekman (February 5, 1901–January 12, 1978) met Groucho Marx in 1926 and a close friendship developed. Within a few years Sheekman became a primary writer for Groucho and his brothers, creating material for books, screenplays, and their singular radio series *Flywheel, Shyster and Flywheel* (1932–1933). Until health concerns sidetracked his career in the 1960s, Sheekman wrote dozens of screenplays and a handful of stage plays.

Source: Sterling.

Shenkin, Ernest

Ernest Shenkin scripted for various shows in the late 1930s and early 1940s including *Alias Jimmy Valentine*.

Sources: *Radio Annual* 1943 p. 822; *Variety* January 25, 1939, p. 26.

Sherdeman, Ted

Ted Sherdeman (June 21, 1909–August 22, 1987) was barely twenty or twenty-one when he entered the young field of commercial radio as an announcer for WOW in Omaha in 1930. After stops in St. Louis and Chicago during which Sherdeman advanced to writing, directing, and producing, he arrived in Hollywood in 1936. On the West Coast he is credited with authoring a number of radio series including *Career Woman* (1938), *Brenthouse* (1939), *Monsieur le Capitaine* (1940), and *Latitude Zero* (1941). Sherdeman left NBC in 1941 to join the Young & Rubicam agency and in 1942 he started a two-year stint with the armed forces.

After World War II Sherdeman returned to radio primarily as a producer with different agencies. By the end of the 1940s and into the 1950s he increasingly penned screenplays and some teleplays in the 1960s.

Television: *Bewitched*; *Flying Nun*; *Hazel*; *My Favorite Martian*; *Wagon Train*.

Sources: *Broadcasting* June 15, 1940, February 17, 1941, p. 34; *NBC Transmitter* February 1939 p. 10; *Radio Daily* March 11, 1938, p. 5; *Radio Digest* April 1930 p. 95; *Variety* July 8, 1936, p. 30; *Los Angeles Times* obituary August 29, 1987.

Sherry, Ed

Little is known of script writer Ed Sherry other than his contribution to *Lincoln Highway* (1940–1942). He also penned a 1942 audition show entitled *Nice Couple*.

Source: *Variety* February 18, 1942, p. 28.

Ship, Reuben

Reuben Ship (1917–1975) was a Canadian writer who penned *Hot Air* (1941) before finding success with a long run scripting *The Life of Riley* in the United States. A victim of the House Un-American Activities Committee, Ship had to return to Canada, where he subsequently produced the scathing anti–McCarthy script *The Investigator*.

Sources: Gross; *Variety* November 5, 1941, p. 37.

Simmons, Ed

Ed Simmons started his professional comedy-writing career at the tail end of radio's Golden Age. Hired to author sketches for *The Martin and Lewis Show* on both television and radio in the early 1950s, Simmons' later television credits include *The Red Skelton Show* (1961–1963) and *The Carol Burnett Show* (1973–1978). Between the two shows Simmons earned eight Emmy nominations and five awards.

Sources: *Broadcasting* February 18, 1952, p. 92; *Los Angeles Times* obituary May 23, 1998.

Simmons, Richard "Dick" Alan

Canadian Richard Alan Simmons (October 11, 1924–November 13, 2004) found employment as a scriptwriter at NBC after serving in World War II and matriculating from the University of Toronto. Simmons is remembered in radio primarily for his years adapting stories for *The NBC University Theatre* (1948) and *The Screen Director's Playhouse* (1949–1951). Simmons found screenwriting to be more lucrative through the 1950s and only in the 1960s engaged in authoring teleplays and television movies. His dramatic work was recognized with two Emmy nominations in 1962 and 1978.

Other Radio: *Emotion* (1949); *If Fight We Must* (1951).

Television: *The Dick Powell Theatre* (1961–1963).

Sources: *Variety* January 12, 1949, p. 22; *New York Times* obituary November 20, 2004.

Simon, Neil

Playwright Neil Simon (b. July 4, 1927) spent two or three years writing radio scripts for *The Robert Q. Lewis Show* (1947) and *The Texaco Star Theater* with Milton Berle (1948–1949), while also breaking into television penning *The Phil Silvers Show* (1948). Fame would come later in the 1960s on Broadway and in motion pictures adapted from his plays. Simon's writing has been recognized with Tony Award, Emmy Award, and Academy Award nominations

Sources: *Variety* May 7, 1947, p. 52, December 1, 1948, p. 30.

Singer, Ray

Ray Singer (October 24, 1916–November 16, 1992) moved to Hollywood in the late 1930s and enjoyed a long career in radio and television thereafter. For his first years on the air Singer reportedly wrote for such comedians as **Fred Allen**, Milton Berle, and Bing Crosby. Programs with which he is credited include *Three Ring Time* (1941), *The Rudy Vallee Show* (1942), *The Sealtest Village Store* with Jack Haley (1943–1944, 1947), and *The Charlotte Greenwood Show* (1944). While writing *Village Store* Singer began teaming with **Dick Chevillat** and the pair continued to collaborate on their most popular series, *The Phil Harris–Alice Faye Show* (1948–1954).

Singer co-created television's *It's a Great Life* (1954–1956) with Chevillat and later wrote many episodes for Lucille Ball both for *The Lucy Show* (1964–1968) and *Here's Lucy* (1968–1974).

Sources: *Broadcasting* September 15, 1941, p. 32, October 12, 1942, p. 36, December 31, 1945, p. 46, February 25, 1952, p. 29; *Variety* October 8, 1947, p. 25; *Los Angeles Times* obituary November 12, 1992.

Sklar, Michael

Michael Sklar, a staff writer for WMCA for most of the 1940s and a freelancer on the side, wrote for *Grand Central Station* (1941), *New World A'Coming* (1944–1947), *Inner Sanctum* (1945–1946), *The Whistler* (1947), *You Are There* (1948–1950, originally *CBS Is There*), *Cavalcade of America* (1950), *Tales of Tomorrow* (1953), and *Time Capsule* (1953).

In 1949 Sklar was hired as a senior writer by ABC to script for their television and radio networks. For most of the 1950s Sklar worked as a television producer and executive.

Other Radio: *Five Star Final* (ca. 1945); *Headlines on Parade* (ca. 1945); *Inside New York* (1948).

Sources: *Radio Daily* December 21, 1949, p. 5; *Variety* April 23, 1941, p. 34, August 1, 1945, p. 28, April 16, 1947, p. 26.

Sloane, Allan E.

Allan Sloane (June 24, 1914–April 29, 2001), a newspaper reporter in the 1930s who started writing radio scripts in 1943 and in earnest after World War II, earned a reputation for his broadcasts that raised awareness of different social issues. Representative of his work were scripts for United Jewish Appeal about a girl in Nazi Germany, the United Nations about post–War hunger in Europe, and the Cerebral Palsy fund. Sloane found work on more commercial fare as well such as *The Man Behind the Gun* (1943–1944), *Radio Reader's Digest* (1944–1945), *The Big Story* (ca. 1947–1956), and *Indictment* (1956–1959).

Sloane was named in 1950's *Red Channels* and within two years network writing assignments had dried up. He persevered, however, and returned to scriptwriting under his own name in the late 1950s on radio and then television for another three decades. Between 1964 and 1972 Sloane was nominated for three Emmy awards (winning one), and broadcasts for which he wrote were nominated for and won Peabody awards (though Sloane himself was not).

Other Radio: *Bulldog Drummond, Green Valley U.S.A.* (1943).

Sources: Allan Sloane Collection; *Broadcasting* November 24, 1952, p. 50; *Variety* April 9, 1947, p. 30; *New York Times* obituary May 12, 2001.

Sloane, Robert

Robert Sloane (July 21, 1912–April 3, 1955) was a man of many talents who put them all to use in a show business career that ended tragically young. Originally a playwright and Broadway actor in the 1930s, Sloane appears to have moved into radio around 1941 when he began auditioning material to various ad agencies along with collaborator Leonardo Bercovici. One of his earliest efforts was the serial *Mr. Jonathan* (1941, revived in 1943 by the Compton agency).

Within two years Sloane's freelance writing was appearing over the networks on a regular basis on series such as *Commandos* (1943), *Inner Sanctum* (1944–1952), *The Fat Man* (1946–1951), *Radio Reader's Digest* (1947–1948), and *Casey, Crime Photographer* (1947). He continued to display his acting talent with occasional roles and ongoing narrator duties on *The Big Story*. Sloane was writing, directing, and producing television's *Treasury Men in Action* (1953–1955) when he passed away at 42 from a heart attack.

Sources: *Broadcasting* February 1, 1943, p. 16, April 11, 1955, p. 44; *Radio Mirror* June 1949 p. 71; *Variety* January 15, 1941, p. 53, December 24, 1941, p. 34, January 23, 1946, p. 26, January 1, 1947, p. 23, June 18, 1947, p. 26.

Slon, Sidney

Chicago native Sidney Slon (May 27, 1910–January 21, 1995) developed his acting bug in high school, studied at Northwestern University and the Goodman Theater, and then relocated to New York in 1933 to pursue a full-time acting career. The Depression squelched the young Slon's stage dreams and he returned briefly to Chicago before moving to Cincinnati in 1935 for a job with station WLW. Initially hired for announcing and acting roles on shows including *The Life of Mary Sothern* (ca. 1936) and *Famous Jury Trials* (ca. 1936–1937), Slon also claims to have started writing some of the programs in which he was featured. This led to his hiring by Ruthrauff & Ryan to script *The Shadow* (1939–1943) until he grew weary of the series.

During World War II Slon worked for the Overseas Radio Branch of the Office of War Information and subsequently wrote for programs such as *Eternal Light* (1944), *Dick Tracy* (1946), *The Molle Mystery Theatre* (1946), and *Cavalcade of America* (1946, 1948). Though Slon occasionally cranked out a *Shadow* script in the late 1940s, he joined Ruthrauff & Ryan during that time as a script editor for radio and, increasingly, television.

By the 1960s Slon decided a new life direction was in order and he left broadcasting entirely to work for his family's contracting business. He briefly returned to his earlier profession in the mid–1970s to contribute stories to *The CBS Radio Mystery Theater*.

Sources: Grams *Shadow*; *Radio Annual and Television Yearbook* 1950 p. 198; *Radio Mirror* November 1936 p. 8, February 1937 p. 6; *Variety* May 8, 1935, p. 61; *Chicago Tribune* April 26, 1928, p. 27; *New York Times* obituary January 23, 1995.

Smith, Alan

Alan Smith's radio career remains very much a mystery. His only known work at this time was the summer series *The Gracie Fields Show* (1944) and a multi-year stint with the perennially popular *Chase & Sanborn Hour* featuring Edgar Bergen & Charlie McCarthy (ca. 1941–1947).

Sources: Shearer; *Broadcasting* August 21, 1944, p. 63; *Variety* June 14, 1944, p. 26, August 27, 1947, p. 24.

Smith, David Frederick "Fred"

Fred Smith (d. 1976) was a director and program manager for WLW from 1922 to 1928 where he developed a unique feature called *Musical News*, an innovative mixture of news and music, both content staples of the airwaves. Around 1928 Smith moved to New York where he wrote continuity for *The Majestic Hour* (1929) and began to collaborate with staff from *Time* magazine on a ten-minute syndicated feature called *NewsCasting*. This led to his development of a news entertainment genre and the creation of scripted reenactments of news headlines. Smith's show was eventually christened *The March of Time* (originally *Magazine of Time*). In 1930 Smith also began writing radio transcriptions used by United Artists to promote their upcoming films.

Smith departed *March of Time* in 1932 to devote more time to authoring novels only to return to the broadcast news-entertainment genre by the mid–1930s scripting *New Magazine of the Air* for *Newsweek*. Building on his experience with *Time* and *Newsweek*, Smith created a new series in 1936, *Next Week*, that attempted to dramatize stories that he felt would become big news in the coming week.

The radio industry eventually passed Smith by and in 1941 he assumed the role of director of Cincinnati's College of Music. He left the position in 1956 to focus on writing books and articles for the remaining two decades of his life.

Books: *The Broadcast Murders* (1931).
Sources: *Broadcasting* March 15, 1935, p. 45; *Exhibitors Herald* August 2, 1930, p. 24; *Radio Daily* July 1930 p. 90; *Radio Digest* May 1931 p. 26, February 1932 p. 57; *What's on the Air?* May 1931 p. 10; *Variety* May 27, 1936, p. 41; *New York Times* obituary August 15, 1976.

Smith, Robert Tharp

A distinguished fighter pilot during World War II, R. T. Smith (February 23, 1918–August 21, 1995) spent the early 1950s writing for a number of radio series including *Lum 'n' Abner*, *The Phil Harris–Alice Faye Show*, *Hopalong Cassidy* (1950), and *The Clyde Beatty Show* (1950–1952), the latter two for Commodore Syndication. Until the time of his death Smith capitalized on his interest in aviation and his service with the Flying Tigers during the war.

Television: *Ding Howe and the Flying Tigers* (1950).
Film: *Perils of the Jungle* (1953).
Sources: *Broadcasting* October 30, 1950, p. 53; *Los Angeles Times* obituary August 24, 1995.

Snyder, Howard

Howard Snyder (May 24, 1909–April 13, 1963) was an early comedy writer on the airwaves, earning a spot on Jack Benny's program with collaborator **Hugh Wedlock, Jr.,** in 1936. Snyder earned a contract with 20th Century Fox in 1937 before joining Eddie Cantor's *Texaco Theatre* show and *Jack Oakie's College* that fall. In 1938 he moved on to *The Laugh Liner* with Billy House and to Walter O'Keefe's broadcasts the following year.

Snyder's screenwriting career gained momentum in the early 1940s and after some additional work later in the decade on series such as *The Lady Esther Screen Guild Theatre* (1944), *That's My Pop* (1945, based on **Milt Gross'** comic strip), *Lum 'n' Abner* (1948–1950), *Hallmark Playhouse* (1948), *Sealtest Variety Theatre* (1948), and *The Ford Theatre* (1949), focused increasingly on television. There he contributed scripts to his old boss Jack Benny through the 1950s and early 1960s.

Theater: *Popeye* (1936); *Betty Boop* (1936);
Sources: *Broadway* September 15, 1937, p. 46, November 1, 1937, p. 42, July 15, 1938, p. 29; *Variety* July 1, 1936, p. 34.

Soderberg, Robert

Active as a writer primarily in the 1950s and 1960s, Robert Soderberg (June 22, 1915–April 9, 1996) was active in radio, television, and motion pictures. His aural credits include *Meet Me in St. Louis* (1948), *The Penny Singleton Show* (1950), *Cavalcade of America* (1951–1952), and *Junior Miss* (1948–1953). Much of his later television writing was with his wife, **Edith Sommer,** for the daily soap operas such as *The Guid-*

ing Light (where he served as head writer), *As the World Turns*, *Another World*, and *One Life to Live*.

Sources: *Radio Mirror* July 1949 p. 22; *Los Angeles Times* April 4, 1980, p. G3.

Sommer, Edith

Edith Sommer (August 21, 1917–February 1, 1994) gave up her hope of becoming an actress in 1943 and turned to script writing, an area in which she would have considerable success in the ensuing years. Her first radio stories were sold to *Dr. Christian* and *Molle Mystery Theatre* in 1943. Afterwards, Sommer's work appeared on *Cavalcade of America* (1943), *Words at War* (1943–1944), *We Came This Way* (1944), and *Lux Radio Theatre* (1946) among others. After some screenplays in the 1940s and early 1950s, Sommer concentrated on teleplays and found her niche co-writing serials such as *The Guiding Light* and *As the World Turns* with husband **Robert Soderberg**.

Theater: *A Roomful of Roses* (1956).
Sources: *Variety* December 29, 1943, p. 20; *Sarasota Herald-Tribune* October 15, 1976 5D.

Sommers, Jay

While studying to be a chemist and the City College of New York, Jay Sommers (January 3, 1917–September 25, 1985) decided to try writing at the encouragement of a girlfriend's father, a Bristol-Myers executive. Sommers got his opportunity to break into radio writing for Milton Berle in 1940. Soon he was hired by the Blue network as a staff writer where he authored *The Allen Prescott Show* (1942), *The Chamber Music Society of Lower Basin Street* (1942–1944), *Duffy's Tavern*, and *The Lion's Roar* (ca. 1943).

Throughout the rest of the decade Sommers scripted for a range of comedy shows including *The Alan Young Show* (1944, 1945), *The Danny Kaye Show* (ca. 1945), *The Joan Davis Show* (1945–1947), *The Jack Kirkwood Show* (1946), *The Victor Borge–Benny Goodman Show* (1946–1947), *The Eddie Albert Show* (1947), Eddie Cantor's *Pabst Blue Ribbon Show* (1947–1948), *The Spike Jones Show* (1947–1949), *Lum 'n' Abner* (1948–1950), and *Granby's Green Acres* (1950, creator, producer, and director).

Turning to television in the 1950s, Sommers scripted for numerous series that had their origins on radio including *The Amos 'n' Andy Show*, *Great Gildersleeve*, *My Friend Irma*, and *Our Miss Brooks*. After a notable stint on *The Adventures of Ozzie and Harriet*, Sommers gained experience with rural humor on **Paul Henning**'s *The Beverly Hillbillies* and *Petticoat Junction*. This led to his opportunity in the mid–1960s to turn his *Granby's Green Acres* program into a television series, *Green Acres*, that became one of several CBS hits with a rural theme, running from 1965 to 1971.

Other Radio: *Gang Busters* (1946).
Sources: *Broadcasting* September 25, 1944, p. 30, August 27, 1945, p. 74; *Variety* July 29, 1942, p. 25, August 25, 1943, p. 35, April 11, 1945, p. 30, June 18, 1947, p. 28; *Los Angeles Times* obituary September 28, 1985.

Stafford, Gene

Gene Stafford was a well-traveled radio manager by the mid–1930s, having spent time on staff at NBC, CBS, and the American Broadcasting System, as well as working as a program manager at WMCA, KSD, WLW, and WHN before signing as a scriptwriter for the Langlois and Wentworth agency. Between 1935 and 1938 Stafford is credited with authoring *Front Page Drama*, *The Girl from Reno*, *Jungle Jim*, *Treasure Adventures of Jack Masters*, *We Want a Touchdown*, and *Wings Over the World* for the agency.

Other Radio: *K-7*; *Quite by Accident*; *You the Jury*.
Sources: *Broadcasting* June 15, 1935, p. 30; *Film Daily* August 11, 1934, p. 2; *The Radio Annual* 1939 p. 651; *Radio Daily* February 15, 1937, p. 8, January 26, 1938, p. 1–2; *Variety* September 25, 1935, p. 53.

Stagg, Jerry

Jerry Stagg has been identified as the author of *Hop Harrigan* (ca. 1942) and *In Time to Come* (1943) before spending years as a television producer.

Sources: *Broadcasting* October 25, 1943, p. 10; *Variety* September 2, 1942, p. 40.

Stander, Arthur (Artie)

Arthur Stander (January 7, 1917–July 20, 1963) spent his entire professional career penning comedy for some of the industry's biggest names. His earliest known work was *Laugh Liner*

(1938, with **Sid Zelinka**) but he moved on to *The Bob Hope Show* (1939, with Fred Williams) and other new shows nearly every season. Among his identified work during the 1940s is *Hap Hazard* (1941), *The Ransom Sherman Show* (1941–1942), *Grapevine Rancho* (1943, with Chet Castellaw and Hank Garson), Groucho Marx's *Blue Ribbon Town* (1943–1944), *The Amos 'n' Andy Show* (1945–1946, which was interrupted by a brief period of military service), *Sad Sack* (1946, an adaptation of George Baker's cartoon from the Army's *Yank* newspaper), *The Bob Burns Show* (1947), *The Jack Paar Show* (1947), *Joan Davis Time* (1947–1949), and *Baby Snooks* (1949–1951).

Stander's skill led to plentiful television work on shows including *I Married Joan* (1952–1953), *The Jimmy Durante Show* (1954–1955), *The Andy Griffith Show* (1960, including the pilot), and *Make Room for Daddy* (1959–1963). Stander died at 46 at the height of his career of a cerebral hemorrhage.

Other Radio: *Life With Luigi.*
Sources: *Broadcasting* February 1, 1939, p. 38, December 29, 1941, p. 29, March 15, 1943, p. 34, May 14, 1945, p. 46, November 7, 1949, p. 69; *The Radio Annual* 1944 p. 730; *Variety* November 1938 p. 36, July 30, 1947, p. 31; *Newsday* July 23, 1963, p. 20.

Stark, Sheldon

Writing for the Kiesewetter agency in the late 1930s, Sheldon Stark (August 7, 1909–February 6, 1997) penned *Famous Jury Trials* (1937) and *CBS Radio Workshop* (1937). In 1939 he joined WXYZ's writing staff to work under **Fran Striker** on *The Green Hornet* (1939–1942) and within two years was also scripting for *The Lone Ranger* and *Ned Jordan, Secret Agent*.

Stark became a writer for the powerful J. Walter Thompson agency in 1943 and was immediately placed on *Amos 'n' Andy* and *What's New?* followed by *The Fannie Hurst Show* (1944) and an early televised quiz show, *The Queen Was in the Kitchen* (1945). Over the next few years Stark was responsible for stories for *The American School of the Air* (1945), *Forever Tops* (1946), *Tennessee Jed* (1946), *Listening Post* (1947), *Adventures of Col. Flack* (1947), and *Studio One* (1948). At the end of the 1940s Stark joined Wilbur Stark-Jerry Layton Productions in New York during which time he authored *Straight Arrow* (1948–1951).

Blacklisted during the early 1950s, Stark made a comeback later in the decade and remained a working writer into the 1980s, scripting dozens of teleplays for a wide variety of series, from *Batman* to *Rawhide* to *The Fugitive*. In his later years he taught screenwriting at UCLA and Santa Monica City College.

Other Radio: *Escape*; *It Can Happen to You*; *Love Story Theatre* (1946); *Police Blotter*; *Spotlight on Crime* (1945, audition).
Sources: Grams *Green Hornet*; *Broadcasting* February 3, 1941, p. 32, November 15, 1943, p. 61; *Motion Picture Daily* July 30, 1937, p. 10; *Variety* January 20, 1937, p. 37, May 3, 1939, p. 25, October 3, 1943, p. 26, January 31, 1945, p. 22, January 23, 1946, p. 26.

Starr, Ben

Ben Starr (October 18, 1921–January 19, 2014), the son of Russian immigrants, spent his childhood in New York before moving with his family to Los Angeles when he was about twenty. His studies to become an accountant were interrupted by World War II during which Starr served on a bomber.

After the war Starr wrote his first script on a whim and submitted it to *The First Nighter Program* where it aired, somewhat to his surprise. Only after many years in the industry did he realize how improbable that occurrence was. Starr went on to write for Al Jolson, Dean Martin and Jerry Lewis, and George Burns on radio before moving to *Sara's Private Caper* (1950), co-written with **Larry Klein**. His short time in radio was just a warm-up for three decades in television during which he contributed to many episodes of *Mr. Ed* (1961–1963), *The Brady Bunch* (1971–1973), and *All in the Family* (1975–1978). Starr was behind two 1980s hits, *Silver Spoons* (co-creator) and *The Facts of Life* (developer).

Sources: *Broadcasting* June 26, 1950, p. 44; *Variety* April 13, 1949, p. 26; *Variety* obituary January 20, 2014; Ben Starr interview Archive of American Television.

Stein, Joseph (Joe)

Joseph Stein (May 30, 1912–October 24, 2010) studied at City College of New York and Columbia to be a social worker, a career he pursued until 1945. Stein fell into writing for radio programs in the mid–1940s after meeting Zero Mostel. His earliest identified work was *The Hildegarde Show* (1945–1947, with Norman Barasch) followed by *Story from the Stars* (1947), *The Henry Morgan Show* (1948), *Big Talent Hunt* (1948), *The Ethel Merman Show* (1949), and *The Robert Q. Lewis Show* (1949). As early as 1948 Stein began to test the television waters writing for Phil Silvers' *Laugh and Learn*, and *School House* in 1949.

By 1948 Stein had teamed with **Will Glickman** and in addition to broadcasting scripts the duo wrote some sketches for the stage production *Lend An Ear*. In time, Broadway would be Stein's road to fame, most notably for his book for 1964's *Fiddler on the Roof*. Two Tony Award wins and three additional nominations between 1960 and 1987 demonstrate Stein's sustained career of writing excellence.

Theater: *Mrs. Gibbons' Boys* (1949); *Take Me Along* (1960); *Zorba* (1969); *Rags* (1987).

Sources: *Variety* May 1, 1946, p. 44, May 14, 1947, p. 34, March 24, 1948, p. 34, January 12, 1949, p. 22.

Sterling, Stewart (see Winchell, Prentice)

Stern, Len (Leonard)

Emmy Award-winning writer Leonard Stern (December 23, 1923–June 7, 2011) spent a very few years writing for radio before embarking on a career in television that would span four decades. Stern's first scripts were written during World War II where he wrote shows to encourage military recruitment. The variety of celebrity guests available to Stern gave him the opportunity to author stories for a range of genres depending on the performer.

After the war Stern's first professional gag writing was for Milton Berle and his entry to radio came on *The $64 Question* followed by *The Dinah Shore Show*. Stern's break came after being hired by Bud Abbott and Lou Costello for their radio show (1947–1949) that led first to a contract with Universal Pictures and eventually television. Late in his career Stern, who co-created the Mad Libs franchise in 1953 with **Roger Price**, credited radio for his sense of comedic structure and timing.

Other Radio: *The Comedy Writers Show* (1948).
Theater: *Confetti* (1946, sketches).
Sources: *Showmen's Trade Review* February 26, 1949, p. 32; *Variety* October 8, 1947, p. 24, June 9, 1948, p. 26; *New York Times* obituary June 9, 2011; Leonard Stern interview, Archive of American Television.

Stevenson, Rick

Rick (Richard) Stevenson was a scriptwriter on *Wilderness Road* (1944) and *Gene Autry's Melody Ranch* (1947) among other programs.

Sources: *Variety* June 21, 1944, p. 36, February 26, 1947, p. 34.

Stirling, Nora

Mary Nora Stirling proved herself adept in many areas of radio, from acting to writing to producing. She developed an early interest in acting and studied at the Alberti School for drama at Carnegie Hall after high school. Stirling spent several years gaining experience in stock theater and by 1929 was appearing on New York radio shows such as *Mary and Bob* and *Johnson & Johnson Musical Melodrama*.

Stirling expanded her duties to penning aural stories and in 1932 was providing scripts for *Ladies and Gentlemen*, *Mary and Bob*, and *The Old Home Town* as well as *North Woods Adventure* in 1933. In addition to authoring episodes for *Meet Miss Judith* (1939), CBS provided Stirling the opportunity to create her own shows, notably *Funny Things*, a children's show that aired from 1937 to 1938. Stirling joined NBC's script division in 1942 and subsequently worked on *The March of Mercy* (1943) and *Words at War* (1943–1945). Her post-war credits include *American Portrait* (1946), *Good News* (1948), and *Yours for a Song* (1948–1949).

Sources: National Broadcasting Records; *Broadcasting* October 5, 1942, p. 38; *Radio Digest* March 1930 p. 47; *Radio Mirror* September 1937 p. 50; *Variety* June 7, 1939, p. 18, July 17, 1946, p. 36; *What's on the Air?* March 1930 p. 22.

Stone, Gene

Gene Stone (October 14, 1905–April 28, 1997) graduated from UCLA in 1933 and subsequently landed a job overseeing Los Angeles' Federal

Theatre Project for the Depression-era's Works Progress Administration. He frequently wrote plays with **Jack Robinson** who would become his long-time collaborator both for stage and radio works. Stone managed to work his way into radio after World War II on such series as *The Great Gildersleeve* (1947–1949), *Sealtest Variety Theatre* (1949), *The Halls of Ivy* (1950), and *Honest Harold* (1950–1951). His writing career ground to a halt after appearing before the House Un-American Activities Committee in 1952 though he was able to return to authoring plays and books in the 1970s.

Sources: Gene Stone Papers; *Broadcasting* September 18, 1950, p. 70; *Variety* August 27, 1947, p. 26, September 15, 1948, p. 31; *Los Angeles Times* obituary May 3, 1997.

Stone, Lynn (Marilyn)

Lynn Stone was a coveted scriptwriter for a succession of daily serials for fifteen years. Her earliest known work was *Hilltop House* (1937–1941, revived 1948–1949), that was written under the pseudonym Adelaide Marstone with longtime co-writer **Addy Richton**. This series was followed by *Keeping Up With Rosemary* (1942), *Woman of Courage* (1942), *This Life Is Mine* (1943–1945), and *Valiant Lady* (1945), all with Richton.

Other Radio: *Studio One* (1947).

Sources: *Radio Daily* October 28, 1937, p. 12; *Variety* March 18, 1942, p. 30, August 26, 1942, p. 3, March 24, 1943, p. 32, September 19, 1945, p. 34.

Striker, Fran

Fran Striker (August 19, 1903–September 4, 1962) is one of the legendary writers of old-time radio programs because of his impact on creating the immortal *The Lone Ranger* program. Striker was only slightly less influential in developing two of WXYZ's other juvenile hits, *The Challenge of the Yukon* and *The Green Hornet*.

A budding chemist, Striker dropped out of the University of Buffalo in the 1920s to work at the city's WEBR. During a brief stint with WTAM in Cleveland Striker wrote his first radio script and upon returning to Buffalo he found his niche as a scriptwriter. Striker historian Martin Grams has identified nearly a dozen shows for which Striker scripted during the earliest days of his writing career. These series included *Crystal Gazer*, *Drums of Kali*, *Headlines*, *Lights and Shadows*, *Mad Hatter*, *Mort Manor*, *Rhinestones*, *Sands of Time*, *The Sky Boat*, *Steppin' Out*, and *Temple Bells*.

Striker ultimately saw more potential in pursuing freelance work and quit WEBR to author episodes for Phillips H. Lord's *Seth Parker* and then for James Jewell of WXYZ. For the next couple years Striker dashed off scripts for *Crimson Fang*, *The Lone Ranger*, *Manhunters*, *Thrills of the Secret Service*, and *Warner Lester, Manhunter*, before accepting full-time employment from WXYZ in 1934. The station's crown jewel, *The Lone Ranger* was the product of Striker's collaboration with George Trendle and Jim Jewell, despite attempts by parties involved to claim individual credit for the hero. Striker's contribution was adapting an old script from his WEBR series *Covered Wagon Days* and devising much of the Ranger's lore including the silver bullets and Tonto.

Described once as "the greatest hack writer who ever lived," Striker produced a reported 60,000 words per week by the late 1930s. One account indicates that in one year Striker cranked out 312 radio episodes (*The Lone Ranger*, *The Green Hornet*, and *Ned Jordan, Secret Agent*), 355 Lone Ranger comic strips, twelve Lone Ranger novels, and scripts for two Lone Ranger serials. Though all this work earned him upwards of $10,000 per year, a healthy sum for the time, financial security eluded him. As part of his contract with WXYZ Striker waived all rights to his work, thus ensuring he would never profit from his work beyond its original use.

Sources: Francis Hamilton Striker Papers; Grams *Green Hornet*.

Strong, Paschal

Paschal "Pat" Strong was a West Point graduate and career Army officer who scripted *Jack Armstrong, All-American Boy* in his spare time in the years before the outbreak of World War II. He reportedly started writing scripts in 1933 while stationed in the Philippines and took over *Armstrong* in the 1940s. The job was subsequently turned over to other authors in 1943 so Strong could turn his full attention to the United States' entry to the war. Strong penned many short stories and books for juveniles, often under the nom de plume Kennedy Lyons. Trade magazines suggest he returned to the series for at least a short time ca. 1947.

Sources: *Variety* May 26, 1943, p. 38, February 26, 1947, p. 34; *Philadelphia Enquirer* obituary January 6, 1988.

Sullivan, Norman

Before getting hired by WLW in 1937 for a continuity position Norman Sullivan (December 11, 1909–June 21, 1984) worked as a doorman at the Loew-Poli Theatre in Bridgeport, CT. Within a year Sullivan had moved on to *The Pepsodent Show* with Bob Hope (1938–1948, 1951–1953), for whom he wrote on and off for the next four decades. Sullivan's most notable sabbatical from Hope was a two-year stint on Dean Martin's and Jerry Lewis' highly touted show (1948–1949).

Sources: Faith; *Billboard* December 25, 1948, p. 4; *Broadcasting* January 19, 1953, p. 15; *Variety* August 25, 1937, p. 62, February 1, 1939, p. 24, September 20, 1944, p. 34.

Susann, Jacqueline

Jacqueline Susann (August 20, 1918–September 21, 1974) was a minor actress in the late 1940s who did a bit of writing as well. Her work was used on radio's *It's Always Albert* (1948) and *Texaco Star Theatre* (1948–1949) as well as an unsuccessful theater production and some obscure television broadcasts. Susann's biggest hit was the 1966 novel *Valley of the Dolls*, a commercial smash that was panned by many of her contemporaries. At the time of her death, Susann's book was the best-selling novel of all time.

Sources: *Variety* July 7, 1948, p. 22; *New York Times* obituary September 23, 1974.

Sutton, Vida R.

Vida Sutton, a specialist in diction and speech, had her own show for many years, *The Magic of Speech* (1929–1937).

Source: *Radio Digest* March 1932, p. 31.

Swanton, Harold

Harold Swanton was a talented author of mystery and crime tales whose work appeared regularly on various radio series, some of those scripts eventually being adapted into motion pictures. Among his credits were *The Whistler* with **Joel Malone** (1944–1952), *Suspense* (1945, 1949, 1950), *Hopalong Cassidy* (1948–1949), *The Phillip Morris Playhouse* (1949), *Murder by Experts* (1950), *Hollywood Star Playhouse* (1951), and *A Crime Letter from Dan Dodge* (1952). Swanton wrote for two air versions of Dashiell Hammett characters, *The Adventures of Sam Spade* (1950–1951) and *The Fat Man* (1951). On television Swanton continued to author dozens of teleplays in those genres but also became adept at Westerns as well, including *Buckskin* (1958–1959) and *Wagon Train* (1959–1962).

Sources: French & Siegel; *Variety* March 19, 1947, p. 34.

Swart, Howard

After spending his childhood and formative years in Michigan and Ohio, Howard Swart spent a dozen years performing on vaudeville circuits around the country before landing in California in the early 1930s. Though only his much later work has survived in recorded form, Swart entered radio as early as 1933 acting on Los Angeles-area programs. Early on he understood the importance of a good story and opened a script service in 1936 in Hollywood and started penning his own stories as well such as *The Gravelpit Courtroom* (ca. 1934) and *The Newlyweds* (1936–1938), first over KHJ and then KNX. Over a decade later records show Swart also scripted *The Anderson Family* (1947) and *Hopalong Cassidy* (1948–1952).

Sources: *Broadcasting* October 1, 1936, p. 44; *Radio Daily* March 8, 1938, p. 5; *Radio Mirror* June 1937 p. 71; *Variety* May 23, 1933, p. 28.

Sweets, Bill (William)

Bill Sweets was a pioneer in broadcasting, reportedly entering the industry in 1925 as a studio manager at WRC and then as a continuity editor for NBC. Sweets had a long and illustrious career writing and directing programs over a quarter century. One of his earliest writing jobs was *Detective Story Magazine Hour* (ca. 1930), the show that featured the original Shadow character. Sweets was also the creative mind behind *Dangerous Paradise* (1934), *The Court of Human Relations* (1934–1939), *Big Sister*, and *The Story of Bess Johnson*. After returning to NBC for directorial duties in the early 1940s, Sweets had to give up his writing due to a network policy that discouraged directors from such tasks. Sweets' career slumped after being accused of Communist sympathies during the McCarthy era.

Sources: Grams *Shadow*; *Radio Mirror* May 1934 p. 51, September 1935 p. 14; *Variety* March 26, 1941, p. 26; *What's on the Air?* November 1930 p. 37.

Tackaberry, John

John Tackaberry (October 9, 1912–June 24, 1969) joined the writing staff of *The Jack Benny Show* in 1943 after his first radio job authoring *The Jack Carson Show*. Tackaberry wrote for the program for over a decade as Benny transitioned from radio to television in the 1950s. In 1947 he continued to work with the Benny writing team who handled writing chores for the summer replacement *The Jack Paar Show*. Tackaberry contributed to non–Benny television projects including *The Garry Moore Show* (1958) and *The Joey Bishop Show* (1963–1964).

Other Radio: *Elmer and Elsie* (1948).
Sources: *Broadcasting* October 13, 1958, p. 18; *Variety* June 23, 1948, p. 27.

Tallman, Robert (Bob)

Robert Tallman (December 15, 1914–September 10, 1995) proved himself adept at not only crafting an entertaining radio tale but surely-exaggerated accounts of his childhood as well. Tallman authority Jack French relates how Tallman fancied himself a successful fifteen-year-old poet despite dropping out of high school soon after. Similarly, he often described himself as the chief editor of the *March of Time* in the late 1930s despite being fired as a copyboy by the *New York Herald Tribune*.

Nevertheless, Tallman clearly had writing talent as demonstrated by a 1939 screenplay for *Slightly Honorable* and well over a decade of regular commercial broadcast writing. Tallman proved to be a workman writer, churning out quality stories over a variety of CBS series for more than a decade. Some notable shows with which Tallman is associated are *Cavalcade of America* (1939–1944, 1949–1951), *Readers Digest* (ca. 1942–1943), *Suspense* (1943–1946, 1948), *Inner Sanctum* (1944), *This Is My Best* (1944–1945), *The Sea Has a Story* (1945), *Theatre of Romance* (1946), *Intrigue* (1946), *Voyage of the Scarlet Queen* (1947–1948), *Escape* (1947, 1954), *Mr. I.A. Moto* (1951), *Mystery Theatre* (1952), *Best Plays* (1952–1953), and *NBC Star Playhouse* (1954).

Tallman's most famous assignment may have been *The Adventures of Sam Spade* (1947–1949), a hardboiled detective program based on Humphrey Bogart's iconic investigator in the immortal *Maltese Falcon*. Along with co-writer **Jo Eisinger** and director William Spier, Tallman developed one of the air's most beloved (and most spoofed) private eyes, both mining Hammett's work for story inspirations and devising original plots. After just a few months on the air Eisinger left the show and was replaced by **Gil Doud**, a prolific writer across radio, television, and film. Tallman's regular writing duties on *The Adventures of Sam Spade* ended in June 1949 when he and Doud burned out on the show and decided to step away. During the ensuing decade Tallman penned teleplays for series such as *Omnibus* (1952–1953) and *Hawaiian Eye* (1961–1962).

Sources: Abbott "Best D**n Writers"; French "Bob Tallman"; *Broadcasting* July 1, 1939, p. 199; *Variety* May 6, 1942, p. 37, September 9, 1942, p. 26, July 4, 1945, p. 26, July 31, 1946, p. 26, February 26, 1947, p. 34.

Tarkington, Booth

Booth Tarkington (July 29, 1869–May 19, 1946) was one of the nation's premier authors during the first decades of the twentieth century, among audiences as well as critics. Two Pulitzer Prizes and multiple honorary degrees attest to his literary influence, especially in the years following the first World War.

Born just after the end of the Civil War, Tarkington was well into middle-age when radio technology was developed and over sixty by the time he penned his first (and only) radio series. Entitled *Maud and Cousin Bill* (1932–1933), the show's approximately 100 episodes represent the majority of Tarkington's work in the field, save for a handful of scripts written primarily during World War II to promote the war effort.

Sources: Tarkington Papers; *Variety* October 17, 1932, p. 60.

Taussig, Frank Hart

After graduating from the University of Chicago in 1936, Frank Hart Taussig (d. April 11, 1985) became a professional writer, first in Chicago radio and then later in Hollywood for radio, television and film. Two programs to which he has been connected as scriptwriter are *The Clyde Beatty Show* and *The Modern Adventures of Casanova* (1952), featuring Errol Flynn. Taussig is also credited with at least two B films from the 1950s, *Perils of the Jungle* (1953) and *Giant from the Unknown* (1958). The last decade of his life was spent in Oklahoma City where he worked for a time at the Children's Memorial Hospital.

Sources: *Broadcasting* September 1, 1952, p. 79; *The Oklahoman* obituary April 14, 1985.

Taylor, Lawrence E.

While Lawrence E. Taylor has nearly a dozen screenplays to his credit between 1941 and 1950, so far he has only been connected to one radio series, 1944's *Results, Inc.* (as Larry Taylor).

Source: *Billboard* October 7, 1944, p. 9.

Taylor, Samuel

Samuel Taylor was an obscure writer of radio comedy (and one of two scriptwriters with this name) who is known to have scripted for *The Adventures of Maisie* (ca. 1945, with **Bob Sloan**) and *Tales of Willie Piper* (1946–1948).

Other Radio: *Henry Aldrich*.
Sources: *Variety* July 18, 1945, p. 46, October 23, 1946, p. 30.

Taylor, Samuel

Screenwriter and magazine author Samuel Taylor took over penning *Shorty Bell* in 1948 when original writer Frederick Hazlitt Brennan left the series.

Source: *Variety* April 28, 1948, p. 26.

Tazewell, Charles

Charles Tazewell (June 2, 1900–June 26, 1972) had his first experiences with radio in the mid–1920s while working as the director of the Des Moines Community Drama association during which time the group performed weekly plays over station WHO. After a stop at WQAM in Miami Tazewell landed in New York where he joined the continuity staff for CBS around 1931.

Over the next two decades Tazewell penned episodes for many different series, first as a CBS staff writer and later as a freelancer. One of his earliest identified programs was *Wilderness Road* (1936–1937) that won Best Children's Show Award from the Women's National Radio Committee in 1936. His other aural credits include *The Columbia Workshop* (1937, 1938), *The Silver Theatre* (1938), *Your Hollywood Parade* (1938), *The Gulf Screen Guild Theatre* (1939–1941), *Mayor of the Town* (1942–1949), *The Matinee Theatre* (1944), *Philco Radio Time* (1946–1948), *Family Theatre* (1947–1952), and *Prudential Family of Stars* (1948–1950).

A 1939 script Tazewell wrote was published as the book *The Littlest Angel* in 1946 and became his most famous work, going through numerous reprintings and adaptations in various media. In 1954 Tazewell and his wife left California to live permanently in their longtime vacation destination of Chesterfield, NH. Tazewell spent his later years involved in all aspects of the Little Theater in Brattleboro, VT.

Other Radio: *Paducah Plantation*; *The Tom Mix Ralston Straight Shooters*.
Sources: Ellett "Wilderness Road"; *Broadcasting* January 15, 1932, p. 18, November 15, 1939, p. 80; *Radio Daily* June 3, 1937, p. 3, January 14, 1938, p. 8; *Variety* October 20, 1926, p. 94; data.desmoinesregister.com.

Teichmann, Howard

Howard Teichmann (January 22, 1916–July 7, 1987) was a broadcasting freelance writer for about a decade, penning radio's *Campbell Playhouse* (1940–1944), *They Live Forever* (1942), *Valiant Lady* (1942–1946), *Road of Life* (1944–

1948), *Young Doctor Malone* (1945), *Great Scenes from Great Plays* (1948), and *Theater USA* (1948–1949).

Outside of radio, Teichmann left behind a rich library of writings that included television scripts during the 1950s, dozens of articles, screenplays, short stories, plays, and biographical books on Henry Fonda, George S. Kaufman, Alice Roosevelt Longworth, and Alexander Woollcott. He was a professor at Columbia's Barnard College for forty years, from 1946 to 1986.

Other Radio: *Cavalcade of America; The Fighting Senator.*
Sources: Howard Teichmann Papers; *Variety* September 9, 1942, p. 1, February 24, 1943, April 2, 1947, p. 35.

Tepperman, Emile C.

Little of Emile Tepperman's life has been uncovered outside of his writing accomplishments. After many years writing pulp stories during the 1930s Tepperman sold many scripts as a freelancer to programs such as *American School of the Air* (1944), *Suspense* (1944–1945, 1947), *Bulldog Drummond* (1945), *Counterspy* (1945), and *Inner Sanctum* (1945–1947, 1950).

Sources: *The Radio Annual* 1945 p. 833; *Variety* February 14, 1945; vintagelibrary.com.

Thomas, Cliff

Cliff Thomas, husband of writer **Mona Kent**, spent years as one of the many unidentified writers of serials in the 1930s, often for Blackett-Sample-Hummert. He recalled scripting many series during the era including *A Woman of America, Betty and Bob, Captain Midnight, The First Nighter Program, Roads to Adventure, Those Happy Gilmans* (1938), and *Valiant Lady*. Thomas was hired to write the long-running *Myrt and Marge* serial ca. 1941 while regular author **Stuart Hawkins** was absent for a year. Thomas is also known to have scripted a syndicated run of *Myrt and Marge* in 1946 and *The Adventures of Ted Drake, Guardian of the Big Top* in 1949.

In 1948 Thomas relocated to Nashville and some work on an Eddy Arnold network program introduced him to country-western broadcasting. Within a decade he had become the writer and producer of the legendary program *Grand Old Opry*.

Sources: Slate "Ted Drake"; *Billboard* October 31, 1960; *Variety* February 9, 1938, p. 31, January 21, 1942, p. 22; *St. Petersburg Times* October 10, 1943, p. 23.

Thomas, Gilbert

Gilbert Thomas worked for a number of stations, including WBDO (Orlando), WCPO, and WGR (Buffalo), in the early 1940s as an announcer before turning his focus to writing in middle years of the decade. After a short time with Allied Agencies, Thomas joined KQW's (San Francisco) continuity staff and then KFI (Los Angeles) a year later in 1945. During the last half of the decade Thomas' work could be heard on West Coast shows such as *The Whistler* (1948–1950), *Suspense* (1950, 1959), *Jeff Regan* (1950), and *Rocky Jordan* (1950).

Other Radio: *Are These Our Children?* (1946–1948); *O'Hara* (1951, audition).
Sources: Cox *Crime Fighters*; Grams *Suspense*; *Billboard* April 21, 1951, p. 14; *Broadcasting* December 11, 1944, p. 44; *Variety* September 24, 1941, p. 35.

Thompson, Rob

Rob Thompson was the writer behind a handful of fondly remembered juvenile programs during the 1930s including *Tarzan and the Diamond of Asher* (1934), *Tarzan and the Fires of Tohr* (1936), and *The Shadow of Fu Man Chu* (1939).

Sources: *Broadcasting* September 1, 1939; *Radio Daily* November 10, 1937, p. 7.

Thorne, Richard

Richard Thorne (d. February 12, 2007) was a man of many talents for WGN in the late 1940s and early 1950s. He announced and acted on a 1949 version of *Hall of Fantasy* and three years later also wrote and produced the 1952–1953 edition of the same series for Mutual. Thorne went on to write, direct, and produce many training films, teach at Chicago's Columbia College, and serve as the press secretary for Illinois governor Otto Kerner, Jr., in the 1960s.

Sources: *Telecasting* May 25, 1953, p. 92; *Chicago Tribune* December 10, 1949, p. 10; *Chicago Tribune* obituary February 19, 2007.

Todd (Kagel), Elizabeth

Elizabeth Todd (ca. 1907–December 26, 1965) joined NBC's staff in 1928 as a typist immediately after graduating from New York University. She soon started authoring her own radio plays, the first called *Margie, the Steno*. Some of Todd's other early programs were an adaptation of *Winnie, the Pooh*, *Dot and Will*, and *Sue Blake*. Todd found her niche in the daily serials where she also worked on *Love and Learn* (1937) and *Mother-in-Law* (1938).

By 1942 Todd had worked her way up to the position of senior staff writer for NBC's Blue network and was in charge of scripting for *Amanda of Honeymoon Hill*. Through the 1940s Todd wrote for numerous other soap opera series including *The Thatcher Family* (1942), *Young Widder Brown* (1942–1947), *David Harum* (1942–1943), *Lora Lawton* (1947), and *The Maxwells* (1947).

Other Radio: *Mary Noble, Backstage Wife*; *Second Husband*.

Sources: *Broadcasting* March 23, 1942, p. 34, January 3, 1966, p. 134; *NBC Transmitter* May 1938 p. 18; *Variety* March 10, 1937, p. 35, March 18, 1942, p. 34, April 2, 1947, p. 35, November 26, 1947, p. 24.

Tokar, Norman

After taking over the role of Henry Aldrich in *The Aldrich Family* when previous actor Ezra Stone enlisted in the Army in 1941, Norman Tokar (November 25, 1919–April 6, 1979) also wrote some scripts on the side. His stories were used on *Manhattan at Midnight* (1942) and then his former show *The Aldrich Family* (1945–1947) after his time in the service. In television Tokar worked primarily as a director on shows including *Leave It to Beaver* (1957–1960) and *The Donna Reed Show* (1960–1962) followed by many films for Disney in the 1960s and 1970s.

Sources: *Variety* October 7, 1942, p. 28, November 7, 1945, p. 40.

Tovrov, Orin

Orin Tovrov made a long and melodrama-filled career in soap operas, first on radio and then television. One of his first efforts was *Manhattan Mother* (1938–1940) followed quickly by a nearly two decades-long run on *Ma Perkins*, interrupted by two years in the Navy from 1943 to 1945. An attempt to bring a serial of his own creation, *The Searching Heart*, to the airwaves in 1948 was ultimately unsuccessful.

Other Radio: *The Brighter Day*.

Television: *The Doctors* (creator, 1963–1982).

Sources: *Broadcasting* April 15, 1938, p. 56, April 5, 1943, p. 24; *Radio TV Mirror* December 1958 p. 55; *Variety* February 26, 1941, p. 25, August 18, 1948, p. 28.

Tugend, Harry

Harry Tugend (February 17, 1897–September 11, 1989) was a *Motion Picture Herald* critic before he became one of **Fred Allen**'s early main writers, joining the show in 1934. He stayed with Allen until 1938 after which he pursued more screenwriting opportunities. Dozens of Tugend's screenplays were made into motion pictures from the 1930s to the 1960s.

Sources: Allen *Treadmill* p. 12–13; *Variety* July 10, 1934, p. 38; *Los Angeles Times* obituary September 16, 1989.

Tunick, Irve

Irve Tunick's (July 27, 1912–September 5, 1987) first radio work came with the WINS continuity department before he joined the radio staff of the Department of Interior in 1938. After some time scripting for the Office of Education, Tunick returned to the private sector in 1942 to organize a production company with Robert L. Cotton. After World War II much of Tunick's writing was done on a freelance basis. Among his aural credits are *The World Is Yours* (1936–1940), *Democracy in Action* (1939), *Gallant American Women* (1940), *Freedom's People* (1942), *The American School of the Air* (1944–1945), *CBS Is There* (1947–1948), *The Eternal Light* (1947–1950), *You Are There* (1947–1950), and *Cavalcade of America* (1949–1953). Tunick wrote teleplays for shows such as *The Witness* (1960–1961) and *Daniel Boone* (1968–1979) up until the time of his death.

Other Radio: *Cowboy Tom's Roundup*;

Sources: National Broadcasting Records; *Broadcasting* June 15, 1938, p. 46, September 1, 1938, p. 38, March 23, 1942, p. 38; *The Radio Annual* 1941 p. 973; *Variety* December 1, 1948, p. 22; *New York Times* obituary September 10, 1987.

Tyler, Ed

A writer for John Guedel Radio Productions in the late 1940s, Ed Tyler is credited with penning scripts for Grouch Marx for at least six years on *The Groucho Marx Show* (1948), *The Railroad Hour* (1949), and *You Bet Your Life* (1949–1954).

Sources: Coniam; *Billboard* November 12, 1949, p. 9; *The Radio and Television Yearbook* 1949 p. 740; *Variety* October 6, 1948, p. 24.

Vail, Myrtle

Myrtle Vail (January 7, 1888–September 18, 1978) fell in love with show business and left home at 15 to join her first show. Vail met a tenor during one tour, married him a year later, and had two children, Donna and George. The four spent the first two decades of the 20th century traveling from town to town as a performing family. The family's lifetime investments in real estate was lost in the economic crash of 1929 and Vail returned to show business, this time making a foray into radio.

Vail approached chewing gum giant the Wrigley Company with a prospect modeled on the emerging serial format in the early 1930s. Her pitch featured a mother and daughter, Myrtle Spear and Margie Minter, a play on Wrigley's Spearmint gum. The resulting show, *Myrt and Marge*, ran over a decade, from 1931 to 1942.

After Vail's series came to an end she created a new program, *Myrt, Ltd.*, for the fall 1942 season but it failed to find an audience. *Myrt and Marge* was briefly revived as a transcription feature in 1946 and Vail freshened up old scripts for the new run. Listener interest had passed years before, however, and the revival disappeared quietly. The series' decade of popularity was not easily forgotten by sponsors and as late as 1948 Vail was in discussions for yet another version of her classic program.

Sources: *Radio and Television Mirror* November 1939 p. 48, June 1948 p. 19; *Radio Digest* December 1931 p. 16–17; *Variety* July 15, 1942, p. 28.

van Cronkhite, John

A manager for Transradio ca. 1935, John van Cronkhite later had his own agency and worked in various executive positions around the industry for many years. Van Cronkhite is credited with authoring at least one series, *Mortimer Gooch* (1936–1937).

Sources: *Broadcasting* July 1, 1935, p. 48; *Variety* November 18, 1936, p. 44.

van Hartesveldt, Fran

Fran van Hartesveldt (1912–June 29, 1970) spent many years as a radio director, first for Young & Rubicam from the mid–1930s until 1945, then for Needham, Louis & Brorby, and finally for Benton & Bowles until the early 1950s. As a director van Hartesveldt contributed scripts to various shows over many years including *Suspense* (1944), *Great Gildersleeve* (1947–1949), *Sky King* (1951), *Father Knows Best* (1952–1953), and *The Roy Rogers Show* (1952–1953). In the early 1950s he walked away from directing to concentrate solely on writing where he found modest success on programs such as *CBS Radio Workshop* (1956), *Family Theater* (1956), and *Luke Slaughter of Tombstone* (1958). Van Hartesveldt's television credits include scripts for *Leave It to Beaver* (1958) and *Bat Masterson* (1959–1961).

Sources: *Broadcasting* May 28, 1945, p. 54, October 1, 1951, p. 10, August 25, 1952, p. 76; *Variety* October 1, 1941, p. 40; *Christian Science Monitor* May 28, 1956, p. 11.

Vendig, Irving

Irving Vendig (October 11, 1902–January 7, 1995) started writing serials in his early 30s and successfully wrote and created programs for the genre for thirty years. Among his radio credits are *David Adams—Son of the Sea* (1936), *Judy and Jane* (1936–1955), *Houseboat Hannah* (1936–1955), *Helpmate* (1943–1944), *The O'Neills* (1943), and *Perry Mason* (1946–1955). Vendig recrafted *Perry Mason* into television's *The Edge of Night* (1956–1965) and also scripted *Search for Tomorrow* (1951–1956), *Three Steps to Heaven* (1953–1954), and *Hidden Faces* (1968–1969).

Sources: Irving Vendig Collection; *Broadcasting* June 28, 1943, p. 34, October 22, 1951, p. 80; *TV Radio Mirror* September 1956 p. 83; *Variety* April 14, 1943, p. 31.

Victor, David

At 13 David Victor (August 22, 1910–October

18, 1989) immigrated with his mother from Russia and in his 20s began authoring scripts for the airwaves. Victor penned for a wide variety of shows though serials were regularly on his workload. Among his credits are *Her Honor, Nancy James* (1938, with **Herbert Little, Jr.**), *Wheatana Playhouse* (1940–1942 with Little), *Hilltop House* (ca. 1941, with Little, augmenting the scripts of regular writers **Lynn Stone** and **Addy Richton**), *The O'Neills* (1941–1943, with Little), *Cohen the Detective* (1943), *Mary Small Show* (1944), *Joanie's Tea Room* (1945–1947), (1946–1954), and *The Mel Blanc Show* (1946–1947). Later, Victor served as writer and producer on many television series, notably *The Man from U.N.C.L.E.* and *Marcus Welby, M.D.*

Other Radio: *Let George Do It; Lincoln Highway.*

Sources: *Broadcasting* August 27, 1945, p. 74; *Variety* August 17, 1938, p. 36, November 20, 1940, p. 25, April 23, 1941, p. 24, March 4, 1942, p. 26, September 1, 1943, p. 34, September 11, 1946, p. 34; *New York Times* obituary October 24, 1989.

Vittes, Louis

In the 1930s and early 1940s Louis Vittes (April 18, 1911–April 21, 1969) authored a number of plays including *Comes the Revelation* that were produced on stage. During the 1940s and early 1950s Vittes became a prolific scriptwriter of detective and mystery stories for many series. Among the programs for which he wrote during more than a decade on the ether were *Mr. & Mrs. North* (1944), *Two on a Clue* (1944), *Inner Sanctum* (1946, 1948–1949), *The Shadow* (1948), *Sealtest Variety Theatre* (1948), *The Adventures of the Lone Wolf* (1949), *The Saint* (1949–1951), *The Affairs of Peter Salem* (1949–1953), *The Man from Homicide* (1950–1951), and *Barrie Craig, Confidential Investigator* (1951–1955).

Other Radio: *The Adventures of the Thin Man; The Amazing Nero Wolfe.*

Sources: Barer; Grams *Shadow*; *Variety* June 10, 1942, p. 51, April 19, 1944, p. 23, October 4, 1944, p. 24.

Vollmer, Lula

Lula (Louisa Smith) Vollmer (March 7, 1889–May 2, 1955) was a native North Carolinian playwright whose work often reflected the rural Southern region of her youth. Some of her notable plays include *Sun-Up* (1923), *Trigger* (1927), and *The Hill Between* (1938). During the 1930s even as she continued to write for the stage, Vollmer penned radio shows such as *Moonshine and Honeysuckle* (1930–1933), *Grits and Gravy* (1934), *The Widow's Son* (1935–1937), Gabriel Heatter's *A Brighter Tomorrow* (1945–1947), and *It's Your Business* (1949).

Sources: Lula Vollmer Papers (Appalachian State); Lula Vollmer Papers (NYPL).

Walpole, Helen

Helen Walpole (Brower) (b. February 1, 1915) wrote and acted in school plays as a young girl and followed this passion into adulthood. After a short time on stage in the early 1930s, Walpole found steady work as a writer-actor in radio. Her work spanned the heart of the era of dramatic radio, from the mid–1930s to the early 1950s. Early in her career Walpole's acting was featured on *Eno Crime Clues* (ca. 1936), *Just Plain Bill* (1938), and *Lorenzo Jones* (1938).

In 1938 Walpole teamed with **Margaret Leaf** to create a 30-minute radio script about Mark Twain that was submitted to NBC editor Lewis Titterton. This first known scripting effort by Walpole became *Adventures in Reading*, an educational program that ran two years (1938–1940). Walpole added the commercial serial *Our Gal Sunday* to her writing load in 1939 and joined NBC's writing staff that same year. Throughout the 1940s Walpole returned to freelancing and had stints authoring a number of serials including *Amanda of Honeymoon Hill* (ca. 1941), *Stella Dallas* (1941–1949), *Mary Noble, Backstage Wife* (1942), *Second Husband* (1942), *Katie's Daughter* (1948), *Lora Lawton* (1943–1949), and *Nona from Nowhere* (1950). Walpole occasionally created new stage plays during this time but radio remained her main creative outlet.

Sources: *Radio Mirror* April 1938 p. 43; *Variety* April 15, 1936, p. 40, June 1, 1938, p. 39, August 9, 1939, p. 2, November 1, 1939, p. 27, October 8, 1941, p. 25, May 12, 1943, p. 40.

Wang, Eugene (Gene)

Gene Wang (April 4, 1914–July 7, 1971) was a prolific writer for over twenty-five years, specializing in mystery and private investigator shows for much of that time. *Sky Blazers* (1940), *It's the Navy* (1942), *The Adventures of the Falcon* (1943–1954), *The Adventures of the Thin Man* (1943–1944), *Creeps by Night* (1944), *Quick as a Flash* (1945–1951), *The Amazing Mr. Malone* (1947–1951). Wang scripted a number of these shows as they transitioned to television in the 1950s but was still authoring stories well into the 1960s for *The Third Man* (1964–1965) and *The Trials of O'Brien* (1965–1966) among others.

Other Radio: *Perry Mason.*

Sources: Gene Wang Papers; *Broadcasting* June 15, 1953, p. 36; *Radio & Television Mirror* June 1940 p. 52; *Variety* January 13, 1943, p. 35, April 14, 1943, p. 41.

Ward, Shirley

A CBS employee in the 1930s and later with the J. Walter Thompson agency, Shirley Ward joined the writing team for Edgar Bergen's *Chase & Sanborn Hour* in 1937.

Source: *Variety* April 14, 1937, p. 75.

Ware, Harlan

William Harlan Ware's (July 14, 1902–May 7, 1967) writing career began inauspiciously as a police reporter in Chicago but he started publishing articles and short stories in the early 1930s. Ware's radio work is represented by two years scripting *The Bartons* (1939–1942) and **Carlton E. Morse's** *One Man's Family* (1944–1959). Though responsible for very few screenplays, a number of Ware's original stories were adapted to the big screen.

Sources: Harlan Ware Papers; Cox *A to Z*; *Broadcasting* January 1, 1940, p. 50.

Watt, Kenneth

Kenneth Watt joined Blackett-Sample-Hummert in 1938 as a director and writer. He provided stories to *Second Husband* (1938), *One Minute to Go* (ca. 1939), and *Tsar of Stars* (ca. 1939).

Sources: *Variety* September 21, 1938, p. 36, May 31, 1939, p. 24.

Webb, Ken

Ken Webb spent much of his career as a director but he served as one of the primary writers for *Cavalcade of America* during its first four years (approx. 1935–1939).

Source: Grams *Cavalcade.*

Webb, Nancy

Author Nancy Webb is credited with writing *Nick Carter, Master Detective* (1943), *Chick Carter, Boy Detective* (1943–1945), *Cosmo Tune Time* (1945), *Blackstone, the Magic Detective* (1948–1949) during her years in the industry.

Sources: *Variety* March 22, 1944, p. 28, October 3, 1945, p. 36.

Wedlock, Hugh, Jr.

Hugh Wedlock, Jr., (February 15, 1908–December 13, 1993) had an extensive career writing comedy that spanned nearly fifty years across radio, film, and television. His earliest known scriptwriting was for Jack Pearl and his Baron Munchausen character in the early 1930s under Lucky Strike's sponsorship. With long-time writing partner **Howard Snyder**, Wedlock joined Jack Benny's program in 1936 and stayed for one year before signing with Eddie Cantor's *Texaco Town Hall* in 1937. Soon after they added *Jack Oakie's College* to their workload as well.

Wedlock moved on to programs featuring Billy House (*Laugh Liner*) and Walter O'Keefe as well as scribing for *Lady Esther Screen Guild Theatre* (1944), *That's My Pop* (1945, based on **Milt Gross'** comic strip), Jack Benny (mid–1940s), and *Lum 'n' Abner* (1948–1950). However, much of his work during the 1940s was for the motion pictures studios.

On television Wedlock wrote regularly for *The Jack Benny Program* (1953–1961), *The Red Skelton Hour* (1962–1963), and Rowan & Martin's *Laugh-In* (1968–1969). His scripts were still used as late as 1981 on shows such as *Diff'rent Strokes.*

Animated Shorts: *Betty Boop* (1930s); *Popeye* (1933).

Sources: *Broadcasting* September 15, 1937, p. 46; *Variety* May 1, 1935, p. 31, July 1, 1936, p. 34; *Los Angeles Times* obituary December 18, 1993.

Weinrott, Les

Les (Lester) Weinrott wrote motion pictures in Hollywood in the early 1930s before moving to radio around 1933 upon joining the Don Lee network's Thomas Lee Artist Bureau. By 1937 Weinrott had relocated to Chicago where he worked on radio shows for the powerful Blackett-Sample-Hummert agency. Among his earliest writing assignments were *It Can Be Done* (1937), *Aunt Jemima's Cabin at the Cross Roads* (1937), *Margot of Castlewood* (1938), and *Rural Crime Reporter* (1939).

Within three years Weinrott opened his own production company where one of his series provided to clients was *Anne Thomas, Career Wife* (1940). As head of L. A. Weinrott and Associates he was allowed the freedom to also take on freelance production work in New York. One of his original creations, *Meet the Meeks*, aired as early as 1942 and reappeared later in the decade (1947–1949). During the latter years of World War II Weinrott scripted and produced *America in the Air*, featuring stories of the Navy and Army air forces.

After the war most of Weinrott's attention was focused on production work, though he scripted a handful of other series including *Five After the Hour* (1945) and *The Peabodys* (1945–1946). He had a close working relationship with the Wrigley company during the last half of the 1940s and Weinrott produced and packaged several programs for them. After a short time producing in New York, Weinrott returned to Chicago where he produced television programming through the 1950s.

Film: *The Hot Shot* (ca. 1933); *Confidential Adviser* (ca. 1933).

Sources: *Broadcasting* June 29, 1942, p. 37; *The Film Daily* March 8, 1933, p. 1; *The Radio Annual* 1940 p. 661, 791; *Radio Daily* February 19, 1937, p. 8, December 29, 1937, p. 1; *Variety* October 17, 1933, p. 39, January 21, 1942, p. 23, December 26, 1945, p. 31.

Weiskopf, Bob

Bob Weiskopf (March 13, 1914–February 20, 2001) was a friend of **Norman Panama** and **Melvin Frank** at the University of Chicago where they regularly listened to radio comedians such as Jack Benny and **Fred Allen**. After college, Weiskopf was comfortably working in advertising when his old pals convinced him to quit that job and come to the West Coast to try radio.

Chicago's prominence in the radio industry was declining at the time so Weiskopf took up the offer. He first worked for Eddie Cantor in 1941 for a partial season before moving on to Rudy Valley, Joan Davis, *The Sealtest Variety Theatre* (1942), and Fred Allen before his induction into the service. Weiskopf scripted for Fred Allen again later in the decade before he moved into television. On the small screen his credits include *I Love Lucy*, *All in the Family*, and *The Red Skelton Show*.

Other Radio: *The Chesterfield Supper Club*; *Our Miss Brooks*.

Sources: Young; *Motion Picture Daily* May 11, 1943, p.1; *Variety* September 2, 1942, p. 29.

Welch, William

William Welch is known to have scripted for at least two 1940s series, *Words at War* (1943) and the stories of juvenile hero Frank Merriwell on *The Adventures of Frank Merriwell* (1946–1949). Later Welch was a producer and script advisor for many shows on NBC until the late 1950s.

Sources: *Broadcasting* March 12, 1956, p. 91; *The Film Daily* October 29, 1945, p. 12.

Wells, Billy K.

Billy Wells was the gag writer in radio's early days behind Jack Pearl's Baron Munchhausen character. Munchhausen's catchphrase "Vass you dere, Sharlie?" was a sensation with listeners but quickly wore out its welcome.

Sources: Allen *Treadmill* p. 12; Jack Pearl obituary *The Spokesman-Review* December 26, 1982.

Wells, George

For approximately nine years George Wells had the Herculean task of adapting a Hollywood film into a 60-minute radio script every week for *The Lux Radio Theatre*. In the mid–1940s Wells signed with a motion picture studio to author screenplays though he did return to radio at least once to pen stories for *Silver Theatre* (ca. 1945).

Sources: *Variety* December 15, 1943, p. 29; June 20, 1945, p. 30.

Werris, Snag

Solomon Samuel "Snag" Werris (August 9, 1910–February 27, 1987) earned a living as a vaudeville performer and magician before spending some years in the 1930s writing comedy scripts. His gags were used by **Fred Allen**, Burns and Allen, Eddie Cantor, and Ed Wynn among others. Werris authored *Quixie Doodles* (1939–1941), a show featuring F. Chase Taylor, one half of the famous Stoopnagel and Budd comedy team. After writing screenplays during the 1940s, Werris worked on a number of comedy television shows in the 1950s.

Other Radio: *Rookies* (1941).

Sources: Berard & Englund; *Variety* July 21, 1943, p. 33.

West, Jane

Jane West was the author of *The O'Neills* (1934–1943), described by critics as an Irish version of the popular Jewish serial *Rise of the Goldbergs*. West also starred in her show that followed its characters as they aged in real time. West penned the daily episodes until 1941 when she fell ill and writing chores were taken over by **David Victor** and **Herbert Little, Jr.** After her recovery she continued to supervise the script writing until the show left the airwaves in 1943.

Sources: *Radio Mirror* July 1936 p. 64; *Variety* May 22, 1934, p. 38, October 28, 1942, p. 28.

West, Paul

Starting as a continuity writer for CBS's Hollywood station in the mid–1930s and then the network's San Francisco outlet ca. 1940, Paul West (August 27, 1911–June 15, 1998) found his niche authoring comedy and light dramatic fare for radio and, later, television. Among his radio credits are *Sally of the Star* (1935), *Hollywood Showcase* (1941), *Mischa, the Magnificent* (1942), *Raffles* (1942–1943), *The Billie Burke Show* (ca. 1945), *Stars Over Hollywood* (1945), *The Adventures of Ozzie and Harriet* (1947–1948), *Family Theatre* (1948), *The Great Gildersleeve* (1949–1951), and *Father Knows Best* (1952–1953).

West's television credits are even more extensive, including shows that transitioned from radio such as *Amos 'n' Andy* (1955) and *Father Knows Best* (1954–1960) to small screen originals including *The Brady Bunch* (1969–1970) and *The Waltons* (1975–1978).

Book: *It's a Living* (1941).

Sources: *Broadcasting* June 1, 1939, p. 46, October 27, 1941, p. 32, June 29, 1942, p. 28; *Radio Mirror* February 1945 p. 33, August 1946 p. 13;

Wheaton, Glenn

Glenn Wheaton spent a quarter-century penning gags and scripts for various comedy programming on radio and television. During his career Wheaton wrote for *Command Performance* (1942, which he later produced), *The Bob Burns Show* (1943), Dinah Shore's *Birdseye Open House* (1943), Bob Hope's *The Pepsodent Show* (1944–1947), *Songs by Sinatra* (1945–1946), *The Tony Martin Show* (1946–1947), *The Jack Smith Show* (1949, later *The Oxydol Show*), *The Jo Stafford Show* (1953), and *The Johnny Mercer Show* (1953–1954). Wheaton's television work in the 1950s and 1960s included scripts for *The Colgate Comedy Hour* (1950–1955) and *My Three Sons* (1961–1964).

Sources: *Broadcasting* April 6, 1942, p. 12, August 30, 1943, p. 18, September 11, 1944, p. 60, December 10, 1945, p. 95; *Variety* October 1, 1947, p. 26.

Whedon, John

After graduating from Harvard but before getting into show business ventures, John Whedon wrote for *The Forum* in the early 1930s and worked as *The New Yorker*'s managing editor as well. Working for the Lord & Thomas agency, Whedon's early radio scripts appeared on *Royal Desserts Hour* (1936), *The Columbia Workshop* (1937), *The Rudy Vallee Hour* (1938), and *The Chase & Sanborn Hour* (1939).

Whedon, "a quiet man with a twinkle," wielded his pen deftly in writing one of radio's most beloved programs, *The Great Gildersleeve*, for five years from 1942 until 1947 with **Sam Moore**. Despite the success that came on the show, a friend recalled that even during the heady days of *The Great Gildersleeve* at which time he was "making a small fortune," Whedon, his wife Carroll, and children Tom and Jill continued to live in a modest house with a small garden.

In 1949 Whedon was appointed to the CBS television writing staff in along with Robert Fine and their first assignment was an hour-long variety show with original music and sketches. His television credits include *Lux Video Theatre*

(1951–1955), *The Donna Reed Show* (1958–1961), and *The Andy Griffith Show* (1963–1964).

Over his long career Whedon wrote for just about every entertainment format including radio, film, television, and the stage and is recognized as the first of the Whedon line of writers that includes his son Tom who wrote for television's *Alice* and *Benson* and grandson Joss who created *Buffy the Vampire Slayer*.

Other Radio: *Forecast* (1940).

Theater: *Life's Too Short* (1935); *Texas Lil' Darling*, book written with Sam Moore, music by Robert Emmet Dolan, lyrics by Johnny Mercer.

Film: *Island at the Top of the World* (1974); *The Bears and I* (1974).

Other: Three sets of Great Gildersleeve records released by Capitol between 1944 and 1947. Co-written with Sam Moore.

Sources: John Whedon Collection; Billips & Pierce; Stumpf & Ohmart; *Billboard* December 21, 1946, p. 92, November 22, 1947, p. 116, October 10, 1949, p. 49; *Broadcasting* May 2, 1949, p. 40; *Radio Daily* June 18, 1937, p. 3; *Variety* September 18, 1935, p. 75; *New York Times* May 6, 1931, p. 32, April 24, 1961, p. 59, November 27, 1991, p. B10; *Los Angeles Times* April 6, 1956, p. B6, May 2, 1956, p. 14, May 4, 1973, p. F13.

White, Andy

Andy White isn't known to have written widely in radio, but his primary credit—eight years penning *The Great Gildersleeve* (1947–1955)—is an impressive one. With the departure of the original *Gildersleeve* writers **Sam Moore** and **John Whedon** in 1947, White was called in to work on the 1947 summer replacement series *Summerfield Bandstand*. That fall he joined *Gildersleeve*'s new writing team and stayed on board for the remainder of its radio run. White worked on television's short-lived version of *The Great Gildersleeve* (1955–1956) but went on to write and produce for many more widely remembered programs including *Bat Masterson* (1958–1961) and *The Waltons* (1975–1978).

Sources: Schulz *Gildersleeve*; *Variety* June 18, 1947, p. 26.

White, Bob (Robertson)

Bob White (February 24, 1900–November 29, 1985) was a screenplay writer in the 1930s before moving to radio in the 1940s where he worked as writer and director, keeping one foot in Hollywood with the occasional screenplay. White created and supervised the script creation for *Deadline Dramas* (1941), a show that used audience submissions to craft short scripts for impromptu performances. White concurrently authored *The Sea Hound* and directed *Dick Tracy* until 1943 before giving up the serials to focus solely on dramas. In the 1950s White went to work for Charlotte, N.C.'s WBT and WBTV.

Sources: *Broadcasting* January 13, 1941, p. 48, August 16, 1954, p. 103; *Variety* December 22, 1943, p. 32.

White, Kenneth

Kenneth White was responsible for at least four episodes of the war-time series *Words at War* in 1943.

Source: NBC Records.

Wilkinson, Richard Hill

Richard Hill Wilkinson, author of pulp fiction under several pen names, a few screenplays, and some stage productions, authored for a handful of known radio series, primarily in the mid–1940s such as *Crime Is My Pastime* (1945), *Murder Is my Hobby* (1945), *Danger, Dr. Danfield*, and *Family Theatre* (1948).

Other Radio: *California Caravan*.

Sources: *Saturday Review* February 10, 1962, p. 60–61; *Variety* July 25, 1945, p. 34, October 31, 1945, p. 36, February 26, 1947, p. 34.

Williamson, Mel

An announcer and jack-of-all-trades in Los Angeles radio in the early 1930s, Mel Williamson scripted a few series early in his career before most of his time became focused producing radio programs for a number of agencies over the 1930s and 1940s. In 1935 Williamson wrote a series for Federal Housing Administration that aired in Southern California before he joined the Federal Radio Theatre Project in 1936. Two of his other series include *The Marines Tell It to You* (1937) and *Wings of Destiny* (1940–1942).

Sources: *Broadcasting* August 1, 1935, p. 39, December 1, 1936, p. 58; *Radio Daily* November 17, 1937, p. 8; *Radio Mirror* October 1934 p. 43.

Wilson, Frank

Frank Wilson worked as an NBC staff writer beginning around 1933 during which time he is known to have authored a serial based on Paul Bunyon (ca. 1935). While with the network Wilson created *The Bishop and the Gargoyle*, a series he reprised in 1938 and again in 1941 after joining Lord & Thomas in 1937 as a script editor. During this time Wilson penned for Kay Kyser (ca. 1941–1942).

After five years with the agency Wilson joined the Office of Facts and Figures where one of his first efforts was *Stage Door Canteen* (1942–1944). Returning to the commercial sphere, Wilson proved a versatile writer, authoring comedy, musical, and dramatic programs with equal success. Shows on which he worked included *Starlight Serenade* (1944), *Songs by Sinatra* (1945–1947), *Academy Award Theatre* (1946), *Mystery in the Air* (1947), *Hollywood Star Time* (1948), *Spotlight Revue* (1948), and *The Hartmans* (1949).

Seeking to revitalize its ratings in the face of both television and competing radio networks, NBC assigned **Goodman Ace** to head the writing of *The Big Show* (1950–1952). Wilson was added to Ace's scripting team but ultimately this weekly 90-minute collection of NBC talent failed to attract the audience so desperately desired.

Sources: Cox *Crime Fighters*; *Broadcasting* March 16, 1942, p. 16; *Variety* April 3, 1935, p. 40, March 18, 1942, p. 30, March 25, 1942, p. 24, July 22, 1942, p. 25, February 26, 1946, p. 28, July 9, 1947, p. 73, February 4, 1948, p. 37.

Wilson, Jack C.

A continuity writer for WLW in the late 1930s, Jack C. Wilson joined NBC's Hollywood writing staff in 1945. Wilson worked for the network for at least twenty years on shows such as *The Jimmy Edmondson Show* (1946), *Music America Loves Best* (1946), *Your United Nations* (1946–1947), *NBC University Theater* (1948–1951), *Roy Shield and His Orchestra* (1951), *Radio City Previews* (1952), *The All-American Sports Show* (1953), *Five Star Matinee* (1956–1957), and *Theatre Five* (1964–1965).

Sources: NBC Records; *Broadcasting* March 15, 1939, p. 82, September 15, 1952, p. 75; *Motion Picture Daily* February 26, 1945, p. 6; *Variety* February 6, 1946, p. 34.

Wilson, W. Ray

W. Ray Wilson scripted serials such as *Red Mackenzie* (1936) and *Jack Westaway Under the Sea* (1938) for Chicago-area stations while also writing for the industry magazine *Variety*. Wilson joined CBS in early 1938 and then WLW after just a few months. One of his first assignments with WLW was scripting *Man of Mars* and then *My Lucky Break* (1939) and *Gateway to Hollywood* (1939). After going to work for Wrigley's radio division in the early 1940s Wilson earned credits on *The Wayne King Show* (1940), *Dear Mom* (1941), and *The Winner* (1941). Wilson also scripted numerous other series over his lengthy career including *Flight Nurse* (1944), *Mystery Is My Hobby* (1947), *All-Star Western Theatre* (1948), and *The Roy Rogers Show* (1951–1952).

Other Radio: *Romance of the Ranchos*; *Your Movietown Radio Theatre*.

Sources: *Broadcasting* January 1, 1938, p. 34, October 1, 1939, p. 16; *Motion Picture Daily* February 23, 1944, p. 6; *Radio Daily* January 5, 1938, p. 2; *Variety* July 8, 1936, p. 32, May 25, 1938, p. 38, January 25, 1939, p. 42.

Wiltten, Virginia

Virginia Wiltten is best remembered for a series of adaptations of Edgar Allen Poe stories scripted for *Black Night* (1937–1938) over WBAP in Fort Worth, TX. She later joined the continuity staff of Oklahoma City's KOMA in 1940.

Sources: *Broadcasting* December 1, 1937, p. 53, August 15, 1940, p. 58.

Winchell, Prentice

Stewart Sterling was the broadcast penname used by Prentice Winchell (1895–1976), a former New York-area journalist and fiction writer. Outside of radio Winchell used a number of other aliases while publishing in various pulp magazines. Winchell's radio credits stretch back to the early days of radio drama, when scripting forms were still being crafted. His works include *Eno Crime Clues* (ca. 1932–1936), *Maverick Jim* (1933), *Red Trails* (ca. 1935), and *The Spider's Web* (1938, audition).

For a few years Winchell's radio involvement turned more to production and oversight for various agencies including N. W. Ayer & Son and Douglas F. Storer. While Winchell continued to pen some radio scripts including *The Adventures of Bill Lance, Results, Inc.* (1944), and *The Whistler* (1947) during the 1940s, he was increasingly focused on his crime novels of which dozens were published into the 1960s.

Sources: *Broadcasting* February 15, 1935, p. 6, July 1, 1938, p. 30, December 1, 1938, p. 45; *Variety* December 27, 1932, p. 33, December 19, 1933, p. 40; gadetection.pbworks.com.

Winston, Irene

Irene Winston (July 18, 1916–September 1, 1964) originally dreamed of being a physician but when she missed taking the licensing exams Winston decided to try acting instead. The decision worked out and she was a busy broadcast actress through the 1930s and 1940s. However, Winston also took time out to pen the occasional aural story, too. Her authorial credits include *Fighting Senator* (1946), *Molle Mystery Theatre* (1946), and *Romance* (1956). Winston wrote a handful of teleplays as well before her premature death.

Book: *If Words Could Kill* (1943).

Sources: *Radio Mirror* April 1939 p. 52; *Variety* July 31, 1946, p. 26.

Wishengrad, Morton

Morton Wishengrad worked as a scriptwriter for NBC on some of the network's more prestigious programs including *Cavalcade of America* (1944–1945, 1949–1951), *The Eternal Light* (1944–1950, 1953), and *NBC University Theatre* (1944–1950).

Other Radio: *Music in American Cities* (1944); *They Call Me Joe* (1944); *Words at War*.

Sources: Segal; *Broadcasting* February 28, 1944, p. 44; *NBC Transmitter* August 1944 p. 3.

Wolfe, Winifred

Winifred Wolfe (May 29, 1923–October 27, 1981, not to be confused with the *One Man's Family* actress of the same name) wrote scripts for a number of dramatic series during the postwar era. Among them were *Suspense* (1945), *Carrington Playhouse* (1946), *Murder at Midnight* (1946), *Marriage for Two* (1949), and *Dangerous Assignment* (1950). She also contributed stories to *Cloak and Dagger* (1950), *Five Star Matinee* (1957), and *Theatre Five* (1965).

In television Wolfe worked as a lead writer for *As the World Turns* in the 1970s. She wrote dozens of stories, two of which were adapted to feature films ("Ask any Girl" and "If a Man Answers") and penned two plays for summer theaters, *Man on the Stairs* and *Three Stories High*.

Sources: NBC Records; *Billboard* December 28, 1946, p. 9; *Variety* October 31, 1945, p. 40, April 24, 1946, p. 38; *New York Times* obituary October 29, 1981.

Wolff, Nat

Nat Wolff worked primarily as a director and producer through much of dramatic radio's Golden Age from the 1930s into the 1950s. Moving between various agencies and even running his own talent agency for a time, Wolff is credited with authoring scripts for a number of series, often series for which he had directorial duties as well. Some of those programs included *Flying Red Horse Tavern* (1935), *Silver Theatre* (1945), *Presenting Charles Boyer* (1950), and *Mr. and Mrs. Blandings* (1951), based on Eric Hodge's novel *Mr. Blandings Builds His Dream House.*

Sources: *Variety* October 30, 1935, p. 40, October 10, 1945, p. 34.

Woodman, Ruth Cornwall

Ruth Cornwall Woodman (November 26, 1894–April 2, 1970), a native of England, Vassar graduate, banker's wife, and mother of two children, was approached to write radio scripts in 1928 based on the strength of some of her published articles. Cornwall asked to create a program for the Pacific Borax Company that was wanting to create a Western series ca. 1930. At the time, Cornwall was an advertising copywriter when she created *Death Valley Days* to promote 20 Mule Team Borax, a show that ran for two decades. From 1930 until 1944 the series aired as *Death Valley Days*, for one year (1944–1945) as *Death Valley Sheriff*, and then until 1951 as *The Sheriff*. Reruns of the program were broadcast under numerous monikers including *Call of the West, Frontier Adventure,* and *The Pioneers.*

Cornwall scripted the first five years of stories for the television adaptation of *Death Valley Days* (1952–1970) and served as a script supervisor after writing chores were turned over to other authors. In addition to writing for other radio shows on the side, Cornwall continued to contribute articles for publications such as *The New Yorker* and *Reader's Digest*.

Other Radio: *Armstrong Theatre of Today*; *Cavalcade of America*; *Dr. Christian*; *Ripley's Believe It or Not*; *Suspense*.

Sources: Ruth Cornwall Woodman Papers; *Radio Digest* March 1933 p. 18–19.

Wouk, Herman

Herman Wouk (b. May 27, 1915) entered radio after graduating from Columbia University. His first job was with classmate **Arnold Auerbach** working for comedy writer **Dave Freedman**. Freedman had cabinets full of cross-referenced jokes that Wouk and co-writers strung together into some semblance of a monolog, Freedman refined, and was then sold to some of radio's prominent comedians.

Wouk eventually grew tired of this routine and, looking for new challenges, worked up an original script with Auerbach that they sent to **Fred Allen**'s staff. Allen later claimed to immediately recognize their talent and hired them for his show. Wouk enjoyed an approximately five-year run with Allen before enlisting in the Navy at the beginning of World War II.

During his time serving on a minesweeper Wouk began imagining grander stories to write than topical jokes for radio and after the war focused on penning novels. He won the Pulitzer Prize for 1951's *The Caine Mutiny* that was also made into a film. In the 1970s Wouk published his two most popular works, *The Winds of War* (1971) and *War and Remembrance* (1978).

Other Radio: *Millions for Defense* (1941).

Sources: Allen *Treadmill* p. 70–71; *Variety* October 5, 1938, p. 34, June 25, 1941, p. 24; interview NPR.org.

Young, John M.

As an NBC continuity writer in the 1930s, John M. Young (b. 1906) scripted for *There Was a Woman* (1937), *Woman Behind the Man* (1937), *The Zenith Show* (1937), *Attorney at Law* (1938), and *Woman in White* (1938–1939) among others. His experience with serials during this time paved the way for nearly three decades of work scripting soap operas on radio as well as television. Young's other radio credits include *Second Wife* (1940), *Michael* (1941), *Bright Horizon* (1941–1944), *The Right to Happiness* (1942–1960), *The Second Mrs. Burton* (1946–1947), *Road of Life* (1948–1952), and *Theatre Five* (1965).

Television: *Golden Windows* (1954–1955); *From These Roots* (1961).

Sources: John M. Young Papers; *Broadcasting* November 15, 1940, p. 53, April 20, 1942, p. 33; *Radio Daily* November 8, 1937, p. 1, 8; *Variety* August 13, 1941, p. 37, December 31, 1947, p. 19.

Zelinka, Sydney (Sid)

Sid Zelinka (November 2, 1906–January 17, 1981) headed to California after a chance meeting with Ira Gershwin during which the lyricist complimented Zelinka's humor. With new wife in tow in 1935, Zelinka found work writing for *Jack Oakie's College*. Within just a few years Zelinka was working steadily in the industry and over the course of 25 years scripted for some of the top comics on the airwaves.

Among his radio credits over the next fifteen years were *Laugh Liner* (1938, with **Arthur Stander**), *Sealtest Variety Theatre* (two runs on the show between 1942 and 1949), *The Rudy Vallee Show* (1942), *The Fred Brady Show* (1943, a summer replacement for Bob Burns), *The Jimmy Durante–Garry Moore Show* (1944), *Birds-eye Open House* (1944–1946), and *The Phil Silvers Show* (1947, with **Selma Diamond**).

After the radio comedians abandoned radio for television, Zelinka had little trouble finding work in the new medium. He scripted consistently in the industry until about 1970, including for a number of Jackie Gleason programs and for Phil Silvers.

Sources: *Broadcasting* October 12, 1942, p. 36; *Variety* November 9, 1938, p. 36, October 14, 1942, p. 36, October 11, 1944, p. 32, August 13, 1947, p. 34; *New York Times* obituary January 19, 1981.

Zimm, Maurice

Maurice Zimm (June 19, 1909–November 17, 2005) moved to Los Angeles in the 1930s from his native Iowa and spent the next decade writing for radio dramas, first for companies such as the Dan B. Miner Co. and the Edward Sloman Productions and then later as a freelancer. In 1942 Zimm won the opportunity to script *Dan Dunn, Secret Operative* after winning a CBS script contest.

After time in the armed forces (1944–1945) Zimm returned to broadcasting, contributing scripts to *Suspense* (1946), *Family Theatre* (1947, 1949), *Your Movietown Radio Theatre* (1947), *The Man Called X* (1950), and *Hollywood Star Theatre* (1951). Highlights of Zimm's decade writing for motion pictures and television include *Creature from the Black Lagoon* (1954) and *Perry Mason* (1959–1963).

Other Radio: *The Adventures of Bill Lance.*
Sources: *Broadcasting* December 28, 1942, p. 11; *The Radio Annual* 1940 p. 224, 659.

Bibliography

Books

Ace, Goodman. *Ladies and Gentlemen—Easy Aces.* New York: Doubleday & Company, 1970.

Adir, Kanin. *The Great Clowns of American Television.* Jefferson, NC: McFarland, 1988.

Allen, Fred. *Much Ado About Me.* Boston: Little, Brown and Company, 1956.

_____. *Treadmill to Oblivion.* Boston: Little, Brown and Company, 1954.

Anderson, Arthur. *An Actor's Odyssey: Orson Welles to Lucky the Leprechaun.* Albany, GA: BearManor Media, 2010.

Ansboro, George. *I Have a Lady in the Balcony: Memoirs of a Broadcaster in Radio and Television.* Jefferson, NC: McFarland, 2000.

Association of Documentary Film Producers, Inc. *Living Films: A Catalog of Documentary Films and Their Makers.* NY, 1940.

Auerbach, Arnold. *Funny Men Don't Laugh.* Garden City, NY: Doubleday & Co., 1965.

Balakian, Nona. *The World of William Saroyan.* Cranbury, NJ: Associated University Presses, 1998.

Bannerman, R. LeRoy. *Norman Corwin and Radio: The Golden Years.* Tuscaloosa: University of Alabama Press, 1986.

Barabas, Suzanne, and Gabor Barabas. *Gunsmoke: A Complete History.* Jefferson, NC: McFarland, 1990.

Barbas, Samantha. *The First Lady of Hollywood: A Biography of Louella Parsons.* Berkeley: University of California Press, 2005.

Barer, Burl. *The Saint: A Complete History in Print, Radio, Film and Television of Leslie Charteris' Robin Hood of Modern Crime, Simon Templar, 1928–1992.* Jefferson, NC: McFarland, 1993.

Bassior, Jean-Noel. *Space Patrol: Missions of Daring in the Name of Early Television.* Jefferson, NC: McFarland, 2005.

Berard, Jeanette M., and Klaudia Englund. *Radio Series Scripts 1930–2001, a Catalog of the American Radio Archives Collection.* Jefferson, NC: McFarland, 2006.

Bird, William L., Jr. *"Better Living": Advertising, Media, and the New Vocabulary of Business Leadership, 1935–1955.* Evanston, IL: Northwestern University Press, 1999.

Bradley, Edwin M. *The First Hollywood Sound Shorts, 1926–1931.* Jefferson, NC: McFarland, 2005.

Brecher, Irving, as told to Hank Rosenfeld. *The Wicked Wit of the West: The Last Great Golden Age Screenwriter Shares the Hilarity and Heartaches of Working with Groucho, Garland, Gleason, Burns, Berle, Benny, and Many More.* Teaneck, NJ: Ben Yehuda Press, 2008.

Brunsdale, Mitzi M. *Icons of Mystery and Crime Detection: From Sleuths to Superheroes.* Santa Barbara, CA: Greenwood, 2010.

Buhle, Paul, and Dave Wagner. *Hide in Plain Sight: The Hollywood Blacklistees in Film and Television, 1950–2002.* New York: Palgrave Macmillan, 2003.

Buxton, Frank, and Bill Owen. *The Big Broadcast, 1920–1950: A New, Revised, and Greatly Expanded Edition of Radio's Golden Age.* New York: The Viking Press, 1966.

Coniam, Matthew. *That's Me, Groucho! The Solo Career of Groucho Marx.* Jefferson, NC: McFarland, 2016.

Cowgill, Rome. *Fundamentals of Writing for Radio: Drama, Talks, Continuities, and Nondramatic Features with Guidance in Program Planning, Production, and Marketing.* New York: Rinehart & Company, 1949.

Cox, J. Randolph, and David S. Siegel. *Flashgun Casey, Crime Photographer: From the Pulps to Radio and Beyond.* Yorktown Heights, NY: Book Hunter Press, 2005.

Cox, Jim. *Frank and Anne Hummert's Radio Factory: The Programs and Personalities of Broadcasting's Most Prolific Producers.* Jefferson, NC: McFarland, 2003.

_____. *The Great Radio Sitcoms.* Jefferson, NC: McFarland, 2006.

_____. *The Great Radio Soap Operas.* Jefferson, NC: McFarland, 1999.

_____. *Mr. Keen, Tracer of Lost Persons: A Complete History and Episode Log of Radio's Most Durable Detective.* Jefferson, NC: McFarland, 2004.

_____. *Radio Crime Fighters: More than 300 Programs from the Golden Age.* Jefferson, NC: McFarland, 2002.

_____. *Radio Journalism in America: Telling the News in the Golden Age and Beyond.* Jefferson, NC: McFarland, 2013.

Cox, Stephen. *The Munsters: A Trip Down Mockingbird Lane.* New York: Back Stage Books, 2006.

Davidson, Randall. *9XM Talking: WHA Radio and the Wisconsin Idea.* Madison: University of Wisconsin Press, 2006.

DeRosa, Steven. *Writing with Hitchcock: The Collaboration of Alfred Hitchcock and John Michael Hayes.* New York: Faber and Faber, 2001.

Bibliography

Drew, Bernard A. *The 100 Most Popular Young Adult Authors: Biographical Sketches and Bibliographies.* Englewood, CO: Greenwood, 1997.

Dunning, John. *On the Air: The Encyclopedia of Old-Time Radio.* New York: Oxford University Press, 1998.

_____. *Tune in Yesterday: The Ultimate Encyclopedia of Old-Time Radio, 1925–1976.* Englewood Cliffs, NJ: Prentice-Hall, 1976.

Ellett, Ryan. *Encyclopedia of Black Radio in the United States, 1921–1955.* Jefferson, NC: McFarland, 2012.

_____. *The Texas Rangers: Two Decades on Radio, Film, Television, and Stage.* Albany, GA: BearManor Media, 2014.

Epstein, Lawrence J. *George Burns: An American Life.* Jefferson, NC: McFarland, 2011.

Erickson, Hal. *From Radio to the Big Screen.* Jefferson, NC: McFarland, 2014.

Etter, Jonathan. *Quinn Martin, Producer: A Behind-The-Scenes History of QM Productions and Its Founder.* Jefferson, NC: McFarland, 2003.

Everitt, David. *King of the Half Hour: Nat Hiken and the Golden Age of TV Comedy.* Syracuse, NY: Syracuse University Press, 2001.

Faith, William Robert. *A Life in Comedy.* Cambridge, MA: Da Capo Press, 1982.

Fein, Irving A. *Jack Benny: An Intimate Biography.* New York: G.P. Putnam's Sons, 1976.

French, Jack. *Private Eyelashes: Radio's Lady Detectives.* Boalsburg, PA: BearManor Media, 2004.

Froug, William. *How I Escaped from Gilligan's Island and Other Misadventures of a Hollywood Writer-Producer.* Madison: University of Wisconsin Popular Press, 2005.

Godfried, Nathan. *WCFL: Chicago's Voice of Labor, 1926–78.* Urbana: University of Illinois Press, 1997.

Grams, Martin. *The History of the Cavalcade of America.* Kearney, NE: Morris Publishing, 1998.

_____. *The Shadow: The History and Mystery of the Radio Program, 1930–1954.* Churchville, MD: OTR Publishing, LLC, 2011.

_____. *Suspense: Twenty Years of Thrills and Chills.* Kearny, NE: Morris Publishing, 1998.

Hall, Randal L. *Lum & Abner: Rural American and the Golden Age of Radio.* Lexington: The University Press of Kentucky, 2007.

Harmon, Jim. *The Great Radio Heroes, Revised Edition.* Jefferson, NC: McFarland, 2001.

_____. *Radio Mystery and Adventure and Its Appearances in Film, Television and Other Media.* Jefferson, NC: McFarland, 1992.

Havig, Alan. *Fred Allen's Radio Comedy.* Philadelphia, PA: Temple University Press, 1990.

Hayde, Michael J. *My Name's Friday: The Unauthorized but True Story of Dragnet and the Films of Jack Webb.* Nashville, TN: Cumberland House Publishing, 2001.

Heilbut, Anthony. *The Fan Who Knew Too Much: Aretha Franklin, the Rise of the Soap Opera, Children of the Gospel Church, and Other Meditations.* New York: Alfred A. Knopf, 2012.

Hetherington, John T. *Vic and Sade on the Radio: A Cultural History of Paul Rhymer's Daytime Series, 1932–1944.* Jefferson, NC: McFarland, 2014.

Higby, Mary Jane. *Tune in Tomorrow: Or How I Found the Right to Happiness with Our Gal Sunday, Stella Dallas, John's Other Wife and Other Sudsy Radio Serials.* New York: Cowles Education Company, 1966.

Hollis, Tim. *Ain't That a Knee Slapper: Rural Comedy in the Twentieth Century.* Jackson: University Press of Mississippi, 2008.

Horne, Gerald. *Class Struggle in Hollywood, 1930–1950.* Austin: University of Texas Press, 2001.

Hyatt, Wesley. *Short-Lived Television Series, 1948–1978: Thirty Years of More than 1,000 Flops.* Jefferson, NC: McFarland, 2003.

Kallis, Stephen A., Jr. *Radio's Captain Midnight: The Wartime Biography.* Jefferson, NC: McFarland, 2000.

Kanter, Hal. *So Far So Funny: My Life in Show Business.* Jefferson, NC: McFarland, 1999.

Kleber, John E., Ed. *The Kentucky Encyclopedia.* Lexington: University Press of Kentucky, 1992.

Laurents, Arthur. *Original Story by Arthur Laurents: A Memoir of Broadway and Hollywood.* New York: Alfred A. Knopf, 2000.

Lee, Mordecai. *Promoting the War Effort: Robert Horton and Federal Propaganda 1938–1946.* Baton Rouge: Louisiana State University Press, 2012.

Leszczak, Bob. *Single Season Sitcoms, 1948–1979: A Complete Guide.* Jefferson, NC: McFarland, 2012.

Levering, Marijean. *Detroit on Stage: The Players Club, 1910–2005.* Detroit: Wayne State University Press, 2007.

Macfarlane, Malcolm, and Ken Crossland. *Perry Como: A Biography and Complete Career Record.* Jefferson, NC: McFarland, 2009.

Marks, Jeffrey A. *Who Was That Lady? Craig Rice: The Queen of Screwball Mystery.* Lee's Summit, MO: Delphi Books, 2001.

McCarthy, Todd. *Howard Hawks: The Grey Fox of Hollywood.* New York: Grove Press, 1997.

McLeod, Elizabeth. *The Original Amos 'n' Andy: Freeman Gosden, Charles Correll and the 1928–1943 Radio Serial.* Jefferson, NC: McFarland, 2005.

McNeil, W.K. *Encyclopedia of American Gospel Music.* New York: Routledge, 2005.

McQueen, Neile Adams. *My Husband, My Friend: A Memoir.* Authorhouse, 2006.

Mott, Robert L. *Radio Live! Television Live! Those Golden Days When Horses Were Coconuts.* Jefferson, NC: McFarland, 2000.

Nevins, Francis M., and Martin Grams, Jr. *The Sound of Detection: Ellery Queen's Adventures in Radio.* Churchville, MD: OTR Publishing, 2002.

Ohmart, Ben. *Don Ameche: The Kenosha Comeback Kids.* Albany, GA: BearManor Media, 2007.

Oppenheimer, Jess, with Gregg Oppenheimer. *Laughs, Luck ... and Lucy: How I Came to Create the Most Popular Sitcoms of All Time.* Syracuse, NY: Syracuse University Press, 1996.

Paar, Jack. *P.S. Jack Paar.* Garden City, NY: Doubleday & Company, 1983.

Parker, Stephen. *Bertolt Brecht: A Literary Life.* London: Bloomsbury, 2014.

Payton, Gordon, and Martin Grams, Jr. *The CBS Radio Mystery Theater: An Episode Guide and Handbook to Nine Years of Broadcasting, 1974–1982.* Jefferson, NC: McFarland, 1999.

Reed, Alan, with Ben Ohmart. *Yabba Dabba Doo! ...*

or Never a Star: The Alan Reed Story. Albany, GA: BearManor Media, 2009.
Rideout, Walter B. *Sherwood Anderson: A Writer in America, Vol. 2*. Madison: University of Wisconsin Press, 2007.
Rimler, Walter. *George Gershwin: An Intimate Portrait*. Urbana: University of Illinois Press, 2009.
Royce, Brenda Scott. *Hogan's Heroes: The Unofficial Companion*. Jefferson, NC: McFarland, 1998.
Schulz, Clair. *Tuning in the Great Gildersleeve: The Episodes and Cast of Radio's First Spinoff Show, 1941–1957*. Jefferson, NC: McFarland, 2013.
Segal, Eli. *The Eternal Light: An Unauthorized Guide*. Newtown, CT: Yesteryear Press, 2005.
Shearer, Stephen Michael. *Beautiful: The Life of Heddy Lamarr*. New York: St. Martin's Press, 2010.
Shnayerson, Michael. *Irwin Shaw: A Biography*. New York: Putnam, 1989.
Skutch, Ira, editor. *Five Directors: The Golden Years of Radio*. Lanham, MD: Scarecrow Press and Directors Guild of America, 1998.
Sterling, Christopher H., Ed. *Encyclopedia of Radio, 3-Volume Set*. New York: Taylor & Francis Group, 2003.
Takamoto, Iwao. *My Life with a Thousand Characters*. Jackson: University Press of Mississippi, 2009.
Taylor, Robert. *Fred Allen: His Life and Wit*. Boston: Little, Brown and Company, 1989.
Taylor, Timothy. *The Sounds of Capitalism: Advertising, Music, and the Conquest of Culture*. Chicago: University of Chicago Press, 2012.
Terrace, Vincent. *Radio Program Openings and Closings, 1931–1972*. Jefferson, NC: McFarland, 2003.
Tucker, David C. *Joan Davis: America's Queen of Film, Radio and Television Comedy*. Jefferson, NC: McFarland, 2014.
_____. *Shirley Booth: A Biography and Career Record*. Jefferson, NC: McFarland, 2008.
Vermazen, Bruce. *That Moaning Saxophone: The Six Brown Brothers and the Dawning of a Musical Craze*. New York: Oxford University Press, 2001.
Weaver Tom. *Interviews with B Science Fiction and Horror Movie Makers: Writers, Producers, Directors, Actors, Moguls and Makeup*. Jefferson, NC: McFarland, 1988.
Wertheim, Albert. *Staging the War: American Drama and World War II*. Bloomington: Indiana University Press, 2004.
Wertheim, Arthur Frank. *Radio Comedy*. New York: Oxford University Press, 1979.
Westkaemper, Emily M. *Martha Washington Goes Shopping: Mass Culture's Gendering of History, 1910–1950*. Dissertation, Rutgers, The State University of New Jersey, 2009.
Williams, Sonja D. *Word Warrior: Richard Durham, Radio, and Freedom*. Urbana: University of Illinois Press, 2015.
Young, Jordan R. *The Laugh Crafters: Comedy Writing in Radio and TV's Golden Age*. Beverly Hills, CA: Past Times Publishing Co., 1999.

Articles

Abbott, John C. "The Best D**Mn Writers on Radio: Gil Doud and William Tallman." *Radio Recall*, February 2013.
Adcock, Thomas. "Who's Afraid of a Paf? Dead End for the Red Bogeyman." culturmag.de, 2014.
Bowie, Stephen W. Interview with Norman Katkov. Archived at classictvhistory.com, 2007.
Bryson, Lyman. "The American School of the Air." *Music Educators Journal (30)*, 1 p. 19, 1943.
Cagle, Maury. "In the Air on the Air: Radio Captured the Thrill of Flying." *Radio Recall*, February 2006.
Corliss, Richard. "The Credits You Never Read." *Film Comment* 15.4 (July/Aug) p. 45–47, 1979.
Cox, Jim. "Daytime Diary: Soap Opera Superwriters." *Nara News*, Summer, 1998.
_____. "Drama! Thrills! Action! Fbi Narrative Proffers Convincing Pretense." *Radiogram*, June 2011.
_____. "Same Time, Same Station" *The Illustrated Press*, December 1996.
_____. "Same Time, Same Station" *The Illustrated Press*, February, 1997.
_____. "Young Dr. Malone." *The Illustrated Press*, March 1997.
Drake, Bob. "Ted Drake, Guardian of the Big Top." *Radio Recall*, April 2005.
Ellett, Ryan. "Bradford Browne: Cellar Knight, Nit Wit, and More." In press.
_____. "Dethroning Ma Perkins: The Radio Career of Caroline Ellis." *Radiogram*, January 2012
_____. "From Jungles to Dog Shows." *The Old Time Radio Digest*, Spring 2011.
_____. "*Wilderness Road*: Another Tame Children's Serial." *The Old Radio Times*, January—February 2016.
French, Jack. "Bob Tallman: Radio's Man of Mystery." From author, 2010.
_____. "Keep 'Em Flying: Radio Aviators." www.otrsite.com, 1997.
_____. (2011). "Radio's 'Land of the Lost': Good Clean Fun Under the Water." *Radio Recall*, April 2011.
Grams, Martin. "Duffy's Tavern." www.otrr.org.
Gross, Gerry. "A Palpable Hit: A Study of the Impact of Reuben Ship's the *Investigator*." *Theatre Research in Canada*, Fall 1989.
Hayde, Michael. "Martin & Lewis on Radio, Part 2: The 1951–53 Series." *Radio Recall*, April 2003.
Hopkinson, Doug. "The Evolution of Og, Son of Fire." sperdvac.com
Isaac, Dan. "Ethiopia: The First 'Living Newspaper.'" Introduction. *Educational Theatre Journal* 20(1), p. 15, 1968.
"The Many Lives of Herbert O. Yardley." www.nsa.gov
Robinson, L.J. "Enterprise at Harvard College Observatory." *Journal for the History of Astronomy* 20 (1) p. 89–103, 1990.
Rouse, Morleen Getz. "Daytime Radio Programming for the Homemaker, 1926–1956." *Journal of Popular Culture* (12) p. 315–327, Fall 1978.
Taves, Brian. "Reconstructing Talbot Mundy's Jack Armstrong Radio Serials." *Radio Recall*, August 2006.
Vitty, Cort. "Tommy Riggs and Betty Lou." *Radio Recall*, June 2007.
Wright, Stewart. "Gunsmoke's Forgotten Writer." *Radio Recall*, October 2014.
_____. "Produce It Again, Sam: The Reuse of Scripts During the Golden Age of Radio." *Radio Recall*, April 2006.

_____. "Kathleen Hite: Radio Writer Pioneer." *Radio Recall*, August 2014.

_____. "The Line-Up: Anatomy of a Police Procedural." *Radiogram*, January 2014.

Websites

Catalog of Copyright Entries
emmys.com
ibdb.com
imdb.com
oscars.org
radiogoldindex.com

Collections Finding Aids

Abe Burrows Papers, 1904–1993, The New York Public Library Archives & Manuscripts.

Al Lewis Radio and Television Scripts, 1943–1954, Charles E. Young Research Library, UCLA.

Albert Lewin Papers, 1938–1991, Charles E. Young Research Library, UCLA.

Aleen Leslie Papers, University of Wyoming, American Heritage Center.

Allan Sloane Papers, Hargrett Manuscripts, University of Georgia.

Anne Nichols Papers, Billy Rose Theatre Division, The New York Public Library.

Arthur B. Church KMBC Radio Collection, LaBudde Special Collections, University of Missouri—Kansas City.

Arthur B. Church Papers, RS 21/7/31, Special Collections Department, Iowa State University Library.

The Ben Hecht Papers, The Newberry Library, Chicago.

Bernard Dougall Scripts, *T-Mss 2001-077. Billy Rose Theatre Division, The New York Public Library.

Bob and Esther Mitchell Collection, Writers Guild Foundation.

Booth Tarkington Papers, 1812–1956. Department of Rare Books and Special Collections, Princeton University Library.

Brice P. Disque, Jr. papers, Ax 291, Special Collections & University Archives, University of Oregon Libraries, Eugene, Oregon.

Bruce Geller Papers, UCLA Library Special Collections.

Carlton Morse Copyright Script Collection, The Library of Congress Recorded Sound Research Center.

Charles Isaacs papers (Collection 80). Performing Arts Special Collections, Charles E. Young Research Library, UCLA.

Charles R. Jackson Papers, Ca. 1920–1992. MS-1070 Rauner Special Collections Library, Dartmouth College.

Collection of Scripts for Death Valley Days (PASC Collection number 250). UCLA Library Special Collections, Charles E. Young Research Library, UCLA.

David P. Harmon Papers, 1941–1964. Wisconsin Historical Society.

Donald T. McNeill Collection, 1913–1979, Raynor Archives, Marquette University.

Doris Frankel Papers, 1922–1993, *T-Mss 2002-023 Billy Rose Theatre Division, The New York Public Library.

Dudley Dean McGaughey Collection, American Heritage Center, University of Wyoming.

E. Jack Neuman Papers, 1935–1982. Wisconsin Historical Society.

Edith Meiser Collection, Sherlock Holmes Collections, Special Collections and Rare Books, University of Minnesota Libraries.

Edith Meiser Papers, *T Mss 1993-041, Billy Rose Theatre Division, The New York Public Library for the Performing Arts.

Edward Jurist Papers (Collection PASC 122). UCLA Library Special Collections, Charles E. Young Research Library, UCLA.

Elaine Carrington Papers, 1903–1959, The New York Public Library for the Performing Arts

E.P. Conkle papers, Collection #C0157, Special Collections and Archives, George Mason University Libraries.

Ernest Kinoy Papers, 1948–1987. Wisconsin Historical Society.

Francis Hamilton Striker Papers, 1929–1986, University Archives, The State University of New York at Buffalo.

Frank and Doris Hursely Papers, 1942–1969, American Heritage Center, University of Wyoming.

Gene Stone Papers, UCLA Library Special Collections.

Gene Wang Papers, 1943–1956, American Heritage Center, University of Wyoming.

George Oppenheimer writings, *T-Mss 1978-001. Billy Rose Theatre Division, The New York Public Library.

Gilbert Seldes Papers, Kislak Center for Special Collections, Rare Books and Manuscripts, University of Pennsylvania.

Hal Goodman papers (Collection 344). Performing Arts Special Collections, Charles E. Young Research Library, UCLA.

Hal Kanter Papers, 1937–1977, University of Wisconsin–Madison.

Harlan Ware papers, 1939–1966, Ax 565, Special Collections & University Archives, University of Oregon Libraries, Eugene, Oregon.

Harry Crane Papers (Collection 203). Performing Arts Special Collections, UCLA Library.

Hattie and Sam McDaniel Papers, 1900–1957, Margaret Herrick Library

Hector Chevigny Scripts, *T-Mss 2013-120. Billy Rose Theatre Division, The New York Public Library.

Henry Garson Collection, Writers Guild Foundation.

Howard Koch Papers, 1937–1976, Wisconsin Historical Society.

Howard Teichmann Papers, 1857–2001, Library of Congress.

Irna Phillips Papers, 1931–1997, Wisconsin Historical Society.

Irving Vendig (1902–1995) Collection, Howard Gotlieb Archival Research Center, Boston University.

Jack Douglas Papers, Special Collections Research Center, Syracuse University Libraries.

Jack Rubin papers, *T-Mss 2015-003. Billy Rose Theatre Division, The New York Public Library.

Jackson Gillis Papers, Writers Guild Foundation.

Jerome Lawrence—Robert E. Lee Collection, Collection ID: L&L, Jerome Lawrence and Robert E. Lee Theatre Research Institute, The Ohio State University.

Jerry Devine Papers, 1938–1973, American Heritage Collection, The University of Wyoming.
Joe Quillan Papers (Collection PASC 133). UCLA Library Special Collections, Charles E. Young Research Library, UCLA.
John Dunkel Radio Scripts (Collection 191). Performing Arts Special Collections, Charles E. Young Research Library, UCLA.
John M. Young Papers, 1937–1965. Division of Rare and Manuscript Collections, Cornell University Library.
John Pickard—Frank Provo Collection, American Radio Archives, Thousand Oaks Library Foundation.
John Roeburt Collection, Howard Gotlieb Archival Research Center, Boston University.
The Kendell Foster Crossen Collection. Howard Gotlieb Archival Research Center.
Larry Klein Papers, 1946–1973. University of Wyoming Heritage Center.
Lawrence and Lee Papers, *T-Mss 1967-003, Billy Rose Theatre Division, The New York Public Library for the Performing Arts.
Lawrence M. Klee Papers, 1936–1957. University of Wyoming Heritage Center.
Lou Derman Papers (Collection PASC 99). UCLA Library Special Collections, Charles E. Young Research Library, UCLA.
Lula Vollmer Papers, *T-Mss 1977-005. Billy Rose Theatre Division, The New York Public Library.
Lula Vollmer Papers, W.L. Eury Appalachian Collection, Appalachian State University, Boone, North Carolina.
Mac Benoff Papers, 1938–1972. University of Wyoming Heritage Center.
Margaret E. Sangster, Jr. Collection, Brooklyn College Archives and Special Collections.
Martin A. Gosch Papers. Margaret Herrick Library. Academy of Motion Picture Arts and Sciences.
Max Simon Ehrlich Papers, 1939–1964. Wisconsin Historical Society Archives.
Mel Shavelson Collection, 1946–2007.Writers Guild Foundation Archive.
Milt Gross Papers (Collection 109). Department of Special Collections, Charles E. Young Research Library, University of California, Los Angeles.
Milton and Barbara Merlin Collection, Thousand Oaks Library.
Milton Geiger Papers 1932–1973, CSU Northridge Oviatt Library Special Collections.
Milton Merlin Papers, Margaret Herrick Library, Academy of Motion Pictures Arts and Sciences.
Mona Kent Papers, University of Maryland Special collections.
Morris Freedman Collection, Thousand Oaks Library.
Nat Hiken Papers, 1932–1968, Wisconsin Historical Society.
National Broadcasting Company Records, 1921–1976, University of Wisconsin.
Nila Mack Papers, *T-Mss 1953-002, Billy Rose Theatre Division, The New York Public Library for the Performing Arts.
Orson Welles Materials, Lilly Library, Indiana University.
Paul Green Papers, #3693, Southern Historical Collection, The Wilson Library, University of North Carolina at Chapel Hill.
Paul Rhymer Papers, 1928–1972, Wisconsin Historical Society.
Peg Lynch Papers, 1944–1976, University of Oregon Libraries, Special Collections and University Archives.
Peter Lyon Papers, 1884–1998, Wisconsin Historical Society.
Phyllis Merrill Papers, *T-Mss 1998-004, Billy Rose Theatre Division, The New York Library for the Performing Arts.
Robert Hardy Andrews Collection, 1908–1999, Howard Gotlieb Archival Research Center
Robert Hardy Andrews Papers, 1945–1966, UCLA
Ruth Cornwall Woodman Papers, Ax 690, Special Collections & University Archives, University of Oregon Libraries, Eugene, Oregon.
Seaman Jacobs Scripts, Special Collections Research Center, Syracuse University Libraries.
Screen Guild Players Recordings, PA Mss 28, Department of Special Collections, University Libraries, University of California, Santa Barbara.
Ted Malone Collection, LaBudde Special Collections, University of Missouri—Kansas City.
Television and Radio Scripts of Kathleen Hite, Wichita State University
Vin Bogert Papers, 1964–1967, UCLA
Will Glickman Papers, University of Alabama.
William Fifield Papers, 1891–2005, Whitman College and Northwest Archives
William Froug Papers (Collection 150). Performing Arts Special Collections, Charles E. Young Research Library, UCLA.
WPA Radio Scripts, *T-Mss 2000-005. Billy Rose Theatre Division, The New York Public Library for the Performing Arts.

Periodicals

Abilene Reporter-News
Atlanta Constitution
Baltimore Sun
Billboard
Boston Daily Globe
Bridgeport Sunday Herald
Broadcasting (Later Broadcasting—Telecasting)
Brooklyn Daily Eagle
Bulletin (CT)
Chicago Tribune
Christian Science Monitor
Educational Screen
Ellensburg (Wa) Capital
Eugene (Or) Register Guard
Exhibitors Herald-World
Exhibitor's Trade Review
Film Bulletin
Film Daily
Free Lance-Star (Va)
Hartford Courant
Hollywood
Hollywood Filmograph
International Photographer
Lakeland Ledger
Lewiston Daily Sun

Los Angeles Times
Milwaukee Journal
Milwaukee Sentinel
Motion Picture Daily
Motion Picture Herald
Motion Picture Magazine
Movie Makers
Moving Picture World
Nbc Presents
Nbc Transmitter
New York Herald Tribune
New York Times
Pittsburgh Post-Gazette
Pittsburgh Press
Radio Annual
Radio Broadcast Advertiser
Radio Daily
Radio Digest
Radio Fanfare
Radio Life

Radio Mirror
Radio Review
Radio Romances
Radio Showmanship
Radio Varieties
St. Petersburg Times
Sarasota Herald-Tribune
Screenwriter
Sherbrooke Telegram
Showmen's Trade Review
Spartanburg Herald-Journal
Sponsor
Swing
Television Digest
Tryon Daily Bulletin
Variety
The Washington Post
What's on the Air?
Wow News Tower

Index

Abbey, Elinor 27
Abbott, George 27, 89
The Abbott & Costello Kid Show 77
The Abbott and Costello Show 33, 48, 54, 72, 73, 77, 90, 95, 96, 126, 134, 157, 161, 164, 173, 183
Abbott Mysteries 10
ABC Mystery Time 19, 172
The ABC of NBC 113
The Abe Burrows Show 40, 54
Abie's Irish Rose 152
Absolutely Free 21
Academy Award Theatre 196
Academy of Art (Chicago) 119, 161
Ace, Goodman 9, 15, 61, 74, 77, 102, 113, 196
Ace in the Hole 152
Acree, Chuck 10
Across the Sport Page of the World 59
Adair, Lynn 10
Adams, Gerald Drayson 21
Adams, James Truslow 76
Adams, Paul 10
Adamson, Ed 10
Adamson, Hans Christian 10, 11–12
Adamson, Helen Lyon 12
The Addams Family 78, 107, 125, 134
Admiral Thunderbolt 12
Adventure Comes to Mr. Timothy 39
Adventure, Inc. 128
Adventure of Captain Courage 69
Adventures by Morse 148
Adventures in Exploration 11
Adventures in Reading 122, 191
Adventures in the Land of the Lost 102
The Adventures of Archie Andrews 109, 141
The Adventures of Babe Ruth 81
The Adventures of Big Bill Baker 140
The Adventures of Bill Lance 45, 140, 141, 167, 197, 199
The Adventures of Christopher London 174
The Adventures of Christopher Wells 176
Adventures of Col. Flack 63, 182
The Adventures of Dari Dan 168
Adventures of Don Renegale 18
The Adventures of Ellery Queen 35, 57, 122
The Adventures of Frank Merriwell 36, 193
The Adventures of Frank Race 18, 149

The Adventures of Helen and Mary 119, 131
The Adventures of Jungle Jim 63
The Adventures of Leonidas Witherall 141
The Adventures of Maisie 25, 34, 38, 158, 187
The Adventures of Michael Shayne 59, 69, 70, 134, 137, 172
The Adventures of Omar 84
Adventures of Ozzie and Harriet 54, 57, 63, 78, 86, 92, 100, 139, 150, 160, 172, 173, 175, 181, 194
The Adventures of Philip Marlowe 61, 85, 86, 102, 125, 145
The Adventures of Polly Preston 139
The Adventures of Robin Hood 74, 182
The Adventures of Sam Spade 7, 26, 63, 68, 75, 98, 151, 156, 185, 186
The Adventures of Sinbad 103
The Adventures of Sterling Holloway 56
The Adventures of Superman 81, 88, 95, 110, 129
The Adventures of Ted Drake, Guardian of the Big Top 188
The Adventures of the Abbotts 144
The Adventures of the Lone Wolf 191
The Adventures of the Thin Man 91, 98, 120, 127, 151, 191, 192
The Adventures of Wild Bill Hickok 39
Aeropagus 75
The Affairs of Anthony 142
The Affairs of Dr. Gentry 64
The Affairs of Peter Salem 169, 191
African Trek 134
The A-G Musical Grocers 49
Against the Storm 142, 143
Ahern, Gene 42, 124
The Air Adventures of Jimmie Allen 13, 40, 41, 146
Air Features, Inc. 27, 144
Air Youth for Defense 145
The Al Jolson—Monty Woolley Show 125, 161
The Al Jolson Show 39
Al Pearce and His Gang 33, 54, 75, 97, 98, 100, 108
The Al Pearce Show 73, 101, 161, 169
The Alan Young Show 76, 84, 88, 101, 135, 156, 174, 175, 181
Albert the First 144
Alberta Food Co. 24
Albertson, Jack 12

Album of the Week 121
Alcoa Theatre 172
The Aldrich Family 67, 89, 111, 187, 189
Alexander, Harmon J. 12–13, 21
Alexander, Martha 13
Alexander, Michael 13
Aley, Albert 13
Alfred Hitchcock and the Three Investigators 19
Alfred Hitchcock Presents 149, 174
Alias Edward Taylor 146
Alias Jimmy Valentine 18, 35, 57, 94, 177
Alias John Doe 98, 151
Alias John Freedom 24, 62
Alias the Deacon 128
Alice 76, 108, 195
Alison, Joan 39
All Aboard 93, 165
The All-American Sports Show 45, 124, 196
All Hands on Deck 159
All in a Lifetime 80
All in the Family 60, 111, 113, 119, 122, 133, 166, 173, 182, 193
All My Children 80
All Quiet on the Western Front 16
All-Star Western Theatre 137, 196
Alland, William 14
Allen, Fred 14–15, 20, 22, 33, 41, 77, 78, 80, 84, 102, 108, 109, 117, 127, 143, 170, 171, 178, 189, 193, 198
Allen, Gracie 35, 48, 78, 79, 100, 127, 139, 157, 164
Allen, Steve 144
The Allen Prescott Show 181
Allied Agencies 188
Along Life's Highway 160
Alsberg, Arthur 15, 113
Amanda of Honeymoon Hill 189, 191
The Amazing Mr. Malone 166, 192
The Amazing Mr. Smith 90, 95
The Amazing Mr. Tutt 157
Amazing Nero Wolfe 191
Amazing Stories 19
Ameche, Don 113, 140, 153, 164
Ameche, Jim 24, 26
Amen 111
America in the Air 95, 193
The American Comedy of the Air 99
American Communist Party 77, 146
An American Family Saga 148
American Holiday 23

Index

An American in England 31, 52
An American in Russia 31, 52
The American Jewish Caravan of Stars 56
American Jewish Committee 67
The American Music Hall 63
American Paradise 24
American Pilgrimage 133
American Play Company 94
American Portraits 72, 157, 169, 183
American Radio Features 24
The American Radio Newsreel 110
American School of the Air 11, 20, 97, 130, 133, 157, 169, 182, 188, 189
American Women 107
Americans All, Immigrants All 175
Americans at the Ramparts 87
Americans at Work 126
America's Grandma 68
America's March on Crime 136
The Ammident Show 62
The Amos 'n' Andy Music Hall 49, 148
The Amos 'n' Andy Show 3, 26, 49, 51, 54, 75, 80, 88, 90, 91, 96, 98, 100, 108, 113, 139, 148, 170, 181, 182, 194
Anacin 9
The Anacin Hollywood Star Theatre 95
The Anchorman 42
And Sudden Death 34
Anderson, James Maxwell 16, 17, 105
Anderson, Sherwood 16–17
The Anderson Family 185
Andrews, Bob 118
Andrews, Charles Robert Hardy Douglas 17–18
Andrews, Julie 67
The Andy Devine Show 83
The Andy Griffith Show 37, 79, 87, 92, 109, 170, 171, 182, 195
Angel, Buckley 18
Angels in Blue 146
Ankles Aweigh 59
Ann of the Airlanes 40
Ann Worth, Housewife 63
Anne Thomas, Career Wife 193
Annie Oakley, Woman At Arms 50
Another Case for Quest 140
Another World 45, 70, 159, 181
Appointment with Adventure 71
Appointment with Crime 137
Appointment with Life 19, 56, 61
Arabesque 119
Arabian Nights 119
Arch Oboler's Plays 153
Archie Bunker's Place 158
Arden, Eve 15, 115
Are These Our Children? 37, 188
Are You a Genius? 156
Are You a Missing Heir? 130
Are You with It? 22
Arent, Arthur 18
Arizona Adventure 137
Armed Forces Radio Service (AFRS) 25, 34, 56, 85, 121, 123, 126, 140, 175
Armstrong Theatre of the Air 13, 31, 144
Armstrong Theatre of Today 23, 95, 137, 198
The Army Hour 50, 71
Army Nurse 134
Army Play-By-Play 150
Arnaz, Desi 68

Arnold, Eddy 188
Arnold Grimm's Daughter 173
The Arnold Stang Show 102
Art for Our Sake 65
Arthur, Robert A., Jr. 19, 117
Arthur Hopkins Presents 50, 103
Arthur Kudner Inc. 54
Arthur's Place 54, 133
As the Twig Is Bent 23, 29
As the World Turns 159, 181, 197
Ascot, Rita 19
Ashkenazy, Irwin 19
Ashman, Jane 20
Ashman-Ferrin Productions 20
Assignment Foreign Legion 67
Assignment Home 120, 157
Associated Releases 134, 141
Astaire, Fred 155
At Home Abroad 116
Atkins, Lee 20
Atkins, Violet 20
Atlantic Family 78
Atlantic Flight 122
Atlas Radio Corp. 54
Attorney at Law 92, 198
Attorney for the Defense 118
Attorney John J. Malone 166
Auerbach, Arnold 15, 20, 113, 198
Aunt Jemima's Cabin at the Cross Roads 193
Aunt Jenny 13, 18, 37
Aunt Jenny's Real Life Stories 107, 117
Aunt Mary 54, 72, 173
Aunt Zelena 28
Auntie Mamie 121, 123
Author! Author! 57, 122, 176
The Author Meets the Critic 103
Author's Playhouse 93, 105
Autumn in New York 10
Avalon Time 126
The Avenger 36, 187
Ayers, Stuart 20
Ayers-Prescott 110

Baby Snooks 30, 62, 76, 108, 155, 172, 175, 182
Bacall, Lauren 74, 82
Bachelor Father 15, 82, 128
Bachelor's Children 76
Bacher, William 21, 118
Back from Eternity 45
Back Home 25
Backus, Georgia 12, 13, 21
Backus, Jim 88
Baffling Detective Mysteries 55
Bagni, Gwen 21
Bagni, John 21
Bailey, Harry 22, 85
Bailey, H.C. 140
Baker, Art 93
Baker, George 182
Baker, George Pierce 116
Baker, Herbert 15, 113
Baker, Kenny 61
Baker, Phil 30, 34, 154, 155
Bakers of America Program 32
The Bakers' Theatre of Stars 56, 69
Ball, Lucille 22, 44, 57, 68, 78, 154, 155, 162, 178
The Ballad of Will Rogers 163

Ballard, Aline 22
Balzer, George 22, 105, 111, 157
Bambi 137
Bandwagon 111
Banjo Eyes 162
Bank of Montreal 60
Bankhead, Tallulah 95
Banner Mysteries 55
Banning, Margaret Culkin 76
Bannister, Albert 22
Banyon 11
Bar X Days and Nights 71
Barasch, Norman 183
The Barbara Stanwyck Show 18
Barbara Wayne 146
Bard College (MA) 161
Barker, Al 13, 22–23
Barley, Ann 23–24, 29
Barley, Bennett 55
Barnaby 149
Barnaby Jones 13
Barnard College 176, 188
Barnard School for Boys 155
Barnes, Beth 24
Barnes, Forrest 24
Barnes, Howard McKent 25
Barnett Sanford 25
Barney Blake—Police Reporter 67
Barney Miller 114
Barnouw, Erik 18, 25–26, 143
The Barnstormers 24
The Barrett Outfit 114
Barrie Craig, Confidential Investigator 112, 169, 191
Barry, Peter 26
Barry Cameron 33
Barrymore, John 24
Bartell, Harry 12
Barth, Ruth 26, 100
The Bartons 192
Bassett, John 26
Bat Masterson 190, 195
Bates, Barbara 27
Batman 182
Batten, Barton, Durstine & Osborn 64, 144
Battle, John Tucker 27
Battle Cry 20
Battle Stations 93
Battles of the Philippine Sea 12
Baumer, Marie 27, 41
The Beachcomber 151
Beacon Syndicate 116, 166
The Bears and I 195
Bearson, Lawrence 27
Beasley, Irene 28
Beat the Band 62
The Beatrice Kay Show 109, 141
Beatrice Lillie Show 64
Beattie, Dan 28
Beck, Jackson 91
Becker, Bob 28
Becker, Don 23, 28–29, 33, 76
Beckmark, Peggy 29
Behind the Mike 127
Behold a Woman 148
The Bell Telephone Hour 26, 106, 171
Bellaman, Henry 23
Beloin, Ed 29, 147, 154
Beloit College 28

Ben Bernie and All the Lads 143
The Ben Bernie Show 166
Ben Casey 148
The Ben Hecht Television Show 99
Benet, Stephen Vincent 29
Bennett, Jay 29–30
The Bennetts 148
Benny, Jack 9, 22, 29, 35, 48, 82, 89, 104, 113, 133, 154, 157, 163, 180, 192, 193
Benny Rubin's Whirligig 98
Benoff, Mac 30
Benson 195
Benson, Sally 88
Benton & Bowles 108, 136, 190
Berch, Jack 33
Bercovici, Leonardo 30, 179
Berg, Gertrude 24, 30–31, 141
Berg, Lewis 30
Bergen, Edgar 9, 32, 44, 49, 54, 55, 56, 77, 108, 116, 131, 150, 164, 170, 180, 192
Berger, Hal 31
Berger, Sylvia 31
Bergman, Teddy *see* Reed, Alan
Berle, Milton 10, 15, 20, 34, 37, 39, 48, 60, 79, 81, 105, 109, 117, 137, 146, 170, 174, 175, 177, 178, 181, 183
Bernie, Ben 22, 126, 127, 128
Berns, Larry 163
Best from Fantasy and Science Fiction 36
Best Music 45
Best Plays 45, 115, 123, 170, 186
Best Sellers 134
The Best Things in Life 167
Bester, Alfred 31–32
Betty and Bob 17, 50, 188
Betty Boop 180, 192
Between the Bookends 133
Between You and Me 56
Beulah 75, 80, 111, 113, 123, 150, 172, 175
The Beverly Hillbillies 101, 187
Bewitched 38, 56, 68, 83, 92, 111, 172, 177
Beyond Laughter 39
Beyond Reasonable Doubt 168
Beyond the Street 42
Beyond These Valleys 29
Bible Dramas 133
The Bickersons 54, 164
Bierstadt, Edward 32
Big Broadcast 133
The Big Carnival 152
The Big Guy 26
Big Jim McClain 125
The Big Payoff 105
Big Red 156
The Big Show 9–10, 61, 77, 114, 149, 196
Big Sister 33, 83, 96, 98, 120, 136, 151, 152, 186
The Big Story 67, 95, 107, 108, 115, 157, 179
The Big Talent Hunt 88, 183
Big Town 7, 17, 18, 39, 46, 50, 61, 67, 96, 111, 118, 137
Bigelow, Joe 32, 49, 148
Bigelow-Sanford Carpet Co. 12
The Bill Bendix Show 57
The Bill Goodwin Show 33, 84, 92, 111, 161
The Bill Thompson Show 43
Billboard 147

The Billie Burke Show 38, 49, 194
Billy and Betty 30
Billy Bachelor Sketches 116
Billy House's Wrigley Laughliner 126
Bing Crosby—Rosemary Clooney Show 147
The Bing Crosby Show 147
Bingham, Harrison 32
Biow Agency 56, 117, 154
Bird of the Iron Feather 66
Birds Eye Open House 96, 172, 194, 198
The Bishop and the Gargoyle 196
The Bishop's Wife 30
Bixby, Carl 29, 33
The Black Chamber 56
Black Chapel 46
Black Mask 19
The Black Museum 134
Black Night 196
Black Saddle 69
Blackett-Sample-Hummert 9, 35, 41, 54, 56, 61, 94, 108, 135, 139, 149, 150, 176, 188, 192, 193
Blacklist 30, 45, 77, 83, 102, 130, 141, 167, 168, 182
Blackouts of 1949 77
Blackstone, Harry 87
Blackstone, the Magic Detective 87, 192
Blake, Howard 33
Blake, Peggy 33
Blazing Travel Trails 64
Bless You All 20
The Blind Spot 27
Block, Hal 33
Block & Sully 81
Blocki, Fritz 34
Blonde from Brooklyn 122
Blondie 92, 147, 175
Blood and Fire 127
Blood on the Midnight Sun 12
Bloodbrothers 152
The Blue Frolics 104
Blue Monday Jamboree 132
Blue Ribbon Town 54, 60, 61, 96, 182
Blue Theatre 30
The Blue Veil 53
Boardman, True 25, 34, 56
Boasberg, Al 34–35
Bob and Victoria 54
The Bob Burns Show 96, 108, 138, 175, 182, 194
The Bob Crosby Show 81
The Bob Cummings Show 90, 101
The Bob Hope Show 33, 79, 90, 110, 115, 119, 137, 170, 182
The Bob Newhart Show 114
Bobby Benson of the H-Bar-O Ranch 25, 62, 177
Bogart, Humphrey 74, 82
Bogert, Vincent 35
Bold Venture 55, 74, 82
Bolton, Guy 38
Bonanza 34, 72, 141, 149
Bond Wagon 34
The Bookworm 112
Booraem, Hendreick 56
Boots and Saddles 83
Borden, Ruth 35, 139
The Borden Show 54, 113
Boretz, Allen 12

Borge, Victor 49
Born in a Merry Hour 97
Bostic, Joe 35
Boston Blackie 140, 141, 162
Boston University 116
Boucher, Anthony 35–36, 57, 91, 122
Boulette, Leo 36
Bourban Street Beat 88
Box 13 100, 106, 145, 150
Boyd, William 18
Boyle, Betty 36
Boys' Life 55
Bracken, Eddie 104
Bradley, Vi 17
Brady, William A. 87
The Brady Bunch 21, 38, 80, 87, 95, 166, 175, 182, 194
Braun, J. Gilbert 36, 87
Braun, Ruth 36, 87
Brave New World 83, 174
Brave Tomorrow 117
Break the Bank 112
Breakdown 56
Breakfast at Tiffany's 67
Breakfast Club of the Air 138
Breakfast with Burrows 40
Brecher, Irving 36–37
Brecher, Jack 37
Breen, Richard 37
Brennan, Frederick 85, 187
Brenner, Ray 36
Brenthouse 177
Breslin, Howard 37, 105
Brice, Fanny 30, 55, 56, 81, 82, 114, 155, 164
The Bridge on the River Kwai 77
Bright Horizon 83, 97, 98, 136, 145, 152, 198
The Brighter Day 79, 94, 159, 169, 189
A Brighter Tomorrow 46, 171, 191
Bristol-Myers 181
British Broadcasting Corp. 34, 53, 102
The Broadcast Murders 180
Broadway Is My Beat 74, 82, 130, 171
Broadway Matinee 71, 85
Broadway Melody of 1936 48
Broadway Merry-Go-Round 138
Broadway Showtime 72
Brody, Lee 12
Brooklyn College 64, 74
Brooks, Albert 68
Brooks, Margo 37
Brooks, Matt 38
Brooks, Ruth 38
Brown, George Frame 38
Brown, Himan 30, 64, 83, 127, 129
Brown, Russ 59
Brown, Wally 171
Brown & Williamson Tobacco Co. 93
Bruce Eels & Assoc. 149
Bublick, David 38
Bublick, Judith 38–39
Buck, Ashley 39
Buck, Frank 80
Buck Benny Rides Again 82
Buck Rogers of the 25th Century 54, 63, 110, 125
Buckskin 185
The Buddy Rogers Show 39
Buena Vista Film Distribution Co. 177

210 Index

Buffum, Ray 39, 91
Buffy the Vampire Slayer 195
Bulldog Drummond 30, 124, 148, 157, 169, 179, 188
Bullet Trenton, C.D. 173
Bunce, Alan 129
Burch, Bill 39
Burke, Billie 127
Burnett, Murray 39–40
Burning Gold 18
Burning Questions 107
Burns, Bob 22, 134, 198
Burns, George 35, 40, 48, 78, 79, 100, 109, 127, 139, 164, 182
Burns, Willie 40
The Burns & Allen Show 12, 22, 34, 40, 44, 56, 62, 78, 84, 89, 97, 101, 115, 127, 156, 157, 171, 194
Burrows, Abe 40, 84
Burt, Frank 40
Burton, Laverne 40
Burtt, Robert 13, 40–41, 146
Buss, Carl 27, 41
The Busyman Program 166
By Kathleen Norris 62, 152
By the People 39, 67, 169
Byrne, Brian 41
Byron, Ed 41–42, 60, 176

Cab Calloway's Quizzicale 103
Cabin B-13 43, 144
Cady, Jerry 42
Caesar, Sid 10
Cagney, Jeanne 101
The Caine Mutiny 198
California Caravan 24, 98, 169, 173, 195
Call for Music 121
Call Me Mister 20
Call Northside 777 42
Call of the West 197
Call the Police 26, 112
The Callahans 34
Calling All Cars 63, 168
Calling America 126
Calloway, Cab 118
Calmer, Ned 42
Calvin and the Colonel 49, 170
Camel Caravan 72, 108, 128, 145, 171
Camel Cigarettes 25
Camel College 112
Camel Program 127
Camel Quarter Hour 25
Campbell, Kane 42
The Campbell Playhouse 14, 50, 187
The Campbell Room 88
Campbell Soup 14, 50
Campbell's Soups Show 63
Canadian Holiday 103
Canadian National Railway 60
Candy Matson, Yukon 2–8209 135
Caniff, Milton 17
Canteen Quiz 112
Cantor, Eddie 38, 44, 48, 58, 68, 72, 77, 81, 88, 112, 115, 117, 119, 134, 156, 162, 164, 170, 180, 181, 192, 193, 194
Capra, Frank 149
Captain China 21
Captain Flagg and Sergeant Quirt 16, 139
Captain Midnight 13, 40, 41, 146, 175, 188

Captain Starr of Space 105
Captain Video and His Video Rangers 114
Car 54, Where Are You? 88, 102
Career Woman 177
Carefree Carnival 132
Careless Love 149
Carl Wester & Co. 104
Carleton, Henry Flake 133
Carlton, Sam 42–43
Carmer, Carl 43
The Carnation Contented Hour 95
Carnation Family Party 33
Carnival 30
Carnochan, Frederic Grosvenor 12
The Carol Burnett Show 115, 173, 178
Caroline's Golden Store 70
Carr, John Dickson 43
Carrington, Elaine 43
Carrington Playhouse 145, 197
Carroll, Bob, Jr. 43–44, 161, 162
Carroll, Carroll 22, 44, 49, 72
Carroll, Jean 44
Carroll, Richard 44–45
Carson, Jack 62, 63, 79, 86, 96
Carson, Lee 45
The Carters of Elm Street 114
Carton of Cheer 127
Casa Cugat 99
Casablanca 39, 117
A Case for Mr. Fortune 140
The Case of the Seven of Calvary 36
The Casebook of Gregory Hood 35, 39, 91, 170
The Cases of Eddie Drake 68
The Cases of Mr. Ace 68
Casey, Crime Photographer 107, 112, 118, 179
Cashman, Ed 33
The Cass Daily—Frank Morgan Show 95
Castellaw, Chet 45, 182
Cat Ballou 152
Cataline Swim 20
The Catholic Hour 137
Cavalcade for Victory 163
Cavalcade of America 12, 13, 16, 18, 23, 25, 26, 29, 31, 43, 45, 46, 53, 60, 64, 72, 79, 80, 84, 92, 95, 98, 103, 106, 114, 117, 120, 126, 130, 137, 143, 160, 164, 167, 171, 172, 178, 179, 180, 181, 186, 188, 189, 192, 197, 198
Cavalcade of American Aviation 165
Cavalcade of Stars 54
CBS Is There 9, 31, 67, 128, 143, 177, 178, 189
CBS Radio Adventure Theater 151
The CBS Radio Mystery Theatre 32, 39, 56, 70, 129, 145, 151, 179
CBS Starlight Theatre 13
CBS Workshop 41, 46, 69, 83, 96, 110, 152, 172, 182, 190
Ceiling Unlimited 123
Celebrity Theatre 127
Cenedella, Robert 45
Cervantes 53
Chaber, M.E. 155
The Challenge of the Yukon 28, 63, 91, 104, 111, 121, 136, 141, 164, 184
Chamber Music Society of Lower Basin Street 113, 159, 181
Chambrun, Jacques 16

Chandu the Magician 56, 154
Chapin, Martha 45
Chaplain Jim 115
Chaplin, Charlie 13
Charles, Lucile 16
Charles Michelson Inc. 36
Charlie and Jessie 50
Charlie Chan 32, 38, 39, 42, 46, 76, 164
The Charlie McCarthy Show 164
The Charlie Ruggles Show 131
Charlie Wild, Private Detective 26
Charlie's Angels 37, 144
Charlot, Harry 45
Charteris, Leslie 45–46, 91
Chase, Kay 46
The Chase 56, 75, 106, 111, 115
The Chase & Sanborn Hour 32, 38, 45, 47, 49, 54, 55, 56, 59, 75, 78, 85, 108, 127, 131, 138, 146, 150, 151, 153, 155, 164, 167, 170, 180, 192, 194
Chase Me, Charlie 13
The Cheaters 143
Cheers from the Camps 158
Chesterfield Music Shop 148
Chesterfield Supper Club 95, 100, 193
Chevigny, Hector 46
Chevillat, Dick 46–47, 178
Chevrolet on Broadway 34
The Chevrolet Tele-Theatre 118
The Chicago American 166, 168
Chicago Central School of Commerce 168
The Chicago Daily News 17, 118
The Chicago Defender 65
Chicago Herald-Examiner 118
The Chicago Sun Times 36
The Chicago Tribune 28
Chick Carter, Boy Detective 34, 87, 92, 192
Children of Divorce 170
Children of the Wind 155
Children's Theatre of the Air 131
Chimney House 87
Chinatown Squad 147
The Christian Herald 173
Christian Science Monitor 177
Christmas Roundup 34
Christy, Floyd 47, 175
Cimarron Tavern 104, 144
Cincinnati's College of Music 180
The Cinnamon Bear 100
The Circle 44, 47, 72, 85
The Cisco Kid 98
The Cities Service Program 75
Citizen Kane 14, 21
Citizen of the World 53
The City 24, 40, 102, 128, 137, 150
City College of Los Angeles 150, 168
City College of New York 57, 150, 181, 182
City Desk 39, 56, 91, 98, 140
City Hospital 83
City of Angels 86
City of St. Francis 64
Clark, Marian 47
Classroom for Democracy 50
Cloak and Dagger 90, 95, 197
The Clock 115
Club Aluminum Products Co. 25
Club Car Special 92

Club Embassy 100
Club Fifteen 44, 92
Club Hollywood 98
Club Time 25
Club Zero 109
The Clyde Beatty Show 79, 180, 187
Coast to Coast on a Bus 158
The Cobbs 84
Coca Cola 64
Cohen, Sam 14
Cohen the Detective 128, 191
Cole, Alonzo Deen 47
Cole, Beatrice 47
Cole, Phil 12
Coles, Stedman 47
The Colgate Comedy Hour 75, 80, 122, 194
Colgate Sports Newsreel 59
Collier's 37, 77, 117, 126
Collins, Ted 103
Colman, Ronald 44, 121, 153, 163
Columbia College (Chicago) 188
Columbia Phonograph Co. 142
Columbia Pictures 68, 75, 102, 139
Columbia Presents Corwin 53
Columbia School of Journalism 57
Columbia String Trio 121
Columbia University 20, 25, 75, 91, 105, 115, 120, 141, 168, 182
The Columbia Workshop 29, 31, 37, 41, 43, 52, 56, 60, 75, 80, 83, 85, 87, 91, 92, 96, 97, 98, 111, 117, 121, 126, 128, 131, 141, 143, 144, 151, 162, 169, 171, 173, 176, 187, 194, 198
Colwell, Bob 47–48
Combat! 18
Come Up and See Me Sometime 95
Comedy Capers 60
Comedy of Errors 83
The Comedy Writers Show 72, 161, 183
Comic Page of the Air 62
Command Performance 54, 79, 86, 108, 121, 123, 127, 156, 175, 194
Command Theatre 71
Commandos 23, 30, 156, 179
Commodore Syndication 180
Community Sing 37
Como, Perry 10, 61, 77
Compton Advertising 38, 62, 119, 174, 179
Conan Doyle, Arthur 35, 139
Concerning Miss Marlowe 161
Confetti 183
Confidential Adviser 193
Confidentially Yours—Jack Lait 95
Congo Square 20
Conkle, E.P. 48
Conlon, Paul 48, 75
Conn, Harry 48, 157
Connecticut Players 144
Connee Boswell Presents 63
Connelly, Joe 48–49, 148
Connor, Herbert 49
Conover, Harry 94
Constance Hope Associates 114
Consumer Time 20
Continental Celebrity Club 88
Cook, Dwight 49
Cook, Phil 126
Cook, Virginia 49

Cool, Gomer 49–50, 170
Cooper, Courtney Ryley 50, 59
Cooper, Fenimore 114
Cooper, Jackie 76
Cooper, Wyllis 50–51, 153
Copy 117
Corcoran, Robert 51
Corley, Bob 124
Cornell University 75, 120, 170
A Corner of Chicago 18
Correll, Charles 49, 51, 90, 163, 170
Corwin, Norman 3, 25, 31, 51–53, 72, 85, 130
Cosentino, Nicholas 39, 53
Cosmo Tune Time 192
Cosmopolitan 17, 85, 117
Cotton, Robert L. 189
Could Be 53
Counselor-at-Large 110
Counterspy 10, 67, 71, 112, 118, 144, 152, 169, 188
County Fair 164
County Seat 85
The Couple Next Door 129
Courage for Love 64
Court of Human Relations 25, 186
Court of Missing Heirs 134
Cousin Willie 107
Cover Girl 94
Covered Wagon Days 184
Cowboy Tom's Roundup 189
Cowgill, Rome 4, 54
Coxe, George Harmon 23, 47
C.P. MacGregor 54, 97
Cramer-Krasselt Co. 142
Crandall, Perry 54
Crane, Frances 10, 141
Crane, Harry 54
Crazy Quiz 106
Cream of Wheat 131
The Creature from the Black Lagoon 14, 199
Creeps By Night 46, 192
Cresta Blanca Hollywood Players 106
Crime and Peter Chambers 112
Crime Cases 47
The Crime Cases of Warden Lawes 67
Crime Classics 69, 74, 82
Crime Club 47, 50
Crime Correspondent 86
Crime Doctor 134
Crime Does Not Pay 134
Crime Fighters 144
Crime Is My Pastime 195
A Crime Letter from Dan Dodge 185
Crimson Fang 184
Crimson Trail 64
Crisis in War Town 67
Cronman, Happy 34
Cronyn, Hume 26
Crosby, Bing 22, 44, 79, 108, 113, 147, 156, 178
Crosby, Bob 44
Crosby, Leigh 54
Crosby, Virginia 54
Crosley, Powel, Jr. 52
Cross, Joe 54–55
The Cross-Eyed Parrot 147
Crossen, Kendall 55, 83
The Croupier 85

The Crucible 143
Crump, Irving 55
Crusade for Children 152
Crusinberry, Jane 55, 76
Crutcher, Jack 55
Crutcher, Robert 55–56
Crutchfield, Les 56
Crystal Gazer 184
Cub Reporter 62
The Cuckoo Hour 116
Cuckoo Newsreel 116
Cugat, Xavier 94
Curious Trials & Criminal Cases 32
Curtain Time 19, 25, 105, 175
Curtin, Nathaniel 56
Curtin, Tom 56
Cut the Cards 13
Cuthbertson, John 61
The Czar Is Far Away 46

Dagmar 161
Dahm, Frank 56–57
Dailey, Cass 83
The Daily News (Miami, FL) 23
Dale, Frances 22
Daley, Cass 111
Dallas 176
Dalt & Zumba 42
Damon Runyun Theatre 97, 106
Dan B. Miner Co. 93, 199
Dan Carson 34
Dan Dunn, Secret Operative 48 101, 199
Dan Harding's Wife 168
Dana, Richard 56
The Dancer 83, 127
Danch, Bill 56
Dancing Party 71
Danger 95
Danger, Dr. Danfield 195
Danger Is My Business 128
Dangerous Assignment 80, 72, 197
Dangerous Paradise 33, 186
Dangerously Yours 103
Daniel Boone 189
Daniel Boone Kissed Me 104
Daniels, Bebe 127
Dann, Sam 56
Dannay, Frederic 35, 56–57, 122
The Danny Kaye Show 9, 40, 42, 74, 89, 97, 113, 127, 173, 181
The Danny Thomas Show 54, 84, 146, 156, 174, 175
The Dark Goes Mad 23
Dark Memory 169
Dark Venture 134, 171
Darling and Dearie 47
Dartmouth University 142, 156
Darts for Dough 138
A Date with Judy 69, 121, 124, 162
Davenport, Bill 57, 78
Daves, Delmer 21
Davey and Goliath 145
David, Marvin 57
David Adams—Son of the Sea 190
David Harum 33, 61, 110, 176, 189
Davidson, David 57
Davidson, Ron 82
Davis, Eddie 38, 58–59, 73, 112
Davis, George W. 84
Davis, Joan 54, 97, 128, 165, 193

Davis, Mac 59
Davis, Owen 59
Davis, Phil 59
Davis, Stanley 75
Dawson, John 59, 151
Dawson, Ronald 59
Day, Robert 11
A Day at the Races 155
A Day in the Country 146
A Day in the Life of Dennis Day 15, 57, 78, 84, 133, 162
Days of Our Lives 94, 159
Dayton's Teachers College 158
DC Comics 32
Deadline Dramas 195
Deadline Mystery 152
Dear Adolph 29
Dear Mom 196
Death at Midnight 136
Death of a Salesman 143
Death Valley Days 18, 39, 98, 117, 161, 162, 197, 198
Death Valley Sheriff 197
DeBall, Patricia 147
December Bride 126, 173
Decision! 26
The Deerslayer 114
The Defenders 67, 115
Defense Attorney 149, 171
Defense for America 130
de Graffe, Richard 59
Demling, Bill 46, 59–60
Democracy in Action 60 189
Democracy USA 65
The Demolished Man 32
Denison, Merrill 60
Denker, Henry 60
Dennis the Menace 69, 75, 78
The Denver Post 69, 150
Derman, Lou 60
Desilou Productions 152
Destination Freedom 66, 138
Destination Unknown 38, 103
Destiny Trails 114
Detect and Collect 109
Detective Fiction Weekly 54
Detective Story Magazine Hour 186
The Devil and the Deep Six 18
The Devil Bird 28
The Devil's Marchioness 73
Devine, Andy 83
Devine, Jerry 60–61
Dewey, Thomas E. 53
DeWitt, John 61, 110
Diamond, Selma 61, 198
Diamond Dust 59
Dick and Jeannie 173
The Dick Haymes Show 118, 135
Dick Powell Theatre 178
Dick Tracy 82, 92, 100, 129, 137, 176, 179, 195
Dickson, Sam 61
Did They Ask You? 146
Dietz, Howard 50
Diff'rent Strokes 109, 111, 123, 127, 192
Dimension X 65, 115, 123, 169, 170
The Dinah Shore Show 37, 144, 164, 171, 183
Dinelli, Mel 61

The Dinglebenders 98
Disque, Brice, Jr. 61–62
Dissette, E.F. 12
Dixon, David 62
Dixon, Peter 62
Do You Want to Be an Actor? 131
Doc Corkle 76
Doc Savage 92
Dr. Christian 32, 96, 97, 117, 137, 181, 198
The Doctor Fights 75, 85, 128, 156, 171
Dr. Paul 54
Dr. Sixgun 115, 123
Doctor Standish, Medical Examiner 94, 104, 144
The Doctors 160, 189
Doctor's Hospital 148
Document A/777 53
Dog Chats 28
Dog Club of the Air 28
Dolan, Robert Emmet 146, 195
The Don Ameche Show 104, 138, 169
Don Winslow of the Navy 13, 23
The Donald O'Connor Show 73
Donavan, Hobart 62
Donlevy Development Co. 172
Donna Curtis 85
The Donna Reed Show 89, 97, 122, 189, 195
Donner, Dick 11
Don't Throw Glass Houses 80
Don't You Believe It 43
Doorway to Life 14, 149
Dorfman, Sid 62
The Doris Day Show 79, 92
Dorsey, Tommy 44, 154
Dot and Will 89
Double Detective 55
Double or Nothing 22, 44, 167
Doubleday Award 73
Doud, Gil 37, 62–63, 64, 69, 70, 186
Dougall, Bernard 63
Dougall, Tom 63
Douglas, Jack 56, 63–64
Douglas, Melvyn 90
Down Mexico Way 137
Down to Rio 28
Down to the Sea in Subs 12
Downey, Morton 46
Dragnet 37, 40, 83, 148, 172
Drake, Elliot 64
Dramalogues 85
The Drene Show 61, 164, 168
Drene Time 113
Driscoll, David 64
Driscoll, John 64
Droodles 161
Drummond, David 64
Drums 154
Drums of Kali 184
Du Barry Success Magazine 20
Dudley, Paul 64–65
Duff, Howard 26
Duffield, Brainerd 65
Duffy's Tavern 12, 30, 35, 38, 40, 54, 62, 75, 80, 81, 86, 109, 126, 128, 133, 134, 135, 140, 165, 166, 172, 173, 181
Dunkel, John 65
Dunning, John 69
Dunninger 74
Dunsany the Dramatist 32

Durante, Jimmy 54, 81, 97, 119, 133, 165
Durham, Eddie 73
Durham, Richard 65–66, 103
Dusty Pages 21
Dutton, Myron 66

Earaches of 1938 48
Earl Carroll's Sketch Book 77
Earnshaw-Young 154
Easton, Harvey 66
Easy Aces 9, 77
Echoes of History 67
Ed and Zeb 97
Ed McConnell and the Buster Brown Gang 62
Ed Wolf Associates 88
The Ed Wynn Show 64, 78, 89, 109
The Eddie Albert Show 89, 181
The Eddie Bracken Show 56, 104
The Eddie Cantor Five-Year Plan 81
The Eddie Cantor Show 35, 47, 60, 68, 82, 86, 89, 105, 127, 154, 162
The Eddie Garr Revue 26
Eddie Rickenbacker 12
Edgar Allen Poe Award 19, 30, 36, 117, 148
The Edgar Bergen & Charlie McCarthy Show 44, 77, 115, 116, 131, 148
The Edgar Bergen Show 156
Edge of Night 33, 144, 190
Edgley, Leslie 66
The Education of Emily Adams 161
Educational Comics 102
Edward Sloman Productions 199
Edwards, Blake 66–67
Edwards, Jack 61
Effie and Laura 30
Egad—the Gadsbys 108
Ehrlich, Ma 67
Eight Is Enough 21
87th Precinct 18
Einstein, Harry 67–68
Einstein, Robert 68
Eisinger, Jo 63, 68, 186
Elaine Carrington Playhouse 43
Electric Hour 45
The Electric Theatre 45
The Elephant Valley 71
Elgin Watch 44
Elinson, Irving 68
Elizabeth the Queen 16
Elizabethan Radio 97
Ella Cinders 78
Eller, Herman 68
Ellery Queen's Mystery Magazine 57
Ellington, Richard 69
Elliott, Bob 100
Elliotte, John 69
Ellis, Antony 69
Ellis, Caroline 69–70
Ellis, David 70
Ellis, Herb 70, 101
Elmer and Elsie 186
Embarrassing Moments in History 116
The Emerald Trap 172
Emmy Awards 20, 22, 31, 35, 38, 77, 80, 83, 86, 90, 109, 113, 114, 115, 119, 124, 137, 143, 145, 149, 151, 158, 164, 166, 169, 171, 175, 178, 179, 183
Emotion 178

Index   213

Empire Builders 32, 116
The Empire of the Snakes 12
Empires of the Moon 103
Encore Theatre 103
Eno Crime Club 143
Eno Crime Clues 191, 196
Entrikin, Knowles 37
Epic of America 76
Epstein, Jerome 70
Eric, Elspeth 70
Erskine, Gladys 21
Erthein, James 70
Erwin, Wasey Agency 25
Escape 21, 55, 56, 63, 65, 69, 70, 74, 82, 83, 84, 98, 103, 123, 142, 149, 150, 151, 162, 165, 167, 168, 170, 172, 182, 186
Esquire 71
Estabrook, Howard 163
The Eternal Light 18, 31, 72, 115, 128, 130, 143, 157, 179, 189, 197
The Ethel Merman Show 88, 183
Ethiopia 19
Ettinger, Ed 70
Everitt, Arva 71
Everitt, Tom 122
Everybody Comes to Rick's 39
Everybody's Inn 70
Everyman's Theater 153
Everything for the Boys 121, 140, 141, 153
Everything Happened to Him 154
Excursion 102
Experience Speaks 56
Experimental Theatre 106
Experiments in Symphonic Drama 97
Exploring the Unknown 26, 38, 56, 74, 95, 144
Exploring Tomorrow 108
Eyes Aloft 36, 165
Eyes and Ears of the Air Force 63, 126
Eyes of the Air Force 171

The Fabulous Dr. Tweedy 56, 108
Faces in the Window 57
Fact or Fantasy 102
The Facts of Life 123, 182
Fairbanks, Jerry 98
Fairfax, Beatrice 120
The Falcon 26, 30, 63, 70, 169, 192
Falk, Lee 32
Family Affair 84
Family Circle 63
The Family Doctor 94
The Family Goes Abroad 176
Family Skeleton 148
Family Theatre 18, 21, 24, 34, 49, 95, 125, 135, 136, 140, 141, 148, 149, 151, 187, 190, 194, 195, 199
Famous First Facts 112
Famous Jury Trials 23, 29, 47, 55, 74, 118, 121, 137, 119, 182
Famous Loves 176
Famous Operas 24
Fanchon & Marco 76
Fang and Claw 80
The Fannie Hurst Show 182
Fantasy 62
Fantasy Island 37, 104, 125
Far Journeys 145
Farber, Les 71

The Farmer Rusk Hour 162
Farr, Finis 71
Fashions of the Times 38
The Fat Man 69, 112, 115, 174, 179, 185
Fathers Knows Best 69, 101, 109, 169, 190, 194
Faulkner, George 71–72
Faust, Gil 72
Favorite Story 83, 121, 123
Fay, Frank 127
Faye, Alice 49, 148, 164
The FBI in Peace and War 10, 75, 156
FDR 53
Fear Is the Parent 72
Federal Housing Authority 76
Federal Theatre Project 18, 19, 21, 134, 168, 183–184
Federal Theatre Radio Division 39, 41, 195
Fein, Bernie 10
Fennelly, Parker 37
Ferrin, Ralph 20
Ferro, Mathilde 72
Ferro, Theodore 72
Fibber McGee & Molly 26, 56, 57, 78, 100, 110, 123, 124, 125, 140, 150, 162
Fiddler on the Roof 157, 183
Fiddlesticks 84
Field Museum (Chicago) 28
Fields, Gracie 134
Fields, Sidney 72–73
Fields, W.C. 78, 111
Fifield, William 73
The Fifth Wheel 31
The Fighting AAF 78
Fighting Senator 128, 157, 171, 188, 197
Fimberg, Hal 68, 73, 75
Final Edition 134, 172
Fine, Lupan 12
Fine, Morton 73–74, 82
Fine, Robert 194
Fine, Sylvia 9, 74
Finesse 23
Finger, Len 74
Finke, Jack 75
Finn, Herb 75
Fireside Theatre 21, 26
The First Nighter Program 13, 19, 24, 33, 104–105, 114, 130, 135, 154, 156, 167, 173, 174, 182, 188
First Stop to Heaven 171
Fischer, Marvin 75
Fisher, Robert 15, 75–76
Fisk University 149, 168
The Fitch Bandwagon 46, 49, 83, 148, 164
Five After the Hour 193
Five Star Final 178
Five Star Jones 167
Five Star Matinee 196, 197
Five Star Theatre 56, 115
Flash Gordon 92
Flashback 123
Flashgun Casey 39, 47
Fleischmann's Yeast Hour 16, 25, 78, 81, 84, 151
Fleming, Van 138
Fletcher & Ellis Agency 42
Flight Nurse 196
Flight to the Pacific 162

The Flintstones 75
Flip 173
The Flip Wilson Show 115
Flippen, Jay 33
Flow Gently, Sweet Rhythm 159
The Flying Nun 89, 177
Flying Red Horse Tavern 197
Flying Time 50
Flynn, Bernadine 166
Flynn, Bess 76, 84
Flynn, Errol 56, 170, 187
Flywheel, Shyster, and Flywheel 138, 154, 157, 177
Fogarty, Paul 28
Folgers Coffee 41
Folies de Paris 37
Folks from Dixie 149
Follies Girl 47
Folliott, Doria 76
Follow Me Boys 156
Follow the Girls 59
Follow the Moon 27
Fonda, Henry 188
Fonda, James 165
Fontaine, Leo 76–77
Football Fables 59
Foote, Cone & Belding 117, 132
For All Time 108
For Distinguished Service 104
For Men Only 29
For Services Rendered 34
For Us the Living 130, 167
For Valor 62
Ford, Glenn 68
Ford Festival of American Music 72
Ford Motor Co. 72
The Ford Road Show 44
The Ford Show 40, 108, 146
The Ford Summer Show 97
The Ford Television Theatre 18, 106
Ford Theatre 31, 57, 65, 72, 99, 136, 145, 146, 174, 175, 180
The Ford Theatre Hour 58
Forecast 27, 30, 34, 71, 74, 77, 78, 84, 104, 195
Foreign Assignment 158
Foreman, Carl 77
Forever Ernest 160
Forever Tops 182
Forge of Freedom 31
Forman, Ed 77
Forster, Robert 11
The Forsythe Saga 147
Fort Laramie 56, 63, 65, 103, 151, 168
Fortune and Death 140
Fortune Stories 25
The Forum 194
Forum of Liberty 25
Foster, George 77
Foster, Lewis R. 21
Foster, Richard 55
Foster, Royal 77
Foster's Corner 23
Four for the Fifth 168
Four Star Playhouse 21, 85
Four Star Productions 10
Fowler, Keith 77, 78, 124
Fox, Frank 57, 78, 89
Fox, Fred 78, 104
Fox, Fred S. 79

214 Index

Fox, Gibson Scott 78–79
Fox-Educational Pictures 126
Franchey, William 79
Frank, Harriet, Jr. 165
Frank, Melvin 79, 155, 193
Frank Hawks 143
The Frank Morgan Show 49, 148, 171
The Frank Parker Show 78
The Frank Sinatra Show 44, 47, 65, 123
Frankel, Doris 79–80
Franklin, Paul 80
Frankly Mr. Feebish 104
Fraser, Ferrin 80
Freckles and His Friends 78
The Fred Allen Show 15, 38, 114, 135
The Fred Brady Show 198
Fred Wittner Advertising Agency 98
Free Company 16, 17, 29, 52, 92, 131, 173
Free World Theatre 36, 121, 153
Freedman, Benedict 80, 81
Freedman, Bill 80
Freedman, David 20, 31, 80, 81, 82, 99, 190
Freedman, Hy 81
Freedman, Morris 81
Freedom's People 189
Freedom's Workshop 30
Freeman, Ben 81
Freeman, Everett 81
Freiheit 92
French, Jack 186
Frey, Helen 82
Friedkin, David 73, 74, 82
Frivolities 86
From These Roots 161, 198
Front and Center 56
Front Page 73, 82
Front Page Detective 144
Front Page Drama 63, 181
Front Page Farrell 35, 115, 176
Front Row Center 65
Frontier 74
Frontier Adventure 197
Frontier Gentleman 14, 69
Froug, William 73, 82–83, 151
The Fugitive 182
Full Circle 144
Fuller, Muriel 117
Fulton, Lou 83
Fun Factory 100
Fun in Swing Time 113
Fun with Dunn 156
Fundamentals of Writing for Radio 54
Funeral of General Von Blatz 37
Funny Men Don't Laugh 20
A Funny Thing Happened on the Way to the Forum 86
Funny Things 183
Funt, Julian 83, 127, 151
Furness-Beattie Radio Productions 28
Futran, Herb 83–84

Gabel, Martin 26, 53
The Gabriel Horn 104
Gabrielson, Frank 84
The Gale Storm Show 80
Galen, Frank 40, 77, 78, 84
Gallant American Women 20, 189
The Gallant Heart 49
The Galley Cookbook 12

Galsworthy, John 147
Gang Busters 56, 62, 77, 112, 144, 152, 176, 181
Gangway for Tomorrow 154
Gardner, Ed 30, 40, 128, 131, 165, 166
Gardner Advertising 135
Garland, Judy 141
Garr, Eddie 40, 84
The Garry Moore Show 35, 186
Garson, Hank (Henry) 12, 84, 182
Gaslight Gaieties 88, 165
Gasoline Alley 42
Gateway to Hollywood 62, 196
Gay 90s 196
The Gay Nineties Revue 141
Gebhart, Lee 84–85
Geiger, Milton 22, 85
Gelbart, Larry 85–86
Gendot, Adrian 86
The Gene Autry Melody Ranch 44, 62, 87, 183
General Electric Theater 19
General Hospital 72, 107
General Mills 54, 70, 159
General Spanky 93
Generation 31
Gentle Ben 69
The Gentleman Adventurer 71
Gentleman from Athens 90
The George Gobel Show 64, 113
George Jessel's Jamboree 42
George White's Scandals of 1939 38
Gershman, Ben 86–87
Gershwin, George 71
Gershwin, Ira 198
Gerson, Sidney 87
The Gertrude Berg Show 31
The Gertrude Lawrence Theatre 26
Geyer, Morey, Madden & Ballard 28
The Ghost and Mrs. Muir 103
The Ghost of Benjamin Sweet 87
The Ghost Walks 102
G.I. Jive 14
G.I. Journal 108, 127
Giant from the Unknown 187
Gibbs, John 142
Gibson, Pauline 87
Gibson, Walter 87, 92
The Gibson Family 50, 59
Gidget 38
Gilbert, Doris 87–88
Gilda 68
Gilligan's Island 75, 83, 95, 96, 107, 131, 150, 175
Gillis, Jackson 88
Gilman, Don 147
Gilsdorf, Frederick 187
Gimme a Break! 119
The Ginny Simms Show 66, 85, 140, 141, 148
Girl Alone 118
The Girl from Reno 181
Girl Trouble 56
Gitterman, Gayle 23
Give 'Em the Heat 29
Give Me a Sentence 104
Givot, George 81
Glad 105
Glad Tidings 130
Gladd, Art 159

Glamour Manor 61, 105, 137
Gleason, Jackie 54, 68, 175, 198
Glickman, Will 88, 165, 183
Goff, Norris 88–89, 119, 120
Going My Way 18
Gold If You Find It 96
The Gold Spot Pals 116
The Goldbergs 31
Golden Rainbow 115
The Golden Treasury of Song 159
Golden Windows 198
Goldsmith, Clifford 89
Goldstein, Jess 78, 89
Goll, Ralph 89
Gomer Pyle: USMC 37, 156, 171
Gone with the Wind 87–88
Good Listening 144
Good Neighbor 50
Good Neighbors 20
Good News of 1937 146
Good News of 1938 146
Good News of 1939 55, 146
Good News of 1940 55, 146
Good Time Guy 78
Good Times 156
Goodman, Benny 89
Goodman, Hal 90
Goodrich, Tom 46
Gordon, Gale 91
Gordon, Jack 90
Gordon, Shirley 90
Gosch, Martin 90, 95
Gosden, Freeman 49, 51, 90–91, 163, 170
Gould, Frank 56, 91
Goulding, Ray 100
Grace & Bement 42
The Gracie Fields Show 179
Grams, Martin 63, 137, 184
Granby's Green Acres 97, 81
Grand Central Station 13, 27, 30, 33, 64, 112, 129, 135, 157, 173, 178
Grand Hotel 22, 105, 129–130, 134, 153
Grand Marquee 56, 57, 130
Grand Old Opry 188
Grand Slam 28, 174
Grandma Beale's Story 22
Grandma Travels 22
Granlund, Nils Thor 44
Grant, Cary 30, 151, 173
Grant, James Edward 21
Grant, Maxwell 87
Grapevine Rancho 182
Gravedigger's Funeral 19
The Gravelpit Courtroom 185
Great Americans 50
Great Artists 65
The Great Escape 151
The Great Gildersleeve 69, 111, 125, 129, 145, 146, 168, 181, 184, 190, 194
Great Gunns 24
Great Moments in History 133
Great Moments of Music 126
Great Plays 103, 130
Great Scenes from Great Plays 96, 144, 157, 188
The Great Talent Hunt 165
Greater Than the Bomb 53
The Greatest 66
The Greatest Story Ever Told 60

Green, Bob 91
Green, Denis 35, 91
Green, Paul 92
Green Acres 47, 181
Green as Grass 72
The Green Hornet 28, 36, 63, 89, 104, 121, 136, 164, 182, 184
The Green Lama 55, 83
Green Valley, U.S.A. 30, 64, 83, 179
Greenbrier Military Academy 161
Greene, John L. 92
Greenfield Recorder (MA) 51
Gregory, David 79, 92
Griffin, Frank 92
Grimy Gazette 154
Grits and Gravy 191
Gross, Milt 92, 180, 192
The Grouch Club 102, 114
The Groucho Marx Show 190
Growing Pains 137
Gruskin, Edward 92
Guadalcanal Diary 92
Guedel, John 79, 93
Guedel, Walter 93
Guerrilla Submarines 12
Guess It and Win It 68
Guess Where? 134
Guess Who Show 164
Guest Star 82, 130, 145
Guiding Light 45, 54, 159, 176, 180–181
Gulf Screen Guild Theatre 46, 53, 63, 78, 82, 84, 94, 118, 155, 157, 187
The Gumps 76, 176
Gun Smoke Law 94
Gunderson, Robert 27
The Guns of Navarone 77
Gunsmoke 47, 56, 63, 65, 69, 70, 73, 82, 103, 118, 129, 142, 145, 149, 151, 162
Gus and Louie 133
Gussman, Charles 93–94
Guys and Dolls 40
Gypsy 120

H-Bar-O Rangers 27
Hagen, Harry 94
Haggart, John 94
Hal Nichols and His School Kids 107
Haley, Alex 157
Haley, Jack 58, 73 112, 165, 166, 169, 178
Hall, Cliff 96
Hall, Wilbur 94
Hall of Fantasy 188
Hall of Fun 75
Hallelujah, Baby! 120
Halliday, Brett 59, 172
The Hallmark Charlotte Greenwood Show 12, 45, 98, 124, 139, 178
Hallmark Hall of Fame 40, 69, 74, 82, 83, 85, 103, 121, 128, 151, 167, 172
Hallmark Playhouse 37, 85, 103, 121, 123, 149, 171, 172, 180
The Halls of Ivy 46, 121, 123, 140, 141, 151, 163, 168, 172, 184
Halls of Montezuma 98
Halman, Doris 23, 41, 94
Halsey's Typhoons 12
Hammer, Richard 90
Hammett, Dashiell 26, 29, 68, 98, 115, 127, 185, 186

Hammil, Joel 76
Hammond, Lawrence 87, 94
Hampton, Bill 94–95
The Hand of Man 159
Hank McCune Show 60
Hanna, David 95
Hannibal Cobb 63
Hansen, Albert 95
Hansl, Eva 20
Hap Hazard 97, 182
Happiness Is Just a Little Thing Called a Rolls Royce 15, 76
Happy Days 111
Happy Hollow 132
The Happy Home 70
The Happy Homemaker 70
Happy Island 34, 60, 116, 165
Hardy, Oliver 93
The Hardy Family 171
A Harlem Family 110
Harlem on Parade 35
Harmon, David 95
The Harold Peary Show 56
Harrigan and Son 105
Harris, Howard 90, 95–96
Harris, Phil 19, 49, 148, 164
Harris, Stanley 22
Harrison, Paul 96
Harry O 169
The Harry Von Zell Show 49, 149
Hart, Elizabeth 96, 97
Hart, Evelyn 96
Hart, James 96, 97
The Hartmans 196
Hartogensis, Harold 97
Harvard University 56, 116, 125, 167, 194
Harvest of Stars 32, 65, 79
Harvey, Helen Gould 97
Harvey, Jack 97
Hashknife Hartley 129
Hasty, John Eugene 97–98
Have a Thrill 130
Have Gun, Will Travel 13, 14, 47, 59, 65, 107, 139, 151, 168
Haven MacQuarrie Ideas 131
Haverdill Musical Conservatory 119
Hawaiian Eye 79, 152, 186
Hawk Durango 137, 157
Hawk Larabee 49, 137, 150, 155, 168
Hawkins, Ruth 98
Hawkins, Stuart 98, 188
Hawkins Falls, Pop. 6200 110
Hawks, Howard 20
Hawks Sky Patrol 151
Hawthorne House 24, 39, 61, 64, 136, 161
Hay, Bill 56
Hayes, Helen 45, 137
Hayes, John Michael 98
Hayes, Larry 99
Hayworth, Rita 68
Hazel 56, 125, 177
Headlight and Crown Mfg. Co. 29
Headlines 184
Headlines of 1936 113
Headlines of 1940 113
Headlines on Parade 178
Hearst Radio Inc. 41, 92, 168
Heartbeat Theatre 85

Heartbeats in Sport Headlines 59
Hearthstone of the Death Squad 35
Hearts in Harmony 115
Heatter, Gabriel 38, 144, 191
Heavenly Days 163
Hecht, Ben 73, 82, 99
Hector in Hollywood 23
The Hedda Hopper Show 165
Hediger, Ted 99–100
Heider, Fred 100
Heidt Time for Hires 161
The Heinz Magazine of the Air 43
Heisch, Glanville 100
The Helen Hayes Theatre 102, 140
Helen Holden, Government Girl 28
Hell at 50 Fathoms 12
Hell Bent for Election 146
Hellcats of the Sea 12
Hellinger Stories 140
Hellman's Mayonnaise 15
Hello, Americans 27, 66
Hello, Mars! 116
Helm, Harvey 100
The Helping Hand 35
Helpmate 30, 107, 126, 190
The Henn House 97
Henning, Paul 26, 49, 100–101, 163, 181
The Henry Morgan Show 88, 145, 183
Her Honor, Nancy James 128, 191
Her Honor, the Judge 85
Hercule Poirot 38
Here Comes Elmer 98
Here Comes Tomorrow 65
Here We Go Again 77, 163
Here's Babe Ruth 38
Here's Looking at You 73
Here's Lucy 60, 111, 158, 178
Hermann, Cleve 70, 101
Hermann, Harry 70, 101
The Hermit's Cave 49, 69, 106, 107
Hero of the Week 64
Heroines of the Santa Fe 22
Hersholt, Jean 97, 142
Herzinger, Carl 101
Hewson, Isabel 101–102
Hey, Jeannie! 108
The Hickock Program 116
Hidden Faces 190
Higby, Mary Jane 13
High Adventure 39, 64, 145
High Noon 77
The High Places 41, 117
Highway Patrol 107, 129
Highway U.S.A. 95
Highways in Melody 126
Higley, Philo 102
Hiken, Nat 102, 114, 171
Hilda Hope, M.D. 83
Hildegarde 88
The Hildegarde Show 183
Hilltop House 128, 167, 184, 191
Hines, Joe 67
His and Hers 81, 130
His Honor, the Barber 148
Historic Trials 32
A History of Broadcasting in the United States 26
Hit and Run 168
Hit Parade 159

216 Index

Hit the Hay 104
Hitchcock, Alfred 16, 98
Hite, Kathleen 47, 102–103
H.N. Swanson Agency 24
Hobby Lobby 71
Hodapp, William 103
Hodge, Eric 197
Hodge Podge Lodge 132
Hoff, Harry 23
Hoffa, Portland 14
Hogan's Daughter 146
Hogan's Heroes 111, 135
Hold On to Your Hats 38
Holes in a Stained Glass Window 53
Holiday and Company 40
Holland, Gerald 103
Holland Productions 56
Holloway, Jean 95, 103–104
Hollywood Half Hour 21
Hollywood Hotel 34, 46, 50, 77, 80, 118, 136
Hollywood Love Story 115
Hollywood Mardi Gras 101, 155
Hollywood Mystery Time 70, 128
Hollywood Players 45
Hollywood Premier 118
Hollywood Radio Theatre 21, 90
Hollywood Reporter 95, 149
Hollywood Showcase 103, 133, 194
Hollywood Silhouettes 97
Hollywood Soundstage 118
Hollywood Star Playhouse 40, 85, 128, 170, 172, 185, 199
Hollywood Star Time 85, 165, 196
Hollywood Story 13, 145
Hollywood Tomorrow 99
Hollywood Writers Mobilization 146
Hollywood's Open House 174
Holt, Felix 104
Holton, Leonard 92
Home Fires 27
Home Is What You Make It 114
Home of the Brave 120
Home Run Derby 97
Home Town 62
Homicide Squad 64
Honest Abe 48
Honest Harold 168, 184
Honeymoon Cottage 86
The Honeymooners 54, 75
Honolulu Bound 30
Hoople, Henry 104
Hop Harrigan 13, 41, 129, 146, 181
Hopalong Cassidy 10, 18, 19, 79, 137, 162, 180, 185
Hope, Bob 34, 45, 63, 75, 78, 79, 86, 104, 109, 113, 115, 119, 120, 124, 135, 150, 155, 156, 161, 170, 174, 175, 176, 185, 194
Hope, George 104
Hope Alden's Romance 173
Hopkins, Neal 104
Hopkins, Pauline 104–105
Horatio Alger's Stories 36
Horatio Hornblower 102
Horne, Lena 118
Horror Inc. 127
Horse in the Gray Flannel Suit 157
Hot Air 177
The Hot Shot 193

Hotchkiss, Barbara 105
Hour of Charm 126
House, Billy 180, 192
House by the River 61
The House Detective 62
A House in the Country 116
House of Glass 30
House of Mystery 45, 67, 169
House of Myths 147
House on Q Street 173
House Party 93
House Un-American Activities Committee 21, 144, 146, 177, 184
House Undivided 49
Houseboat Hannah 190
How Do You Know? 103
How To? 161
How to Marry a Millionaire 81
How to Succeed in Business Without Really Trying 40
How to Write for Radio 176
How to Write Jokes 165
Howard, Cy 105, 118, 126
Howard, David 37, 105
Howard, Eugene 37, 127
Howard, Tom 81
Howard, Willie 37, 127
Howdy Stranger! 156
Howell, Bob 106
Howell, Ruth 106
Howie Wing 146
Howlett, Eric 106
Hubbard, Tom 106
Hugh, Herbert F. 101
Hughes, Don 106
Hughes, Langston 16
Hughes, Rupert 136
Hughes, Russell 106–107
Hugo Award 32
Hula Honeymoon 90, 96
Human Adventure 128
The Human Angle 169
Hume, Benita 163
Hunter Is a Fugitive 66
Huntley, Lester 107
Hursley, Doris 107
Hursley, Frank 107
Hurt, Marlin 124
Huston, Lou 107
Huxley, Aldous 83

I Ain't Talking 95
I Challenge You 55
I Cover the Waterfront 63
I Deal in Crime 99
I Dream of Jeannie 15, 76
I Fly Anything 56, 157
I Know the Enemy 26, 144
I Led 3 Lives 40
I Love a Mystery 147, 148, 160, 174
I Love Adventure 135, 174
I Love Lucy 44, 155, 162, 173, 193
I Married a Communist 18
I Married Joan 89, 172, 175, 182
I Remember Mama 84
I Spy 74, 82, 141
I Want a Divorce 34
I Was a Convict 39
I Was There 40, 65, 169
Ice Box Follies 161

Ideas That Came True 130
If Fight We Must 114, 178
If I Had the Chance 127
If This Be My Harvest 20
If Words Could Kill 197
Illinois Bell 86
Illinois Writers Project 65
Impossible Pictures 125
The Impossible Years 76
Impulse 134
In Care of Maggie Horn 34
The In-Laws 31
In One Head and Out the Other 161
In Time to Come 181
Incredible But True 175
Indiana University 103, 137, 161
Indictment 51, 179
Industrial Commission of Wisconsin 107
Information Please 143, 159
Ingram, Gail 107–108
Ingram, Harry 107
Inheritance 124
Injunction Granted 19
Inner Sanctum 10, 46, 64, 85, 127, 134, 143, 148, 151, 169, 178, 179, 186, 188, 191
Inside Detective 140
Inside New York 31, 178
Inside the Movie Kingdom 53
Inside the Rackets 168
Inside U.S.A. 20
Inspector Stevens & Son 135
Institute for Radio Education 82
International Airport 169
Into the Light 27
Intrigue 186
The Investigator 178
I.O.U. 117
Irene Rich 154
Ironside 13
Irving, Peter 108
Irving Fogel Radio Productions 46
Is That Your Best Offer? 20
Isaacs, Charlie 168
Island at the Top of the World 195
Island Boat Club 140
Island Venture 168
It Can Be Done 193
It Can Happen to You 182
It Could Happen to You 23
It Pays to be Ignorant 72, 107
It Shouldn't Happen to a Dog 84
It Takes a Thief 114
It Takes a Woman 44
It's a Great Life 43–44, 162, 178
It's a Woman's World 105
It's About Time 115
It's Always Albert 47, 185
It's Always Sunday 78, 89
It's Higgins, Sir 96
It's Maritime 59, 136
It's Murder 169
It's the Berries 148
It's the Navy 192
It's Up to You 19
It's Your Business 191
Ives, Burl 82
The Ivory Tower 27

Index 217

J. Walter Thompson 19, 25, 32, 44, 47, 48, 49, 70, 71–72, 88, 95, 98, 99, 101, 131, 145, 148, 156, 164, 182
Jack and Ethel 147
Jack Armstrong, All-American Boy 17, 55, 138, 149, 184, 185
The Jack Benny Show 15, 22, 37, 42, 84, 105, 111, 147, 155, 157, 186, 192
The Jack Carson Show 54, 64, 75, 83, 96, 125, 186
The Jack Haley Show 165
The Jack Haley Variety Show 48, 73, 108
The Jack Kirkwood Show 54, 60, 165, 181
Jack Oakie's College 175, 180, 192, 198
The Jack Paar Show 62, 64, 86, 109, 111, 113, 135, 157, 182, 186
Jack Paar Tonite 64
The Jack Smith Show 194
The Jack Webb Show 37
Jack Westaway Under the Sea 196
Jackie Gleason: American Scene Magazine 72
The Jackie Gleason Show 75, 96
Jackson, Shirley 65
Jackson and Jill 129
Jacob and the Indians 115
Jacobs, Morris 108
Jacobs, Seaman 108–109
Jacoby, Coleman 109
Jacqueline Susann's Open Door 47
Jaeger, Pete 23
Jalopy 55
James, Ed 109
James, Harry 121
James, Jason 68
The James and Pamela Mason Show 153
James Dean: His Tragedy, His Life, His Films 95
Jampel, Morton Carl 109
Jane Arden 103
Jason and the Golden Fleece 70, 101
Jax Cavalcade of Sports 59
Jean O'Neill Show 121
Jeannie 61
Jed Snowden 72
Jeff Regan, Investigator 73, 83, 86, 88, 150, 170, 172, 188
Jeffers the Butler 138
The Jeffersons 122
Jergens Co. 24, 27
Jessel, George 42, 43, 47, 143
Jessup, Richard 109
The Jetsons 15
Jewell, Jim 184
Jigger Moran 169
The Jim Backus Show 60
Jim Rogers, Claims Agent 112
Jim West of the Mounties 79
The Jimmy Dean Show 88
The Jimmy Durante–Garry Moore Show 54, 64, 72, 96, 165, 198
The Jimmy Durante Show 34, 54, 81, 108, 150, 173, 182
The Jimmy Edmondson Show 196
Jimmy Hughes, Rookie Cop 51
The Jimmy Stewart Show 113
Jo and Vi 133
The Jo Stafford Show 194
Joan and Kermit 85

The Joan Davis–Jack Haley Show 46
The Joan Davis Show 40, 54, 62, 86, 96, 151, 162, 181
Joan Davis Time 45, 54, 135, 182
Joan of Arc 16
Joan of Lorraine 16
Joanie's Tea Room 97, 128, 191
Joanne Taylor's Fashion Flashes 69
Joe and Mabel 104, 150
Joe Bren Producing Company 51, 90
The Joe E. Brown Show 60, 101
Joe Palooka 21
The Joe Penner Show 48, 112
Joe Powers of Oakville 97, 114
The Joey Bishop Show 68, 186
Johansen, Al 109
John A. Clements Associates 174
John Guedel Radio Productions 81, 190
John J. Malone for the Defense 166
John Steele, Adventurer 64, 145
Johnny Fletcher 73
The Johnny Mercer Show 194
Johnny Mercer's Music Shop 125, 168
Johnny Modero: Pier 23 37, 134, 147
The Johnny Morgan Show 109
Johnny on a Spot 126, 128
Johnny Presents 110, 134
The Johnny Thompson Show 100
John's Other Wife 35, 94
Johnson, Doug 110
Johnson, Jack 71
Johnson & Johnson Musical Melodrama 183
The Johnson Family 47, 175
Johnston, Johanna 110
Johnston, Joseph 110
Johnstone, Jack 110
Jolson, Al 20, 39, 44, 48, 58, 59, 68, 70, 80, 81, 108, 182
Jonathan Trimble, Esq. 127
The Jonathan Winters Show 55, 111, 117
Jones, Arthur 110
Jones, Grover 110
Jones, Spike 33, 79
Jones, Venzuella 110
Jordan, Jim 124, 162, 163
Jordan, Marian 124, 162, 163
Josefsberg, Milt 105, 110–111, 157
The Joseph Katz Co. 126
Journeys Out of the Body 145
Joyce, Betty 111
Joyce Jordan, M.D. 64, 83, 159, 173
The Jubilaires 59
Jubilee 108, 175
Judd for the Defense 58
The Judge 83
Judgement: The Court Martial of the Tiger of Malaya 53
Judson Radio Program Corporation 45
Judy and Jane 17, 41, 190
The Judy Canova Show 48, 60, 78, 104, 119, 158, 161
The Judy Holliday Show 96
Julia 113
Julian, Arthur 111, 113
Julliard 82
Jumbo 81
The Jumbo Fire Chief 99
June Moon 144

Jungle Animals 80
Jungle Jim 181
Junior Miss 84, 88, 118, 180
Junior Partners 174
Junior Thriller 10
Junkin, Harry W. 111
Jurist, Edward 111
Just Five Lines 19
Just Outside Hollywood 125
Just Plain Bill 17, 27, 33, 57, 96, 114, 191
Justice 156

K-7 181
Kane, Frank 112
Kane, Henry 112
Kane, Joseph 112
Kane Furniture Co. (Boston) 67
Kansas City Journal-Post 9
Kansas City Post 69
Kanter, Hal 15, 112–113
Kate Hopkins, Angel of Mercy 136
The Kate Smith Show 19, 30, 55, 89, 103, 111, 118, 142, 167
Kate Smith Variety Hour 60
Katie's Daughter 191
Katkov, Norman 10, 11
Kaufman, George 188
Kay Fairchild, Stepmother 22, 136
Kay Kyser's Kollege of Musical Knowledge 56, 63, 84, 94, 161
Kay Thompson and Co. 156
Kaye, Danny 9, 15, 74
Kaye, Sammy 70, 109
KDKA 111, 167
KECA 24, 42
Keene, Day 113
Keep 'Em Rolling 85, 90, 95, 174
Keep Healthy 38
Keepers of the Lights 12
Keeping Up with Rosemary 167, 184
Keith-Albee 138
Kelk, Jackie 88
Kelley, Welbourn 113–114
Kellogg 44, 47
The Kellogg Hour 72
Kelsey, John 114
The Ken Murray–Oswald Show 77
The Ken Murray Show 77
Ken-Rad Unsolved Mysteries 29
Kent, Mona 114, 188
Kent, Priscilla 114
Kermit-Raymond Radio Productions 174
Kerner, Otto, Jr. 188
KEX 63
Keystone Broadcasting System 137
Keystone Chronicles 166
Keystone of Hollywood 46
KFAB 28
KFAC 31
KFDM 74
KFI 24, 34, 42, 61, 100, 188
KFOX 48, 107
KFRC 86, 119, 132, 140, 155
KFRC Breakfast Club 86
KFSO 79
KFWB 24, 39, 60, 106
KGB 54, 99
KGO 61, 147
KGW 64

218 Index

KHJ 34, 62, 64, 140, 185
Khyber Pass 18
Kibbee, Roland 114
Kiesewetter Agency 182
King, Frank 42
King Features 54, 62
King Features Presents 62
King of the Khyber Rifles 149
King Size Weekly 80
King-Trendle Broadcasting Corp. 36
The King's Men 110, 124
King's Row 23, 114
Kings Jesters 94
Kings School of Dramatic Arts (Pittsburgh) 110
Kinoy, Ernest 114–115, 123
Kirkland, Roslyn 12
Kirkwood, Jack 86, 174
Kiss and Make Up 60, 105
Kiss and Tell 101
A Kiss for Peter 53
Kitty Foyle 23, 26, 33
Kitty Keene, Inc. 107, 113, 152
Klee, Lawrence 115
Klein, Larry 115, 182
Klem, Per 12
Klinker, Zeno 115–116
Klondike 46
Klondike Mike 60
KMBC 9, 26, 28, 49, 69, 100, 132
KMOX 28, 103, 159
KMPC 24, 107, 121, 168
KMTR 169
KNBC 61
Knickerbocker Holiday 16
Knickerbocker Playhouse 85, 105, 135
Knickerbocker Press and Evening News (Albany, NY) 67
Knight, Raymond 116
Knight, Ruth 116–117
Knight, Vick 117
KNX 24, 39, 46, 47, 65, 71, 73, 100, 156, 161, 169, 172, 185
KOA 112
Koch, Howard 117
Koehler, Joseph 21
Kogan, David 19, 117–118
Kohnhorst, David 12
KOIL 104
KOL 46, 161
KOMA 196
KOMO 46
Kosco, G. F. 12
Kostelanetz, Andre 72, 175
KOTA 27
KPO 24, 39, 56, 61
KQW 188
Kraft, Hy 118
Kraft Music Hall 22, 32, 44, 45, 61, 79, 81, 99, 108, 113, 125, 127, 138, 147, 163
Kramer, Milton 118
Kress, Fred 33
Kronman, Harry 118
Krum, Fayette 118
KSD 181
KSFO 97
KSRO 98
KTAR 137
KTAT 74

KTHS 88, 89, 120
KTM 99
KTRH 105
KTSB 160
KTTV 36
KUJ 73
Kurtzman, Joel 119
Kurtzman, Samuel 119
KWK 99
KYA 61, 79, 86
Kyser, Kay 83, 94, 196

L.A. Weinrott & Associates 193
Labor for Victory 92, 130
Lachman, Morton 119
Ladd, Alan 100, 106
Ladd, Hank 119
Ladies and Gentlemen 183
Ladies Courageous 88
The Ladies Home Journal 71
Ladies in Linen 23
La Dievere, Lucien 12
Lady Be Beautiful 147
The Lady Dances 56
Lady Editor: Careers for Women in Publishing 117
The Lady Esther Screen Guild Theatre 53, 94, 163, 180, 192
The Lady Esther Show 137
Lady of Millions 46
Lady on a Train 154
Lamp This 26
Land o' Make-Believe 119
Land of Plenty 16
The Land of the Lost 101–102
The Land We Live In 103
Lang, Jeannie 42
Lang-Worth Feature Programs 104
Langford, Frances 33, 164
Langworthy, Yolande 119
Lansworth, Lew 119
Laramie 13, 39, 85
Lassie 62, 71, 85, 92
The Last of the Mohicans 114
The Last Testament of Lucky Luciano 90
The Last Wagon 21
Latitude Zero 177
Lauck, Chester 88, 119–120
Lauferty, Lillian 120
Laugh and Learn 183
Laugh Liner 180, 181, 192, 198
Laughing Moon 21
Laurel, Stan 93
Laurents, Arthur 120
Laven, Paul 120
Laverne & Shirley 111
Lawes, Lewis E. 32, 67
Lawless Twenties 112
The Lawless Years 68
Lawrence, Jerome 120–121, 123, 141
Lawrence, Jim 121
Lawyer Tucker 37, 105
Lazarus, Erna 121–122
Leaf, Margaret 122, 191
Lear, Norman 122
Leave It to Beaver 21, 49, 72, 76, 84, 87, 89, 111, 124, 131, 148, 170, 189, 190
Leave It to Joan 54, 97
Leave It to Mike 141
Leave It to Papa 53

Lederer, Francis 142
Lee, Earl 61
Lee, Leonard 122
Lee, Manfred 35, 56, 57, 122
Lee, Margaret 20
Lee, Robert E. 120, 121, 123, 141
Lee, Spike 157
The Lee Sweetland Show 174
Leeds, Howard 113, 123
Leeson, David 123
Lefferts, George 123–124
Legend of a Lady 18
Legends of Illinois 65
Lehr, Lew 126, 128
Lend an Ear 183
Lend-Lease Library 59
Leo Boulette Agency 36
Lerner, Al 70
Leslie, Aleen 124
Leslie, Leonard 124
Leslie, Phil 124–125, 163
Lesser, Julian "Bud" 125
Lesser, Sol 125
Lest We Forget 143
Let Freedom Ring 131
Let George Do It 73, 88, 105, 128, 191
Let Yourself Go 34, 60
Let's Get Associated 147
Let's Get Together 33
Let's Pretend 13, 110, 119, 131
Levinson, Leonard 49, 83, 125
Levitt, Gene 125, 144
Levy, Parke 125–126, 128
Lewerth, Margaret 126
Lewi, Jack 126
Lewin, Al 126–127
Lewis, Al 127
Lewis, Cathy 74
Lewis, Elliott 74, 82, 91
Lewis, Milton 127
Lewis, Mort 127
Lewis, Robert 24
Lewis, W.B. 52
Lewis, William 153
Libbott, Robert 128
Library of Congress Radio Project 128
Liebman, Max 74
The Life and Love of Dr. Susan 140
Life Begins 76
Life Can Be Beautiful 29, 33
A Life in Your Hands 110, 138
Life Is What You Make It 107
Life of Edison 54
The Life of Mary Sothern 29, 179
The Life of Riley 30, 37, 62, 128, 131, 136, 160, 166, 175, 177
Life of the Reillys 136
Life on the Red Horse Ranch 49
Life with Henry 89
Life with Luigi 30, 60, 105, 118, 182
Life with Tena 29
Life's Little Problems 116
Life's Too Short 195
The Light of the World 29, 107, 136, 175, 176
Lightning Jim 104
Lights and Shadows 184
Lights Out! 50, 110, 124, 153
Lil' Abner 93
Lillie, Beatrice 164

Index 219

Lincoln Highway 41, 98, 112, 177, 191
Linda Dale 113
The Line-Up 63, 66, 74, 82, 125, 135, 145, 151
The Linit Bath Club Revue 115
Linkletter, Art 93, 166
Lions After Slumber 30
The Lion's Roar 181
Lippe & Lazarus Productions 121
Lipscott, Alan 126, 128
Liss, Joseph 128
Listen Carefully 26
Listener's Playhouse 30, 130
The Listening Post 79, 182
Little, Herbert 128–129, 191, 194
Little Blue Playhouse 134
Little Immigrant 105
Little Mother Mag 29
Little Old Hollywood 165
Little Orphan Annie 23, 56, 80, 113, 135, 152
Little Orvie with Skippy 127
Little Rascals 93
Little Show 9
The Little Things in Life 129
The Littlest Angel 187
Littletown, U.S.A. 83
Lives of Harry Lime 49
Lives of the Great 42
Living Diary 95
Living Dramas of the Bible 173
Living History 52
The Living Newspaper 19
Living—1948 62
Lockwood, Charles A. 12
Loesser, Frank 40
Loew-Poli Theatre 185
Log Cabin Jamboree 58–59, 73, 112, 169
Log Cabin Show 166
Log of the Black Parrot 63, 69
Logan, Janet 22
Lomax, Alan 128
Lone Journey 142
The Lone Ranger 28, 36, 63, 65, 78, 89, 91, 104, 111, 136, 164, 182, 184
The Lone Wolf 98
Lonely Women 159
The Long Count 169
Longworth, Alice 188
Look 73
Look Who's Laughing 163
Looney Tunes 108
Lootville 80
Lopez, Vincent 74
Lora Lawton 189, 191
Lord, Phillips H. 41, 47, 56, 62, 71, 152, 184
Lord & Thomas 64, 119, 159, 194, 196
Lorenzo Jones 72, 191
The Loretta Young Show 62
The Los Angeles Daily News 95
The Los Angeles Record 42
Lost Empire 46
Lost in Space 88
Lost in the Stars 16
The Lost Legion 50
The Lottery 65
Louis, John Jeffry 162
Louisiana Hayride 48
Louisville Courier-Journal 138

Lovaire, Ruth 87
Love Ahoy 33
Love and Learn 189
The Love Boat 79, 109
Love Me Long 80
The Love of Life 160
Love Story Magazine 22
Love Story Theatre 26, 182
Love Time 45
Lovely Me 47
Lover Come Back 101
Loves of Southern Seas 29
Lowry Field Theatre of the Air 112
Lowther, George 129
Lucky Stars 123
Lucky Strike Hit Parade 64, 112
The Lucky Strike Hour 56
Lucky Strike Theatre 13
The Lucy–Desi Comedy Hour 173
The Lucy Show 29, 68, 84, 111, 138, 173
Luddy, Barbara 24
Luke, Fred 129
Luke Slaughter of Tombstone 190
Lum 'n' Abner 36, 88–89, 101, 119, 132, 169, 180, 181, 192
Luncheon at the Waldorf 140
Luncheon with Lopez 74
Lunchtime Follies 143
Lust for Life 53
Lux Radio Theatre 16, 18, 25, 80, 85, 120, 144, 156, 172, 181, 193
Lux Summer Theatre 103
Lux Video Theatre 25, 111, 194
Lynch, Peg 129
Lynne, Virginia 129
Lyon, Ben 127
Lyon, Peter 130, 167
Lyons Agency 156

Ma Brown 27
Ma Perkins 17, 56, 65, 85, 107, 189
Mabley, Edward 130
Mac Davis Features 59
MacArthur, Charles 73, 82, 99
Macdonnell, Norman 56, 142
MacDougall, Ranald 130
MacGillan, Dan 130
Mack, Dick 131
Mack, Helen 124
Mack, Nila 131
Mackeral Skies 94
MacLane, Roland 131
MacLeish, Archibald 128, 131
MacQuarrie, Haven 131
Mad Hatter 184
The Mad Hatterfields 104
Mad Libs 161, 183
The Mad Masters 135
Madison Avenue 53
Madison Square Garden 19
Madison, That's Me 83
The Magazine of Fantasy & Science Fiction 36
Magazine of Time 150
Magazine Theatre 95
Magic Island 54
The Magic Key of RCA 52, 137
The Magic of Speech 185
Magic Waves 103
Magnificent Lady 142

The Magnificent Montague 102
The Magnificent Seven 151
Maguire, Arnold 131–132
Mail Call 121, 123, 127, 175
The Main Line 119
Main Street Music Hall 144
Main Street Sketches 38
The Majestic Hour 180
Major Hoople 42, 124
Major North, Army Intelligence 151
Major V 93
Make Believe Town 70, 83, 144
Make Me Laugh 101, 161
Make Room for Daddy 68, 84, 182
Makers of History 42
Making the Movies 116
Malone, Joel 132, 185
Malone, Pick 127
Malone, Ted 132–133
Maltese Falcon 186
The Maltine Story Hour 21
Mama Talks 31
Mame 121, 123
Man About Harlem 35
Man About Hollywood 121
Man About Town 101
Man Against Crime 115
The Man and the City 169
The Man Behind the Badge 95
The Man Behind the Gun 24, 95, 120, 130, 156, 177, 179
The Man Called X 40, 56, 128, 135, 140, 141, 199
The Man from Blackhawk 55
The Man from G-2 151
The Man from Homicide 160, 191
The Man from Laramie 40
The Man from U.N.C.L.E. 69, 191
The Man I Married 29, 33
Man in Dress Clothes 128
The Man Inside 55
A Man Named Jordan 39, 172
Man of Mars 196
Man on the Stairs 197
The Man Who Wouldn't Talk 71
Mandrake the Magician 32, 54
Manhattan at Midnight 30, 56, 70, 111, 129, 172, 189
Manhattan Matinee 21
Manhattan Mother 89
Manhattan Playhouse 145
Manhoff, Bill 13
Manhunters 184
Manley, William Ford 133
Manning, Marie 120
The March of Mercy 114, 137, 148, 183
The March of Time 18, 23, 26, 43, 49, 56, 62, 64, 71, 96, 97, 130, 141, 144, 160, 167, 180, 186
Marcin, Max 133–134
Marcus, Lawrence 134
Marcus Welby, M.D. 171, 191
Mardi Gras 21
Margie, the Steno 189
Margolis, Herbert 134
Margot of Castlewood 193
Marie, the Little French Princess 64
The Marines Tell It to You 195
Marion, Charles 134
Marion, Ira 134

Maris, Herbert L. 96
Mark Trail 13, 36, 81
Marks, Larry 134–135
The Marlin Hurt and Beulah Show 124
Marquette University 138
Marquis, Arnold 135, 163
The Marriage 115
Marriage for Two 43, 197
Married for Life 56
Marschalk & Pratt 62
Marshal, Sidney 135
Marston, Adelaide 167, 184
Martha Mears 121
Martha Webster 76
The Martha Wright Show 100
Martin, Charles 154
Martin, Dean 54, 158, 182
The Martin and Lewis Show 45, 64, 90, 108, 115, 119, 122, 158, 161, 165, 170, 178, 185
Martin Kane, Private Eye 65, 71, 99
Martinek, Frank 23
Martini, Roland 135
Marx, Groucho 61, 68, 78, 114, 168, 177, 182, 190
Marx Bros. 37, 44, 81, 114, 138, 155, 157, 170
Mary and Bob 87, 183
Mary Noble, Backstage Wife 18, 22, 27, 34, 35, 42, 94, 115, 145, 189, 191
The Mary Small Show 128, 191
Mary Small's Junior Revue 63
*M*A*S*H* 62, 86, 111, 135
Masquerade 144, 159
Massachusetts State College 98
Massey-Harris 60
Masters, Edgar Lee 142
Masters, Monty 135
The Matinee Theatre 19, 72, 103, 128, 187
Maud and Cousin Bill 187
Maudie's Diary 143
Maverick Jim 196
Maxwell, Ted 24, 135–146
Maxwell House 55
Maxwell House Iced Coffee Time 49, 103, 164
The Maxwell House Show 118
Maxwell House Showboat 18, 63, 154
The Maxwells 189
Mayberry R.F.D. 148, 170
Mayehoff, Eddie 76
The Mayers Co. 169
Mayfair Productions 106
Mayo Clinic 129
Mayor of the Town 33, 37, 90, 95, 103, 121, 172, 187
Maypole, Roy 136
McCambridge, Mercedes 73
McCann-Erickson 65, 79, 97, 100, 110
McCarran, Pat 53
McCarthy, Charlie 32, 55, 131, 170, 180
McCarthy, Joe 130, 143, 186
McCarthy, Steve 136
McClain, John 136
McConnor, Vincent 136
The McCoy 74, 82
McCracken, Chester 136
McDaniel, Hattie 113
McDonagh, Richard 137

McGaughey, Dudley 137
McGill, Jerry 137
McGreevey, John 137
McHale's Navy 37, 150
McKay, Ted 137
McKean, Eddy 138
McKee, Bob 138
McKnight, Tom 138, 139
McLeod, Victor 138
McNeill, Don 138–139
McQueen, Steve 11
Meadow, Herb 139
Meadow, Leon 139
Medbury, John 139
Medicine U.S.A. 130
Meet Corliss Archer 44, 45, 101
Meet Me at Parky's 68, 96
Meet Me in St. Louis 37, 84, 180
Meet Millie 54, 81, 84, 131, 133
Meet Miss Judith 183
Meet Miss Sherlock 150
Meet Mr. McNutley 49, 96, 148, 172
Meet Mr. Meek 92
Meet Mr. Music 121
Meet Mrs. America 105
Meet the Folks 174
Meet the Meeks 193
Meet the Missus 33
Meet Your Navy 19, 87
Meetin' House 149
Meiser, Edith 139–140
The Mel Blanc Show 30, 128, 173, 191
The Mel Torme Show 12
Melody and Madness 101
Melody Lane 21
Melody Madness 80
Melody Roundup 83
Meltzer, Louis 140
Memo from Lake Success 56
A Memo from Molly 49, 83
Memoirs of Mischa, the Magnificent 101, 194
Memories of Buffalo Bill 50
Memory Lane 136
Men Against Death 27, 97
Men at Sea 22, 85, 118
Men in Black 95
Men, Machines, and Victory 30, 141
Men with Wings 165
Menken, Helen 81
Menkin, Larry 140
Mercer, Johnny 121, 146, 148, 195
The Mercury Summer Theatre of the Air 27
Mercury Theatre of the Air 117
Merdith School (NH) 105
Meredith, Burgess 16, 43
Meredith Wilson's Musical Review 146
Merlin, Barbara 140–141
Merlin, Milton 140
Merrick, William 141
Merrill, Howard 141
Merrill, Mildred 141
The Merry Merriweathers 146
Meston, John 142
Metro Good News Show 164
Metropolitan Opera Auditions of the Air 134, 74
MGM 25, 54, 141, 145, 155
MGM Good News Hour 37

MGM Theatre of the Air 114
Michael 198
Michael, Sandra 76, 142–143
Michael and Kitty 143
Mickelson, Gunnar 142
Mickey Finn 22
Mickey Mouse Theatre of the Air 100
The Mickey Rooney Show 66, 80
Midstream 105
The Mighty Casey 60
Mike Hammer 112
Mike Malloy, Private Cop 106
Mildred Pierce 130
Miller, Albert G. 92, 143
Miller, Arthur 143
Miller, Peg 143
Miller, Sigmund 143–144
The Millionaire 18, 108
Millions for Defense 34, 198
Milton, Paul 144
The Milton Berle Show 102, 108, 111, 115, 164, 171
Milwaukee Journal 138, 166
The Mindy Carson Show 144
The Minneapolis Journal 17
Minnie's Boys 76
Mirror, Mirror on the Wall 114
The Misadventures of Si and Elmer 54
Mischa, the Magnificent 101, 194
Miss Pinkerton, Inc. 134
Mission Trails 132
Mr. Ace 68
mr. ace and JANE 9
Mr. Adams and Eve 172
Mr. Aladdin 160
Mr. and Mrs. 133
Mr. and Mrs. Blandings 119, 123, 151, 197
Mr. and Mrs. North 46, 66, 70, 90, 95, 115, 144, 191
Mr. Blandings Builds His Dream House 79, 119, 156, 197
Mr. Chameleon 27, 44, 115
Mr. District Attorney 41, 42, 47, 60, 71, 101, 111, 120, 137, 176
Mr. Ed 40, 60, 68, 154, 166, 182
Mister Feathers 103
Mr. I. A. Moto 111, 186
Mr. Jonathan 179
Mr. Keen, Tracer of Lost Persons 13, 18, 27, 41, 44, 47, 57, 94, 111, 112, 115, 148, 170, 176
Mr. Lucky 66
Mr. Magoo 100
Mr. Moto 42, 50
Mr. President 56, 63, 103, 134, 140, 141, 144
Mr. Strauss Goes to Boston 125
Mr. Tuff Goes West 40
Mitchell, Bill 71
Mitchell, Esther 144
Mitchell, John 71
Mitchell, Margaret 71
Mitchell, Robert 144
Moby Dick 53
The Modern Adventures of Casanova 56, 170, 187
A Modern Girls' Romance 41
Modern Romances 51, 134, 174
Modigliani: The Biography 73

Mole, John 144
Molle Mystery Theatre 30, 36, 55, 85, 96, 97, 107, 139, 140, 151, 156, 171, 179, 181, 197
Molly 31
Molson Brewing Co. 60
Monig, Christopher 55
Monitor 124, 129
Mono-Drama Theater 30
Monroe, Charles 144
Monroe, Robert 145
Monsieur le Capitaine 177
Montgomery Ward 69
The Monticello Party Line 142
Monty Masters Variety Show 135
Moon Over Mulberry Street 53
Moon River 41
Moonshine and Honeysuckle 191
Moore, Carroll, Jr. 145
Moore, Garry 61, 128, 165
Moore, Grace 33
Moore, Nancy 145
Moore, Sam 12, 145–146, 194, 195
Moore, Wilfred 13, 40, 41, 146–147
Moore, William 147
More By Corwin 53
The Morey Amsterdam Show 140
Morgan, Frank 56, 164
Morgan, Gilbert 61
Morgan, Helen 147
Morgan, Henry 109, 137
Morgan, Johnny 72
Morheim, Louis 147
Mork & Mindy 111
Morning Almanac 126
Morning Market Basket 101
Morrison, Bret 24
Morrow, Bill 29, 147
Morse, Carlton E. 72, 147–148, 174, 192
Morse International, Inc. 150
Mort Manor 184
Mortimer Gooch 130, 190
Morton Salt 8
Morwood, William 148
Moser, James Edward 148
Mosher, Bob 49, 148–149
Moss, Carlton 149
Mostel, Zero 183
Mother and Dad 10, 101
Mother-in-Law 189
Mother o' Mine 137
Motion Picture Herald 189
Mountainville True Life Sketches 119, 141
Moustache by Jonathan 37
The Movie Man 9
Movie Matinee 152
Movie Pilot 61
Mrs. Gibbons' Boys 88, 183
Mrs. Mike 80
Mrs. Minivera 83
Mrs. Wiggs of the Cabbage Patch 18, 170
Much Ado About Doolittle 55
Muddy Waters 110
Muhammad Speaks 66
Mullen, Virginia 149
Mulligan's Travels 20
Mulroy, James W. 118
Mundy, Talbot 149
Muni, Paul 16

Munsey's Magazine 54
The Munsters 49, 148
Murcott, Joel 18, 149
Murder and Mr. Malone 166
Murder at Midnight 67, 139, 143, 148, 151, 171, 197
Murder By Experts 19, 118, 127, 144, 171, 185
Murder Clinic 26
Murder Is My Hobby 195
Murder, She Wrote 88
Murder Will Out 119
Murphy, Nan 150
Murray, Dave 150
Murray, John 150
Murray, Ken 12, 77, 78
Murrow, Edward R. 52
Music America Loves Best 196
The Music and Musings of Dr. Mu 38
Music By Gershwin 42, 71
Music in American Cities 197
Musical Cookbook 126
Musical News 180
My Best Girls 114
My Favorite Blonde 79
My Favorite Husband 44, 55, 57, 73, 78, 98, 155, 162, 172
My Favorite Martian 68, 80, 92, 127, 177
My Friend Irma 84, 92, 105, 126, 131, 181
My Little Margie 45, 78, 97, 107
My Lucky Break 196
My Man Godfrey 128
My Prayer Was Answered 49
My Secret Story 115
My Sister Eileen 140
My Son and I 103, 161
My Son, the Chimp 163
My Three Sons 29, 34, 90, 108, 123, 194
My True Story 173
Myrt & Marge 98, 188, 190
Myrt, Ltd. 190
Mysteries in Paris 140
The Mysterious Traveler 19, 117
Mystery Harbor 18
Mystery House 71
Mystery in the Air 151, 196
Mystery Is My Hobby 196
Mystery of the Week 32
Mystery Theatre 186
Mystery Time 23
Mystery Without Murder 32
Mystery Writers of America 36, 117
Naked City 169
The Naked Maja 53
Name's the Same 161
Napoleon was Right 27
The National Air Travel Club 12
National Association of Gag Writers 122
National Congress of Parents and Teachers 87
The National Enquirer 141
National Public Radio 53
National Radio Forum 30
National School of Broadcasting 169
Native Sons 92
The Naughty Nineties 73
The Navy Hour 102

NBC Comedy Hour 75
NBC Comedy Theatre 171
NBC Minstrels of 1938 23
NBC Presents 169
NBC Presents: Short Story 115, 123, 136
NBC Radio Theatre 123
NBC Star Playhouse 45, 115, 186
NBC Symphony Orchestra 170
NBC University Theatre 65, 85, 103, 115, 123, 136, 170, 178, 196, 197
NBC's Short Story 87
The Nebbs 69
Ned Jordan, Secret Agent 182, 184
Needham, Louis & Brorby Inc. 100, 190
The Negro Art Group Hour 149
The Negro Business Hour 35
The Negro Soldier 149
Neiman, Irving 150
Neisser-Meyerhoff 168
Nellie Bly 162
Nelson, Ozzie 113, 150
The Nelson Eddy Show 170
Neuman, E. Jack 24, 150–151
The New Adventures of Martin Kane 65
The New Adventures of Nero Wolfe 32
The New Adventures of Sherlock Holmes 35, 91
The New Beulah Show (also *Beulah*) 45, 109
The New Frontier 143
New Magazine of the Air 180
New Millennium 53
The New Penny 140
The New Swan Show 174
The New Theater 115
New World A' Coming 93, 115, 134, 178
New York Daily News 110
New York Evening Post 57
The New York Herald Tribune 36, 98, 102, 114, 186
The New York Morning Telegraph 76, 102
The New York Post 134
The New York Press 133
The New York Times 81, 142
New York Times Book Review 36
The New York Times Goes to Press 113
New York University 133, 189
The New York World 133
New Yorker 88, 194, 198
The Newlyweds 185
Newman, Robert 67, 151
Newman, Walter 151–152
News from Home 43, 151
NewsCasting 180
Newsday 155
Newsstand Theater of the Air 63, 154
Newsweek 180
Next Week 180
Niagara 37
Nice Couple 177
Nichols, Anne 152
The Nichols—Family of Five 96
Nick Carter, Master Detective 19, 32, 47, 67, 77, 80, 87, 92, 112, 118, 137, 140, 175, 192
Night and the City 68
A Night at the Opera 155
Night Club Romances 131

Night Court 61
Night Editor 161
A Night in Casablanca 114
Nightcap Yarns 121, 132
Ninety Years of News 113
Niss, Stanley 152
Nit Wit Court 12
No Birds Sing 66
No Man Is Single 98
No Place to Hide 53
No Sense of Guilt 27
Noah Webster Says 131
Nocturnes 21
Nona from Nowhere 104
Non-Royalty Radio Plays 172
Nonsense and Melody 60
Norman, Wallace K. 152
Norman Corwin Presents 53
Norman Corwin's Journal 52
Norman Corwin's Letters 53
Norris, Kathleen 152
North Woods Adventure 183
Northwestern Daily 172
Northwestern University 38, 65, 158, 170, 179
Nosserman, Dick 152
Nothing But the Truth 127
Now Hear This 95
Now Is the Time 114
NTG and His Girls 44
The Nurses 160
N.W. Ayer & Son 98, 101, 143, 150, 197

Oakie, Jack 145
Oboler, Arch 22, 24, 121, 152–154
O'Brien, Robert 154
Occident Flour 27
Occidental College (CA) 172
O'Connor, Donald 133
Odd Bodkins 78
The Odd Couple 127
O'Dea, John 15
O'Donnell, Judson 68
The Odyssey of Runyon Jones 53
Off the Air 37
Off the Record 37, 128
Office of Price Administration 102, 108
Office of Strategic Services 90, 95
Office of War Information 22, 48, 52, 56, 57, 79, 100, 125, 128, 153, 166, 174, 179
Official Detective 143
O'Flaherty, Maggie 154
Og, Son of Fire 55
Oh, God! 86
Oh, Mr. Dinwiddie 135
Oh Say! Can't You See? 28
O'Hara 69, 188
O'Henry Prize 73
O'Henry Stories 140
Ohio State University 120, 124, 145
O'Keefe, Walter 48, 143, 180, 192
The Old and the New 94
The Old Gold Show 44, 70, 140, 146
The Old Home Town 183
Old Time Prize Fights 56
Oldham, Vera 154
Oliver, Edith 154
Oliver, Edna Mae 96

Olsen & Johnson 112, 162
Omar the Swingmaker 87
Omnibus 186
On a Note of Triumph 53
On Broadway 98, 141
On Guard America 114, 117, 173, 176
On Jungle Trails 80
On Stage 69, 74, 90, 151, 152
Once in a Lifetime 59
Once Upon a Midnight 24
Once Upon a Time 177
One Bright Day 144
One for the Book 102
One Life to Live 181
One Man's Family 145, 147, 192, 197
One Man's Story 30
One Minute to Go 192
One Out of Seven 148
1001 Wives 23, 118, 142
The O'Neills 128, 190, 191, 194
Orloff, Arthur E. 155
The Orson Welles Show 160
Osborne, Innes 155
Oscar Awards 37, 42, 49, 53, 67, 77, 79, 86, 98, 99, 101, 117, 120, 130, 134, 149, 151, 165, 170, 173, 176, 178
Ottley, Roi 93
Our Barn 158
Our Boarding House 42, 124
Our Gal Sunday 27, 35, 44, 61, 94, 191
Our Man Higgins 96
Our Miss Brooks 15, 60, 92, 111, 127, 162, 181, 193
Our Town 110
Out of Africa 12
Out of the Deep 136
Out of This World 94
The Outer Limits 10, 171
Over Here 44, 63, 72, 157
Overkill and Megalove 53
Overnight 23
Owen, Dean 137, 155
Owen Vinson & Co. 175
The Owl 125
The Owl and the Pussycat 133
Oxford University 137
The Oxydol Show 194

Pabst Beer 74
The Pabst Blue Ribbon Show 68, 115, 139, 156, 168, 181
Pacific Borax Co. 197
Pacific Story 135
The Packard Hour 60
Padgett, Pat 127
Paducah Plantation 187
Page, Gale 24
Painted Dreams 46, 76, 158
Paley, William 53, 131
Palmer, Nancy 105
Palmolive Party 105
Palmolive Revue 170
Pan American Holiday 137
Panama, Norman 79, 155–156, 193
Panhandle 67
The Paperchase 13
Parade of Stars 77, 78
Paramount 27, 41, 144, 165
Paris & Peart Advertising 105
The Paris Review 73

Parker, Frank 126
The Parker Family 114, 154
Parson, Louella 118
Pasadena Community Playhouse 161
Passed by the Censor 64
The Passing Parade 64
Passport for Adams 52, 130
Pat Novak, for Hire 37
Pathe News 110
Pathways to Yesterday 86
Patrick Calls Me Mother 23
Patti Page Show 51
Patton, Gilbert 36
Patton, Mary 22
Paul, Norman 156
Paul Whiteman Club 63
The Paul Whiteman Show 127, 174
The Pause that Refreshes on the Air 175
The Pay-Off 134
Peabody Award 14, 53, 86, 130, 142, 163, 179
The Peabodys 193
Pearce, Al 97, 124
Pearl, Jack 96, 107, 126, 192, 193
Pearson, Ben 156
The Peggy Lee Show 144
Pegler, Westbrook 71
Pelar & Ryan 71, 141
Pelletier, Louis 75, 156
Penner, Joe 38, 39, 48, 58, 73, 125, 126, 131, 161, 169
Penny Arcade 27
The Penny Singleton Show 55, 88, 180
Penrod 141
Penrod and Sam 135
People Are Funny 79, 93
The People Next Door 102
The People's Choice 76, 128
The Pepper Pot 138
Pepper Young's Family 43, 76
The Pepsodent Show 45, 63, 79, 115, 155, 161, 170, 174, 176, 185, 194
Perenchio, Lee 20
Perils of the Jungle 180, 187
Perkins, Kenneth 156–157
Perl, Arnold 67, 157
Perrin, Nat 157
Perrin, Sam 22, 34, 111, 157–158
Perry, Ben 12
The Perry Como Show 51
Perry Mason 34, 35, 85, 86, 106, 144, 174, 190, 192, 199
Personal Album 121, 123
Pete and Gladys 15
Pete Kelly's Blues 15, 37, 68, 148
The Peter and Mary Show 97
Peter Gunn 66
Peter Lind Hayes 51
Peter Lind Hayes and Mary Healy Show 64
Peterson, Jean 158
Petticoat Junction 89, 96, 101, 107, 109, 163, 181
Petticoat of the Air 101
Peyton Place 72, 98, 159
The Phantom 32
The Phantom of Crestwood 71
Phantoms at Sea 147
Phares, Frank H. 158
Phenomenon 132

Index 223

The Phil Baker Show 33–34, 95, 138, 157, 158, 164
The Phil Harris–Alice Faye Show 37, 46, 60, 64, 75, 91, 109, 174, 178, 180
The Phil Silvers Show 20, 35, 102, 109, 165, 178, 198
Philco Radio Hall of Fame 85, 172
Philco Radio Show 82
Philco Radio Time 40, 127, 147, 187
Philco-Variety Hall of Fame 34
Philip Marlowe, Private Eye 68
Philip Morris 82, 134
Philip Morris Playhouse 73, 82, 85, 154, 167, 185
Phillips, Arthur (Artie) 25, 34, 113, 157, 158
Phillips, Irna 46, 54, 65, 76, 84, 158–159
Phillips, Paul 159
Philo Vance 176
Pickard, John 160
Pickerberry, John 105, 161
Pickford, Mary 42, 145
Pictorial Review 71
Pierre the Trapper 138
Pilgrimage of Poetry 133
The Pink Panther 67
Pinon Players 144
Pins and Needles 19
The Pioneers 46, 197
Pioneers of Science 39
Pipe Smoking Time 127
Plainclothesman 118
The Player 156
Playhouse 90 80
Plays By Ear 46
Plays for Americans 153
The Play's The Thing, Inc. 96
Playwright Producers 130, 167
Poe, Edgar Allan 24, 196
Poems from Arabesque 119
Poetic License 52
Poetry Recital 79
A Point of Honor 68
Point Sublime 165
Police Blotter 71, 182
Police Line-Up 74, 82
Pontiac Varsity Show 143
Popeye 180, 192
Popular Detective 55
Popular Playhouse 111
Porter, Garrett 160
Portia Faces Life 46, 114
Portrait By Proxy 23
Portraits 104
Portraits for Americans 154
Posner, Henry 160
Post Toasties Time 42
Pot O' Gold 64
Potluck Party 43
Powell, Dick 10, 66, 73, 156
Powell, Dick (writer) 160
Power 19
Practical Radio Writing 176
Pray, Rupert 160
A Present Is a Present 71
Presenting Charles Boyer 34, 121, 140, 141, 168, 172, 197
Presnell, Robert, Jr. 160
Pretty Kitty Kelly 56

Price, George 164
Price, Roger 160–161, 183
The Price of Glory 64
The Prince on Center Street 10
Princeton University 56
Principal Productions 24, 31
Prindle, Don 48, 161
Private Files of Matthew Bell 169
The Private Files of Rex Saunders 10
Private Hal Kanter of Lowery Field 112
Private Life of Josephine Tuttle 95
Private Lives of Elizabeth and Essex 16
The Private Lives of Ethel and Albert 129
The Private Practice of Dr. Dana 86, 102, 172
The Private War of Major Benson 49
Proctor & Gamble 26, 50, 98, 135, 159
Production Five 115
Professional Father 81
Professor and Mrs. O'Reilly 126
Promenade, All 168
The Promised Land 76
Promoting Priscilla 24
Prosecuting Attorney 41
Prouder, Doris 112
Proudly We Hail 95
Provo, Frank 160, 161
Prowl Car 39
Prudential Family Hour of Stars 163, 187
The Prudential Hour 60, 72
Prudential Show 107
Public Life of Cliff Norton 166
Public Pigeon No. 1 163
Pugh, Madelyn 161–162
Pulitzer Prize 29, 40, 92, 118, 131, 143, 173, 186, 198
Pull Over, Neighbor 93
Purdum, Herb 162
Pursuit 63, 69, 74, 82, 151
Pursuit of Happiness 23, 25, 43, 52, 61, 72, 173
The Pursuit of Peace 53

QM Productions 11
Quaker Oats 89, 120
The Quartermaster Quarter-Hour 24
The Queen Was in the Kitchen 182
The Queen's Mark 169
Quicks as a Flash 192
Quiet, Please! 50
Quillan, Joe 162
Quinn, Don 12, 22, 100, 121, 123, 124, 125, 140, 151, 162–163
Quinn, Stanley 164
Quite By Accident 181
Quixie Doodles 194
Quiz Kids 154

R-Bar-O Ranger 62
Racket Squad 122
Radcliffe, Virginia 164
Radio Almanac 171
Radio Charades 93
Radio City Playhouse 34, 111, 115, 123
Radio City Previews 196
The Radio Edition of the Bible 25
Radio Enterprises 42
Radio Events, Inc. 12, 21, 119
Radio Free Munich 113

Radio Guild 130
Radio Guild on the Air 113
Radio Hall of Fame 60, 72, 127
Radio Minstrel Tales 21
Radio News Week 62
Radio on the Range 41
Radio Productions, Inc. 108
Radio Proudly Presents 85
Radio Reader's Digest 45, 60, 75, 95, 179
Radio Recorders Inc. 42
Radio Schoolhouse 70
Radio Screen Actors Guild 37
Radio Sketches 62
Radio Transcription Co. 106
Radio Waves 103
Radio Writers Guild 19, 23, 24
Radio Writing 62
Radioaids Inc. 46
Radio's Biggest Show 108
Raffles 65
Raft, George 68
Ragaway, Martin 164
Rags 183
Rah! Rah! Rhythm 126
The Railroad Hour 103, 121, 123, 190
Raising a Husband 174
Raising Junior 62, 116
Raison, Milton 97
Randolph, Amanda 80
Randon, Lee 164
The Ransom Sherman Show 108, 127, 182
Rapp, John 164
Rapp, Phil 42, 168, 139, 146, 164
Rare Detective Cases 55
Ravetch, Irving 165
Rawhide 13, 129, 182
Ray Knight's Cuckoo Clock 116
The Ray Milland Show 81
The Rayburn and Finch Show 51
Raymond Scott Show 144
Reader's Digest - Radio Edition 33, 186, 198
Ready! Aim! Fire 168
Real Folks 38, 116
The Real McCoys 68, 79, 92, 133
Rear Window 98
Reasonable Facsimile 96
Rebellion in Missouri, 1861: Nathaniel Lyon and His Army of the West 12
Red Adams 43
Red Book Dramas 80
Red Channels 53, 179
Red Cross 67, 100
Red Cross Show 113
Red Davis 43
Red Mackenzie 196
Red Ryder 46, 80
Red Scare 19, 53
The Red Skelton Hour 79, 80, 81, 89, 100, 111, 123, 158, 173, 175, 178, 192, 193
Red Trails 196
Redd, Robert 165
Reed, Alan 12
Reeves, Mary Watkins 165
Reg'lar Fellers 60
Reincarnation in Venice 67
The Reincarnation of Peter Proud 67
The Remarkable Miss Crandall 90, 95
The Remarkable Miss Tuttle 90
Rendezvous in Paris 92

224 Index

Reno 94
Report Card 144
Report to the Nation 75, 128, 143
Request Performance 121, 123, 127
Resnick, Sidney 165
The Restless Gun 40
Results, Inc. 172, 187, 197
Return to Peyton Place 45
Revere All-Star Revue 66
The Rex Allen Show 83
Reynolds, Ed 165
Rhine, Larry 166
Rhinestones 184
Rhymer, Paul 166
Rhymes and Cadences 52
Rhythm Road 72
Rice, Craig 166
Rice, Ed 146
Rice, Gerald 167
Richard Diamond, Private Detective 10, 66, 98, 106, 151, 162
Richards, Clay 55
Richards, Robert 130, 167
Richards, Silvia 167
Richton, Addy 167, 184, 191
Rickenbacker, Eddie 12
Rickey's San Francisco Hour 61
Ridgeway, Agnes 167
The Rifleman 10, 13, 95, 118, 129
Riggs, Tommy 56, 157, 167
Right This Way 126
The Right to Happiness 94, 159, 198
Riley, Donald 4
Riley, James Whitcomb 25
Rinehart, Mary Robert 76
Ripley's Believe it or Not 123, 198
Rise of the Goldbergs 24, 30–31, 194
The Rise Stevens Show 170
The Rivalry 53
Rivers of America 95
R.J. Potts-Calkins-Holden 27
RKO Pictures 168
Roach, Hal 93
The Road Ahead 118
The Road of Life 54, 94, 148, 159, 187, 198
Road to Bali 113
Roads to Adventure 114, 188
Robert Monroe Productions 145
Robert Montgomery Presents 72, 76, 143
The Robert Q. Lewis Show 60, 178, 183
Robert S. Taplinger Inc. 39
Robinson, Edward G. 50, 52, 67
Robinson, Jack 168, 184
Robinson, Ken 168
Robinson Crusoe, Jr. 62
Robison, Carson 71
Robison, David 168
Robson, William N. 120, 130, 146, 168
The Rochester Show 90, 108
Rockhill Radio 13, 15
Rocky Fortune 45, 115, 123
Rocky Jordan 49, 65, 73, 83, 86, 88, 98, 125, 128, 145, 150, 170, 172, 188
Roddy, Lee 168–169
Rodman, Howard 169
Roeburt, John 169
Roger Kilgore, Public Defender 47
Rogers, Buddy 42
Rogers, Roswell B. 36, 169

Rogers of the Gazette 56, 103, 151
Rogue's Gallery 39
Roman, Lawrence 169–170
Rolfe, Sam 139
Romance 56, 65, 69, 74, 75, 82, 83, 94, 103, 130, 135, 142, 144, 151, 156, 162, 168, 172, 197
The Romance of Canada 60
Romance of Evelyn Winters 27
Romance of Helen Trent 13, 17, 35, 37, 46, 59, 65, 165
Romance of Oil 62
Romance of the Ranchos 71, 196
Romantic Ancestors 21
Rooftops of the City 140
Rookies 194
A Roomful of Roses 181
Rooney, Mickey 45, 141, 151
Roosevelt, Franklin 52, 53
Roots 115
Ros S. M. Durstine Inc. 79
Rose, Jack 170
Rose, Ralph 170
Rose, Si 170
Rose of My Dreams 33
Rosemary 43
Roses and Drums 27
Ross, Bob 170
Ross, Claris 170
Ross, Jerome 170–171
Ross Dolan, Detective 99
Ross Roy Inc. 28
Rosten, Norman 171
Route 66 169
Rowan & Martin's Laugh-In 64, 192
Roy de Groot Consultants 56
The Roy Rogers Show 80, 125, 170, 190, 196
Roy Shield and His Orchestra 196
The Royal Desserts Hour 78, 85, 194
The Royal Gelatin Hour 78
Royal Welcome 30
Ruben, Aaron 171
Rubin, Jack 171
The Rudy Vallee Show 32, 46, 48, 60, 78, 79, 87, 89, 101, 108, 117, 127, 151, 153, 155, 158, 164, 167, 171, 176, 178, 194, 198
Rudyard Kipling Stories 140
Ruggles, Charlie 134
Rural Crime Reporter 193
Ruscoll, Joseph 171
Russel M. Seeds Co. 79
Russell, Joseph 172
Ruth, Babe 42
Ruthrauff & Ryan 39, 70, 179
Ryan, Quin 56
Ryf, Robert 172

The Sacred Flame 10
Sad Sack 108, 182
The Saint 19, 45, 55, 70, 111, 119, 123, 135, 160, 170, 191
St. Clair, Gordon 172
St. Clair, Leonard 172
St. Louis Amusement Co. 124
St. Louis Blues 59
St. Matthews College (CA) 131
Saks, Sol 172–173
Sal Hepatica 15

The Sal Hepatica Revue 15
The Salad Bowl Revue 15
Sally of the Star 194
Salt of the Earth 94
Salute to Youth 95
Salvation Army 85
Sam Benedict and Mr. Novak 151
Sam 'n' Henry 51, 90
Sam Pilgrim's Progress 30
The Sammy Kaye Show 45
The San Francisco Chronicle 36, 132
The San Francisco Examiner 148
San Francisco Final 82
San Jose State University 103
Sanders, Albert 58
Sands of Time 184
Sanford and Son 122, 171
Sangster, Margaret 173
Santa Monica City College 182
Sara's Private Caper 74, 82, 115, 182
Saroyan, William 173
Saturday Evening Post 37, 81
Saturday Morning Party 121
The Saturday Review 10, 177
Saunders of the Circle X 61
Savage, Courtenay 173
Savoy, Harry 59
S.C. Johnson & Son 162
Scandal at Scourie 53
The Scarlet Pimpernel 149
Scattergood Baines 103, 127
The Scene of the Crime 91
The Scent of Roses 124
Schiller, Bob 173
Schlichter, Karl 24, 173
Schoen, Lillian 28, 174
Schoenfeld, Bernard 174
Schofield, John 174
School House 88, 183
School Teacher 174
Schuffman, Dan 174
Schulberg, Budd 121
Schwartz, Albert 174–175
Schwartz, Arthur 50
Schwartz, Dave 26, 59
Schwartz, Sherwood 174, 175
Science Fiction and Fantasy Hall of Fame 32
Science Fiction Theatre 88, 107
Science Fiction Writers of America 32
Scofield, Louis 175
Scotland Yard 26
Scott, Ashmead 175
Scott, Joy 20
Scott, Tom 20
The Scoundrel 99
Scramble 145
Scramby Amby 33
Screen Director's Playhouse 85, 171, 178
Screen Test 145
Scribner, Jimmy 47, 175
The Script Library 12, 59
The Sea Has a Story 186
The Sea Hound 56, 195
The Seadon Fortune 172
The Sealed Book 19, 118
Sealtest Variety Theatre 40, 56, 96, 104, 107, 149, 180, 184, 191, 193, 198
The Sealtest Village Store 46, 62, 64, 75, 86, 115, 165, 178

Search for Beauty 144
Search for Tomorrow 80, 83, 94, 107, 176, 190
The Search That Never Ends 38
The Searching Heart 189
Sears Radio Theatre 53, 65, 83, 90
Second Breakfast 169
Second Cup of Coffee 71
Second Husband 27, 33, 35, 57, 93, 145, 189, 191, 192
The Second Mrs. Burton 13, 46, 110, 114, 198
Second Wife 198
Secret Agent 78
Secret Legion 164
The Secret Life of Walter Mitty 82, 140
Secret Missions 47, 141
The Secret Storm 32, 33, 45
Secret Three 135
Secrets of Beauty 122
See America First 116
Seeing It Through 71
Seldes, Gilbert 175
The Sellout 143
Seneca, U.S.A. 169
Sennett, Mack 109
Sergeant York 117
Service to the Front 107
Service Unlimited 67
Seth Parker 184
77 Sunset Strip 55
Seymour, Katharine 29, 175, 176
The Shadow 18, 19, 26, 32, 38, 41, 47, 57, 60, 67, 70, 79, 87, 97, 107, 112, 118, 122, 129, 137, 138, 140, 148, 179, 191
The Shadow (magazine) 19
The Shadow of Fu Man Chu 188
Shafter Parker and his Circus 31
The Shaggy Dog 143
Shaitan 67
Shapiro, Stanley 101
Sharp, Henry 163
Shavelson, Mel 176
Shaw, Irwin 176
Shaw, Robert 176
Shayon, Robert 176–177
Shean, Jim 177
Sheekman, Arthur 177
Shell Chateau 44, 60
Shelton, George 81
Shenkin, Ernest 177
Sher, Jack 143
The Sheriff 197
Sherry, Ed 177
Sherwood, Jane 9
Shevelove, Burt 86
Ship, Reuben 177–178
Shirley Temple Time 118
Shoe Leather Sonata 161
Shoestring Castle 23
Shore, Dinah 40, 96, 121, 172, 194
A Short Short Story 50
Shorty Bell 45, 85, 151, 187
The Show Goes On 140
Showboat 184
Shriner, Herb 145
Shuler, Marjorie 117
Shumer, Henry 61
Signal Carnival 48, 75, 101
Signpost to Murder 76

The Silent Men 21, 149, 172
The Silver Eagle 79
Silver Spoons 123, 182
The Silver Theatre 25, 34, 53, 55, 63, 78, 94, 110, 187, 193, 197
Silvers, Phil 20, 61, 183, 198
Simmons, Ed 122, 178
Simmons, Richard Alan 11, 178
Simon, Neil 178
Sinatra, Frank 20, 64, 65, 123, 147
Sing It Again 110
Singer, Ray 46, 178
Singer Four Star Playhouse 66
The Singing Marshal 46
Sinners Holiday 27
Sisters of the Skillet 104
Six-Gun Justice 94
The Six Million Dollar Man 169
The Six-Shooter 40, 56
The $64 Question 183
Skelly Oil 40, 146
Skelton, Red 22, 63, 80, 137, 150
Skipper Storm 121
Skippy 17, 135
Skippy Hollywood Theatre 34
Sklar, Michael 178
Sky Blazers 80, 192
The Sky Boat 184
Sky King 41, 146, 190
The Sky Parade 41, 146
Slapsie Maxie Show 109
Sleep No More 39
The Sleeping City 68
Slightly Honorable 121, 186
Sloan, Bob 30, 156, 179, 187
Sloane, Allan 67, 178–179
Slon, Sidney 26, 30, 179
Slott, John 46
Slums Cost You Money 41, 76
Smackout—The Crossroads of the Air 162
Small Town Hotel 107
Smarty Party 39
Smith 156
Smith, Alan 179–180
Smith, David Fred 180
Smith, Joseph 65
Smith, Kate 103, 112
Smith, Robert 180
Smith & Dale 48
The Smiths of Hollywood 152, 160
The Smiths of San Fernando 160
Smoke Dreams 29
Smokey Rogers: Fire Chief 166
The Snow Leopard 144
Snow Village 133
Snyder, Howard 112, 180, 192
So This Is Radio 52
Society Girl 57, 170
Socony Hour 133
Soconyland Sketches 133
Soderbert, Robert 180–181
Soldier Town 144
Soldiers of the Press 95
Solomon and Sheba 65
Somebody Knows 135
Somerset Maugham Theatre 13, 108
Something for the Boys 84
Something to Talk About 10
Sommer, Edith 180, 181

Sommers, Jay 89, 181
Son of Frankenstein 50
Sondheim, Stephen 86
Song of the Stranger 94
Song Sheet 121, 123
Songs By Sinatra 121, 194, 196
Sons of the Pioneers 83
Sound-O 62
Space Patrol 107
The Sparrow and the Hawk 41, 94, 140, 144
Speaking of the Devil 13, 21
Special Agent 71
Speed Gibson of the International Secret Police 49
The Spider's Web 196
Spier, William 186
The Spike Jones Show 181
Spillane, Mickey 10
Spin & Win with Jimmy Flynn 104
The Spiral Staircase 61
The Spirit 144
Spirit of '41 150
Split-Second Tales 147
Sports Views, Reviews, and Interviews 64
Sportsman's Game and Fish Cookbook 12
The Sportsmen's Club 103, 111
Spotlight Bands 64
Spotlight on America 144
Spotlight on Crime 182
Spotlight on Youth 99
Spotlight Playhouse 135
Springfield Republican (MA) 51, 52
Squad Room 108
Squib Show 126
Stafford, Gene 181
Stagg, Jerry 181
Stage Door Canteen 34, 77, 196
Stagestruck 51
Stampede 67
Stand By for Crime 20
Stand By for the Ladies 117
Stander, Arthur 76, 118, 181–182, 198
Standish, Burt 36
Stanford University 16, 125, 155
Stang, Arnold 61
The Star and the Sword 114
Star Performance 69
Star Spangled Theatre 47, 112, 113, 171
Star Trek 95
Stark, Sheldon 182
Starlight Serenade 196
Starr, Ben 182
Starr, Ken 115
Stars and Stripes 104, 173
Stars Fell on Alabama 43
Stars Over Hollywood 33, 121, 125, 130, 168, 172, 194
Startling Stories 55
Static 136
The Steeper Cliff 58
Stein, Joseph 88, 182–183
Stella Dallas 13, 20, 27, 165, 170, 176, 191
Step Down to Terror 61
Steppin' Out 184
Stern, Bill 59
Stern, Len 183
The Steve Allen Show 48
Steve Canyon 63, 65
Stevenson, Rick 183

Stewart, Jimmy 40, 52
Stirling, Nora 183
Stockton Field Army Show 104
The Stolen Husband 17
Stone, Ezra 89
Stone, Gene 168, 183–184
Stone, Lynn 167, 184, 191
Stop and Go 77
Stop or Go 121, 138, 156
Stop the Music 15
Stories America Loves 126
Stories to Remember 143
Storm Over Lisbon 88
Stormy Weather 118
Story Behind the Story 22
Story from the Stars 183
The Story Lady 82
The Story of a Thousand Dollars 62
The Story of Babe Ruth 53
The Story of Bess Johnson 50, 126, 186
The Story of Dr. Kildare 56, 80, 98, 103, 148, 149, 151
The Story of Ellen Randolph 154, 173
The Story of Holly Sloan 136
The Story of Mary Marlin 55, 76, 136, 142
The Story of Rita Martin 18
The Story of Sandra Martin 66
The Story of Terry Reagan 85
Story Shop 100
Straight Arrow 182
Strange 87
Strange Bedfellows 114
The Strange Dr. Weird 19, 118
The Strange Land 42
Strange Romance of Evelyn Winters 33
The Straw Hat Review 74
Streamlined Shakespeare 24
Street & Smith 87, 92
Strictly from Dixie 159
Strike It Rich 105
Striker, Fran 28, 63, 111, 182, 184
Stroke of Fate 72, 127
Strong, Paschal 184–185
The Stu Erwin Show 125
Studebaker 154
The Studebaker Show 127
Studio One 33, 65, 102, 136, 169, 182, 184
The Stuntman 134
Sue Blake 189
Sullivan, Norman 185
Sullivan, Stauffer, Colwell, & Bayles 48
Summer Holiday 104
Summerfield Bandstand 195
The Sun Beats Down 79
Sunbrite Junior Nurse Corps 84
Sunbrite Smile Parade 63
Sunday Barnstormers 67
Sunday Night Revue 74
Sunday Playhouse 83
Sunday Serenade 111
Sunny Side Up 31
Superman 13
Superman, Inc. 129
Sure as Fate 102
Susann, Jacqueline 47, 185
Suspense 3, 18, 19, 21, 25, 26, 43, 45, 46, 51, 55, 56, 60, 61, 63, 65, 66, 68, 69, 70, 73, 74, 75, 80, 83, 84, 90, 98, 99, 103, 107, 111, 123, 130, 132, 134, 135, 137, 139, 143, 148, 149, 150, 151, 156, 164, 165, 167, 168, 169, 170, 171, 172, 185, 186, 188, 190, 197, 198, 199
Suspicion 19
Sutton, Vida R. 185
Suzie 109
Swanton, Harold 132, 185
Swap Shop 86
Swart, Howard 185
The Sweeney and March Show 55, 57, 62, 78, 90, 98, 127, 173
Sweet City 90
Sweets, Bill 185–186
Swenson, Carl 87
Swerling, Jo 37
Swift, Mack 13
Swift Reviews 163
Swop Night 103
Sycamore Street 54

T-Man 56
Tackaberry, John 111, 157, 186
Take It or Leave it 34, 154
Take Me Along 183
A Tale of Today 172
Tales from an Antique Shop 160
Tales from Harlem 35
Tales of Fatima 107, 169
Tales of the Foreign Legion 50
Tales of the Foreign Service 103
Tales of the Texas Rangers 86, 106, 149, 172
Tales of the Tuna Clippers 54
Tales of Tomorrow 178
Tales of Willie Piper 187
Tallman, Bob 63, 68, 130, 167, 186
The Tamarack Tree 37
Tangee Varieties 109
Tapestries of Life 42, 95
Tarantula 14
Tarkington, Booth 141, 186–187
Tarzan 125
Tarzan and the Diamond of Asher 188
Tarzan and the Fires of Tohr 188
Taussig, Frank 187
Taylor, Bruce 91
Taylor, F. Chase 194
Taylor, Lawrence 187
Taylor, Samuel 187
Tazewell, Charles 37, 187
Ted Bates Inc. 39
Ted Steele 130
Teentimers Club 103
Teichmann, Howard 121, 187–188
Tell It Again 170
Tell Me a Story 148
Tell Your Story 149
Temper the Wind 130
Temple, Shirley 88
Temple Bells 184
Temple University 125
Ten Biggest News Stories of 1939 113
Ten Thousand Public Enemies 50
Tena and Tim 29
Tennessee Jed 182
Tenney, Jack 146
Tenth Row Center 64
Tenting Tonight 191
Tepperman, Emile 188
Terry and Mary 18
Terry and the Pirates 17, 23, 32, 129
Tetley, Walter 62, 116
Texaco Star Theatre 25, 34, 40, 43, 54, 61, 77, 78, 80, 84, 85, 92, 102, 108, 109, 118, 127, 133, 158, 170, 175, 178, 180, 185, 192
Texaco Town 38, 68
The Texan 18
Texas Lil' Darling 146, 195
Texas Rangers 49
The Textron Theatre 45
That Brewster Boy 105
That Girl 38
That Hammer Guy 10
That They Might Live 67
That's a Good Idea 162
That's Baseball 59
That's Life 24, 33
That's My Pop 92, 180, 192
That's Rich 60, 81, 96, 107, 174
That's the Way Money Goes 144
The Theater of Famous Radio Players 170
Theater of Today 27
Theater USA 188
Theatre Five 19, 39, 45, 53, 70, 108, 129, 143, 151, 164, 167, 196, 197, 198
The Theatre Guild on the Air 16, 18, 25, 45, 84, 130, 164, 171
Theatre of Romance 31, 69, 103, 132, 171, 186
Theatre of Today 80, 117
Theatre Time 33
Then and Now 84
There Was a Woman 66, 130, 198
There Were Such Moments in Sport 59
There's Always a Woman 145
These Are My Children 159
They Call Me Joe 197
They Live Forever 121, 187
They Live in Brooklyn 53
They Say Today 93
The Thin Man 29, 56
Think 82
The Third Man 192
Thirteen By Corwin 53
The Thirteenth Hour 66
The Thirteenth Juror 135
Thirty Minutes in Hollywood 42
This Day Is Ours 29, 33
This Is Adventure 39
This Is Helen Hayes 104
This Is Hollywood 95, 171
This Is Judy Jones 66
This Is My Best 34, 38, 56, 186
This Is My Story 21, 73, 106, 129
This Is New York 40
This Is Nora Drake 83, 127
This Is Our America 34
This Is Our Enemy 96
This Is the Truth 127
This Is the Underground 175
This Is War! 16, 29, 52, 71, 130
This Is Your FBI 40, 60, 120, 158
This Is Your Home 61
This Life Is Mine 167, 184
This Nation At War 103
This Our Enemy 174
This Small Town 107
This Way Please 163
This Week 37

Thomas, Cliff 188
Thomas, Gilbert 188
Thomas Lee Artist Bureau 193
Thompson, Don 39
Thompson, Maggie 41
Thompson, Rob 188
Thompson, William 49
Thorne, Richard 188
Those Calloways 156
Those Esmonds 72
Those Happy Gilmans 188
Those Sensational Years 32
Those We Love 117, 167
Those Websters 107, 114, 143, 154
Those Young Bryans 39
Three After Three 126, 128
Three Blind Mice 78
The Three Doctors 166
Three Girls Lost 18
Three Musketeers 160
Three Ring Time 146, 178
Three Steps to Heaven 190
Three Stories High 197
The Thrill Quiz 59
Thriller 18
Thrillers 56
Thrilling Wonder Stories 55
Thrills 24
Thrills of the Highway Patrol 160
Thrills of the Secret Service 184
Thunder Adams 61
Thunder and Lightning 172
Thunder Bay 63
Thurber, James 42
Thurlow Wade 71
Thus We Live 176
Till the Clouds Roll By 104
Tim Thompson in the Jungle 80
Tim Tyler's Luck 54
Time 23, 43, 71, 160, 180
Time Capsule 178
A Time for Love 97
Time for Women 71
Time to Smile 68, 134
Timid Tiger, Lusty Lamb 15
Tip Top Show 38, 73, 125, 131
Tish 76
Titanic 37
Titterton, Lewis 122, 153, 191
To Catch a Thief 98
To the Land of the Takatu 28
Toast to the Town 136
Tobago 18
Tobin, Lu 61
Today 50
Today's Children 49, 54, 158, 159
Todd, Elizabeth Coe 113, 189
Together Tonight! 53
Tokar, Norman 189
Tokyo Rose 113
Toledo Times 117
Toledo University 116
Tom Corbett, Space Cadet 13, 36, 81, 106, 109
Tom Dixon Meets the Enemy 87
The Tom Mix Ralston Straight Shooters 129, 135, 187
The Tommy Dorsey Show 138
Tommy Get Your Fun 34
Tommy Parker, G-Scout 129
Tommy Riggs and Betty Lou 22, 56, 60, 63, 126, 146
Tomorrow the World 127
Tomorrow's Children 76
Tonight in Hollywood 70
Tonight on Broadway 90
The Tonight Show 115, 165
Tony and Baby 104
Tony and Gus 38
Tony Award 40, 86, 120, 121, 123, 143, 178, 183
The Tony Martin Show 133, 156, 194
Too Close for Comfort 61
Tootsie 86
The Top Guy 69
Top Secret 111
Top Secrets of the FBI 47
Topical Times 127
Tornado 93
Tovrov, Orin 189
Town and Country 71
Town Hall Tonight 15, 41, 48, 143
Trade Winds 85
Tragedy at Honda 12
Transamerican Broadcasting & Television Corp. 23, 29, 106, 176
Transradio Press 76, 113, 190
Travel Is So Broadening 22
Travelaugh 139
The Travels of Mary Ward 69–70
Treasure Adventures of Jack Masters 181
Treasure Chest 64
Treasure Island 55
Treasure of Last Canyon 65
Treasury Agent 144
Treasury Hour 34, 64
Treasury Men in Action 67, 179
Treasury Salute 25, 40, 46, 56, 87
Treasury Star Parade 20, 34, 85, 95, 96, 104, 153, 171
Trendle, George 111, 184
Triadors 116
Trial of Harry Morley 87
The Trials of O'Brien 192
Triple-A Plowed Under 19
Triple Bar X Days and Nights 27, 80
Trivializing America 53
Trouble House 43
The Trouble with Marriage 22
True Air Adventures 54
True Confessions 144
True Crime Detective 36
True Detective Mysteries 39, 45, 108
True or False 94
True Stories from Britain 60
True Story Theatre 79
True Story Time 87
The Truitts 107
Truth or Consequences 39, 59, 109, 127
Try and Do It 33
Tsar of Stars 192
Tugend, Harry 15, 189
Tune Out Time 132
Tunick, Irve 189
Turning Point 120
Tuttle, Wilbur C. 129
Twain, Mark 122, 191
Twelve Players 39, 70, 98
20th Century Fox 42, 52, 145, 180
20th Century Radio Productions 31
21st Precinct 152
The 22nd Letter 130
Twenty Thousand Years in Sing Sing 32
20 Years in Sing Sing 140
2000 Plus 38
Two Yanks in Trinidad 45
Tydol Jubilee 27
Tyler, Ed 190

Ugly Dachshund 13
Ultimate Journey 145
The U.N. Story 169
An Uncensored Biography of Mae West 95
Uncle Charlie's Tent Show 138
Uncle Judge Ben 148
Uncle Sam 72, 157
Uncle Walter's Doghouse 172
The Uncrowned King 106
Under Arrest 144
Under the Boardwalk 171
Under Western Skies 121
Underworld 99
The Unexpected 40, 121, 128
Union Holding Co. 39
Union Oil Co. 24
United Artists 140, 180
United Nations Radio 53, 56
United Packinghouse Workers of America 66
United Press 85, 160
U.S. Department of Agriculture 19
U.S. Office of Education 20, 87
U.S. Recording Co. 28
The United States Steel Hour 19, 84
United States Treasury Department 26
United We Fight! United We Give! 24
Universal Studios 18, 79, 183
University of Alabama 24
University of Arkansas 88, 119
University of Buffalo 184
University of California–Berkeley 156
University of California–Irvine 149
University of California–Los Angeles 53, 80, 83, 120, 151, 165, 166, 173, 182, 183
University of California–San Francisco 147
University of Chicago 33, 79, 81, 155, 174, 187, 193
University of Florida 137
University of Illinois 77, 158
University of Michigan 19, 63, 67, 111, 123, 144, 161
University of Minnesota 129
University of Missouri 150
University of North Dakota 16
University of Oklahoma 88
University of Pennsylvania 15, 143, 175, 177
University of Pittsburgh 73
University of Southern California 53, 100
University of Texas 48
University of the Air 95
University of Toronto 178
University of Vienna 168
University of Washington 119
University of Wisconsin 54, 82, 105, 107, 158, 176
University of Wyoming 125, 144

228 Index

Unlimited Horizons 135
The Unseen Enemy 173
Untamed Frontier 21
The Untouchables 10, 118, 171
Up for Parole 45, 157
The Upper Room 148
The Urgent Air 160

Vail, Myrtle 190
Valentine's Day 113
Valiant Lady 13, 35, 46, 115, 142, 167, 184, 187, 188
Vallee, Rudy 27, 40, 61, 72, 78, 81, 82, 84, 85, 89, 95, 131, 155, 156, 167, 168, 193
Valley of the Dolls 185
van Cronkhite, John 190
van Hartesveldt, Fran 190
van Harvey, Art 166
Vanity Fair 145
van Ronkel, Rip 152
Varsity Varieties 68
Vassar College 197
VD Radio Project 25
Vega$ 13
Vendig, Irving 190
Vic and Sade 166
Vick Chemical 85
Victor, David 128, 190–191, 194
The Victor Borge–Benny Goodman Show 191
The Victor Borge Show 89
Victor Victoria 67
Viking Press 155
Vinson, Owen 105
The Virginian 10, 34, 82
Vittes, Louis 191
Voice from Nowhere 126
A Voice in the Night 118
Voice of America 54
The Voice of the Army 75, 156
Voice of the Red Cross 67
Vollmer, Lula 191
Volume One, Numbers One to Six 50
Vox Pop 108
The Voyage of the Scarlet Queen 63, 186

WABC 21, 38, 96, 126, 136
Wagon Train 72, 103, 111, 177, 185
Walk, Don't Run 173
Walk the Proud Land 63
Wallace, Henry 153
Walpole, Helen 122, 191
Walter K. Neill Inc. 49
The Waltons 103, 194, 195
Wang, Eugene 191–192
Wanted: Dead or Alive 10
War and Remembrance 198
WARD 136
Ward, Shirley 192
Ward Tip Top Club 21
Ward Wheelock Agency 44
Ware, Harlan 192
Waring, Fred 139, 140
Warner Bros. 18, 24, 38, 64, 79
Warner Lester, Manhunter 184
Warriors of Peace 74
Waterfront Wayside 29
Watt, Kenneth 192
Watts News 39

Way Down Home 25
The Wayne King Show 196
Wayne St. University 59
The Wayside Theatre 129
WBAP 196
WBBM 50, 73, 105
WBDO 188
WBK 117
WBT 195
WBTV 195
WBZA 51, 52
WCAE 59, 167
WCAU 7, 85
WCCO 28, 29, 99, 129
WCFL 136, 175
WCHS 59
WCLO 166
WCLO Syndicate Serials 166
WCPO 188
WDAN 36
We Are Always Young 39, 53
We Are Four 76
We Believe 114
We Came This Way 67, 95, 181
We Hold These Truths 52
We Live Again 105
We Love and Learn 23, 29, 76, 136
We, the Abbotts 76, 98
We, the People 10, 23, 46, 50, 56
We, the People, at War 26
We Want a Touchdown 181
We Who Dream 85
WEAF 62, 71, 104, 176
Weak-end Satires 29
Weapons for Victory 157
Webb, Jack 37, 40, 68, 83, 134, 147, 148
Webb, Ken 192
Webb, Nancy 192
WEBR 184
Wedding Ring Party 94
Wedlock, Hugh, Jr. 112, 180, 192
Week-End Pass 59
Weill, Kurt 16
Weiner, Henry 78
Weinrott, Les 192–193
Weiser, Norman 12, 26
Weiskopf, Bob 193
Welch, William 193
Welcome, Neighbor 142
Welcome Valley 140, 159
WELI 106
Welles, Orson 14, 52, 117, 153
Wellesley College 70
Wells, Billy 193
Wells, George 25, 156, 193
Wells, H.G. 117
Wendy Warren and the News 160, 161
WENR 22, 162
Werris, Snag 193–194
West, Jane 194
West, Mae 153
West, Paul 194
West Point 121
West Side Story 120
Western Dakota Technical Institute 27
Western Gold 25
Western Reserve University 85
Westinghouse Salute 32
WEVD 100, 149
WFDF 109

WFIN 96
WGAR 117, 123
WGN 9, 28, 40, 42, 46, 51, 56, 65, 90, 146, 158, 188
WGR 188
WHA 182
WHAS 28, 138
What a Life 89
What Big Ears 68
What Makes You Tick? 71
What Price Glory? 16
What Would You Have Done? 140
What's in a Name? 22
What's My Line? 34
What's My Name? 41, 54, 55, 85
What's New? 32, 182
WHBF 136
Wheatana Playhouse 128, 191
Wheatanaville Sketches 116
Wheaton, Glenn 194
Whedon, John 27, 146, 194–195
Whedon, Joss 195
Whedon, Tom 195
Wheeler, Bert 119
When a Girl Marries 43
When a Man Marries 43
Where Do We Stand 74
Which Is Which 73
While America Sleeps 173
While the City Sleeps 104
Whispering Streets 173
The Whistler 18, 24, 39, 40, 49, 65, 66, 73, 75, 83, 86, 88, 90, 98, 102, 106, 107, 114, 125, 128, 132, 134, 137, 144, 149, 150, 156, 169, 170, 172, 178, 185, 188, 197
White, Andy 195
White, Bob 195
White, George 38
White, Kenneth 195
White Christmas 79, 156
White Fires 46
White Magic 86
Whitehall 1212 50
Whiteman, Paul 84, 127, 172
Whitman, Walt 142
Whitman College (WA) 73
WHK 145
WHO 70, 187
Who Knows? 85, 110
Whodunit? 119
WHOM 111
WHY 54
Wicker, Ireene 158
Wide Horizons 169
The Widow's Son 191
Wilbur Stark–Jerry Layton Productions 182
Wild Bill Hickok 98
Wild Waves 133
Wilder, Thornton 110
Wilderness Road 59, 183, 187
Wilkinson, Richard 195
William Esty Company 63, 79, 125, 145, 147, 165
Williams, Fred 182
Williamson, Mel 195
Willow Cottage 13
Wills, Sy 46
Willy 128

Wilson, Don 42
Wilson, Earl 71
Wilson, Frank 195–196
Wilson, Jack 196
Wilson, James 163
Wilson, W. Ray 196
Wiltten, Virginia 196
Winchell, Prentice 196–197
Winchell, Walter 174
The Windfall 124
Window on Main Street 169
The Winds of Montauk 42
The Winds of War 198
Winesburg, OH 17
Wing and a Prayer 42
Wings for the Martins 87
Wings of Dawn 25
Wings of Destiny 172
Wings of the Hawk 195
Wings Over America 137
Wings Over the World 97, 181
Wings to Victory 80
The Winner 196
Winnie, the Pooh 189
Winning the West 61, 161
WINS 189
Winston, Irene 197
WIRE 161
Wishengrad, Morton 197
WISN 138
The Witch's Tale 47
Without Warning 71
The Witness 189
The Wizard of Oz 37, 84
WIZE 36
WJBK 104
WJR 69, 106
WJZ 98
WJZ Takes the Cake 104
WKNY 106
WLS 36, 161
WLW 19, 28, 29, 41, 52, 71, 84, 93, 105, 106, 145, 167, 175, 179, 180, 181, 185, 196
WMAQ 51, 65, 158, 162
WMAS 52
WMBS 111
WMCA 30, 48, 126, 140, 159, 178, 181
WNAX 27
WNEW 13
WNLC 106
WOL 59
Wolf, Ed 87
Wolf, George 27
Wolfe, Winifred 197
Wolff, Nat 197
Woman Behind the Man 198
Woman in Love 115
The Woman in My House 72, 148
Woman in White 84, 136, 143, 159, 198
A Woman of America 60, 76, 114, 188
Woman of Courage 27, 41, 167, 184
A Woman to Remember 94
Woman with a Past 114

Woman's Club 97
A Woman's Life 82, 152
Women in the Making of America 20
Women of the Day 77
Women Shoulder Arms 23
Women's Army Corps 82
Wonder Child 66
Wonder Woman 88
The Wonderful Wileys 156
Woodbury's Hollywood Playhouse 46
Woodman, Ruth 197–198
The Woody Woodpecker Show 138
Woollcott, Alexander 188
WOR 47, 65, 117, 177
WOR Summer Theatre 177
Words and Music 52, 104
Words at War 38, 67, 103, 104, 111, 113, 114, 137, 140, 181, 183, 193, 195, 197
Works Progress Administration (WPA) 20, 27, 55, 76, 97, 174, 184
The World and America 43
The World and David Lee 136
World Broadcasting Co. 87
The World Is Yours 174, 189
World News Parade 79
The World of Carl Sandburg 53
World of Song 74
World Parade 79
World Service 102
The World We're Fighting For 121, 123
The World's Best 130
The World's Greatest Novels 138
The World's Most Famous Flights 12
The World's Most Honored Flights 12
Wouk, Herman 15, 20, 198
WOV 136
WOW 27, 104, 177
WPAT 10
WPCH 79
WQAM 187
WQXR 52, 71
WRC 105, 185
WRHM 99
Wright, Burton 22
Wrigley Co. 11
The Wrigley Show 165
Writers Bureau, Inc. 33
Writer's Radio Theatre 12
WRNY 38
WROL 39
The Wrong Man 16
WSAI 29
WSB 24
WSOO 109
WSPR 67
WTAM 167, 184
WTMJ 138
WTTW 66
WWJ 93, 136
WXLE 113
WXLI 113
WXYZ 28, 36, 63, 78, 79, 89, 104, 111, 121, 136, 140, 141, 164, 182, 184
Wylie, Max 4, 5, 75, 85, 94

Wynn, Ed 34, 48, 60, 88, 113, 116, 126, 127, 128, 165, 194
The Wynn Show 109

X Minus One 115, 123

Yale University 116, 144, 168
Yancy Derringer 163
Yank 75, 182
Yankee Doodle Doo 34
Yankee Press & Dakotan 27
Yardley, Herbert O. 56
Yarns for Yanks 121, 123
Yes Speak Out Yes 53
Yoo-Hoo, Prosperity! 81
You Are There 9, 31, 45, 128, 130, 141, 143, 148, 177, 178, 189
You Bet Your Life 81, 96, 190
You Can't Take It with You 56
You Decide 131
You Have to Go Out 112
You the Jury 181
You Wanna Fight? Here's How 24
Young, Chic 92, 147
Young, John 159, 198
Young Dr. Malone 64, 83, 94, 123, 160, 161, 188
The Young Lions 176
Young Love 123
Young Mr. Gabriel 165
Young Widder Brown 27, 44, 150, 189
Young Widder Jones 10, 18, 80, 94, 108
Your Blind Date 66
Your Dubonnet Date 99, 100
Your Family and Mine 120
Your Happy Birthday 128
Your Hit Parade 56, 75
Your Hollywood Parade 80, 153, 187
Your Marriage Club 131
Your Movietown Radio Theatre 19, 196, 199
Your Neck of the Woods 43
Your Three Wishes 109
Your United Nations 196
Your Unseen Friend 104
Your Witness 175
Yours for a Song 183
Yours Truly, Johnny Dollar 3, 56, 59, 62, 64, 66, 70, 80, 86, 98, 110, 135, 149, 150–151, 172

Zacharias, Ellis M. 141
Zachary, George 56–57
The Zane Grey Show 80
Zanities of 1943 128
Zelinka, Sydney 96, 182, 198
The Zenith Show 198
Zero Hour 143
Ziegfeld Follies 81, 127
The Ziegfeld Follies of the Air 31
Zimm, Maurice 198–199
Ziv Productions 9, 77, 82
Zoomies, Subs, and Zeros 12
Zorba 183

www.ingramcontent.com/pod-product-compliance
Lightning Source LLC
Chambersburg PA
CBHW081553300426
44116CB00015B/2864